Acclaim for

Katharine Graham's Washington

"A glorious volume. You don't have to love the capital . . . to be caught up in her varied glimpses of grandeur, novelty, and complexity of life at the center of political power." —*Houston Chronicle*

"Engaging. . . . Includes charming, instructive essays . . . and some happy surprises." —*The New Yorker*

"A first-rate book. . . . Wise. . . . Addictive. . . . Wide-ranging. . . . For the reader who wants to get a good overview of this country's capital, *Katharine Graham's Washington* is a fine place to start." —*The Times-Picayune*

"Delightful, informative, often moving. . . . Well-organized and annotated. . . . Eminently readable. . . . An almost bottomless cornucopia." —*The Baltimore Sun*

"A terrific read. . . . Packed with fascinating social history, behind-the-scenes details of the lives of the powerful in our nation's capital. . . . The book is [Graham's] own Proustian time regained." —*Vogue*

"Remarkable. . . . Graham . . . offers a balanced perspective of the city and its politically obsessed denizens. . . . [Her] lineup of authors is impressive." —*Fort Worth Star-Telegram*

"Marvelously readable. . . . Wonderful. . . . There's substance here and thoughtfulness." —*The Buffalo News*

"A massive, though wonderfully evocative, collection of vignettes. . . . The book allows readers to share a truly personal love story about the city." —*The Columbus Dispatch*

"Delightful and insightful. . . . Sharp, witty, and carefully chosen. . . . A worthy follow-up to her Pulitzer Prize–winning autobiography." —*Booklist*

"A pitch-perfect anthology that captures the nuances of life in the nation's capital. . . . Vibrant, affecting. . . . Graham's selections yield a rich blend of viewpoints. . . . The real treats in this book are Graham's vignettes introducing each piece. . . . [They] add considerable zing to the volume."   —*BookPage*

"Excellent views and tales about the city. . . . Sprinkled with cogent comments."   —*The Indianapolis Star*

KATHARINE GRAHAM

Katharine Graham's Washington

Katharine Graham served as the publisher of *The Washington Post* from 1969 to 1979, and as the president and chairman of the Washington Post Company for much longer, piloting the paper through the crises of the Pentagon Papers and Watergate. In 1998 she won a Pulitzer Prize for her bestselling autobiography, *Personal History*. She died at the age of eighty-four in July 2001.

ALSO BY KATHARINE GRAHAM

Personal History

Katharine Graham's
WASHINGTON

Katharine Graham's
WASHINGTON

Vintage Books
A Division of Random House, Inc.
New York

FIRST VINTAGE BOOKS EDITION, NOVEMBER 2003

Copyright © 2002 by The Library of Congress

All rights reserved under International and Pan-American Copyright Conventions. Published in the United States by Vintage Books, a division of Random House, Inc., New York, and simultaneously in Canada by Random House of Canada Limited, Toronto. *Katharine Graham's Washington* was originally published in hardcover in the United States by Alfred A. Knopf, a division of Random House, Inc., New York, in 2002.

Owing to limitations of space, all permissions to reprint previously published material may be found on pages 809–813.

Vintage and colophon are registered trademarks of Random House, Inc.

LCCN: 2002111640

ISBN: 1-4000-3059-5

Book design by Virginia Tan

www.vintagebooks.com

Printed in the United States of America
10 9 8 7 6 5 4 3 2 1

CONTENTS

PERIOD PIECES   183

WARTIME WASHINGTON   248

WORLD WAR I

WORLD WAR II

EDITOR'S NOTE

A FTER the unflagging work she put into writing her autobiography, *Personal History*, and the excitement surrounding its publication, Kay Graham was eager to move on to other activities; she wasn't one to rest on her laurels. Another book seemed a possibility, but she had no interest in writing more about herself. As we talked about possible subjects, she kept coming back to Washington, the city she loved, and particularly what had changed and what had remained the same in the more than eighty years since 1917, the year she was born, which was also the year her parents first came to live there. Indeed, a frequent point of reference was the full and forthright diary her mother had kept from her first days in the city, filling in for Kay the Washington she herself was too young to know.

Slowly the idea of an anthology emerged—a big collection of the best writing we could find that would reflect her own sense of Washington: its flavor, its history through her lifespan, its great characters, its great events. Her own library of Washington books was extensive, and her brilliant assistant and collaborator, Evelyn Small, who had been so crucial to the success of *Personal History*, set to work to track down countless other books and magazines and newspapers for all of us to poke through, looking for treasure. Kay immediately began reading what she herself had found and what Ev served up to her, pouncing on material here, rejecting it forcibly there. She knew what she liked, and she knew why.

Anthologies generally grow into their structure, but we agreed from the start that this one should gather itself around certain themes: Social Washington, President Watching, Mr. and Mrs. Smith Come to Washington, etc. She would write general introductions (there would be twelve sections in all), and shorter introductions to each of the hundred-plus pieces. And they would be personal—indeed, they could only be personal, since she was a witness to so much that had happened in Washington, and was often a *part* of what had happened. Many of the writers, too, were friends of hers (Arthur Schlesinger Jr., Dean Acheson, the Alsop brothers, Henry Kissinger, Nancy Reagan, among others) or with whom she had been close when they worked for *The Washington Post* (Herblock, Meg Greenfield, Art Buchwald, Ben Bradlee, Sally Quinn). She and/or her parents had known all the presidents since Woodrow Wilson.

Her goal was to present *her* Washington, hence the title; this was never intended to be a policy book or a full history or a survey. She simply wanted to share her excitement about her city, her own fascination with it, through the best writing she could find. Early on, she decided that she couldn't and wouldn't try to cover all the bases—there were subjects that didn't seem to have stimulated first-rate writing, and those she would ignore. Nor did she want to present political analysis or extended biography. Not surprisingly, she found that on the whole, the past provided more interesting writing than the present, and she made no apology for representing the Harding or Coolidge or Roosevelt or Kennedy eras more fully than the Ford or Carter or Clinton years. (No doubt the best writing on those is yet to be done.)

At the time of her death, in July 2001, the book was unfinished. It had been structured, specific writers and passages had been chosen, and she had written many of the introductions and left notes on most of the others. And of course she had talked about the pieces with Ev Small, who completed anything and everything Kay had left undone.

I have never worked with a writer more generous to her collaborators than Kay Graham. She never ceased giving public credit to me and to Ev for *Personal History*, more, certainly, than I deserved; Ev deserved it all. And I know what Kay would have said about Ev's contributions to this new book: that there would have been no book without her. To that I can testify. Ev's superb research, her capacity for organization, her editorial intelligence, and most important, her profound understanding of, and sympathy for, Kay's cast of mind are what brought *Katharine Graham's Washington* to final fruition. Where Kay hadn't actually written text, Ev was able, given her seventeen years' experience of working with her, to piece together from notes, discussion, and intuition what was required. It was a labor of prodigious capability as well as a labor of love. The proof of her success, as anyone who knew Kay or read her earlier book will attest, is that what we have here is indisputably Katharine Graham's Washington.

—Robert Gottlieb

Katharine Graham's
WASHINGTON

FOREWORD

FOR MORE than eight decades, Washington has been my hometown. My whole orientation is toward this place. It is a city that offers me more people—more different *kinds* of people—than I could otherwise possibly have come to know in a lifetime: the native Washingtonian, the local merchant, the foreign diplomat, the ever-present tourist, the public servant, the journalist, the president, the friend.

It is a city whose geography is embedded in my mind: the sidewalks on which I skated to and from school through the cool shade created by arching branches of overhanging trees; the streets on which the too-full trolley cars and buses took me back and forth to work; the houses, great and small, in which dramas played themselves out publicly and privately; all the places to which I was always ready to go.

It is a city whose industry—first and foremost politics, both local and national—got into my blood early and stayed there: the arguments generated by all sides of any given question; the intense issues that sparked countless actions and reactions; the gossip created and contributed to by memorable characters; the events around which swirled high hopes and rich dreams; the presidents who have both molded and been molded by all that happens here.

In short, in Washington I've always found people to see, places to go, things to do.

ALTHOUGH I was born in New York City, my parents moved to Washington in the fall of 1917, just a few months after my birth. I'm not sure why I was the only one of the five children in our family for whom Washington became home. All of us grew up here, for the most part, although my older siblings did go to school in New York before my parents made a more permanent move here; but once each went away to college, no one but me came back.

I came home again and remained here always. Washington held me. I cannot imagine living anywhere else. I love the Virginia countryside where my husband, Phil, and I bought an old place in the early 1950s. I love Martha's Vineyard, where I have had a house for thirty years. I have loved visiting countries around the world. But I always come home to Washington.

My mother was more ambivalent about Washington, although she lived here for the better part of half a century. She kept a diary from the time she moved here, beginning it only a few days after her arrival, in October 1917. She continued to write in it (often only sporadically, sometimes skipping whole years) until the summer of 1933, right after my father resigned from his government position as governor of the Federal Reserve Board and just before he bought *The Washington Post* at a bankruptcy sale on the steps of the dilapidated building in which it was housed.

I don't remember when I first read this diary (at her request), but it was certainly when I was an adult. Any daughter reading her mother's diary has reason to hold her breath the first time through, but what I found there interested me from the start. When I was working on my own memoir, I reread the diary. What comes through very clearly is not only what a contrast this new city was to the New York she was in part leaving behind, but also what a rich tapestry Washington is, for the observer and for the participant in the life of the place, both of which she most definitely was.

In my rereading, I came across one little paragraph in which Mother tells of riding to Rapidan, President Hoover's camp in the Blue Ridge of Virginia that was his equivalent getaway to today's Camp David, with Mrs. Hoover at the wheel and two other ladies in the car, chatting the whole way, Mrs. Hoover's foot heavy on the gas pedal. This impossible scene clearly could not take place today.

As I thought about this and so many other scenes that my mother wrote about, I reflected on how much Washington has changed over the years. But while change has been a constant, it is also true that the more things change, the more they stay the same. Because Mother's diary reflects both of these realities, it got me to thinking harder about this city in which I've lived and worked for so long. And I thought it would be fun to look back on these years for what they tell us about the development of this place from the "small town" my mother found when she arrived, and to which she brought me as a baby, to the world capital Washington is today.

It's natural, but not always easy, for someone of my age—eighty-three—to look back. I have no desire to live in the past, yet so many people who read my memoir, *Personal History*, wrote me that it was for them a form of "popular history"—that learning more about the history of Washington was something that rang bells for them.

I was privileged to have been so often over my many years in Washington if not in the center of the rich life of the city, then at least hovering near. My father always taught me that with privileges come responsibilities, and I began to think that my unique perspective over eight decades might be of some interest to others who love our capital and would like a fuller glimpse into the constituents of this place we call Washington.

Nonetheless, I was reluctant to write another book, however different it might be from my memoir. I became a convert to the notion of doing some kind of book focusing on Washington when two relevant bits of information were pointed out to me: 1) this city has just marked the two hundredth anniversary of the government's arrival in Washington as the capital of the nation, and I have been here for 40 percent of those years; and 2) I have been connected—either indirectly through my parents, or directly—with more than a third of all the presidents who have served the United States. Of the forty-two different men who have served as president—one served twice—I have "known" sixteen of them. Even I was awed when faced with the facts.

As I read more Washington history, to give flesh to some of the events my mother described in her diary and to others I myself remembered, I came across many books and articles that either amused me or taught me something and gave me a reason to want to share them. In addition, I've always been intrigued by the real-life characters who peopled my mother's diary, as well as those who were often in my father's stories and conversations. Many of these people came and went during my child-hood—right through my parents' living and dining rooms, in many cases—but I was aware of them only remotely. It has been enlightening to learn more about them, and to see what others, particularly those writing contemporaneously, thought of them.

Finally, having retired from active direction of The Washington Post Company nearly a decade ago, I knew that it's not in my nature to stop working.

For all of these reasons, I decided to spend time reading and thinking more about my hometown and see where it led me. What I decided was that I was too old to write the kind of book I might like to, but not too old to share some of what I'd come across. Hence, the idea of a kind of anthology of Washington pieces began to take shape.

My selection of entries from books about Washington and its people is highly arbitrary—one of the prerogatives of age, perhaps. It's focused on my own interests, on what amused me, and on what made me pause to reflect. It's a book that could easily have been doubled in size; I've left out a great deal in order to keep it to a manageable length. What is here is what I know best, and I'm aware of how much is left out. It's unfortunate in many ways that in the first years that this book covers, those who wrote—whether diaries or memoirs or even letters—tended to be those who had the leisure time and money to devote to writing. Consequently, what is presented here, at least for the early years, is mostly a view of one aspect of Washington. Much that makes this city all that it is was not a part of the public record and isn't easily accessible to us looking back. That is a pity, because the full richness of life here in the past deserves to be known.

But the world in which my parents moved when they first came to Washington—and the world I knew as a child—was circumscribed in many ways, and I can only write about what I know. In addition, I can only reprint excerpts of what has come to light in our search for the best writing about the city from the time of my birth, during World War I and the Wilson administration. I hope that my sins of omission are greater than my sins of commission.

What follows are the more interesting pieces, vignettes, stories, articles, and excerpts from books about Washington that I've come across over the years. These tend to fall into the "popular" category—that is, they are mostly written for the general reader. They are often of the "I was there . . ." variety, whether *Backstairs at the White House* or *My Studio Window, Sketches of the Pageant of Washington Life*. They are not historical treatises or academic accounts and renderings of public events. I've chosen what I enjoyed reading: pieces that amused me, that gave me some new information, that informed and entertained at the same time.

In all cases, I've introduced the pieces with some prefatory comments of my own. In some cases, I wasn't able to resist writing a little personally about the authors represented here, so they have a chance to speak for themselves while at the same time I comment on their commentaries and add some of my own and others' observations. But I am not a historian, nor am I an "authority" on Washington, and, in many ways, neither were the authors selected for inclusion here. Whatever authority they may have stems from their personal experience of this city and the strength of their opinions and attitudes, positive or negative. Whatever authority I have stems from my love of the city and my longevity here and my good fortune in having been present—Forrest Gump–like—at so many public and private events that define the essence of this place.

Some of the stories and anecdotes that these authors repeat may be apocryphal. Especially from the Wilson-Harding-Coolidge-Hoover years, most of the principals have long departed the scene and can't come forward to speak for themselves, deny what was said, or set the record straight. And with each day that passes, and with the loss of even more of the "older generation" of Washingtonians, this is increasingly true. There are fewer and fewer of us who personally remember the FDR years in this town, and Harry Truman and the mark he left on this place. Even Eisenhower's presidency, which I experienced from the vantage point of what I thought of as middle age—I was thirty-five when Ike took office, had been married for thirteen years, and had my four children by then—began nearly a half century ago.

I, in turn, may be adding to Washington mythology by putting many of these stories back into circulation, but in the best spirit of oral and written tradition, some of these stories are just too good not to repeat—whether they are totally true or not.

IN THE very first entry in my mother's diary, back in 1917, she wrote, "The march of events has been much too rapid." That simple sentence holds true for the entirety of my life as well. I believe that the fast pace was exacerbated by living in Washington, and by all the drama that that involved. From my mother, this statement seems more of a lament than something to cheer about. For me, it has always been only the latter. One of the happy results of my backward glance at this city that I love is that, despite all the changes, it reminds me of some of what lasts in Washington, what endures—including society, civility, great men and women (and some colorful rascals), and devotion, respect, and good work.

One of the most interesting and amusing books I found while looking into the city's past was a journal kept by Ellen Maury Slayden—wife of a Texas congressman from 1897 to 1919—and published in 1962 as *Washington Wife*. Mrs. Slayden's wise and witty commentary never ceases to amaze and stimulate me. In one of her journal entries, she wrote, "I am so glad to have spent my life largely where the figures and events of history stir the dullest scene as in . . . Washington, which, if it has little history behind, is at least engaged in the daily manufacture of more." This could easily have been a sentence from the pages of Mother's diary, or from the pages of most of the books excerpted here. The sentiment, so true of that long-ago Washington, remains true of the Washington of today.

What fun I've had with these bits of this historical record of sorts, of a time long gone, people long forgotten or misremembered, and a place, Washington, where the march of events continues at its much too rapid pace, leaving ever more history behind it and still engaging in making more each day.

WASHINGTON OVERVIEW

The Washington experience with its bigness and its novelty ends in a deep, grateful happiness.

—my mother, Agnes Ernst Meyer, from her diary

MOTHER was right: Washington is indeed a big experience. This is a place where novelty is nothing new. As Isabel Anderson, a social light here from 1897 to 1919, wrote in her book, *Presidents and Pies*, "In Washington there is always something new under the sun."

So how does one begin to tackle a topic as big as Washington? My friend Stewart Alsop once wrote that, after years of observing Washington, he "understood why John Gunther had never written *Inside Washington*, although he at one time firmly intended to do so. There are just too many Washingtons to get inside of."

Clearly, this city cannot be reduced to any single dimension. During the New Deal, FDR, as part of the Federal Writers' Project of the Works Progress Administration, set Americans to work writing guides to great American cities. In the guide to the nation's capital, WPA writers made so bold as to speak of "the fundamental fact about Washington." Their "fact" was that Washington "was created for a definite purpose and has been developed, with many modifications, according to a definite plan. Therein lies its unique distinction among American cities, and among all existing capitals in the western world."

All of my experience relating to this place, however, leads me to the conclusion that there is no one "fundamental fact" about Washington. It's not just *one* thing—it's one thing and its opposite at the same time. The contradictions inherent in this place are evident everywhere: it's formal and informal; it's public and private; it's social and political; it's a small town and the capital of the world. It's a city that's a symbol of democracy and yet thoroughly undemocratic, since it remains the only place in America where the people are taxed without

Looking west toward the Washington Monument from one of the arched windows in the Senate wing of the Capitol (1936)

representation in the very bodies that make the policies that govern them.

In Washington, the public and the private intertwine in such a way that they can't be easily separated. This is the city where the personal and the political are most closely linked. Part of the "bigness" that Mother must have had in mind is that this is a town where principles and passions are writ large. The climate here—by which I mean the feel of the place, its heat in a non-meteorological sense—is just right for people who like drama with all its figurative thunder and lightning.

Washington is certainly the best city in the world for someone like me, who thinks that there just is nothing more exciting than news. To me, involvement with news is absolutely inebriating. It's what makes my life exciting. And even if the news doesn't originate here, it's often commented on here, or enlarged here, or explodes here. Something said in Washington comes boomeranging back in an even bigger way.

Washington is more than a place. It's the best example I can point to of the old English-class concept of personification. People say, "Washington knows this . . . thinks this . . . says that," and everyone seems to know what or who is meant.

Frank Carpenter, a syndicated writer and correspondent for the *Cleveland Leader* in Washington in the late 1800s, called this city a "living curiosity, made up of the strangest and most incongruous elements." Henry James called it the "City of Conversation, pure and simple, and positively of the only specimen, of any such intensity, in the world." Others have variously referred to Washington as "Democracy's home town," the "city of magnificent distances," and "at once the most and the least American city in America."

Alice Roosevelt Longworth, the daughter of Teddy Roosevelt and the wife of House Speaker Nicholas Longworth, once wrote about Washington: "Anyway, it is always an entertaining spectacle . . . the show is there for us, and we might as well get what entertainment we may out of it." I certainly have, and most Washington watchers, including the following writers, have, too.

EDWARD G. LOWRY

The Washington Scene

Washington Close-Ups (1921)

I don't know much about Edward Lowry except that he was a friend of my parents. Mother first met Mrs. Lowry at the home of Mrs. Mark Sullivan in November 1921, shortly after his book was published—a book that, at the time of its appearance, created a lot of buzz in Washington. Mother considered Mr. Lowry "very clever" and described him in her diary as "one of the oldest of the Washington newspaper crowd."

Over the next decade or so, Lowry and his wife, Elizabeth, were often guests at our house—both in Washington and in Mount Kisco. In a guest book that my parents kept for a few years, Lowry wrote a little ditty on July 14, 1923: "Rest little booklet rest, bearing this honored name, And may we hear when I come back, 'I'm glad that he has came.' "

What he did in the chapters of Washington Close-Ups, *several of which appeared in magazines and journals of the time, including* The New Republic, Collier's Weekly, *and the* Weekly Review, *was—in Walter Lippmann's words—to "shine the light" on twenty-six of Washington's best and brightest men of that era, and some of the less than best. While his writing is old-fashioned, the portraits he paints of these long-gone (and, in some cases, long-forgotten) public figures are vivid and incisive. No doubt, many were controversial at the time of publication. The chapter on then Vice President Coolidge, for example, is titled "Coolidge: Foster-Child of Silence," and within the first two paragraphs, Lowry describes the VP as "a politician who does not, who will not, who seemingly cannot talk," and says of him, "It appears from the meager record that he thinks of himself as Peter Pan, the boy who never grew up to be a man."*

This selection from Washington Close-Ups *introduces the Washington scene within which all these public figures made their mark.*

AEONS upon aeons agone, when the bat-winged pterodactyl
swooped down relentlessly upon its prey,—I mean to say a long
time ago,—this humid cup in the hills that is now the Washington scene may have been different; it must have been. With that we have
no present concern.

But Washington itself; the Washington of the organic act, of the
Adamses, John and Quincy, of Martin Van Buren, Millard Fillmore,
Rutherford B. Hayes, Benjamin Harrison, William H. Taft, and
Woodrow Wilson, is the Washington of Warren G. Harding. Regard the
eternal changelessness of the two stone legs of King Ozymandias in the
desert of Egypt and attune your mind to the tale I have to tell.

Come with me into Mr. Harding's front yard and let us sit under a
flowering magnolia and leisurely, as becomes the pure in heart and
detached in mind, talk about the familiar apparitions who inhabit these
pleasant walks and tinker with our destiny.

It passes belief how little is known about Washington by the country
at large, and yet no city is more written about. Still, it is hardly ever justly
appraised by the people at home. They seem to see it through a refract-
ing and magnifying haze. New York and Chicago and San Francisco and
St. Louis and New Orleans they know and can justly estimate. They are
visualized clearly, but it is curiously true that almost every newcomer to
Washington and every visitor suffers a sort of stage fright.

O. Henry in one of his stories tells about a cowboy going to New York
and being diffident before New Yorkers, until he discovered they were
people "just like Grover Cleveland and Geronimo and the Watson boys."
No citizen of Danville, Illinois, or Pike County, Missouri, or Springfield,
Massachusetts, would make any average American tongue-tied or step on
his feet with embarrassment. Yet those three places have furnished the
last three Speakers of the House of Representatives, and the Speaker of
the House is a great personage in Washington. Tourists to the Capitol
peer into his room with awe, and nudge one another furtively and say,
"That's him," when they pass him by happy chance in a corridor. Then
they go home and talk about it for days and days.

I do not know why it is that individually the Senators and Representatives and Cabinet members are always so awe-inspiring to their fellow
countrymen, while collectively it has always been the fashion to disparage them. The late Henry Adams was the very greatest of Washington
correspondents, though I should have been afraid so to describe him in
his presence. He spent a lifetime, from Lincoln's administration through
Roosevelt's, looking at the Washington scene with clear eyes and inter-
preting the marionettes with the coolest, most detached mind that has
ever been brought to that occupation. When I used to talk with him in

the latter years of his life I found to my dismay that all of my slowly acquired discoveries he had known since the sixties, and some of them were known to his grandfather before him. Some of his impressions gathered between 1840 and 1869 might have been written to-day looking at the present assemblage here.

It is as true now as it was in President Taylor's administration that Senators are a distinct species, and that continuous service in Congress produces—a Congressman. They have their own easily discernible vocational stigmata. They are a distinct sort of human being and as easily distinguishable, once you know them, as a raw oyster from a cup of tea. The type reproduces with astonishing fidelity, despite the greatest moral, social, and political convulsions.

Our system is so arranged that Congressmen must necessarily spend two thirds of their time making arrangements to endeavor to ensure their reelection. I do not make any outcry against the system, but it is a thing to be pointed out. Six thousand night telegrams properly distributed will agitate Congress like a strong wind blowing over wheat, so sensitive is it to the possible political effect of anything it may do or leave undone.

I remember that President Wilson, who never got on with Washington easily, never fitted into the scene, and, to me, always seemed rather afraid of its allure and subtle charm, once said:

> The city of Washington is in some respects self-contained, and it is easy there to forget what the rest of the United States is thinking about. I count it a fortunate circumstance that almost all the windows of the White House and its offices open upon unoccupied spaces that stretch to the banks of the Potomac and then out into Virginia and on to the heavens themselves, and that as I sit there I can constantly forget Washington and remember the United States. Not that I would intimate that all of the United States lies south of Washington, but there is a serious thing back of my thought. If you think too much about being reelected, it is very difficult to be worth reelecting. You are so apt to forget that the comparatively small number of persons, numerous as they seem to be when they swarm, who come to Washington to ask for things, do not constitute an important proportion of the population of the country, that it is constantly necessary to come away from Washington and renew one's contacts with the people who do not swarm there, who do not ask for anything, but who do trust you without their personal counsel to do your duty. Unless a man gets these contacts he grows weaker and weaker. He needs them as Hercules needed the touch of mother earth. If you lifted him up

too high or he lifts himself too high, he loses the contact and therefore loses the inspiration.

Washington cries aloud to be written about in an intimate, amusing way. It is somehow different from other social settlements on the broad expanse of our continent. The town has a distinctive social life of its own with a flavor and quality slightly tinctured with the modes and manners of "abroad." It has, too, a seductive charm and glamour all its own. The oddity and part of the charm of the Washington condition is just this, that while it has the social framework of a world capital the chief official personages who people the scene are villagers with a villager's outlook and a villager's background. This makes for unexpected ellipses and provides conversation. Henry James called Washington the "City of Conversation": "Washington talks about herself, and about almost nothing else: falling superficially, indeed, on that ground, but into line with the other Capitals. . . . It is in positive quest of an identity of some sort, much rather—an identity other than merely functional and technical—that Washington goes forth, encumbered with no ideal of avoidance or escape: it is about herself as the City of Conversation precisely that she incessantly converses; adorning the topic, moreover, with endless ingenuity and humor. But that, absolutely, remains the case; which thus becomes one of the most thorough, even if probably one of the most natural and of the happiest, cases of collective self-consciousness that one knows."

I couldn't refrain from quoting that bit of rich and experienced condensation and observation because it is precisely the whole story. People take such dreadful risks when they venture to approach or touch a subject that a master has laid a benevolent and passing hand upon, even if ever so lightly and in passing. Henry James stopped with Henry Adams when he was last in Washington. These two are the only men who have ever written about this national capital with a sureness and skill that illumined and interpreted their subject. Many others have been conscious, but, as it proved, vaguely and dimly, of the scene they have sought to portray.

It all comes down to this: Washington is a curious and delightful place; it is so full of the most refreshing and striking contrasts. The capital of a country of a hundred million, and the center of statesmanship, diplomacy, and high politics, its citizens write hot and hasty letters to the powers that be, protesting that hawks devour their Pekin ducks, and that rabbits come after their corn. They argue gravely the constitutionality of their right of defense against these depredations.

Washington is the most feminine of all cities. It has grace and loveliness and many wanton wiles, and, above all, that elusive quality and ors in history in the final examinations at Oxford, stores it all away in his well-disciplined mind, and a German diplomat, who has one hundred dollars in gold concealed in a money belt round his waist in case *der grosse Krach* should begin tomorrow, listens with half an ear and broods on the long train of consequences ensuing from the result of a battle on the north German plain five hundred years ago, in which an early Hohenzollern defeated his very-great grandfather, because the early Hohenzollern had a cannon and the diplomat's very-great grandfather had not.

In the little brothels which dot the city, the madams take counsel with the pimps on the question of what return may be expected from an extra outlay of capital before the tourists arrive for the Washington Bicentennial. In the hotels and embassies and legations, lobbyists from every state in the union and every nation in the world are gathered at the doorstep of the headquarters of representative government, each with his demands in one pocket and his little *apologia pro vita sua* in the other. Some are the boys that make no noise and others give constructive statements to the newspapermen and some will fail and be shamefully exposed and others will become leaders of industry or cabinet ministers or champions of the rights of the people. On Lincoln's Birthday the big movie houses make a special feature of throwing the Gettysburg Address on the screen. The usher at the door wearily tears up the tickets, saying to each ticket holder as he has been taught to say, over and over again, "RKO welcomes you. RKO welcomes you." Travelogue, newsreel, Mickey Mouse, *Spring Symphony* by the orchestra, with color effects, big picture, portrait of Lincoln, "Men will not long remember . . . Shall not perish from this earth." "This is where we came in" . . . and now it is time to see the Washington Monument. One tourist, early American, with long beard and cotton umbrella, had only one hour in Washington, between trains. No movie, no Washington Monument; rather go straight to the headquarters of representative government on Capitol Hill. He went to see his congressman from New York. "You don't know me, but I helped elect you. My four sons and I took off our coats and pitched right in the first time you ran."

"Sit down, sir, sit down. And how are your sons?"

"They're not doing so well now, since we moved to Flatbush."

"Flatbush? You say you live in Flatbush?"

"Yes, and as I was saying, I just have an hour or so in Washington, so . . ."

"Well, Flatbush isn't my district and you're not my constituent any more and I'm sorry I haven't any time to waste, I'm very busy. Good day." The old man walked out with time still in hand to see the Washington Monument. And the representative from the great Empire City of New

attribute that for want of a better name we call charm. Its seductiveness and glamour have drawn many a good, homespun citizen away from the hay, grain, and feed business, where he belonged, into the political morass of office-holders. It has the same effect on small-town people that Cleopatra had on Anthony; it makes them forget their homefolks and have dreams which do not come true.

Politicians are great men in Washington and get their names in the newspapers, and hold their jobs just so long as they remember their home towns. When they forget their origins; when they begin to think of themselves as being "big men" in and of themselves rather than as delegated spokesmen for their constituencies, they wither and die. I often think of Washington as being like a flower show. Nothing grows here, but every community sends what it deems at the moment to be its choicest product. So long as these budding, flowering plants remember that their tap-root is in Augusta, Maine; or Terre Haute; or Red Oak, Iowa; or Tuscaloosa, Alabama, and must be watered and nourished there, they thrive; but when they forget it, they become just cut flowers and their end is at hand.

So in this scene life proceeds from one crisis to another. But do not despair of the Republic. The only thing one can be sure about in a crisis or situation or condition at Washington is that it is not unprecedented; it has happened before. Washington cannot be seen intelligently or to any effect without a background. It produces crises and periods of welter and confusion in such regularly recurring cycles as to be almost susceptible to the formulation of a law of natural phenomena. Certainly the sons and descendants of Jeremiah have rended their garments, beat their breasts, and made loud lamentation before the Capitol and the White House after each of our war periods. They sat about in bewilderment as they sit now, and will again, saying to one another, "Was there ever such an extraordinary situation? Was there ever such another mess as we find ourselves in now? Was there ever such another set of dolts, knaves, and incompetents in command of our destinies?" The answer is: There was. This is not the first time that the wind has moaned through the rigging.

30–32

City of Magnificent Intentions

High Low Washington (1932)

30–32 was the chosen byline for two writers who, for reasons unknown to me, wanted to remain anonymous—or who wanted to be much talked about (as were Drew Pearson and Robert S. Allen, when they published Washington Merry-Go-Round *anonymously in 1931, the year before* High Low Washington*). The only clue to the authors' identity that the publisher gives is a paragraph facing the title page that is more like a blurb than an author's note. It reads, "Two writers of unique experience both in Europe and America here present the last word on the national capital."*

Whoever these two men were, there is evidence throughout that they were journalists. The whole book has the contemporary feel of two knowledgeable men discussing Washington issues out loud, commenting on then-current events, and deciding to share their thinking.

The picture of Washington that emerges is an insightful one, and farsighted as well. In "Grand Old Parties," the authors indicate that the tradition of being either Republican or Democratic is "tending more and more to fall into obsolescence." Such a simple sentence as "The election of a President is always to some extent a confession on the part of the public of its hopes and beliefs" is lovely and perceptive. The authors talk about their period as one of "economic revolution" and note the irony of history in Hoover's taking office when he did, when his political philosophy was so at odds with reality: "At the best, all that remained of it was a sort of dimly mystical ideal unsupported by any discernible body of facts, like a grin without a Cheshire Cat."

This excerpt, from High Low Washington*'s introductory chapter, takes its title from an old description of Washington as the "City of Magnificent Distances," which Charles Dickens suggested should be amended to "City of Magnificent Intentions." There seems to me nothing very bad about a nation's capital having good intentions—and when the intentions are magnificent, so much the better.*

LIKE VERSAILLES and Angora [Ankara] and Canberra and Potsdam, Washington is the product of a deliberate plan. But unlike Versailles and Potsdam, it is still in the business for which it was originally designed, and unlike Angora and Canberra, it is old enough to have been subjected to a series of historical upheavals not foreseen by its founders. Thus architecturally and politically too, it presents today, as Vienna does and London does, the spectacle of a stage production in which, by some extraordinary pressure of haste or by negligence on the part of the stage hands, scenery and properties from all the previous acts of a long and varied drama are found to have been left standing unremoved as the curtain rises on the latest scene. More confusing still, a number of characters from earlier acts seem to have been left on the stage too, there to wander about, tripping over the unaccustomed properties, interjecting unrehearsed and unsuitable lines, interfering with and often obscuring altogether the actors properly cast to play the leading roles in this particular phase of the drama.

In a red house on Massachusetts Avenue, near one of the *ronds points* designed by Major L'Enfant to prevent revolutionary mobs from erecting barricades in the streets, the unofficial representatives of the unrecognized Soviet Union are conferring in a room dominated by a bust of Lenin with the representatives of the General Motors Company. On the table a clipping from the *Automobile Engineer* announces that the newest machine for cutting steel parts for automobiles, invented in the United States by American technicians, has had to be shipped to Russia because that is the only place where the demand is likely to be large enough to permit economical operation of this machine of vast capacity. Around the corner, at one of the only two fashionable night clubs in town (the other is patronized exclusively by the negro smart set) the white débutantes are dancing, balancing the uncertain social prestige and dubious sexual tastes of the European upper classes against the moneyed present and doubtful future of the native Americans. Some achieve prominence by actually witnessing a gang shooting. Gang war in Washington, my dear, how thrilling! And Mr. Tompkins actually saw Capone; my dear, how too thrilling! And undeterred on a neighboring hilltop, Mrs. Borden Harriman continues to conduct her political salon where Democratic bankers and Republican government officials, with authentic period senators, guaranteed genuine unrestored products from the Jefferson period, Bryan period, trust-busting period, are earnestly discussing the effect of the unemployment problem on the Presidential election. Will the unemployed vote Republican? Or will they possibly vote Democrat? It is agreed that anything may happen, and a British diplomat, first-class hon-

York, nerve center of the western world, financial capital of the richest nation on earth, had time to go on with his dictation. For like Lourdes, Washington is full of pilgrims with a purpose seeking cures for their political and economic afflictions. As at Lourdes they are often disappointed. And as at Lourdes they keep on coming. No piece of land in the world, except the island of Manhattan, is so full of immigrants as the city of magnificent distances. There are the visitors for pleasure and the visitors for profit and there is the whole army of the bureaucracy recruited by civil service examination from all over the United States. The personnel of this army have no political power and they have no money. Some of them, arriving full of enthusiasm at the nation's capital, sit down at the heart of men and things and type and type and type till thirty years of typing bring a pension. Except when they commit suicide or shoot their husbands their names do not appear in the newspapers. Others, safe in the happy obscurity of governmental laboratories, are busy conducting researches which, as the whirligig of time soon or late brings in its revenges, are observed to exercise a more revolutionary effect upon the economic and political destiny of America and the world than all the financial juggleries of the bankers, all the memoranda of the diplomats, and all the laws voted on Capitol Hill. If it had not been for certain tests of steel and concrete carried out in the Ordnance Department and in the Bureau of Standards in discovering new and more efficient methods of standardizing the multifarious products of American industry before the industries of other nations did the same thing, there might never have been any boom in the nineteen twenties.

Between one end of the scale and the other there are thousands of government workers whose work is a good deal more than routine and a good deal less than revolutionary. The cheap apartment houses and boarding houses all over the city are full of them and at five in the afternoon the street cars bulge with them as the subways of New York bulge with the workers of Wall Street. Some are there because there is nothing else that they can do, and most because, at least when they were young, to be in the government service was what they wanted. The pay starts very low and the prospects never rise very high. So what? So despite our "business civilization," to scores of thousands of people a government clerkship in Washington is more desirable than a broker's clerkship in Wall Street or La Salle Street, or a job with a real estate office in Wichita or Cedar Rapids. It seems to them a nicer way to live. For though some people call it a racket and some call it a dead end, there are people, especially in the Middle West—that breeding ground of simple enthusiasms and extravagant ideals—who grow up with a picture of a Washington possessing some of the qualities of Plato's *Republic*; a place where a person can work to good purpose in the service of the state and employ leisure delightfully. The lectures at George Washington University are thronged at evening with the government workers, and at night the streets of the capital are lined with their ramshackle flivvers, for those of them that can afford automobiles cannot afford garages too. Some, when their work is over, illegally stick "For Hire" signs on their windscreens and ply as taxis. They skim the dinner-hour trade and the theater trade and the supper trade, and enrage the regular taxi drivers, who have already been reduced to penury by the frenzied rate-cutting of competing automobile companies scrambling for the profits of the taxi business in the City of Magnificent Distances. Charles Dickens, most eminent and disgruntled of all the eminent and disgruntled Englishmen who have visited the city, suggested the title be corrected to "City of Magnificent Intentions." Since his day a good many of the intentions, magnificent and otherwise, have been realized. Some have been thwarted, perhaps permanently, perhaps only for a hundred years or so, by the real estate operators who, in an age when it was supposed possible for a government to plan a city successfully without controlling the price of real estate, managed to keep the price of land in the neighborhood of Capitol Hill so high that the place was left deserted and the residential district grew up in the northwest district instead. The real estate men overstayed their market, and the surroundings of the Capitol, intended to be so fine, are today squalid and disorderly. One of the few cities in the world entirely devoted to government, it is one of the few in the world and the only city in America entirely dominated by its public buildings. Since governmental architecture always lags a long way behind political history, they tend outwardly to suggest monuments to the memories of vanished institutions rather than the places of business of a going concern, a series of vivid but slightly incoherent historical reminiscences recounted in stone and marble to the America of the nineteen thirties. In the midst of it all is the White House, its pillared façade a model of Jeffersonian dignity admirably suited to the days when the tobacco lands on the other side of the Potomac, subsequently ruined by over-exploitation for quick profit, were dotted with similar housings for gentlefolk. Kisch, that irreverent little person from Prague who came and looked at it in 1928, described it as a sort of Tusculum "as though made for the dalliance of a charming Roman youth and his Lavinia." In one part of its cellars are still lying the remains of the charred beams left there by Admiral Cockburn in 1814 when he burned the place to the ground and thus contributed his simple effort to the history of Anglo-American relations. In another, only a few yards away, stands the loudspeaker through which, at the beginning of 1930, the President of the United States heard for the first time the voice of the King of England expressing his hopes for the success of the International Conference on Naval Disarmament. Upstairs in the executive offices (artificially cooled in summer by General Electric system), one of the President's secretaries is at work on a speech of which the keynote is to be an appeal to American individualism, while all around the tourists, arriving in motorcars produced en masse at Detroit and clad in suits produced en masse at New York, are taking snapshots with cameras produced en masse at Rochester. And in the President's office sits Wilson or Harding or Coolidge or Hoover or Franklin Roosevelt. It makes some difference which, it makes in many respects a big difference, but never a difference big enough to solve or obscure the continuing basic paradox of a man's situation who for one reason or another has been put in charge of a piece of governmental machinery designed to carry out the purposes of the American ruling classes of the eighteenth century, with the understanding that he shall use it to bring satisfaction and prosperity to the classes dominant on this continent one hundred and fifty years later. Wilson and Hoover, each after his fashion, was conscious of this fundamental and ineluctable dilemma, and each tried to do, as the saying is, something about it. Wilson lost his health at the job and Hoover lost his reputation. Harding managed to pass through and out without much idea of what it was all about anyway. And Coolidge, who realized better than his supporters that a capacity for not rocking the boat is something different from seamanship, was safe ashore in the insurance business before the rapids began, and is today much admired by many. Like some other leaders during the boom period, he resembled that young man in the story whose behavior exemplified the valuable quality of presence of mind. When fire broke out in the theater, he sprang to his feet and in loud clear tones assured the uneasy audience that there was no danger whatsoever, they should keep their places and avoid at all costs panic and stampede. Impressed by his calm and his air of authority, they resumed their seats, with the result that the sagacious young man was able to reach the exit unimpeded before the roof caved in on their heads.

JAY FRANKLIN

Main Street-on-Potomac

Vanity Fair (1933)

For some reason, I had this March 1933 issue of Vanity Fair *on my shelves. I can only guess at why my parents saved it over the years; certainly, in 1933, as a high school junior, I wasn't the one reading Vanity Fair on a regular basis. Mother may have saved this particular issue because it includes a photographic portrait of Fritz Kreisler, "the music master," who was her paragon for my sister Bis's "fiddle-playing." Or she may have wanted to keep the caricature drawing and word portrait of her friend Oliver Wendell Holmes, "first citizen of the land," who had recently resigned after thirty years of service on the Supreme Court. It seems more likely that Dad may have kept this issue to read Milton Mayer's affecting piece on "Moving day at the White House," recounting the importance of March 4, which back then was when, every fourth year ("or, at the most, every eighth"), "the United States of America changes hands." The Mayer article was accompanied by a two-page print by Miguel Covarrubias of the most important personages involved in the inauguration of FDR—which, by the way, was for sale by* Vanity Fair *for a mere dollar.*

What struck me most in the issue was Jay Franklin's vision of Washington as a "political village." He seems to have been what we would now call a "frequent contributor" to Vanity Fair, *often writing on Washington and on political issues that were naturally centered in Washington. Here he gives us his take on "the home city of our political Babbittry where cliques and cocktails dominate the social scene."*

WASHINGTON is a political village which has become a world capital, without becoming a metropolis. This is what gives it a peculiar charm, at the same time that it inflicts innumerable annoyances upon its inhabitants. It is both representative of America as a whole and unlike anything else in the United States. Its climate in summer is sub-tropical to the point of danger; in winter, it is cold and damp.

Its population is half political and half Negro, intersected by Sinclair Lewis's Main Street and dotted with Booth Tarkington's small Indiana towns, with a liberal seasoning of suave diplomats, self-important administrative officials, hordes of government clerks, and the bull-voiced, fishy-mouthed tribe of professional politicians and lobbyists. It is the only community in a nation which was founded on the theory that taxation without representation is tyranny which has no voice in its own government and is taxed—and heavily taxed—without its consent.

More people inhabit the District of Columbia than live in Arizona, Delaware, Idaho, Nevada, New Hampshire, New Mexico, Utah, Vermont, or Wyoming, yet this population not only goes without representation in the federal government but has no voice in managing its own affairs. However, the District takes it all calmly in view of the fact that nearly a third of the population is Negro and that it would be difficult to set up a Jim Crow government in the national capital. As a result, the whole city functions on a live-and-let-live basis, with what was until recently one of the least efficient police forces in the country and with a tax-rate which reflects the lively desire of Congress to make the District pay for the most elaborate system of public parks in the country, for the benefit of visiting constituents.

This situation lends both dignity and flavor to the life of Washington, but what gives the city its distinctive touch is the fact that politics and not money is the main interest of its inhabitants. This difference is so subtle that it is not at first realized, especially since money and politics both represent a form of power. There are plenty of millionaires in Washington, for this is the town which harbors the successful pork-packers, oil-men and *nouveaux riches* who have enough sense to realize that they wouldn't make the grade on Park Avenue or in Mayfair. But it is true that money does not matter much in the capital. A man with political brains or political power may be as poor as Borah or as bumptious as Brookhart, yet he will achieve general recognition in this republican encampment. The poor man—or more accurately speaking—the man of modest means gets a better break in Washington than anywhere else this side of the Seine. Here poverty is no disgrace and even political defeat—which is the equivalent of bankruptcy in the financial world—is no permanent handicap. For a man may be out in politics but he is never down until the daisies are nodding their heads above his grave.

THIS IN TURN means that Washington is a city of homes. The federal payroll is the greatest local industry, and the federal payroll is carefully designed to give the lowest average salary to the largest possible number of people. Seventy-two thousand civil service employees in the District of

Columbia, paid on a scale which regards $3,600 a year as a good salary, are bound to live a quiet life at home. The city consists of small, partially purchased houses, equipped with radios, automobiles, automatic furnaces, electric ice-boxes, wives, beds, and large numbers of small children. There is not much room for social life, after the monthly bills are paid, and a trip to the movies or a visit to the ball park represents the upper limits of the intellectual life of the great mass of the Washingtonians.

As a result, the city is conspicuously lacking in what might be described as intelligentsia. Interest in literature, art, music, and the world of ideas—except for political schemes—is practically non-existent. There is a small group composed chiefly of newspaper correspondents, who live in Georgetown and aspire to create a sort of Greenwich Village or synthetic *rive gauche* on the right bank of Rock Creek, but hitherto they have failed to produce anything but malicious gossip and political muckracketeering. The only indigenous magazine of any pretensions has failed and the Washington newspapers are, with the exception of the *Evening Star*, beneath contempt.* Outside of a couple of mangy dance-restaurants and a flock of seventh-rate speakeasies, Washington's night-life is conspicuous by its absence, and the profession of illicit amour is largely confined to a few kept ladies and to colored girls in back-alleys.

The other side of Washington's home-life is rather more creditable. There is still a tradition of entertaining. Thanks to a superb system of bootlegging, it is possible to get excellent Maryland rye whiskey and peach brandy in your own home at a reasonable rate. The grain alcohol trade is brisk and a small outlay enables the average man to reproduce the essential features of genteel exhilaration at low cost. Cocktails, highballs, and mint-juleps predominate, except in Embassy circles, where Scotch and soda, cordials, and champagne assuage the thirsty. In consequence, Washington offers a maximum of pleasantly lubricated personal contacts, friendships, and conversation. Where you can live for years in a city like New York or Chicago and, unless you have a large income or are socially registered, have only a handful of friends, in Washington you can accumulate an almost embarrassing number of intimate acquaintances. You live at what is, possibly, a low mental plane, in which good food, drink, gossip, and exercise loom bigger than sonnets, the Theatre Guild, the Five-Year Plan, and the importance of Harlem's nightlife.

Unfortunately, these Washington friendships exist under the curse of impermanence. The normal administrative and political turnover in the District is high, and in time of elections becomes almost catastrophic. All diplomats, State Department officials, Army and Navy officers live under

---

*This was three months before my father bought the *Post*.

the sword of Damocles in the shape of a transfer. Three or four years is, generally speaking, the limit of a period of assignment to the capital. Politicians are likely to be defeated and officials have a habit of resigning to accept better paid jobs in time of prosperity or of being discharged in time of depression. Hence there is a continual coming and going, in every part of Washington's society. One year your best friend may be sent to Tegucigalpa or to the Presidio or to his ship. Your pet Congressman may run foul of the liquor issue and your favorite Senator may get tangled up in a roraback* or spite campaign. Your charming friend in the Polish Embassy may be transferred to the Legation at The Hague or to the Foreign Office at Warsaw. The man who has sat across the desk from you for four years may suddenly announce that he has taken a position with the National City Bank and the man in the next room may have his job amputated as a result of that terrible disease known to bureaucrats as contraction of the budget.

For example, four years ago the social activities of the State Department were dominated by a group of worldly, hard-drinking, clever young snobs, who went everywhere and knew everybody. Today they have vanished like the host of Sennacherib and an entirely different group, both inside and outside of the department, has replaced them at the dinnertables and cocktail shakers of the capital. Every Representative and Senator who came up for reelection this autumn faced so serious a risk of defeat, that today the flock of lame ducks in Congress is the largest in history. The need for drastic economy in administration threatens to decimate the official ranks of the Army and the Navy, while the Civil Service Commission is working up a list of political appointments, the spoils of Democratic Victory.

As a result of all this, Washington is a city of cliques. Despite all of the friendliness and all of the ease of society in the District, the tendency is for every man to stick to his game and to make his friendships count in the circles where it will help his career. So the Army goes around with the Army, the Navy sticks to the Navy, the various government departments have their various little sets and circles—Agriculture, Commerce, Treasury, all the way down to the Federal Trade Commission and the Shipping Board. Even the members of the Prohibition Unit of the Department of Justice take pleasure in each other's company and there is,

*This is one of those great eponymous words, more commonly spelled roorback or roorbach, and meaning (according to the *Random House Dictionary of the English Language*): "a false and more or less damaging report circulated for political effect." It derives from Baron Van Roorback, "pretended traveler in whose alleged book of his experiences in the U.S. occurred an account of an incident damaging to the character of James K. Polk."

no doubt, the liveliest camaraderie among the personnel of the Light-house Inspection Service and the Public Health Service. Representatives flock with Representatives, Senators with Senators, and the Diplomatic Corps spend a great part of their time buzzing around with each other. Except in the highest reaches of officialdom, the Cabinet members and the Ambassadors of the Big Powers, there is little osmotic mingling of the liquor-tight little compartments into which the city is divided. When you consider that the wife of a Congressman is expected to pay about 434 calls on the wives of her husband's colleagues, and that they all call on the same day, you will realize that there are difficulties involved in reaching out of your own circle in the capital.

One exception to this rule is found among the lobbyists. Washington is the home of causes, lost or otherwise. There is no business of any importance which does not find it expedient to keep or to put a man on the spot. There is no moral spasm so absurd as not to rate Washington headquarters of some sort. These range all the way from the United States Chamber of Commerce and the Federation of Labor down to the Anti-Saloon League, the Methodist Board of Temperance, Prohibition and Public Morals, and the Women's League for Peace and Freedom, of which it has been said that the men get peace and the women freedom. Pacifists, veterans, the "Power Trust," the banks, the brokers, the Manu-facturers Association, the "wets" and the "drys," the pleaders for a single tax, the pink economists of the Brookings Institute, the rag-tag and bob-tail of a great country which thinks it can get anything by asking for it, all circulate, undulate, ooze, and perambulate throughout the city. Now they rush up to Congress with a petition, now they slip into a govern-ment bureau with a request, sometimes they walk into political head-quarters with a few weighty remarks about the difficulty of getting campaign funds unless—sometimes they threaten Congress or the Presi-dent with masses of phantom or only too existent voters.

And finally there are the journalists, who still labor under the impres-sion that the typewriter is mightier than the ballot-box and the headline more than the cheque book. They scamper around, weighted down with mimeographed hand-outs, burdened with personal friendships, cramped by editorial policies, and they grind out, day by day, year by year, the mass of dull and misleading information, facts and opinions, which has made Washington journalism conspicuous for its irresponsible and stupefying inertia even in an age when the entire press is becoming a device to enable advertisers to peddle their goods. A few exceptions, such as Paul Anderson, Ray Tucker, Elliot Thurston, Arthur Krock and the vehemently independent Bill Hard and the vindictive little coterie of Washington Merry-Go-Rounders cannot atone for the soggy and unsalubrious character of Washington journalism. For the plain fact is that the correspondents have swallowed Washington whole and have watched the country plunge into one political crisis after another without a sustained or intelligent note of journalistic warning from the men who think that the freedom of the press can survive in an era of chain newspapers, tons of official data, and high-pressure advertising.

The result is a city like nothing else in these rather Disunited States—the pleasantest small town in America and the most immature of world capitals: a government which denies to its capital the fundamental assumption of American politics, a population which doesn't care, a city which lives by the federal payroll and understands politics as some people understand the stock market, a community of homes, of limited intellectual range, with a sound taste in liquor and seafood and horses, a knack for friendliness and hospitality, and practically no knowledge of what it is all about, how we got that way, or where we are going. Main Street enshrined on the Potomac, Middletown surrounded by public monuments, politicians, and the vilest climate on the Atlantic seaboard. That's Washington—the spot where the accident usually occurs, but what of it?

Natural Setting

The WPA Guide to Washington (1942)

A promise of the New Deal was putting people back to work. One revolutionary way FDR did this was to create jobs for thousands of people, by paying them with public federal dollars. For the first few years of its existence, the Works Progress Administration (later called the Work Projects Administration) was headed by Roosevelt's friend and adviser Harry Hopkins. Most prominent among the WPA's projects in the arts were the Federal Art Project, the Federal Music Project, the Federal Theatre Project, and the Federal Writers' Project, the last of which hired out-of-work writers and white-collar professionals to create a series of guidebooks to American states, regions, and individual cities and towns. Known as the American Guide series, these books—nearly four hundred of which were created—are still in demand today, more for their historical significance than for their practical guidance to any particular town or region. The guidebooks had the added advantage at the time of helping to promote patriotism as well as travel and tourism.

Like the other WPA guidebooks in the series, this one on Washington covered the waterfront—from the city's history to a special section on "The Negro in Washington." Within the introductory pages, the authors wrote, "The natural situation of Washington has dignity, distinction, and beauty." When it comes to Washington, most people tend to think first of politics. But Washington is also a geographic and physical place. It is, for instance, one of the few cities of the world where you can talk endlessly about trees. It is a city filled with trees, and I've been fortunate that the house I've lived in for nearly fifty-five years has enough land surrounding it to support a number of them. From the Jackson magnolia at the White House to the flowering cherry tree that my son Don gave me recently for my front yard, I love the trees of Washington.

One doesn't soon forget the natural beauty of Washington, although those of us who live here do sometimes take it for granted. This excerpt from the WPA guide to Washington is strangely evocative of the natural beauty of the place. I myself have reveled in the "sheer beauty" of Washington for more than eighty years, and continue to do so today.

V IEWED from the air or from the top of the Washington Monument on a clear day, salient topographical features of the District stand out: to the south, the Potomac, nearly a mile wide at this point, low marshy lands along its borders; the Anacostia River to the south and east, edged by reclaimed flats; the Potomac Parks and, across the river, Washington National Airport, on filled-in swamp-lands; the artificially created Tidal Basin; Rock Creek winding down through magnificent scenery from the northwestern plateau region; and a gentle roll of hills encircling the city to the north. Wooded suburban areas, parks, and tree-lined avenues merge softly with each other in a seemingly continuous mass of vegetation. . . .

The edges of four different zones of plant and animal life extend over the District and its environs, giving the area a singularly abundant and varied wildlife. There are approximately 1,800 varieties of flowering plants and 250 different native shrubs and trees; more than 300 varieties of birds, 94 of fishes, and 68 amphibians.

Washington's thousands of trees, though many of them are native, probably include a higher percentage of exotics than those of any other American city. Many a Government official traveling abroad has contributed to the number of introduced specimens, but most exotics have been provided by Federal plant introduction agencies. The best known exotics are the Japanese cherry trees, around the Tidal Basin. In any event, whether native or introduced, the trees intercept, with green aisles and arches, and intervals of shade, the hard white light reflected from limitless façades of stone.

Although L'Enfant's original sketches included plans for tree planting, little attention was paid to this or to the preservation of natural groves until the beginning of the nineteenth century. Thomas Jefferson, while President, was outraged by the cutting of trees on the Mall, and did much to save and restore the natural beauty of the city. He planted Lombardy poplars, because of their "most sudden growth," along Pennsylvania Avenue, and often gathered and planted seeds and seedlings in other spots. In 1815, the city made its first appropriation expressly for trees, stipulating 400 English elms to replace the poplars along Pennsylvania Avenue. These, in turn, were replaced by lindens, oaks, maples, sycamores, and other varieties.

Until the middle of the century, small appropriations were made annually for tree planting, and Washington began to be known as one of the few capitals of the world distinguished for sylvan beauty. No really important step, however, was taken after Jefferson's time until about 1872, when the first systematic municipal tree planting was begun under Alexander R. Shepherd.

Many native shade trees may be seen at their best in the parks, squares, and gardens of Washington, and along the principal streets. American elms on Q Street, New Hampshire and New Jersey Avenues, around the Ellipse and Lafayette Square, and arching over several sections of New York Avenue; sycamores on Florida Avenue and approaching the White House; the pin oak and red oak, colorful in all seasons, along upper Connecticut Avenue and on Pennsylvania Avenue, S.E.; Massachusetts Avenue's American lindens; and old willows around Hains Point and by the Potomac.

The Oriental ginkgo, found in innumerable places, dates back farther than any other tree. With its fan-shaped leaves and gesturing branches, it is scarcely changed from what it was in the age of the dinosaurs. Ginkgos are planted along Lafayette Square, 5th Street, 14th Street, and elsewhere. Other exotics are the ailanthus, acacia, locust, cedar of Lebanon, European elm, willow, hornbeam, holly, and linden, and the Asiatic magnolia, in the wood between the Tidal Basin and the Lincoln Memorial. The Japanese Paulownia, with lilac blossoms, is naturalized throughout the region and, likewise, the Chinese scholar or pagoda tree, with greenish-yellow flowers.

There are several varieties of magnolia, perhaps the handsomest being the great-flowered, with lustrous dark leaves and large lemon-scented ivory blossoms. This tree is in flower late into the summer in Lafayette Park, the Cathedral Close, the grounds of the Department of Agriculture, around the Capitol and other public buildings, and in many private gardens. Another and smaller magnolia blooms in early spring even before it is in leaf.

The squat Camperdown elms in Thomas Circle and a great copper beech in Lafayette Park are of unusual interest. Over Lafayette Park's 7 acres are planted 97 varieties of trees, including spruce, fir, basswood, hornbeam, redwood, bronze beech, magnolia, cherry, ash, holly, yellow-wood, yew, Japanese cryptomeria, the Paulownia, sawtooth zelkova, and bald cypress.

Evergreens are numerous: American holly, of which there are fine stands in the Capitol Grounds, in Cathedral Close, and at St. Elizabeth's Hospital; boxwood, around the Supreme Court and the Lincoln Memorial; English yew, in Meridian Hill Park, the White House grounds, and Grant Circle; and Irish yew in the grounds around the Smithsonian Institution and the White House, and in two groupings in front of the lodge in Lafayette Park.

Dogwood in profuse bloom, especially in Rock Creek Park, is one of the sights of the Capitol, rivaling the cherry blossoms around the Tidal Basin and at Hains Point. The native wild-crab flowers along the sea-wall drive, and fragrant native honeysuckle covers uncared-for areas in an almost tropical tangle.

In Rock Creek Park, along the Potomac trails, and in other wooded areas, all the native species are represented and many naturalized ones, such as the Paulownia and white-flowered black locust. In Rock Creek Park alone, 63 out of 66 kinds of trees are native. The soaring black walnut with its bright green crown of leaves, the ample sycamore, the basswood, cottonwood, pignut, willow and various oaks, beeches, and pines, make the splendor of these groves, with honeylocust, wild-crab, dogwood, and hawthorn flowering among them.

The trees of the District contribute a bright procession of flowers, beginning with those which bloom before or with the leaves, like the early magnolia, dogwood, white June-berry, and the exquisite Judas-tree. The red cedar, golden with catkins in early spring, the red and silver maple, white ash, and boxelder, the fragrant linden and white-flowered locust, the Paulownia in purple panicles, the catalpa, horse-chestnut, and persimmon, and the tuliptree with greenish-yellow flowers, are conspicuous. . . .

Among the birds, Washington's three most conspicuous specimens are all introduced—the pigeons, loved and fed by many habitués of the city's parks; the ragamuffin English sparrow; and chattering hordes of starlings (both of the latter species, the English say, were well-behaved before they left home). Rock Creek Park, in addition to being a natural woodland well suited as a habitation for native birds, draws an additional increment of bird-dwellers through a strange, but apparent, feeling of kinship for the captive birds in Rock Creek Zoo. Seagulls wheel gracefully about the water front. To the waterfowl sanctuaries at Roaches Run, Rock Creek and elsewhere, come gallinules, herons, bitterns, coots, egrets, sandhill cranes, and numerous ducks and geese. The District is generally the habitat for songbirds native to the region.

Washington's greatest panhandlers, the gray squirrels, have adapted themselves to a sleek and lucrative existence, garnering peanuts begged from park-bench people, and nesting comfortably in large-boled trees. Cottontail rabbits survive on the lawns and in the hedges of suburban Washington having apparently learned the nuances of escape from neighborhood dogs. There are numerous chipmunks, a few opossums, and an occasional skunk. The remaining small mammals of the District come mostly in the class for which traps are set at night.

JOHN DOS PASSOS

Washington Evening

State of the Nation (1943)

WALT WHITMAN, during the Civil War, wrote about being in Washing-
ton and what he saw. In Specimen Days, *he wrote, "The White House*
by moonlight: the White House of future poems, and of dreams and dra-
mas, there in the soft and copious moon . . . the White House of the
land, and of beauty and night—sentries at the gates, and by the por-
tico, silent, pacing there in blue overcoats. . . . To-night I have been
wandering awhile in the Capitol, which is all lit up. The illuminated
rotunda looks fine. I like to stand aside and look a long, long while, up
at the dome; it comforts me somehow."

John Dos Passos, twenty years shy of a century later, came to Wash-
ington and wrote about the city in an equally beautiful and personal
way. This excerpt evokes the city in another wartime. There is a palpa-
ble sense of immediacy and reality. Henry James once said, "Summer
afternoon, summer afternoon; to me, those have always been the two
most beautiful words in the English language." I think that the two
words "Washington Evening" rank right up there for the beauty they
bring to mind.

FOR THE first time in my life I was finding Washington beautiful.
On a hot afternoon in June I was sitting on a bench in the backyard
of one of the houses built on the edge of the low house-crowded
ridge that cuts across the northwest section of Washington to form the
rim of the shallow bowl in which the downtown city stews. The grass in
the sloping yard was very green. The sky over the rooftops in front of us
was very blue. A few big tattered white clouds shaded at the base stood
motionless in the midst of it.

When I was a very small child I used to hear my elders talk about the
beauty of Washington and never could figure it out. There had been, to
my infant mind, a certain cozy dilapidation about Georgetown, vine-
grown brick walling in the little lives of elderly female relatives sitting in
parlors behind drawn shades; there'd been the stately degradation of

Alexandria, "the deserted city," as the colored people used to call it; there'd been Rock Creek and the false feeling of being in the mountains it gave you, and green swampy meadows and the haze over the mud-colored Potomac. My parents used to talk about the beauty of Washington. To me it had seemed stifling and hideous. Now I was discovering that I was old enough to find Washington beautiful. Or maybe it was the city that had got old enough.

The old Washingtonian who was sitting beside me on the bench was working as a checker on the street cars. He'd never done a job of that kind before, but he was enjoying the work. He liked the idea that he was being useful in the war effort. As we looked out at the grassy yard and the ailanthus trees and the nondescript bushes along the fences and the backs of brick buildings, he told me with cheery enthusiasm about his days standing on street corners or in the flailing sun on traffic islands, noting the times the cars passed and the number of people in them.

Sizing up the number of people in a car at a glance was a trick it took some time to learn. The work made him feel busy, useful, and in an odd way, free. He was enjoying the life of the streets, the varieties of people he saw, the change in personnel as the day wore on: the early workers less well-dressed, the old-fashioned American mechanics who worked at the Navy Yard or the Bureau of Printing, the floodtide of office workers between eight and nine, the housewives going shopping, the school kids, the random specimens in the afternoon, fashion plates from embassies, tourists, soldiers and sailors on leave, young women going to the movies s; the great flood of tired heat-wilted clerks struggling to get home five and six; the evening life of the town; people in fresh clothes ose, city-sized crowds in search of places to eat, in search of ses they could find a seat in, cocktail bars they could get a table so drink beer, aimlessly, hopelessly roaming about in what was bely overgrown small Southern town in a stagnant hollow Potomac River and Anacostia Creek.

a wh came home at night, often very late, my friend said he'd sit dampn is bench smelling the rankness of wilted leaves that the neighin ught out from the heat-trampled vegetation, listening to with men out of darkened windows, girls' voices making fake dates all, this wa g men's voices yodeling that they'd be right over. After

We deci itially a town of lonely people.
fragment of a go downtown to eat supper at Hall's to renew a torn foliage against llection that lingered in my mind—of the shadow of tains in embroit brick, and curlicued gilt mirrors, and tow-boat cap-against a black wa ed suspenders drinking beer in their shirtsleeves
t bar, and powdered necks of blowzy women, and of

a great-aunt of mine, a lame old lady in her seventies who wore a black silk dress with a lace yoke and used to like to shock her daughters by saying that her idea of heaven was sitting in Hall's beer-garden eating deviled crabs and drinking beer on a Sunday afternoon.

We walked out through the lodging-house, a big old place that had been a family mansion not so long ago, now partitioned off into small cubicles where lived a pack of young men and women clerks, most of them in government jobs. The house was clean but it had the feeling of too many people breathing the same air, of strangers stirring behind flimsy walls, of unseen bedsprings creaking, and unseen feet shuffling in cramped space, a feeling of private lives huddled lonesome and crowded. As we walked out the front door it occurred to us that it might be in Washington that the Greenwich Village of this war would come into being. Around the period of the last war it had been in the slums of downtown New York that young Americans, fresh from the uneventful comfort of one-family homes in small towns, had holed up like greenhorn immigrants in sleazy lodging-houses to get their first taste of a metropolis. In this war it might be in Washington. Maybe Washington was a metropolis in the making. . . .

WE WALKED, sweating prodigiously, clear on down to the river. There we found a heat-wilted crowd of men in shirtsleeves and girls in light dresses filing up the gangplank of a rusty old excursion steamer. We walked out to the edge of the wharf to look at her. There was a faint freshness off the water but no breeze. Out on the greenish brown stream the sails of some little racing boats hung limp. The trees across the water were oozing intense green as the day drowned in hot pearly haze. In west the haze was flushed with sunset.

We both had recollections of Potomac wharves. We stood a whi the edge of the piling beside the excursion boat talking about the when people in Washington used to buy oysters right off the sch at two dollars a barrel.

Talking about this old river life, remembering the cranky whe the ragged Negroes who sold steamed crabs and the shaggy lark from Tangier Island with tobacco in their cheeks and all as a Twain's world I used to scurry through with my heart in mon how child because it was so rough and rank and noisy, and excla ept away the old dilapidated coal wharves and oyster wharves had b ers and the and with them the bugeyes and the white Chesapeake sch and crab-old colored men sculling skiffs and the stench of rotti as as I remem-shells and flies, we walked up the street to Hall's. Hall m the street by a bered it; the bar was there, and the garden fenced off f wooden paling, and the gaslit look of green trees against red brick. We walked past the great painting of a very undressed looking Adam and Eve being told to get out of the park, it's closing time, by a rosy and ineffectual angel and settled down in the yard to eat deviled crabs and drink beer. Across the frame for the awning over our heads yellow cats scampered back and forth and snarled at each other and caterwauled. . . .

BY THE TIME we had finished our cheese and washed it down with a last glass of beer my friend the old Washingtonian had to start off for home. He was to be on duty at five the next morning. Meanwhile I'd found sitting alone at a table a reporter I knew. He was a small precisely dressed man with deepset eyes and a preacher's forehead. I sat down to have another last glass of beer with him while he finished his supper.

"Well, how's it stacking up?" he asked me.

"There are the people who tell you sob stories and there are the people who think it's wonderful here. . . . After all, a whole lot of them have better jobs than they ever had in their lives."

"Termites. They are eating out the structure of the government like termites in an old house. My people are farmers. I get an idea from their letters of how things look from the outside, from the Nebraska side. There's the darnedest rift widening between Washington and the country."

"Here when they talk about the rest of the country they talk about 'out in the field.'"

"Sure. The farmers, storekeepers, small business men of this country are just natives. . . . I can tell you one thing. They don't like it."

He wiped his mouth decisively with his napkin. "Now I'm through. Want to walk around the town some more?"

We walked out southeast toward the Navy Yard. This was still the Washington I remembered: the shadowy streets choked with trees where all the life seemed to be going into the vegetation, the streetlights shaded and muffled in green leaves, families sweltering till bedtime sprawled out on their front stoops or hunched on chairs in tiny dooryards; men in undershirts, dank little half-naked children sitting out in swings, stout women fanning themselves on settees, old women panting in rockers under lowhanging branches, light filtering through green leaves, the shadows of branches thrown on brick walls, the young men and girls and boys lined up limply at the dingy soda fountains dimly lit on the corners, the feeling of slack life stagnant in a jungle.

We walked for blocks and blocks under the trees through wilted white neighborhoods of narrow brick houses with elongated windows, through colored blocks where the pavements were littered with squirming black children and where well-setup yellow girls in slacks with black hair slicked smooth against their heads sauntered beside young bucks in open-necked short-sleeved shirts and trousers cut tight to their narrow hips, where dark lodgers were thick in the hallways as peas in a pod. Four and a Half Street was one of the streets I wanted to find. In the old days it had been full of pool parlors and bars and honkytonks, the main stem of waterfront characters and fishermen and Chesapeake Bay boatmen. "As I was walkin' up Four and a Half Street" was how the tow-boat captains and brackish-water sailors used to start their more scabrous tales of night life ashore. I was disappointed. So far as I could make out it had been swallowed up in Fourth Street. It was surprising to find the Navy Yard so immensely enlarged. The old building with the 1830 look of the pediment over its arched entrance was lost in the midst of a great industrial plant, shoebox-shaped concrete sheds spilling greenish violet light.

By the time we were abreast of the stately old entrance that had always made my heart beat faster with thoughts of Ericsson and the *Monitor* and "Damn the torpedoes" Farragut when I saw it as a boy, we were all in from walking so far through the steamy night in heat so dense that it was like pushing your way through a swamp. We turned into various bars but found no beer. At last we stumbled, dripping from every pore, into a small beer parlor and lunchroom. We were still asking each other what made Federal office-holders different from other people.

As a small child, I was trying to explain, I dimly remembered a boarding house where my mother's father and mother lived, a place that smelt of camphor and chicken dinners, full of very old people whose youth dated from before the Civil War. They were all "in office." I used to wonder what the words meant. There was Colonel this and Major that and General so and so, relics of both war bureaucracies, old fellows with white goatees and bushy mustaches who went to work ceremoniously at ten and vegetated in their offices until four. It was hard to explain the peculiar lack of verve or sense of importance or ambition with which they performed the routine that furnished them with room, board, tobacco, and an occasional suck out of a whiskey bottle when their wives weren't looking. In those days nobody ever imagined those duties meant anything to the world or the nation or were other than a tedious method of obtaining a small addition to an old soldier's pension. "I guess it was Wilson brought righteousness into Washington," the reporter said. "Roosevelt's ardor for social reform means righteousness multiplied by itself. We get the self-righteousness and we don't get the reform." . . .

WE WENT on slogging up the street. In the old brick residential blocks every house looked as if it had been turned inside out like an overripe pod. Men, women and children crouched elbow to elbow in drowsy huddles on brick steps. Elderly people were sitting at open doors in dim-lit hallways. Women were leaning out of windows. It was a long walk.

We had come out into the open spaces of trees and grass and shrubbery in front of the Library of Congress before we noticed that there was a moon. My friend the reporter was telling me that the Capitol grounds these days were the place where service men went to pick up girls, like a small town cemetery full of couples rolling in the shadows. The white uniforms of sailors walking across the gardens stood out bright in the moonlight. There were girls' voices giggling in the shrubberies. A soldier was asleep on the grass. The Capitol looked immensely quiet. The dome slept solid as a mountain in the moonlight. The red and green lights of a plane droned bumbling across the powdered sky overhead.

The reporter hailed the sentry who was walking back and forth half way up the steps on the House side. "Howdy, soldier?" The sentry brought his gun up to attention. "At ease, soldier. I'm just a newspaper man."

The soldier looked at us suspiciously from under his bulbous tin hat. "I'm not rightly supposed to talk," he said.

"I won't let anything happen to you," said the newspaper man in a Napoleonic tone.

"I got a furlough comin' up. I want to git home to see my wife."

"I'll see you get your furlough; what do you think of that?" The sentry had walked down the steps toward us and stood with his gun at rest looking at us. He kept running his tongue over his lips. He was a quiet-voiced man with a ruminative air.

"Married?" asked the reporter.

He nodded. "I married me a little girl down South."

"When you went for training?"

The soldier nodded.

"How long have you been in?"

"Two years. They let me out once and I got married. Then they hauled me back in again. I been all over this country. I trained down South. Then I was out in Oregon guarding forests.... I liked that ... out in the woods three months at a time."

"They say there's a lot of monkey business goes on at night around the Capitol."

"I wouldn't know that. I only been here a week."

"Where are you quartered?"

"I don't rightly know the street yet. We march down here in formation." The soldier had a leisurely, quiet voice.

"What do you think about the anti-strike bill?"

"I guess it's all right. I don't think much about it."

"How do you like Washington?"

"I guess it's all right. When you're in the Army you take what comes."

"Do you think Congress is doing a good job?"

The soldier ran his tongue over his lips. "Mister," he drawled after a pause, "when a feller's in the Army he don't think much about what's going on outside."

"Well, I'll bet you a bottle of beer I can get you a furlough." The reporter took down his name and address and we walked on. "Nice fellow," he said.

"Say," I asked him, "did you suddenly have the feeling that there was no date to that conversation? It might be during the Civil War."

"Don't tell me that. My business is getting news."

Suddenly we remembered there was a concert going on in Meridian Park. At the corner of the Senate Office Building we found a taxi. We tumbled into it and sat back and waited for the breeze the car made to chill through our wet shirts.

"Have you been reading about the high-class call house up on Connecticut Avenue that's been running as a massage parlor all these years? No article on Washington will be complete without that," the reporter was saying.

The husky blond young man who was driving the car let his breath out through his teeth with a whistle.

"If they asked me," he said, "I could write a book. Washington's a wide open town. The cops don't know they're alive. Just the last few days I've seen about fifty of those girls. They've all taken jobs as waitresses till this blows over. When they start investigatin' these things they won't never ask nobody who knows about it. They never ask the cab drivers."

"Do you think they ought to stop things like that?" asked the reporter.

"How can they? Ain't everybody has the luck to be happily married. If they shut up the professionals the amateurs take over. Look at all these nice girls from small towns with no place to go in the evenings. Look at all these boys away from their families. I call this the city of lonely hearts."

Out on Sixteenth Street hill it was cooler. Meridian Park, where the concert was, turned out to be opposite Mrs. Henderson's castle, a building that since childhood had given the locality a faintly comic flavor for me. We said goodnight to our cab driver and walked up the steps toward the music. Beyond the trees pale shapes of tall apartment houses glimmered in the moonlight. The small park was crowded. People, white-faced and dark-faced, were sitting in rows of chairs and standing in banks behind them on three sides of an oblong piece of water. At the far end in the white orchestra shell a violinist was playing. You could hear each note perfectly. The sound of the violin came unusually sweet across the water. The crowd was quiet. There was little light in the park except flood-lights that picked out the black figures of the violinist and his accompanist and the black shape of the grand piano against the white shell. Reflections from the water lit up very dimly white faces and dark faces, a pair of glasses, the white of an eye. All were motionless, listening. When the piece was over there was immense applause from the darkness packed with people under the trees. "Have you ever thought," the reporter asked me, "that if Washington were Rio everybody would say it was a very picturesque place?"

ISA KAPP

Living in Washington, D.C.

Commentary (1957)

This is a piece written by a New Yorker in exile. It may be a bit provocative to include it, but I think it's instructive to have something written by a real outsider. Isa Kapp, a regular contributor to Commentary, *had been living in Washington for a few years at the time of this report, which appeared in the magazine as part of a series of "informal reports on American places"—Detroit and Chicago had been reported on already, but I don't know how they fared. She has a good point when she says that "the impression this city makes depends a great deal on what a person is doing here," noting that it offers a dismal fate for some and a promising one for others. Perhaps, having come with her husband and not of her own volition, her experience was not altogether a happy one.*

*What I like about Kapp's piece—even if I don't agree with all that she says—is the very idea of comparing Washington with other cities, especially New York. This is a different place, and people draw contrasts all the time. Vera Bloom (also from New York), whose title for her book on Washington—*There's No Place Like Washington*—gives away her view, makes this comparison: "While in New York it's more important to 'do something,' in Washington it's more important to 'be someone.'" That may have been true at one time, but I hope it's not anymore. In any case, here is Kapp's somewhat jaundiced view of living in Washington, a place, as she writes, with "open vistas and limited views."*

A WEEK after I came to live in the suburbs of Washington, I began to miss the effrontery of New York. In this city of protocol and triplicate forms, even the bus drivers manage a certain amount of formality. I thought at first it was a surface polish that glittered here, the sum of deferential "yes, ma'ams" and supermarket decorum, the omnipresence behind real estate desks of ceremonious Southern colonels. But one learns more than the outer and perfunctory ways of being civil in the service of the government, and no one can live here very long without acquiring some education in the inner rhythm of diplomacy. At the least, one learns to put things in their most palatable form, and to keep people and ideas at a comfortable distance.

To some extent, Washington politeness is only the legacy of small-town manners; the round of office birthday parties, coffee breaks, and solicitous inquiries is meant to ward off the impersonality of urban life. Even a negligent New Yorker can easily pick up such minor cues from the provinces. But what really awes him is the underlying tone of well-lubricated easy intercourse in the capital, so unlike the sudden confidences and quick retreats he was accustomed to. A good deal of the affability in this white-collar city is brewed by government workers with some small administrative responsibility or the middle officer corps of the armed forces—the natural bureaucrats who ask only security of their jobs and have found it here without too much effort or frustration. But the note of urbanity, the more cultivated layer of civil behavior, is established by the ivy-leaguers who have gravitated to Washington out of a family tradition of public service or a reluctance to get embroiled in commerce. Such well-bred, well-educated, sometimes ambitious men in gray flannel suits staff the State Department, the Central Intelligence Agency, and International Cooperation Agency—those government branches that offer the bait of foreign assignments.

If I resented the temperamental smoothness of D.C. when my husband's job brought us here two years ago, I could not avoid thawing out in the city's physical ease. There may be something dispiriting in the marble gleam and compromise-square pillars of the Neo-Classical government buildings, but the presence of Federal architecture does keep commercial enterprise at a respectful distance. After the dense pallor of New York, it is pleasant to be in populous urban surroundings and look toward a horizontal instead of a vertical skyline, walk along avenues of lindens and oaks, and move from a bus stop into a convenient green square. Though the fountains of Washington seem to splash with more pomp than vitality, they at least guarantee the public occasional refreshing wet moments that New Yorkers, if they are to get any at all, must steal from their fire hydrants.

In New York people live as they can, but in these functional and official quarters we are more at liberty to live as we like. A family from Stuyvesant Town now boasts of the creek behind their modestly priced four-room garden apartment. Some friends of ours who used to live in Greenwich Village have rented a plain rambler in the woods near Alexandria; they have put an old hand-hewn coffee table in the center of their living room, and their most comfortable chair is a huge airplane tire cov-

ered with soft cloth. In New York such furnishing stiffens under its
bohemian banner, but here it is only one element of a pliable environment. In our own case, inertia would have kept us in a city apartment, but
once in Washington we ventured to a roomy house on a Virginia hill-top,
and are surrounded by fruit trees and English ivy. Almost everyone we
know has in some way acquired the space and comfort that New Yorkers,
in their worry for convenience, can hardly ever demand for themselves.

Most government workers with families live in the close-in suburbs,
and though the Washington area is not without its share of treeless, bar-
becuing new suburbia, many of those who settle just across the bridges in
Virginia or beyond the District line in Maryland are getting the best of
two worlds: quiet small-town streets, and the culture and privacy of a
city. Encouraged by the turnover in military and foreign service personnel and government administrations, lower-middle-class Washington
families buy and sell their houses quite casually and move out of town
without that sense of anxious commitment that oppresses emigrant New
Yorkers. The shock of change is absorbed by Washington's conciliatory
disposition. Just as it breaks down the lines between city and country life,
and leaves the devotees of each dimly thwarted, the capital softens the
distinctions between natives and strangers. Art galleries and restaurants
are always filled with newcomers, and foreign languages buzz in the
stores. In New York a sari or a Spanish hair-do is either lost in the crowd
or stared into exoticism, but Washington takes the presence of a great
variety of foreigners as a matter of course. However provincial it may be
in other respects, the capital is not likely to fall prey to xenophobia. New
York is full of private cases, difficult for outlanders to find; Washington is
a common property, relaxing and kind to everyone.

This ingratiating city keeps holding out a democracy of small luxuries
and urging us to live well. "Down to the Puritan marrow of my bones!
There's something in this richness that I hate," wrote Elinor Wylie in a
poem describing the fruitful countryside just north of Washington. Living well can slip from a happy accident into a major vocation, and it is
with this mild apple that Satan makes his most successful bid for souls
from the capital. In this connoisseur's city one is not surprised when
friends give candle-lit dinners that begin with shrimp-filled pastries and
end with mocha-vodka drinks and glazed grapes. Of course, gourmet
dishes and virtuoso hospitality are not really regional weaknesses; but the
conditions of life in Washington conspire to make one seek a subtler
wine and nurse one's fireplace into a more lavish blaze. All this is part of
a holiday existence that does a lot to smooth out jagged, uncomfortable
manners. Because of its civil service paternalism, its lack of commerce,
and its gentility, a place like the capital becomes a temporary harbor from

the pressures of the market place—and the imagination. Except in the case of political office holders, it soothes the competitive, envious impulses and erases the wrinkles of ambition. But a native New Yorker winces at the prospect of life-long sedation; he begins to long for his own nervous city where food is bolted and conversation interrupted, and graciousness has to be condensed to a lucky gesture or a considerate phrase.

Unfortunately, the suitors that press the refinements of life upon the capital are constantly growing more insistent and crude. Washington is reputedly the most air-conditioned and among the most gadget-ridden cities in the world, and the daily newspapers continue to proposition their readers shamelessly with discount and easy credit offers of TV sets, freezers, fans, garbage disposals, and other electrifying treasures in white enamel. To visitors, D.C. looks like a city reprieved from commerce, but its few businesses—beer brewers, auto dealers, and discount houses— have expanded to fill the breach, and they produce as strident and incessant an advertising clamor as all the multifarious enterprises of New York.

My husband and I were not eager to come to this well-organized city where almost everyone worked for the same employer. As cynical natives said, Washington was a company town. We would constantly be running into civil servants with pensions in their futures, and a very gradual, predictable range of salaries and opportunities: there would be few robber barons or experimental poets around the corner. It turned out that since the New Deal years, the bureaucracy had become much roomier than we imagined, and had created niches for a large number of capable lawyers, economists, writers, and policy-makers. There are also several government-contracted research organizations located here that attract serious scholars. Nevertheless, despite all the talk about bringing brain power into the government, it is hard to keep intellectual mavericks in an atmosphere clogged with memoranda, clearances, and channels.

Even more than most Americans, Washingtonians seem to make their social distinctions in a very literal and naive way: big money meets big money or big names, intellectuals consort with their peers, and Federal employees move within their own salary brackets. As a lady who has lived in D.C. for a long time pointed out with some satisfaction, everyone she knows has an income within a thousand dollars of her husband's, and this seemed to her a very reasonable state of things. Both the city and its suburbs are full of discrete recognizable areas, easy to price-tag, and one is likely to keep bobbing up to one's own social level.

The lower-salaried military personnel often move into rows of semidetached houses in the scrubby lowlands of South Arlington, while in the hills just above, among old trees and English stone fronts, are the families of captains and colonels and several Congressmen. South of Alexandria, there is a community of new gleaming Charles Goodman houses ("contemporary homes in a contemporary setting," says the language of real estate). Panels of brick or knotty pine draw nature into the living room, and two complete walls are made of glass. These structures were meant for clean, outdoor communal living, but because of high fuel costs and some natural instinct for privacy, the owners have barricaded themselves behind miles of cloth. As one passes through the raw lanes, swoops of abstractly designed draperies completely blur together the indoor and outdoor landscapes—a plaintive defense against the imperatives of modernism. Someone once claimed that it was impossible to start an argument in this community, as its inhabitants were all Stevenson supporters. Whoever chose his home here had a strong premonition of "belonging." If they were not precisely drawn by the architecture, its very presence must have somehow guaranteed them a majority of up-to-date, well-adjusted, college-bred neighbors. Yet almost around the corner, there has sprouted a rougher-hewn, woodsier, less durably built community. In it one can find some conservatives, a few eccentrics, and even an occasional wife-beater.

The city itself is also laid out in a similar social geography, but when it actually gets down to social practice, a few breaks show up in its otherwise tidy seams. Several years ago, *Life* magazine did a story on a young government worker who made a pastime of crashing diplomatic parties and was pictured shaking a number of prominent hands. Even without such maneuvering, barriers are often unofficially let down because of the rather intimate nature of the Washington diplomatic scene. Unassuming employees may find themselves welcome at the affairs of foreign legations, and there is no doubt that such democratic accidents have their charm for people who like to be in on big things. In general, living in or near Washington gives us a domesticated sense of political life. We see a Congressman painting his screened porch and begin to think of our national officials as local citizens rather than representatives of special interests. The daily society sections of the *Washington Post* and the *Evening Star* open vicarious doors to embassy bazaars, Presidential regattas, and smiling receptions. And it is very possible that this false familiarity, this aura of local patriotism and community bustle, contribute to the lack of any real political consciousness in Washington's general population. It is true that there are bursts of ardor for school and sanitation problems, strong feelings about civil liberties (especially when they affect the job rights of government employees). But such enthusiasms do not usually extend to national issues like farm and labor legislation or to international issues that agitate ethnic and religious groups elsewhere.

Washingtonians tend to forget the pressures they felt in their home towns. For most of them, politics in the capital means the brief cases in Union Station and that decorative air of cosmopolitan excitement that is more flattering than real.

Though Washington is so close to past and present history, though it seems nearer to Europe than New York ever did (a young man recently announced his plans for a trip: "I've got to go! Everyone in my car pool except me has been to Paris!"), though it is in continuous political motion, the thought of living here for more than a few years throws some of us into intermittent panic. A number of grievances keeps the hope of exodus alive. Some people don't like the idea of working indefinitely under the constraints of government policy. For others, the fact that the District of Columbia does not have the vote is a reminder that they live in an administrative cubicle cut off from the local political bustle in the rest of the nation. (The political liveliness of Washington is mainly concentrated in the hallways and elevators of Congress.) The confirmed metropolites resent the condition of being outside commercial life— sheltered from factory dirt and gross values, from the contrasts of wealth and poverty, and the boisterous street life one can find in New York's garment center at lunch-time. It sometimes looks as if the capital, with the exception of that relatively small group which makes policy, is a large secretariat fixed in a career pause, momentarily released from the enterprise and success pull of other cities. For one reason or another, the business of getting ahead has pretty much come to a halt here.

But the most crushing restrictions are those imposed on the capital's intellectual life. It is quite true, as Richard Rovere pointed out in a *New York Times Magazine* article a while back, that Washington is one of the four or five most cosmopolitan cities in America. It is also true, as any loyal native can tell you in a hurry, that Washington has more than its share of concerts, that its "Good Music" radio station rivals New York's WQXR (or at least did until recently, when its AM station was bought out by the Mutual Broadcasting Company), that Marcel Marceau and Broadway shows come here too, and can be more cheaply and conveniently attended. Certainly, there is no shortage of books, lectures, art galleries, even excellent amateur theatrical groups, like the one at Catholic University. What Washington does lack is cultural impetus and something more than moderate quality in its intelligentsia and its universities. Even its few serious publications are responsible rather than vigorous. This is a middlebrow city, hostile to extremes, seeking stimulus within the bounds of safety, always keeping an indulgent eye on its own urbane image. I do not mean that no high intellectual standards exist in Washington. But minds are mainly at work on "projects," are concerned with immediate goals, and with getting jobs done. Not much time is spared for the pursual of knowledge or ultimate wisdom. The best intellects are astute, alert, and judicious, rather than creative or imaginative. One of our friends, however, has protested that a competitive city where writers are forced into high-pressured publicity jobs to earn a living can wreck a literary talent more speedily and irrevocably than gentle, paternalistic Washington ever would. But whether potential artists are lulled by the serene atmosphere or simply avoid government quarters by instinct, the fact remains that Washington has not harbored many distinguished poets or novelists or painters. It is our dissonant cities and prying small towns that have produced our best artists.

Another friend of ours has described the fraternity-house camaraderie of his suburban Maryland car pool, which includes a wit, a serious scholar, and several other ebullient conversationalists. At its best, this city, which rather resembles a large university campus, achieves a sort of collegiate liveliness. The internal office jokes are not very different from those that made the varsity shows, and the low-priced government cafeterias look and smell like school lunchrooms. But shorn of the susceptibility and expectations of college years, such institutional pleasantries are really not enough to content postgraduates. Maybe these complaints are only a sample of the New Yorker's gluttony. People we have spoken to from various states tell us that Washington is the most exciting place they have ever known. As for myself, as long as I can remember New York, I don't expect to be altogether at home in this muted, foggy, lovely city. The welcoming lawns that lead to the Capitol, the white granite of Union Station—this tourist's Washington is not too far from the real city, which never seems quite as civilized and inviting as when it shows you the way in and the way out.

RUSSELL BAKER

It's Middletown-
on-the-Potomac

The New York Times Magazine (1965)

*Russell Baker is best known to most of us for his classic American
"Observer" column, written for the* New York Times *for thirty-six
years, until his retirement—at least from column writing—in 1998.
Others know him as the host of* Masterpiece Theatre *or for his
memoir,* Growing Up, *read and loved by hundreds of thousands. He
won the Pulitzer Prize both for commentary (in 1979) and for biography (in 1983).*

*I think of him as someone who has watched Washington with a
gentle-hearted humor for a long time. In fact, he started off with the*
New York Times *by writing a feature called "Random Notes in
Washington." In this piece written in 1965, nearly fifteen years into his
observations of this place, he captures the rhythm of Washington life
and gives an inviting description of our very own Middletown. It's easy
to see why he's so often quoted.*

*Don't let the witty manner in which he writes about Washington get
in the way of noting how his observations are completely on target.
Irreverent though he may be, he's also right.*

WASHINGTON is my home town. It dies at sundown; it is too
hot in the summer, too damp in the winter, too dry on Sundays and more interested in politics than it is in sex, but I
like it.

It is civilized in a square, middle-class way, which is to say, urbanely
dull. It is ideally suited for the middle-aged family couple, being perhaps
the last great city in which middle income can afford a house, a tomato
patch and a canopy of dogwoods within fifteen minutes of the office.

Its society is democratic, unstartling, cosmopolitan and notably
free of the small-town chauvinism of New York or San Francisco. The

Washingtonian is unruffled by New York's insistence upon being thought
the most thrilling city on earth or by San Francisco's claim to be the
loveliest.

Being tolerant and well-traveled, he is unlikely to point out that London, Paris, Hong Kong and Tokyo have equally valid claims, but being
perfectly satisfied that his own town is a bit of a drag, he would surely
never argue the case for Washington's superiority.

He may feel sorry that the New Yorker cannot afford to rear his children among Manhattan's splendors or that the San Franciscan must live
out his days at the far edge of Nowhere, but it pleases him to see these
unfortunate people making a virtue of necessity, for he is, above all, a
man with the politician's devotion to the status quo.

He might—just might, mind you—prefer to live in New York if he
were rich, or in London if he were more adventurous, or in Paris if he
were at ease in the language. But with all problems judiciously weighed—
he is a very judicious fellow—and his own middle-class limitations faced
up to and conceded, Washington seems the best of all possible cities.

What we Washingtonians cannot for the life of us understand is the
relentless American urge to turn the town into someplace else. The
Kennedys tried to make it into a cultural capital—a sort of instant Lincoln Center–Vienna–Paris–London. President Johnson's blueprints seem
to call for Augustan Rome. . . .

Scarcely a week passes without a new plan to turn Washington into a
"showcase" for this or that, and there are as many schemes for converting
it into a "truly great world capital" as there are sociologists, art critics,
architects and city planners.

This passion for reshaping the town rests on a naïve misconception.
The fact which the reshapers fail to grasp is that Washington is no longer
the child capital in the wilderness, waiting to be molded by loving
parental hands. It is not only fully grown now, but well on into maturity,
set in its ways, committed in its habits and hardened in its vices. With the
inner city filled to capacity and a metropolitan population of 2,300,000,
its growth is substantially complete and, though the "slums" will doubtless continue to spread through outlying Maryland and Virginia, the
city's character is well formed and no longer pliant.

This explains why the Kennedy effort to implant a taste for the arts—
the "culture bit," as local cynics called it—was always doomed. You can
lead a middle-aged burgher to the "Mona Lisa," but you cannot make
him surrender the martini hour for Couperin. Faced with the challenge
to do something about culture, Washington's response has been characteristic. It will build another marble monument—the National Cultural

Center—isolated from everyplace that has to do with living, and unreachable except by the most daring expressway pilots.

It is the natural middle-class response to Kultur which will be appropriately venerated in stone but kept at comfortable arm's length from daily life. It is this instinctive middle-class reflex which distinguishes Washington from all other American cities and accounts for the placid charm that is the special quality of life here. It is the urban triumph of the middle class, the apotheosis of Zenith. No more appropriate capital could be envisioned for the nation that made a mass blessing of capitalism, and it is time for the rest of the country to stop fretting about what the city is not and to accept it as it is.

It is first of all a city of civil servants—250,000 of them. The society-page myth has it that the tone of Washington life is set by the President and his lady. It is true only for the privileged few in the orbit of official society. In the vast sprawl of suburbia, the tree-shaded side streets of the Northwest and the huge Negro ghettos north and east of the White House, it is the 250,000 civil servants who dominate the patterns of Washington life.

The bureaucratic passion for order, safety and a neat out-basket is the prevailing force in the Washington temperament. It fears extremes, whether of dress, drink or opinion. The security police are omnipresent, and as the 250,000 must all be certified orthodox by the U.S. government, dullness and the stolid family virtues are at a premium.

The refusal of the big Negro population to explode in protest has troubled some leaders of the civil-rights movement. It is a symptom of how firmly the cautious civil-service mentality has taken hold, for while the Negro is relatively well off in relation to other cities, there remain cruel economic and social disparities between him and the white Washingtonians.

The schools, to cite a case, are overcrowded, out of date and perpetually starved for funds. The school population is predominantly (about 85 per cent) Negro within the city limits. Technically, the schools are integrated; in fact, after a brief period of integration in the mid-nineteen-fifties, most have been resegregated by the mass move to the suburbs by thousands of young white families.

Suburban discrimination against Negro home buyers keeps the Negro population (about 106,000 families) penned within the city limits, and the integrated school system becomes blacker every year. Negro protests against the shabbiness of the schools have been notable for their absence. It is probably no coincidence that the Washington Negro has a long history of civil-service employment or that only one other city has a higher percentage of Negro families earning middle-class income ($6,000 a year or more, by Urban League standards).

The civil-service regard for the proprieties permeates more than race relations. It has eaten into the soul of the city and left it with that well-ordered small-town atmosphere which prevents life from becoming the continual social mess that it is in places like New York.

Proper dinners end at 11 p.m. Proper people bed down by midnight. Proper drinkers have two before dining and a brandy afterward. Proper conversations deal with children, schools and government. Proper opinions range from three degrees left of center to five degrees right. The likelihood of ever meeting a living, breathing anarchist, Communist or pacifist in a proper Washington living room is virtually nil, and Socialists are acceptable only if they are foreign Cabinet ministers on tour.

Occasionally one may come upon a couple living out of wedlock, but they are invariably young and planning to move elsewhere. God only knows what goes on in the suburbs, but in town at least the percentage of men capable of forgetting government long enough to make a pass at a bored wife is negligible. Two or three years ago, a prominent party divorced his wife for another woman, and the town is still talking about it.

There is no liquor sold on the Sabbath. The last restaurant shuts down at 1 a.m. and on the main thoroughfares the traffic lights are shut off or left blinking until dawn. It is all very comfortable, private, quiet, relaxed and free of ugly temptation.

At night, the Washingtonian visits old friends for a proper dinner or goes to a proper reception to discuss children, schools and government with old friends he has seen at proper receptions the night before the night before that. If he is on the town, he may go to the National Theater to see a tryout or a road show, to the Arena to watch the only original theater company in town or to one of a dozen movie theaters where he is certain to run into old friends with whom he discussed children, schools and government at a proper reception recently.

Nighttime excursions downtown, however, are rare. The town center is a marble graveyard after dark, and in the daytime, too, for that matter, unless one enjoys watching footsore tourists struggling from monument to monument.

The rhythm of life is small-town and middle-class, which makes the town comfortable. What makes it yeasty is the cosmopolitan worldliness of its people. The man across the street has just gotten off an airplane from Karachi, and the fellow umpiring the kids' softball game has spent the day over plans for putting a man on the moon. Not long ago I dined with a Middle Eastern gentleman whose government, after harrowing indecision, had decided to send him to Washington rather than hang him after the last political shake-up.

Another woman at the same party complained that her husband had been unbearable all week because "he's been insisting on bringing Vietnam home with him." The cab driver has just delivered three men who, he tells you hootingly, have a scheme for carrying Texas for the Republicans, and the elevator operator has always just taken the British Ambassador up or the Nigerian Ambassador down.

Besides being a town of civil servants, Washington is also a town of specialists who are constantly preoccupied with the burdens of the world. This preoccupation colors their society with a judicious, almost somber respect for the realities.

As a result, conversation is rarely dazzling. The Washingtonian has small time for the brilliant flight of fancy or the freewheeling bull session or even the philosophical gymnastics of abstruse thought. He is a man accustomed to live within the confines of the harsh possibilities and conditioned to the realization that a mistake in judgment may be disastrous. Sagacity, and not creativity, is the city's most cherished quality.

The Washingtonian is too sophisticated to believe any more in solutions. He is bred to the idea that life offers no soluble problems, but only unpleasant alternatives, some of which are less unpleasant than others. This makes him a professional and accounts for the glazed look which quickly betrays him in, say, a typical New York conversation about world problems after someone has announced that everything would turn out happily if only people would love one another.

The Washingtonian does not scorn the psychic virtues of love, but people who believe it to be a viable foreign policy strike him as out of touch with reality and decidedly lacking in urbanity. He is willing to leave such qualities to philosophers, for they are not the business of his city. Reality compels him to understatement and caution.

Caution, moderation, understatement. These are basic qualities of Washington life. It is this prevailing distaste for extremes that has saved the inner city from esthetic ruin. Long ago, some cautious spirit decreed that private construction should not be permitted to overshadow the monumental Federal skyline. Accordingly, the office-building architects are restricted to a maximum height of 12 stories.

What they have done to the city's noblest boulevards within this limitation is bad enough, but the abominations that might have been if the sky had been the limit are all too plain. Connecticut Avenue, which had a kind of Parisian grace 10 years ago, is a case in point. It is now being completely faced with squalid glass real-estate speculations designed solely to cramp the maximum number of drones in the minimum amount of space at the greatest rental profit. It is a bleak period everywhere for architecture, but Washington has at least had the luck of the 12-story limit.

As a result, for three seasons of the year when the trees are leafy, the eyesores are partially softened and the sky remains broad and open overhead.

The trees and the sky. Something must be said about each, for they are the secret charm of Washington. They are its beauty. They fill it with color and air and drama. The city's tree and landscaping division maintains 350,000 trees on public land alone. They include the elm which canopies the broadest boulevard, the red maple, sugar maple, Norway maple, the red oak, willow oak, pin oak, the linden and the honey locust whose sweetness perfumes the spring night, the sycamore, the sweet gum, the Japanese keaki, the Chinese scholartree and the malodorous gingko.

The tourists come in early spring for the fragile and unreliable Japanese cherry blossoms, but the time to see the city at its loveliest is May when the flowering shrubs and dogwood are on the bloom in 10,000 front yards, or in autumn when the sunlight turns it gold and scarlet.

The sky gives the city a sense of openness that no other great American city has. It is a low city, rising from reconverted swampland on a series of encircling hills, and L'Enfant's broad avenues let the light in. London's sky, as V. S. Pritchett has written, "encloses the mind." Washington's sets it free and suffuses it with light.

And yet, it is an unsatisfactory town to walk in. Except in Georgetown, a few areas around Dupont Circle and on Capitol Hill, distances tend to the monumental and streets to monotony. It is not a place of sudden surprises tucked away around unexplored corners but a city of vistas to be viewed from magnificent distances—from the George Washington Memorial Parkway on the Virginia escarpment, the west front of the Capitol, or the steps of the Custis-Lee Mansion in Arlington.

As the triumphal middle-class city, it is ideally viewed from a car. It is, in fact, a city built for cars and a city with extraordinary respect for cars. Its suburbs which, with the exception of Alexandria, Chevy Chase and Silver Spring, are highly forgettable, are basically Los Angeles East.

Magnificent expressways belt and penetrate the city to speed the white middle-class servants between dormitory and parking lot twice a day. New beltways and expressways are constantly springing up to menace the city homeowner and make a hash of L'Enfant's original city plan. Not surprisingly, for this is also the worst-governed city in the country, the private parking-lot operators have one of the few effective political lobbies in town. (The whisky distributors have another.)

The government of Washington cannot be described. It must be lived with for 10 years to be believed. Again, it is the kind of government ideally fitted to the bureaucratic temperament, for basically no one is in charge and no one, therefore, can be held responsible for the mess.

The central feature of the thing is an ingenious system of committees which veto each other's recommendations. This assures that nothing will be done in a hurry and that very little will be done in a single lifetime. One of its more bizarre cogs is a complex of four Congressional committees which feud among each other about how much money can be spent for things like schools.

No one who lives in the city sits on these committees. They are usually dominated by gentlemen of the rural South or by Congressmen from the suburbs whose constituents are not very interested in the city's schools but in a terrible hurry to get a faster highway built through the city's residential district. These Congressmen have just built themselves the most expensive office building in the history of humanity, and this year for the first time the Ben W. Murch Elementary School was assigned a part-time librarian to operate the library supplied by the school parents.

This nongovernment has its virtues. A great many bad recommendations for the city die along with the good. The city drifts inexorably along its placid middle-class way, full of decay and unsolved problems but, on the whole, not so badly decayed or so problem-ridden as smartly governed cities like New York.

Everyone manages to keep his temper and go on behaving with civilized propriety. Yes, the crime is bad, but not so bad as it is painted, and, of course, there are too many people left to feel hopeless and desperate, and something should be done about them, but one must accept the realities of local politics.

On the whole, life is well-ordered and calm. The out-basket could be neater, but it is not out of control. We know how to live properly here, you see. In bed by midnight. No indiscretions. Not too much passion. The Washington Senators will finish tenth again this year, but we are above the bush-league despair of small-town chauvinists like the Mets fans.

In spring the herring will run again in the Potomac, and on the first warm day in April we will walk the C. & O. Canal towpath and listen for a whippoorwill. Or drive out to Dulles Airport and look for new expressways. In May there will be the azaleas and, between now and then, any number of very proper dinners with old friends.

In June the nights will be sweet with white locust blossoms and the sky will wash the city with soft breezes off the Carolinas. There will be visitors from out of town and we will drive them down to the Cultural Center to show how culture stands with us.

What better place could there be to live if you are neither rich, nor adventurous, nor capable in French? In the summer there will be tomatoes in the back yard. Only fifteen minutes from the office.

The Drama of Conflict

The Center (1968)

Stewart Alsop, Joe's younger brother, was my good friend. In many ways, Stew was a more human version of his older brother. While my husband, Phil, and I had known Joe since long before the start of World War II, we met Stew only after the war, when Joe's original writing partner, Bob Kintner, left to go into broadcasting and Joe announced that Stew would be the new collaborator on his column. I asked Joe at the time how he knew Stew could do it, and Joe's response was characteristically sure: "I just know." And he was exactly right. Together they made a very strong team. By the late 1940s, the Alsop brothers' column, "Matter of Fact," had become a major feature in the Post.

Stew had volunteered for service with the British army in 1941 and commanded an infantry platoon of the King's Royal Rifle Corps in Africa and Italy, transferring in 1944 to the American Office of Strategic Services. He returned from the war with a stunningly beautiful, young—I think she was eighteen years old at the time—British wife, Tish. Despite her youth, Tish managed to cope with the Alsop brothers, and eventually had and raised six children. With a modest income, she ran two large houses—one in Washington and another in Maryland—and entertained at both. Stew and Tish shared Phil's and my love of bridge and tennis, so we saw quite a lot of them in the postwar years.

At some point, Stew found he could no longer tolerate being Joe's partner and began writing longer, more thought-filled pieces for the Saturday Evening Post. In 1958, the brothers parted ways as far as work was concerned, and Joe went on writing the column alone. It was only in the mid-sixties that we were able to talk Stew into leaving the Saturday Evening Post, of which he had become Washington editor, to write a column for Newsweek, which he did essentially until his death.

At much too young an age, Stew developed a virulent strain of leukemia. He fought a gallant battle and even wrote a book about hav-

*ing the disease, his last piece of work. I remember sitting with him on
my back terrace the spring before he died, with him knowing he'd likely
never see another Washington springtime, and watching him look wistfully out over the flowers and blooming trees. It was clearer to me than
ever how much he loved this city.*

IT IS BEST for a reporter to admit his bias. My bias is this: I like
Washington. It is not only, after a couple of decades, my home town.
It is also, in all the world, my favorite city.

There are lots of things wrong with Washington, of course. As everybody knows, the summers can be dreadful. There are no really first-class
restaurants, and the parking lot operators practice legal highway robbery.
Persons interested in theater, music, and the like are fed on very thin fare.
The tax laws have encouraged real estate speculators to turn much of
downtown Washington into a characterless mass of flat-faced, steel-
glass-and-concrete office buildings.

There are other things that are more profoundly wrong with Washington. There is too much crime, and there are too many poor Negroes
crowded into too small an area, which is, of course, one reason why there
is too much crime. There are also things that are very wrong with the
government of the United States, which is Washington's only reason for
existence. Even so, the bias is there: I like Washington.

I like Washington for small reasons, like May, or the eleven o'clock
rule, or the occasional whiff of the past. But I like Washington for larger
reasons, too.

The tourists come to Washington in April to see the cherry blossoms,
when Washington is often chilly and blossomless. They ought to come in
May. May is a lovely month, but nowhere in the world lovelier than in
Washington. Washington's May makes up for Washington's August,
which is saying a great deal.

As for the eleven o'clock rule, it is a lifesaver for anyone who has to
dine out a lot, and for most denizens of Political Washington dining out
is part of the job. The eleven o'clock rule is a curious, un-American custom imposed by the fact that Washington is filled with diplomats and
other protocol-conscious persons. The ranking guest leaves the house at
eleven—eleven-fifteen at the latest—which means that everyone can get
to bed sober and at a reasonable hour. And because of the eleven o'clock
rule, a sensible hostess serves dinner within half an hour of the time the
guests were invited, without the eternal standing and guzzling which pre-
cedes dinner in New York and most American cities. New Yorkers who
have lived long enough in Washington to become used to such amenities

never again quite accustom themselves to the barbarities of dining out in New York.

As for that whiff of the past, Washington is a young city, of course, even by American standards. In 1800, when the federal government moved from Philadelphia to the "Federal City" and Abigail Adams first hung her washing in the East Room of the unfinished White House, Washington was not a city at all, but a rather slovenly bad joke. But largely because George Washington's dream of the Federal City (modestly, he never called it Washington) as a busy industrial center never came true, the smell of the past is strong in Washington. . . .

But the best thing about Washington is, quite simply, the people who live here. The people who live in Political Washington—in The Center—are involved in the business of governing the United States, or in the business of dealing with the rest of the world on behalf of the United States, or dealing with the United States on behalf of the rest of the world. In short, they are involved in politics, in its broadest dictionary sense—"the science and art of government . . . the theory or practice of managing the affairs of public policy."

It follows that those who find politics interesting find the people who live in Washington interesting. Mind you, Washington has its generous quota of bores. It is very easy to come across denizens of Political Washington who are only too happy to try out their latest speech on you, complete with gestures. Some of the women, who are in Washington only because they married Senator So-and-so or Secretary Such-and-such in their long-lost nubile youth, are boring quite beyond the bounds of belief. The vivid phrase "I felt as though I were being nibbled to death by a duck" was invented by a male Washingtonian subjected to the dinner-table conversation of such a rapaciously tedious female. But if you are interested in politics, it is not necessary to be bored in Washington.

Just as it is necessary to be interested in automobiles in Detroit, or movies in Hollywood, or insurance in Hartford, it is absolutely essential in Washington to be interested in politics. Culturally minded, nonpolitical persons tend to go mad if exposed to Washington for too long a period. Especially New Yorkers and especially ladies. But if you are interested in the political process, Washington is an interesting, even an exciting, place. There is drama in Washington—more drama, surely, than in making automobiles, or writing insurance, or even making movies.

Washington's drama is, curiously, a recent discovery for the rest of the country. Until recently, for example, the Washington novel, aside from such exotica as Henry Adams' *Democracy* and bits of Edith Wharton, hardly existed. Then Allen Drury wrote his *Advise and Consent*. Since then the bookstores have been flooded with Washington novels, in which generals unleash nuclear war, Senators commit sodomy, Presidents go mad, and beautiful hostesses leap relentlessly in and out of the beds of Very Important Persons. No doubt there is a certain amount of leaping in and out of bed among the town's movers and shakers, but far less than in the novels, for Political Washington is a rather moral town. The drama of Washington is of a different order.

It is of two kinds. First, and rarest, is the ceremonial drama, which can be unforgettable. A Presidential Inauguration is always moving, for it symbolizes the legitimate assumption of great power—and the transfer of power without risk of bloodshed is in itself a great, and historically novel, accomplishment. The Inauguration of John F. Kennedy was peculiarly moving, in part because it also symbolized the transfer of power from one generation to another. And surely no one who witnessed it will ever forget the ceremonial drama of the Kennedy funeral—the rearing riderless horse, the boots reversed in the stirrups, the drums beating to the tempo of the human heart.

But the drama of Washington lies more often in conflict than in ceremony. It is conflict that chiefly produces drama, and conflict is the stuff of which Washington is made—and always has been, back to the time when George Washington's two chief lieutenants became mortal enemies. When conflict concerns vital national issues, as in the case of Jefferson and Hamilton, the drama takes on grandeur. And although Washington has always had its share of squabbles based on personal ambition and petty rivalry, the basic conflict almost always revolves around issues of genuine importance—sometimes, of life-and-death importance. In today's Washington, for example, it is around such issues that the conflict between Lyndon Johnson and Robert Kennedy, as dramatic in its way as any conflict in Washington's history, revolves. . . .

To the occasional visitor, and especially to the foreigner unaccustomed to our disorderly ways, Washington may seem an appalling capital for a great nation. And yet, over a period of years, Washington comes to seem an oddly reassuring place. . . .

The inhabitant of Washington—Political Washington, that is—has his nose rubbed hard and daily in the political realities. He is therefore no perfectionist. The glazed look also betrays the Washingtonian when out-of-towners suggest that all politicians are crooks, thieves, or liars, and all civil servants and officeholders a bunch of lazy bureaucrats. The fact is that the level of ability at both ends of Pennsylvania Avenue is a good deal higher than the American citizenry deserves.

For a good many years, in company with such professionals as Louis Harris and Oliver Quayle, I have been going on polling expeditions to ring doorbells and ask questions of (to quote Mark Sullivan) "the great rancid American people." Public-opinion polling is fascinating in its way, and it makes good copy. But at the end of a long hard day of polling, it is sometimes tempting to succumb to the notion that the American people are a lot of ill-informed louts, filled to the eyeballs with misinformation and wrongheaded prejudice.

It is certainly true that most Americans are much less interested in the processes by which they are governed than in, say, baseball or their favorite television western. Political reporters and commentators are writing for 10 percent of the total population—and that is a generous estimate. And yet by some mysterious instinctive process most of the men the ill-informed citizenry choose to send to Washington are rather able men. Some are very able indeed. And very few are crooks or fools.

Joe McCarthy is the only politician or major public figure I ever really hated. I hated him not because he was a fool or a crook (he was not, at any rate, a fool) but because he came so close to destroying the American political system. . . . He did not play the game according to the rules.

The game, when played according to the rules, can be a rather uninspiring and even, on occasion, a rather sleazy game, with much mutual back-scratching or arm-twisting. But there it is—the system works, not very well, but better than any other. As Winston Churchill said: "Democracy is the worst form of government, except all those other forms that have been tried from time to time."

Democracy is also the most entertaining form of government. What seems to me the most striking characteristic of the Communist form of government is that it is so intolerably dull. As soon as you land in Moscow, or Bucharest, or Prague, or Budapest, or Sofia (but not Warsaw—Poles don't know how to be boring), you are engulfed in a great smog of tedium. Conflict, which is the chief ingredient of political drama, exists, all right, but it is concealed behind closed and locked doors. And everything that makes politics fun—the gossip, the jokes, the predictions about who is going to get whose job, the stories about some awful thing the President said to an amazed lady the other night, the head-counting before a major vote, the freewheeling argument on the issues—all this is wholly lacking.

It is good, too, to live in the midst of great events, to live in history—even as an onlooker, a mere provider of footnotes. And Washington is where most great events either begin or are molded and altered or end. In short, my bias is there: I like Washington.

True Grit
and Imitation Grandeur

"Portrait of the City," *The Washington Post Magazine* (1999)

To say that Henry Allen writes for the Style section of The Washington Post *is an understatement. Henry, who won the Pulitzer Prize for criticism in 2000, after having been a finalist for the prize twice before, knows Washington well. He covered both the White House and the Congress for the* New York News *before joining the* Post *in 1970. He was the central writer of a* Post *series, "What It Felt Like," that ran in 1999, covering each decade of the twentieth century. This particular piece was the lead article of a special millennium issue of* The Washington Post Magazine *called "Portrait of the City"— an issue I was especially proud of, both for the* Post *and for Washington. Here, Henry poetically and elegantly points up the contradictions of this city, a place where "authenticity and fantasy are close companions."*

THINK of ideas of Washington, of notions and sidelong glances, memory snapshots, sounds, smells . . . of this accidental city, this sly encampment with the sad ease, lawns and trees of an old colonial capital—New Delhi, Saigon—a sense that none of us quite belong here, that we're all obituaries waiting to happen; while at the same time the city of Washington feels like a conspiracy we're all in together, and nobody else in America quite understands, even though they pay for it.

Contradictions everywhere: the offhanded magnificence in democracy's real marble temples that have the poignance of the fake marble Parthenons at old-time world's fairs . . . something ephemeral about a city that looks like it's trying to be its own suburb; with avenues stretching out to the dark fields of the Republic, or, if you head back downtown, avenues converging on cautious monuments of office buildings where sentries guard the even darker doors of empire.

How glorious. How wistful. Neighborhoods of brownstones and

bungalows are full of ordinary Washingtonians who've acquired the comfy fatalism of knowing that almost all who come here to be Somebody will end up like those walls of photographs at the Occidental Restaurant—which is to say they will become Nobody with tidy hair and a frank, hopeful and earnest stare that no one recognizes. The Occidental is the Valhalla of former student council presidents.

Meanwhile, there are other true Washingtonians who live their lives with a Buddhistic acceptance rarely found elsewhere. For them, the frenzy of power and the dreams of judgeships or TV talk shows mean nothing, and they can see through the veils of ambition to Washington as the sensual city that outsiders say it isn't.

They savor its heat and its terrible sunsets mounted for hours over Rosslyn; its mornings of old men coming out to sit on old chairs on old sidewalks in old neighborhoods; the Jusserand bench* in Rock Creek Park and other monuments to the forgotten (who was the statued Logan of Logan Circle?); a delicate and convoluted spring as long as a New Hampshire winter; the older generation of taxi drivers who don't so much drive as proceed through the city; the grip 'n' grin congressmen who look like they're wearing wigs even if they aren't; a glimpse of three little girls doing a time step in front of a stoop on Florida Avenue, slide/clap, slide/clap; the exemplary grace of African Americans who know the secret is not merely looking good but moving well, too, through the endless layers of Washington.

In this city of so much imitation glory and grandeur, an authenticity resides in the black community, from its ancient aristocracy to its newcomers. With their old-family sophistication or rural energy, African Americans come closer than most to believing that they belong here. They seem to have a particular knack for being public people in this public city.

Once there was also an authenticity of seediness about Washington—the gritty carpets of the Willard Hotel before its renovation; the frayed comforts of the Fairfax Hotel before it became the Ritz-Carlton and then something else and something else again. Biker bars nestled up to the town houses of Georgetown grandees. Drugstores here may have been among the last in America to close their lunch counters. At Schwartz's at

---

*The Jusserand bench is a granite bench installed in 1938 to memorialize Jean-Jules Jusserand, ambassador to the United States from France. He served here for twenty-three years and was the long-time dean of the diplomatic corps in Washington. When he left in 1925, a banquet was held in his honor at the Willard Hotel, to which a thousand people came. He was awarded the first Pulitzer Prize in history for his book *With Americans of Past and Present Days*. Frances Parkinson Keyes said of him that "he had the perpetual air of being about to commit some act of drollery."

Connecticut and R, Charlie the counterman always knew the score if the Senators were playing.

"How they doing?" you'd shout through the door.

"Two to five, bottom of the eighth," he'd say, always putting the Senators' score first.

White House guards looked like they needed to tuck their shirts in. Families slept in parks on hot nights. Pennsylvania Avenue was a promenade of cafeterias, fireworks stores and souvenir stands.

And there were smells, the most authentic experiences of all. What has happened to them? In Takoma Park, an activist complained about the smell of baking bread exuding from the bakery. The smell of baking bread!

And the vegetable smell of heat-wave Washington, the coolness breathing out of metal cellar doors in old sidewalks, the exhaust from Chinese restaurants; the mown grass of spring down on the Mall (why doesn't it smell as good in summer?); the dankness rising from the Potomac at night, a sort of attar of darkness; the wonderful wind that blows over the bluffs of Anacostia, through the trees of the lawns where you study the finest cityscape to be seen in all Washington, which is the view from St. Elizabeth's mental hospital; the churches with their incense of colognes, powders, perfumes—a scent that seems to arise from the floral magnificence of hats that church ladies for decades bought from a milliner named Vanilla Beane out by Coolidge High School; the earth smell of collard greens at an African Methodist Episcopal church lunch; the long-lost beer-funk and peanut-breath of the stands at Griffith Stadium, the vast mildew chill of empty Union Station back when there were pools of rainwater on the floor and birds flying under the vaulted ceiling; the perfume counter at Garfinckel's—lamps with pleated shades, the Chanel No. 5 in wood-and-glass cases; the smell of tear gas back when riots were coming to seem a way of life, like the 1968 riot after the breakup of Resurrection City on the Mall.

Resurrection City had housed civil rights demonstrators in plywood and canvas, and finally the government tore it down, starting a riot. I remember walking up 14th Street, downtown. On one side of me a skinny black kid was extracting a pair of shoes from a small hole he'd broken in the store window. On the other, white commuters studied their *Evening Star*s while they prayed for the bus that would carry them away from the terror, the anarchy, the Black Power vengeance of one skinny kid. I seem to recall smelling fear, which there's a lot of in Washington.

There's fear of our minorities, fear of our majorities and fear that our myriad police forces won't keep the fears from coming true. Or will help them to.

Ever since the Soviets tested their first atom bomb, we have feared that our city would be turned into a charred crater at any moment. There's also fear of committee chairmen, judges, lawyers and some peevish beta-male assistant at the White House who decides to turn your life into hell because he can; fear of some young man who will decide to shoot you in the back even after he has your wallet because you disrespected him by running away; fear of ending up in the Superior Court holding cells (which smell so rank that lawyers splash themselves with cologne before they talk to their clients); fear of spending the rest of your life eating lunch in government cafeterias where the steam-table Swiss steak and Brussels sprouts etch themselves into your skin like an olfactory tattoo.

Anyway, things don't smell like much now, and fear is treated with prescriptions for anti-anxiety pills. Authenticity wanes and imitation waxes. We have a new and satanic form of imitation we might call Disneyfication, in which things don't imitate other things, they imitate themselves. In other words, the Washington Monument doesn't imitate an Egyptian obelisk, it imitates itself, as if it had been transported to a theme park as "the Washington Monument."

Washington is particularly susceptible to this, because so many people have ideas, notions and memory-snapshots of what "Washington" is, as opposed to our own pleasant, easy, authentic, real Washington.

It's as if Disney had moved in to clean up Pennsylvania Avenue, to give us John Kennedy's dream of a triumphal way between White House and Capitol. And sometime in the last decade or two, the Capitol dome at night, beneath its spotlights, began to look too perfect to me, as if it were made of plastic, like a full-scale model of itself, which is what Georgetown has looked like, too, ever since the rich people drove all the poor people out of it with that modern American relish for economic segregation.

The great halls of governance around the Mall now have the look of memorials to nothing more than themselves, as if there should be quotation marks around them. "The Justice Department." "The Labor Department." "The Lincoln Memorial." All this imitation perfection is unsettling. It looks a little dead. Couldn't we have saved just one fireworks store or cafeteria?

So much to fear. At the same time, Los Angeles traffic jams and New York manners crowd us, hurry us, frustrate us, but still, Washington remains a pleasant place to live—adamantly pleasant, as if pleasantness were a founding principle of the city, like beauty in Paris or money in Las Vegas. It's a city of huge lawns and roomy sidewalks and hallways that provoke an impulse to stroll. We are not intimidated by skyscrapers because we don't have any. The huge trees, the fields of the Mall and the deer-thick forests of Rock Creek Park reassure us that we can live here and still partake of the virtues of the pioneers and Jefferson's yeoman farmers.

How pleasant. Please, God, says the Washington prayer, don't let the voters figure out what a good thing they've given us. Don't let us get caught. In other words, the modesty that some attribute to Washington is in fact slyness. No matter how much money we have, we choose to exhibit suburban taste, not big-city style. Big jewelry and big fur are not necessary or appropriate here. Lawyers have clothes tailor-made to look just like clothes that are off the rack. We walk slowly enough that if you're from up North you think we're small-towners, and we walk quickly enough that if you're from down South you think we're efficient. Jack Kennedy spoke the truth when he said that Washington is a city of Southern efficiency and Northern charm.

At the same time, didn't Duke Ellington derive at least part of his fabulous grace, precision, ease and genius of contradictions from Washington, his native city?

Some Americans don't care about Washington at all. To them, Washington isn't a city as much as a mailing address or a dateline or an abstract principle of power or scandal or foolishness. It isn't even a capital as much as the mother board of the American bureaucratic computer, suitable for class visits by high school students.

One suspects that citizens of New York or Chicago would be insulted if somebody in Pocatello talked about their cities as if they were irrelevant or almost invisible. Yet the true Washingtonian, hearing this dismissal in the speech of taxpayers, rejoices. Yes, we've fooled them again. They don't believe we really exist, so they won't stop sending us money. (It's just crazy enough to make political sense.)

Oh, let's not worry about this too much, this reality/unreality business. Reality has always kept a careful distance here, from the quaintness of notions of importance to the alleys full of shantytown ghosts, the single sculls on the Potomac at dawn, pulsing along with their acute aloofness. . . . But the old unreality depended on our secret knowledge of how transitory it was. The new unreality depends on the insistence of permanence.

Stop it! Why bother? Except to say that Washington does greet undeniable reality with exhilaration, even a reality as life-snarling as a blizzard. On a hot night once at the Carter Barron Amphitheater, I was sufficiently impressed with the reality at hand that I took a note on it: "The spotlights hissing through the humidity, smoky tubes of light, and beyond them the little smears of fireflies—it all seems heroic and

*My parents riding in Rock Creek Park in their first years in
Washington. My mother described this regular habit as "splashing
through the fords ... in that most lovely of parks."*

exhausted, as if the city were under siege and you could hear the artillery in the distance, which you can, sometimes, when the thunderstorms gather over Virginia and Maryland. (And when the thunderstorms hit, we race around closing windows, feeling so exultant. Hail the size of chickpeas! Golf balls! Canned hams!)"

You feel almost grateful for loony Lafayette Square demonstrators and the sullen weariness of neighborhoods so dangerous that whiskey and lottery tickets have to be sold through bulletproof plastic. The sirens reduce the melody of Washington to the lowest common denominator of stolen cars and heart attacks. The transvestite prostitutes are sad comedy, and the streets called the Riot Corridor 30 years ago are still reminders of the frailty of cultures, black and white, in the face of the sins of rage and covetousness.

And we sift through our private snapshots, incomprehensible to some outsiders—the smell of air gliding out of underground parking lots on a summer night, the sound of two companies of Marine rifle butts coming to rest in a crash so perfect it is almost a single crack, the clatter of young heels running down the stairs of the Washington Monument, the private certainties and public fears, the temporary feeling that can become a lovely joke. Sometimes, at 4:30 in the morning, Massachusetts Avenue can be so empty of cars you worry that the moving men are about to arrive and remove the buildings, too.

Then it's morning. Smell the trees! Look at that airliner rising under a morning moon! The old men setting out their chairs and the wind stirring the leaves on the bluffs of Anacostia. With pleasures coming this easily, says the true and enlightened Washingtonian, why worry too much about reality?

MR. AND MRS. SMITH
COME TO WASHINGTON

There are a number of ways of getting to Washington. Some get elected. Some get appointed. Some get drafted. Some get transferred. Some ride a lobbyhorse to this man's town. Many arrive as wives, and some join their kin or their kind. Some come on pilgrimages and remain. I know a man who came on a bonus march after the first World War and stayed to start a sight-seeing service with a car his bonus bought.

—Bess Furman, *Washington By-Line*

THERE are as many reasons for coming to Washington as there are people who've come. Some are sort of born to be here. As Bess Furman also wrote in *Washington By-Line,* "Whole families, such as the Adamses, the Lodges, the Roosevelts, the Bankheads, Tafts, and La Follettes, are born with souvenir spoons in their mouths, of a pattern with a dome on the handle and plainly marked, 'Washington, D.C.' on the bowl." Others clearly worked their way to Washington. Furman herself said she wrote her way in.

In some ways my parents were the quintessential Mr. and Mrs. Smith. When they first arrived in Washington, in 1917, they saw and experienced a big small town. Indeed, in a memoir that my mother was writing in her later years but never finished—*Life as Chance and Destiny*—she described Washington as a village:

Washington as a whole still had a village atmosphere. Connecticut Avenue was lined on both sides by overarching elms. One fashionable old couple did their shopping in a tandem-drawn Hansom cab. When you walked the streets you stopped constantly to gossip with friends. The final proof of small-town atmosphere was the annual parade through the city streets of Barnum & Baileys circus. Seated on the brown stone steps of our house we could enjoy the somber lumbering march of the elephants and envy the lovely ballerinas on their backs, or on those of the glistening white circus horses, all seeming to keep step with the raucous tones of the calliope. The children shuddered at the slender bars on the cages of the lions and tigers but shrieked joyously when the clowns did their best to be frightening when their painted masks were revealed by the bright light of day. And what delightful nonsense to attend the circus in a tent amidst the pop-corn booths, side shows and the screams of joy and fun of innumerable children.

Washington was to be sure a village on a grander scale than Pelhamville [the town just outside the New York City limits where she grew up], which the circus would not have dignified by a parade. But after living in the cold immensity of New York City for many years, it still had the cozy intimacy of village life, of nature and of familiar human beings which always haunted my innermost self. In that early Washington atmosphere I was singularly at home.

Mother also wrote that

> When war was declared Eugene turned the key in the door of his New York office and betook himself to Washington for sundry duties, chiefly that of helping Bernard Baruch organize the War Industries Board, of which President Wilson had appointed him chairman. As our daughter Katharine . . . was born in June, I could not go to Washington to find a house until the beginning of August amidst the torrid heat of Washington. I found that the houses big enough for a family of four children contained enormous ballrooms but sordid little bedrooms. We found temporary shelter in K Street.

Despite the fact that my father had liquidated the assets of his business, my mother, not unnaturally, had assumed that the move was only temporary. In fact, the Smiths who used to come to Washington would mostly also go. Many families, especially those connected with the government in one way or another, thought of this place as transient. At that time, with the buildup of the effort to prepare to fight the war, there was a sense of transience about the whole city—particularly in the circles in which my parents moved. Most people with the kind of resources of my parents maintained summer homes and lived in Washington only during the "season"—a social season that lasted essentially from October through May and corresponded roughly to both the congressional session and the time when the Washington weather was bearable.

Some of the entries in my mother's diary imply that she thinks of Washington as a place she's just visiting. She wrote, "Washington is like an ocean voyage. One spends a short time with people and then good-by, never to meet again." Vera Bloom, whose entire book *(There's No Place Like Washington)* is a kind of extended "Ms. Smith Comes to Washington," expressed the same thought about Washington relationships: ". . . they are friendships, full blown in an amazing moment like the friendships one sometimes makes on shipboard, and probably for the same reason, because you know from the first that they can't last forever. But you know, too, that whenever you may meet again, the friendship will go on as if there had never been a moment's break."

Others also wrote of this transient nature of life in Washington. Marietta Andrews, in her "sketches of the pageant of Washington life," reflected, "Life in Washington is a strain upon genuine friendship as it is upon marital fidelity, for no sooner do we become attached to these delightful transients than fate whips them out of sight, Governments issue new orders, and the place thereof knows them no more—Diplomats, Cabinets, Congressmen, Army and Navy officers—here today and gone tomorrow!"

But my parents were among those who came and stayed, although every year, for my entire childhood, it seemed as if we were always on the verge of moving back to New York.

Many other Mr. and Mrs. Smiths have followed. This section includes a grab bag of people—from congressional wives to an ambassador's wife to the unlikely Bobby Baker. Here is an assortment of Smiths, all of whom made Washington their home for a while.

The Old Order Changeth

Morning and Noon (1965)

Dean Acheson first came to Washington to be Supreme Court Justice Louis Brandeis's law clerk. Like many who come here thinking they're going to stay only for the duration of a given job, Dean got caught up in the Washington atmosphere. He stayed a second year and then another. I remember his wife, Alice, telling me that they both thought each of those years at the start of their Washington sojourn would be their last.

Felix Frankfurter, who had been one of Dean's professors at Harvard, had had a lot to do with Dean's coming to Washington as he did with another generation, with Phil and many of our friends. Later, when Felix himself came to Washington, he and Dean, fast friends, would walk together to work. In fact, according to Alice, Felix, who lived near the Achesons, would walk around to their house, often with his car and driver following him, pick up Dean, and off they'd walk to Dean's office at Covington and Burling, from where Felix would hop in the car for the remainder of the trip to the Supreme Court.

This excerpt comes from a book that I recently pulled off my own shelves. I remember buying it at Savile Book Shop, which was once a Georgetown institution. Its dust jacket has a full-length photo on the back cover of these two great men—Felix and Dean—on one of their walks in the early 1940s. The book itself was dedicated to Felix— actually, "To FF"—with this accompanying quotation from the book of Amos in the Bible: "Can two walk together, except they be agreed?"

Dean and Alice were part of the sort of in-between generation, between mine and my parents'. They became older friends of ours. Every Christmas they invited our family, including the children, for a caroling party, which was a holiday tradition we all looked forward to.

Dean Acheson was one of the very best and brightest of the men who ever came to Washington. He wrote a number of books, the most well *known of which is probably* Present at the Creation, *and several of which deal with some of the important positions he held in Washington, including secretary of state. But I like this book because it's a charming recalling of his early years, and an account of times and people who, as he says in his introduction, "have completely vanished."*

W E CAME to Washington that September (of 1919) when Woodrow Wilson fell "like Lucifer, never to hope again." He had gone to the people with his "solemn referendum" on the League of Nations against the Senate "Irreconcilables" and the reservations of Senator Lodge. The blow fell in Colorado. In silence and mystery the special train sped back to the capital. There mystery grew as the weeks passed, the bland medical bulletins continued, but no word came from the President. Not even the faithful Joe Tumulty saw him. He had simply disappeared. Rumors flew. More weeks passed. The government and the Senate Democrats wallowed rudderless. In Congress wolves tore at the carcass of the Covenant and howled for the blood of the Administration. From the White House, only silence; but for an occasional Sibylline utterance from the High Priestess.*

In the circle in which we moved depression and bewilderment deepened. Justice Brandeis, whose law clerk I was, brushed aside attempts to draw him out, giving the impression that things were so much worse than could be imagined as to be beyond discussion. We went on with our work and our lives, as I imagine people did in Rome in the fifth century with the defenses of the frontiers crumbling. A year passed; the depression grew; the forthcoming election, a bad prospect, turned into a horror in fact. A sack of the city by the victorious barbarians appeared a certainty. It was.

In the fall of 1920 we moved from a small apartment on Vermont Avenue above Thomas Circle, between the Georgian Wylie house, now gone, and Mr. Theodore Noyes's house, also gone, to a minute house on Corcoran Street. The Washington of 1920 was a small, gangling southern city. I remember with nostalgic affection the old Shoreham Hotel at 15th and H Streets, a period piece of southern hostelry, with a most serene dining room decorated in white with mirrors and chandeliers. There Joe Tumulty and a group of friends lunched daily and Joe recited his favorite Shakespearean passages.

*Woodrow Wilson's second wife, Edith Bolling Wilson, whom he had married in December 1915.

The Justice's apartment and also his office were on Connecticut Avenue in Stoneleigh Court, built by and named after John Hay's father-in-law. Every morning at ten o'clock the Justice and Mrs. Brandeis took the air in a smart runabout behind a handsome and spirited hackney. The Justice, a Kentuckian, himself handled Sir Gareth, as Mrs. Brandeis had romantically named their horse. Later on, when automobile traffic made the drives too dangerous, Sir Gareth grew old on our farm in Maryland, mildly pulling a less distinguished buggy.

Poindexter, the messenger, and I constituted the whole office staff; and Poindexter, half the household staff as well. Out of the office window we could see Senator Elkins's mansion on K Street, and Poindexter would talk of the glamorous parties given there when the Duce d'Abruzzi was thought to be courting Miss Katherine Elkins, and of earning nickels as a boy by holding restless horses in the torchlight while footmen handed ladies from their broughams.

Across Connecticut Avenue from Stoneleigh Court the fashionable Magruder grocery furnished the ladies' morning meeting place, while farther up the Avenue they danced in the evening at Rauscher's, the caterer's ballroom. In the basement of Stoneleigh Court Charlie Laudano had his barbershop. For forty years we were to be friends. In those days he was barber to the diplomatic corps. Later I insinuated him into the State Department, where he outstayed me. One day, after I had gone, I said to him, "Charlie, how's my friend Foster?"

"Not so good, not so good," he replied. "I think he's got hold of that damned initiative and can't let go of it." In the old days, the Justice patronized his shop twice a week. Mrs. Brandeis did not like him to have his hair cut. He solved the problem by these frequent visits and his admonition, "Charlie, the invisible haircut!"

North from our office, Connecticut Avenue, its broad sidewalks shaded by double rows of sycamore trees, passed first the Convent and Academy of the Visitation, whose brick wall enclosed the whole block where the Mayflower Hotel is today; then St. Matthew's Cathedral and Chief Justice White's house on Rhode Island Avenue, and on past the British Embassy at N Street, to join Massachusetts Avenue in a traffic and social jumble at Dupont Circle.

While commerce was moving up Connecticut Avenue, society was leaving K Street to settle on Massachusetts Avenue from Scott Circle west. A massive enclave grouped around Dupont Circle—Miss Mabel Boardman's large and somber brick house, the marble palaces of the Countess Gizycka, née Eleanor (Cissy) Patterson, and of the Leiters across the street. On the other side of the Circle came the Henry

Spencers, Speaker Longworth, Mrs. Walsh, Mrs. Townsend, and the Misses Patten. At Sheridan Circle, where the General in bronze perpetually rallies his troops from defeat at Winchester, another wave of mansions and embassies moved—and still moves—westward.

Hidden away above Dupont Circle is a more modest street. Quite properly, Admiral Du Pont on his granite pedestal, himself soon to be replaced by Daniel Chester French's marble fountain, turned his back on it. Corcoran Street runs east from a dead end at 19th to be lost, temporarily, in the broad confluence of 18th Street and New Hampshire Avenue, before again briefly taking up its way, to peter out at 13th Street. On the south side of the street at its west end we lived in one of a row of small identical houses, each with an overhanging bay window on the second floor, giving a slightly Walt Disney impression of a twelfth-century Normandy village. In this area existed what might be called a ghetto of near respectability and intelligence in the midst of high position, wealth, and fashion.

I say "near" respectability because of one of our neighbors whose conduct was unpredictable. One evening we had dining with us a most proper Bostonian, who was a law clerk to Justice Holmes. Not long afterward, distaste for America of the twenties drove our guest to England and British citizenship. On the evening I mention, just as dinner ended, our unpredictable neighbor in fez, false beard, and his conception of the probable clothes of an Armenian rug peddler, and with some of his own unimpressive rugs over his arm, pushed past a bewildered cook and stamped muttering up the stairs, the cook protesting behind him. Surprise, embarrassment, and the torrent of his speech as he laid out his wares and pressed a sale on our guest and my wife, as the householders, carried all before him. The performance was first class, but soon ended as the disguise was penetrated and the peddler revealed as our entertaining and then obscure friend Sinclair Lewis. Our guest was definitely not amused. . . .

THE NEW President paraded down Pennsylvania Avenue on March 4, 1921. The most "striking feature of the parade," *The Washington Post* reported, was "the biggest broom ever made," gilded of handle, topped by an American flag, given to the President by an Oklahoma delegation to typify the "possibilities of change of administration from Democratic to Republican." The day was a rarely auspicious golden one, and the crowds shouted and jumped up and down with frantic enthusiasm at being rid of high endeavor and being led back to normalcy. We and our friends stood with a small group on S Street, bareheaded while a cripple, helped from his car, hobbled laboriously to the door of his new house. At the threshold he turned, took off his top hat to us and disappeared. Again, three years later, we stood there while his coffin was carried out.

Meanwhile, the new Administration developed its own curious blend of piety, vulgarity, and corruption. At first, attention centered on the piety. "I met the President, today," said Justice Brandeis after the Court's official call. "He has a fine face. I have hope of him." This was significant, coming from the Justice, one of whose maxims, adopted from Lincoln, was, "At forty every man is responsible for his face." Justice Clarke, an enthusiast for the League of Nations, found hope in another quarter—"Hughes is our best hope for finding a way into the League."

Soon the gilded broom had swept the White House clean of any lingering taint of professional intellectuality. Poker parties with senatorial pals provided relaxation. There were rumors of a scene at the house on McPherson Square of the publisher of *The Washington Post*, Ned McLean, when Secretary Hughes found that a party for the Cabinet was to be entertained by movies of a Dempsey championship fight, illegally transported in interstate commerce. A young woman of doubtful reputation had her skull bashed in—it was said by a bottle—in an equally doubtful hotel, after a riotous party allegedly attended by some who might more profitably have spent the night gathering strength for official duties.

"The little green house on K Street" was whispered to be the scene of deals, appointments, and payoffs. The word "oil" began to be bruited about. About this time, Mrs. Brandeis being ill and attended by nurses, the Justice for a while slept on a couch in his office. I was no longer his law clerk, and it was then that our former relationship subtly changed. Being lonely, he would send word that, if convenient, he would welcome an evening call on him in the office. There, with no work to stand between us, and all alone, he would say conspiratorially, "Dean, what is the latest dirt?"

The Justice was an arresting figure; his head of Lincolnian cast and grandeur, the same boldness and ruggedness of features, the same untamed hair, the eyes of infinite depth under bushy eyebrows, which in moments of emotion seemed to jut out. As he grew older, he carried a prophetic, if not intimidating aura. It was not in jest that later law clerks referred to him as Isaiah. But it would be wrong to leave the impression here. For more than twenty years I had the great privilege of his friendship and learned much of his mind and spirit at once worldly and austere, severe and loving; of his affections, detached and yet wholly committed. During that time I became assured of his affection and I believe that he never doubted my devotion. One of the greatest honors and hardest tasks which has come to me was to speak at his funeral service.

I started with the advantage of working for him when he had been only three years away from active practice and of knowing two close friends of the old days, Herbert White of the Plimpton Press in Boston, and Norman Hapgood, once the sensational muckraking editor of *Collier's Weekly*, the destroyer with Brandeis of Taft's Secretary of the Interior, Richard Ballinger. These two men and the Justice's sisters-in-aw were the only people whom I ever heard call him "Louis." Mrs. Brandeis's name for him, as nearly as I can render it, sounded like "Leurps."

I shall never forget my first meeting with Herbert White. Answering a ring of the office doorbell, I found a genial and rumpled stranger who asked me whether "Louis" was in. He was not, and I said so, adding that he could be seen only by appointment. If he would give me his name, etc.

"Don't give me that stuff," he said good-naturedly. "I'll come in and wait for him. I see he has you hypnotized, too. Come on in with me and tell me who you are." With that he led casually into the study, with me tagging along. He pulled a chair up to the desk, to my horror swept onto the floor a stack of carefully place-marked *U.S. Reports*, and put his feet up. Surely, I thought, surely a bolt direct from the hand of Jove will strike this impious profaner of the shrine itself.

Instead, he went on imperturbably, "I'm Herbert White. Louis and I used to do a lot of sailing and trout fishing together. I never went along with that fox hunting of his. He was a great guy in those days. Still is. But not much use to his friends since he got sight of the Holy Grail." I was beginning to come out of shock, but he saw me glancing nervously at the door. "Sit down," he said. "For God's sake, relax! He doesn't eat children."

I took a semiseat facing the door, ready to spring to attention, in no way convinced by the last observation. "I remember the day and hour of the conversion," he went on. "We were sitting around a campfire in Maine after a great day's fishing. I wanted to plan for tomorrow. But he started off on the damnedest bellyache you ever heard. The tie-up between government and money; the way the banks used other people's money against their interest; the way big corporations skinned the public and pushed the laboring man around; insurance companies fought savings bank insurance, and railroad management didn't know its own business or interest. On and on it went.

"Finally," he ended, "I'd had enough. 'Louis Brandeis,' I said, 'you've had the best day ever on the river, a wonderful dinner, and your pants are dry. What the hell's the matter with you?' "

I heard the key in the lock and was already on my feet when the Justice came in. "Ah, Herbert," he said, "I see that you are already giving my new law clerk his first lesson."

"Good morning, sir," I murmured and faded through the doorway into my own room.

New Boy on Capitol Hill

Wheeling and Dealing: Confessions of a Capitol Hill Operator (1978)

Not everyone is the Jimmy Stewart variety of Mr. Smith (actually, Dean Acheson comes closer than most), and not all that has been written about Washington has been written by Nature's noblemen. One example of a less than admirable accounting of activities is Bobby Baker's book, whose subtitle, "Confessions of a Capitol Hill Operator," reveals a great deal.

While I cannot pretend to admire or respect Mr. Baker, I do find compelling his account of arriving in Washington as a kid and what it did to him. I think this is probably a unique story, and it certainly carries conviction. Here we have a "Master Smith" who came to Washington and eventually went on to jail.

I ARRIVED in Washington full of trepidation. On January 1, 1943, I reported to the office of Les Biffle, who then held the job I later would hold as secretary to the Senate majority. Biffle was a gentle man from Arkansas I later would know as a friend, but I do not recall whether I reported to him or to some faceless subordinate. Perhaps this is because I was worried about Japanese spies.

A hoary old merchant seaman, recognizing a gullible kid when he saw one, told me in the boarding house we newly shared (at First and Constitution, where the Dirksen Senate Office Building now stands) that fifteen Japanese spies had sneaked up the Potomac River in submarines and were thought to be somewhere in the bowels of the Capitol Building. They were not idle, according to my craggy informant, but even then were working to place explosives which would blow the Capitol to smithereens.

This was not difficult to believe if you not only didn't know anything but didn't even suspect much—and if you had seen through wide eyes the antiaircraft guns, and the military men with bayonets at the ready, which guarded the Capitol grounds. I had heard, too, that only those in possession of security passes—with, I guess, the obvious exception of Japanese spies—were permitted admittance to the Capitol Building. There had to be a reason for that.

Government propaganda, and the messages of potboiler war movies cranked out in Hollywood, had conditioned my mind to the dangers of sabotage; I thus had no cause to doubt the presence of Japanese agents on Capitol Hill. Remember, this was in a time when Uncle Sam had taken his lumps in the Pacific; the memories of Pearl Harbor and the horrors of the Bataan Death March remained fresh. I did not feel any patriotic stirrings to go into the catacombs of the Capitol Building in search of Japanese spies, but I kept a wary eye out in case they saw me first.

Washington represented the frozen northlands to a Southern boy, and so I reported for work wearing old-fashioned long-handle underwear under my outer garments. When I was suffering a beating with brooms from other pages during my initiation rites, these long-handle woolies were discovered by my tormentors amid much laughter and much to my own humiliation.

I was miserably unhappy and homesick during those first weeks on Capitol Hill. My education in Pickens [South Carolina] perhaps left something to be desired and so I found myself having to struggle to keep up academically in the Capitol Page School, which met for daily classes conducted under the big dome.

One of my letters home admitted to my loneliness and disenchantment. This word filtered back to a former teacher of mine, Miss Lucille Hallum, who wrote from Pickens to urge me to reach for the best in myself. Unfortunately for those who love the correct uses of grammar, my letter of response has been preserved and it surfaced some years later during my highly publicized troubles. "Bobby Baker don't quit," I assured my old teacher.

There were times, however, when I wanted to. Pickens, whatever its limitations, had been a warm cocoon where I was nurtured by family and friends. I was accepted there, permitted to grow at my own pace; perhaps, as a budding big duck on a small pond, I had received more praise than was good for me. It was a shock to discover that in Washington I might be just one among the many. In the early months I did not find much camaraderie among my more sophisticated fellow page boys or among the rag-tags with whom I shared a boarding house. I was physically smaller at fourteen than almost all of my associates, I was green, and I was scared. This often caused me to be the target of rough humor and the butt of jokes.

The uniform of a Senate page boy, alone, was hateful to me in the extreme. The knickers we wore implied that we were juveniles, of low rank, less than full citizens. Girls giggled at them and adults often teased us about them. I hated them with a passion difficult to fully measure. Years later, when I had the power, I ordered that page-boy knickers be replaced by long trousers.

The work of a rookie Senate page boy is mundane enough. We filled the traditional inkwells and snuff boxes on each senator's desk, though by the 1940s few senators were snuff addicts. We filled the senatorial water tumblers. We brought the senators public documents, newspapers, telephone messages, or anything they desired. To call us, they'd snap their fingers and we'd scurry to them in a half trot.

I realized early on that the key to being efficient and well liked in the Senate was learning to anticipate what each senator might require. I noted each senator's special preferences: Senator X might prefer Kalak water, a soda-water-like beverage, while Senator Y might insist on Mountain Valley spring water; I did not confuse their tastes. When I learned that a given senator would be making a speech on a given day, I stationed myself nearby to quickly fetch some documents or materials or fresh water as he might need. It was not long until many senators asked for me by name. I took pride in my good reputation among the senators, because it meant that I was successful in what I was being paid to do.

In lax times I enjoyed roaming the Senate chamber to read the names of former senators (many of whom had been only dead figures of history for me) which they had burned or carved inside their desk drawers—a tradition still honored to this day. I recall running my fingers over the names—Daniel Webster, Stephen Douglas, Andrew Johnson—and marveling that I stood where they had stood.

One of my big thrills was hearing the great figures of World War II— Winston Churchill, Madam Chiang Kai-shek—when they came to address the United States Senate. I hustled to the front of the chamber to sit on the carpeted step where alert and ambitious page boys posted themselves; so great was my enthrallment that I even forgot for a few moments that I wore those hated little-boy knickers.

I very early became fascinated with the give and take of Senate debate. Each day I contrived to find an advantageous position from which to listen to the senators, while keeping an eye and an ear open for the sight or sound of snapping fingers calling me to work. I took an early interest in mastering the parliamentary rules. When I did not understand a particular rule, or why something had been done, I sought out Mr. Charles Watkins, the Senate parliamentarian. He was a kindly, gracious man from Arkansas and he patiently educated me. I learned, too, to anticipate how long each individual senator would be likely to talk and to read from the visible parliamentary signs just when an adjournment for the day might come. My favorite pastime was counting noses: long before my job would require that I tell Senate Majority Leader Lyndon Johnson how many votes he might expect for a given bill, I made private tallies and predictions for my own amusement. In retrospect, I suppose one might say that I had a little of Sammy Glick in me. Ambition was honorable in the society I had been raised in, however; I tried constantly to learn, to serve, to improve myself.

One learned, too, the human frailties harbored by each United States senator. Senator Bennett Champ Clark of Missouri, when sober, was a kind and gentle man. When drunk, however, he became an abusive tyrant, one who railed and cussed at his subordinates. Consequently, I danced attendance upon Senator Clark in the early part of the day and then, as the hours passed and he began to show signs of inebriation, I made myself scarce. I learned that Republican Senator Charles McNary of Oregon, an Irishman with a twinkle in his eye and a man I much admired for his friendly countenance and ability, simply could not see a skirt pass by without compulsively chasing it. For a while I distrusted Senator Robert Wagner, Sr., of New York—a truly nice man—because, as part of the normal initiation rites, he once sent me to the Senate Document Room to fetch a nonexistent "bill stretcher." One of my favorites was old Senator Tom Connally of Texas, one of the great characters of American politics. He was so pigeon-toed it was unreal, and we pages sometimes mimed the way he walked across the floor. He was a kind man at heart, though in debate he could become the most partisan, caustic man I would know until Oklahoma's Bob Kerr came along. With long curly hair that flowed over his collar, his old-fashioned high-top shoes, and his bombastic oratorical style, Connally may have been a caricature of Senator Claghorn; to me, however, he was a better show than any Shakespearean actor.

Of all the senators in my early Washington years, my favorite was a small, unassuming man from Missouri. Harry Truman was the most genteel man I ever met. Not once did I see him act imperiously toward lowly page boys. "Young man," he would say—not "Sonny" as so many called us—"Young man, when it's convenient, could you please get me a glass of water?" Or, "Young man, would you mind calling my secretary and asking her to send me such-and-so?" In any popularity contest, among page boys or senators, I think Truman would have won in a landslide.

A minor scandal occurred among Senate page boys in September of 1943, and in recent years I've sometimes had the feeling it portended the darker side of my future. It began well enough—indeed, it began as the biggest thing that had happened to me in Washington—when Mrs. Eleanor Roosevelt invited the congressional page boys and the Supreme Court page boys to the White House for a Saturday luncheon to be followed by a movie. The splendor of the White House dazzled the country kid from Pickens.

After lunch came a surprising bonus. Mrs. Roosevelt escorted us upstairs to the First Family living quarters. I vividly recall her knocking on the door of the president's second-floor office—not the Oval Office, but a secondary one in the living quarters—and saying in that high half-yodel of hers, "Franklin, Franklin, I have some guests for you." President Roosevelt received us with a warm smile and pleasantries I no longer remember. He exhibited a German helmet captured in the North African campaign, and I recall that he spoke at length of America's and of freedom's stake in the war. The remainder of the visit he spent in cordially asking each of us our home states and personal questions. He talked inordinately long of my sponsor, Senator Maybank, saying how much he personally appreciated the senator's having quit the governorship of South Carolina to assist the New Deal in Washington. Perhaps it was merely the practiced prattle of the consummate politician, but it caused me to feel pride and to get the impression that my sponsor might be a bit special. I went back to my boarding house to dash off a letter home describing my big day, and I was delighted when excerpts from it later appeared in the Pickens weekly newspaper.

The Monday morning following our White House visit, however, proved to be embarrassing and scary. Shortly after Capitol Page School convened, Secret Service men appeared to consult with our agitated headmaster, a Mr. Kendall. Soon a general school assembly was called. Mr. Kendall, angry and humiliated, stated the problem: so many souvenir hunters from among us had pocketed so much of the best White House silver that not enough remained to meet the requirements of a state dinner scheduled that night. School would be dismissed and we would return to our homes, on the double, to return the pilfered silver. I felt as embarrassed as Mr. Kendall did; I was not a souvenir hunter to begin with, and, had I been, I would have considered it a breach of good manners to pocket my host's silver. This lack of good manners among my peers caused me to feel a collective guilt and shame. What would President and Mrs. Roosevelt think of such ruffians?

When I became one of the few page boys not to leave the room to return home, Mr. Kendall asked me, "Bobby, hadn't you better be running along?"

"No sir," I said. "I wasn't raised to steal silver, and I didn't steal silver. I've got better manners than that."

I may have said it with a sting in my voice; I'd resented Mr. Kendall since he'd written my parents, shortly after my arrival in Washington, that I might not be high school material. My improving grades, as I advanced through Capitol Page School, were, I imagine, attained by way of showing Mr. Kendall up for a bad prophet.

Not long after Congress adjourned and I returned to Pickens feeling much a man of the world, I attended a South Carolina political ritual known simply as "The Speaking." It was a command performance for all political candidates and officer holders, and each county annually held one. It was obligatory for everyone from the lowliest constable to the congressman to appear and give the voters an account of themselves. I was astonished when Mr. Julien Wyatt, the Democratic county chairman, suddenly said, "Ladies and gentlemen, we are honored to have all these distinguished people on our platform, candidates for many important offices, but we're proudest of a young man who comes from us, is one of us, and belongs to us. He's now making a name for himself in Washington—our own Bobby Baker. Bobby, we'd like to hear you say a few words."

I could not have been more astonished had he asked me to tap dance or announced my engagement. Groping toward the microphone, I was shaking so badly that I only vaguely heard the rustle of applause; I had no more idea than a fencepost of what to say. Somehow it flashed in my mind that someone had once said that if you really wanted to make a good speech you should say: "To be seen, you must stand up. To be heard, you must speak out. To be appreciated, you must sit down." So I recited it and quickly sat down, basking in the laughter and applause greeting my first public speech. It may not have ranked with the best of Churchill, but for a few days you might have had trouble convincing me otherwise. If the political bug hadn't already fatally bitten me, that was the day it did.

BARBARA HOWAR

A Report on a Life Lived in Washington

Laughing All the Way (1973)

I always liked Barbara Howar and admired her spunk. I know that she considered me—and Alice Roosevelt Longworth—an exception to her negative feelings about Washington widows and single women, whom she basically found dispensable.

Howar, at one time a true Johnson insider—her daughter was one of Luci's little bridesmaids—had quite a falling out with the Lyndon Johnsons, which she reports on in this book, and I believe that this got in the way of my relationship with them (or at least the president), not from anything I did, but rather because Johnson believed, as most presidents, and in fact most others, do, that the Post *and I were one and the same, and that I controlled everything that went into the paper.*

Despite several periods of chill in our friendship, I had got back together with the Johnsons in a notable thaw after he left the presidency. However, in the fall of 1970, when Lady Bird's book, A White House Diary, *was published, someone at the* Post *had the unfortunate idea of having it reviewed by Barbara Howar. She began the review by saying, "Can you imagine how it must have felt to face a tape recorder every single day from November 22, 1963, to January 20, 1969. I'm so overwhelmed by Mrs. Johnson's discipline that I can barely get myself together to discuss the resulting book . . . [which] weighs 4¼ pounds, broke the strap of my over-the-shoulder bag twice and caused me to have a recurring dream that I was Fay Wray carrying around King Kong." Howar questioned the book's historical value and faulted its incompleteness. Her somewhat snide (albeit funny) review, which the* Post *ran under the headline "Weak Vignettes Linked by Steel," made LBJ understandably angry all over again.*

Barbara Howar sets the scene at the beginning of her book by saying that her story "is neither a comedy nor a memoir. It is a report on a life

lived in Washington; on a time, a town, and a heroine, all equally fool-
ish." In this excerpt she describes Washington as she found it in the
1950s; for her experiences in 1960s Washington, you'll have to go
to the original. What is clear from this piece is that, however many dif-
ficulties she ran into here, Howar loved "practically every minute in
Washington." On the second page of her book, she offers one reason
why: "Living among politicians has had an enormous effect on me and,
while I am not prepared to think the reverse is true, I believe the city
and I were well met. It is right that I should recount Washington in
the bizarre period of the 1960s. We somehow deserved one another."

I . . . SET OUT to conquer Washington. This was a wild fantasy considering that my qualifications consisted of a vague but cosmetically
encouraged resemblance to Grace Kelly and six years of elocution
lessons at Miss Bootsie MacDonald's School of Tap and Toe. I rode the
midnight *Silver Meteor* north on New Year's Day of 1957, peacefully
squeezed into an upper berth with a squirrel jacket and an enormous
teddy bear with one shoe-button eye. I had two hundred dollars in traveler's checks and all the confidence in the world that I would need nothing more to be the finest thing to hit Washington since Eleanor
Roosevelt. My optimism lasted all the way to Union Station.

The reunion with Washington was less than spectacular. It was not an
easy town for women seeking employment other than typing or strip-
ping. Not being skilled or built for either, I had trouble finding a glamorous, high-paying position with short hours, long vacations, and all the
benefits I thought a girl with a nice, classic face deserved. I presented my
journalistic credentials to Alfred Friendly, editor of the *Washington Post*.
He was not impressed with my résumé or my Grace Kelly profile. There
were, he told the top of his desk, "no places for women with experience,
much less you kids who can't do anything." His policy, and probably the
only one, was shared with several slightly more polite men named Noyes
[family owners of the paper] whom I saw at the *Evening Star*. I was never
able to get an appointment at the *Daily News*, which wiped out my journalistic aspirations and left me curious as to where the cartoonist found
his prototype for Brenda Starr.

Washington, it seemed, was not to be the hot-time-in-the-ole-town I
had envisioned. My money and confidence ran out as fast as my welcome
from an old schoolmate, upon whom I had descended, in her third-floor
walk-up apartment over a Georgetown bar-and-grill. When I passed the
point of no-money-for-a-return-ticket-home, I presented myself, in a

manner of speaking, to Uncle Frank Boykin, whose years in Congress had dulled his interest in women but accrued to him a certain seniority which entitled him to patronage, Capitol Hill slang for welfare. He had won enough elections to enable him to place relatives and constituents on the government payroll as doorkeepers, pages, guards, and elevator operators. Though I was neither kissing kin nor a loyal voter, he was willing to extend his patronage to me; but I was, and still am, the wrong sex to avail myself of congressional handouts.

His younger friend and colleague, Oren Harris of Arkansas, had just become Chairman of the House Committee on Interstate and Foreign Commerce, a coveted position but one that constitutionally stripped him of his patronage. His secretary was married to a man crippled during World War II who lost his appointment as House Doorman when Harris became Chairman; they planned to move back to Arkansas if he did not find a new slot immediately. After much southern haggling it was agreed that Frank Boykin would use his patronage to return Harris' man to his old job, in return for which Harris would hire me on a trial basis to fill a vacant committee job—a transaction which later earned me the Capitol Hill description of "the kid Frank Boykin traded Oren Harris for the one-legged doorman." That exchange of influential favors remains my single soft spot for the existing system of congressional seniority.

Mr. Harris must have had one fine secretary to be willing to go to the extreme of hiring me to keep her, because I was not only an uninterested public servant, but a lousy secretary. Naturally, I was ecstatic. The job paid far beyond my qualifications which, of course, would have been true at any salary. I immediately went out and charged an extensive working-girl's wardrobe and busied myself stalking the halls of Congress looking for the right kind of "gay young men" to spend my evenings with.

This was the 89th Congress, Eisenhower's last, and women who worked on Capitol Hill were aging war horses, sometimes more knowledgeable than the Members they served. They were tough, shrewd, and dowagerlike ladies, most of whom swelled the statistics list that showed women outnumbering men in the nation's capital. Most were maiden ladies content to stay in nights with the cat and a cup of hot Serutan. Others were swingers in the old political sense, seasoned and responsible women by day; by night they were something else altogether. These women knew precisely what they were about, and one was ill-advised to get in their way. It also did not do to have a fancy social background, and I was fast finding that good family connections guaranteed one all the status and welcome of the town hooker at a quilting bee. I became unaffectionately known as the "Hill Debutante," which in truth had been my single qualification for the job in the first place. Later the congressional offices would be as full of pretty girls as a Hollywood sound stage, but then they were as scarce as dedicated politicians.

For a long time I was the only female on the committee staff, my duties being similar to those of the only Negro, Leroy, a splendid man with whom I established an instant and lasting friendship. He and I ate together most days and stayed late nights to run the mimeograph machine or hand deliver bills and committee notices to Members scattered about the two mammoth House Office Buildings. We took turns fetching coffee and running errands, and quickly arrived at the understanding that I was young enough to manage the leg work and that he, though elderly, could do the heavy tasks. He had a knack for knowing where to lay his hands on any Member of Congress during an unexpected roll call vote, and it was some months before I understood that the secret of his clairvoyance lay in his access to the House gymnasium where most congressmen passed their terms. With no more than a third-grade education, Leroy was the canniest politician in the lot. He taught me more about legislating than many political science majors learn in a lifetime. He also showed me a thing or two about feeding the extraordinary egos of politicians that helped take the edge off my brazen candor and left me with an abiding disrespect for the street parlance about Uncle Toms.

My typing and spelling were atrocious, my shorthand nothing more than an ability to write fast. I committed whole paragraphs to memory, and later learned to rephrase correspondence, sometimes more lucidly than it had been dictated. I once wrote a fifteen-page letter to President Eisenhower on the Committee's findings about the International Geophysical Year, a task made impossible by the Chief Clerk's insistence that no White House correspondence leave his office with a single erasure. That letter took ten work days to complete and as many nights to smuggle home the reams of used stationery for secret disposal. It was all a prodigious waste, for it was common knowledge that Mr. Eisenhower never read that sort of report, however well it was typed.

It became an open question between the Clerk of the Committee and myself as to which of us would be fired first. More than seventy and inherited from a previous Republican chairman, he was a nervous, cranky perfectionist who would have fired me outright except that he suspected I was the chairman's doxy when I was not otherwise vamping the entire Democratic membership—lewd suspicions I did not discourage.

The truth was that I never received one undue advance from any congressman of either party in the two years I worked there, an innocence probably believed at the time by no one but myself, who took it as more of a blow to the pride than a star to the crown. During the scandal that followed the Committee hearings on the Oil and Gas Lobby of 1957, Drew Pearson wrote a column alleging that Chairman Harris had so "profanely berated" a colleague who failed to appear for an important vote that "one young lady on the staff had to cover her ears and flee the Committee Chamber." This was an extravagant charge considering I was the only female employee of any vintage and one, moreover, who had never displayed an aversion to any kind of profanity. I also did not know Drew Pearson from a sack of salt, but no one bothered to question my guilt; it was assumed that I was the "leak," a tough charge back in the days when "leakers" were not held in today's high esteem.

I was not fired, I think because it was feared I had strong press connections. It was a power position I shored up with casual references to "Drew," actually getting so good at dropping his name that I took to alluding to him as "ole Droopy"—a nomenclature that worked more effectively at the time than it did years later when I had Mr. Pearson as a dinner partner and titillated only myself by addressing him as such.

I came, after a time, to accept working on the Hill, and made myself indispensable by establishing an elaborate filing system, putting railroad legislation under "T" for Trains, and Committee expense vouchers for congressional summer junkets under "F" for Freeloads. I took care of all the backlog correspondence that accumulated by simply dropping it in the burn-basket when it got ahead of me.

Sam Rayburn had been the Committee's chairman before becoming Speaker of the House, which may have prompted his loyalty in assigning a new Special Subcommittee on Legislative Oversight to us. The subcommittee was established ostensibly to police Congress, to rummage in government closets and then announce to the gullible public that all dealings in high office were above suspicion. A clever, fanatically industrious academician named Bernard Schwartz from Columbia University was hired as chief investigator. Poor Dr. Schwartz, the embodiment of the humorless, political neophyte with an ivory-tower integrity, was no match for wily congressmen whose dedication to the country rarely extended itself beyond the quest for reelection. He did not grasp that he was supposed to be nothing more than an impressively educated front man for the congressional candy store. He settled down to investigating the hands that hired him, found malpractice and influence peddling and promptly took the charges over the heads of his astonished superiors and presented his findings to the press.

Overnight there ensued a tempest so far-reaching that it commanded the front page of every publication in the country. Once begun, the investigations reached into Eisenhower's White House, exposing Sherman Adams, surrogate President of the United States, and his dealings with industrialist Bernard Goldfine. Before Dr. Schwartz was cast back into academe, he had cost Sherman Adams his career, indicted Goldfine, shadowed Republican chances in the coming 1958 elections, and set the vicuña coat industry back a hundred years.

There was the usual angry cry for scalps. Influence peddling came to a grinding, if temporary, halt. Angry exchanges of corruption charges sent politicians running for cover, and there was a brief scare-period when congressmen avoided lobbyists and picked up their own lunch tabs. Republicans and Democrats work together quite congenially when they have something to hide or protect, and Sherman Adams—an over-worked, underpaid presidential assistant with the burdens of high office placed on his shoulders by a seemingly indifferent Dwight Eisenhower—was the public sacrifice. Few people in high office spoke in his behalf, although his deeds were often less reprehensible than those of the men who tossed him to the wolves. Dr. Schwartz was dismissed by congress-men of both parties, who knew they had a tiger by the tail, which if not silenced, would turn and devour them all.

These were exciting weeks on Capitol Hill. The committee office was filled with scoop-happy journalists who thought my desk a convenient place to plant their half-soled shoes, my coffee cup a proper receptacle for cigar butts. While the committee met nervously in secret sessions, I passed endless hours in smoke-filled confusion playing the tricky word game of Botticelli with sassy reporters, and developed a passion for both.

It was during the investigation that I first met Lyndon Johnson, then Senate Majority Leader, friend, protégé, and lackey of Sam Rayburn. He came over from the Senate to deliver a few well-chosen words on behalf of the Speaker, who was infuriated by the Adams hearing. LBJ was the most impressive caller we ever had, leaving not one doubt in anybody's mind that here was a personage to be reckoned with—not only for his personal force, but because he represented the awesomely combined powers of himself and Sam Rayburn, the most powerful twosome in con-temporary congressional history.

I had seen LBJ from afar at Rayburn's massive birthday parties, where Johnson was fond of shoving any woman under forty into the grumpy Speaker's arms to march around the room with him singing "Deep in the Heart of Texas" and "For He's a Jolly Good Fellow," the latter tribute being questionable. Later, I would watch LBJ at cocktail and garden par-ties given by staff members of Johnson's Texas colleagues. LBJ would arrive by limousine in the manner of a Middle-Eastern potentate, parting the crowd as he swept by and gathering around him admiring young con-gressional secretaries. Lyndon Johnson was never a social lion. Rather, he preferred small groups of worshipful Capitol Hill workers whom he frequently treated to an evening on the town in the Shoreham Hotel's Palladium Room. It was to be years before I analyzed his aversion to social and political peers, or made any connection between him and the cocky, ubiquitous Bobby Baker, or for that matter, any of the other men Johnson anointed during his reign.

I once had lunch with Mr. Baker. For reasons I forget, he announced to the group of Hill people with us that I was "a prissy little snob" who would do well "to stay on his better side." The reference to his better nature eludes me still, but he was prophetic on that day about my burgeoning snobbery. I never liked Bobby Baker, a negative reaction I could not ascribe to discriminating ethical standards, but it suggested much about my indifference to bragging fools. In the tawdry game of politics I came to know, the only thing that counted was to be a winner, and Bobby Baker was never that.

I sensed in those congressional days that every public figure had some clay about the feet and ankles. Not then and rarely since would I encounter a politician who was not forced to leave a part of his soul in escrow somewhere on his climb to the top. With a few exceptions, there are no skeletonless congressional closets. Those days lulled me into accepting as calmly as everyone else the simple pragmatic attitude that it did not matter how one acquired power, only that one used it. I developed the awareness of the necessities of this pragmatism from seeing daily in my neophyte days on the Hill that nobody was perfect. It was a comforting rationalization then, and it would be later, ironically, when I turned up as one of Washington's skeletons. But it sure blew a hole in my youthful idealization of the United States Congress.

After two years, it became apparent that if fate had some splendid scheme to set me aside from all the other girls, some cosmic encounter with destiny, it would not be consummated within the gray dreariness of Congress. The plodding pace of legislative government was not for me. I was bored, and boredom would ever be my path to destruction.

I never tired of wild parties, the quest for more wine and louder music. I never wearied of flying on private planes to the Kentucky Derby with groups that included Aly Khan, of first nights of Broadway musicals, or the less exotic satisfactions of the Army-Navy football game. But the tedium of clerical work dulled the excitement of my social life. I started doing bizarre things—my personal indicator of unrest—painting mail boxes shocking pink, leaping fully clothed into the Supreme Court fountain. One day I woke up disposed to do the only thing I had not tried: marriage. It was just that uncomplicated. My mind was made up. All I had to do was choose a man from among the available crowd who was going places, and move on to something new and more fulfilling.

Life Intertwines
Along the Potomac

Marvella, A Personal Journey (1979)

There is a great deal that I like about Marvella Bayh's book, but I espe-
cially like the picture she provides of a newcomer to Washington trying
to cope with extraordinary new pressures. Marvella, who was more than
ten years younger than I, came to Washington at the beginning of
1963, just after her young husband, Birch Bayh, was first elected to the
Senate as a Democrat from Indiana. She experienced Washington in
the 1960s as a "wife of . . . ," as I did before Phil's death and my own
going to work. She worked just as hard as Birch to settle in here—
doing everything from buying and furnishing a house, making a home
for their son, Evan, while her husband flew back and forth to his home
state nearly every weekend, and keeping up with all of the issues that it
was so necessary to understand.

Lady Bird Johnson wrote an introduction to Marvella's book in
which she said something that strikes me as completely true and beau-
tifully descriptive:"Life intertwines along the Potomac as it only can
when you are sharing the hard work of it, the heady successes of it, and
the deep disappointments of it." Marvella died of a recurrence of breast
cancer right after completing this memoir in 1979, but she left a book
that candidly details the ride she had on her own Washington roller
coaster, with all its hard work, successes, and disappointments.

WASHINGTON, in the glamorous days of John and Jacqueline
Kennedy, was like a smorgasbord with exquisite food from all
over the world—and I could not get enough of it.

In the first six weeks, I found myself at home for only two full days.
Katie Louchheim had a Sunday brunch in our honor, where Hubert
Humphrey kept us laughing, telling about his 1960 campaign for the
Democratic nomination. "You can't imagine how many precious cam-

paign hours I lost sitting around airports waiting for commercial flights, while Jack Kennedy's private jet would swoop in and fly him off on a minute-to-minute schedule," he said, without rancor.

I was in awe of Katie, the hostess, vice-chairman of the Democratic party. She had all the style, flair, and polish of a well-to-do Eastern background. In her Georgetown home, she had blended beautiful antiques, Oriental art, and contemporary paintings with a connoisseur's hand. A poet and journalist, well traveled, keenly intelligent, she gathered stimulating people and deftly directed the most mind-expanding conversation around her table. But she was warm and witty, talking to me as if I were her equal, and I was thrilled that she'd remembered me in the play she'd written back in our Indiana law school days. At Katie Louchheim's luncheon that day, Birch and I took a big first bite of the intellectual diet that would soon be our fare at the Washington smorgasbord.

There was a party given by philanthropist Mary Lasker, where I sat between Ted Kennedy and Walter Lippmann and tried to remember every quip to share with Birch. That night I danced with Senator William Fulbright, a longtime hero of mine, and Adlai Stevenson, and Secretary of Labor Willard Wirtz. Then the night before my birthday, February 13, we were invited to the Vice President's home, to a small dinner party, at which Lyndon Johnson made a dinner toast to me—and sang "Happy Birthday." There, once more, I felt at ease—Lady Bird Johnson was the most gracious, kind, unpretentious woman I had ever met, I thought, and very elegant in her formal, French-decorated home. (That night I called Mama, afloat in excitement: "You'll never guess who sang 'Happy Birthday' to me tonight.")

I went to a tea at Ethel Kennedy's, where she asked me to pour, and then to an ice-skating party given by Ted and Bob Kennedy for the New Frontier crowd, where Birch played a fierce hockey game with a broom, winning the respect of the competitive Kennedys.

We went to a small buffet dinner at the Embassy of Luxembourg, and to another at the Russian Embassy (where I developed an immediate taste for caviar) to watch motion pictures of the new Russian cosmonauts. The embassies were so exotic that they whetted my long-suppressed appetite to see Europe. One evening we had accepted an invitation to a small dinner at the Norwegian Embassy, to which I had especially looked forward because of my mother's ancestry. The afternoon of the dinner, we had a call from the White House, inviting us to drop by for a movie that night. "What shall we do?" I asked Birch. He called the Protocol Office. We sent our regrets to the Embassy. In Washington, a White House invitation was a command, we learned.

This was my first visit to the Mansion itself. We drove in through the gate on the majestic south lawn and entered on the ground floor through the Diplomatic Reception Room, where we were escorted by an usher to an elevator, which let us off upstairs at the family quarters. It was like an elegant private house, with a wide hall that was used as a sitting room, filled with antique furniture. Jacqueline Kennedy herself met us at the door of the large oval drawing room. We had cocktails in that lovely yellow room with its Louis XIV furnishings, along with a small group that included Senator Gale McGee of Wyoming and his wife Loraine. And then we took the elevator again to the ground floor, where we entered a large blue room that was set up as a movie theater. We watched *The Ugly American*, which the President seemed to enjoy, propped up in a bedlike chair to ease the discomfort in his back. Afterward, John Kennedy told his wife that I had beaten Birch in a speech contest. "Does that make you nervous?" she asked Birch in her soft, whispery voice. "I'm glad it's not today, she'd run circles around me," he replied gallantly. It was a grand evening, I thought. I remembered sitting in our little living room in Enid during the 1960 Democratic Convention, thinking the Kennedys were the very epitome of glamor and sophistication, never dreaming that I'd know them on a social basis.

Oh, those first heady months. I accepted every invitation—I thought that we were supposed to. Besides, I didn't want to miss anything!

And yet, I was seized with terror at the thought that I'd soon have to reciprocate some of those invitations. Jackie Kennedy set the tone for Washington entertaining, which, in those days, meant intimate seated dinners with silver gleaming under candlelight, fresh flowers, French cuisine, and a formal progression of events, from pre-dinner cocktails to place cards to salad-after-the-main-course to segregation of the sexes for after-dinner coffee (or cigars and brandy).

In all the years from Lahoma to Washington, I'd never had a chance to learn about entertaining. Fried chicken on Sunday or a baked-bean supper for a few friends was just about the extent of my experience. I'd never even lived in Indianapolis! In those glittering Kennedy days of little black-tie dinners and formal embassy affairs, suddenly we were faced with what seemed like a forest of silverware at tables, confronting that great enigma, the fingerbowl. I had confessed to Lady Bird Johnson that Birch and I were babes at sea, and she gave that time-honored piece of advice, "Just keep an eye on your hostess, and follow her lead." Birch came home from a luncheon one day. "Now what do I do?" he asked. "I was seated between the Chief of Protocol and the President of the United States. You told me to watch the leader if I didn't know what to use, right?"

"That's right," I nodded.

"Well, one picked up his fork to eat his first course, and the other picked up his spoon!"

The right fork or spoon, the correct way to answer an invitation, the right dress to wear—all of those details seemed so important to me, back then. I was always calling the Protocol Office with questions: "What do you say when you're introduced to a grand duchess?" "What does it mean when an invitation is marked 'informal'?" (I'm glad I asked that one. I had slacks in mind. The officer answered, however, that "Informal" meant dressy, but not black tie.) "I don't know a thing about protocol," I confessed to Mrs. Johnson. "Oh, my dear, most of that died with the Second World War," she said, soothingly, laughing at the old custom of new Congressional wives running all over Washington to drop engraved calling cards at the door of just about everybody who had seniority, from the White House on down. Yes, a lot of the formality was gone, but a good bit still remained: Husbands preceded their wives in reception lines, for example, and "ranking" guests always left the party first, I noticed. But what I really wanted to know was what was expected of me, as a Senate wife.

On the advice of Mary Day, who worked in Birch's office, I enrolled in Mrs. Gladstone Williams' ten-week course on protocol, which included veritable Emily Post lessons in entertaining. At the beginning of the course, I wrote in my diary, "Am terrified at repaying dinners to these people who are so proper." . . . I knew I'd need new clothes in Washington—those few packable, crushable, unobtrusive candidate's-wife dresses were worn out from the campaign—and I didn't own a long dress. In Terre Haute, I'd bought a "formal" for Washington evenings, a gold-trimmed ivory satin gown. At its first wearing, a dinner for the new Congress at the National Press Club, I saw very quickly that I was overdressed. Mine was a ball gown. Some unspoken signal seemed to be going around: one kind of dress for Saturday nights, another for mid-week; some people's dinner parties were "dressier" than others. I was spending far too much time worrying about what to wear. I needed help.

Dorothy Stead, who owned a dress shop in Georgetown, had sent a welcome-to-Washington note to all the new Congressional wives. "I have been in Washington a long time. Come around and let me advise you on your wardrobe," she wrote. Rather timidly, I took her up on it, and soon had my entire closetful of clothes spread around her shop. "This is worn out, this is too dated, this can be livened by a scarf, this needs to be shortened, this can be remade, this can go to a luncheon at the White House, this to a five-to-seven reception. . . ." Like a wizard, she flipped through my sparse Terre Haute/Bloomington collection, and then told me what gaps needed filling. "A good, all-around coat is very important here," she began. Of course, I couldn't afford a new wardrobe, but as the year wore on, as I could, I'd buy a new dress from Dorothy Stead. Dorothy, like Bea Keller, soon became a trusted personal friend.

In the protocol class, I learned more than who sits on whose right, and how to decline an invitation. "I'm just a plain, ordinary cook," I confessed to Mrs. Williams. "I'm afraid I'd be in the kitchen all night long—even if I served a four-course meal rather than a full formal dinner." "Very few of us in Washington are lucky enough to have the time to spend in the kitchen, even if we have the ability," she answered. "Catering is a very honorable profession here." Bob Keefe, Birch's new assistant, introduced me to a wonderful caterer, Willie Mae Carter, and a butler, Norwood Williams, who served at the White House, and Mabel Taylor, who served at table. "They will come into your home," Mrs. Williams told me, "prepare dinner, and leave you time for conversation with your guests."

Conversation was the one area, I discovered, in which I did not feel woefully inadequate. I had worried about what people were going to talk about during those fabled Washington dinner parties. Art? Ballet? The latest European philosophers? I envisioned enrolling in classes (and still would like to!) on those subjects which had not turned up in my curriculum or my experience. What a happy surprise, from the very first, to hear familiar words being tossed around a table: "Medicare," "Peace Corps," "civil rights," "Nuclear Test Ban Treaty"—and, of course, "Cuba." Washington is a "company town." Most conversations center on the political issues being debated in Congress—in 1963 those issues I had studied so hard for Birch's and my speeches during the campaign. I had no trouble holding up my end of the conversation during a dinner party—in fact, I found these evenings of informal political discussion so informative that when two invitations would arrive for the same evening, I wanted to go to both. (An evening with statesman Averell Harriman, for example, was almost a graduate course in Western Civilization.) I went often to the Senate galleries to hear debate, and continued my clipping service for Birch, becoming almost a *Reader's Digest* of events and opinion that might help him in his work. As I look back, if I hadn't had the experience of campaign partnership, studying the issues so closely, I'd have been 100 percent overwhelmed by this complex capital city, rather than 75 percent overwhelmed.

One strong support system for me and the other new Senate wives was the Tuesday meetings of the Senate Ladies Red Cross group. Since World War I, this group had met to roll bandages for servicemen or, in peacetime, for local hospitals. Those women, of both parties, were sources of much-needed information—the best dentist or dry cleaner, for example—and supportive sympathy to a newcomer. It was there I first came to know Joan Kennedy, who was so much more worldly and sophisticated in many ways, but in others, as lost and timid as I. We worried about our husbands' health holding out, at the frantic pace they were keeping. We worried about raising our children alone. Joan was open, vulnerable, and very, very sweet, I thought. Through her easy acceptance of me, I began to relax around the awesome Kennedys and to look on them as individuals, with flaws and foibles like my own.

But it was the Vice President's wife, presiding over the Senate Ladies group, who was most instrumental in giving me guidance and the assurance that a country-born, small-town girl like me could survive in the heady sophistication of Washington. Mrs. Johnson never ceased to amaze me. I would read that she was in Texas or Norway on Sunday or Monday, but on Tuesday, jet lag or not, there she would be at Red Cross. Lady Bird Johnson took me "under her wing"; she included me in family gatherings, at poolside, sometimes with her daughters Luci and Lynda; she and the Vice President invited Birch and me to a musicale at the Mexican Embassy in the Johnsons' honor, and for a memorable evening drifting slowly down the Potomac River to Mount Vernon and back on the President's yacht, the Honey Fitz. How could I ever hope to reciprocate an evening like that, I worried. (Fortunately, I didn't have to worry just yet. The furniture I had ordered in January still hadn't been delivered by late spring.)

Birch left early every morning for the long drive to the Senate Office Building, totally wrapped up in organizing his staff, learning how the Senate works, finding his way among the labyrinths of the Capitol. At home, a kind woman from Indiana, Bea Smith, was helping me battle my new house, along with her own homesickness, and taking care of Evan while Birch and I sampled Washington's giant smorgasbord in the evenings.

That enchanted spring of 1963 reinforced my feeling that I was in the middle of a dream. I'd always had a pang of homesickness in the springtime. But spring in Washington is a fairyland of cherry blossoms, not just around the Tidal Basin, but also in the family neighborhoods. Then come the bright burst of azaleas, the proud stands of tulips, the greening of a thousand trees. I'd pack Evan in the back seat and drive round and round, discovering a new world of color and life. We had lots of company, old friends from Indiana whom I proudly took sightseeing. Springtime in Washington made the connection: This was my home, and I loved it. . . .

Among the rites every spring are the Senate Ladies' luncheon at the Capitol honoring the First Lady, the Congressional Reception at the

White House, and then the First Lady's luncheon at the White House for the Senate wives. In 1963, however, the First Lady didn't appear at the first two affairs because she was pregnant.

For the Senate wives' luncheon, I had a new dress, and a tiny little hat in which I felt very silly, because I didn't wear hats. But Jackie's pillbox hat had set a fashion, and after all, I was going to Jackie's house. At that time, the doctor had me on a combination of medication, which at that time I didn't even question—thyroid to juice me up, and then some little purple pills to calm me down. I walked into the Oval Diplomatic Reception Room at the White House that day, nervous in my new dress and new hat, clutching a new patent-leather handbag. Suddenly the clasp on my purse popped open, and out spilled the contents, all over the floor. The bottle of medicine hit the fireplace, broke, and little purple pills rolled out in every direction. Immediately one of those terrific White House aides, military men who are skilled in diplomacy, was at my feet, helping me scoop up everything and pull myself back together. I was shattered. As we walked out of the room, headed upstairs to the State Dining Room, I glanced back over my shoulder at the site of Franklin D. Roosevelt's fireside chats. There in the fireplace, tucked away in the corner, were two little purple pills. How significant, I thought. Some women have calling cards, but I leave my tranquilizers.

In the dining room, Mrs. Johnson was receiving, as Mrs. Kennedy was upstairs, not feeling well. I was seated between Mrs. Wayne Morse of Oregon and Mrs. Lister Hill from Alabama. In Birmingham that day, police had turned fire hoses and dogs on civil rights demonstrators, including children; Mrs. Hill seemed ill at ease. Within weeks of that luncheon, our husbands had become adversaries on President Kennedy's bill to combat discrimination in public accommodations, schools, jobs, and voting. I soon learned, through the bipartisan Senate wives' group, how Senate wives managed to remain friends even though their husbands could be locked in what seemed like mortal combat. . . .

Being a new senator had its drawbacks, we were to discover. Our new home was so far out in the suburbs that those late homecomings from the Capitol altered what had been a pattern in our lives prior to the Senate campaign. Evan and I learned to have supper without Daddy. If we were going out in the evening, I'd sit with Evan while he ate, or read to him, then throw a fresh shirt or tuxedo in the car for Birch, and meet him at the reception or the dinner party—sometimes he'd change in the office, sometimes in the car.

There were other domestic changes. On the farm there had been a clear delineation of roles. Birch was responsible for everything outside the house, I was in charge of the house itself—until something broke, of course. Then Birch, like most farmers, would fix it. I'd never had to call a repairman on the farm. Now, I was surprised to find myself in charge of repairs, the yard, the car. Birch simply didn't have the time.

What I hadn't learned about Washington, during all those weeks of eager study, was what heavy demands a senator's job would place on our family life—and just how lonely it was going to be, much of the time. For I had not counted on Birch continuing his campaign in Indiana for six more years.

True, our margin of victory had been very slim, and Indiana is a "swing" state, as likely to vote Republican as Democratic, very conscientious about keeping an eye on its elected officials. Birch was back in Indiana just about every weekend, mending political fences, finding out how folks at home felt about what he was voting on—in other words, paying attention to the fact that he was an elected representative for that state. But as the summer wore on, and I began to miss his easy laugh, his arms at night, his sharing the burden of disciplining Evan (I had become the "heavy"), I began to wish he were senator from Alaska—which was too far away to go home every weekend. (One far-western senator told me his constituents didn't expect him to come home so often. But Birch's did, and he did what they expected.)

On weekdays during those periods when the Senate wasn't in session, it wasn't so bad—I had my various clubs and luncheons, Evan had school. But it was those weekends, those lonely suburban weekends, that were hell for a thirty-year-old and still-in-love woman who couldn't afford to fly out with him. I came to dread those Saturdays and Sundays alone out in McLean, Virginia, even though Evan and I would use them to explore the Smithsonian and the playgrounds. We found friends in the neighborhood, and Birch would phone us every night, from wherever he might be. . . .

I began to have trouble sleeping, in contrast to the happy picture of me that appeared in *Life* magazine on July 25. President Kennedy wrote me a lovely, complimentary note about the piece. I wondered what he or Jane Howard, the reporter, would think if they saw me taking estrogen shots, thyroid medicine, the purple tranquilizers, and now, out of desperation, sometimes sleeping pills.

On August 1, we were at a dinner party at the home of the senator from Alaska. Charming old Senator Gruening had been a pioneer there, not too many years after my grandparents in Oklahoma. I was seated next to Estes Kefauver of Tennessee, who had held me and most of the nation spellbound during his crime hearings in 1951, who had been my candidate for the Democratic presidential nomination in 1952 (although Birch later converted me to Adlai Stevenson), and who had been my candidate for Vice President in 1956. He had finished his first course when he looked over and spied some fish still on my plate. "Aren't you going to eat that?" he asked. "No," I said, and he reached over and started eating right off my plate. It was exactly the kind of thing my Uncle Oren or any others of my family might have done, a "waste not, want not" generation dispensing with formal manners.

Birch was in fine form that night, accepting congratulations from senators right and left about his spectacular performance at the Democrats vs. Republicans baseball game the night before. The day after that party, when he was mowing the steep incline in our front yard, he slipped, cutting off half his big toe and fracturing two more. That put him into Sibley Hospital for two weeks in excruciating pain, and effectively halted his baseball career.

I remember flying to Indiana to make a speech for him, hating all the while to leave him. When I returned, I learned that my mother was in the hospital with nervous exhaustion, and much as I wanted to, I couldn't leave Birch to go to her.

It all seemed to be going by so fast, I couldn't take time to assess my situation or my parents', or to gather strength or to savor what goodness there was in life. Days marched by in staccato: Birch was on crutches. Daddy was worse. Senator Kefauver had died, he who had so recently been my dinner partner. Birch spoke in South Bend, at Purdue, in Rapid City, in Columbia City, in Gary, in Mount Vernon. I spoke in Akron, in Louisville. Birch cosponsored the Freedom of Information bill. Thousands massed at the Lincoln Memorial to hear Dr. Martin Luther King, Jr.: "I have a dream. . . ." Birch was named to the subcommittee that handled civil rights legislation. We met the king of Afghanistan at an embassy reception. Birch was named chairman of the Constitutional Amendments Subcommittee, which Estes Kefauver had chaired, because nobody else on Judiciary seemed to want it. We celebrated Daddy Bayh's seventieth birthday. Birch got word that Studebaker was closing their South Bend plant, that thousands would be unemployed. . . .

Meanwhile, Birch was up to his neck in the Studebaker situation. Since September, we had lived, breathed, eaten, slept, dreamed Studebaker. I had associated it with Indiana ever since Birch proudly drove me around the Chicago lakeshore in that funny little blue car that looked the same coming and going. ("It's made in Indiana," he announced. "And what runs it is made in Oklahoma," I retorted.) Now Studebaker was closing down its American operation entirely, because it was losing money, and its move to Canada was throwing the northern Indiana economy into a tailspin, not to mention the families of the 7,000 workers. Birch had been all over the country seeking help. Delegations of concerned Hoosiers poured into Washington; Birch and John Brademas met with government officials around the clock. Hobbling to the White House on crutches, Birch had asked President Kennedy to help.

Today, November 22, Birch had asked Teddy Kennedy to fill in for him presiding over the Senate. While he was in Texas campaigning with the President, the Vice President had asked Birch to preside, as junior senators are often asked to do, but Birch had to go to Chicago to talk to another company about moving into the Studebaker plant. He flew out of National Airport at about 12:30 p.m.

I had said goodbye at his office, where I was working on correspondence addressed to us. At about 1:30, one of Birch's assistants ran in, crying that the President and Vice President, and Governor Connally, had been shot in Dallas. As I drove home down Constitution Avenue, I looked up at the White House, to see the flag still flying, full mast. I ran into the house, crying, to meet Evan. The phone rang. Birch, from Chicago. The pilot had waited until wheels touched runway to announce the news. There was no way we could speak to each other of how we felt. We were both weeping. I blurted out the first thing that came to mind. "Why is it you are always gone when there's a crisis and I need you?"

The horror, the heartbreak of those days in Washington has been told and retold. It does not dim with memory. Driving over to Bobby Kennedy's that night, finding only the children there. Standing in the White House, looking at the flag-draped coffin in the East Room, where John and Jacqueline Kennedy had danced. Driving to Ted and Joan's, then to the Johnsons', to leave a letter. The new President welcomed us, invited us in. Lady Bird came downstairs, wearing her robe, holding out her arms to me. "It's been a year since yesterday morning," she said.

We left, and on the way home we clung to each other, weeping still. My parents called me. "Life is so short," I said. "I know," said my mother.

SONDRA GOTLIEB

The Unpaid Manager of a Small Hotel

Washington Rollercoaster (1990)

This is from a Washington memoir by someone from another country, on whom Washington made a big impression—and vice versa. Sondra Gotlieb was the wife of Canada's former ambassador to the United States, Allan Gotlieb. Their time in Washington largely coincided with the Reagan administration. The book is breezy, funny, and full of the kinds of stories that pass for gossip in Washington. What Mrs. Gotlieb was probably best known for was the famous slap heard round the world—the slap she gave her social secretary minutes before a dinner at the Canadian embassy for Prime Minister Brian Mulroney and his wife. She gives her own version of the events leading up to the slap in an entire chapter, "The Day of the Slap—Wednesday, March 19, 1986." Because I felt sorry for Sondra, who suffered greatly when the press had a heyday with the story, I, together with Bob Strauss, gave a dinner for the Gotliebs. It at least made her feel better about something that she felt horrible about to begin with, inexcusable though it may have been.

A writer before (and after) she came here as an ambassador's wife, Sondra wrote a much talked about satirical column for the Post, *at Meg Greenfield's invitation, that appeared on the op-ed pages as a letter from Washington titled "Dear Beverly." In the first chapter of* Washington Rollercoaster, *"The Twinkling Hostess," she writes, "In political Washington you are identified by your job." This book gives the background for much of the material she accumulated from her years at her job as ambassador's wife in Washington.*

JUST BEFORE our departure for Washington, the wife of the previous Canadian ambassador to the United States, Carol Towe, gave me a couple of clues about my future life.

"The butler at the residence is a little strange. I thought of firing him. But maybe he'll suit you better."

I wasn't quite sure what butlers did, so I kept quiet.

"Before I came to Washington," she added, "the embassy was actually using typed instead of handwritten place cards." Carol had been an ambassador's wife before and knew about place cards. Until she spoke, my mind had never dwelt upon them. Those were the only hints I had of what was in store.

The plane did make it to Washington, and we were met by a protocol officer and several members of the embassy staff who led us and our luggage straight past the customs officials and immigration lines. It was only then, with this "make-way-for-the-ambassador" procedure, that I realized that life was going to be different. No more passing suitcases through the windows and leaving the train in our pyjamas.

Our entrance into Washington was almost regal. Our chauffeur, Jacques Hèlie, was a Canadian who had been a driver with the embassy for more than twenty years and knew each ambassador's foibles, which thankfully he kept to himself. We were greeted at the door of the elegant official residence on Rock Creek Drive by Pat Thomas, the social secretary at the embassy; the enigmatic Spanish butler Rito, a sombre El Grecoesque figure in black; Ibrahim, the Turkish chef, over six feet tall and weighing more than 250 pounds; Noemi, the downstairs maid from Honduras who was pregnant; Thelma, the Filipino upstairs maid; and a little Portuguese man named Mario, who was described as a houseman. Pat Thomas tried to explain to me what each of them did, but it took me three years to figure out the duties of the houseman. Except for Thelma, the household staff spoke little English, and it was a mystery to me how they communicated with each other. Rito and Mario had related languages, but they loathed each other and never spoke. Noemi and Ibrahim worked well together in the kitchen with their innovative Turko-English-Spanish dialect. A Canadian film called *Quest for Fire*, which opened in Washington not long after we came, showed the beginning of speech in primitive man. It was a little like that at the Residence when I arrived in Washington.

Rito the butler's first act was to hand me a set of keys. I asked him what they were for.

"The downstairs storeroom," he said.

"What's in it?" I asked.

"Fifty cans of peas and two bottles of ketchup."

I asked about another key.

"That locks the thermostat so no one but Madame can touch it."

I made my first decision and told him not to give me any keys.

Although I was too frightened to say anything then, I knew that we would not serve canned peas and ketchup to our guests. As for the other key, my idea of power was not being the only one allowed to fool with the thermostat. As a matter of principle, I stayed away from it during our stay in Washington.

The analogy of primitive man included ourselves. We had never lived in Washington, knew few people and for several months would feel like a Cro-Magnon couple who had been banished from our familiar cave and found ourselves settled near the first of an unknown tribe, the Washington power-seekers and cave-dwellers, whose customs and taboos were foreign to us. We had no understanding of the complexity of the political system or of the importance attached to social activity by the Reagan administration.

The departing British ambassador to the U.S., the extremely sophisticated Sir Nicholas "Nico" Henderson, gave Allan one hint about the byzantine nature of the political system: "If anyone tells you that he knows where a decision was made in this town, he's either a liar or a fool."

Allan said this was the only useful piece of advice he received during all the courtesy calls that diplomatic ritual required him to pay on his ambassadorial colleagues when he arrived.

During our early period of adjustment to Washington I would sit gloomily on the black leather furniture in the Residence's dark library and ask Allan, "What does an ambassador do? And where do I fit into all this?" Allan was playing everything by ear and was stumped for an answer.

My immediate concern had to do with the domestic problems of running a large embassy residence. I had always liked being alone in a house, and I was intimidated by so many people around me, no matter how helpful they were. The first thing I did when I opened my suitcase was hide away in drawers all my dirty underwear left over from my Canadian book tour. I was hoping to wash it late at night in the bathroom sink. My hiding places were discovered and three hours later my dirty laundry was cleaned, ironed and folded back in my secret drawers. This was the first time in my life anyone else had washed, let alone ironed, my panties. Despite this luxury my instinct was to return to Ottawa.

I had no idea how to supervise a staff. They were waiting for orders from their new *patronne*, but little information had been offered to me about their routine. For example, I had no idea who lived in or out of the house and whether they were supposed to be on duty during weekends. Of course I should have asked the butler, but I was reluctant to do so and anyway had already discovered that he didn't usually understand my questions.

Allan left for Brussels on my first weekend at the Residence and I woke early on a cold Sunday morning to a seemingly empty house. I went outside in my kimono to collect the newspapers. The door swung shut behind me and I heard the lock click. I ran around to the front door, also locked, and rang the bell. Nobody answered. I found myself on the front steps in my bathrobe, clutching the *New York Times* and *The Washington Post* to my bosom. A few men jogging across the street looked at me curiously. The houses nearby were large and unwelcoming, and I had no idea who lived in them. I knew the Canadian Chancery in Sheridan Circle was about a ten-minute walk down Massachusetts Avenue, but was reluctant to proceed there given my state of undress and the unusually cold weather. In Ottawa I wouldn't have worried too much about my predicament, but now I was an ambassador's wife and I assumed that more dignified behaviour was to be expected of me. Nevertheless I shuffled along in my slippers for a block down Massachusetts Avenue, holding the papers for warmth, hoping the guard at the Chancery would recognize the new ambassador's wife. Suddenly I heard a shout: the butler, who was fully dressed and had been watching from a window, ran after me and saved me and my country from shame.

The formal presentation of Allan's credentials to President Reagan took place ten days after we arrived. It was my first official event. I was very upset because my hair had shrunk—the result of a bad permanent. Also one of the maids had washed and shrunk the blouse I was supposed to wear with a brown suit. All my life I had done my best to avoid ironing and there I was ironing my blouse while Noemi the maid watched. She was willing to iron, but expected an order from Madame; I didn't know how to give one.

Lee Annenberg, then Chief of Protocol at the State Department, helped me get through the presentation of credentials ceremony with only minor embarrassment. The best part for me was speeding to the White House in a motorcade. It was only a little one, with rather rundown D.C. police cars fore and aft, but it was gratifying to run through a couple of red lights with the sirens going. Lee greeted us at the White House door and told us there was a gaggle of ambassadors waiting to present their credentials that day. Before we went to the Oval Office some anxious young men took us into another room and told us where to stand, how long to speak and when to shove off.

In the official Presentation of Credentials photograph, which was reproduced in the Canadian papers, my hair looked like corkscrews because of the permanent. And my brown suit was so unflattering that my brother didn't recognize me when he saw me on television. He told me later that he thought it was Mrs. Brezhnev standing beside the President. Actually only Mr. Ambassador (as the Americans called Allan) was supposed to have his picture taken with the President. I was told to move out of camera range, away from the fireplace where Allan and the President were standing. After the handshake with the President I backed into the camera crew. Some of the young men began to hiss at me, but the President graciously grabbed my wrist and insisted that I be in the picture too. Mrs. Reagan was not there. All I remember is flashing cameras and that the President was wearing a brown suit too.

Afterwards Lee told me not to worry about the frizzy permanent, for it would eventually come out. In the car I said, "Allan, I hope I didn't humiliate Canada." After so many years of marriage he knew that I get flustered easily and quoted a Newfoundland saying in my honour: "When she rises ups she gets confused."

Allan had another favourite comment for me in those first few weeks. "Assert your authority," he would say when he left for the Chancery in the morning, leaving me alone with Rito, Thelma, Ibrahim, Noemi, and Mario.

It was all very well for Allan to say that. He had been deputy minister of several large government departments including one with 25,000 employees. I had never been the boss of anyone except my cleaning lady in Ottawa, whom I never once contradicted in twenty years. I had arrived in Washington as an ignorant foreigner, used to a middle-class private way of life—little notes pinned on the fridge door and forgetting to put the sprinkler on.

I was also supposed to give orders to my social secretary and her assistant. What do you do with a secretary if you've never had one in your life? My social secretary, Pat Thomas, worked at the Chancery office, but had a direct line to me at the Residence. However, the telephone had five bewildering buttons. Press one, I would get a maid in the laundry room. Press a second and I could dial Disney World in Orlando, Florida. Press a third, I would overhear an argument in Tagalog; that was the staff's personal line—Thelma, the Filipino upstairs maid, was yelling at her ex-husband. Press a fourth and I would get a local line for making calls to people I barely knew and who usually had unlisted numbers anyway.

In Ottawa I had lived in a house with no servants and my children had been away at college for some time. I was used to privacy. But in Washington I was not living in my home. I was living in a place referred to by the Chancery officials as the O.R. At first I didn't know what those initials meant. Did we have an operating room somewhere in the embassy?

I was enlightened by Allan, who told me the O.R. was the Official Residence.

I would wake up in the O.R. and go downstairs in my kimono to face Rito, sullen from the first fight in the morning with Mario, the idle houseman. Then I'd bump into a couple of political officers chatting in the drawing room, who had to come by to talk to Allan. There might be a procurement official waiting around to tell me I shouldn't have bought a dozen (very cheap) champagne glasses from Lord and Taylor because all champagne glasses must be ordered from headquarters in Ottawa. Occasionally there were outside workmen who wanted to come into my bathroom before I had time to get dressed. It was like living in a luxurious dormitory, or a small hotel. The O.R. was an institution belonging to the Canadian government. It was not a home. For the first year I was extremely unnerved by this lack of privacy and would whisper complaints into the telephone to Allan, who had escaped to the office, about "too many people around me all the time." I needed privacy, I said, or I would go out of my mind. . . .

My normal retreat from so many people would have been into a kitchen. . . . Cooking has always been my escape. At home there was nothing better I liked doing than closing myself in the kitchen, shutting out the children, turning on the radio, and trying out a new Julia Child recipe.

In Washington the kitchen was off limits to me. Officials in Ottawa think elaborate second kitchens in many Canadian embassies and consulates are acceptable budget items so that the wife of the ambassador can make toast or reheat coffee in the microwave all by herself. I considered this a futile expense for our O.R. In Washington I soon learned that I would never have the time or energy to use it. One kitchen per O.R. is sufficient.

This meant, however, that my hobby—my escape hatch—had disappeared.

Chefs hate Madame poking around in their kitchen, which in the O.R. belonged to the household staff. If I walked into the kitchen two maids, the chef and the odd chauffeur, with his mouth full, would jump up and ask if Madame wanted something. They would give me anything—tea upstairs on a tray, a steak in the middle of the afternoon—as long as I didn't disturb their private kitchen life. If we arrived home late at night and I wanted to heat up some soup, a maid would hear me and come running downstairs to find a pot. She knew where everything was supposed to go and I would certainly put a spoon in the wrong place.

Later, of course, when we were either entertaining or going out every night, the last thing I wanted to do was boil soup, let alone cook a meal. I tried to escape from the world by shutting myself in the upstairs sun-room, covering my eyes with a hot towel because the whites were tinged acid green. I wasn't suffering from jaundice, merely social overload.

My first test of strength in the kitchen had to do with Ibrahim, our Turkish chef. After about six weeks in Washington I realized that we'd been eating a lot of shishkebab. Ibrahim was good-natured but a little limited in his repertoire. I asked him if he could make a coulibiac for one of our first dinner parties; coulibiac is an elaborate dish, fresh salmon surrounded by a puff pastry.

"No problem, Madame," he said. "I can make anything. I cook for three hundred people when I work for King of Jordan."

He had mentioned his former employer, the King, several times, which had its desired effect on me. Nevertheless, I was a little worried about his capacity for cooking coulibiac, so I asked him if he would make a test coulibiac for Allan and myself the night before the dinner. That evening when we sat down, we were served shishkebab. I still didn't know how to work the telephones or deal with the paperwork coming across my desk, nor how to manage the quarrelling in the household between the servants and the difficulties in the office of my social secretary. Pat Thomas wanted to write out place cards by hand for our first dinner party, but for some reason no one in the Chancery would supply her with nib pens and black ink.

Tumult at the office, tumult at home. When Rito placed in front of me the shishkebab instead of the coulibiac, my eyes filled with tears. Allan asked, "Why are you crying?" I told him about the coulibiac. Apart from shaking hands with the chef on our first day, Allan had never spoken to him, or even gone into the kitchen.

"For God's sake," Allan said, "don't cry. Assert your authority."

"How?" I replied, thinking of the King of Jordan.

Allan rose, walked into the kitchen and backed the 250-pound Ibrahim into a wall.

"Where's the coulibiac?" Allan asked, stumbling over the word (he had never heard of a coulibiac before). Ibrahim muttered something unintelligible.

"When my wife asks for something, you make it," Allan said.

The next morning the two of us ate a huge test coulibiac for breakfast.

In this manner I discovered that unless the household and Chancery staff knew they would get hell from the ambassador, the "wife of" would get nothing at all. The ambassador was the boss and his word was respected. If the ambassador didn't care about things that worried his wife, nobody else would care either. But once word got around that the ambassador actively supported his wife in all her reasonable decisions (and my decisions, of course, were always reasonable), "wife of" got her way, sooner rather than later.

But Allan warned me I still hadn't got a grip on things when I had my second to-do with Ibrahim. I opened one of the refrigerators in the kitchen (a rather daring act for me at that time) and saw huge bags of frozen shrimp.

"What's this?" I said, "I want only fresh shrimp."

"No fresh shrimp in Washington," Ibrahim informed me.

"Nonsense," I said firmly. Someone had told me they sold fresh shrimp down by the wharf.

"No fresh shrimp down by the wharf, Madame."

I made Jacques Hèlie drive me and the silent Ibrahim to the wharf, where we saw shrimp piled high in front of the vendors. There were even fishing boats behind the stalls. I was triumphant. Ibrahim poked a few fish uninterestedly while I spoke to a vendor.

"Give me three pounds of fresh shrimp."

"Lady, we don't have fresh shrimp."

"What's that in front of me?"

"Defrosted shrimp. They freeze them on the boats in Carolina."

Ibrahim spoke only once on our way home. "No fresh shrimp in Washington, Madame."

As WITH redecorating, shopping for the O.R. might have been an engrossing experience, but somehow it ended up the least satisfying of my duties. Thankfully, I could count on the assistance of Glen Bullard, our maintenance official in the Chancery. Glen had been with the embassy "since the beginning" and would entertain me with stories about the foibles of my predecessors and their families. He pointed out the window box where someone's child had grown marijuana during the sixties, showed me the spot where an embassy dog had chewed the brand-new drawing room carpet and told me which ambassador's wife had maintained perfect discipline in the Residence with her exemplary English butler. "He was just like a lord, and he was the only servant she spoke to in the household. It was the silent treatment for the rest." . . .

When I made my first shopping foray for the Residence, to purchase a Mr. Coffee machine ($21.95), there were dark rumblings from shadowy administrators in the Chancery. Apparently I was supposed to ask an embassy procurement officer from the Chancery if there was money for a Mr. Coffee machine. If he wasn't on vacation and if there was money in that particular budget, he might then go out and buy something resembling what was needed—in a couple of months. Only he knew, or claimed to know, how much money I was allowed to spend on a Mr. Coffee machine. The embassy procurement officers were mostly ex–military people who bought office equipment in large quantities—not single coffee makers or upholstery for dining room chairs.

The sunroom downstairs needed new couches, and the embassy procurement officers gave me the good news that the sunroom decorating budget for the O.R. hadn't been depleted by our predecessor. I had been in Washington about two weeks and didn't know where to buy furniture. After the Mr. Coffee episode, the embassy procurement official told me to go and buy a sofa all by myself. He designated two discount warehouses in the wilds of Bethesda as suitable places from which to buy a sofa for the Canadian Residence. I went with Jacques Hèlie, my driver, who had been given only a sketchy idea where they were located. After a wild goose chase of three hours we found them barred and empty—gone bankrupt years before.

The Mr. Coffee incident and the bankrupt warehouses brought me to a new reality. I became aware of the anomalous position of the wife of an ambassador. I lived in the world of bureaucratic diplomacy: every embassy employee—the ambassador, the press attaché, the embassy procurer and the downstairs maid—had a job description and official classification. Butlers were not butlers: they were house managers, W.S.4.

But nobody knew what to do with that quaint, old-fashioned figure, the wife of the ambassador. She was the only person in the embassy without a job description. Yet somehow the "wife of" is supposed to assert her authority over those who are legitimately employed. There she is, this "wife of," this diplomatic remnant from the Congress of Vienna of 1815, powerless because she doesn't control the purse strings, ignorant because she doesn't understand bureaucracy, trying to find out from Chancery administrators—who may or may not tell her—how much money there is to upholster furniture or buy a rug, or at what salary she might employ a chef.

Yet it is clearly she who is supposed to hire and fire maids, social secretaries or butlers, as well as redecorate the embassy. I soon discovered that the wife of an ambassador is in fact the unpaid manager of a small hotel.

Social Washington

Even if Judgment Day is well advertised in advance, I'm quite sure that there will be a party going on in Washington, and that everyone there will feel they had some very good reason why they simply had to go.
        —Vera Bloom, *There's No Place Like Washington*

SOCIAL Washington is a topic that almost everyone writing anything about Washington touches on. Washington's social life—at least at the sort of public level that gets written and talked about—is different from that of other cities, mainly because Washington is the nation's capital. As the unnamed authors of the 1942 federal *WPA Guide to Washington* wrote, "Virtually all that gives society here its distinction, its special color and variety, its individual code, arises in the city's character as the abode of high governmental officials, originating from every section of the United States and from every country of the world." Washington is different socially because it's a one-industry town—less now because it's grown so—but still essentially a government town.

Social Washington has changed greatly in the years I've been watching it and been a part of it. Most of the changes were gradual, but when I look back over my eighty years here, it seems like a sea change. Entertaining in Washington has taken different shapes. When my parents arrived in 1917 they attended and gave formal dinners with forty guests as a matter of routine—usually with one long table laid with the best china, silver, and crystal. Frank Carpenter, a syndicated writer and correspondent for the *Cleveland Leader* in the late 1800s (of whom it was written that his "stories are being copied more widely than those of any other writer in Washington"), wrote in *Carp's Washington* that "the dinners of Washington could not be more expensive if their pepper and salt were grains of gold dust."

Frances Parkinson Keyes gives a good picture of the social temper of the times in my mother's day, and in the period right after World War I, when she writes, "It was not infrequent for me to pledge myself

---

Overleaf: A social event not untypical of dinners my parents attended. The caption reads "Dinner at Anderson House. This was the scene around an impressive horseshoe banquet table last Tuesday when Secretary of State John Foster Dulles hosted his formal dinner in honor of the visiting Uruguayan President and his wife. Secretary Dulles and President Batlle Berres are seated at the flower-banked head of the table. The affair was one of a series of banquets, luncheons and parties which kept official Washington on the go during the three-day visit here last week of the Latin American chief of state and entourage." (1955)

for luncheon engagements twenty days in succession and seven weeks in advance; to pour tea at several different receptions in the course of the same afternoon and 'look in' on at least a dozen others, unless I were at home to hundreds of callers myself; to receive six dinner invitations for the same night; and to tumble into bed at four in the morning after having gone to a private musicale and a ball or two after dinner. The scheme of all this entertaining was carried on in the most sumptuous style." Mother's diary confirms all of this by recording dinners, teas, luncheons, receptions, and musicales too numerous to count—even throughout World War I and during the height of the Depression.

By then it was already getting toward the end of the era of the big houses and the iron grip of the "cave-dwellers," but they still held sway when my parents came to Washington, leaving us children behind in New York as though they were going off to a foreign country. The cave-dwellers were an eccentric lot and were so-called informally because they were the ancient inhabitants of the city, who were socially important, as one writer put it, "by right of birth . . . not the will of the people." Referred to always with a kind of "reluctant reverence," cave-dwellers were defined in Mrs. John King Van Rensselaer's book, *The Social Ladder,* as "the native aristocracy, frequently of unimpressive lineage as most eastern cities rate such matters, but with a background of two or three generations of residence in the capital which gives them an air of hoary antiquity when compared to the rest of the city's transitory Society."

No matter how cave-dwellers have been defined, I fear that many people think I've joined their ranks. Susan Mary Alsop and I were having lunch one day, talking about social Washington and some of the women who were the "hostesses" of the past, and we agreed: we have met the cave-dwellers, and "they is us."

THERE certainly have been different phases in social entertaining in Washington. Frank Carpenter wrote that "A curious feature of the wining and dining of Washington is the craze for giving entertainments of special colors," for example, a pink tea, an orange reception, blue and purple affairs.

Others have tried more daring entertainments through the years, from masked parties to costume balls of one sort or another.

Daisy Harriman used to give dinners that turned into a kind of salon. After dinner, she would rap for attention. There might be forty people in the room, all of whom would turn to Daisy, who would say, "Now we're going to discuss . . ." and she'd lay out the topic for the evening, and everybody would have to get to their feet and discuss it.

Allen and Shannon, in *The Truman Merry-Go-Round,* told of one woman who gave a party to usher in the 1950 social season by asking her guests to come dressed as political problems. She "arrayed herself as Mr. Truman's onetime hotly controversial White House balcony." Others showed up as the devalued British pound, the coal crisis ("black satin dress, bituminous coal necklace"), and the Navajo Indian problem, feather-bedecked.

My friend Joe Alsop once wrote that "there has always been a strong touch of the zoo in Washington social life; everyone in Washington likes to see the lions, who also like to be seen." Joe knew how to entertain well—how to mix people so they had a good time, good food, good wine, and a congenial table. He would often divide people into two tables. People would linger at the tables, enjoying the conversation. There was a good deal of high-pitched political argument and gossip exchanged. All tables at formal dinners let the women separate and kept the men at the table. As more and more women went to work or into politics, there was increasing pressure to stop this quaint custom. Finally, I tipped it after I had been working a few years. I didn't want to make a statement but volunteered that I had work to do and wanted to quietly step out and go home. This distressed Joe to the extent that he kept everyone for the discussions after dinner, and a bad habit was broken all over town.

CERTAINLY one of the biggest transformations in Washington society has been that the rules have changed. We seem to have gone from a time of universally understood and accepted rules of society to an era with occasional feuds over the least resistance to the strictures, to a time of much less rigidity to one of anything goes.

During my senior year in high school, in December 1933, *The Washington Post Magazine* ran an article titled "Capital has a rigid calling card code," whose subhead threatened: "Social ostracism is the penalty paid by women who break it." The article warned the astute Washington wife that "if she would seek her husband's political or official fortunes she must build her house of calling cards most carefully under the code" and pointed up the "potent power the little pasteboards wield in their social failure or success in Washington." I never dealt with calling cards in Washington. I recall being in college at the University of Chicago and consulting with my mother about what was the proper thing to do because I was going to leave a card at the home of Mrs. Fairbank, a noted Chicago society woman and friend of my parents.

Happily for me, calling cards and almost all of the attendant rigors of strict society had fallen by the wayside by the time I was a young adult. It's hard for me to imagine episodes of the kind I read and knew about, of women wearing themselves out dropping cards all day long from house to house. Frances Parkinson Keyes, in her book *Capital Kaleidoscope,* writes of two senators' wives arriving at the home of Eleanor Roosevelt "one Wednesday—the time appointed for Assistant Secretaries' wives to receive—were therefore astonished when the maid who opened the door told them that 'she would find out whether Mrs. Roosevelt would see them.' Such a question had never arisen before. The callers seated themselves in the empty drawing-room, where there were no signs of preparations for tea, and looked at each other in astonishment. But almost immediately the maid returned, smiling reassuringly, and said that Mrs. R would be glad to have them come upstairs. With accustomed cordiality she greeted them from her bed; then she pointed with pride to a brand-new baby which was peacefully slumbering beside her."

Among the many rules I lived under at one time or another were those about having equal numbers of men and women as dinner guests—not always easy in a town known as a haven for rich widows protecting their investments. The need for extra men created great difficulties and pressures on hostesses well into my time. My friend Lorraine Cooper once solved the extra-man problem by calling Jack Kennedy when he was president. He was more than delighted to fill her table. When I expressed surprise at finding him at her small dinner in the garden, Lorraine was very nonchalant and replied, "Well, I thought we needed an extra man and wondered who I could get." I also remember a wonderful story about two of my friends in the early 1960s, Clayton Fritchey and Bill Walton, who were both single men at the time. Clayton, having been out of town for a while, met Bill on the street one day and said, "How are you, Bill?" Bill began bemoaning his plight at once: "You were away and Henry Brandon was sick, and I've had to do it all myself. I'm just exhausted." Generally, the extra-man problem remains only for those unwilling to have uneven numbers among the sexes, but, if the truth be told, I even worried about this peculiar kind of gender inequality just recently when I gave a dinner for President George W. Bush.

I also recall Nancy Reagan's surprise one time when I invited the Reagans for dinner, and she called to say that they would have loved to have come, but that Ronnie was going to be out of town. I asked her to please come alone, and she seemed astonished—but delighted—that I might have suggested such a thing. (She came.)

I DON'T think that many of my mother's feelings about social Washington rubbed off on me—mostly because, like any child, I heard only half (at best) of what my mother was trying to convey, but also because her social life was so very different from mine. She went to all the big dinners and teas and parties, left cards, did all the right things—but not to excess, according to her. Although she often feigned lack of interest, her social antennae were up and receiving. In 1935 when she was in the thick of planning a series of parties involving my "coming out," she wrote my sister Bis, "I am in the throes of Kay's reception, dinner, dance, and what not. As I still feel shaky and as the hectic excitement and competitive spirit of the other mamas strikes me as silly, I can't get up any real interest in the whole business but I try not to let Kay know how it bores me."

She did manage to come up with a Greek theme for my dance, and even thought up the idea of having a local fortune-teller, "whom I shall place in a separate chamber of mystery called the Oracle of Delphi." Also according to Mother in that same letter to Bis, I apparently had 750 people on my tea list and "she goes on adding more." This phrase leapt right off the page as though she were saying, "What's a mother to do?" But I, of course, am quite sure I knew no more than fifty people to begin with, so I'm also sure that a large portion of the remainder had to be social friends of hers and my father's. She further reported that we were having seventy people in for dinner before the big ball, to which 350 were coming, and ended another letter with a lament about another sort of coming-out afternoon reception for me: "Think of Kay and me on Friday shaking some 500 people by the paw. What a life."

What a life, indeed. All I remember is the fun.

ALTHOUGH the White House is viewed as the center of Washington social life, not many people ever get to go there. It's important to recognize that society exists on all kinds of levels: big public (or even pri-

vate) dinners—even White House ones—aren't always the ones most
liked and best remembered. For example, Lady Bird, in the summer of
1964, wrote of one small dinner, a birthday party for Bill Moyers at
the home of the Max Freedmans, where there was "a glorious backyard with a noble tree in it. The tables were spread on the back porch,
where we had supper and enjoyed good talk among the small company
of about twenty—the sort of richness peculiar to Washington and
what I shall miss most when I leave here."

People go where they know they'll have a good time. Yes, it helps if
there's a good dinner and you're comfortable—like being seated, rather
than juggling a plate on your lap—but the important thing is to see the
people you're interested in seeing. It doesn't matter what the amenities
are. Within Washington there's a nucleus of people who know each other
and enjoy each other's company and see each other no matter what's happening politically or who is in or out of power.

So, what can we conclude? The underpinnings of Washington society do seem to be different from those of most other places. Wealth is
only one among many factors important to society here. Power and
position alone may not give you an in. There are lots of lions who roar
in Washington. Despite the much talked about Washington hostesses,
social Washington, at least in my lifetime, has been dominated by men.
At the same time, one of the things I like about Washington society is
that the generations mix it up here. Parties count as more than just fun
in Washington. What Vera Bloom wrote in 1944 holds true today:
"Something beyond frivolity keeps them going . . . they are somehow
altogether a part of carrying on the nation's business."

I believe Washington is an open place. Maybe that's easy for me to
say since I'm looked on as one of the "insiders," but it does seem that
there's a lot of fluidity in the boundaries of social Washington. Frank
Carpenter, again in *Carp's Washington,* wrote that "Lucifer himself will
be welcomed if he will dress well, keep his hoofs hidden in patent
leather, and his tail out of sight."

The Society of the Nation's Capital

The Social Ladder (1924)

The heights of the "society" and "social distinction" described in The
Social Ladder *would have been a tough climb for anyone not born
with the proverbial silver spoon in his mouth.*

While most of The Social Ladder *was written by Mrs. John King
Rensselaer and is focused on society in general and New York society in
particular, three places are singled out for greater attention in separate
chapters: Newport, Southampton (and the rest of Long Island), and
Washington, D.C. Actually, it was Mr. Frederic Van de Water who wrote
the chapter on Washington excerpted here.*

*Although much of what he has to say may sound old-fashioned and
pedagogical, he's quite instructive about a time long gone. And he is
not without humor—for example, he writes, "The chief social use of
U.S. Representatives in Washington is to furnish a class toward which
the rest of Society, Senators especially, can feel superior."*

*In the category of "the more things change, the more things stay the
same" may be his notion that "Nowhere else in America are the prizes to
be won by social distinction so brilliant. The possibility of intimacy
with men who are making history; the chance of entertaining or being
entertained by European aristocracy; the reflected glory that shines
upon all who are close to events in their making, are factors in the
weedlike growth of the capital's social sets. . . . The social ladder in
Washington has innumerable rungs. Some may be too exalted for the
average person to reach at once, but there are always lower levels where
any one can stand who is willing to pay for the privilege."*

THREE years ago, she dwelt in a two-family house in a two hundred
family town. A whim of the voters lifted her husband out of his
law practice and set him down in one of the seats of the politically
mighty in Washington.

Today, she is a leader in the Society of the capital. Custom has decreed that she entertain at her table ambassadors, leaders of the government and the diplomatically great from all quarters of the globe. Her name is sought for inclusion in lists of patronesses. It is included in the roster of the invited at every great social function.

A year from now, the free, enlightened but undeniably whimsical electorate may have removed her husband from his present post. She will return with him to the two-family house in the two hundred family town and, in all probability, resume the life she abandoned when she went to Washington to become one of the temporary rulers of the most temporary Society in America. . . .

Washington Society has as its foundation wealth and an imported aristocracy, either directly or indirectly political. A city that was a marsh until 1800 cannot be expected to produce native genealogies of Biblical length and portentousness. A city whose social life is directly dependent upon its politics, whose Society suffers disruption when Democrats succeed Republicans, or vice versa, cannot build up a rigid, permanent social organization. In the years when political landslides bury the party in power, when lame ducks go hobbling sadly and disconsolately homeward, Society suffers agonies of dismemberment.

No other Society is so uncomfortably dependent upon the whims and convictions of the common or garden variety of American voter. As long as these heartless individuals insist upon voting, first for one party and then for the other, Washington can never hope to have a stable, organized social system. She will have to get along as best she can with the shifting, continually altering groups, linked together by only the most tenuous ties, which constitute her Society. The Washington world of fashion is composed in large part of what might be called camp followers of that executive, legislative, administrative and diplomatic army of which the President of the United States is head. . . .

To the President of the United States, Washington Society and the city itself owe their existence. His presence there drew the community out of the Potomac swamps. Remove him and the government he heads elsewhere, and not only the social system but the town itself would, in all probability, crumble and die.

The first reception held at the White House each winter opens the Washington social season: This affair usually takes place early in December. From then on until Lent, Society entertainments tread upon each other's heels. After Lent "the little season" endures until the first furnace blast of the capital's summer heat drives the last of the faithful to cooler climes.

During the season, the President and his wife give three receptions in all—one to the diplomatic corps, one to the senators and a third to the army and navy. In each of these, procedure is similar. In accordance with tradition, there are enormous preparations and elaborate preliminaries leading up, by solemn progression, to very little.

Twenty-five hundred invitations are issued for each reception. Formerly there was a regrettable tendency upon the part of some unappreciative invited guests to turn their cards of admission over to others who would value them more. The anguish suffered by certain patrician Washingtonians who found themselves standing side by side at these august assemblages with their barbers or butchers caused recent reform. Now, the invitations are absolutely non-transferable.

The invited, in the ultimate in evening dress, are marshaled into the East Room of the White House. The line is so long that it curves back and forth across the chamber in several loops. Its head is thrust through a door in the southwest corner; its tail is continually receiving additions as late arrivals come hurrying upstairs.

Across the Blue Room from one door to the other is strung the receiving line. The President stands at the head of this. Next to him is his wife and beyond them, the men and women who are assisting at the reception—usually nine in all. Behind them stand those fortunates who through special favor are entitled to a place "behind the line." This means that they enjoy the privilege of standing in the Blue Room, gazing at the backs of those on the receiving line, through the entire ceremony. The view may not be inspiring, but their souls are filled with peace. Their names will appear in every paper on the morrow, proclaiming that they have attained, or retained, social prominence.

The patient twenty-five hundred in the East Room shuffle slowly forward, chat half-heartedly with their neighbors and sweat profusely. Their progress is extremely gradual. The greeting of two thousand five hundred persons by nine men and women on a receiving line is not a brief ceremony.

At length, a little disheveled by the jam, more than a little footsore from long standing in patent leather shoes or silver slippers, the average patient guest reaches a weary military aide at the door leading into the Blue Room. In a hoarsened voice, he announces your name to the valiantly smiling President at the head of the line. You pass down its length and forth into the Green Room, thence to the Ball Room where the Marine Band, in the most brilliant of scarlet coats, dispenses brazen harmony. The room is packed. As well try to dance on a New York subway platform during the rush hour. You go home to bed and perhaps by the time you have arrived there, the Chief Executive has shaken hands with the last of the twenty-five hundred and gone upstairs with the same end in view.

The receptions confer social distinction only upon those fortunates "behind the line." The musicales given now and again by the wife of the President are much more exclusive affairs at which the list of invited guests rarely reaches one hundred. Each of them has warrant for feeling that he or she is numbered among the socially elect. The afternoon teas are even more intimate affairs at which the President's wife entertains her friends.

Yearly, each member of Washington Society in good and regular standing pays a formal call at the White House. Here again, tradition rules and imposes enormous preparations leading up to a flat anti-climax. If you are male, you array yourself in a cutaway, silk hat, pearl gloves and spats and all the rest of strictest afternoon regalia. If you aren't, you don your best frock. Then you hire a carriage with coachman and footman— motors for such enterprises of state are frowned upon—and drive to the door of the White House. The footman descends and presents your cards to the servant who appears at the door. Then, he climbs back and you—drive home again, your whole part in the proceeding having been confined to sitting still and looking as aristocratic as possible. . . .

To be among the uninvited to anything is an indignity unendurable to Washington Society. To avoid such a disaster, certain families practice planting what is coarsely termed "the alibi," weeks before some spectacular entertainment. They inform all their acquaintances that upon the date set for the affair they will have to be in New York or Richmond or elsewhere "on business." If an invitation to the affair is received, the "business" is postponed. If the worst comes to pass and they have been ignored, they leave town ostentatiously a day or so before the function. . . .

The diplomatic set and its firm ally, the young married set, represent a brilliance and dash that the rest of the capital envies while it deplores. Europe usually sends to Washington, as embassy attachés, the most attractive unmarried specimens of its gentry classes. To the eyes of a city satiated with gazing upon the simple, rugged examples of American manhood that politicians pretend to be, the courtly members of the diplomatic service seem to have stepped bodily out of the novels of E. Phillips Oppenheim. Their cosmopolitan air is alluring, the faint atmosphere of international intrigue that surrounds them, irresistible. Hence, through the social season, they lead lives of the hunted. Insatiable debutantes and no less determined mammas pursue them through wildernesses of receptions and swamps of teas. Their alliance with the young married set is brought about not only by community of interests but also through yearnings for a haven of safety.

Yet even the diplomatic set is broken up into various cliques. In addition, there are some embassies considered still outside the social pale— chiefly those of a few South American republics whose attachés are too nearly the hue of a well-smoked meerschaum to please the taste of Society.

Beyond the diplomatic and young married sets, anything like social stability or exclusiveness vanishes. Prowling about the shaky walls of the social citadel are all sorts of would-be invaders, among them even folk who have been in trade. That term, in Washington, remains the ultimate in social condemnation. The Society of the republic's capital holds to the conviction that a man who is paid wages by any one but the government is not at all welcome in the social system. But things are not what they were in the good old days! Ideals are withering and ancient standards falling. Even so stalwart and conservative an institution as the Chevy Chase Country Club has permitted its patrician atmosphere to be tainted recently by admitting certain persons "in trade."

Still there are some bulwarks of aristocracy that remain. There is the Grasslands Country Club, with seventy members, that has not taken in anybody, in trade or out of it, for seven years. Since membership therein descends like a patent of nobility from father to son, it presumably can get along without any recruits for the next seventy. The Alibi Club's name is deceiving. It has only fifty members. None of them is in trade.

Yet the old order, as Washington estimates age, is changing. Year by year the climbers in their legions pour into the capital to campaign for social recognition. A few are accepted, now and then, by the more exclusive circles because of native qualities. More get in by purchasing or building a home and setting up a large and expensive establishment. Not a few buy their way into the social system. . . .

Social agents, little brothers and sisters to the climber, have become so common in the capital that their work has almost reached the dignity of a profession. It is no unusual thing for a Washington hostess to consent to launch a debutante in Society for a certain, not at all insignificant, sum. Once launched, the debutante's chance of fulfilling her destiny and marrying well is small. Competition is tremendous. The women in Washington Society far outnumber the men. A wedding in the capital is something more than a ceremony. It is a celebration of the triumph of feminine persistence over tremendous handicaps.

Because of this lack of unmarried men, the pathway into Society of the bachelor who dresses and dances acceptably is smooth compared to the rough road a married man or woman must travel. The average unattached male has been made so welcome that he has come to feel that any dance, however exclusive, is open to him, whether he has received an invitation or not. So aggressive have these "Walk-ins" become that Washington of late has been forced to erect defenses against them. Invitations now are sometimes accompanied by a card of admittance. At other houses, guests are asked to sign a register upon arrival, but in spite of these precautions, the "Walk-in" walks in, calm, debonair with a pose of aristocratic boredom that does not desert him, even when ejected by persons unappreciative of the honor his presence bestows.

Only recently, a Washington family gave a dance for its debutante daughter and surrounded the affair with a particularly intricate system of defenses to keep out the "Walk-ins." It seemed to work, for many were caught and turned away. Toward the end of the evening a youth was escorting the daughter of the house from the dance floor and murmured to her:

"Don't seem to be many 'Walk-ins' here tonight."

"Not a single one," she replied. "We've kept them all out."

"Not all," he corrected. "I'm one. Had such a pleasant evening. Good night."

ANNE SQUIRE

Don'ts in Washington

Social Washington (1929)

Anne Squire's Social Washington—*the 1929 edition that I read was
a revised edition of an earlier work—is a rule book, just like* Robert's
Rules of Order *for parliamentarians. To succeed in Washington
socially, one need only to have followed the rules as set down by Squire.
In fact, following these rules was no doubt necessary for inclusion in
later editions of the Washington "Green Book," or* Social List.

*Miss Squire, well known in her day in Washington, was called by
David Cohn the "Emily Post of the Capital." Vera Bloom, writing that
"Washington social secretaries are really a story in themselves," mentioned Squire as one of the best: "conscientious, conservative . . . usually members of distinguished old Washington families—like Miss
Anne Squire, whose little book* Social Washington *is every newcomer's
bible, if there is still a copy to be had." Miss Squire covered all one
needed to know: how to make calls at the White House, how to address
the president (whether speaking or in writing), who might call upon
the justices, and how to give an official dinner. Her foreword explains
why these rules had to be relied on:*

> The knowledge of [the social rules] simplifies life for every-
> one; the ignorance of which unhappily often brings upon the
> innocent newcomer very humiliating rebuffs; and indifference to
> which calls down stern criticism upon the offender. . . .
>
> This book is intended to . . . familiarize [American women]
> with a code of manners that has resulted from years of adapta-
> tion to peculiar conditions. . . .
>
> We are for the most part Democratic in our ideals; but it is
> well to remember that simplicity is obtained by order in detail,
> and that the affectation which refuses to recognize its own
> rights is quite as deplorable as the affectation which insists
> upon consideration that is not its due.

Here is her simple list of "social don'ts."

A s in all places where there is a particular code there must be inhibitions, I shall give a few that are scattered through the foregoing pages, but are more easily realized—brought together in a list. Of course there are exceptions to some of them. A few are cast iron. All highly to be recommended.

1. Don't delay in answering invitations.

2. Don't change your mind about coming to a party without notifying the hostess.

3. Don't ask people occupying high official positions to dine with you before you have called on them. At least leave cards with the invitation.

4. Don't, when wishing to give a dinner to someone, suggest more than two dates lest your invitation take the nature of a hold-up (this does not apply to dinners given as part of one's official duty).

5. Don't keep prompt guests waiting for tardy ones. Wait ten minutes for a man and fifteen for a woman or a couple, and then go in to dinner. If the persons late are socially important, they know better. If unavoidably detained they will prefer that there is no delay on their account.

6. Don't forget that the above cannot be applied to the ranking guests. It is necessary to wait for them.

7. Don't change people's rank at dinner under the impression that you are giving satisfaction to those whom you move up.

8. Don't say to a friend that you are "so sorry that I could not dine with you on Tuesday" unless there is no one listening. The one asked to fill your place may be present and while everyone willingly fills a place, there are occasions when it need not be rubbed in.

9. Don't forget that the lady who sits at the right of the host at dinner must make the move to go home. Never mind how the men precede each other. It is the lady on the right of the host who makes the move.

10. When you are the "lady on the right," make the move to go home at ten o'clock for a very formal dinner; at ten thirty for a less formal one, and always at three o'clock for a half-past-one luncheon.

11. Don't substitute guests. If Mr. and Mrs. X. are invited it is not permissible for Mr. X. to go and take a daughter; or for Mrs. X. to appear alone and say that her husband was detained at the last moment. Write and explain the situation, or if necessary call

up over the telephone. Then let the hostess decide if she wishes a substitute or prefers to have you both drop out. Remember it is often a question of reseating a large dinner which is almost impossible at the last moment, and gives endless trouble.

12. Don't bring prejudices to other people's houses. Your worst enemy must be treated with special courtesy when you meet him or her at dinner. It will be all the more fun to cut him the next day.

13. Don't start anything at a dinner party. During President Monroe's Administration the French and British Ministers got into an altercation at dinner at the White House and retired into the hall to fight a duel. For the host and hostess such episodes even in mild form do not increase one's popularity as a guest.

14. Don't think that the Man from Home must precede officials at dinner. Jefferson says in his "Canon of Etiquette" that "6th: Our Ministers to foreign nations are as private citizens while here." An added reason for making no exceptions even for very distinguished people who come unofficially.

15. Don't regret invitations for dinner. That is wrong. Accept or regret invitations to dinner. Remember that they have saddle of mutton for dinner. Guests are asked to dinner.

16. Don't give a luncheon and follow it up by an unannounced program of music or anything else. Announce the program with the invitation.

17. Don't make such a program long. Make it short. Afternoons are very busy.

18. Don't wear afternoon costume when you go to evening parties at the White House. The President will not care, but you will—awfully.

19. Don't forget to always give your name to anyone making introductions (Mr. A., Mrs. A., Miss A.).

20. Don't fail to put an address on your visiting cards.

21. Don't use the word "house guest." It is an unpardonable social lapse. "A visiting friend," "someone stopping with me," or even a "guest" is explicit enough.

22. Don't ask people "to pour" when you mean "to pour tea" or "to receive" with you.

Please don't forget these Don'ts.

ANONYMOUS
(Drew Pearson and Robert S. Allen)

Boiled Bosoms

Washington Merry-Go-Round (1931)

Those in the know in Washington still know about the Washington
Merry-Go-Round *books. The first one was published in 1931 completely anonymously, with no byline on the title page. Its sequel,* More
Merry-Go-Round, *appeared the next year, by which time it was
clear to nearly one and all that the men behind the trenchant pens creating this picture of Washington were Drew Pearson, then Washington
reporter for the* Baltimore Sun, *who focused his attention on covering
the State and War Departments, and Robert Allen, a correspondent for
the* Christian Science Monitor. *Allen was let go by the* Monitor
right after publication of the first book. The Sun *held on to Pearson
until just after the second one landed, when he, too, was discharged. In
one article about Pearson's dismissal, the* Sun's *managing editor was
quoted as saying, "We felt that as a result of his work on this book he
had destroyed his usefulness to this newspaper." He seems to have had
plenty of opportunities to continue to work in Washington, however,
which he did. These books were big bestsellers at the time. In 1931,
when Pearl Buck's* The Good Earth *headed the fiction bestseller list,*
Washington Merry-Go-Round *was close to the top for nonfiction.*

Together the Merry-Go-Round *books shone the light on some of
Washington's hypocrisy and demagoguery. With individual chapters
like those on the House of Representatives—"The Monkey House,"
which the authors called the "greatest organized inferiority complex in
the world"—and the newly forming group of presidential aides—
"The Vestal Virgins"—Pearson and Allen exposed the "political and
social foibles of Washington life." One reviewer suggested that "If every
college student of American Government could have the 'Washington
Merry-Go-Round' placed in his hands as the foundation of a course in
American Federal Government, interest in political science would
increase by several hundred per cent. Intelligent insight into how we
are actually governed would also pick up by comparable leaps and*

bounds. . . . [This material] is the real flesh and blood of politics. . . .
I doubt if anything since the publication of 'The Federalist' has done so
much as these books to educate the American public relative to our governmental affairs."

Although The Federalist would not have been my first point of
comparison, these books are full of insight from the period and are
classic Washingtoniana.

WITH THE exception of Peking, no other capital in the world
equals Washington for the relentless brilliancy with which the
spotlight of public attention is fixed upon the comings and
goings, the cocktail parties and the amours of the petty people who run
the official and social life of the capital of these United States.

If Nick Longworth came back from Cincinnati unexpectedly one
autumn night to find himself locked out of his house on Massachusetts
Avenue; should Dolly Curtis Gann stop to adjust a slipping stocking
before a crowd of shoppers at Woodward and Lothrop's; or should Mrs.
Hoover have a dispute with her secretary, Polly Randolph, over flowers
for the White House table, most of the dinners and tea parties of Washington are buzzing over the incident twenty-four hours later.

There are two reasons for this. In the first place, Washington is small,
and the group which runs its social and official life is even smaller. In the
second place, Washington has only one industry—politics.

London, Berlin, Paris, Rome, Moscow, Vienna—all the other great
capitals of the world are also vast industrial and commercial centers in
which the pompous preening of society is almost swallowed up. Were the
capital of the United States located in New York, much of the material
for the merry-go-round of Washington would be non-existent. But the
capital is not in New York. Instead, it has been plumped down in a placid
agricultural community, surrounded by the remnants of a Southern aristocracy which still prides itself on its hounds, hunters and mint-juleps,
and which boasts no industry other than the Bureau of Printing and
Engraving plus a few river boats which chug sleepily up the Potomac,
bringing oysters, Norfolk honeymooners and split pine logs.

Not only is the sole industry of the capital politics, but this industry is
concentrated among a very few. Fifty percent of Washington's half million population is of a race which, except when it gathers to cheer Paul
Robeson or its lone congressional champion, Oscar De Priest, is neither
interested [in] nor admitted into high society.

Of the remaining quarter million people, most are government clerks
and the trades-people who support them, leaving the capital's social life

almost exclusively in the hands of those who live in the fashionable northwest. This is an area, which, socially speaking, begins at the White House and stretches out Pennsylvania Avenue and Sixteenth Street toward ancient Georgetown to the west and toward *nouveau riche* Chevy Chase on the north.

Within this orbit, divided into many cliques and schisms, throbs a social life as gay, as superficial and as futile as in any capital of Europe.

Broadly speaking, Washington society can be divided into two classes: Those who want to get their names in the papers and those who want to keep them out.

The Cabinet members, the congressional climbers, the Army and Navy, and the professional pushers are all more or less in the first category, while the Young Set, the intellectuals and the fast-riding, hard-drinking poker players are in the second.

There are in Washington a half dozen middle-aged or aging ladies who absolutely dominate the social stage. Their arrival in the fall and their departure in the spring is the order for the ringing up or down of the curtain for the social season. They put the social lions through their tricks—pull them in and out of the social ring. They crack the whip, and they crack it with all the grimness of the tamer who must inspire fawning obedience or retire from the ring.

Most fawned upon among Washington's social whip-crackers are:

MRS. JOSEPH (Juliette) LEITER, big, blonde, and the most domineering whip-cracker of them all. Just after the turn of the century she married Joe Leiter, whose boast is that he was "the largest individual holder of wheat in the history of the grain trade," but who, finding it easier to control wheat than his wife, now leaves his enormous mansion on du Pont Circle entirely to her and to the fabulous parties which she gives in the manner but not the quality of the Vanderbilts.

MRS. JAMES F. (Laura) CURTIS, patron saint of those who play for a thousand-dollar limit. She has swallowed her pride just once. Although she left her husband, only to take him back again, Jimmie has gone to live in New York, from which point of vantage he supplies the cash and watches her crack the whip over her little clique as relentlessly as she once cracked it over him.

ELEANOR MEDILL PATTERSON, formerly Mrs. Eleanor Schlesinger, formerly Countess Gizycka, formerly Eleanor Medill Patterson, one of the most gifted women in Washington but who has dissipated her gifts, for the most part on trivialities.

ALICE ROOSEVELT LONGWORTH, brilliant if not gifted, who

through the prestige of her position and the vitriol of her tongue dominates Washington's ultra-fashionable official group more completely than any other whip-cracker in the capital.

One of the most charming things about Washington is that it is almost never without a social, diplomatic or matrimonial war, and as in all one-industry villages these feuds are waged so earnestly that before they are over they line up on one side or the other almost every one in town. Within less than the past twelve months there have been:

The EDWARD B. MCLEAN–PRINCE DE LIGNE WAR over an alleged dinner-table prank, as the result of which the Belgian Ambassador, although later forced to retire, received a personal apology from Secretary of State Stimson, and the publisher of the *Washington Post* got a personal apology from the *Philadelphia Record*.

The PRADO-POINDEXTER WAR over a servant imported from Lima by the wife of the American Ambassador to Peru, which resulted in Counselor Prado, of the Peruvian Embassy in Washington, resigning his post and taking the servant off with him to London.

The TOTÒ MACIA–ITALIAN EMBASSY WAR over the unimportant question of incompatibility, which resulted in the beautiful Signora Macia rising up in all her Canadian wrath, fleeing her house at midnight, and secreting her baby in Baltimore.

The SIAMESE LIQUOR WAR over the right of a legation to transport beverages from Baltimore, which resulted in the entire Diplomatic Corps rebelling against the capital police, with the exception of the gentle British Ambassador, Sir Esme Howard, who promptly announced he would import no more liquor.

The SALVADOREAN LEGATION–POLICE WAR over the failure of the latter to prevent hi-jackers from absconding with seventeen cases of liquor, and which caused Don Carlos Leiva, having been severely beaten over the head with a flashlight, to sit up in bed and issue scathing statements about repeated attempts to rob his Legation, against which the police offered no protection.

The DAISY HARRIMAN–RAY BAKER WAR, between two of the most charming and once friendly Democrats of the capital, which resulted when the former came back from Bermuda to find that the latter had dumped 5,000 tons of dirt from the cellar of his new house in the middle of her front lawn.

None of these, of course, could compare with the Dolly Curtis Gann–Alice Roosevelt Longworth precedence war, a war which stirred

Washington to the depths of its sensation-loving soul. Unfortunately, this feud, except when Edward Everett Gann calls up the *Washington Daily News* to complain that he is not a "meek" husband, is in a completely comatose stage. Fortunately, however, its place was taken, just before it breathed its last, by the Patterson-Longworth War.

This was not a new battle. Intimate friends of both Eleanor Patterson and Alice Longworth knew that it had been smoldering ever since their debutante days when they had competed for the most eligible men in town. One of them married a young Congressman from Cincinnati, and the other Count Joseph Gizycka, a dashing young Polish cavalryman in Emperor Franz Ferdinand's army.

Later, Cissie Gizycka came back from Warsaw once again to cramp Alice's style and in later years to tell a story on herself—which may or may not be true—about a young nobleman who sat at Alice's right at dinner one evening. After dinner Cissie monopolized him in an upstairs library. The following morning she received a note from her hostess which read as follows:

Dear Cissie:
Upon sweeping up the library this morning, the maid found several hair-pins which I thought you might need and which I am returning.

Alice

To which Cissie says she replied:

Dear Alice:
Many thanks for the hair-pins. If you had looked on the chandelier you might also have sent back my shoes and chewing gum.

Love,
Cissie

It was at the Republican National Convention of 1920, held in Chicago, that the first real breach occurred. Cissie Gizycka had taken a house for the period of the convention, and had invited as one of her guests William Edgar Borah, shaggy-maned and shaggy-browed Senator from Idaho. She was writing a series of human-interest stories on the convention for the Hearst papers and devoted one of them to a more than laudatory sketch of Borah. Her house-guest explained that this was highly embarrassing and cautioned her against any repetition of her flattery. A day or two later and with all the ear-marks of having been inspired by an irate Countess Gizycka, her brother's newspaper, the *Chicago Tribune*, published a scathing editorial, headed "Borah and Blah." Borah's hostess had no connection with the editorial, but both he and Alice

Longworth, even then one of his most intimate friends, thought she had. They never forgave Cissie.

Simultaneous with her marriage to Elmer Schlesinger, five years later, Countess Gizycka shook Washington out of its usual slumber by publishing her first book, *Glass Houses*. In it she painted, so deftly that no one could mistake them and so brazenly that every one gasped, her old friend and her arch-enemy, Borah and Alice. This widened the breach beyond all repair.

The climax came after Cissie Schlesinger, widowed, always too active to be idle and too intelligent to be content with the routine of society, became editor-in-chief of Hearst's *Washington Herald*. A few weeks later there appeared tucked away at the bottom of the first page an insignificant looking box which brought the *Herald* more circulation in one week than it had ever gained before in years. The box read:

INTERESTING BUT NOT TRUE

The news is that Mrs. Alice Longworth will not only be the confidential advisor to Mrs. Ruth Hanna McCormick, but that she will campaign publicly for her lifelong friend. Interesting but not true.

Mrs. McCormick takes no advice, political or otherwise, from Mrs. Longworth.

Mrs. Longworth gives no interviews to the press.

Mrs. Longworth cannot utter in public.

Her assistance will, therefore, resolve itself, as usual, into posing for photographs.

Letters of approval and protest followed. Washington beamed. A sequel to the Gann-Longworth War had broken out. Editor Patterson, who by that time had resumed her maiden name, tried it again. The majority of her friends frowned and her enemies raved. But as a circulation-getter it was a wow.

It had only one fault. In order to create a first-class row there must be two parties to a dispute. In this case, however, there was only one. Alice refused to hit back. She continued to grant no interviews, make no speeches. She confined her activities to the thing she has always done best, posing for photographs. There is no fun in punching a deflated punching-bag, and Editor Patterson quit.

Since then she has had to be content with giving pretentious dinner parties for Mrs. William Randolph Hearst, interviewing Al Capone and Dr. Einstein, and pretending to enjoy coarse newspaper revelries at which she tries hard to be one of the gang.

ALICE ROOSEVELT
LONGWORTH

Innocence and Mischief

Crowded Hours (1933)

I know I first read Mrs. Longworth's memoir long ago—so long ago, in fact, that I hadn't remembered it. But when I looked at it again and read the first sentence of her last chapter, I put the book down and said, "Exactly!" What she wrote was: "Washington, where I have spent the greater part of nearly every year since I was a child, is such a habit, has become so much a matter of course to me, that it is difficult to see it in proper perspective." I, too, find it difficult to see Washington objectively.

Alice Roosevelt Longworth was only a few years older than my mother but outlived her by a decade, dying in 1980. From the time they met, in 1917, they were lifelong friends of sorts, though each was a bit wary of the other. At one point Mother felt distanced from Mrs. Longworth because she felt she had become an adherent of America First. But even though politics separated them at times, Mother admired Mrs. Longworth, particularly the way she enjoyed herself and how she bore up under the hardships of the death of her husband Nick and the too-early death of her only child, Paulina.

My father was much closer to her. They played cards together often, and she found him charming and witty. She admitted that once when she was pontificating on something or other, he said, "Alice, you say things with more finality to less foundation than anyone I know." She loved it and laughed harder than he did.

By the time Alice Longworth became a friend of Phil's and mine and our friends of our generation, she had an established position in Washington as an older prominent figure whom we all adored. She was so established that she was known as "Washington's other monument." In social matters, she helped break Washington out of a straitjacket, often setting the precedent or social standard rather than adhering to it.

No one ever called her Alice, as I remember, except Lorraine Cooper, who was a little older than we were, and Joe Alsop, who was related. The rest of us called her Mrs. L. The story did go around, however, of how Joseph McCarthy had come up to her once at a party, put his arm around her, and said, "Here's my blind date. I'm going to call you Alice." Her response: "Senator McCarthy, you are not going to call me Alice. The trashman and the policeman on my block may call me Alice, but you may not."

Mrs. L. had a distinguished aquiline face and long hair tucked up somehow, but not neatly. She was highly intelligent, witty, sharp, and irreverent. She had a caustic and quick wit. She didn't take credit for some of the many things she supposedly said, but it was she who was known to have said, "If you can't say anything good about someone, sit right here by me."

She often spoke negatively of Eleanor Roosevelt, her distant relative, but she adored Franklin and went often to the White House. In fact, she went to the White House through eighteen administrations. Michael Teague's book Mrs. L., Conversations with Alice Roosevelt Longworth, quoted her as saying, "Somebody once calculated that I had been to an average of 2.7 dinners a year at the White House over a sixty-year period. That's an awful lot of dinner." Teague also quoted her as noting that LBJ, whom she called "an engaging rogue elephant of a man," complained that "he couldn't kiss me under my hat and I told him that was why I wore it." As for LBJ, he was smitten with her; he once said that, even in her eighties, Mrs. L. was more fun to talk to than anybody else.

She was conservative, as my mother had discovered, and very much enjoyed Richard Nixon—admiring something stubborn in him, I think. But somehow she related more closely to us and all our friends, especially to her distant cousins Joe and Stew Alsop.

She was everybody's favorite dinner guest. We all exchanged dinners, which she gave at her beautiful period house near Dupont Circle on Massachusetts Avenue. She always served what Joe described as good solid American food, such as crabmeat soup and a roast of meat. Her house had the living and dining rooms on the second floor. The walls were lined with the skins of animals shot by her father, Teddy, while hunting—I seem to remember tiger skins and others.

The Gann-Longworth feud, the topic of this excerpt from Mrs. L.'s memoir, turns up in practically every book on Washington from the period, with many of them clucking on about it at some length. According to accounts of the time, it became a veritable social war. The main combatants were Dolly Gann, the sister of Hoover's vice president,

Charles Curtis, and Mrs. Longworth, as wife of the Speaker of the
House. Mrs. Gann was someone to be reckoned with, formidable. She
was known to be so helpful to her brother that during one vice presi-
dential campaign tour, as Vera Bloom reports in There's No Place
Like Washington, *"the handshaking got so strenuous that before it*
was over the candidate simply couldn't shake another hand. Mrs. Gann
used to stand behind him and unobtrusively slip her hand through his
exhausted arm, offering it cordially to unsuspecting handshakers, who
went away pledged by this 'personal contact' to vote for Curtis."

One of my favorite stories about Mrs. Gann happened at a time
when certain colors were being associated with prominent women—
like "Alice blue" for Alice Roosevelt. Someone had asked Mrs. Gann if a
color was to be named after her. It was Vera Bloom herself who piped
right up with, "How about 'Gann green?'"

In any case, few incidents in twentieth-century Washington caused
more stir than this feud. Here's Mrs. Longworth's take on it.

I F O N E has anything like a real interest in politics, one does not have
to be in an official position to know and take a part in what is going
on. Of course it is the greatest possible fun, and most interesting, to
be on the "inside" and hear about, if not horn in on, the course of legislation and policies. On the other hand, there is a great deal in the routine
of official life which seems a penalty rather than a reward from the point
of view of the wife of an official. For one thing, there is the making calls
and being called on. As I had never done it, I did not take it up when Nick
became Speaker.

He and I had long before decided that I was more a liability than an
asset to him along those lines, that if the wives of his fellow politicians
were going to be affronted by my inactivity in assuming "social obligations" he would have to make the best of it. He did not think, any more
than I did, that a successful political career depended on such perfunctory and conventional activities. It was not as if I had an aversion to people, such was far from the fact, there is nothing I like better than meeting
and communicating with my fellow man and woman, but to shake a hand
and chatter for a few minutes in the course of receptions and at homes
certainly cannot be called communication.

Then there were the Washington dinner parties. When one has a certain rank, one can tell in advance which of half a dozen among the other
guests one is bound to draw as a dinner companion; I recollect that after
sitting beside the same ambassador at a dozen dinners in succession, I did

not feel that I could stand another meal at his elbow and thought that he probably could not either. One of our friends was giving a dinner and happened to tell me where I was to be seated and there were he and I together again. I struck. I asked to be let come in after dinner, or if I did come to dinner, might I not be put "out of my rank," just a little, or below the salt, if she only would. At first, after some argument, she reluctantly agreed to put me elsewhere, but when I got to the dinner, she said that she had thought it over, and discussed it with several people, and it really was impossible to do as I had asked, that I must sit where I belonged. People in Washington seem as hypnotized by precedence as though they were hens with their beaks on a chalk line.

A jealous interest as to their seat at table seems to spring up in the temporary holders of official positions. I believe that it was in the '90's that there was a great row about whether or not the Vice-President should out-rank the representatives of foreign nations, a battle that was won by the Vice-President. During Father's administration, Admiral Dewey developed ideas about where his position entitled him to sit and Miss Helen Cannon, the daughter of the Speaker, thought she was entitled to the rank of her father.

The only row of that sort that I ever found myself involved in was what the newspapers called the Gann-Longworth feud. In one way I was completely innocent of any participation in it, in another I made a little mischief which had the most unforeseen results. When Charlie Curtis became Vice-President, it became known, or was announced, in the jargon of the newspapers, that his sister, Mrs. Gann, was to be his "official hostess." It seems to me the word "hostess" has lost its meaning, or acquired a new one, since it has become associated with night clubs and hotels. The label "official" seemed unnecessary, it would be only natural that the sister who lived with him should sit at the head of his table. Then to the delight of gossip-loving Washington it was realized that official hostess meant official diner-out—that at all functions she was to take the rank of her Vice-Presidential brother.

At that there was a cackle of excited discussion about the propriety of designating any one not a wife to hold the rank of one. Nick did not approve of it at all. He thought that to put the sister of the Vice-President ahead of the wives of the representatives of foreign nations was an act of discourtesy, and eventually his disapproval extended to her out-ranking the wives of American officials, though so far as out-ranking me was concerned, he never specifically alluded to that though as he was an official, and I his wife, I was of course in the category.

The immediate cause of the torrent of newspaper publicity on the subject was a dinner given by the Eugene Meyers. The Meyers, much to

Nick's disapproval, had, after years of serving things to drink, decided to have a dry house. That aroused Nick's wrath. He had little sympathy with those who were dry from conviction, but if they went dry from what he considered political expediency, it exasperated him. He had not dined with the Meyers for some time but had told me I might accept for him this particular dinner. A few days before, Mrs. Meyer and I were talking and she happened to mention who were coming and how she was going to seat her party. There were to be many potentates, the Vice-President, a selection of ambassadors, and other lesser lights. When she said that Eugene was to take in Mrs. Gann, I remarked that when Nick heard that, I did not believe he would come; that the combination of a dry house and Mrs. Gann out-ranking the ambassadorial wives would probably be too much for him.

Then I regret to say the temptation to make trouble became too strong for me. Instead of saying nothing and letting Nick go to the dinner, I told him the horrid news of the seating, whereat he promptly said he would not go, that he was very glad to get out of the despised dry dinner, using as an excuse "the slight" to the foreign ladies. The next day he had a large lunch party in the Speaker's dining room of the House, and made a good story about how he had managed to dodge doing what he did not wish to do. Within less than three hours he, the Meyers, and I were being called up by the press and the whole ridiculous episode was attributed to my having "taken a stand" against the pretensions of Charlie Curtis and Mrs. Gann.

Of course, obviously, there never was any row; any one who knew me was aware that rank and conventionality were things I always fled from and shirked. I could not very well tell the true story—that Nick had seized a straw to avoid a dry dinner, so all I could say was, "I have really nothing to do with it." It was fantastic, the interest that was taken in the so-called row. People took sides, not so much in Washington, where many knew the truth, but out in the country. I used to get letters demanding how I could be so snobbish as to "snub Mrs. Gann" and others saying "stick to your guns." The first time she and I were seen in public together in the Senate gallery, the rustle in the press gallery across the way was like leaves in an autumn wind. And I really think a great many people never believed that Charlie Curtis and Dolly Gann were just as good friends of mine as they had always been.

JOSEPH W. ALSOP

Dining-Out Washington

I've Seen the Best of It (1992)

I love this book, and I don't think it's just because it was written by my friend Joe Alsop. When I read it, it creates a mental picture for me of so much that illustrates Washington over the decades—the "ancient downtown centers" of the White House and Treasury Building (where my father's office was for so many years), the heat that forced men to wear Panama hats and seersucker suits, the "intoxicating atmosphere that settled over the capital" during the early months of the Kennedy administration, including "oddly enough, glamor, which is not a quality usually associated with Washington."

I believe that Joe Alsop, over time, became a brilliant reporter. He certainly had a unique perspective on Washington, as he had on everything to which he turned his watchfulness, but he was especially fascinated by this place. Joe held firm opinions and held them vociferously. He was eccentric—there's no doubt about it—but he once wrote that it seemed to him that all the formidable people in Washington were rather eccentric.

While our relationship was close, loving, and lasting, it was not without its storms. Some of those storms came from political disagreements. Phil walked out of Joe's dining room more than once, but he always went back. When Joe had first arrived in Washington, journalists were not major social factors, but in some ways he helped change that. That there are no more of the raging fights that used to take place around Joe's table is a great loss to Washington. They represented an important melding and fusion around social interaction, and helped to create a certain state of mind in Washington that no longer exists.

Joe Alsop (and his brothers, Stew, who came to Washington also, and John, who didn't) came from a New England family. Joe was the oldest child. The whole family talked with what can only be described as stentorian voices, and an accent perhaps picked up either at home or at Groton School. I deduced the mother was the greater influence on them.

Joe first came to Washington as a young man in 1935, almost as though he were setting out to see the world. Before coming here, he hadn't even much read the papers. But he had connections. Being related to the Roosevelts helped him from the beginning. The relationship was that his grandmother was Theodore Roosevelt's sister, so Eleanor Roosevelt was his mother's first cousin. Alice Roosevelt Longworth was a cousin as well, and she took a fancy to him from the moment he arrived. All of these connections, as Joe wrote, "were suitable enough to win me a New Year's Eve invitation to the White House shortly after my arrival in Washington."

I think it was Joe's charm that won him everything else. Even with his connections and his early entry onto the social circuit, Joe felt that he was so much on the fringes of Washington society when he first came here that he once described it to me as being "three quarters of the way to the men's room."

In many ways it couldn't have been easy for him. In the very earliest days that I knew him, I was appalled by his appearance and couldn't cope with his maturity. He was enormously fat and extremely sophisticated. Later, when his health was threatened by his excess weight, he took himself off to Johns Hopkins Hospital and was put on an eating regimen that probably saved his life. In any case, I still thought he was ancient, although he wasn't that much older than I. Despite not having an auspicious beginning, we became devoted friends.

Joe always seemed so much more worldly and socially advanced. When Phil and I were leading the lives of young New Dealers, Joe was already busy writing a column with Bob Kintner and giving Washington-type dinners. He lived for the better part of fifty years in one house or another on Georgetown's Dumbarton Avenue, which were run beautifully. He had exquisite taste and collected Chinese antiques and French furniture. His laugh, like his voice, was earsplitting. He had firm, generally informed opinions, which he voiced at the top of his lungs.

Joe was a constant visitor both at Glen Welby, our country house in Virginia, and at my parents'. At one Sunday springtime lunch, around the time that the Marshall Plan was being proposed, Bernard Baruch was apparently going on at some length about the situation in Europe. As Joe remembered, "Baruch had an enormous cigar and your father had an even bigger cigar, either one of which could have been a baseball bat, for a Little League game anyway." Baruch held court for quite a while, and then ended his pontification by saying to my father, "Well,

Gene, I'll tell you what I'm going to do. I'm going to make a study of what this country can afford to do, and I'm going to go tell the president."

My father, obviously annoyed both by Baruch's having gone on for so long and by his comment, shook his cigar menacingly in the direction of Mr. Baruch, and responded, "What you ought to do is make a study of what this country can't afford not to do, and then you go and tell the president."

Joe said that that struck him as one of the few really wise political remarks he'd ever heard.

Joe Alsop was a real friend, and we continued to keep each other company until his death, in 1989, which left a large vacuum in my life. When you are single and alone, as Joe and I both were for so many years, close friends are doubly important.

When he died, the incredible loss I felt was not just for me personally, but for the world of Washington, of which he was such a central character. More than those of us who preferred to look ahead, Joe looked back to his first years in Washington as being about as "enjoyable as any time in my professional life." He explained, "The old prewar Washington was the backdrop of everything that happened to me in my young professional life and had its influence on my every idea as it developed. . . . This noble, congenial, curious old world became a kind of personal benchmark for all that came after it."

In a simple sentence in I've Seen the Best of It, Joe wrote, "Washington has been my base, my home, and the place that shaped my viewpoint for considerably more than half a century." This excerpt helps explain why.

I AM NOT at all sure that anyone fifty years old or under would be able to survive a full year of life in the Washington of the second half of the 1930s, the first year I lived there. Despite its standing in the nation, despite the monuments and the lumpish federal architecture that had come up in Hoover's time, prewar Washington was not like a city at all. Downtown, instead of street upon street of identical façades and the avenues of storage warehouses for government clerks so prominent today, there were just the ancient centers: the White House, the Treasury, and the endearing old State, War, and Navy Building—now known as the Old Executive Office Building—at one end of Pennsylvania Avenue, and the Capitol, the House and Senate office buildings, and the congressional Library and Supreme Court at the other.

Air-conditioning was, of course, totally unknown except in a small number of especially luxurious movie theaters, where a cruelly dank cold was maintained all summer to draw in gasping customers. The absence of air-conditioning had its advantages, however. First, because all but the very rich senators and congressmen lived in small, desperately hot apartments, it made it almost impossible for Congress to stay in Washington through much of the summer. The lack of air-conditioning also gave the city a special look in summertime because by mid-May, when the heat began to set in, wardrobes changed dramatically. Women wore large, shade-giving hats and dresses of brightly colored cotton. The more respectable men favored white linen suits or even cream-colored silk suits or, if they were economical about it, cotton suits made from seersucker. The men also wore straw hats, generally Panama.

In that old summer Washington, before the days of daylight saving time, it was possible to dine outdoors coolly and comfortably when the night air came down into the Potomac river valley after sundown. The river, itself, was so free of pollution that people quite regularly swam in it. Radio was a curiosity and television unknown, so one could think, talk, and, indeed, work in relative serenity. Only the very rich owned motor cars, but trolleys were plentiful, and, if one was in a hurry, there were also plenty of taxis. Nor were there any suburbs to speak of, so that a trip to the country was still, in those days, a bona fide and welcome event.

Normal Washington life proceeded in neighborhoods, the rhythms of which were seasonal and decidedly southern. Indeed, after the bustle of Manhattan, the pace of the place was very engaging and pleasant, for no one hurried and few ever worked later than 5:00 p.m. There were more jokes in those days; and there was less pretense in the daily routine of the capital and decidedly less show. The great security apparatus so common today had never been heard of or imagined anywhere in government, and almost everybody could know everyone else if they just made the effort. Cultural diversions were few, and there was no really great restaurant in Washington, nor was it missed, although I suppose the forerunners of that grey mass of lobbyists who now inhabit Duke Zeibert's on Connecticut Avenue may have pined for one.

Beneath this easy, pleasant exterior, however, Washington was a deceptively complicated place, for the town was endlessly divided by a series of tall, unseen barriers. The most important of these was the barrier that separated white Washington from black Washington. As is still the case today, the wealthier, white neighborhoods were located in the northwestern section of the city, although when I first moved there, Georgetown—now among the very wealthiest and most exclusive sections of town—was home to many middle- and lower-middle-class black

families. The larger black community, however, occupied the neighborhoods that spread south and east of the Capitol building, and, much as
today, there was very little crossover between the residents of the black
community and the white men and women who made their lives on the
opposite side of the city.

On the professional side, too, the small world of newspapermen I
entered was only one Washington among many. The Senate Washington, which I also inhabited when I first arrived in town as a reporter, was
paralleled by congressional Washington; and there was an army Washington, navy Washington, and business Washington. Then, as government grew larger and more powerful under Franklin Roosevelt, there
was an embryo lobbyists' Washington, which now has grown into a monstrously large, monstrously rich, and monstrously sleazy community.
These professional barriers were far more pronounced than today, for
the government moved along at a slower, more regional pace. The great
government agencies were not the giant competing institutions they
are now, and there was no need, especially among the small troops of
civil servants, to know how fiefdoms in other areas of the kingdom were
operating.

However, the most curious divisions in the city (and in many ways the
most rigid) were to be found in the realm of society and entertainment.
In nineteenth-century novels and in reminiscences of perfectly intelligent persons a generation older than I, one finds regular mention of an
unexplained body named "society." Even a person as careless of worldly
opinion as Eleanor Roosevelt admits in her informative autobiography
that it was a long while before she ceased to worry over the approval of
what she called "New York Society." "Society" is a word that had already
all but gone out of use in Eleanor Roosevelt's day, and we, in our time,
were brought up not to use it. However, we also were brought up to be
aware of a large, recognizable, semiorganized body of style and etiquette
to the fringes of which, at least, it was important to cling.

Dining-Out Washington, as I will call it, was the remnant of this
organized body called "society" that had enjoyed itself and made fools of
many of its members ever since Washington became a city in the early
1800s. Its members were connected to one another not by their proximity to power (as is the case in what passes for social fashion in the capital
today) or by fantastic wealth, but by a certain longevity, a modicum of
breeding, and a decidedly southern sense of grand style. Their world
contained an astonishing number of large houses through which
revolved the same three or four hundred full members of Dining-Out
Washington all autumn, winter, and spring. Dinners usually seated no
less than forty of these three or four hundred, an arrangement that

insured that everyone in the group saw everyone else in the group about once a fortnight. In consequence, each member came to know the others only too well, and if the company was not always invigorating, the ritual of dinner, dance, and bridge offered to each member a certain comforting permanence. The permanence proved an illusion, however, for this world vanished soon after the second war, and I am not so sure this was a bad thing.

I arrived in Washington just after Christmas 1935, and although my income did not justify it, my family connections and friends launched me immediately into the Dining-Out Washington of the rich. A Harvard friend had asked his mother to put me up for a week or two until I could find my feet in the city. As a result, the first house I stayed in was that of Mrs. Dwight Davis, the former Mrs. Charles Sabin. . . . The house she occupied when I came to Washington was in Georgetown and had been rented to her by Mrs. Ruth Hanna McCormick, a considerable Republican personality in her own right and the widow of Joseph Medill McCormick, the former senator from Illinois. This was the only Georgetown house Mrs. Davis ever occupied, although until the end of her life she had the odd and expensive habit of moving from one enormous Washington residence to another, each time making the new house ravishingly pretty at what must have been very substantial cost, and each time moving on again in a year or so to repeat the process.

I learned soon enough that in coming to Washington I had made a step back into the American past, for Mrs. Davis's first rather stern instruction to me was that after attending a dinner, I must leave a calling card with my hostess on the morning following the event. I told Mrs. Davis I could not possibly leave calling cards, that, to begin with, I had none and, moreover, I would have no time to tour the city, dropping squares of cardboard at people's houses instead of covering the Senate, which was to be my beat for the *Tribune*. Mrs. Davis suggested that whenever I went to dinner at a new house, I write a little letter that explained my working situation, gave the hostess my warmest thanks for her hospitality and said in passing that I hoped she would accept this explanation of my situation as a substitute for possible calling cards in the future.

The first of these letters went to Mrs. Henry Keep, who invited me to dinner as soon as she heard I was coming to the city. Mrs. Keep was an old family friend—my father had very nearly married her sister, Mrs. Winthrop Murray Crane, long before my mother came along, in the dim, dark, distant past, during the time of Theodore Roosevelt. Mrs. Keep's invitation filled me with considerable uneasiness—first of all, because guests to the gathering were instructed in no uncertain terms to wear white tie and tails. In New York and Boston, dining out in white tie was unknown for anyone under the age of forty and considered rare even among the aged. Possessing only the dinner jacket customary for those of my age, I, therefore, had to rent a white tie, tails, and evening coat, with all the proper accessories. I dutifully did so, but because of my unusual heft the whole getup fitted very badly, although Mrs. Davis was polite enough not to offer any comment on my appearance.

This odd costume, plus the fact that the city was completely unfamiliar, filled me with trepidation as I made my way at the appointed hour to Mrs. Keep's large, pseudo-Adams house on Sheridan Circle. When I rang the bell and the door opened, the first thing I discovered was a table covered with small envelopes, one of which had my name on it. When I opened it, I discovered the instruction "Please take in Lady Rumbold." I had no notion of who Lady Rumbold was; worse still, I had no notion of what "take in" meant; nor did I have time to inquire because Mrs. Keep greeted me warmly and led me into a huge, rather ornate living room, the interior of which was all late eighteenth-century pastiche, except for a cavernous pseudo-medieval fireplace. From the fireplace, where he had been warming himself, an immensely elegant old gentleman promptly advanced on me in an alarmingly purposeful way and said in crisp and almost accusing tones: "You Joseph Wright Alsop?!" I replied in the affirmative. "Well, Alsop, your great-grandfather was my godfather." It turned out that this indeed was true; for the elegant old gentleman was the son of General George Brinton McClellan. McClellan, of course, had commanded the Army of the Potomac with no great distinction during the first years of the Civil War. Prior to battle, as his son happily explained to me, the general had served as the engineer for the Illinois Central Railroad, which my grandfather, on the Alsop side, had controlled.

For a young, overly impressionable man, this was a disconcerting beginning. It was even more disconcerting when I learned, first, that it was just as well that I had come early and, second, what "take in" meant. Both these important facts were imparted to me by Felicity Rumbold, who turned out to be an enchanting girl, younger than I and married to the third secretary of the British embassy, Sir Anthony Rumbold. Felicity began by congratulating me on my promptness and warning me, as a newcomer to Washington, that no drinks were served in most of the big houses until the last dinner guest had arrived. This meant, of course— and it happened to me more than once because of an unfaithful taxi—that if a guest arrived even so much as ten minutes late, he or she could expect to be met with looks of blackest hatred from the rest of the assembled party. The unfortunate miscreant would also come close to being trampled by the rush of footmen bearing silver trays of delayed cocktails, which consisted in those days, when no choices were offered, of rather weak, tawny-looking martinis and even more awful Manhattans (a drink that tasted to me like sweet varnish and is happily now nearly extinct).

As for the matter of being "taken in," Felicity informed me that in most big Washington houses guests still went into the dining room like the animals going into the ark—two by two. Invariably, the procession, which, for obscure reasons, was called a crocodile, proceeded in strict order of rank, with the exception of the hostess, who brought up the rear with the male guest of honor. As Felicity and I were the lowest ranking persons present, our place in the procession was directly in front of Mrs. Keep and her principal guest, the impossibly grand and imposing chief justice of the United States, Charles Evans Hughes. As befitted his position, Chief Justice Hughes wore a splendid thatch of white whiskers. So it was an odd sensation for me, all of twenty-five years old, straight off the train from New York, and wedged into my elaborate costume, to march in to dinner as if on parade, just ahead of a man who looked remarkably like an early Renaissance painter's portrayal of God Almighty.

The dinner table itself was also a considerable surprise to me simply because of the fact already underlined by my ill-fitting white tie—that pre–Second World War Washington maintained much more of the old pre–First World War style than was the case in New York. As our procession wound into the dining room, I heard Mrs. Keep explaining to the chief justice, "I always like a simple dinner." Our "simple dinner" consisted of a consommé that must have cost the lives of innumerable chickens and perhaps some animals, too, followed by two impressively large salmon, accompanied by a generous vat of hollandaise sauce, and a cucumber-and-tomato salad on the side. These delights, in turn, were followed by roast guinea hens with fried bread crumbs and bread sauce, served with hot vegetables. Then came two mousses of foie gras with green salad, and, at long last, an ice-cream bombe wreathed in the peculiar spun-sugar hay that I remembered from children's parties. This plus three wines were enough to send one away comfortably full. But it was nothing, I must add, to Washington's grander dinners (for Mrs. Keep's table was thought to be simple by the city's standards). . . .

Mrs. Keep's table was seated in rigid accordance with protocol, with the most important man placed to the right of the hostess and the most important woman to the right of the host. Guests of uncertain rank like myself were always "bout de table," set fast in the middle ground. While the identity of those guests at the tops of table tended to vary, few young people were asked to big dinners, so those of us who had passed the unwritten tests for admission tended to sit next to one another over and over again at the grand houses. So it was that I sat next to Felicity that evening and would do so for many evenings after that, or at least until Mrs. Davis and her friends decided to expose me to Mrs. Davis's stepdaughter, young Helen Davis.

Helen was the youngest of three beautiful Davis daughters. During one summer abroad, in Germany, she had fallen deeply in love with a German officer of uncertain origin who was rumored by the ladies of Washington to be handsome in a tiresome Germanic sort of way. Young Helen came sadly back to Washington, where she remained very attached to her lover, so much so, all the ladies agreed, that drastic measures had to be taken. By this time, I was thought to be a coming young man, hard-working to be sure, and, at 240 pounds, looking not at all like a member of the Prussian military aristocracy. I soon found myself seated next to poor, bereaved Helen at dinner after dinner over the course of several weeks. She, I think, was equally shocked at this development, although we both carried on politely as best we could. However, our topics of conversation were exhausted after the first few seatings to the point where I finally turned to her and said: "You know, Helen, I am just as aware as you are as to why we are sitting together. You don't have to worry. You don't have to marry me. I don't intend to marry you. So let us both just keep up appearances until these tactics are recognized as futile." Helen agreed with evident relief, and so we finished the remainder of our dinners together in peace.

At any rate, Felicity Rumbold and I passed our first seating together in great good spirits, enjoying the marvelous food and convivial conversation. When the last course had been cleared, however, the group rose as one, whereupon the men, led by the venerable chief justice, separated from the ladies for about half an hour of talk. Later on in my Washington life, I, too, would adopt this odd custom of separation, although I was persuaded to end it finally by my great friend Katharine Graham, publisher of *The Washington Post.* By the late 1960s, Kay had suffered the experience called "having your consciousness raised." She let my wife, Susan Mary, and me know that if we persisted in separating after dinner, she would leave our dinner as soon as the last woman left the room after supper. Since Kay's friendship meant a great deal to both of us and since the almost nightly separations had begun to seem irrational anyway, we agreed to her request.* However, there were others, like Averell Harriman, who insisted on this ritual until the day they died.

---

*This is not quite the way I remember it. Joe has made me more of a heroine than I was.

Separated from the ladies after dinner, the gentlemen would talk of politics and sundry topics of the day over cigars and brandy. In grand houses, one sometimes was served scotch and soda, after which time—usually between 10:30 and 11:00—the servants arrived bearing pitchers of orange juice and trays of boiled eggs. The eggs were already peeled, in silver platters, resting on beds of crushed ice, ready to be dipped into little dishes of mixed salt and pepper. The guest of honor was required to leave the party promptly at 11:00 p.m., and if he or she overstayed, it was very much resented by the rest of the party. Those grand guests who played bridge and loved sitting around and drinking the champagne that flowed freely later on in the night would sometimes feign departure. Following elaborate farewells, they would walk around the block once or twice only to return, with a wink to the hostess, to the bridge table, thereby releasing the other guests to go home to bed.

I do not remember how the chief justice departed that first dinner at Mrs. Keep's, although I am inclined to think a bridge game never materialized in deference to such an august and formal guest. I myself ended the evening feeling giddy and somewhat dazed, happy to have witnessed such an archaic gathering but glad, all the same, to have survived the event without precipitating some sort of social disaster.

Perhaps I should not have been so surprised to find the old ways—and leaving calling cards after dinner really was one of the old ways—still preserved in the city I had come to live in. The truth is that Dining-Out Washington had existed for a very long time without any break except on the celebrated occasion when the British put the torch to the White House in 1814. Within my own business, I should add, there was not much crossover into Dining-Out Washington, for, as I have said, newspaper Washington was again a semiseparate community within the city and had its own order of precedence based, in those days, on seniority of membership in the Gridiron Club. Besides a few columnists, I was the only reporter I can recall who frequented Dining-Out Washington. The first time I ever met *New York Times* Washington Bureau chief Arthur Krock, he said to me, "You know, Alsop, the first thing you have to realize is that in Washington newspapermen have no place at table." Arthur was absolutely dead right. Newspapermen in Washington now have a great deal of leverage, but in those days they had no place in society. Then the high seats belonged, as they still do, to members of the cabinet, ambassadors, Supreme Court justices, and members of the Senate.

Even in my day, admission to this world was subject to the city's ancient and peculiar snobberies. If one reads the papers and diaries of Henry Adams, one finds that he saw very few people socially who were not foreigners, a tendency, I am sorry to say, that can be laid to straight old-fashioned snobbery. However, it was not so much that Adams admired foreigners as he disparaged the dubious locals who failed to pass his unwritten social tests. These tests, although greatly diminished and diluted, still had some importance in the Dining-Out Washington that I knew, although the accepted group was still thought by some society-minded outsiders to be decidedly mixed. Often, old-fashioned New Yorkers, like my friends Martha and Ducky Harrison, came down from Manhattan, spent a year on the Potomac, and crossed so many people off their lists that they ended up living in a very reduced city.

The great Washington houses in those days were the last to preserve grand, old-style American cookery. They depended, first of all, on the possession of farms near the city or acquaintanceships with nearby farmers. The results were marvelous milk, real cream that hardly poured, butter with little relationship to the sad substance that now carries that name, and mountains of fresh vegetables and fresh fruit in season. The vegetables were always picked when they were still tiny, and I am bewildered to this day as to how those ladies managed to persuade their cooks to shell peas hardly bigger than pinheads in quantities sufficient for forty people.

To these basics were added delicacies: shad in season, not boned but so slowly cooked in a sealed container that the bones melted, giving it ten times the taste of the flannellike fish we get today; shad roe in mountains; soft-shell crabs; oyster crabs, which are tiny parasite crabs that inhabit oysters and have the tastes of both animals, not exactly in mountains because they were too expensive, but as a recurrent prize dish; in the autumn, turkey broilers (meaning specially fed, very young turkeys that were literally small enough to split and broil); reed birds, the pride of southern houses; all sorts of game as well as guinea hen; then, too, there were the game birds one sees no more like plovers and wild turkey; and there was, above all, terrapin* in season.

This creature—halfway between a sea turtle and a land tortoise—was, to me, the greatest of American delicacies, and since it had inhabited the Maryland estuaries in great numbers, it became a staple of grand Washington dinners. Properly made (without cream sauce), terrapin appeared on the dinner table as an unctuous, even gelatinous stewlike dish, with the tenderest bits of the terrapin's meat plus its liver and the female ter-

---

*In fact, when President Kennedy appeared on Joe's doorstep on the night he was inaugurated, saying he could find no one in the White House who could give him anything to eat, Joe offered the new President champagne and terrapin soup. JFK partook only of the former, needing, as Joe wrote, "no more than a glance to reject what had formerly been the greatest delicacy in the United States."

rapin's eggs all floating gently in an enormously rich sauce made by end-lessly boiling down the broth derived from the rest of the terrapin, plus fresh butter in huge quantities, sherry and cayenne pepper. I don't know how to describe the taste except to say that although its aroma reminded one a bit of the way feet sometimes smell, it was absolutely delicious.

Terrapin had been a principal American delicacy for so long, however, that it had come close to extermination. As it grew harder to get, the price had soared. Hence, only a few very rich houses still offered terrapin by the time I arrived in Washington. The best known of all of these rich houses was that of the old chief of the Southern Railroad, Mr. Henry B. Spencer, who had a terrapin pen in his cellar, where the beasts that would eventually be consumed on his table were fed to happy repletion on a diet of cornmeal. About half-a-dozen terrapin cooks used to perambulate rather profitably from one house to another when terrapin was in season, their services being much in demand.

Properly cooked and aged Virginia ham, now just as unobtainable as terrapin, was not then such a rarity as terrapin had already become, but it was not easy to find, and no wonder. Ideally, the finest Virginia ham was four years old when eaten, and the haunch was as hard and dry as a board when initially taken in hand for the dinner to come. The first step was to set aside a guest-room bathroom or a large tub in which the ham was soaked in water that had to be changed twice a day. The person charged with the duty of soaking the ham had to watch the ham carefully, too, for the haunch would begin by floating with the heavier bone side down, but would prove its readiness for consumption by turning over of its own volition when the meat side had absorbed enough moisture.

After this preliminary, which might take four days, the ham was removed from the bath and boiled, quite often in wine. After boiling, the surface of the ham—the fat, of course—was skinned, rubbed with brown sugar and spices, carefully scored in a diamond pattern, and decorated with a clove in each diamond. After that, finally, the ham was baked and was then ready to be cut into very thin slices and offered cold at the din-ner table, accompanied by salad. The fat, which was eaten, was sherry-colored and rather sweet, while the flesh was mahogany-colored, moist, and astonishingly rich-tasting. Some foreigners found our Virginia hams a bit salty, but for me they had a flavor I have never experienced before or since. If offered a Virginia ham of the old sort today, I think I could go on eating nothing else for a week.

By now, it will be clear how important food and society were in Wash-ington. As for me, I have always enjoyed company, and, as a curious, amply fed young man, I soon developed a taste for my new Washington life.

Washington Parties
Are Serious Affairs

Washington Tapestry (1946)

Olive Clapper was one of the women in Washington generally referred to as "wife of . . ." In this case, she was the wife of Raymond Clapper, one of the most famous reporters of his day, who began reporting from Washington in 1917. A radio commentator as well, Raymond Clapper was among the legendary newspeople who worked for UPI, nicknamed the Unipressers, a group that included at one time or another David Brinkley, Walter Cronkite, Westbrook Pegler, Harrison Salisbury, William Shirer, and Howard K. Smith. Even the redoubtable expert-at-everything Frances Parkinson Keyes thought him one of the best commentators of the time. Writing in Capital Kaleidoscope *at a time when he was working for the* Washington News, *she said that his column was so valuable that it alone could maintain the newspaper's circulation. Raymond Clapper was killed in World War II, in 1944, in an airplane crash over the Marshall Islands.*

In a one-page explanation at the beginning of chapter one of her book, Olive Clapper refers to her husband as "one of those rare reporters" who kept detailed notes and descriptions of important events and people, adding, "He had intended to write a book someday that would have been his honest accounting of the historical period in which he lived."

Considering her husband her coauthor, Mrs. Clapper took up the challenge and produced this entirely readable book. She confesses that her own "most vivid memories of Washington political life and social life started with the election of 1932," and so she focuses particularly on the Roosevelt years. Here is her view of the serious side of Washington parties.

IT IS TRUE that social life in Washington frequently influences the business of government—seldom in a sinister way, but in the manner of congenial friends meeting often who like to do favors for each other. Therefore it is usually important to entertain and be entertained by people in influential positions, if you want to succeed in politics.

Although the average newspaperman and his wife are not usually invited to diplomatic parties, chiefs of newspaper bureaus and columnists are often included. When Ray and I first began to see the inside of some of those magnificent houses on Sixteenth Street or on Massachusetts Avenue, where Ambassadors and Ministers from foreign countries live, work and entertain, I could not feel at home or at ease. These fabulous houses are beautiful and filled with old world treasures. I hated the dull, stilted protocol that went with dinners and luncheons. My excuse to myself for slackness in social duties was that we held no official position, were just plain midwestern newspaper people and could add no distinction to formal parties. I didn't know that often diplomats and their staffs are lonely, or that only through their contacts with Americans do they learn about our country. I too could benefit and increase my acquaintance of the world by knowing them and, through them, something of other countries.

At first we went shyly to the large receptions at the embassies. The first dinner we attended was at the Italian Embassy. I paraded into the dining room on the arm of a young diplomat who had arrived in the United States only two days before. At the table I chatted in English to my dinner companion, who seemed very dumb because all he did was smile and nod. I had just concluded that he didn't speak English, when he burst out, "Have you ever seen bananas growing?"

No, I admitted, I had not. I could not figure out what that question had to do with my conversation about the elegant new marble Supreme Court Building on Capitol Hill.

Pompously and very slowly, he launched into a detailed account of how bananas grow, their uses, the climate most satisfactory for them, and shipping methods. When the ladies retired, leaving the men to their coffee and cigars, another lady asked me, "Did you learn about bananas, too? I sat beside that new attaché at dinner last night." She told me then that the young man spoke no English but, in preparation for his diplomatic duties in the United States, had memorized an English translation of an article on bananas.

Latin American hospitality was showered upon me one morning when I went with Mabel Vernon, Chairman of the People's Mandate Committee, to talk with two different South American diplomats about peace and Western Hemisphere friendship. Appointments had been made for us a week ahead of time. When we were ushered in to the first legation, at 10:15 a.m., we saw, to our horror, that their idea of American hospitality was to serve American cocktails at that time in the morning. To show our appreciation we felt we must drink at least two. We managed that but were completely overcome when we found the same hospitality at the next legation. When we escaped after two additional cocktails, we fuzzily decided we had contributed our share to good neighborliness, and went home to sleep it off.

It was somewhat difficult for me to become accustomed to the objective attitude sometimes displayed in Washington social life. Hostesses in Washington who are ambitious for social success often do strange things. I shall never forget a telephone call a friend of mine received from one such ambitious lady who chirruped: "I hear your husband is about to be appointed to a Cabinet post. If that is true, won't you both come to dinner next Tuesday evening? If it isn't true, do come in for coffee afterward."

Officials particularly, and sometimes even newspaper people, have to be careful about accepting invitations from propagandists and lobbyists of special interests. We once accepted an invitation from a stranger in town because she mentioned a Senator who was a good friend of ours. He and his wife would be present, the hostess said, as well as an outstanding Justice of the Supreme Court and a prominent Congressman. We all accepted and enjoyed a delicious dinner. Later, several of us happened to drive home together. The Senator said, "Say, exactly who are these people who entertained us? They invited me, saying the Clappers were coming, so I was sure it must be all right." One by one, we all confessed to the same bewilderment. These particular strangers turned out to be fine people, but it was a little terrifying to think how effective the technique could be in unscrupulous hands.

On the other hand, a hostess can often bring together people of divergent views to a more rational attitude toward each other. This is the theory that motivates Evalyn Walsh McLean, whose wealth and fame are well known. She believes that friendship is the greatest force on earth. Unhesitatingly she will invite to her dinners people of violently opposed viewpoints. They are then seated together in the belief that if they can really get to know each other they are bound to be more tolerant. During the bitter isolationist fight, Senators Burton K. Wheeler and Robert Taft were seated alongside Senators Pepper, Guffey, and Congressman Sol Bloom, ardent interventionists.

Evalyn McLean's dinners are real events in Washington. It is exciting to see one or two hundred guests of prominence assembled in her great drawing room. Flower-bedecked tables seating eight to twelve are spread throughout several rooms. The many-coursed dinners are served by caterers on gold plates and exquisite china while an orchestra plays soft music. It is all done in the grand manner and you feel as if your generous-hearted hostess wants nothing else in life except to have you attend her dinners and enjoy yourself. She accepts almost no invitations in return, and since she has everything in the world money can buy, the only thing her friends can do to please her is to accept her invitations.

I know from personal experience, however, that promoting tolerance by making antagonists dinner companions does not always work. It happened that several times at Mrs. McLean's dinners, I had been seated beside a southern gentleman who expressed violent opinions against the Negro race, was opposed to education and equal employment opportunities for them, and advocated that the southern states of the United States should again secede from the Union if the north continued its misunderstanding of the place of the Negro as a slave. We argued violently. I became so upset by his undemocratic attitude that I found it difficult to be polite.

When for the third or fourth dinner I found myself again beside him, I turned to the man on the other side of me, who was a mild little stranger, and said: "Do you mind if I talk to you all the time during the dinner? I thoroughly dislike the man on my right and do not wish to talk to him."

He looked astonished, but gallantly agreed to accept my undivided attention. We talked for several minutes, until suddenly the lady on his left said to him, "Do you mind if I talk to you the remainder of the dinner? I hate the man on my left so much that I refuse to talk to him at all. We disagree so violently I am apt to pick up this squab and throw it at him."

Our poor little Mr. Milquetoast gulped a couple of times. However, he met the challenge and kept both of us in good spirits during the rest of the dinner until we dispersed to the drawing room where Mrs. McLean usually entertains her guests with a first showing of a moving picture.

Evalyn McLean does do a great deal of good. You hear about her great society dinners, but you seldom know of her generosity to a multitude of civic and charitable projects which could not function without her help and her personal attention. Every week since our war casualties started to come to Walter Reed Hospital, she has entertained one hundred wounded servicemen at her home. Each man is asked to bring his wife or sweetheart. They are entertained just as lavishly as are the brass-hats at her other parties.

At one White House formal dinner, I had the pleasure of being seated beside Alexander Woollcott. He was a great tease. "Missy" Le Hand, whom he adored, sat opposite him. Woollcott started to light a cigarette after the soup course. "Missy" leaned over to tell him he was not allowed to smoke at State dinners until coffee was served.

"Who says I can't smoke?" thundered Woollcott. "Who'll stop me?"

Poor, lovely "Missy," embarrassed, said, "It just isn't done, Alec. Be a good boy, please! This is the White House."

"Well, who'll stop me? Will the President come over here and take it away from me? There is not another house in this country where I can't smoke if I want to. It is barbaric. . . . Or will one of the flunkeys snatch it from my mouth. . . . Or will one of the Secret Service arrest me? I'm going to do it just to see what happens."

All through dinner he kept a cigarette out, frequently making threatening movements to light it. "Missy" was miserable in anticipation, but he never actually lit it. . . .

A hostess in Washington whose invitations we never declined is Mrs. J. Borden Harriman. Born in old New York's Four Hundred, she never played the society game; but her influence among the powerful in Washington for 40 years is incalculable. At her famous Sunday Night parties we found only those who were doing worthwhile things. Brilliant, imperious, a powerful and handsome woman, she used to announce after the servants had cleared away the dessert, "There is Scotch and water on the sideboard. Please help yourselves. And now, Mr. Ambassador, do tell us what you think of the debt moratorium." From then on, the evening would be dazzling as Senators, diplomats, writers, and artists argued under her inspired questioning.

She has a genius for drawing people out of their conversational shells and because she knows everything that has happened in Washington in 50 years, she can always pin down a man or an idea. They seldom escape her vivisection. Her keen interest in life and people make her irresistibly loved.

Mrs. Harriman began dabbling in politics as one of McAdoo's willing workers at San Francisco in 1920 and at Madison Square Garden in 1924. Because of her interest in politics, she often is bracketed with the other famous hostess of Washington, Alice Roosevelt Longworth. But they are not much alike. Alice was born in politics. Mrs. Harriman acquired her interest in it. Alice is a playful spectator who was just frivolous enough to run up to Elihu Root after the 1912 Republican Convention and shout, "Toot! Toot!" to remind him of the steamroller which he had helped drive in reducing her redoubtable father, Theodore Roosevelt, to the proportions of a corn fritter. . . .

In 1937 President Franklin Roosevelt appointed Mrs. Harriman

United States Minister to Norway, "land of goddesses and heroes." Her popularity there was climaxed by her courageous actions when the Germans sailed up the Skagerrak and the lights of Norway went out. Mrs. Harriman drove into exile with the King and his government. Later, she escorted Princess Marthe and her children to the United States.

We used to be invited frequently to fashionable Crescent Place for dinners or Sunday luncheon at the magnificent home of Eugene Meyer, owner of the *Washington Post*. Once Mrs. Meyer kindly asked us to bring our children, Janet and Peter, to Sunday luncheon. Peter was only seven years old, and his red head barely topped the dining room table. I was talking to Mr. Meyer when he suddenly arose hastily, dashed around the table, knelt down, and put his arm around Peter. Silent tears were coursing down Peter's face as he contemplated a huge pink lobster that had been placed in front of him. Peter had never had a lobster to eat before, and he was frightened about how to eat it. Mr. Meyer said, "I don't like them either, Peter. Take this away," he ordered the butler, "and bring in some roast beef for this boy. We are having ice cream for dessert," he comforted Peter as he wiped away his tears.

I never paid any attention to protocol when I wanted to entertain any one. It is a regrettable fault. To me, these people were interesting in their own right as individuals, and I liked to invite them, not because of rank, but because they were friends who would enjoy a couple of carefree hours together. Such was my intention when I invited a group to a picnic luncheon on our outdoor terrace one Sunday in early June.

I asked that scholar and philosopher, Dr. Hu Shih, who was at that time the Chinese Ambassador. I had also asked two Justices of the Supreme Court, Harlan Fiske Stone, with his kindly, wise little wife, and the delightful bachelor of the Court, Frank Murphy. That was bad, my protocol experts told me. You could never seat the Justices properly with an Ambassador present.

"But it is a picnic," I said; "they'll sit at scattered tables, wherever they please to light."

"A picnic," chorused my horrified social experts. "You can't mean a picnic—so informal for such distinguished guests. It is unthinkable. You'll find they won't come."

To further confuse everybody, I asked a Cabinet member, Attorney General Robert Jackson, and his charming wife, Irene. Also there were present two members of what might be called the secondary Cabinet—Paul V. McNutt with his wife, Kathleen, and Thurman Arnold, with his wife, Frances. There were others, too: among them, the former Governor of Pennsylvania, Gifford Pinchot, and Lelia Pinchot, the Eugene

Meyers and Stanley Hornbeck, Adviser to the State Department on Far
Eastern affairs (now Ambassador to Holland), and his energetic wife,
Vivien.

To my delight, picnic or not, all those invited came. The first
headache I encountered was that the extra servant I had expected failed
to show up. Lelia Pinchot rescued me by bringing in her chauffeur, who
helped with the serving. The plates were served from the buffet in the
dining room, then the guests walked out to sit wherever they chose.

I was the last to step out onto the terrace. There were no place cards,
no orders at all to any one as to his place at the tables, but to my astonishment I saw that every person had seated himself or herself exactly
according to protocol. A place had discreetly been left for me at the hostess end of the first table, and on the right of that, sure enough, there sat
the Ambassador. The Supreme Court had accommodated itself at a small
table seating only four people. Unquestionably correct. The Cabinet and
sub-Cabinet had discreetly appropriated another table out under the
trees. In short, those who really ranked had automatically taken their
correct places.

ROBERT S. ALLEN
and WILLIAM V. SHANNON

Rumblossoms on the Potomac

The Truman Merry-Go-Round (1950)

As the name implies, The Truman Merry-Go-Round *does for the Truman administration what the two earlier* Merry-Go-Round *volumes did for the Hoover administration, maybe to possible less effect only because there was less to bring to light. Robert Allen, of course, was one of the original Merry-Go-Rounders. By 1950, Drew Pearson was on to other things, and Allen, who had suggested the idea in the first place, found another writing and reporting partner in William Shannon. Here again, the authors made the rounds of government, looking through doors that others might have wanted to keep closed.*

It's interesting that Allen had edited a volume in 1947, Our Fair City, *in which seventeen cities around the country were written about—New York City, Cleveland, Los Angeles, Miami, Chicago, St. Louis, and the other usual suspects—but not Washington. Maybe he thought he'd covered the city by focusing on the political side in the* Merry-Go-Round *books.*

This selection is from the chapter called "Rumblossoms on the Potomac." Allen and Shannon define rumblossoms as "A New England colloquialism applied to those who imbibe too freely and acquire red noses. Washington has long been famous for its cherry blossoms. But these can be seen only very briefly in the spring along the banks of the Potomac tidal basin. Washington's rumblossoms are far more numerous and long-lived. They can be seen in the best drawing rooms all the year round."

WASHINGTON society is like lemon meringue pie without the filling: all fluff and a lot of crust.

Any connection between entertaining and fun is purely coincidental. The endless parties, shindigs, and various other gatherings are made up of four kinds of people: those who come to see, those who come to be seen, those who hope to be seen, and those whose job requires that they be seen. And, every once in a while, there are those odd persons who invite people they like. Washington society is thus a mixture of fourth estate, celebrity collector, social climber, and the weary dispenser of expense-account good cheer.

This incredible social merry-go-round has no parallel anywhere else in America, and probably not in the world. It exists in Washington because it is an artificial city. If it were not that the center of the federal government is here, there would be no Washington. . . .

Washington is like a giant Grand Central Terminal. People are constantly arriving or departing. There is ceaseless activity, people moving from here to there and from there to here. But despite all this hustle and bustle, all the unending motion and commotion, there is no genuine community spirit, morale, or social pattern. Everything is artificial, pretentious, and fleeting.

The city seems always to retain the graceless, vacant, strictly utilitarian, and almost featureless character of a huge waiting room, where all the seats are taken but everybody sits alone. Even the residential areas are rows of houses, not neighborhoods. Most people look upon them as they do depot rest rooms—places to change clothes and rest their feet. Even people who suddenly discover they have been in Washington twenty or thirty years are constantly talking about leaving and "going home." The reason for all this is the same core of reality that dominates life in a depot: the important thing is what flashes up on the train dispatcher's giant board. The arrivals and departures are important and not the stopover. The people in Washington share in the big events because they buy and sell the tickets, but the nature of these events is determined elsewhere. . . .

Washington's peculiar social make-up, thickly infiltrated with outsiders who expect to leave, or like to think they will, robs the city of civic spirit. This is gravely accentuated by the lack of home rule. Washington is run by three District Commissioners appointed by the President (usually, it would seem, in a fit of absent-mindedness or obscene jesting) and answerable only to God. These three gentlemen are considerably circumscribed by various agencies of the federal government on the one side and by the House and Senate District of Columbia Committees on the other. . . .

Only one man has ever been able to pep up Washington's community spirit. He is Bucky Harris. When his Washington Senators baseball team won the American League pennants in 1924 and 1925, the town for once in its listless life went wild.

But Washington is more than listless. It is insecure. Throughout the whole District of Columbia, and from the bleak bungalows of Maryland's Silver Spring, which has become that State's second largest city, to the manufactured colonial quaintness of Falls Church, Virginia, Washington is just one big settlement of camp followers—divided, restless, and uneasy. Rumors run like wildfire. Gossip is incessant. Factions, cliques, coteries spring up, flourish, fall, form, and re-form. Personal feuds and vendettas go on interminably. Men rise or hope to rise, but all is dependent on the turn of the cards at the next election. Even when a party has been in power a long time, a key official may plummet from favor and take his personal "empire" of secretaries, assistants, protégés, and hangers-on crashing down with him.

It is against this background of ceaseless insecurity and fierce competitiveness that the giddy social whirl goes on. For those at or near the top, it has some of the element of the "drink and be merry for tomorrow we die" spirit. Also, since there is no clear social structure, no traditional hierarchy or established social pace setters, each officeholder—or, more important, each officeholder's wife—feels she must put up a big front to prove she and the old man are really right up among them.

"Front" requires only two things—gall and money.

This makes it easy for the ambitious social climber to imitate the real thing and eventually get accepted as part of the real thing. Rich old women with rings on their fingers, time on their hands, and greenbacks in their bank account, lead the chase. Mrs. J. Borden Harriman, a witty and charming octogenarian, frankly calls herself and her rivals "fifty overage destroyers." . . .

THOSE who do the entertaining in Washington fall into certain broad categories. There are the big-timers who make a career of it; the embassies who make a business of it; the proud parents of panting debutante daughters who make a virtue of necessity; and the "young set" who pretend they hate the stuffy affairs but who actually are only in training for more strenuous efforts later.

There are some fifty hostesses in Washington who entertain frequently in what is invariably called "the grand manner." The most prominent of these are:

> Mrs. J. Borden Harriman—the grand old lady who set the pattern—as Democratic fund raiser in the 1920's and later as Minister to Norway—that Madame Minister Mesta is trying to follow. Mrs. Harriman, at eighty-two, recently bought a new house in Georgetown because her old dining room was too small to permit her to entertain more than forty guests at a time.

Mrs. Perle Mesta—who is now so busy holding open house for GI's and steel barons in Luxemburg that she keeps only one eye on her old stamping grounds and on her former foremost guest, Harry Truman.

Mrs. Gwendolyn Cafritz—who scheduled her biggest party the day after Mrs. Mesta, her archrival, was sworn in as Minister to faraway Luxemburg.

Mrs. Joseph E. Davies—the former Marjorie Post of the Post Toasties millions, who finally realized her ambition to be the chatelaine of an embassy when she married the Wisconsin lawyer, Joe (*Mission to Moscow*) Davies. Mr. Davies' daughter by his first marriage is the wife of Senator Millard Tydings of Maryland. Mrs. Davies enjoys all the conspicuous success that such awesome amounts of money and political connections can bring.*

Mrs. Alice Roosevelt Longworth—the political golden girl of two generations ago, the No. 1 whipcracker of the last, and now a somewhat jaded but still acidulous observer of the passing scene. She prefers to do her entertaining behind silken curtains, but occasionally some of her remarks filter through, such as "Tom Dewey is like the man on the wedding cake."

Mrs. Robert Low Bacon—widow of a very rich Long Island Republican congressman, she hoped to become the queen of Washington society until "the man on the wedding cake" blew his chance and hers.

Mrs. Truxtun Beale—wealthy widow who lives in solitary splendor at historic Decatur House, diagonally opposite the White House. She is proud of two things: her dinners are always served exclusively by candlelight, and, unlike some of her competitors, she never phones her list of guests to the society editors.

Mrs. Lawrence Wood Robert, Jr.—the inimitable Evie who is the daughter of a staunch Republican dowager, Mrs. Harold Walker, and the wife of the irrepressible "Chip," who was once secretary of the Democratic National Committee and is now partner in one of the country's largest contracting firms. Evie was playing up her Republican ancestry in the fall of 1948, but Chip saved the day by sitting up the night of the election with Democratic Chairman J. Howard McGrath. The Roberts are wealthy, daring, and ambitious, but Evie's more effusive friends mourn the fact that she won't stay put long enough to nail down the honors as

---

*You can read more about Mr. and Mrs. Davies and Senator and Mrs. Tydings in Eleanor Davies Tydings Ditzen's *My Golden Spoon, Memoirs of a Capital Lady*.

ranking hostess. She is always off to Palm Beach or Nassau just when congressmen get thirstiest.

When Gwendolyn Cafritz and her husband, a local realty magnate, moved into their big estate at Foxhall, overlooking the Potomac, Mrs. Cafritz called up Mrs. Mesta, who was then living in that swanky suburb. Gwen had met Perle but had never entertained her. So she called her up and very sweetly observed that, now that she had a home in Foxhall, "I suppose we'll be seeing you soon."

To which Mrs. Mesta replied very tersely, "I don't think so."

This anecdote illustrates the difference between the two women. Mrs. Cafritz has the suave, Continental touch and a talent for manipulating even her thorniest opponents, while Mrs. Mesta is the old-fashioned Oklahoma Indian-fighter type who achieves her ends by brute force and gouges the other gal's eye out if necessary.

Gwendolyn Cafritz is the leading claimant for the title of Washington's foremost hostess.

She laughingly denies having any such ambitions. "Heavens," she exclaimed when asked, "why, I'd much rather be on the board of the Smithsonian Institution." But her deeds contradict her, and, after all, as one society writer pointed out, for her to confess such a goal would be "as unrestrained as a debutante advertising for proposals!"

Mrs. Cafritz was born forty-five or more years ago in Budapest, Hungary, the daughter of a wealthy physician named Dr. László Detre de Surany. As a youngster, Gwen Detre hit the culture circuit pretty hard. She studied and traveled in Budapest, Rome, Paris, Los Angeles, and back to Budapest again before she was twenty. She studied art, learned five languages, and acquired a useful air of cosmopolitan sophistication. She speaks English with a broad "a" and a slight foreign accent.

In the late 1920's, she accompanied her father to Washington when he went there to work for the United States Public Health Service. The somewhat impoverished young European with the large dark eyes, gay smile, and ingratiating manner won the attention of Morris Cafritz, a moderately-well-to-do real-estate salesman on the make. They were married in 1929 and now have four sons. In the last twenty years, Cafritz has built a lot of houses and profited hugely from Washington's bloated size and stringent housing shortage. Now a baldish, sharp-nosed, nondescript man of late middle age, whose most noteworthy contribution in 1950 was to act as a glad-handing prop for the rapacious real-estate lobby, Cafritz has plenty of money to subsidize Gwendolyn's desire to buy her way to the top of the social ladder. They own a magnificent ultramodern house surrounded by gardens and landscaped grounds and equipped with all the necessities for big-time partying, including the inevitable swimming pool.

The Cafritz drawing room is muraled with ancient Egyptian queens. Gwendolyn is undoubtedly eager to play a somewhat queenly role herself. But, like Cleopatra, she occasionally guesses wrong as to the outcome of political battles in this modern imperial Rome.

In the fall of 1948, Gwen figured the Republicans were sure to win, and she was anxious to prevent such old-time elephant followers as Mrs. Robert Low Bacon from getting the jump on her during the Dewey administration. Consequently, the Cafritzes made a fat contribution to the GOP and practically snubbed the penniless Democrats. Gwendolyn also captured every stray Republican within hailing distance and dragged him off to dinner.

But then came the election, and the Cafritzes were out in the cold. Gwendolyn's archrival Mrs. Perle Mesta had not only contributed to the Truman cause but had helped raise money from others. She was in more solidly than ever before. Madame Cafritz spent the whole ensuing winter ruing her bad luck and trying desperately to cuddle up to the Democrats. Finally, when Mrs. Mesta collected a diplomatic appointment as her campaign reward and departed for the pleasant wilds of Luxemburg, Gwen got into high gear again.

The very next day after Madame Minister was sworn in at the State Department and given her credentials, the Cafritzes roared into action. They threw a lavish steak party for one hundred and fifty of Washington's top-flight figures. The affair was ostensibly to celebrate their twentieth wedding anniversary; actually, it was the opening gun in a carefully calculated comeback campaign.

During the 1949–50 season, Gwen made good her ambitious bid. She entertained fiercely and purposefully almost every day in the week. By the end of the year, she seemed to have clinched ownership of the party-giver crown. Toward the end of the spring season, however, Perle Mesta returned from Europe, supposedly to report to the State Department. But her visit stretched on and on for weeks. In the mind of the Capital socialites, she had come back to keep an eye on her rival and maintain a foot in the door.

This soft-shoe jostling for position created difficulties for all the others trying to give parties during this period. It would be most indelicate for both to appear at the same dinner table, or even to run into each other at the same cocktail buffet. Yet, if one were invited and the other were not, the slighted party would unquestionably retaliate. What to do! Hostesses struggled along as best they could. Finally the blowup came.

At a huge semiofficial function in late May, both ladies were invited.

They both arrived purposely late—and almost simultaneously. The President and Mrs. Truman were at the head of an informal receiving line. Each contender wished to greet them first. The two ladies edged forward furtively, attempting to maintain dignity and cover ground at the same time.

Mrs. Cafritz, perhaps because she is the younger of the two, beat Mrs. Mesta to the President's side by the margin of an ostrich plume.

She chatted amiably with him and his spouse while her rival cooled her heels at a respectable distance. Then she moved on with head high. Onlookers are convinced that they noticed just a hint of a proud, arch smile flit across Mrs. Cafritz's handsome Grecian features as she turned away.

Gwendolyn Cafritz really has one up on Mrs. Mesta in the race for Washington society's mythical bauble. She is a tall, slender (118 pounds), graceful brunette with dazzling dark hair and eyes. She goes in strongly for low-cut gowns and plunging necklines, and she has something worth plunging to.

Of Mrs. Mesta, it cannot be said that she is beautiful. She does look younger than her age. She could pass for fifty, though she is actually pushing seventy. She is a diminutive five feet tall, has bright blue eyes, wrinkle-ringed and darkly shadowed, and weighs, like her taller rival, about 118 pounds. Her hair is brown without a trace of gray, her jawline is firm, and she smiles readily with lips that are razor-thin and almost nonexistent. As one cat put it, "She is remarkably well preserved—considering her age."

Perle Mesta is no fashion plate and makes no bones about it. She fits exactly the crack once made by a writer in *The New Yorker:* "We in New York love to laugh at the dowdiness of women in the provinces. Take Washington, a town notorious for its frumpiness."

But Mrs. Mesta takes the attitude that she is so rich she doesn't have to show it off with diamonds and Parisian gowns like some women. "I get a laugh," she says, "when they call me the 'worst-dressed woman in Washington.' I detest fancy clothes. And neither do I need fancy cars." Up to her departure for Luxemburg, Mrs. Mesta continued to use a 1941 Packard.

If Perle Mesta is not fashionable, neither is she witty. She tosses off no bons mots, presides over no political salon. She does have definite ideas on subjects like women's rights, but she couches them in prosaic terms. Her parties are big, loud, long, and expensive. Often she is able to prevail on her guests to perform some eye-catching (and ear-rending) feats. At one of her parties, she inveigled General Eisenhower to sing "Drink to Me Only with Thine Eyes." And, of course, she can get such old hams as former Ambassador Pat Hurley to give his Comanche war whoop and Chief Justice Fred Vinson to sing "My Old Kentucky Home" at the drop of a hat. A unique feat was her persuading Mrs. Cornelius Vanderbilt to whistle a duet with a writer.

Champagne and Scotch always flow freely at Mesta parties, but she herself is a teetotaler and confines her drinking to soft drinks. Her abstinence—she is also a nonsmoker—stems from religious views. Mrs. Mesta is a devout Christian Scientist and contributes heavily in time and money to church activities.

A Mesta menu may not match the unique delicacies of such culinary show places as the French Embassy, but it is pretty flossy just the same. The following is one of them:

Crisp, chilled celery, and olives nearly as large as golf balls.

Salad of mangoes, avocados, midget plums, and blood-red pitted cherries drenched with a tangy lemon sauce.

Thick French white soup, brewed from choice fowl, milk-enriched veal, ham, carrots, parsley, cream, eggs, butter, onions, salt, thyme, and peppercorns.

Suckling pigs, from three to six weeks old, roasted to a succulent turn, gleaming mamey apples in their mouths, cranberries stuck in their eye sockets, their browned carcasses glazed and adorned tastefully with patterns of pimiento and green peppers, sprays of water cress, a dressing of bread, celery, nuts, and sage—all in a pool of sauce made of vintage wine.

Pheasant or quail basted with smooth Madeira wine and stuffed to delight the keenest gourmet. Vegetables prepared in candylike Oriental and European style.

Royal diplomatic pudding, candied cherries and angelica, wine jelly, and rich, thick cream of fruit.

Perle Mesta has many of the same qualities as the President whose rise to power gave her her opportunity. Like Harry Truman, she is vigorous, lively, blunt, and basically plain and ordinary. Entertaining the low-brow Trumans gave her "the big chance."

She became friendly with them when Truman was a senator. When he became Vice-President, she took him up in a big way. In the spring of 1945, she threw a party in his honor that was one of the most glittery in Washington's long history of glittery parties. It had all the charm of an English court tea, the sparkle of a Viennese ball, and the razzle-dazzle of a Hollywood premiere. The best names in officialdom and society attended. Shirt fronts gleamed with star-ruby studs. Evening gowns fairly dripped with diamonds and pearls. Champagne, at $20 a bottle, flowed in cascades. Kingly delicacies were endless.

Exactly two weeks later, Roosevelt was dead and Mrs. Mesta's guest of honor was President of the United States. Overnight, society editors acclaimed her "queen of Washington society."

At long last, she had attained the swooshy throne she had sought so long. It had been a long, arduous, and expensive pull from the time she first arrived in Washington in the early 1920's. She had come from Oklahoma, where her father was oil-rich and where her bachelor brother is still a well-known figure. She also had the wealth she inherited from her husband, a Pittsburgh tool manufacturer. She came as a Republican, which was advantageous in that Republican era. In 1931, a good friend of hers, Vice-President Charles Curtis, the bachelor brother of the famous Dolly Gann, saw to it that she was presented to the King and Queen of England when she visited London.

Throughout the New Deal, Mrs. Mesta still remained a Republican, but she steadily broadened her social ties to include many top Democrats, particularly of the "regular" ilk. It was not until the war, when the GOP refused to go along with Wendell Willkie, that she jumped the fence and became a Democrat. Her enemies have ever since derisively called her "Two-Party Perle." Mrs. Mesta is unperturbed. But, while a loyal Democrat, she does not slight her old Republican friends. When she was entertaining in Washington, her favorite "extra man" was House Republican Floor Leader Joe Martin, who for a while showed up at her parties so regularly that he acquired the nickname "Marryin' Joe." The sad-visaged Yankee has remained, however, a wary object of prey.

Naturally, Mrs. Mesta's favorite guest remained Harry Truman. He usually accepted her invitations, and, when he came, he often played the piano. "Mr. Truman," Perle says, "is an excellent musician—for a man who is too busy to practice."

Mrs. Mesta never lacks for willing guests. One year, she opened her home to the public for the benefit of charity. She also served tea to the visitors. As she sat at the serving table, a businesslike man came up to her and remarked briskly, "You give parties and must need extra men. I'm unattached and very agreeable. Here's my name and address."

Turning to go, he added, "I hope you don't think me presumptuous!" Mrs. Mesta had a little difficulty concentrating on her tea for the next few minutes.

Mrs. Mesta had one lively experience in the conduct of international affairs before she became a diplomat. This was the celebrated "Battle of the Brassiere."

The controversy arose out of a talk American-born Lady Astor gave before a women's club in Washington, during which she indulged in her favorite indoor pastime of deriding American women. On this occasion, her freewheeling Ladyship complained that American women spend too much time "worrying about uplift."

Mrs. Mesta was present. Her strong sentiments regarding women's rights were outraged, and, springing to her feet, she coldly admonished the speaker as follows, "I'm tired of hearing Lady Astor constantly criticize American women. It is true our women are interested in uplift, but it is uplift of their minds and culture, and not their bosoms."

With that, Mrs. Mesta gathered up her cloak and stalked out.

It was inevitable, of course, that Lady Astor would reply. In fact, the genteel, Virginia-born ex-belle sought out the reporters to make sure that they got her reply.

"Mrs. Mesta," she declared haughtily, "is just a social climber who is using me to get some publicity. I have proof she didn't really walk out. She stayed for every word."

That did it! Then the battle really was on.

Mrs. Mesta insisted that she had really walked out and that her position had been correctly stated in the press.

"Position?" snorted Lady Astor. "Why, she has no position."

To which Mrs. Mesta slammed right back, "Lady Astor's tactics are not surprising. She has made a career of achieving a certain dubious international notoriety by such methods. Lady Astor no longer likes or understands the habits or thoughts of the country from which she expatriated herself a half century ago. I seriously question whether the people of the land of her adoption have ever reciprocated her misplaced devotion. I also question very much if she has ever really understood the American people. It was because of my doubts on these matters that I followed the American privilege of taking a walk."

The delighted reporters dashed back and forth between the two contestants with exuberant enthusiasm and appreciation. It was a tumultuous fracas, and everyone enjoyed it, especially the two ladies.

Bigwigs, Littlewigs, and No Wigs at All

Perle, My Story (1960)

Perle Mesta was one of the very few Washington women who seems never to have minded being called a hostess. She and Gwen Cafritz—her "archenemy"—were both Washington hostesses whose reputation went beyond the bounds of the city. Occasionally called "Perlie-Whirly," Perle was certainly hardworking. She came from wealth and acquired even more when she married George Mesta, a Pittsburgh manufacturer. The couple came to Washington during World War I and in the thirties took up politics and political work almost as an avocation. She used her money to support Democratic candidates, Harry Truman among them, who appointed her minister to Luxembourg in 1949, where she served more than ably until 1953. Perle was immortalized in Irving Berlin's Call Me Madam, which hit Broadway in 1950, with her friend Ethel Merman playing the thinly disguised "Sally Adams," a big, brassy imitation of a "hostess with the mostes'."

It was recalling the Washington parties of Mrs. Mary Henderson and of Evalyn Walsh McLean and how they had been useful politically that decided her "that the way I was best equipped to serve the Democratic Administration was by bringing important people together." So Mesta looked for a house large enough for entertaining, set up shop, and hung out her sign. In this book, she wrote that "it is impossible to determine precisely how much is actually accomplished at Washington social gatherings."

Here, she explains some of the secrets of her success—which hardly seems as simple as suggested by her onetime quip that "all you have to do to draw a crowd to a Washington party is to hang a lamb chop in the window."

ALMOST every time I am interviewed, the question is asked, "What is the secret of your parties?" Really, there's no secret. I'm willing to work hard at the preparations, that's all. When it comes to business affairs, I loathe details, but in organizing a party, I enjoy seeing to even the smallest detail.

Once I have decided to have a party, the first step, of course, is to set a date. And that isn't always as simple as it sounds, especially if I am planning a spring or summer party on the terrace at Les Ormes. Some of my friends laugh at me when they see me studying my *Farmer's Almanac* and *Hagerstown Almanac* to help find a day that is the least likely to have rain. I don't think this is so silly in Washington, where the weather is so unpredictable. I usually consider two or three dates and then let my guest of honor choose the most convenient date. Important people are busy people; they usually have to fit parties in when they can.

Then I start making up my guest list. I like to get just the right blend of guests—to mix Republicans and Democrats, and the bigwigs, the littlewigs, and the no wigs at all. As I have said before, I have found that bringing together people of differing positions and opinions gives a party a kind of chemical reaction that makes it interesting.

If I am planning the party several weeks ahead, I always send out written invitations. But most of the time these days my parties spring up on short notice, and then I telephone. It may not be proper according to some of the etiquette books, but I see nothing wrong with a telephoned invitation. It is in keeping with the present speed-up and informality of our lives. And with a telephoned invitation, I always know immediately whether or not my guests can come. A few days after I have telephoned, I mail a reminder card giving the date and time and place. Even when I invite my guests by mail, I like to send reminder cards to those who have accepted.

Once the guest list is completed, I arrange for the extra help that will be needed, work out a table decoration plan, call the florist to make sure the flowers I need will be available, and engage the music. If the party is to be at Les Ormes, I then get together with my cook, Augusta France, and we plan the menu. I also talk with my No. 1 party helper, Jean Anderson, about the china and linens to be used. Next, I work out the seating arrangement and have my secretary make place cards and escort cards. I do not use escort cards at all my parties. Occasionally, at small affairs, I just go around and tell each gentleman the name of the lady he is to escort to the table. When it is a larger or more formal party, each gentleman is given an envelope containing his escort card. And on a table in the foyer I have a chart which shows where everyone is to be seated.

The seating at a formal dinner party or luncheon is different in Washington than any place else in the nation because of the observance of protocol. Anywhere else you can seat your guests where you please. But in Washington, practically every American and foreign official has a fixed ranking determined by the position he holds. The rankings are determined by the State Department and the White House, although no official list is ever published. As might be imagined, the placing of officials is often a troublesome business. Some of the basic plan is mysterious enough, and then occasionally positions are shifted.

For instance, during the Truman administration, when Fred Vinson was made Chief Justice, the place of the Chief Justice was elevated to the No. 3 spot, just below the Vice-President. This put him above ambassadors, the Speaker of the House, and former Presidents. When President Eisenhower took office, governors were ranked ahead of senators, but at an early White House dinner where there were both governors and senators, the senators were seated above the governors. From then on, Washington hostesses adopted this change. And in 1957, the position of Assistant to the President (then held by Sherman Adams) was boosted over both senators and governors to a place just below Cabinet members.

This is the way the ranking goes today:

The President
The Vice-President
The Chief Justice
Former Presidents
The Speaker of the House of Representatives
Ambassadors of Foreign Powers
Widows of former Presidents
The Secretary of State
United States Representative to the United Nations
Heads of Legations with rank of Minister
Associate Justices of the Supreme Court
The Secretary of the Treasury
The Secretary of Defense
The Attorney General
The Postmaster General
The Secretary of the Interior
The Secretary of Agriculture
The Secretary of Commerce
The Secretary of Labor
The Secretary of Health, Education and Welfare
The Assistant to the President
Chairman of the Atomic Energy Commission
Director of the Bureau of the Budget
Director of Defense Mobilization

United States Senators	Former Vice-Presidents
Governors of States	Members of the House of
Acting Heads of Executive	Representatives
Departments	

The list goes on and on. If I am ever in doubt about seating a table, I consult with Wiley Buchanan's protocol office at the State Department or with Carolyn Hagner Shaw, whose *Social List of Washington* (always called "The Green Book") gives a complete Table of Precedence. Sometimes, when having more than one ambassador, it is necessary to find out when their credentials were presented, since this is what determines precedence. The Dean of the Diplomatic Corps is automatically the ambassador who has been in Washington the longest. It is also necessary, when inviting two or more military men of the same rank, to find out which was given this rank first, as seating depends on this. . . .

Under certain informal conditions, the hostess can dispense with protocol if she so desires, as I did at my Thanksgiving Party. Or if there is some unusual protocol problem, a hostess can have several small tables, designate a host and hostess at each table, and work the protocol around that host and hostess.

On the day of a party, I always help the florist in making the arrangements, talk over the music with the leader of the orchestra, and go in and out of the kitchen seeing how Augusta and her assistants are getting on. Just before the arrival hour, I try to check and recheck every single detail. By the time the first guests have arrived, the running of things is entirely in the hands of wonderfully capable Jean Anderson and Day or Domenic, who are my favorite head butlers. I keep the cocktail period short. An eight o'clock dinner means eight o'clock arrival, and by eight-thirty we are in the dining room. In Washington, it is definitely not fashionable to be late.

From the moment my first guest arrives, I play the party by ear, and my byword is "flexibility." Sometimes at the table, I try to start the conversation going, but I never attempt to direct its trend. And contrary to advice in the etiquette books, I like to bring up controversial subjects at the table. An excellent way to keep a party alive is to seat political opponents near each other.

Once I invited Senator Alexander Wiley and the late Senator Pat McCarran to a dinner party, knowing perfectly well that they were not even on speaking terms. I had seated Senator Wiley at my right and Senator McCarran at my left. During the first course, Senator Wiley leaned toward me and whispered in his gentle way, "Why have you got that McCarran here?" Before long, Senator McCarran nudged me and said,

"What in hell have you got Wiley here for?" For a while things remained pretty frigid. Finally I looked straight ahead and said good and loud so that I could be heard the length of the table, "Well, Perle, I guess you'll just have to talk to yourself all evening." And do you know?—at the end of the evening those two men left the house arm in arm.

Another time a few years ago, I placed Democratic Speaker Sam Rayburn next to Alice Longworth, knowing she was firmly opposed to most of Sam's policies. The two of them were arguing politics all through dinner. At one point, Alice started in on the Democrats' proposed twenty-dollar across-the-board tax reduction plan. When she took a twenty-dollar bill out of her purse and started waving it in front of the Speaker, he grabbed it.

"Give me back my money!" cried Mrs. Longworth.

"A Republican shouldn't be carrying around a picture of Andrew Jackson, anyway," chided Sam, and proceeded to put the bill in his wallet, where he carried it all evening before finally giving it back to Mrs. Longworth just before the party broke up.

As a dinner is ending, I generally rise and propose a toast to my guest of honor. At dinners outside of Washington, I seldom do this unless I feel the situation really calls for it. But in Washington it is the custom and seems appropriate, since my guest of honor is usually someone who deserves to be commended for his or her achievements.

After dinner, the men go into one room and have coffee and liqueurs while the women go to another room. I have no set length of time for this to go on. After a while I take a peek into where the men are gathered. If I find they are in deep conversation, I let them alone, but if it looks as if nothing much is going on, I send the butler to ask them if they would please come in and join the ladies.

From then on, the party is on its own. I never know just what turn it is going to take. If I see that my guests are interested in talking, I signal to my musicians to keep the music soft and low. If I sense that they are in a dancing mood, I choose one of the men and start dancing in the foyer, and all those who want to dance follow suit. Those who want to continue their conversation can go into one of the smaller rooms. Sometimes one of the guests will start to sing, and then maybe the whole group will join in. Or sometimes, when expert dancers like Betty Beale and playwright Speed Lamkin, or Mrs. Dale "Scooter" Miller and Jack Logan start a mambo or a Charleston, everyone gets off the floor to watch them and clap in time to the music. If some of my guests want to play canasta or bridge, they are free to go up to the library where a table and cards are always available. It's their party, really, so I let people do as they please.

Ordinarily, the guest of honor at a Washington party leaves around eleven, because many of the guests dine out nearly every night of the week and have to arise early to be at their offices. After the guest of honor leaves, everyone else is free to go. Often, though, the dignitaries who leave early miss the best fun when we littlewigs and no wigs start cutting up. Sometimes we gather around the piano and sing old-time songs. Or we may square dance or put on impromptu entertainment of one sort or another. I always keep my music until the last guest has left, which sometimes is early in the morning.

Another question interviewers ask me is how much my parties cost. Though I am aware that my style of entertainment is doubtless out of the reach of numerous party givers, I would like to point out that I have been to many parties—and indeed have given them myself—where the cost has been comparatively small. Whether it is a lavish party . . . or a simple party like one I attended recently in a tiny Georgetown apartment, it is the atmosphere of warmth and friendliness more than the elegance of the food and service that spells success. If the details are worked out systematically and thoroughly beforehand, the hostess can then greet her guests calmly and graciously. On the other hand, if she is fretting and worrying over things, and has a pained expression on her face, the guests immediately feel her tension and the party is off to a bad start.

I am often asked to list my basic rules for party-giving. Though I fear there will be no sensational disclosures in the following, I offer these few points. Most of them apply to any kind of party, no matter the size or the underlying purpose.

1. Like the people you invite.
2. Make every one of your guests feel wanted. Don't let anyone stand around looking lost.
3. The quality of the food served is more important than the quantity. Be sure that the hot food is hot, and the cold food is cold.
4. Do not urge people to eat more than they desire. Some may naturally have small appetites; others may be on diets.
5. Try to have some kind of music, even if it is recorded. If there is a lull in the conversation, music fills in the gap.
6. Do not ask your talented guests to perform. If your entertaining has put them in a good mood, they undoubtedly will.
7. The hostess should always look her best because it is a compliment to her guests.
8. Don't fret. Tell yourself before the first guest arrives, "I've done all I can—now let's enjoy things and see that everyone has a good time."

JOHN KOBLER

She Teaches Washington
to Put on Airs

The Saturday Evening Post (1953)

My thought when I first read this piece was "Help springs eternal in Washington." It still holds true today. In 1953, when this Saturday Evening Post *writer turned his attention to Mrs. Parker and her Parker School of Personality, Mrs. Parker was just one of hundreds of people who found their niche in serving the various needs of Washingtonians—or those passing through, as in the case of the Soviet diplomats trying to learn Washington ways. Of course, these kinds of social helpers are to be found in every city and small town across America, but whether they are dance-class instructors or caterers or valet parkers or social secretaries, they take on a certain distinction in Washington that differentiates them from their counterparts elsewhere.*

I N T H E Soviet Army there are today twelve high-ranking officers who speak English with the accents of Kelvinside, a residential district of Glasgow, Scotland, noted for its ultragenteel diction. The responsibility for this linguistic anomaly, as incongruous as a commissar in kilts, falls squarely upon the elegantly draped shoulders of one Mrs. Agnes McCall Parker, a native of Kelvinside, who runs the Parker School of Personality and Speech in Washington, D.C. During most of 1950, Mrs. Parker—a trim, erect woman in her fifties, with a seamless complexion and hair tinted jonquil yellow—visited the Soviet Embassy twice a week to teach the twelve officers, military attachés, refined English diction, an accouterment which she considers indispensable to a well-developed personality.

For the last twenty years, Mrs. Parker, whose own refinement of personality and diction no stage duchess in a Mayfair comedy of manners ever surpassed, has striven to elevate to the same lofty plane more than 13,000 people whom circumstances thrust upon the Washington scene. Assisted at present by a faculty of nine men, she offers a curriculum designed to smooth the climb up the sociopolitical ladder of the nation's capital. "Parkerization," the process is sometimes called by those who have gone through it. "An uncouth gesture, a gauche remark," says Mrs. Parker, her tone glacial with disdain, "may wreck a Washington career at the start."

In addition to such orthodox courses as public speaking, parliamentary procedure, English grammar and dress fashions, the curriculum of the Parker School, as described in its latest prospectus, includes Potomac Routine, or How to Create and Hold a Social Position in Washington; and The International Salon, Dealing with the Subtle Forces That Influence Statesmanship and High Finance.

These courses were introduced last year, following the Republican victory, with what Mrs. Parker terms "the Powerful New People" in mind. A Republican herself, she announced at the time: "With social reformers and leftist lawyers in power, the Old Guard drew back into their shells. With an administration of business executives and a supporting cast from the Social Register, the social life of the capital will come back to normalcy. The time is now propitious to develop the hostess of the century—the hostess who will go down in history, just as certain hostesses of the recent era went down in burlesque."

To encourage newcomers of modest background, she added: "Some of our most successful residents have been recently self-developed. Several of our most impressive legislators arrived as cowboys. One of our most lavish hosts started here as a butcher."

Attendance at the Parker School, she pointed out, casts no reflection upon the student's standing in the environment he came from. "But life in the hub is different from that along the spokes. An initial mistake takes years to live down. The Parker School is here to apply a stitch in time."

Tuition is $2.50 per hour for courses held in open classroom, and most courses consume at least thirty-six hours; for private instruction, which about a third of the students prefer, ten dollars an hour.

Though the bulk of the student body is usually composed of minor Government employees and foreign-embassy underlings, it has from time to time numbered heads of Government agencies, congressmen and senators of both parties—Mrs. Parker does not permit her political sympathies to stand in the way of her proffering guidance wherever it may be needed—Army and Navy officers and officials of almost every embassy and legation in Washington.

The Chinese ambassador, Wellington Koo, though otherwise a paragon of the social graces, felt he could do with a refresher in English speech, and studied privately with Mrs. Parker. To vanquish her shyness, Madame Ispahani, wife of the former Pakistani ambassador, took an extensive personality course, also privately. Frank J. Wilson, ex-chief of the Secret Service and the man who arrested Al Capone, took public speaking. "He needed more self-confidence," Mrs. Parker says. Congressman Victor Wickersham, Dem., Oklahoma, recently completed the same course, and at last reports was thinking of signing up for the entire curriculum.

Among the alumni whom Mrs. Parker regards as her greatest successes is still another Democratic legislator, Sen. John L. McClellan, of Arkansas, who came to her complaining that he had never felt comfortable in a drawing room. According to Mrs. Parker, the senator now not only feels comfortable in a drawing room but positively scintillates there.

Upon hearing a Jackson Day speech by Harry Truman, Mrs. Parker once deemed it her patriotic duty to let him know through his aide, General Vaughan, that his delivery sorely needed, as she expresses it, "rehabilitation." The general replied, thanking Mrs. Parker and intimating that the President might send for her. But Truman's term expired before he got around to it, and probably he will now retain his Missouri speech undiluted to the end of his days.

It was the patronage of the Soviet diplomats, a group not normally prone to seeking instruction from capitalist instructors, which provided the ultimate proof that the reputation of the Parker School had traveled far. Mrs. Parker still quivers with mingled pride and horror at the memory of the telephone call she received that morning in 1950.

"Berezny here," said a basso-profundo voice with a Slav accent thick as blintzes, "military and naval attachés' office." It was desired, he explained, that Mrs. Parker personally give diction lessons on the premises to a number of English-speaking officers.

"Alone with the Reds—I was appalled!" Mrs. Parker relates. "I told him I never gave lessons outside the school."

But curiosity got the upper hand, and after determining from various investigative agencies, including the FBI, that she could proceed with a clear conscience, she repaired to the Soviet Embassy annex at 2552 Belmont Road.

Berezny turned out to be squat, bald and totally deficient in those little amenities so dearly prized by Mrs. Parker. With scarcely a greeting, he waved her into a sparsely furnished antechamber.

"I go now get the people," he said. "There is something you wish?"

It was late November and the heat had not been turned on. "Isn't it a trifle chilly in here?" Mrs. Parker ventured.

"Next time I bring electric heater," Berezny promised. "Now I get the people."

He ducked out, reappearing almost immediately, followed by twelve enormous officers in full regalia and encrusted with medals, two of whom, Mrs. Parker learned later, were generals by the names of Kuvinov and Sizov. They filed up to her in parade formation, bowed curtly and took seats facing her on a bench against the wall. Berezny nodded as if to say, "You can begin now."

"Repeat after me, gentlemen," said Mrs. Parker in her flutiest Kelvinside tones, "Good morning, Mrs. Parker. How are you this morning?"

"Good morning, Mrs. Parker," they chanted in unison.

Berezny was always present thereafter, occasionally taking part in the lessons, but mostly keeping his eyes and ears peeled. The officers learned fast. They had to. Berezny demanded a weekly progress report from Mrs. Parker on every pupil. He would then pay for the lessons in cash—at his insistence Mrs. Parker had spotted the embassy a 10 per cent discount—and present twelve receipts for her signature.

Midway through the course, Berezny suddenly shot at Mrs. Parker, "Enough of the cultural English. You teach us now how they talk on the docks."

"I gasped," declares that monumentally ladylike person. "I looked the little man straight in the eye and I said to him, 'My good sir, if that is the sort of English you prefer, I suggest you go down to the docks. Certainly, you shall not hear it from me.' "

Looking back on her experience with the Russians, Mrs. Parker regrets that no opportunity arose to administer the full personality treatment, for it is her conviction that the dangers threatening mankind would be greatly reduced if only the diplomats of all nations would cultivate tact, poise and charm.

The institution which seeks to instill those qualities in its pupils inhabits a large house in fashionable Phelps Place, from whose history Mrs. Parker derives infinite gratification. That dazzling Washington hostess, the late Evalyn Walsh McLean, once lived there. In fact, it was the first property that her father, Thomas F. Walsh, bought after striking it rich in the gold fields of Colorado and coming to Washington. A hulking, three-story, yellow-brick structure with eighteen rooms, it combines several ornate styles of architecture and decor, notably Italian Gothic, Georgian and Victorian. Hand-carved paneling and brocade cover the massive walls; painted cherubs cavort on the ceilings.

The house, which Mrs. Parker refers to simply as "the Mansion," is a recent acquisition. She moved in last summer from more modest quarters. She paid $47,500 for it, which was $10,629.91 less than Walsh paid in 1899. It probably could not be duplicated today under $500,000.

Before transferring the school there, however, Mrs. Parker had to win a stiff fight before the Zoning Commission against some of her neighbors, who protested that if a commercial school were to be tolerated in Phelps Place, then why not a boardinghouse? At this comparison Mrs. Parker's demeanor was, according to those who witnessed it, a majestic and awesome sight. She carried the day by the sheer weight of her dignity. As a parting shot, she fired at the socially prominent attorney who represented the dissenters, "You, sir, could do very nicely with a few diction lessons yourself."

WHETHER a student chooses private or classroom training, the initial step is a two-hour personality analysis conducted behind closed doors by Mrs. Parker. It takes place in what is formally called the Agnes McCall Parker Room, a velvety retreat, under flights of cherubs bearing garlands of roses. The student is ushered thither by Mrs. Parker's secretary, Marie Annette McLean—no kin of Evalyn Walsh McLean—a pretty, auburn-haired young woman who formerly sang with a Navy band.

Be the student male or female, Mrs. Parker rises from behind her bric-a-brac-laden desk and advances, shoulders back, diaphragm pulled in and flat as a board. She attributes this posture to a stretching exercise which she performs at odd intervals throughout the day and which she prescribes for every student. She claims to receive spiritual as well as physical benefit from it. "Imagine," she tells the student, "that you are reaching upward, ever upward."

To describe a recent personality analysis, in which only the name of the analysand has been altered, Miss McLean announced, articulating clearly as she had been carefully trained to do "This is Mrs. Parker. Mrs. Parker, this is Congressman Doe."

"How very nice to see you, Congressman Doe," said Mrs. Parker, lightly gripping his hand. "Won't you sit down?"—gesturing toward an easy chair in front of the desk. "Stifling today, is it not? But perhaps you don't mind the heat, is that it?"

"No, I don't mind too much," said the congressman.

"I thought not. . . . Thank you, Miss McLean, dear. You may leave us now."

She studied the congressman a moment in silence. "You're looking extremely well," she commented finally.

She then began to read off questions from a list. There were forty-seven of them, such as "Do you like flowers?"; "When were you last deeply hurt by someone?"; "Had you a happy childhood?"

No matter what the congressman replied, even to the most routine questions, Mrs. Parker found some cheery observation to make. His Christian name, for example, happened to be William. "Ah, my favorite name!" she cried. Of his home state: "So beautiful, so like England, with

all those undulating hills!" When it emerged that he was happily married, she beamed upon him and trilled: "That's quite, quite wonderful! So
very few people are."

Presently, having thus fortified the congressman's ego, she launched
into the analysis proper. ("I always analyze the student at the first meeting," she says. "I'm afraid if I wait until I know him well, I may lose my
detachment.")

"To relieve your mind," she said, "I may assure you that there is nothing serious amiss. However, there are a few things which are not quite
perfect. None of us is perfect, of course, are we, Congressman? One little point—the way you walk. You slump. It makes you look years older
than you are. You're a very nice-looking man, you know. I shall recommend a few exercises. Then at times you seem a wee bit uninterested in
what the other person is saying. I'm sure you're not. You have far too
alert a mind. It just seems so. A show of lively, unselfish interest would be
most helpful."

She concluded, "I suggest you let us have you two hours a week for
our regular personality-development class—that is, unless you insist on
private consultation. And, by the way, your diction is a little run-down.
Could you spare us an hour a week on that?"

Approximately 350 people a year take Mrs. Parker's advice. Among
the courses she may prescribe for them is The Art of Thinking. A series
of lectures designed to stimulate the brain cells and furnish the student
with conversational ammunition, it was conducted last year by a retired
newspaper reporter and ghost writer named Hayden Talbot, who
proudly proclaims himself a radical. "I believe that schools should be
closed to all children and made compulsory for adults," he says.

Under Talbot, the course bore the subtitle The Fi-Vaze—Affirmative
Altruists Association (American Affiliates), and adhered to what he maintains was the true Socratic method of teaching. By this he means never
uttering a direct statement. The entire series of twenty-eight lectures,
each lasting an hour, is composed exclusively of questions. "Is anything
more worthless than that which costs nothing?" he asked, for example, in
Lecture No. 8. "Is the beauty of the female form an inspiring force that
kindles the sculptor's flame of genius? Do you think these things are accidental or are they the result of that ceaseless struggle whose other name
is—Life?"

Most of the classes are held at night. An exception is Psychology for
Leadership, which takes place Sunday afternoons—the only time the
teacher, a lay psychologist from Missouri named Frederick Indorf, can
get away long enough from his public and private mental-hygiene activities. Indorf has also dabbled in politics. In his native state, during the last

primaries, he was defeated as a Republican nominee for Congress. He is a vigorous speaker in the evangelist tradition ("Very Midwest, very breezy," Mrs. Parker says of him. "Oh, so different from me!") who transmits a smattering of the Freudian ABC's through many an earthy image and homely parable.

Mrs. Parker pays her faculty either a salary, from twenty-five to fifty dollars a week, or a commission. Indorf, who is in the latter category, retains 50 per cent of the regular classroom tuition fees and 60 per cent of any private-counseling fees.

Next to Mrs. Parker, the most compelling presence on the faculty is Gabor de Bessenyey—pronounced "Bessenay"—a towering figure of Hungarian birth, who claims kinship to the noblest Magyar families. Standing six-feet-four and weighing 195 pounds, totally hairless above the eyebrows, De Bessenyey suggests a professional wrestler of the Stanley Zbyszko era. Before he became an American citizen twenty-five years ago he bore the title of baron, and a few of the Washington hostesses who entertain him still address him so. Mrs. Parker calls him Doctor De Bessenyey in public—he left the University of Budapest in 1925 with doctorates in philosophy and the law—and "Brian" in private. "Brian," she says, "means 'manly' in Celtic."

Mrs. Parker met De Bessenyey for the first time last December, when he approached her in his capacity of publicist for educational institutions. Previously he had worked as a free-lance correspondent and a lecturer on international affairs. He not only got Mrs. Parker's account but remained to create and teach Potomac Routine and the International Salon. "I have always been fascinated by protocol, precedence and diplomatic usage," he says by way of stating his qualifications, and he mentions among the famous salons where he has been a guest those of Evalyn Walsh McLean; Eleanor ("Cissy") Patterson, the late publisher of the *Washington Times-Herald;* and the formidable Philadelphia dowager, the late Mrs. Edward T. Stotesbury. "In 1942," he recalls blissfully, harking back to what must have been his social apotheosis, "Mrs. Stotesbury invited me to dinner at her estate, and when it came time to enter the dining room, she bade me offer her my arm."

The ex-baron opens his Potomac Routine course with an illustration from Washington social annals of what disasters can befall the uninitiated. He cites the early experience of another favorite hostess of his, Mrs. A. Mitchell Palmer, the widow of Woodrow Wilson's Attorney General. "There was an unwritten agreement in those days," he says, "whereby the wife of a senator who wished to hold a big reception would do so on, let us say, a Monday, the wife of a Cabinet member on a Tuesday, and so on through all the branches of the Government. I believe the practice will come back. Mrs. Palmer, in her innocence, had the misfortune to give her first reception on a day reserved for judiciary wives. Naturally, many of the most important people she had invited declined."

Recently, Mrs. Palmer, who, despite this faux pas, rose high in the ranks of Washington society, has signed a contract with Mrs. Parker to teach a special orientation course for the Powerful New People.

"To succeed socially in Washington," De Bessenyey tells his Potomac Routine class, with baronial flourishes which leave many of them open-mouthed, "you must have at least one of six things in excess plus a pinch of some of the others. They are, first, money—at least fifty million dollars. The days are gone when one could say, as James Gerard, the former ambassador to Germany, did, 'A man with a million can live as if he were really rich.' Next comes political power. A Republican senator can scarcely miss at present. Then hereditary social distinction. A title is still a priceless social asset in Washington. Then personality, culture and talent—in that order."

In the International Salon, a course concerned more specifically with diplomatic usage, the students learn: "One does not entertain communist diplomats nowadays, unless one happens to be a communist oneself. An occasional exception may be made for the Yugoslavs, provided no representatives of the Catholic countries are present.

"When seating diplomats at the dinner table, seniority of tenure determines who shall occupy the place of honor—that is, the hostess's right. At the same time the relative importance of the diplomats' governments cannot be ignored. Thus, an extremely delicate situation would arise should one invite both the British and the Haitian ambassador. The British represents the more important government, but the Haitian has been in Washington longer. The only way to avoid such a dilemma, of course, is to entertain each ambassador separately."

Of all the courses offered by the Parker School none approaches in popularity those taught by Mrs. Parker herself, regardless of what subjects she chooses—diction, table manners or, her great specialty, personality development. The frequent talks she gives at social clubs, before church and civic groups and on the radio fetch equally enthusiastic response. The secret of her success, however, does not reside in the intellectual content of her lectures and writings. To quote a few typical excerpts:

"Life is a game, the biggest, greatest of all. . . .

"How do you look when you go to bed? Does the charm of your daytime appearance disappear? Real charm is constantly on duty. Going to bed should be as much of a 'parade' as going to the dinner table. . . .

"When women, and men, too, are not getting along so well where they work, and waking up in the morning depressed at the thought of having to go through another day, there's something wrong somewhere." But what Mrs. Parker says is of minor importance compared to her manner of saying it. The majority of her listeners would probably be enthralled if she simply recited the alphabet, for hers is a triumph of, appropriately enough, personality, one of the greatest performances to be seen today off the stage and screen. Moreover, she exerts upon many people an emotional and mystical appeal similar to that which Aimee Semple McPherson had upon her flock. Students and employees alike continually address her by such endearments as "little angel," "dearest angel," "angelita" and "light of my life." Wrote one graduate: "You are all that is beautiful, one of God's rare jewels, your life always scattering beautiful rays of sunshine thru the gloom." Mrs. Harley Kilgore, the wife of the Democratic senator from West Virginia, who attended the Parker School to acquire self-confidence, testifies: "With my eyes closed, I'd know if Agnes Parker was passing"; while Mrs. Wilbur Carr, whose late husband was once United States minister to Czechoslovakia, found Mrs. Parker's lectures to be "not only interesting and instructive, but spiritually uplifting." Another student was moved to compose the following poem:

> *God bless you, gentle Agnes*
> *For so many, many things.*
> *For love and charm and happiness*
> *And social teething rings.*
> *For beauty visioned in the mess*
> *Of people dancing "swings."*
> *God bless you, gentle Agnes,*
> *When you hit, the jack pot rings.*

Not long ago a group of students and graduates formed the Agnes McCall Parker Association. The members, who pay a membership fee of five dollars, meet once a month in the Mansion, ostensibly for a dance, dinner or bingo game. A good deal of the evening, however, consists of a love feast, at which Mrs. Parker bestrews each AMPA with praise ("You've never looked lovelier, my dear," she will assure the plainest of them. "You deserve the highest credit for the way you've improved"), and they express passionate devotion to their "little angel." . . .

CISSY PATTERSON was so impressed by a talk Mrs. Parker gave at a club-women's luncheon that she engaged her to write a daily column on charm. "Friday is fish day," ran a representative specimen of the series, which lasted a year, "and we must watch our fishy manners. I suppose all of us have to struggle with a fishbone at times. The removal is not a pleasant sight, and a few suggestions may help. . . ."

For four years she dispensed *savoir faire* over Washington's Station WOL. ("Hello, everybody! It's delightful to start out again with you on one of our little journeys toward more effective, gracious living. . . .")

But neither journalism nor radio ever yielded Mrs. Parker the satisfaction she gets out of personal contact with individuals. Among her happiest memories are those of pupils she has been able to rescue from social catastrophe, like the wife of the State Department economist from Iowa who couldn't understand why her dinner invitations were not being returned. "A little gentle probing," says Mrs. Parker, "revealed that she was serving red wine with the fish."

For a woman who devotes so much time to helping other Washingtonians achieve a full social life, Mrs. Parker leads a remarkably inconspicuous one. Neither the *Social Register*, the *Blue Book* nor *The Social List of Washington* lists her name. Rarely is she to be seen at embassy receptions or in the homes of the city's elite. "I do not care to gad about," she says primly.

On the other hand, she is a Daughter of the British Empire and a member of the National League of American Penwomen. In 1947 the Penwomen chose her to be Hospitality Chairman of their Washington convention. Mrs. Truman agreed to receive the delegates in the White House, and what ensued left Mrs. Parker with a glowing opinion of the former first lady. "A Secret Service man came out and said, 'Mrs. Truman is ready for you,' " Mrs. Parker recounts. "I thought she meant all of us, but not at all. She wanted just me alone at first. She took both my hands and said, 'I want you to receive with me, my dear.' My heart stopped, as she indicated that I was to stand at her right. Though an extremely shy person, she gave a magnificent performance. Even the most difficult names she pronounced correctly, like 'Mrs. Tryphosa Bates-Batchellor.' I award her full marks."

Mrs. Roosevelt, whom she met at a Penwomen's luncheon, got a lower score. "She has a blanket smile for everybody," Mrs. Parker says, "but you feel she hasn't noticed you personally. She gives a good performance, however, even when she hasn't much to say."

After lecturing at the Army & Navy Club in Arlington some years ago on The Things That Make a Woman Charming, Mrs. Parker received with Mrs. Dwight Eisenhower. "I think Mrs. Eisenhower has become a charming and vivacious lady," she says somewhat cryptically.

At mention of the woman who was Washington's leading party-giver before Truman appointed her minister to Luxembourg, Mrs. Perle Mesta, Mrs. Parker tends to freeze. "She nearly knocked me over once, pushing past me at Elizabeth Arden's," she says. "I expect her tour of duty abroad has probably done her a lot of good."

There is no hostess in Washington today who fully meets Mrs. Parker's high standards. Her beau ideal, and one whom she constantly holds up as a model to her pupils, has long since faded into retirement. She is Mrs. Grace Coolidge, wife of the thirtieth President. "Gay, but not giddy" is the way Mrs. Parker remembers her.

Washington abounds in self-help schools of various sorts, but Mrs. Parker considers none of them a competitor. "We are," she insists, "unique." She refuses to concern herself even about the local branch of the Dale Carnegie Institute, which in its last fiscal year taught 800 students "how to make friends and influence people" at $135 each. "I suppose the Carnegie people accomplish some good," she concedes, "but, really, they are quite different from us—so commercial."

PERIOD PIECES

What Washington is at any period it has been and fearfully will be again.
—Edward Lowry, *Washington Close-Ups*

WHAT I mean by a "period piece" is writing that evokes a special time, a moment in Washington's history or in our lives that we remember as something apart from the next moment and the one that came before. Certainly, how any given period is defined depends on who's doing the defining. And what we consider particular periods also depends on our age, class, race, and any of our other defining characteristics. Maybe because I've lived most of my life with newspapers, front-page people and events and stories come to mind to help me define certain periods in my life. But I also think in terms of blocks of time—my childhood, the growing-up years of high school, being a young adult, my early married years, and so on. Sometimes a period is as short as a few months or less, sometimes as long as several years.

In my parents' time, when they first came to Washington, they found a scene that would have intimidated lesser mortals. In fact, Frances Parkinson Keyes wrote of the period around 1917 and the next few years in Washington as presenting a "prospect so crowded and complex that the outsider, suddenly hurled into the midst of it, was inevitably bewildered, dazzled, and somewhat overpowered." I think my parents made the best of that time.

I remember the Washington in which I grew up as a genuine small town. Maybe this is true for everyone, that we all feel that the times in which we grew up were simpler, less complex.

Yet Washington *was* different then. My friends and I had fun all over the city. We ice-skated on the reflecting pool in front of the Lincoln Memorial; we rode horses on the bridle paths throughout Rock Creek Park; we rollerskated to and from school; we went to Georgetown for bags of doughnuts from a great-smelling bakery, driven by our chauffeur, Phillips. Friends from school did spend the night with each other,

Ice skaters enjoying the frozen reflecting pool on the east front of the Lincoln Memorial, just as my friends and I did for many years (1928)

but only rarely at my house. There seemed to be something sort of intimidating about my house, and I think it may have been my mother. For one thing, she ate so fast that no one else was ever able to finish their meal before she was done and had signalled for the plates to be taken away. One of my sister Bis's friends actually called her family on the first day of a visit to our house and said she was coming home. When she was asked why, she replied, "Because I don't get enough to eat. As soon as I start to eat my soup, the footman snatches it."

But despite chauffeurs and butlers, all in all I think we had a very simple, normal childhood, so that Washington "period" was a happy memory for me.

IN *There's No Place Like Washington,* Vera Bloom described the Washington of the twenties as "a quiet place: like an island of lighthearted existence one has sailed away from and can recall but not really see again through intervening weather." Even by the time I reached high school, in 1930, Washington was still a small town. George Allen wrote of the place: "Washington in 1929 was still an overgrown American country town dangling in limbo between North and South, between metropolitan urbanity and rural parochialism, between the nineteenth and the twentieth centuries. The pace of life was a slow trot."

The Depression didn't hit Washington the way it did the rest of the country, as is still true for depressions and recessions. For my own family, life in Washington fell into a series of period pieces, often defined by my father's work and my mother's moods. Mother and Dad kept busy in different ways. Our life took a new turn when my father purchased the *Post,* in 1933. For him, it was a different form of public service. Although I was away at college from the fall of 1934 until I returned from my first real job (in San Francisco) in the spring of 1939, my parents kept me up-to-date on their Washington life and the life of the paper through constant letters. Mother was doing some of her best work on several fronts at once, including working on welfare issues in the District. She gave lectures and speeches—on everything from the future of the American family to why Catholic girls didn't want to be nuns. She wrote for the paper and, still in her high Republican, anti–New Deal period, prodded my father to "pull a few tail feathers out of the Blue Eagle editorially. Our country needs an intelligent critique if not a polite opposition and it needs it now. Ask 'em a few leading questions at least."

Mother kept up with everything. She wrote us girls in 1936 of the latest fashion in stockings, which struck her as just the thing for my sister Bis: "They are transparent—henna red—to be worn with black dresses—the newest fad as it makes the legs look sun-tanned. Can you bear it?" She was busy translating and reviewing the books of her then new friend Thomas Mann, and sending him pep talks "because it is very important that he should keep himself above the battle." She was, as she said, "writing for the Post with both hands" and helping organize a concert series at the Library of Congress, speaking on the radio, and generally, as she wrote, being "whirled along here like helpless chips on the swift current of time." She also was actively involved in bolstering my father in those first few years of his stewardship at the paper. She supported him 100 percent in what he was trying to do in Washington.

WHEN I CAME back to Washington for good, it was to an altogether new period in its life and mine. The New Deal had intervened while I was away and had transformed the sleepy town in which I'd grown up into a vibrant city. The staid old Washington I'd known had been enlivened by the New Deal, made fresh by the energy of the young people who swarmed into Washington to help the cause. Chal Roberts, who wrote a history of the *Post,* and who had come here in the early 1930s, remembered New Deal Washington as fascinating and full of life: "the lights were on late in every building, and it wasn't just the charwoman at work; it was a jiving, jumping period."

With the end of Prohibition, the town became less straightlaced. Liquor flowed, and there was a great deal of drinking. Washington was still a segregated city, though with pockets of integration (notably the streetcars), and racism was an ugly aspect of the city. It was under Russ Wiggins's editorship, in the late 1940s, that the *Post* published the first picture of a black bride. Russ had especially selected two people with Ph.D.s from Howard to break that particular barrier, hoping to keep the protests to a minimum, and he personally took all the protest calls that came through the switchboard.

Even the installation of air conditioning in many buildings in the late 1930s changed the city, quickening the pace and allowing people in offices throughout Washington to stay at their desks later into the night and throughout the moisture-laden heat of summer.

This period in Washington was one of the most important for me personally, and one of the happiest. I'd come back from San Francisco to what seemed a changed city from the one I'd left. But I must have seemed like a changed person, so maybe it was all in the different eyes through which I was seeing the city. For me, it was the first really wonderful time I had had. Young people—including Phil Graham—had flocked to Washington to help with all the New Deal projects and experiments, and they kept coming in the years before America entered the war. There was an atmosphere of great patriotism, and the "best of breed" wanted to be here. This was a time when young people could have a very important impact on the processes of government. Many of these men and women, newly excited about government, and public service and public issues, came to Washington and couldn't leave. Phil was certainly one of these.

As the 1940s turned into the 1950s, things slowed down in Washington. People didn't work all the time anymore—they might be home from work by 4:30, and go away for weekends and certainly the summer. There was less traffic (although no fewer complaints about it), and little fear. Our front door was open all the time, with football in the front yard in the fall and baseball in the spring. Once, when our station wagon was stolen by a young kid, I was reprimanded by the police, who said it was my fault for leaving the keys in the car.

Despite the presence of the atomic bomb and worries about the Soviet Union, the 1950s were a feel-good period, except for the atmosphere of rancor and distrust brought us by Senator McCarthy.

The Kennedy era of the early 1960s is another period that glows in my memory. There was this extraordinary Kennedy ambience, which many of our friends were right in the middle of, and we were at least on the periphery of. But this period of heightened fun and interest ended for me forever when Phil committed suicide in 1963, in the midst of a desperate spell of depression. The rest of the 1960s, after his death and then JFK's three months later, was a time of turmoil, full of controversy and compassion, the blur of the war on poverty and racism, a war in a distant land that affected Washington daily, a time of demonstrations and protest marches. The war in Vietnam produced bitter arguments in Washington. At least for a while, Washington became, as Stewart Alsop wrote, "an unhappy place."

The decade of the 1970s was a period highlighted for me by the two years of Watergate. Meg Greenfield captured some of the spirit of this period when she wrote about the skyjackers, streakers, snaildarters, quotas, and indictments of the time, concluding, "We are beyond shock. . . . We have already devalued the dollar (unheard of) and had a President tell us 'I am not a crook' and awakened to news that the girl friend of an august House committee chairman had jumped into the Reflecting Pool off the Mall in a bit of drunken razzmatazz."

The Watergate period was the most extraordinary political period I lived through. Elizabeth Drew wrote that "For many of us it was both a national experience and a personal one. We went through things we had never gone through before and had never imagined we would go through. We struggled with questions that had never previously occurred to us and with anxieties that it would have been impossible to anticipate. More major political events took place than we had ever believed could happen in such a brief period. Even now, looking back, we have some difficulty believing that it happened, that it was real." Drew also wrote that the passage of time might lead us to forget what the period was really like. I don't think I ever will forget it. The threats to the paper and to me, the sense of potentially cataclysmic change, the constant tension, the slowly unraveling stories all still seem quite real and immediate.

THERE'S nothing "neat" and structured about period pieces; no historical time can be easily defined and bookended. But the ones I've chosen here all seem to me richly suggestive of specific moments in Washington's—and my own—past, and I hope they manage to evoke these "periods" both for those who lived through them and for those who can only know about them through the testimony of others.

Washington Portraits

Life as Chance and Destiny   (unpublished)

The period when my parents first came to Washington was a time of truly great men. Mother wrote in her diary that "one knows personally all the public figures that stalk across the news and one's life takes on a breadth that is not possible in any other occupation." She especially admired men she considered "big" men—those who could get things done and command attention, and it was this kind of man she sought out.

Three of the "big men" who had a real impact on her in her first years here were members of the Supreme Court, although she was quick to note that "they made a lasting impression on me not because of their eminent positions but as exceptional personalities."

Justice Louis D. Brandeis served on the Court from 1916 until 1939. My father had known him for a while and had got to know him even more intimately when Brandeis—the first Jewish member of the Court—asked him to take financial charge of Zionism, which, according to Mother's diary, he refused to do. She added, "I have a feeling, however, that Brandeis will have his way to a great extent. I shall not interfere for or against. Eugene's feeling in the matter [Zionism] is sure as always to lead him in the right direction."

Mother did feel that the atmosphere at the Brandeis home had "no spontaneity, no freedom," as she wrote in her diary. She loved her walks with him, however. She also wrote in her diary that on one walk they talked about my father. The justice had liked her remark "that Eugene is temperamentally not a democrat but a benevolent despot and that his marriage was the only experience of democracy that he had ever endured."

Mother also saw quite a bit of and became friends in this period with Justice Oliver Wendell Holmes, who served on the Court from 1902 until 1932. Later, she got to know Benjamin Cardozo, who served on the Court from 1932 until his death, in 1938.

Here are Mother's portraits of some of the most memorable Supreme Court justices, about whom she is tellingly and charmingly indiscreet.

I MET Justice Brandeis as an old acquaintance of Eugene's soon after we arrived in Washington. My diary reports that we went for walks together; this I do not remember, only the stimulating conversations that took place wherever we met. He had a wide vision of national and international affairs, which raised the tone of his conversations. The future of what was then called Zion interested him profoundly, more from a large political than from a specifically Jewish point of view. I was skeptical about its future, I insisted, because the Jews were too individualistic. As proof I described a meeting on Zionism in New York to which Eugene had taken me soon after we were married when he was trying to make up his mind what he thought about the question of its feasibility. There were some 150 Jews present—all committed Zionists—but there were at least 150 different solutions in that audience. I laughed harder and harder as the meeting became more and more heated, everybody shouting, nobody listening to anyone else.

The justice was not amused. I fear he lacked any sense of humor. He insisted even in those early days that necessity would create a Jewish state, preferably in Palestine, the appointed site of Biblical history.

I confess I was flattered that this brilliant man singled me out for many conversations. I felt less flattered when Eugene reported that Brandeis had sent for him and told him he ought to go to Zion at once to take charge of its financial problems. When Eugene replied that he could not leave his wife and four children, the justice replied that he had found me a competent woman who could readily take care of the children without him. Somewhat amazed, Eugene settled the matter by stating, "Like you, Mr. Justice, I prefer to serve my own country rather than a nascent Jewish state."

Justice Brandeis was known to have advised many young men what they should do, at times very much to their benefit. Gradually he developed something like a Jehovah complex, which saw the human scene like a chessboard on which he liked to move people around like so many pawns.

It made no difference in his friendliness when Eugene refused to do his bidding, but I discerned that he considered me the real obstacle to his wishes—that the conditioning process to which I had been subjected had misfired. In other words, this modern Jewish prophet was not without some of the guile which has always amused me in his biblical forebears.

I admired him nonetheless for it. On the contrary, it seemed a worthy play in the strategy of a farsighted statesman. And what made one see everything he did as a part of his greatness was a totally unselfish, moral grandeur which was inherent in his personality.

In addition, Justice Brandeis was a sincere ascetic, the only one I ever encountered. His bare—for anyone else unlivable—home surroundings, his complete indifference to the abominable food served at his table, his contempt for comfort of any kind were genuine manifestations of self-imposed restraint. One would suppose that I, who had been brought up in an atmosphere of Lutheran puritanism, would find this trait admirable. It interested me to discover that the moral self-control of puritanism is hostile to the deliberate self-punishment of the ascetic. The former does not exclude a positive, joyous acceptance of life, as in itself a great good, whereas the latter is suspicious of life and often bitterly hostile to it.

Mrs. Brandeis only increased my aversion to this tendency in the justice because she imitated it without his sincerity. The one chicken she served at dinner regardless of the number of guests could just as well have been decently prepared. The house furnishings need not have been more expensive to be attractive or the chairs comfortable. Her authoritarian sense of superiority made it a penance to call on the Brandeises' Monday at homes. The atmosphere was all wrong—stifling. If I tried to join in talk with the men in the justice's corner of the room, she would command, "Agnes Meyer, come over here with the ladies where you belong." "The trouble with you, Agnes," she added one day, "is that Washington has spoiled you and it's gone to your head." My aristocratic friend Mrs. Frederick Keep (one of the Boardman sisters) was then heard to say in a soft voice, "If Washington has been kind to Agnes, Mrs. Brandeis, it is because they enjoy her." I was sorry not for myself but for the younger Brandeis daughter, who was present. She seemed crushed by the maternal presence.

The justice himself rose serenely above all of his wife's eccentricities. He lived at a different moral altitude, which made him oblivious of petty things and surrounded him with an aura of impenetrable dignity.

I saw more of Holmes and saw him more informally, as he lived on I Street just around the corner from our K Street residence. He was gayer, more the ladies' man, and sprightlier in his conversation than the patriarchal Brandeis. Both men were tall and handsome, strong of feature; both faces had been molded by the profundity of their lives. Both came from Boston, but Holmes was an elegant New England cavalier of such pervasive charm that it made him far more attractive than the more austere Brandeis to the general public. Holmes was too gifted to trade on his personality, as many charming men and women do, but it gave him a following of sycophants, who overdid the Holmes cult and hurt rather than helped his place in history.

Without any judgment of legal matters, I have often wondered whether he was not overrated as a man of law because of his overwhelming impact as a man of the world. Very little, for example, is known of Mrs. Holmes, largely because her husband's vitality and popularity overshadowed the plain appearance, restraint, and modesty of a brilliant woman who was content to play second fiddle to the maestro. But her subtle mind was to me so beguiling that I felt her death as a personal bereavement.

When Holmes occasionally dropped in to see me on his way home, I tried to interest him in Chinese painting, but this attempt met with total indifference. When I showed him the famous painting of Berthe Morisot by Manet and a glowing Whistler *Nocturne* in Mrs. Vanderbilt's dining room, I again drew a blank. The plastic arts had no meaning for Holmes. Instead he was an avid reader without an interest in literature as form but with a keen evaluation of content. When I preached Chinese art to him, he replied with his momentary absorption in Vauvenargues, whose incisive skepticism was bound to entrance a mind no less brilliant and no less skeptical. He summed up this aspect of his nature when during one of the Monday-afternoon conversations he expressed his contempt for Indian mysticism: "The Indians gave us those frightful gods and goddesses; the West gave us railroad trains; I prefer the latter. They get you somewhere."

I was sufficiently in accord with this turn of mind to profit by the coruscations of his electric mentality, especially when I heard about his incredible bravery during the Civil War, whose memories were as alive to him as when he had experienced them.

One afternoon when we were taking a drive together, he asked the chauffeur to go to a certain road in Virginia. There we got out and scrambled up a hilltop, from which we could see the undulating hills and distant mountains. The justice pointed out the details of an important battle in which he had taken part. Alas, I remember none of it as military strategy depresses me acutely. But I bring up the episode because it was the only time I saw Justice Holmes excited. His eyes flashed with the fire of youth. I was unhappy about the neglect of the wounded, of whom he had been one, but he was thinking of the toil, the effort, the savagery of the hand-to-hand fighting which he so vividly described. I was awed by the idealism which permeated his whole narrative, and I could not but respect the young man who had been wounded three times, once desperately, but had always returned to battle for the preservation of the Union.

What was no less admirable was his courage in facing his declining strength and approaching death. One day when his end was not far off, I found him reading Aristotle's *Grammar.*

"Why are you reading that dry stuff?" I demanded.

"Partly," he replied with the usual twinkle in his eyes, "because the erudite and saintly Cardozo gave it to me. But mainly because I am preparing for my last examination."

I T I S A tragedy that in the untimely death of this unique man—this almost indescribable example of what men can become if they combine virtue and courage—our country, the nation, and the Supreme Court lost one of its most influential members. For Cardozo was remarkable not only for what he had become despite early adversity, but because no sensitive person could meet him without going away a better person.

I saw far less of him than of Brandeis or Holmes, but I knew him better, if by that pretentious word we do not infer an intellectual process but mutual sympathy and, on my part, a feeling of joyousness in his presence. Perhaps the sense of greater intimacy also came into being because he occasionally came to luncheon on Sundays just with the family. His face had the fine features, the straight thin nose often characteristic of the Spanish Jew. His expression had a sweetness—I can find no better word—which was especially marked when he conversed with the children. He never talked down to them when he addressed them directly, and he managed to let them feel that they were not excluded even when he conversed with Eugene and me.

Concerning his position in his profession, I was told by leading members of the bar that nobody could surpass him for sheer knowledge of the law nor equal his passionate sense of justice. It always made me happy to hear this since I had no competence in these matters but knew him well enough to concur enthusiastically in such high praise.

For me personally Justice Cardozo had a very special significance. Better than most great men I have known, with possibly one exception, he gave validity to that ambiguous word "soul." I say ambiguous because in our era of getting and spending, we have become ashamed to use it. In Cardozo it had become personified. Like the poet Keats, he must have seen life as a vale of "soul making"—soul as clearly distinguished from intelligence, soul not as something given but as the gradual result of daily striving toward an ever higher quality of being through constant choice between the worse and the better.

*historic pattern, patronized by the fundamentalists of several genera-
tions as they made their leisurely way."*

*What she sees from her studio window is the movement of time across
a city: "The panorama unrolls as the years go by. The gas-posts and the
old lamplighter, watched for by the children at twilight, have passed
out for aye; some functionary presses a button somewhere, and Sixteenth
Street is flooded with white light bright as day." Andrews was much
more of a feminist for her time than I ever was for mine. She had a vantage point and a viewpoint, and used and espoused both. She was
known for her ability to cut out silhouettes, and her foreword explained
that this book was her way of creating "silhouettes" in words, what she
called the "most unpretentious of pictures."*

*I was drawn to this vignette from her book because I know what it
feels like to be one of the few women in the room, to feel as if everyone
is looking at you, to know that you have to say something, and to feel
uncomfortable about rising to the occasion.*

N O ONE who had ever known that epoch-making Jewish immigrant, Samuel Gompers, one-time cigar-maker in Whitechapel,
the Ghetto of London, could forget him. Certainly no portrait
painter; for his was a physiognomy to register upon the memory with
indelible distinctness, even as his personality has registered with authoritative force in the industrial and political life of his adopted country. . . .
The most memorable occasion on which I have come in contact with him
was a dinner on Lafayette's birthday, a Lafayette-Marne dinner, at the
Chevy Chase Club, at which both of us were on the program, as I had
been invited to write an ode, and sit at the table of honor! At that table of
honor both of us experienced ignominious defeat!

I had found myself as usual without suitable habiliments for an occasion, and had borrowed a gown from a friend. I dress quietly; this gown
was of rather a hectic combination and calling for considerable dash and
beauty on the part of the wearer. It was not only a creation of silver lace
and green brocade, but it was much too tight for me; my shoulders fairly
rippled over in the back; but it had to do. And anyhow, I would be seated
against the wall at the long guest table, and not be seen from the rear.
That was the slender reed on which I leaned.

Thus at the honor table indeed sat I; Admiral Coontz on one side, a
young Belgian Diplomat, Silvercruys, on the other; they making occasional polite remarks, I calmly devouring my food, with the wretched ode
propped up against my wine glass. Further down the table sat General

MARIETTA
MINNIGERODE ANDREWS

One Sits by the Fire
and Surveys the World

My Studio Window: Sketches of the Pageant of Washington Life (1928)

Marietta Minnigerode Andrews, a charming gadfly, lived in Washington in a comfortable home on Sixteenth Street with an artist's studio from which she could look down onto the life of the city. Her husband taught at the Corcoran Art School, and she felt that Mr. Corcoran was Washington's greatest philanthropist. She called Sixteenth Street itself "one long pageant of the life of Washington."

In this book and in an earlier volume, Memoirs of a Poor Relation, *Mrs. Andrews recorded her "observations, impressions and contacts during 32 years of life in a central location in Washington." Interestingly, this book was dedicated to Edith Bolling Wilson, "whose serene influence and example have been the inspirations of noble thought."*

Mrs. Andrews seems to have liked excess in most things. She engages in hyperbole, but does so engagingly. There's something highly readable, even compelling, about her writing. She described herself modestly (and in the third person): "she has not been the delight of diplomats nor the chosen playmate of cabinets and councils. She has never been a shining light in the world of fashion, and her life in the Capital has been one of citizenship rather than one of 'society.'"

She relates wonderfully funny anecdotes about people in Washington history and touches on so many aspects of the history of the city itself—how Sixteenth Street came to be called the "Avenue of the Presidents" and then have its name changed back; the punch she served for her Wednesday afternoons at home that "became a sort of public utility"; the "Four Mile Run" area between Washington and Alexandria, "a picturesque little hot-bed of malaria and mosquitoes in the days before the electric carline, the power houses and the many factories of today existed"; the old herdics, a kind of low carriage with the entrance at the backs and seats at the sides, which she calls "rumbling concerns of pre-

Pershing, guest of honor, the handsome Mrs. Logan Feland, and my dear friend, Mary Rivers. Next to her, the Prince de Bearn; several seats beyond myself, Samuel Gompers; also many French visitors, and officers of our own Army and Navy.

Mr. Gompers was not in conventional evening dress, but wore a white Palm Beach suit, if I remember correctly. He had a great square head, like a Rodin sculpture, ragged and ugly, tremendous and elemental. His hair was coming out in patches, increasing his homeliness by a suggestion of ill health; his neck very short; again a Rodin effect, as a head chiselled out of a shapeless block of granite. He was a symbol, in his physical appearance, as Benjamin Franklin was—of his convictions; an old man with a high blood pressure; his ill-proportioned, squat body made me think of a grotesque frog, and still he fascinated me by some quality far above the physical. Though an honor guest, it was obvious that to many his presence was unwelcome. It was whispered that the Attorney General left the house, on seeing that the President of the American Federation of Labor was present.

From the moment that Gompers arose to speak, the atmosphere was tense and antagonistic. The guests, seated at small tables all over the large room, listened with close attention for thirty minutes, but they were not of his class or of his creed. His argument was that the Federation of Labor had been in favor of war long before war was declared, and labor had done its share toward the winning of the war. He did not touch upon the immense wages, or the profiteering, or enter into any discussion as to the justice of it, had men been drafted for economic service, as for military; he eulogized his own army of toilers, but he never did say once that Labor won the War.

When General Pershing arose one could hardly breathe. The air was electrical. I never saw Pershing so beautiful, so aristocratic, in all the prestige of uniform and rank. His was the adulation of all, and the personal friendship of most persons present. Rage fairly consumed him, his words fell burning and blistering, as with authoritative eloquence on the assumption that Gompers had laid claim to victory he gave the lie to the old man, who, representing American Labor, was also a leader of men and a toiler for humanity. General Pershing denied that organized labor had been loyal to the country in its hour of need and claimed for the soldiery the honor of having won the war in spite of all the handicaps imposed upon the country by enemies within itself. There were persons, he said, whose activities were so pernicious to the National welfare, that they thought only to turn the woe of the world to their personal advantage—vituperative, vitriolic, he poured upon the head of the old man a torrent of passionate contradiction which fairly swept his audience off their feet. Calmly Mr. Gompers sat through this, as he has through public insult and private insult; in this case they were both invited guests and this was a social occasion upon which such controversy was ill-timed.

I was filled with pain for the situation. Everyone entirely forgot my ode—the audience was wild with excitement—the walls shook with applause, there was a hubbub of agitated comment—and the toastmaster failed to call me and the ode. Mary Rivers then reminded the Prince de Bearn, who acted as Toastmaster, that it was expected, and many persons present were there to hear me read it. He immediately hurried to me.

"Mrs. Andrews," he said, "I believe you would like to read a little ode?"

"Prince," I answered, "I was officially asked to prepare an ode."

With apologetic courtesy he announced me, and with determination worthy of a better cause, I arose, but in a general hum of conversation, could make no impression whatever on the company, still discussing the encounter between the leader of the Federation of Labor and the leader of the American Expeditionary Forces.

Standing in my place at the table, I stated as clearly as I could that when Lafayette was but nineteen, he had decided to cast in his lot with the colonists; and that our soldiers of America averaged but nineteen years when they decided to cast in their lot with France; that nineteen is the age of unpremeditated courage and of unselfish impulse. (I was thinking of my grandfather, marched off from the university to prison; of my father, left for dead upon the field of Appomattox; of my son, with the Croix de Guerre twice, all of them lads of nineteen.)

Here Mr. Gompers called loudly to me to go into the middle of the room where I could be more clearly heard. And here I became a victim to the emanations from my borrowed apparel. Squeezing between the wall and the chairs of the honor guests, of whom naturally all the men arose and stood until I passed, I struggled into the center of the ballroom, uncomfortably conscious that there was no hiding my friend's narrow skirt and extreme decolletage, and indeed too angry to care if adipose tissue was rising in globular exuberance over the tight bodice; then I saw Colonel Rivers leave his seat across the room and move toward me. He took his stand beside me, thus commanding silence and attention, and after stamping my foot violently as a relief to my feelings (another emanation of the arbitrary little friend whose frock I wore), I proceeded with considerable fire to get that ode out of my system. It had been asked for, I had prepared it, and I would read it, at any cost!

I suddenly realized that the thing I had written was trite and ordinary, but I was determined to read it through, good or bad. Neither the United States Army nor the Federation of Labor could have forced me to sit down and hold my tongue. The ode opened with an invocation to Democracy, and then:

> *When young Lafayette arose and spoke*
> *In Freedom's name, a mighty stroke*
> *Was struck for Liberty. . . .*

There is no doubt but that I fell down on it; yet a conscientious biographer should record failure too; failures build up character. And were not the emanations from the green and silver brocade partly responsible?

Unfortunate as had been the clash between two great leaders and the agitation it occasioned, inconsequential as my own contribution, it remained for Mrs. Feland, wife of General Logan Feland of the Marine Corps, to relieve the tensity of the situation. Immediately after me she rose, stately, Juno-esque, exquisitely gowned; stood calmly surveying the company (and being surveyed!), then in a powerful, well-schooled voice, without accompaniment, sang the National Anthem. All were instantly on their feet—soon hundreds of voices took up the strain. A common sympathy spread throughout the company; the reaction had come. Happy faces, cordial greetings, polite congratulations, general goodhumor, marked the occasion. The dancing set betook themselves to the ballroom.

I had a little chat with Samuel Gompers, who promised to pose for me, but never did.

Old Washington Vanished, Never to Return

Our Capital on the Potomac (1924)

Helen Nicolay and her book are period pieces in themselves. Miss Nicolay is a prime example of connections that reach deep into history. I remember always thinking that about Mrs. Mary Henderson, for example, our neighbor who lived in the "castle" behind us on Crescent Place, just off Sixteenth Street. Her husband, Senator John Brooks Henderson from Missouri, who was quite a lot older than she, had been born in 1826 and was a strong Unionist who was influential in keeping Missouri out of the Confederacy. He was a close friend of Lincoln's, and, once he was elected to the U.S. Senate in 1862, he became the author of the Thirteenth Amendment to the Constitution, which prohibited slavery. As a child, I remember feeling awe at the fact that Mrs. Henderson was married to someone who was connected to Lincoln.

I felt the same kind of awe about Mrs. Florence Keep, who was a friend of my mother's. She and her sister, Mrs. Mabel Boardman, were two of Washington's greatest grande dames. Mrs. Keep had one of the big beautiful old granite houses on Ward Circle, where everything was perfect—the house, the food, the wine. I recall her telling me about her first visit to the White House, where as a child she went in a horse-drawn carriage to see President Lincoln. As an older woman, she had gone to read out loud to Henry Adams when his sight was failing. These instances of time stretching back into history impressed me then and still do now. Mrs. Keep bequeathed to Mother a set of fish plates that Mother in turn gave to me, and whenever I use these, which I do at many dinner parties, I'm reminded of these connections to the past.

Miss Nicolay represents another of these connections. She was the daughter of John George Nicolay, who became one of Lincoln's private secretaries. (His close friend, John Hay, was the other.) Twenty-five years after Lincoln's assassination, Nicolay and Hay published a ten-

volume authorized biography of Lincoln, titled Abraham Lincoln: A
History, *and Miss Nicolay used her father's original source materials
to write (in 1906) a biography of Lincoln for children,* The Boys'
Life of Abraham Lincoln, *a book that is still cited today as important both for her own connection to a biographer who knew Lincoln
personally and for her success in inspiring children with the idea that
someone like Lincoln, from humble origins, could succeed so fully. She
also wrote an adoring biography of her father.*

*Miss Nicolay, who was born the year after the Civil War ended, lived
a long life. By the time of her death, in 1954, she had written many
books, most geared to children, and boys in particular. The book
from which this excerpt is taken is almost a biography of the city
of Washington.*

IN THE last weeks of President Wilson's administration the White
House was a strange, silent, baffling place. A few officials came and
went; many rumors flew about; but of what was really taking place
within its walls the public knew no more than if it had been situated in
Tibet instead of a stone's throw from Pennsylvania Avenue's hurrying
throngs. A reporter who gained permission to enter the East Room, at
the very end of Wilson's term, found it dark almost as the tomb, with a
moving-picture outfit installed, where the distinguished patient had been
allowed to witness on the screen shadows of events to which he had
become as a shadow himself—an impotence after great power that must
have been more bitter than death.

An odd manifestation of mass psychology occurred when Wilson left
the White House and Harding entered it. The grounds were thrown
open, and for several days carriages and motors rolled in at one gate,
swept up the semicircle of driveway to the north entrance and out by the
other, making no effort to stop and for no purpose whatever except to
enjoy a privilege long denied. Perhaps this expressed a feeling that
throwing open the gates was a forerunner of happier days and ways of
peace.

Washington has never returned to its pre-war habits. It never can, any
more than it can shrink again to its pre-war size. For a time we hopefully
looked forward to the day when all would be as it had been. But after
khaki had become the exception and not the rule upon the streets, and
dollar-a-year men and war workers had departed, we realized that the
leisurely town we loved had changed to a busy city, with motors enough
in its wide streets to contract them, seemingly, to narrow ones.

Old Washington vanished, never to return, when its skyline changed from one of dormer windows and aspiring chimneys to the great impersonal apartment-houses of tile and light-colored brick, with their square outlines, and the private houses of French Renaissance or modified colonial types, also light in color, that have replaced the deep-red brick beloved of Mr. Corcoran and his contemporaries. On the whole, these newer dwellings give a tone of greater gaiety to the streets.

Pessimists bewail the passing of old Washington, but it is not likely they would be overjoyed to see it return. No one would welcome the Potomac water of uncertain color, verging toward dark cloudy amber, with which we were familiar before the deep-sand filtration plant was installed. Nor should we care to return to the horse-drawn street cars crawling along at snail's pace. Their only advantage was that if you entered one, paid your fare, and possessed your soul in patience, you arrived ultimately at the end of the route, the one fixed goal of the cars in those days. Now each one bears a different label, and in some mysterious way branches off from the main line on a tangent of its own.

Nor would we give up our taxis for the jogging old herdic cab, with its two wheels and crimson-lined, smelly interior, in which those not fortunate enough to own carriages went to parties. They were so safe and so slow that we used to call them the "Washington chaperon."

Gone with jingling horse-car bells are many of the old street cries. "Fresh strawberries" are still with us, from January to June, but we no longer hear, "Deviled crabs!" sung in a high, explosive staccato that made it hard to decide whether they were "Democrats" or shell-fish. Nobody died from eating these dainties, sold on the hot streets from push-carts the size of toy express wagons; but in what dark and unhallowed spots they were prepared, was a fathomless secret. This was a cry that began with the blossoming of the first syringa bush and was heard until the exiled oyster returned to its own. The song of the oyster man has also been stilled. It was one of infinite variety. One vender, who had an anthracite complexion and the manner of a jovial opera tenor, used to chant in a sort of recitative:

> "Here's your oysters, fresh and fine
> All read-dy for sup-per time;
> Little ones for the ladies
> Big ones for the babies
> An' some for ole men an' young men too!"

The ash-man carried a tin horn of prodigious size, shaped like Gabriel's trumpet in the old paintings, and used to perform marvelous solos upon it in the early morning hours. He too was relegated to the limbo of silence, about the time winter residents began to build their homes in Washington. Now nothing really violent is heard except the tooting of their motors all day long and a large part of the night. Occasionally, through this heavy bombardment of sound, sweet and far off as though heard from a great distance (as indeed it is chronologically) comes the wail of a barrel-organ. There is one whose tunes date back to "Silver threads among the gold."

The shops are not what they used to be. In the old days you did your serious fall shopping in Philadelphia or New York on the way home from your summer vacation, or saved up errands until they warranted the outlay of a railroad journey to Baltimore. Yet when, pressed by necessity, you visited Madame Delarue's tiny place of business on Pennsylvania Avenue in search of party gloves or a bit of "real" lace, she or Miss Elise or Miss Rose, waiting on you with the manners of one gentlewoman aiding another, brought forth from secret boxes really surprising treasures. At Perry's, where you went to buy merino or table linen, the clerk who served you knew your great-aunt personally. Entering a bookshop has become—alas!—a mere business transaction. It is no longer good form to drop in socially and browse along the shelves for a half-hour and come out again without spending a cent; and the stock has become sadly distended and diluted by the addition of expensive knick-knacks and cheap postcards by the acre.

Window-dressing has become a profession. On a discordant day in February, when slush and ice dog the streets and wind and watery sunshine contend in the air, the shop-windows array themselves like wantons to catch the Southern trade. Filigree edges of lace and artificial orchids surround groups of wax figures in sport clothes, holding tennis-rackets at unconvincing angles; and wire frames display bathing-suits that no self-respecting wax figure could wear without melting with shame.

Out on the curb the leavings from yesterday's stock in the florists' shops still make a first-class appearance as they are offered at temptingly reduced rates. A Salvation-Army lassie takes up her stand near them to put silently the question, "Luxury or Giving?" and a street faker strolls by with his satchel full of whistles. Motors roll up in endless succession, and pedestrians, thin and plump, short and tall, pass or enter. Most of the women wear fur coats and the latest cut of shoes, and the latest shade in face-powder. It is a crowd such as could not have been seen in Washington ten years ago, or even five. Like the apartment-houses, it is bigger and gayer-looking and more impersonal.

But sometimes a bit of old Washington shows itself, even on F Street and in business circles. Only three years ago a notice announcing the opening of a new banking house assured the public, "There is nothing stiff and formal about this bank." At our shopping corner Mrs. Secretary Blank has scarcely been helped out of her motor by the carriage-opener (it is not many years that we have had carriage-openers in the business section of Washington) when two little women of middle age, in hats that were never fashionable and coats that may have been made over by superhuman cleverness from army overcoats that took part in the siege against Richmond, come out of the big shop and cling to each other in a way that shows their presence on that busy corner to be in itself an adventure.

Their faces are the only things about them that have not been made over, and for that reason alone they are conspicuous. They bear the lines care cuts into the brows and cheeks of women who get the maximum of hard work and the minimum of fun out of life, but momentarily their expression is one of rapturous wonder. For them frothy laces and shameless bathing-suits do not exist. They do not even see the shop-windows; their gaze is lifted toward the bare treetops, where they search with delight and incredulity for the bird whose trills and warbles assail their ears. The bird is really only a toy whistle in the mouth of the fat grimy little street vender in his ulster, walking near the curb with his stock in trade in a satchel strapped over his shoulder. But for them a miracle has happened. On a February afternoon, with snow on the ground and a wind that is no respecter of persons tugging at their faded coats, they have heard, actually heard, a mocking-bird!

ANONYMOUS

(Drew Pearson and Robert S. Allen)

The Capital Underworld

More Merry-Go-Round (1932)

This selection is from Pearson and Allen's sequel to Washington
Merry-Go-Round. *One reviewer preferred this second volume, finding it "just as entertaining as the original and rather more important,
since it gives less attention to society and gossip and more to the actual
processes of government." Its first chapter, "Dance of the Depression," he
called a "staggering indictment of the Hoover Administration with its
evasions, denials and petty puttering in the teeth of grave calamity."
Pearson went so far as to use as an example of Washington with its head
in the sand the fact that his former mother-in-law, Cissy Patterson, was
advocating boxing "to relieve the monotony of life."*

*It's interesting to read about some of the ways in which people got
around Prohibition in the very place where the laws regarding it had
been made. Except for serving ice water at the White House, neither
Harding nor Coolidge ever really worked to enforce the law, and, by
1924, it was estimated that more than five thousand bootleggers were
operating in the Washington area. George Abell and Evelyn Gordon, in*
Let Them Eat Caviar, *wrote of this time, "The water-cooler which
stood in the State Dining Room during Mr. Hoover's occupancy of the
White House was a glaring eyesore but entirely typical of the Volstead
era."*

*Some people had thought that Prohibition would be the death knell
for social activities in Washington, believing that without the necessary
loosening up for an informal exchange of ideas there was little reason
to get together, but cocktail parties remained, and diplomats had their
own stashes on their own "soil," as embassies and diplomatic residences
were considered "foreign soil" in Washington.*

*Although my parents did at times maintain a "dry" house—at least
so Nick and Alice Longworth thought—they seem to have quite easily
got through Prohibition while still obeying the law, because they had*

an enormous wine cellar to begin with, made even larger by their hav-
ing acquired the remainder of Paul Claudel's wine when he returned to
France. Claudel had been the French ambassador to the United States
from 1926 to 1933, and was a great friend of Mother's. She wrote
about her excitement in her diary:"The one really bright spot just now
is the feeling of wealth it gives me to acquire all Clau's wine-cellar
before he leaves. I see the boxes and bottles going into my store-room
with Robinson Crusoe's emotions when he landed his supplies from the
boat on his raft."

Here, the focus is on the distinctiveness of Washington's underworld
in the late 1920s and early 1930s, when Washington boasted "more
small, independent bootleggers per capita than any other city in the
country and has established a unique and universal system of liquor
distribution." Such was the teeming life beneath the surface of our som-
nolent city in the third winter of Herbert Hoover and the third year of
the Depression.

COMPARED with New York and Chicago, Washington is not a
wicked city. . . . The nation always has taken a genuine pride in
the charm and beauty of its capital. This began back in the days
when Washington was merely a muddy suburb of Georgetown, a dream
in the mind of Major L'Enfant. To-day its stately White House, its Lincoln Memorial, its Corcoran Art Gallery, its extensive beautification program have made it the Mecca of sightseers from all over the country,
comparable in beauty to Paris, Budapest and Rome.

Secreted among these historic landmarks are quiet unobtrusive places
where, if the right word is spoken, one may enter a guarded door, place
one's foot on a rail, and partake of Maryland rye, cut Scotch or beer, usually spiked, but sometimes the genuine article brought from Baltimore.
Across the street from the Veterans' Bureau and within a stone's throw of
the White House there was, until recently, one of the most sumptuous
and prosperous of these. In an alley behind the Court of Claims, and just
across the street from the State Department was another. Its old-
fashioned bar and sawdust floors attracted an overflowing clientele until
its proprietor became too ambitious. An act between a Follies girl and a
derelict newspaper man brought bigger crowds—but also the police.

On the south side or front of the White House—for the Executive
Mansion really turns its back on Pennsylvania Avenue and faces the
Potomac—is a fence. It was designed by Major L'Enfant, and tradition
has it that the aristocratic French architect felt that it should be a stout

stone wall of respectable height and capable of giving privacy even to the Chief Executive of a democracy. However, the mansion which it surrounds was to house not a king or emperor, and so, no matter how far George Washington privately may have leaned toward the idea of royalty, the fence finally was built of the plain post-and-picket variety.

But had L'Enfant known the use to which his fence would be put, probably a stone wall would have prevailed. For the White House fence of to-day, rebuilt of steel pickets, has been reënforced by a thick privet hedge which gives to the Chief Executive all of the privacy he could desire. In addition it also gave profitable privacy for a considerable period to a clique of the bootleg brotherhood who cached in its thickness their supplies of corn and bath-tub gin.

No one ever thought of looking for contraband in so respectable a place, and the dapper gentlemen who used it as a base became so prosperous that they began to complain about walking the distance from the hedge to the District of Columbia Building where they stood waiting for their customers.

But eventually a local reporter with a sense of humor and no taste for stimulants wrote a funny story about it for his paper. Though the article drew no official comment, it caused a small furore in Cabinet circles, and the cache in the hedge is no more.

The bootlegging fraternity then resorted to the shrubbery at the base of the Alexander Hamilton monument, quite unperturbed by the fact that the office of the prohibition enforcement chief in the south wing of the Treasury looked down upon the scene. However, morale had sunk so low that they began stealing each other's liquor, and the end came when the rival bootleggers—perhaps inflamed by reading of Al Capone's exploits—retired to the Highway Bridge to fight it out. A couple of penknives were drawn and in the mêlée, an intoxicated citizen, who had come along as spectator, was wounded. Terror-stricken at the sight of blood, the others jumped into their cars and "scrammed."

But the most successful site of operation for a long time was the corner of Fourteenth Street and Pennsylvania Avenue, just a block from the Treasury and directly opposite Detective Headquarters. Two or three unobtrusive trash cans stood alongside the modest fruit stand of Nick the Greek. Near by, as it became dark every evening, stood two or three young men. As an automobile loaded with merrymakers drew up to the curb, one of the young men stepped forward, his eyebrows raised inquiringly.

"Two," was the laconic order from the car.

The young man stepped back. To have kept his supply in his pockets was an invitation to be "frisked." So, like the operations around the

White House hedge, he went over to his base. Negligently leaning against the trash cans for a moment, he pulled out "two" and took the order nonchalantly back to the car.

For a long time this corner enjoyed a reputation among the fraternity as a "good stand." Then a nosy cop developed a penchant for sniffing around trash cans, and the police, with a simple but tactful technique, bankrupted the business. Two of them, "Monkey Face" Barnes and "Bad Sam" Davis, were assigned to stand on the corner for shifts of twelve hours each. Their orders were merely to stand there. That did the trick.

Police occasionally interrupt these too-obvious law-breakers, but the great rank and file of bootleggers and petty criminals who ply their trade in the nation's capital enjoy an immunity almost unsurpassed even in New York and Chicago. This is due to three factors. The first is the influence of Henry Mencken's Free State of Maryland, which surrounds the District of Columbia on three sides. The second is the natural laziness of the capital police. The third is the prestige and pull exercised by so large a number of those enjoying official status, a factor which makes convictions difficult and disrupts police morale.

Probably the most lawless rural district in the United States is that strip of Southern Maryland which lies just south of Washington, between the Chesapeake and the Potomac. Here live the lineal descendants of those who came over with Lord Baltimore, settled in the inlets and creeks of the Chesapeake and Potomac and have been raising tobacco and minding their own business ever since. Cut off by water on all but one side, they have preserved traditions to be found in few other parts of the United States. In the court of Leonardtown, village metropolis of Southern Maryland, the judges still pay tribute to the first ladies of the land who sit with them as court convenes. But the courts and police of Southern Maryland are jealous of their rights, and one of the traditions they most carefully preserve is that of freedom from Federal interference and especially the right to drink where and when they please.

The result is that revenue agents seldom penetrate very far into St. Mary's, King George's, Prince George's and Charles' counties; and on occasion the local constables have given them a blunt warning to stay out. As a result, the peninsula is saturated. For most of the farmers there are two chief money crops—tobacco and rye whisky. And on Saturday afternoon they bring their newly distilled whisky, pure white in color, into town almost as if it were any other crop. That part of the crop which is not consumed by the farmers themselves, while en route, comes up to Baltimore and Washington, contributing materially to the gayety of life in the capital. . . .

"Tea Rooms" is the cloak of respectability given to a chain of houses just a few miles from Washington which for years have been carrying on an organized traffic in Philadelphia and Baltimore girls. Two of the most notorious, Green Gables and the Old Colonial Tea Room, finally brought the wrath of an outraged citizenry about their heads after recent difficulties. The trouble at Green Gables started over "Hot Shot" Ruth Bradley and a dope transaction. Green Gables usually closes at three in the morning, but on this occasion some of the Philadelphia gang, who keep Southern Maryland's road-houses supplied with pretty women, were present and they started fighting over "Hot Shot." The shooting began at five. The lights went out. Neutral guests dove out of the windows. Some months later, Jens Christensen, a Coast Guardsman, and his brother Lauritz visited Green Gables, were recognized by rumrunners who had crossed their trail previously and a knock-down drag-out fight resulted. After that the more righteous citizens of the county marched on Green Gables and pulled it to pieces.

The same Philadelphia gang caused trouble at the Old Colonial Tea Room just across the District line. Bursting into the place in the early morning, they lined up the "guests"—actually members of a rival gang—against the wall, killed one and wounded several others. The only penalties meted out were two years to Chester Renzulli of Philadelphia and one month to Anna Lutz of Baltimore for violation of the Mann Act. Several girls who appeared against them testified that they had been shifted around on a regular circuit of Maryland road-houses, the places being advertised by cards given to Washington taxi-drivers.

It is from these adjacent areas in Maryland and Virginia that Washington recruits most of its police. They come from poor white families who have lived on the land for years and never got anywhere. They are slow, not particularly intelligent, reasonably honest, and when they resort to graft it is of a small and petty type rather than the big deals put over by their confreres in New York and Chicago.

Even were they the most upright individuals, however, their morale eventually would be sapped by the barriers which confront them in dealing with the privileged persons of official Washington. The most untouchable of these are the diplomats who enjoy complete immunity under international law. They cannot be arrested, and if an officer does so by mistake, he is subject to three years' imprisonment, while the State Department is in for a formal apology.

Diplomats, however, are relatively law-abiding people and it is the large and privileged class of Congressmen and high government officials who sap police morale. They are not entitled to immunity but get it through pull and influence.

Police were furious, for instance, over the case of Mrs. Bertha Huddleston, dashing young wife of Representative George Huddleston, Alabama Democrat. She was arrested on a charge of reckless driving while intoxicated after she had careened across West Virginia Avenue and crashed into another automobile. With her at the time was Mark Middleton Penn, a salesman. Mrs. Huddleston was brought into the Ninth Precinct station and the officer who arrested her testified that she "reeked with the fumes of liquor and talked foolishly."

It happens, however, that Mrs. Huddleston's husband is not only a member of Congress, but a bone dry representative from one of the dryest districts in the South. He is sixty-three. Mrs. Huddleston is forty. The story did not go down well in Alabama where Mr. Huddleston is up for reelection. So at this point the Corporation Counsel for the District of Columbia came into action. Despite the testimony of the police, Mrs. Huddleston was allowed to plead guilty only to reckless driving. All she had to face after that was the threat of Mrs. Penn for a damage suit for the alienation of her husband's affections.

WASHINGTON'S most select drinking is done in the diplomatic corps and by those who profit through friendships with diplomats. Every embassy and legation can order an unlimited amount of liquor, which comes by ocean freight to Baltimore and then must be hauled by truck to Washington under special diplomatic convoy. During the early days of Herbert Hoover, one truckload of rare wines and liquors assigned to the Siamese Legation was seized by the police, but the State Department intervened, and ever since then the diplomatic corps has enjoyed an uninterrupted flow of alcoholic beverage. . . . the Honorable R. Beecher Howell, Presbyterian Senator from Nebraska who prides himself on research into the capital's prohibition conditions, estimates that [one] firm "unlawfully delivered in Washington, by virtue of executive permits and protection, some 13,000 quarts of diplomatic whisky within a period of three months, the equivalent of twenty quarts for every diplomatic official and the members of his family, including also maids, cooks, laundresses, chauffeurs and janitors enjoying diplomatic status in the city."

Some diplomatic liquor unquestionably finds its way into illicit channels. But the percentage is small. One or two envoys have been known purveyors in days past.

The next most select drinking set is that which, five cases out of ten, drinks wet while at the same time voting for a stricter enforcement of the Prohibition Act. The congressional supply comes from a whole retinue of small bootleggers who operate on Capitol Hill, the most famous of them being the "Man in the Green Hat," who for two years was almost an official purveyor of liquor supplies to the solons on the Hill. Although in private life he bore the name of George B. Cassiday, his distinctive headgear, like the white plume of Henry of Navarre, became a sort of symbol and the rallying point for thirsty law-makers.

Cassiday was caught as the result of a "buy" made by a Federal stool-pigeon, who worked for weeks as a clerk in the folding-room of the Senate Office Building before success crowned his efforts. With the arrest of Cassiday, the authorities got possession of the famous "little Black Book" in which the bootlegger kept the names and addresses of his customers. A shudder passed down the spine of official Washington when prohibition authorities threatened to make public its contents. This, however, they never did, and the "Man in the Green Hat" got off with a comparatively light sentence.

Lower down the rungs of the drinking ladder come a host of small-time government employees who resort to all sorts of liquid refreshments. It is a matter of official record that at one time the Smithsonian Institution found its reptile exhibit, pickled in glass jars containing alcohol, suddenly decaying because the alcohol had been drained off. Since then guards have been placed in the exhibit rooms. At one time also it was discovered that printers working in the Government Printing Office and the Bureau of Printing and Engraving were ordering twice as much alcohol for type cleaning as in pre-Volstead days. Their supply was cut down. But since then there have been cases where the alcohol, dirty from the cleansing of type, has been re-cooked and sold to an unsuspecting public.

It was to the Bureau of Printing and Engraving that Federal agents traced dope peddlers when they exposed a drug ring described as one of the largest ever caught operating in this part of the country. Seven members of the ring were arrested when Federal agents, after six weeks of mingling with the gang as alleged addicts, discovered an extensive dope doctoring plant near the Raleigh Hotel on Pennsylvania Avenue. Here narcotics were wrapped, packed and labeled, under a system whereby heroin purchased in New York for $25 an ounce was mixed with an ounce of sugar and sold to capital customers for $25 an ounce.

BUT THE industry of which the Washington underworld is most proud is its quiet, steady, year-in-and-year-out bootleg business. Major Edwin B. Hesse, retired chief of police, once estimated there were 3,500 speakeasies and bootleggers operating in Washington. That was in 1929. Since then city officials have uncovered no evidence to indicate a decrease in the number. On the contrary, police maps of the District, ornamented with pins marking suspected locations of speakeasies and bootlegging establishments, indicate an increase.

Despite the huge volume of illicit liquor sold in the capital, the product is of fair quality. Health records show that Washington ranks far down the list of cities in the number of deaths resulting from poison liquor. Seven is said to be the maximum for a single year, and these for the most part resulted from drinking "canned heat" or other substitutes for "legitimate" liquor. In these figures local bootleggers take an honest professional pride. They are out to maintain, or even improve their record.

In another major respect, Washington differs from other cities of similar or greater size. Though bootlegging ranks as the District's second industry, being exceeded in importance only by politics, it is not dominated by the feudal or gang rule which controls the industry in New York, Chicago and many smaller cities.

Speakeasy proprietors are not under the thumb of lordly gang heads. The racket is open to any one who is financially able to establish himself in the business of dispensing liquor—whether by bottle or over the bar— and who is industrious enough to annex a clientele without resorting to the unfair practice of stealing his competitor's customers.

As a result of this open-shop policy, the city is swamped with the small-time variety of bootlegger and speakeasy proprietor, whose net profits average as low as $50 a week and seldom as high as $150. These, for the most part, are gentlemen who have worked as "runners" or delivery men for more pretentious dealers, and being imbued with the old pioneer spirit, have saved enough to rent an apartment or a back room, and install a telephone. Usually they obtain their liquor from the same source as their former employer but in somewhat smaller quantities.

There are, of course, some dealers who have gone into the liquor business in a big way. They are few in number, but their profits are correspondingly high. There is, for example, the late "Alky Queen," who recently retired to a palatial home in Chevy Chase with her limousines, her blooded saddle horses and pedigreed dogs.

At one time virtually every bootlegger in Washington bought alcohol from the Queen at prices ranging from $6 to $11 a gallon, according to quantity purchased. She had scores of employees and many trucks and automobiles, one of them having been known to bring enough alcohol over from Baltimore in a single night "to keep all Washington tight over the week-end." Not long ago she retired, having made all the money she wanted—and with the unique record of never having been arrested for a liquor-law violation.

The most pretentious of Washington's speakeasies, operated on a club membership plan and frequented by the "big shots" of the business and professional world until recently, did a $100,000 business a stone's throw from the White House, when United States marshals closed it under a padlock injunction. Several others are operated on the same basis, but their intake is said to average less than $50,000 a year.

In the spring of 1931, Federal officials became exercised over the operation of a million-dollar liquor ring, with headquarters in Washington. The city was being flooded with alcohol, which sold for a price well under that ordinarily prevailing for the product.

A dozen Federal undercover agents were assigned to the case and the investigation continued for weeks. One Alfred Mendelson, who operated a malt, hops and bottle establishment in the capital, and one Milton J. Lerner were the reputed heads of the ring.

After weeks of patient effort, Herbert Johnson, an undercover agent, managed to ingratiate himself with the gang. Posing as an unemployed bootlegger from a distant city, he cultivated suspected members of the ring, drank with them, and eventually got a job at one of the two re-cooking plants maintained at Riverdale and Hyattsville, just outside of Washington.

Perfume and disinfectants, sent from a clearing house in Philadelphia, were hoarded at the two Maryland plants, passed through the re-cooking process, and distributed on the Washington bootleg market.

Approximately $300,000 had filtered into the coffers of the ring before government agents closed in. Twenty-two persons, including Mendelson, Lerner and two women, were indicted for conspiracy to violate the prohibition laws. The two ringleaders were given two-year sentences. Nine others were given shorter terms. With the ring smashed, Washington bootleggers have been forced to get their alcohol through the old channels, which lead principally to Baltimore.

Adopting the general policy of "live and let live," Washington bootleggers and speakeasy proprietors have effected a certain camaraderie which has kept the city relatively free from gang battles and other pranks of the underworld. Those who cut in on the other fellow's clientele, or consider it easier to replenish diminishing supplies by hijacking, usually wake up with aching heads, discolored eyes, cut lips and other painful but not very serious bodily injuries.

In most cases, a sound thrashing is sufficient to induce an erring bootlegger to mend his ways. But guns have belched their death-dealing slugs even in Washington's comparatively mild-mannered underworld. Squealers have been put on the spot, and "rats" have been given the works on occasion. . . .

Despite . . . sporadic outbreaks, Washington's bootlegging gentry are not bad people with whom to do business. In general, they are out to make an honest dollar as quickly and inoffensively as possible. They may, in fact, be said to hold a unique position among lawbreakers. Because of their almost uniform gentleness of manner and willingness to accommodate, they have worked their way up the ladder of success. They have become a necessary adjunct of the family, like the corner druggist or the chain-store grocer. And like the latter, they have been stuck with many an unpaid bill.

With competition keen and government clerks paid on a semi-monthly salary basis, the liquor venders have found it practically impossible to get along without doing some business "on the cuff"—bootlegese for selling merchandise on credit. It is only the old and steady customer who is permitted to run an account. Thousands of dollars worth of business is transacted "on the cuff," however, and the gentlemen estimate that approximately eighty per cent of these accounts are settled in full.

But the fraternity has a wholesome fear of checks—especially third-party paper. It is axiomatic that a bootlegger would rather put an order "on the cuff" than have it paid for by check.

The speakeasies, with few exceptions, are foul joints. Those in the downtown districts are harassed in particular by the police vice squad. Nearly all are operated behind heavy oak doors with steel trappings. Close at hand is a waiting cesspool into which the liquor stocks are dumped in case of a raid.

It is the perhaps laudable ambition of every speakeasy proprietor to approximate as nearly as possible the appointments of the saloon of pre-Volstead days. He insists on a bar, if only a smooth pine board nailed across a couple of packing cases. An old-time bar, with a back-fixture, mirrors and an oil painting of Venus, is of course devoutly to be desired, but the pièce de résistance is a brass foot-rail. A few of the higher class speakeasies are fully equipped with orthodox furniture of the older and happier pre-war period, and one or two establishments also operate a really good restaurant.

Many of the raids staged by the police squad result in no liquor being found. This is due to two reasons:

First, it is difficult for the police to batter down the heavy barricades before the speakeasy proprietor and patrons can dispose of their contraband. Frequently there is time to rinse out the receptacles, so that not even "sniffing evidence" can be obtained.

Second, the proprietors sometimes are "tipped off" by friends. The police themselves often warn the intended victim. They have a habit, when on a raid, of racing through the city in high-powered automobiles, sirens shrieking. The clamor can be heard for blocks, and there is quick action on the part of every speakeasy proprietor within earshot. Of course, much liquor is dumped needlessly—and at considerable loss. But the proprietors figure that liquor down a cesspool is better than a term at Occoquan, and they soon recoup their losses.

LIQUOR-RUNNING into Washington, chiefly from Baltimore and Southern Maryland, has become a tame affair in recent months. In the old days, when the police motor corps patrolled the highways, it was a hazardous undertaking. The rumrunner had to have a car capable of carrying at least one hundred gallons, and fast enough to outstep the police. Good drivers—those who hit a seventy-mile clip, and with courage enough to run the gauntlet of waiting police—were at a premium in the early days of liquor running. The driver's pay for a night's work was usually $50, but he earned it. The police were quick on the trigger and, with Congress in one instance actually applauding the shooting of a rumrunner by a prohibition agent, the police saw to it that all their shots didn't go astray.

During the first few years after the city went dry, police and rumrunners figured in no fewer than fifteen running battles. Three of the smugglers were killed. Later, with the evolution of the smoke screen, the rumrunners had more than an even chance against the police. At the first warning from the pilot car, which usually preceded the liquor machine by a short distance, the bootlegger sitting beside the driver would get the "pump" ready. They called it the "pump" because the apparatus used to disseminate the eye-filling, nostril-biting smoke resembled the old-time device for forcing air into a tire.

Two developments put a curb on the use of the smoke screen. First, Congress passed a law making it a felony even to have a smoke-screen apparatus in one's possession. Second, the need for smoke screens passed when the police liquor patrols were brought in from the near-by highways.

The business of running liquor into Washington thus has degenerated from a thrilling evening's job to one about as hazardous as carrying a half pint in the hip pocket.

FRANCIS BIDDLE

The President and His Cabinet

In Brief Authority (1962)

Francis Biddle was Franklin Roosevelt's attorney general from 1941 to 1945. This book was the second installment of his reminiscences, which he began with A Casual Past. *Biddle had been Justice Holmes's secretary thirty years before this second stint in Washington, and although the Biddles were closer to my parents in age than to us, Phil and I saw them around Georgetown where they too lived. In fact, Biddle described his house much as I would later come to think of mine: "Like so many Georgetown houses, under a great maple, it was a part of a small friendly world, breathing the air of a village, linked to a more serene century of a hundred and fifty years ago, tidy, informal."*

This was a time when, in some ways, Phil and I and our friends were sort of on the outside of the inside, but we certainly had our noses pressed up against the window. If we didn't know all of these people personally, we knew them all by reputation, since their names were constantly in the news.

In Brief Authority *is a book we had on our shelves. And this particular piece is a kind of anatomy of FDR's wartime cabinet—one moment in one important cabinet, overseeing policy development and decisions in a time of crisis. This was the height of one of the great, exciting times of my life—a time of constant conversations, of real discussions about how the world worked, or didn't work. Biddle's is a succinct, canny, no-holds-barred view of the central people in the government at a specific moment in time. These personalities ring true. I like it because it's gossipy in an elevated way. What could be more fun?*

THERE hangs in my study a photograph of the Second World War Cabinet, signed by each of the eleven members, plus the President, above his likeness. Next to it is an engraving by Currier & Ives, published in 1876, slightly larger than the photograph, portraying President Washington's Cabinet of four, in which Jefferson and Hamilton had been so hostile, and Edmund Randolph so discouraged because his associates were not able, as Washington had fondly hoped, to form a privy council of advisers, patterned on the British model, who would be *au dessus de la mêlée*. President Washington sits next to his Secretary of War, General Henry Knox, who looks not unlike his namesake at our table. Alexander Hamilton is standing, a hand on Knox's chair, the other tucked in his waistcoat below his ruffled shirt, concentrated and determined, his look suggesting irritation below the slight frown. On his other side sits Thomas Jefferson, holding a piece of paper, his smock very simple and without frills, as became a Republican, his unpowdered hair curly, a line of worry between the eyes. At the other end of the little table is Edmund Randolph, the first Attorney General, my mother's great-grandfather, his right hand separating the pages of a book, his hair brushed away from his forehead and caught in a "horse's tail" back of his neck, a serious young man.

In the photograph of the war Cabinet, Frank Knox, Secretary of the Navy, is at the corner of the long table next to me—short, stocky, straightforward, more prepared to be friendly than hostile. He had been a Rough Rider during the Spanish-American War, and followed his colonel, Theodore Roosevelt, into the Bull Moose Party in 1912. Nineteen years later as owner of the *Chicago Daily News* he became one of the leading critics of the New Deal, and was the Republican vice presidential candidate in 1936, when Alfred Landon was so disastrously beaten for the presidency. Knox and Landon were much alike—amiable, middle class, friendly, with a sort of sturdy averageness about them. When his appointment to the Cabinet was announced, Frank repeated a cliché that every one could understand: "I am an American first, and a Republican afterward!" He was the kind of person on whom you could count for that sort of sound, safe platitude. He died before the war was over, on April 28, 1944. I liked Frank Knox. He was not subtle, but he was healthy and decent to the core.

I sat on Knox's right; and Henry Morgenthau, Jr., the Secretary of the Treasury, was on my other side—we took our places in the order in which our Cabinet positions had been created. Henry had been a gentleman farmer, a neighbor of Roosevelt's in Dutchess County, and had served under him in various state and federal positions. I never could feel close to Morgenthau, although I respected his courage, singleness of purpose, and devotion to the President, a bit doglike at times. The President was fond of Henry, patted him when he looked hurt, teased him in public without striking a spark of humor—humor there was none—and protected him as far as possible against the annoyance which his missionary zeal in fields not the Treasury's occasionally caused the rest of us. He had a tendency to send memoranda to F.D.R. about the work of others—which doubtless touched his own, for almost everything was related by the war effort—instead of first discussing it with them.

I hasten to add that his sights were high, his probity impeccable, and the efficiency of his department well above the average, for on the whole he chose good men to serve under him, and leaned over backward, sometimes unnecessarily far, it seemed to me, to keep away from politicians. We shared the same aims, even if the means chosen to accomplish them, or, more precisely, the method of going about the choice, did not on all occasions lead to a warm sense of team play. One could trust him, except where consideration for the feelings of others entered the picture. How could one be at ease with a man who, suspicious of the present and concerned with the future, recorded your telephone talk with him—"wait a minute, Francis, I would like to put on my secretary to make a record of what you are saying"—to be collected for eternity in those endless volumes of the diary that recorded the minutiae of his daily career?

To Henry Morgenthau's right, at the center of the table sat the President, then came Secretary of State Hull and Secretary of War Henry L. Stimson. Beyond Stimson was Frank Walker, the Postmaster General, and next to him Harold Ickes, Secretary of the Interior, looking belligerently at the photographer. I remember one occasion when Harold was away and his Under Secretary, Abe Fortas, sat in his place. Fortas was a recent appointee and the President, unable to place him immediately, asked Morgenthau about him, who in turn passed the question on to me. "Fortas," I whispered, and his name was relayed to the President, who then wrote on a pad: "not his last name, his first name?" And when, going around the table, he came to Abe, the President asked, "Well, Abe, what's been going on in Interior?"

By tradition, the Postmaster General was the political representative of the party in power, and usually chairman of the National Committee at the same time. Although Frank Walker became Postmaster General in 1940, he was not chairman of the National Committee until 1943, and served for a year only. He disliked his political job, but always did what the President wanted him to do, and just then the President wanted the politicians off his back, so that he could get on with the war. Frank was never a professional politician in the sense that Jim Farley was professional or Ed Flynn (who succeeded Jim as chairman) or Bob Hannegan, who followed Walker. Frank was too mild, too decent, too gentle to fill that toughest of all political jobs. But he could and did protect his friend, the President.

Harold Le Claire Ickes was a very different type. If Frank Walker was not a professional politician by temperament there was nothing amateurish about him. People instinctively understood and liked him. Harold Ickes, on the contrary, was the opposite of the politician—a reformer, a liberal (few politicians on either side are liberal by conviction) and an independent—witness his activity as a Progressive from 1912 to 1916. A good cabinet minister should be a competent administrator, and there was none better than Ickes, who sat all through the Roosevelt Cabinet and for a year under President Truman, until he resigned in 1946 with a clarion blast against that President—who was no unworthy opponent himself. He spent the next six years wasting his talents on a syndicated newspaper column that gave him narrow scope for his fierce invective, and occasionally lending his now mild influence to back some liberal measure. Harold Ickes was not a man who, having tasted the satisfactions of public office on a high level, could bear the narrower existence of a critic and gadfly.

I had not fully realized what a suspicious and thwarted human being he was until his secret diaries were published after his death. He had no heroes, and his friends—Tom Corcoran, Ben Cohen, and I were among the closest—remained so only as long as they did not oppose him. Obversely his enemies were those who stood against his strong urges to increased official dominion. Such, for instance was David Lilienthal. They were both Democrats, both New Dealers, both appointed by President Roosevelt in the same administration. And yet during the Truman administration, when Lilienthal was up for confirmation by the Senate as chairman of the Atomic Energy Commission, and needed all the strength he could muster, Harold Ickes, obviously without realizable ambitions in the public field, attacked Lilienthal in his column, and in private talk, with an unfairness equal to that of Senator Pat McCarran, who suggested that Lilienthal was a Communist, because years earlier Lilienthal would not give him political appointments. Lilienthal had fought for the independence of the Tennessee Valley Authority. Harold wanted it put under the Interior Department—and that opposition was enough to make him the eternal foe of the younger man.

In spite of his faults I liked Ickes, although when he asked me I always refused to be a member of any of the interdepartmental committees on which he sat—committees that the President was delighted to set up in an effort to "solve" the problems that arose when several departments were concerned, and which Harold tried to dominate whenever Interior was involved. I liked to lunch with him in his office in the Interior Department, where, looking like an angry and belligerent Donald Duck, he would let go as much at the Democrats as at the Republicans. I can see him on a particular occasion when he was wartime petroleum and solid fuels administrator. Striding up and down, his hands clasped behind his back, his lower lip protruding, he announced that he had won a terrific victory over some oil barons whom he had persuaded that it was more advisable to play the game, to co-operate with him. Under such circumstances one must either kiss a woman or have a drink: would I join him in a martini? . . .

I had first come into personal contact with him in 1938, when I was counsel for the committee investigating TVA. He called me in Knoxville to ask if I would give him professional advice about whether a political speech he was going to make in Philadelphia was libelous. I flew from Knoxville to Washington—I had some TVA business in the Capital— and read the speech, the secretary's gimlet eyes watching me from behind his desk. The speech was libelous, and so I told him. "Very well then," he quacked, "I'll make it." I remember his last sentence. After denouncing two Republican stalwarts in the city, Moe Annenberg, the owner of the *Philadelphia Inquirer,* and one of the Pews, he ended, "Pew! Annenberg! Annenberg, phew!"

A striking characteristic of Harold's was his ability to fire a subordinate without the slightest qualm or hesitation if he thought him disloyal or incompetent—there was no beating around the bush or trying to place the man elsewhere. Once, after a row in which an Under Secretary of the Interior was involved, the Secretary had decided to get rid of him promptly. Ickes gave instructions that after the incumbent had left for the day the lock on his office door was to be changed—he was not to be admitted to his office or given access to his personal files, or even allowed to get his hat! The controversy had been going on for months, and Ickes' ruthless order made it impossible for his subordinate to get at the material he might need to state his side of the argument when the press took it up.

Ickes was combative, shrewd, belligerent. He was a very effective radio speaker—he did not ad lib—and he had a genius for what Justice Holmes called "hitting the jugular." He was disliked by many of his subordinates, feared by members of Congress, and highly respected by the public, who regarded him with a mixture of amusement and admiration. He could not have been a happy man. He took too much and gave too little to have understood what love or friendship could mean. Yet the grains of suspicion and malice in his nature, mixed with fearlessness, gave him a sharpness of character, which was a relief after so much that was soft and sentimental floating on the placid surface of American life. Harold was never a bore.

Jesse Jones, Secretary of Commerce, sat between Harold Ickes and Henry A. Wallace, Vice President from 1941 to 1945, three men as unlike as it is possible to imagine. Frances Perkins, in her invariable dark dress with two strings of pearls, and three-cornered felt hat planted firmly and low over her forehead, came next; and finally Claude Wickard of Indiana, who had succeeded Wallace as Secretary of Agriculture, reflecting in his amiable person all the sunny, smiling, and friendly, if somewhat tasteless, qualities of the great corn and wheat states.

The Cabinet was not a group of outstanding men. But they were competent and offered an experience which reflected the diversity and range of America. Cordell Hull—he was then seventy-one, but seemed older—had been in politics for forty years. He had fought in the Spanish-American War, practiced law, served in the Tennessee legislature, and had been a judge, a representative, and a senator before appointment to the Cabinet. As the terrible strain of war built up he tired easily and had to leave Washington for increasingly longer rests, while Sumner Welles, the Under Secretary, would run things.

Welles was Hull's opposite in every way. A career man, he had been admirably trained in the old school of diplomacy. He spoke French and Spanish fluently, had some Italian and German, and knew thoroughly the involved intricacies of Latin American politics and our relation to them. When a foreign diplomat came to Washington, he made a formal call on the Secretary; and then spent two hours with the Under Secretary, who was usually at home in the visitor's tongue. Welles was under fifty, robust, a tireless worker, with correct and formal manners, intelligent rather than imaginative, instinctively "liberal" in a department where that quality was not often apparent. He never walked from the State Department to the Metropolitan Club without his Malacca cane, and in summer wore an impeccable Panama.

Although as a rule a member of the Cabinet consulted only his opposite number in another department when a problem arose, it was accepted that one did not disturb Mr. Hull, but called Welles, who was quick to understand and to act. The Secretary disliked administration and turned over its daily manifestations to others. This choice left him free for the planning of policy. Yet it involved a weakness inherent in our system; no permanent civil servant, reaching to the highest level below the head of the particular government unit, can altogether relieve his principal of the ceaseless grind of administrative decision. Mr. Hull suffered from partial abdication of power.

Secretary Hull stood in high repute throughout the country for his rugged honesty and independence and was looked upon by members of the Congress with something approaching veneration. He was not very subtle or original. The President counted on him to be his chief liaison with Congress when the time would come to sell the United Nations to the Hill. President Roosevelt was determined not to make the same mistakes that President Wilson's idealistic and obstinate temperament, making co-operation so difficult, had invited after the First World War. From the beginning, Congress was thoroughly and continually informed of the shape that the new union was taking in the minds of the President and his Secretary of State.

I saw very little of Secretary Hull outside of Cabinet meetings. We almost never met socially, and then usually for a meaningless exchange of amenities at one of the formal and solemn dinners that the Secretary gave when the arrival of a visiting potentate made it appropriate, and the President had completed the first gesture, or the visitor did not rank a reception at the top. These dinners took place at the Carlton Hotel—it was before the government had purchased Blair House—and they were not gay. The Secretary was usually tired and worried, but he would not forgo what he considered his duty, impelled, perhaps, by his dislike of his Under Secretary—he did not enjoy Welles stepping into his shoes even on the social side.

I particularly remember a dinner given for General de Gaulle. The President had disliked the general since their first meeting at Casablanca; felt that his bosom harbored the ambition to be a Man on Horseback; and was insistent that we should never "recognize," however indirectly, anyone whom the French people had not themselves freely chosen. We should wait for the time when they could make the choice. Eisenhower was ordered not to sign any agreement with him, nor should there be any with De Gaulle from which a suggestion of "recognition" might be squeezed, nothing formal to which he could later point as conferring authority. . . . De Gaulle, the President said, thought of himself sometimes as General Foch, sometimes as Jeanne d'Arc. He was a bore. . . .

At this dinner for the French general the American Secretary had little opportunity to judge, for he spoke no word of French and his guest was totally deficient in English. No interpreter was present—I suspect that the Chief of Protocol, George Thomas Summerlin, little "Summy" as he was affectionately known, doubtless thought that an interpreter would have introduced an undesirable note of formality. So the Secretary and the general sat stiffly in informal silence, the American drooping a little, the Frenchman solemnly and forbiddingly erect, all the six feet six of him, balancing a chip like an epaulette on each martial shoulder because he had not had his twenty-one guns on arrival.

After dinner Bill Bullitt, the ex-ambassador to France, who spoke the language fluently and had known the general in France, brought up several of us to be introduced to him as he sat in isolated dignity, unsmiling and showing no interest in our tentative remarks. Sol Bloom, chairman of the House Committee on Foreign Affairs, was among the first, and Bill must have murmured in his ear a word or two about the desirability of breaking the ice, an exercise for which Mr. Bloom was eminently qualified, having, in his career as professional entertainer, introduced the lovely Fatima as a belly dancer to the American public. He could be counted on to do his best. Bill stated the congressman's name very clearly to the guest of honor and indicated his importance. Mr. Bloom, bent at all costs on a rapprochement, produced a trick cigar from some inner recess, and offered it to the general, who for a moment hesitated. "Take it, take it," the New Yorker insisted. But when General de Gaulle put out his hand the cigar disappeared up Sol's sleeve, withdrawn by some invisible elastic mechanism—"Now you see it, General, now you don't. . . ." Puzzled, suspecting that he was being laughed at, the general turned to his aide. "What does the American statesman wish?" he inquired. The other did not seem to know, and no one dared to laugh. It was not a successful evening. . . .

Although I rarely came in contact with him except at Cabinet meetings, the member of the Cabinet I most admired was Henry Stimson. He was then seventy-four, in his "tough and tranquil old age." He was as loyal to the President as Morgenthau, but stood up to him, which Morgenthau did not. He tired easily, under the new strain of war, and left the office early each day, to keep fit; and he always looked ruddy and clear-eyed. If you had to see him, it was wise to go in the morning—by five o'clock he was weary and peevish. He had no small talk. On those few occasions when we did not talk shop—for instance, when I went to see him and stayed for lunch at the Pentagon when we had not finished our discussion—I found him difficult, rather shy, not forthcoming.

I never thought of calling him by his first name, as did Morgenthau, a familiarity which I felt he resented. I suppose he was old-fashioned. He did not particularly welcome the views of others on matters in his field. He had the Elizabethan sense of humor of a sturdy man, but though not often revealed, it came like a gust of wind when stirred. I remember his telling a story about General George Patton, when our troops were moving into Germany. Patton detested rules and regulations, Army forms, and Army reports. After General Eisenhower had warned him that he should pull himself together and follow the fitting formulas, the first of Patton's reports showed that he had taken the suggestion to heart; it was impeccable—succinct, objective, impersonal, strictly according to Army Hoyle—until the last sentence: "P.S. I have just pissed in the Rhine. . . ."

Mr. Stimson used strong language with the men he was fond of, an intimation that to them he could let go. In Washington he was closer to Jack McCloy, who was his Assistant Secretary throughout the war, than to anyone, often dining with him. Once, when Mrs. Stimson had not been feeling well, Jack and his wife went over to spend the night with them. The next morning Mrs. Stimson, entirely recovered, was having breakfast with the McCloys. The Secretary's voice, suddenly rising from an adjoining room, broke into the peaceful meal. "I'll be damned if I will," he shouted. "I'll be God damned if I'll do anything of the sort." "It's nothing," said Mrs. Stimson. "Mr. Stimson likes to dictate his journal in the morning, and he often gets rather excited." They could hear him striding up and down the room, as the expletives burst on the air. Then he came in for his soft-boiled egg, relaxed and smiling. . . . To me he was a heroic figure of sincerity and strength.

IT HAS BEEN customary for critics and historians to discount the changing role of the Cabinet, as it developed with the times, charging it with ineffectiveness because it had not fulfilled the original function for which it was intended. But what of that? The Cabinet was thought of by the first President as an advisory and authoritative body, an American privy council, to form policy and decide major questions as they arose. Today it is composed of a dozen administrators heading vast departments, who generally meet once a week to discuss their problems and report to the President what they are doing. Though the members are not primarily there to shape policy, their decisions often do. For policy can never be wholly separated from operation and often is developed and defined by the cumulation of action rather than by a reasoned decision taken before the event. And operation down the line, sometimes far down the line among the NCOs of government, can change and modify the original plan or even create a new one, which in the ultimate view is hardly recognizable. The American Cabinet gives some unity to this vast, sprawling, uncoordinated system and keeps the President informed of what his chief administrators are doing. During my three and a half years there was of course a single overriding consideration which created a sense of unity, the successful prosecution of the war.

The View from E Street

A Cartoonist's Life (1998)

I once called my friend Herb Block, known to the world as Herblock,
"one of the greatest ornaments to the Post *and to all of journalism,"*
and happily wrote an introduction to an updated version of the book of
Herb's from which this piece is excerpted. That introduction was itself
an abridged version of an appreciation I had written for the Post's
Outlook special section in 1995 that marked Herb's half century with
the paper. Everything that I said there and in the introduction to A
Cartoonist's Life *still holds, particularly my conclusion: "The* Post
and Herblock are forever intertwined. The Post *is his forum. He*
helped create it, and he has been its shining light."

Herb tells a story I love about my husband, Phil, taking him to the
Supreme Court for lunch with Felix Frankfurter, for whom Phil had
clerked the first year we were married. During the conversation in
Frankfurter's chambers, the matter of how much Herb was working
came up. He was then still on a seven-day-a-week schedule, which he
had started with my father, who had hired him. It was a demanding
schedule, and Herb admitted to "chafing under this routine." As he tells
the story, "Phil put it to Frankfurter, who rendered a decision that was
certainly agreeable to me. He said, 'There must be leisure for ideas to
stroll into the mind,'" and Phil conceded to having Herb knock off a day
a week. However many days a week he has worked, he has kept it up for
fifty-five years, and I am grateful to him in more ways than I can say.

THE ORIGINAL *Post* building on E Street evoked memories of the
Chicago News "old building." Its similarities included a single passenger elevator operated by an attendant, and patchwork additions requiring steps up and down from one part of a floor to another. Up
a couple of steps on one floor was a small room that served as a studio,
where broadcasters conducted interview programs for the *Post's* radio
station, WINX.

Phone calls went through a switchboard staffed by a few operators
who knew everyone and who could even recognize voices of *Post* people

who had been away for years. Less experienced operators filled in on weekends, and in those simpler times they occasionally woke me on Saturday mornings to say I had a phone call that was long distance! Such calls were usually from people I didn't know phoning from as far away as Baltimore.

Next door to the *Washington Post* building was the Munsey Trust Company—the bank most convenient for employees to cash paychecks or keep accounts. A lot of things of that period seem strange today, but an incident at this bank, where I had checking and savings accounts, remains one of the strangest. It had a policy that money deposited in savings accounts should not exceed a certain modest figure—maybe $100 or $200 at any one time—without approval of a bank official. Flush with some extra money, I wanted to deposit more than the limit, and a polite bank teller referred me to a vice president of the institution. This official asked rather sternly why I wanted to deposit this money—say $250—to my savings account, and I said I thought it might be a good idea to put aside something for taxes. To this he responded, as one who has cleverly seen through a despicable ruse: "Taxes—hah! What you want on that money is our interest!"

That bank, along with the old *Post* building, has long since gone. But after years of seeing banks offer gifts and better-than-other-banks interest rates to attract depositors, and thinking of how investments in a booming stock market would have paid far more handsomely than the modest bank rates then, I am still baffled. Well, at least the Munsey bank officials didn't ask me to give them a toaster.

Less than a block away from the *Post* was the old Willard Hotel, complete with the original marble sinks in the bathrooms. And even closer was an old-fashioned white-tiled Thompson's restaurant, one of a national chain. It was later to become famous in a Supreme Court decision on the "Thompson restaurant case," involving the seating of blacks in restaurants.

At Constitution Hall, the Daughters of the American Revolution banned blacks from the stage but allowed them in the audience. The National Theater, a few doors the other side of the *Post* building, allowed blacks to perform but not to sit in the audience.

I did cartoons on the DAR ladies when they held their annual conventions in Washington and passed resolutions expressing their fears about admitting refugees. I liked FDR's reminder, in addressing one of their conventions: "All of us are descended from immigrants."

In the early 1950s, the National Theater was being picketed for its segregation policies and the *Post* urged it to change. I had a cartoon ready to run on the subject when the editor asked me to hold it. The theater had agreed to end its policy if it could do so quietly without further confrontation or publicity. It made good on its promise, and theatergoers of whatever views never knew just when it happened.

But even after the early '50s, when segregation officially ended in the capital of the United States, the sentiment persisted among some members of Congress, who continued to make racial or ethnic slurs. Some from the South spoke of "nigras" in a way that made it difficult for listeners to know exactly how the word was spelled.

Not long ago a college student asked if I had ever drawn "stereotype southern congressmen"—hoping that I had not. I explained that the "Senator Claghorns" of Congress were not stereotypes or made-up characters. There really were legislative bigots, and through safe seats and seniority quite a few held positions of power in Congress. It's a mark of progress that most of the southern congressmen of today are so different that a newer generation can hardly believe another kind ever existed.

Segregation in Washington was not only by race but by gender. Even the journalistic clubs had no women members, and generally not even women guests. The National Press Club, recognizing that its luncheon speakers made news, permitted women journalists to sit in a balcony. Oh boy!

Washington, D.C., a city where residents pay all taxes and where they can be drafted into the armed forces, had not even a glimmer of home rule. It had no vote for local or federal offices of any kind. It was run largely by city commissioners appointed by the president—and by Congress.

Now it elects local officials, but the president and Congress still can overrule actions of the city government, deciding even how the city spends its own tax revenues. These revenues come from one of the highest state or local income tax rates in the country—as well as from sales and property taxes. And while District residents also pay federal income taxes, they are denied full voting representation in Congress. The early American colonists had a stirring slogan about that kind of taxation.

In the 1940s, before air conditioning was widespread, Washington summers had such a sticky reputation that some governments listed it as a hardship post. Streetcars still operated, quietly and efficiently, among the best in the country. This convenient form of public transportation was later discontinued and the tracks eliminated at considerable expense. By the 1990s, with traffic gridlocks and energy and pollution problems, some cities were actually installing new trolley lines.

No barricades or concrete stanchions ringed the White House. The street between the White House and the Treasury building was open to auto and pedestrian traffic.

Since then, there has been more and more security for officials, if less for residents, who are aware of daily muggings and homicides.

The Secret Service and its functions have become vastly enlarged, not to say bureaucratically bloated. In its determination to protect Vice President Dan Quayle in 1992, these agents blocked off the entire Capitol plaza—until an outraged Speaker of the House Tom Foley sent them packing.

Foley told me of his own more direct experience with protection at a time when the president and vice president were both away. Since the Speaker is next in line for the presidency, a Secret Service delegation suddenly descended on him. They asked what kind of car he used to go to and from the Capitol. When Foley told them that he biked to work, they stared at each other with a wild surmise, visualizing a cycling squad of protective agents around the biking Speaker, making its way from Foley's home to the Capitol. He took them off the hook by acceding to their request that, until one of the two top executives came back, he would ride in a car. When the president or vice president returned to the Capitol, the Secret Service left the Speaker as suddenly as they had come—without his bike to ride home.

Among other things different in post-war Washington was Watergate—not then a building, much less a scandal. It was a place on the riverbank where there was a good restaurant, and firmly moored in the river was a concert stand. On moonlit evenings canoeists would glide by, gently paddling their way between the musicians and the audience. Once when a canoe overturned, the couple in the water, anxious to avoid disturbing other music lovers, very softly called "help."

Under even more congressional rule than now, there were odd Washington regulations. One was a ban on vertical drinking. Drinks could be ordered and served at tables, but you could not even hold a glass in your hand while standing or walking. A waiter could move it for you from one table to another, where you could resume seated consumption. Perhaps Congress was trying to prevent the return of the old-fashioned foot-on-the-rail bar—or maybe these legislators felt that a sloshed slide from a seated position to the floor was less unseemly than falling flat on the face from the upright position. This restriction was later repealed.

With World War I–vintage temporary buildings lined up along sections of Constitution Avenue, a saying was that nothing was more permanent than a "tempo." Another saying was that Washington, D.C., combined all the charm of the North with the efficiency of the South.

Washington, D.C., whatever its faults—many of them national faults—was an exciting place to work. It still is. Trips to the Capitol were as good as going to baseball openers. And for a young cartoonist to see up close and sketch some of the figures he drew, and to think that they saw his work in the paper, was even more exciting. Unlike the situation at NEA in Cleveland, where the cartoons went to many papers but seldom appeared in that city, the work here was seen every day and the response was immediate. It was like watching the fellows on the bus looking at one of my first cartoons in Chicago. But here many of them were government officials.

Attending a White House Correspondents' Association dinner was an occasion, made more so by a senator who was sitting at the same table as some of us *Post* people. One of the big issues the *Post* had fought for editorially was civilian control of atomic energy, which this senator, Styles Bridges of New Hampshire, had strongly opposed. Like many long-settled issues, it may now seem amazing that it was once a burning question. But with the atom bomb still new and tension with the USSR increasing, the struggle between civilian and military control was vigorous. Eventually, civilian control won.

At the correspondents' dinner, Alfred Friendly, who had written many of the *Post*'s articles on the subject, asked Bridges if he thought the *Post* editorials or articles had made a significant difference in the outcome. Bridges nodded and, gesturing in my direction, said, "The cartoons." This was pretty heady stuff.

But I had learned a lesson from *Washington Post* editor Herbert Elliston shortly after I arrived at the paper. He took me along to a party where, as we were about to enter, a Cabinet member on the way out warmly greeted him with "Hello, Herbert." Elliston replied with an equally warm and friendly greeting, and almost in the same breath, he said to me, "I'm giving him hell tomorrow." Elliston felt that the *Post* should use all the advantage of being at the center of things in Washington, but being civil or even friendly with public officials did not interfere with his editorial judgment. . . .

Back on E Street, an office had been created for me when I signed on at the *Post*. I was later moved into a kind of broom closet and then from pillar to post—sometimes behind *Post* pillars. Finally, I got a little office that provided an excellent view of parades. When President Truman was inaugurated, friends came downtown to share this space and leaned out the open window—in that old building the windows actually opened—to shout greetings to people they knew in the parade cars. Truman smiled and waved as he passed by. . . .

It's often said that whatever we think of any current occupant at 1600 Pennsylvania Avenue, we should "respect the office." I feel that respect for the office should begin with the person who occupies it—or who campaigns to occupy it—and his respect should extend to the other branches of government too.

But the Big Name incidents are almost Cinderella stuff. The usual routine has always been working over a hot drawing board, hearing "Yer late" from engravers, and, at the old building where everything seemed to be held together by wire and tape, having occasional hassles with building supervisors and production people. We recall not only the little triumphs, but the sometimes more frequent little indignities.

The *Post* put out a "bulldog edition" to boost street sales and to mail out of town early. On those deadlines, I not only went down to the wire but frequently tripped over it. And the production manager, who used to stick his head in the door to complain, threatened that if the cartoon was not in sufficiently early, he would run it in halftone—like a photograph, with overall dots producing a gray effect, rather than as a "line cut," where the blacks and whites were etched sharply. Line cuts took longer.

The first cartoon on which he made good this threat was one about a gubernatorial election in Georgia in which Eugene Talmadge triumphed over the more progressive incumbent, Gov. Ellis Arnall. In this drawing of a youngster being taken back down Tobacco Road, the gray tone didn't look too bad—it even gave a kind of appropriate nightfall quality to the picture.

But with deadlines moved still earlier, the halftones appeared more frequently, sometimes with the cartoons only partly done. The drawings were given back to me to be finished for later editions. Since this first edition was the one that was mailed around the country, I began hearing from other cartoonists, who commented on this bold, innovative technique in which parts of the drawing were sketched in, parts shaded, and the entire cartoon given an unusual tone.

I hated those halftones. And eventually the *Post* early edition and I got on schedules that meshed. To this day, when I am unusually late, some engraver with a long memory will cry "Halftone!"

CONSTANCE CASEY

Memoirs of a Congressman's Daughter

The Washington Post Magazine (1992)

I first read Connie Casey's memoir about Washington when it appeared in The Washington Post Magazine *in 1992. I was then in the throes of writing my own memoir, and hers struck me as ringing just the right bells with the right tone. Although Connie was in the generation behind me, her account of growing up in Washington jogged some of my own memories.*

Connie's father, Joe, was a Democratic congressman from Massachusetts, elected in 1934 and serving until January 1943. He hadn't been a candidate for renomination in 1942 because he chose to run for the Senate against Henry Cabot Lodge—unsuccessfully, as it turned out. Like so many others who have come to Washington and become so entrenched that they stayed, Joe Casey put out his law sign again and continued to live here until his death, in 1980. The Caseys were close to a lot of journalists, including Walter Lippmann, Drew Pearson, William V. Shannon, and our friend Alfred Friendly of the Post. *Connie admits that "Journalists appreciated my father because he was a good storyteller, and one who verged on indiscretion."*

Joe was a hail-fellow-well-met, live-it-up ex-congressman, and he and his wife were friends of mine and Phil's. Joe went on a lot of pleasure trips, so frequently that I remember asking him one day, "Joe, why do you take so many vacations?"—to which he responded, "What do you remember? The vacations or the times between?" I always recalled his response whenever I began to think that my vacations were too few and far between.

I lived somewhat the life that Connie Casey describes—and resents. But I accepted most of it and didn't fight it. I adored Phil Graham and our children and living in Washington.

This piece gives an engaging view of a pretty typical life in Washington in the 1950s, at least for families of a certain class. It's hard to

*separate growing up in D.C. from growing up anywhere, but I do agree
with Connie that growing up in Washington was different from growing up elsewhere. Connie puts it this way: "A childhood in any American city in the '50s might seem foreign to the rememberer, but there is
something distinct about Washington." That distinction, I think, arose
in part because there were criteria other than money. Certainly wealth
counted, but your job defined your Washington position, and women
assumed their husband's title. The social hierarchy was based on the
political.*

WHEN I WAS 9, in 1954, I began to ask questions about the city
where I was growing up. Till then I had accepted Washington
as the only possible reality; hot, green summers succeeded by
cold, bare winters, ruled with perfect fairness by my parents and their
friends.

I asked my father, Joseph Casey, a lawyer who'd been a member of
Congress before I was born, this question:

Why are all the people at Burning Tree golf club men?

I'd wondered why my mother never went to Burning Tree. Women
played golf; why else would they wear spiked brown-and-white shoes
with fringed flaps?

Why couldn't I go to Burning Tree? (A place, incidentally, where one
caddie made the flattering and sage mistake of regularly addressing my
father as Senator Casey, and sometimes Justice Casey.)

After a short pause, my father explained that no women, no girls,
could ever go to Burning Tree because the men there were naked. Naked
all the time.

I had known for a few years, since I'd grown into shame and begun
wearing more than underpants when running through the front lawn
sprinkler, that Burning Tree men were naked in the locker room. My
father had described the visiting Duke of Windsor, revealed in the locker
room as skinnier than Gandhi, and regular member Clark Clifford, who
stood in front of a mirror in the buff, slowly molding the crimps back
into his damp hair. But I had not imagined that Burning Tree members
were naked from the first tee to the 18th hole—naked under the cherry
blossoms and the red maple leaves. No wonder they so rarely played golf
in the snow.

For weeks I tried to picture Cabinet officers, senators and particularly
Burning Tree's most famous member, President Eisenhower, striding
down the fairways. Did golf bags chafe the senatorial thighs? How careful did Ike have to be when teeing off?

When, a couple of months later, after a Sunday at a River Road farm, my mother stopped to pick up my father at Burning Tree, I scrunched down in the baize back seat of our 1951 Cadillac, head well below window level, so as not to see what I shouldn't.

Maybe I was a particularly credulous little girl—a fourth child who found it politic to believe her elders. But I think now that I fell for this whopper because a man said it. Being a girl in '50s Washington made me unlikely to question a male statement. Directly, anyway. . . .

I THINK being female had a lot to do with my seeing the privileges of Washington social life as a mixed blessing.

As a preteen I got the message from my mother and from the world that the achievements that counted in Washington were men's achievements. Odd small events, like going for square-dancing classes at, incongruously enough, the Cosmos Club, conveyed the lesson. On the way to the cloakroom before do-si-doing with St. Albans and Landon boys, we girls, in ruffled skirts we wouldn't ordinarily be caught dead in, would pass a line of framed photos of those clubmen who had won Pulitzer or Nobel prizes. Though the occasional clubman we saw in the halls came fully clothed, women seemed to stay away from the Cosmos Club.

The most impressive male achievements were political, of course, with the presidency the biggest of all. So at 9 or 10, I tried to get straight which presidents I was supposed to like. Which were the good ones, I asked my mother. She was sitting on the library sofa, a picture of Harry Truman (inscribed "To Constance Casey, a beautiful woman") hanging on the wall near her, and one of FDR over the desk. There she explained that Franklin Roosevelt was something close to God, and that she had slapped the man in the elevator who said, on April 12, 1945, "Thank God that man is dead."

Harry Truman was a nice man in his way, my mother said, but not quite proper. She had been vastly grateful, the night the liquor cabinet key couldn't be found, when Truman had gone to his car to share the case of Wild Turkey from the trunk, but the incident still hadn't put him solidly in her favorable impression column. And Eisenhower was a very nice man, but we couldn't like him as president because he had gone over to the other side.

My brothers had more direct experience with presidents. My brother Joe, four years older than I, remembers his contact with then-General Eisenhower as a religious experience, something like being blessed by the Dalai Lama would be for him today. Joe, an adorable, blond 6-year-old, sat on the general's lap at our house one evening during the period after the war when my father was one of those pleading with Eisenhower to run for president as a Democrat. ("How could I explain it to my Republican friends from Kansas?" the general said, and my father knew he was out of luck.)

My brother John, six years my elder, sat on the Truman lap as well as the Eisenhower lap. He was also photographed at 7 or so, in 1946, leaning against the knees of J. Edgar Hoover at a Miami Beach hotel. "Hoover I didn't like," John remembers. "Eisenhower talked to me. Truman talked to me. Hoover didn't talk."

My sister Jane remembers sitting on no famous laps, ditto my sister Caroline. I sat on Abe Fortas's lap (his suggestion; no chairs left on the terrace) when I was 19.

Though they weren't presidents, only lawyers and lobbyists, the men in the neighborhood around my father's office at 18th and M streets, meeting over shirts in Lewis and Thos. Saltz or strolling in the Mayflower lobby, were obviously the people in charge.

From observing which of my friends' fathers seemed most at ease, I worked out a concept of the best kind of man to be. Six feet tall; neither heavy nor thin; Southern but not too Southern (Virginia and Tennessee were fine, Mississippi and Texas were not fine); a graduate of an Ivy League college and law school or the University of Virginia; not Catholic, not Jewish; the owner of a house in Georgetown or Chevy Chase and a rural second home in the Blue Ridge or Maine or on the Eastern Shore. Having a sailboat didn't hurt.

Some men managed to gain power who didn't fit my mother's standards or mine, who were, in our view, villains. The prime villain lived about ten blocks away in Wesley Heights, one neighborhood over from our Spring Valley house. One night a woman came to our door with a petition against the clause in W. C. and A. N. Miller covenants that barred homeowners from selling any of the Millers' Spring Valley or Wesley Heights pseudo-Georgians or pseudo-Tudors to people of African or Semitic ancestry.

My mother listened with mild approval until the punch line: The originator of the anti-discrimination petition was our distinguished neighbor, Vice President Richard Nixon. Getting ready to turn our ravening dachshund on the woman, my mother said, "I don't care what the petition says; if he's for it, I'm against it."

In my mother's bridge set, it was famous that the terrier of Marie Harriman had thrown up while watching Nixon's Checkers speech.

THE WOMEN'S world had more of an immediate effect on me than the men's, since women spent time with children. Until her forties, when my mother became more at ease with herself (she became president of the

Women's National Democratic Club, then went to George Washington and earned the BA she had started trying for in 1931), she worked harder at developing alliances than on maintaining friendships, a tendency fostered by Washington life. Was it Truman who said it? "If you want a friend in Washington, buy a dog."

At 10, I became friends with a really nice girl (though she went to Holton Arms, not Potomac) named Joanna Sturm. My mother encouraged this alliance, initially forged over a love of horses, in a way that was different from her usual laissez-faire reaction to her children's friendships. Joanna's mother was mysteriously absent, and Joanna lived with her grandmother in an amazingly large house near Dupont Circle.

It turned out that the zebra and tiger skin rugs dotting the slippery floors and the mounted animal heads looming in the dark hallways had been violently acquired by Joanna's great-grandfather, Theodore Roosevelt. Her grandmother was Alice Roosevelt Longworth. I honestly didn't know how much to care about Joanna's presidential forebear, or her imposing grandmother, but the pressure to care was there, so instead I let the friendship dwindle.

Janet Auchincloss, who went to Potomac with me, first grade through ninth, suffered when her friends' parents reacted overapprovingly to invitations to visit her at Merrywood, a place that felt like the setting of a Daphne du Maurier novel. Janet was much happier as an adult, living in Hong Kong, than as a child in Washington.

Her school years didn't get any easier when one agonizing day a French teacher at Potomac, a woman alive to the existence of class distinctions in a way that unhappy private school teachers tend to be, made us spend a class period looking at the *Life* magazine picture story on the marriage of Janet's half-sister Jacqueline Bouvier to Sen. John Kennedy. It was probably better than memorizing the pastoral odes of Joachim du Bellay, but the result was to make us resentful of Janet.

Janet and I once wandered away from a school outing and, on a mutual dare, lapped up a couple of pints apiece of murky water from Pimmit Run. Worried that it might have been 50 percent sewage, as we'd been warned, we confessed, together, to a teacher. The teacher's response was to cry, "Janet, are you all right?" while hustling her off to the infirmary. "Me too," I said, without effect on the departing pair.

It was certainly the case in any town at the time that women—teachers or mothers—made connections through children. But in Washington, such connections led to social events that could shape your fate. Being seen *chez* Longworth or with the president or your home state senator supplied you with added force; perceived connections could lead to a job or another useful invitation.

"Do you write this way because you grew up in Washington?" a friend recently asked. What way? "Cynical," she said. "Maybe not cynical, ironical. With an awareness of three levels of motives, even if there aren't three levels of motives?"

A WOMAN could not, of course, fall into a social event straight from the car pool or the tennis court. To be polished to the correct finish, Washington women spent three hours getting a shampoo and set, manicure and pedicure, at Per or Guilbo. These penultimate hours were preceded by days spent shopping at Julius Garfinckel or Dorcas Hardin or Dorothy Stead—establishments that became de facto women's clubs.

There is a way of dressing that still says Washington to me and brings back memories of sitting on a plush chair watching my mother have an evening dress or a suit fitted. Washington women's suits had to have structure, manners, backbone, character. Three decades later, Barbara Bush is still wearing such suits.

The Washington suit (sometimes this was true too of a dress) was often outlined at cuff or jacket bottom or skirt hem in a band of a different color, frequently black. These suits had well-defined boundaries, suggestive of treaties negotiated. The clothes of women in Washington in the '50s and early '60s did not drift, they had no loose ends. They looked not unlike a Chevy Chase or E. C. and A. N. Miller house, good material crisply defined by a black door and shutters and conservative evergreen foundation planting.

In the early '60s, Guillaume Bosser, whose salon, Guilbo, was at Connecticut Avenue and R Street, gave fashionable Washington women a stiff little sprayed cage of hair whose shape was echoed in a stiff little cage of a dress.

On those occasions for which a woman was supposed to look attractive as well as reputable—a dance, the queen's birthday party at the British Embassy—Washington women ages 15 to 75 struggled unsuccessfully with the balance between pretty and proper and ended up resembling the Mother of the Bride in champagne beige or dusty rose. I retain a vivid image of myself trudging home along 49th Street from the air-conditioned, densely carpeted Spring Valley branch of Julius Garfinckel with the corded handles on the blue-and-white shopping bag digging into my sweaty palm. In the shopping bag is a dress that I know is right but is wrong, a dress that makes me look as though I am married to the secretary of commerce although I am 15 years old.

A woman's house, party site as well as home, also had to be manicured. There were a number of styles in which this could be done.

One friend's mother had a 34th Street drawing room filled with Louis the Somethingth chairs covered in blue-gray silk, a style that has stayed with me as an unachievable ideal. The blinds in her drawing room were always closed, to protect the silk brocade and the mother. Pale and frail, she hated light or noise, especially in the mornings. She was not too frail, however, to grab Bobby Darin by the lapels at the Casino Royale and demand he sign autographs for her daughter and me.

The Francophile brocade stood in contrast to the style I think of as Georgetown Comfortable: authentically child-worn slip-covered sofas, squashed pillows and books heaped on 120-year-old tables. The Georgetown Comfortable mothers I remember as warm, sometimes plump and noisy, at ease enough to stretch the rules.

Many of my friends lived, surrounded by the most subdued and neutral styles, in Chevy Chase Careful. Another lived in a style I think of retrospectively as Kenwood Pompous, which was Chevy Chase Careful with wall-to-wall carpets and fake flowers. There was also Suburban Virginia Expensive Comfortable, which reached its peak in the early '60s with the boom in Ethel Kennedy fauna and flora—dog hair and chintz.

My best friend lived in Fairfax in a house with a less transient style. Her mother's Spartan Southern was characterized by bare polished floors, imposing bureaus with silver-backed brushes and sofas with severe wooden trim on the arms and backs. The heirloom Heriz would be rolled up for the summer, replaced with sisal matting. Air conditioning was tacky, and the family had done fine without it in Richmond; the back door was opened to catch a draft, and sometimes a fan turned.

But the majority of my preteen friends lived in Cleveland Park Messy. It may be hard for people who've bought there recently to conceive of this, but in the late '50s and early '60s, Cleveland Park was bohemian verging on Appalachian, with rusty porch swings, screen doors banging on crippled hinges and sumac filling up the backyard.

In one Cleveland Park house, which I loved for its small front lawn with a parasol-shaped hawthorn tree in the middle, lived a close friend, her bookish sister and father and her determinedly chic mother. For as long as I'd known her, my friend's mother had been yearning to move to Georgetown. Finally, in 1960, she moved her family to P Street, to the sorrow of her bike-riding daughters. The mother was completely vindicated when, during their first Halloween there, the doorbell rang and the small voice saying "trick or treat" was that of Caroline Kennedy.

Georgetown houses were mostly too small for my family to fit into, and all too expensive for my father, whose income could be high one year and nonexistent the next. (One year he was an attorney for Howard

Hughes; the next his clients included a woman who slipped on spilled olive oil at the Safeway.) Temptation thus removed, we stayed firmly in Spring Valley, where the Danish modern living room and library furniture coexisted nervously with sort-of-British sideboards and chests of drawers. The house felt very padded; almost every floor was cushioned with wall-to-wall carpet and almost every window swathed with what you'd have to call drapes rather than curtains. . . .

THERE was a saying that I often heard women, rarely men, repeat when I was growing up: "Washington is full of great men, and the women they married before they became great."

Even the nicer women told mean stories on each other. The mother of one friend found it amusing to tell about evenings at Hickory Hill when Robert Kennedy would invite some top-seeded intellectual to talk to a group of New Frontierites. From the back of the room Ethel Kennedy would often pipe up with a comment. The punchline of this story was a correctly accented rendition of the then-attorney general's response to his wife, which was to yell, "Can it, Ethel!"

It's a truism that most women's lives in the '50s were lived vicariously (my mother's club work was real, though unpaid, but very tied up with being married to a former member of Congress). But the state was more pronounced in Washington, where a man without a title could be a non-person and a woman without a man with a title would be something less. At night, wives waited for their husbands. Together they waited for those substantial cream-colored envelopes from embassies or the State Department or the White House. It would be an exaggeration to say that my mother suffered from a very specific anhedonia—an inability to experience pleasure except when dining at the White House. But not much of an exaggeration.

It was a cure, that White House invitation, that was hard to come by for anyone, and gradually withdrawn from her. She and my father went to the White House frequently in the FDR years (Lady Bird Johnson made an entry in her diary about a White house dinner at which she had the good fortune to sit next to Congressman Casey), but the invitations dwindled after the high point of the Kennedys' Pablo Casals dinner and concert.

As a grown-up, I have a California friend who says Washington selects for parents who are going to pay more attention to invitations from the White House than to their children. He believes that the children of people who need the approval of the Great White Father above and anonymous voters below more than they need the love of individuals must be a neglected bunch. This is obviously too simple; even when I was growing up, there was as large a proportion in Washington of what could be called normal families as you could find in Kansas City or Albany or Philadelphia. And there were many prominent men, elected or appointed or promoted, who were good parents. There were houses, however, in which you felt as though the children were stifled—as if the father, living some grander version of existence, used up more oxygen than anyone else. These were not homes in which the family's hopes were riding on the children.

Sometimes a child's house turned from being a home into something like an ambassador's residence. Many of my friends have, as I do, a memory of jokes, references and hors d'oeuvre trays continually passing above their heads. It's a feeling that children anywhere have—that there are adult jokes you'll never get and references you'll never know the full significance of—but it seems tougher on Washington children, because the jokes, the references, the murmurs seem to matter more.

Three hours before a party there would suddenly be six or seven strangers from Ridgewell's caterers in the house, one or two of them working at the stove where three days ago you had learned to boil an egg. "I've got to be nice to you, but don't get in the way, kid. I've got work to do," their looks said. Which was the same expression you'd get from some of the guests at the party. My first vote was cast for Hubert Humphrey in 1968, but he almost lost it when I remembered the mechanical way he worked our living room, throwing people past him after he'd said "Hiya."

Reading the recent biography of Edward Bennett Williams, I remembered the famous lawyer on the sofa being jolly to us children, but in a bullying way, especially to the boys. Skimming the index, my brother Joe found another Washington lawyer who was often at our house, mentioned briefly as being defended by Williams on a "routine case of bribery." Joe also remembered Averell Harriman snapping at him—Harriman about 65 and Joe about 10—and felt better when he read that Harriman was known to colleagues as "the crocodile." When Joe tried to remember which famous friends of our parents he felt comfortable talking to, the first name he came up with was William Brennan.

My friends and I took a long while to catch on to what these parties were about, and what each other's fathers did for a living. It was hard to know what lawyers, the majority of the fathers, actually spent their work days on, but we slowly came to know which ones were partners in Covington & Burling. The few doctor-fathers were heroes to us because we could understand their jobs.

There was one Georgetown father whom I remember sitting reading, unruffled, as four cats and three daughters pounced around him. When I asked, other parents said his occupation was "import-export." Twenty years later when he fell, jumped or was pushed to his death, I felt a painful jolt over how much I didn't know about him. Yet I now know more than I want to about another friend's father who signed off on the Bay of Pigs invasion, not to mention the failed plot to de-beard Fidel Castro.

PART OF growing up anywhere involves accepting the things your parents foist on you. But in Washington, where there are well-defined Greater Lives and Lesser Lives, parental authority seems to last longer and be harder to resist than in other places.

When friends of mine with parents in power did ordinarily bad adolescent things, their actions had an added edge. The knowledge that their parents' reputation was fragile, vulnerable and crucial to being effective gave extra weight to rebellious acts that might become known.

Sometimes, because of their positions, my friends' parents would urge them to do certain things that were supposed to be wonderful treats but were often not wonderful treats. Such a privilege, unearned and unwanted, was to be a Cherry Blossom princess. One friend forced to wave from the back of the Texas Cherry Blossom Parade car was the teenaged daughter of a Dallas lobbyist who probably hadn't been back to the state for more than a week at a time since his graduation from SMU law school. It was my good fortune to escape this fate. But I couldn't escape the college summer job my father got me in the office of a congressman who referred to Eleanor Roosevelt as a "nigger lover" and told me, at the end of my two months, "I wish I'd known you were such a good typist. I wouldn't have had you waste your time writing speeches."

The worst treat parents imposed on their children, however—worst because it wasn't a one-time event like the Cherry Blossom Festival—was the year-long cycle of coming-out parties and the six years of dancing school that prepared you to know what to do when Lester Lanin began to play "Mountain Greenery" or the cha-cha version of "Hawaiian War Chant."

At Mrs. Shippen's Dancing School (where most of my friends went from sixth grade through junior year in high school) we came in touch with the social world's agents of repression. While the grown-ups were written about and apparently kept in line by the *Washington Post*'s society editor, Hope Ridings Miller (whom I always pictured as an optimistic woman in jodhpurs), Mrs. Lloyd Parker Shippen rode herd on the children. Selected children. A friend from the National Cathedral School, class of '65, told me she was barred from Shippen's because she was Jewish. Her mother called and got the reason, unabashedly delivered, straight from Mrs. Shippen. Two years later, her brother was invited. When the mother asked why her son was less Jewish than her daughter, Mrs. Shippen told her the school needed boys more than girls.

The person who actually taught dancing at Mrs. Shippen's (her one joke: "Every time you hear the word tango, bend your knees") was Miss Reed. But Mrs. Shippen, who stood in the background at Linthicum Hall with an imposing bosom and sagging dress out of the Coolidge administration, was the real power. The subteen male response to being under her control and being trapped in a room with members of the opposite sex was, for those into ordnance, to set off cherry bombs or, for those into psychological warfare, to toss fake throw-up into the girls' cloakroom. The female response was either fearful decorousness or complete paralysis. The reason some of us were paralyzed was that we feared that none of the boys jumping up from their wooden folding chairs would choose us. I can still name, and bless, the few who rescued me from loneliness and humiliation.

When we moved up to deb parties, which were a sort of dancing school with all expenses picked up by the fathers, the arbiter was Mrs. Hetzel. Mrs. Hetzel kept, and I believe sold to deb-party-giving mothers, The List. Someone pointed her out to me at a dance once, a crow-like figure in black, a sort of Madame Defarge, who occasionally came to watch. You could be taken off Mrs. Hetzel's List, our parents warned, and then you would be deceased, socially. Drunkenness or, I presume, pregnancy could get a girl bounced, but it was very rare for a boy to behave so badly that he got taken off. One of the young princes was a perpetually drunk Princeton kid. Though he finally retired the award my brother Joe and his friends gave every deb party night (they called it the Scarlet A), he stayed on The List for a decade.

My brothers went to coming-out parties, drinking some Covington & Burling father's champagne, eating the 2 a.m. omelets, for five or six years. Like most females, I escaped, or was discarded, after one intense year. The June round of dances (which included a quiet tea for me, my parents being emotionally and financially exhausted after the Sulgrave Club ball they'd given my sister Jane) seemed almost logical, if extreme, a celebration of high school graduation. But the other half of The Season—the Christmas series of dances—felt bizarre, since most of us had by then been off to college, where we were expected to behave like adults rather than our parents' representatives at their friends' parties. . . .

HOSTESS work and women's work and mother's work seem to me to have been particularly put down in Washington. I can think of a few happy women then, who were secure in their own qualities, and who loved their husbands. But there were plenty of depressed women, and a lot of wives and mothers who drank heavily. With few exceptions, it would have been unwise for a daughter to want to grow up to be like her mother, even though mothers were the people daughters saw most and loved most.

The solution I evolved at 12 or so was that I would be a loving wife and a wonderful mother to six children, while at the same time so obviously an outstanding human being that an obliging president would appoint me ambassador to the United Nations.

A little later, in my teens, I asked myself, "Well, do I want to be a great man or the woman he married before he became great?" Not easy for me to become a great man; not wise to be the woman he married. The other choice was to be the wicked, though great in her way, woman who's going to break up the first marriage. But I knew that, old wife or new, if I spoke up in a way that got on the nerves of the great man, he would yell the equivalent of, "Can it, Ethel!"

After college I got a job at *Congressional Quarterly*, the first step in becoming not a great man or a first/second wife, but a person with a voice in print. Not long after, I married a scientist, who has stuck with me, his first wife. I support no caterers. My two sons don't go to dancing school. I left Washington behind and I haven't spent the past 36 years brooding about being barred from Burning Tree Club, or worrying that it was those naked men out on the fairways who were really living.

But Burning Tree did come up again a few years ago, the day after my mother's funeral. The five of us, children in our thirties and forties and fifties, were assembled from Oregon and California and Virginia as well as Washington. Sorting through our mother's dresses and hats and gloves, we discovered a cache of Burning Tree caps, yellow high-grade cotton with the distinctive burning fir-tree design on the bill. My mother wore those hats in the seven years between my father's death and hers on her daily walks in Glover-Archbold Park.

Responding to the sudden power given us by possession of these symbols, my brother John suggested that we drive downtown and distribute the hats to the men and women living on benches in Lafayette Park. We laughed. We fell down laughing. But, none of us being in a state that day to execute a brilliant idea, we gave the hats to Goodwill along with her dresses, including the dark red velvet evening gown our mother had worn to the Kennedy White House.

ROBERT G. KAISER

Same Place, Different Frenzy

The Washington Post Magazine (1986)

Bob Kaiser, native Washingtonian and now the associate editor of
The Washington Post, *here provides a boy's perspective of growing
up in Washington in the 1940s and 1950s. His reminiscences of Griffith Stadium brought back for me a time when we cheered on our hapless Senators, whose record was so bad that it led one sportswriter to
quip that Washington was "first in war, first in peace, last in the American League." Actually, in my childhood—1924 and 1925—the
Nats, short for Nationals, as the Senators were sometimes called, won
back-to-back pennants and the World Series in 1925. My identification with the team came later, mainly as a mother of three boys and as
a onetime part owner, although I never quite understood what it was I
owned.*

*Phil loved baseball, and passed that love on to Don. I remember him
coming home from the office one day in 1949 with baseball uniforms
for Lally and Donnie, and being met with a wild reception. He often
went to games in the late 1940s and 1950s, including one with President Truman and one with President Eisenhower and Clark Griffith, the
owner. I know he took Senator Lyndon Johnson to Griffith Stadium at
least once. Mostly he took Donnie to see the Nats, and by 1950, Don
was a huge fan and knew everyone's batting average and pitching
record. Phil once wrote his father that Don "suffers deeply every time
Bucky Harris trades off one of his friends." Bucky Harris was then the
manager of the team, but had earlier, in my childhood, been one of its
stars.*

*We went often to opening-day games—or at least Phil and Don
did—and we were known as such a baseball family that when our
fourth child, Steve, was born in 1952, Herb Elliston, who was then
editor of the* Post, *wrote us to welcome the "new baseball player and
hope for three more to complete the team."*

L YING in sticky sheets under a blanket of hot, humid air, listening to a loud, mechanical "clack-clack-clack" noise in the distance, followed at predictable intervals by female screams—horrific, primal screams, but in me they only evoked jealousy and grins. . . .

Only 35 years later, it is difficult to believe that those are memories of a suburban Washington boyhood and not the exotica of some far-away, long-away dream. The clack-clack-clack was made by a piece of machinery at the top of the third hill of the big roller coaster at Glen Echo Amusement Park; the screams came from passengers who, I knew from experience, were flinging their arms into the air—an act of no real courage, since the safety bar on the seat held you firm—as the old cars dropped like a full water pail down the steep inclines.

I grew up in Washington in the '40s and '50s—only yesterday by any reasonable reading of the calendar, but several epochs ago when measured against the frenetic pace of development in this area and in this country.

Washington and environs have changed so thoroughly in 35 years that if it weren't for the monuments and memorials, a native of my age could fairly wonder if one were still in the same place. That Washington had no Beltway and no shopping malls; much of the Mall we did have was cluttered with "temporary" office buildings; there were four daily newspapers, but no really good restaurants—except perhaps the original Hot Shoppes, which grew into the Marriott Corp.

I raised chickens in my back yard in Bethesda—the neighbors were appalled to discover that the zoning rules did not forbid it. When I ran out of chicken feed, my mother and I mounted an expedition to darkest Virginia—a place called Rosslyn, across Key Bridge. Thirty years ago Rosslyn was famous for its Purina feed store and a long row of one-story loan companies and pawnshops (Washington's usury laws drove them to Virginia). I bought my trombone at one of the pawnshops.

Striking as the physical changes have been, though, I suspect this era will be remembered by historians for the social changes it brought, not for the highways and high-rises. The Washington I grew up in was for whites only. It was a southern town in the era of American apartheid—populated with lots of black people, of course, but they seemed to know "their place."

My first home was an apartment in Arlington off the Arlington Ridge Road. I lived there from 1943 to 1949. Some of my earliest memories involve features of the war—taking bacon fat back to the Safeway with my mother ("They make soap out of it for the soldiers," she told me), and coloring the white margarine with a bright orange dye that came with it in a tiny envelope.

My real introduction to the city of Washington and its black residents came on my visits to Griffith Stadium, a magnificent palace of athletic culture at Florida and Georgia avenues N.W., the site of the Howard University Hospital today. This was a marvelous place to watch baseball or football—just 26,000 seats snuggled around a well-kept field, and a few thousand more for Redskins games in the fall when they moved extra bleachers into right field. I can visualize Griffith Stadium almost as precisely as that house I grew up in on Wilson Lane, a mile from Glen Echo.

The stadium was in what seemed to a suburban kid to be a strange and exotic neighborhood. The bakery on Georgia Avenue that's still there often put a wonderful smell in the air, and on Sundays, before a doubleheader or a Redskins game, you could hear gospel music from the storefront churches. Once I remember peeking inside one of those little churches on Georgia Avenue. I saw a crowd of black people in golden robes, their faces glistening with sweat as they thumped out their love for the Lord.

My identification with the Washington Senators was a central part of my identity as a 10- and 11-year-old. I cared deeply about their fate—a virtually permanent source of frustration. But a Senators fan learned important lessons—for example, the discovery that my heroes were simultaneously wonderful, exciting, truly heroic figures, and also mediocre baseball players. My Mickey Vernon, my Eddie Yost, my Gil Coan could never finish in the first division of the old eight-team American league, let alone at the top of it. This was a lesson in life's limits. I hated it, but I learned it.

My love of sports in those years also introduced me to one of life's more tantalizing possibilities, one I met on the sports page of this newspaper under the title "This Morning." It was Shirley Povich's daily column, an essay on the human condition as often as an analysis of some sporting endeavor. It was the first journalism that spoke to me in a direct, personal way, and it made a permanent impression.

Povich brought the race issue home in a way that a white kid could understand. He devoted many columns to a personal crusade against George Preston Marshall, the owner of the Redskins who for years refused to hire any black football players. Those columns still make marvelous reading. In a typical one, Povich wrote about a black halfback, Bob Gaiters of New Mexico State, whom Marshall refused to draft: "[Gaiters] was born ineligible for the Redskins, whose colors are inflexibly burgundy, gold and Caucasian. Gaiters is a Negro."

On another occasion Povich noted that "The Redskins' end zone has frequently been integrated by Negro players, but never their lineup." Marshall eventually succumbed, not to Povich, but to Stewart Udall,

John F. Kennedy's secretary of the interior, who threatened to ban the Redskins from Washington's new, federally owned stadium unless they integrated. That threat brought Bobby Mitchell to town.

My lifeline to the Big World from Wilson Lane in Bethesda was the Cabin John streetcar, an underappreciated urban amenity that was allowed to die prematurely. For 17 cents originally, if memory serves, and 21 or 22 cents later, we could ride the streetcar all the way to Union Station, a trip of about 40 minutes along the C & O Canal, through Georgetown and down Pennsylvania Avenue.

Occasionally a few of us would take the streetcar downtown to a movie. I don't think we had anyone's permission to do this, we just did it. The first time was to see a movie called *The Robe*, one of the first Cinemascope color spectaculars, at RKO Keith's on 15th Street. Other times we went to the Capitol and the Palace on F Street—two splendid monuments to the baroque age of movies and vaudeville later destroyed in the name of progress.

The Glen Echo Amusement Park was our neighbor thanks to the same Capitol Transit Co. that owned the streetcar line. Like many American amusement parks of its vintage, it was built by the transit company as a way to generate revenue. All summer long the streetcars disgorged city residents (that is, white city residents) outside the main gate to the park.

For us Glen Echo was a neighborhood amenity. We learned to swim in the pool there, though the polio scare kept us away for a couple of years. We drove dodg'em cars the way some kids mastered their scooters, and I learned the bumps and dips on the roller coaster so well that it eventually lost its kick for me—not that I ever admitted this.

Eerily, Glen Echo is still there; only the rides and stands have been removed. (The Carousel still turns, a forlorn reminder of what used to be.) I've walked around the asphalt more than once as a grown man, remembering moments and people in sharp detail, all the time hearing the girls screaming from the now-gone roller coaster.

In 1959, after four years in Albany, N.Y., I returned to a Washington in the throes of racial integration. Like the Redskins, it was still far from succeeding in abolishing the color lines of my youth.

In the summer of 1960 I sporadically joined picket lines around two of my old haunts: one at Glen Echo, the other at the Hiser Theater on Wisconsin Avenue in Bethesda. Both establishments refused to admit blacks, and a lot of my childhood friends from the Wilson Lane neighborhood had joined a group of black kids to picket them. We had a great time yelling back at passing drivers who shouted obscenities at us. That was the summer John F. Kennedy was nominated for president, and we all felt the '60s in the air, though of course we knew nothing of what was coming at the time.

I was talking about this the other day with David Karro, who moved into the Wilson Lane neighborhood in sixth grade and was one of the leaders of the picketing six years later. We recalled how heroic we all felt at the time, standing up for what was Right—and ultimately contributing to the integration of Glen Echo and to John Hiser's decision to sell his movie theater.

David, now a lawyer with the Postal Service, also told me how it felt in the summer of 1966 when he came back to Washington after four years of college and two years in Ethiopia with the Peace Corps: "I was standing in line at the cashier in the Hot Shoppe, when a young black fellow just cut in front of me. He didn't look around to say excuse me—he acted just like any rude white man. I stood there waiting for him to turn around and look apologetic, but he didn't. And I realized that the situation had really changed."

The image of a young black man sufficiently liberated to cut into a line seems appropriately ambiguous. The Washington I live in today is still divided along racial lines; our dreams on those picket lines in the summer of 1960 are still unrealized. But I take comfort from the thought that your skin color no longer dictates how rude you can be. And it is pleasing to see that the city government that I covered just 17 years ago, when it was still almost totally white, is now run at least as well by blacks.

WARTIME WASHINGTON

WARTIME WASHINGTON

War, a couple of oceans away from Washington, marched through this city every day.

— Bess Furman, *Washington By-Line*

IN EACH of the two world wars of the twentieth century, Washington became a changed place. War had an impact on Washington in ways that were quite different from the way it affected the rest of the country, since in both wars, there is no doubt that Washington was the center of the home-front effort. No other place in the country was as much affected as the nation's capital. (This was true also during the Civil War, a phenomenon brilliantly described in Margaret Leech's Pulitzer Prize–winning *Reveille in Washington*.) Indeed, in both world wars, Washington was, as the WPA book on Washington tells us, "the center not only of an embattled nation but to some extent of an embattled world."

The first year that the United States was in World War I coincided with my parents' first year in Washington. Barred from military service by his color blindness—not to mention that he was forty-two in 1917 and had four children—my father was still anxious to serve. Long before the president who had "kept us out of war" actually declared war, my father had read the telltale signs and knew that the European war would soon be directly touching the United States. In the fall of 1916, he began to liquidate his business, asking his clients to transfer their investments to other firms. Eugene Meyer and Company was accepting no new business.

Overleaf: Wartime crowds—military and civilian, old and young, black and white—waiting for trains at Washington's Union Station. The caption for this photo, which appeared on December 23, 1942, reads: "Bound Home for Christmas. This crowd of civilians and servicemen was typical at Union Station today as thousands packed the terminal to await trains taking them home for the holidays. But lines also reported heavy traffic over all routes, some of which were closed last night because of icy roads. The roads reopened today."

Like many others, my father came to Washington as a dollar-a-year man to help the government with the war effort, especially on the industrial side. Initially, Dad worked on everything from cotton duck and shoe contracts to nonferrous metals to the investigation of aircraft production, at the request of Secretary of War Newton Baker. He also helped form the National War Savings Committee. He then moved from the Advisory Committee of the Council of National Defense to the War Industries Board, which had real power and legal authority to enforce whatever decisions were made. Before that, as Dad once said, "we worked by being right in spite of not having authority."

At first, my father served as a sort of right-hand man to Bernard Baruch, who had taken on a number of jobs for the president, as he did in Washington for decades. What Dad did particularly well was to serve Baruch as a trusted adviser who told him exactly what he thought. Once when Baruch suggested to him that he was awfully sour and grumbling and negative, my father shot back, "Well, you've got a big job here. Everybody is telling you you're a wonder and you're blowing up like a balloon. I'm your only friend because I stick a pin in the balloon every once in a while and let out a little of the gas. When things aren't going so well, I'm not going to tell you they are. I'm going to tell you when they're not." It was an important role, one that isn't filled often enough in Washington. When Dad was later appointed by President Hoover to head the Federal Reserve Board, Bernard Baruch said of him, "If President Hoover had taken a thousand good men and rolled them into one, he could not have chosen an abler man." It was a well-earned accolade.

THROUGHOUT that fall of my parents' first season here, the main talk in the drawing rooms of Washington was of the war. A piece on "War-Time Washington" from *Harper's* magazine reported that

> No one has dinner parties now, but everyone has people in to dine. . . . You go out to dinner only secondarily to amuse yourself (though incidentally you do amuse yourself more than of old). You go out to talk about the war and the day's war news and the night's war scandal. . . .
>
> It is out of the question that any one, even the lightest-minded, should talk of anything else. There are, it is true, dark rumors of an old unregenerate gay set, a relic of ante-bellum days, which still meets to talk nonsense and accomplish folly.

But these reunions, if they do take place, are as secret as the meetings of the early Christians in the catacombs of Rome—though doubtless otherwise far different. No, as—thank God!—it should be, the warp of Washington social existence is the war and, more than that, America's part in it.

People were not just talking about the war, of course; they were doing something about it. Everyone did his part. The White House closed its doors to visitors. Mrs. Woodrow Wilson brought a flock of sheep to the White House and set them loose on the lawn so that the people who normally mowed the lawn could enlist, and also to grow a profitable crop of wool to be used in knitting warm woolens for the American soldiers on the fields of France.

As in the second war, women responded, swelling the city and taking the place of men in traditionally "male" jobs. Many of Washington's women—prominent and otherwise—were deeply involved in various activities on the home front: promoting conservation and the Liberty Loan campaigns, "manning" the canteens, tending to sick and injured soldiers who were returned to Washington for convalescence, helping find places to live for the other "army" of clerks and government employees who flocked to the city to help with the war effort. There was "an epidemic of knitting," someone wrote.

In contrast to so many hardworking women—including Eleanor Roosevelt, who wrote about it in *My Story*—Mother later wrote in her autobiography, *Out of These Roots,* about her own inactivity when it came to war work: "At the time my conscientiousness did not reach beyond my own family circle: I took care of our children, now four in number, settled the various houses we rented in Washington and helped my husband by making our home a center for the social gatherings which in Washington are an extension of the working hours. But I was so engrossed in translating Chinese texts and in writing a book on the philosophy of Chinese art that it never occurred to me to make any active contribution toward the war effort. In plain truth I sat out the First World War."

THE CONGESTION in public and private Washington was well documented—and strongly complained about. The demand for living accommodations exceeded the supply. Spare rooms in private homes were put up for rent. Garages were refitted as places to live and rented out. Profiteering was not uncommon.

Surprisingly for wartime, there were still social events every night and days filled with luncheons and teas and dinners. Although many news articles and books from the period reported on the curtailing of social activities, except for formal state affairs given for official visitors, there didn't seem to be much letup, at least as reflected in the pages of Mother's diary. Quite often my parents were out for lunch, tea, and dinner in the same day.

World War I wrought profound changes in the small "village" Mother had first found in Washington and helped propel Washington onto the world stage. As Marietta Andrews wrote,

> With the World War Washington changed its character forever. No longer the leisurely easygoing provincial town, socially pleasant, in which, incidentally, the seat of Government found itself. In a moment, in the twinkling of an eye, it became the heart of the world, the world counting its every pulsation. All eyes turned to Washington, to the enigmatical idealist in the White House whose every syllable was momentous, whose name was on every tongue in every language and in every land. . . .
>
> Before the World War Washington was a southern town, with quite the provincial atmosphere, though the seat of a great government. Since the war it has become more cosmopolitan, but still is unlike New York, London, Paris, or other big capitals. No one is lost, no one need be snowed under, in Washington. Personality registers quickly, wit meets with prompt response. . . . Thus in increasing numbers winter residents flock to Washington, and Washington makes them welcome and shares with them those opportunities which make our life so full of interest.

World War I was my parents' war. World War II was my generation's, and, like my parents before me, I experienced Washington in wartime firsthand. As Vera Bloom wrote in her Washington memoir, published before World War II was over, "There were really two wartime Washingtons: the one when the rest of the world was already at war, but we were still trying to convince ourselves it was no concern of ours; and the one after Pearl Harbor, when everyone had to realize that it was." In that period before Pearl Harbor, Phil was very much involved, because after his years of clerking for Supreme Court Justices Stanley Reed and Felix Frankfurter were up, he had gone to work, in the summer of 1941, for the Lend-Lease Administration. Lindy Boggs wrote in her memoir that "The Lend-Lease hearings were the most popular events in the capital. . . . As soon as the doors of the hearing room were opened each day, people streamed in to take every seat and listen to the arguments. There was always a long line of those hoping to get in, standing for hours in the hall." Although I was work-ing for the *Post,* writing light editorials, among other things, I was often in that crowd, meeting Phil to listen in at the hearings.

The atmosphere in Washington in this second major war of the century was tension-filled. Especially after Pearl Harbor, there were concerns about the city being attacked. Blackout curtains went up everywhere. There were antiaircraft guns on the roofs of government buildings. Helmeted and armed guards with bayonets were stationed at the Capitol. Public shelters were placed strategically around the city. The night lighting of the monuments, which for so long was a bea-con to visitors to Washington as well as us locals, was turned off for the duration of the war. Worry was constant that Germans would contem-plate suicide raids on Washington. There were persistent concerns about what to do about important historical documents and art trea-sures that were housed and exhibited in Washington, not to mention important people. The Pentagon was under construction and seemed to symbolize the entire war effort.

Once Phil enlisted and went off to war, when I wasn't a camp-follower—moving, when I could, to be with Phil wherever he was sta-tioned—I lived in Washington. Phil and I had rented a small house into which we had moved after we were married, but when he went off to the army, I sublet the house to our friends the Steichens and moved back in with my parents.

Again, the character of Washington changed. Just as was the case with World War I, the city grew, mushrooming into a huge and pulsing place. Everything was crowded, and the pace picked up. As Lindy Boggs wrote, "Washington was full of military men and women, and out-of-work civilians from all over the country poured into the capital in search of government and war-supportive jobs." An article in *Life* magazine in January 1943 reported that "If the war lasts much longer, Washington is going to bust right out of its pants." Bess Furman wrote that after Pearl Harbor, "Washington was bedlam," with eighty thou-sand more federal workers pouring in, and "whole cities of war hous-ing" growing up, and "Life in wartime Washington took on a nightmare quality." The newcomers and their families, many of whom were here only for the duration of the war, contributed to the very problems they also complained about, including overcrowded schools, hospitals, streetcars, and other public services.

Crowded conditions and shortages—in food, meat, sugar, chocolate, gasoline, tires, nylons, shoes—were the rule. Lindy Boggs wrote of a phenomenon that occurred at the Safeway store where she shopped, but it occurred as well at stores all over Washington: "Whenever the Safeway store on Connecticut Avenue near Utah got a delivery of meat, everybody at that end of Washington converged on it. You took a number and waited your turn, and there would always be so many people that you had to wait a long, long time."

Gasoline and food rationing helped bring an end to the Washington social tradition of calling on people every afternoon and having weekly "at-homes." Vera Bloom—who described Washington as being "like a sheltered woman suddenly pushed out into a tough world, who tries to put on the veneer of a ruthless woman to convince people that she can hold her own with the best or the worst of them, but the veneer kept chipping off"—wrote, "The before-the-war quota of four or five teas or cocktail parties a day gave way to what Mrs. Roosevelt approvingly called 'parties with a purpose.'" The war affected even Evalyn Walsh McLean, when her estate, Friendship, became a housing development, and she moved down Wisconsin Avenue to R Street, to, as Bess Furman wrote, "a big house with no more grounds than a city block."

Malcolm Cowley, who reviewed W. M. Kiplinger's book on Washington that appeared in 1942, complained that the book gave a "very subdued and incomplete picture of the city in wartime." Cowley explained this by saying that most of the book had been written in 1941 and that he assumed Kiplinger didn't have time to bring it up-to-date, but he also felt that Kiplinger had "lived in Washington so long that he has apparently forgotten what other cities are like or how strange it seems by comparison." Cowley himself described Washington in wartime as "a combination of Moscow (for overcrowding), Paris (for its trees), Wichita (for its way of thinking), Nome (in the gold rush days) and Hell (for its livability)."

Washington was full of wartime refugees from Europe. My parents sponsored a whole group of children and set up a house for them in the Virginia countryside. The Frankfurters, who never had children of their own, took in three children, and dealt patiently with one drama after another with them.

The Washington Post did its civic duty, led by my father, who had the idea for a show to "bring the army to the public" so that the people could see what their war-bond money was buying and how some of that equipment looked in action. The *Post* organized and underwrote a "Back the Attack Show" that lasted eighteen days and attracted 1,724,000 spectators before it closed, helping Washington exceed its war-bond quota in the process. The show was called "the biggest thing that ever happened in Washington." Spread out over twenty-one acres of the open area at the foot of the Washington Monument, the show was a kind of military world's fair, with exhibits and a seven-thousand-seat arena for showcasing special events, like a jeep jamboree, a concert by a forty-piece band of WACs, a "colored" cavalry troop from nearby Fort Myer, and the actual firing of field artillery guns. Evening shows featured searchlights picking out planes over the Washington Monument and antiaircraft guns flashing fire. Children could climb on a captured Nazi tank.

As was also the case in World War I, Washington was transformed. Whereas many people attribute Washington's growth as a city to the influx of people in World War I, others—David Brinkley, for example—say Washington remained essentially a slow and still southern place until World War II came to town. William White marveled at Washington, and, early in 1943, wrote of it as being the new "commercial, political, and spiritual capital of the world." Liz Carpenter put it more poetically when she wrote that "World War II put lines on the face of Washington."

WORLD WAR I

HARRISON RHODES

War-Time Washington

Harper's (1918)

This piece appeared in Harper's *magazine not quite a year after the United States entered World War I. It's full of colorful on-the-spot reporting that gives a real picture of what Washington must have looked and felt like as it led the attack in a world war—even one being waged thousands of miles away. It contrasts in many ways with another article, "Washington in War Time," from a publication called* The World's Work, *which was published in June 1917, reporting that "Washington in war time is still its usual leisurely self, only now every day looks like Washington's Birthday. The crowds in the hotels and groups of women with badges suggest a convention. The flags everywhere betoken a holiday." That piece went on to report that "except for these manifestations there are few signs of war," noting that one could still walk into the State, War, and Navy Building, state one's business, and go off to see whomever one wanted to see.*

Harrison Rhodes's article chronicles the changes wrought on Washington over the next months as World War I helped propel Washington onto the world stage.

THE ARRIVAL by railway at the nation's capital used to take place in a cloud of eager and smiling blacks, cheerfully called "Red-Caps," who competed for the privilege of carrying your handbag. Under the station's portico numerous willing taxicabs, circling like gray doves, waited to bear you to hotels behind the desks of which suave clerks welcomed you with semi-Southern hospitality. "Other times, other customs!" You tote your own grip now. And while you wait, in the far hope of securing a taxicab, or a part of one, you can make acquaintances and swap stories concerning the incredible difficulties, dangers, and delays of the pilgrimage Washingtonward. It was here recently that two happy youths were encountered who had come back to the station for their suitcases, having, after a four hours' search through twenty-two hotels and boarding-houses, by the grace of God, found a room in a Turkish Bath which they had to share with only three others! Those who actually sleep in bedrooms of their own in Washington hotels seem like a race apart, fabulous, like the gods. Important arrivals often only secure cots in the ladies' parlor or under the telegraph counter, while less great people are glad of a go at the billiard-table when the balls are silent and the lights low.

The congestion in private houses is equally notable. A friend in need is always a friend indeed, but a friend in Washington—Washingtonian hospitality is stretched almost to the breaking point. Exhausted hostesses rush to the peace and quiet of New York for a few days' rest and come back, only to find that in their absence friends have occupied all the spare-rooms, having forced themselves upon defenseless butlers left in charge, who had known them as honored and welcome guests in earlier less aggravated days, and scarcely dared turn them out to sleep in the near-by parks or gutters. There is a story—doubtless untrue—of one woman at bay who is actually having the workmen in to tear down partitions and reduce radically the number of bedrooms in her house. She expresses the fear, however, that her friends will merely convert the enlarged quarters into dormitories and come in even greater numbers. Every American who can must now live at the capital, every one who cannot must constantly visit there. Washington is now the nation's housing problem, its congested district.

There is a feeling in Washington that if the excess tax upon war profits is properly adjusted it will be the real-estate agents of the capital who will bear almost the greatest part. They themselves admit that a month's business now is worth what a decade's was. The crush for houses, furnished or unfurnished, and the prices paid for them, have been astounding. One Washingtonian who had just moved into a charming but modest new residence which cost her $30,000 to build, was sorely tempted by an offer of $15,000 for it for this past winter's season! Prices were not so fantastic last spring; *terque quaterque beati* those who heard the call of the capital in April and closed with the owners then. As winter set in and in a passionate November the whole nation determined to live in Washington, house-hunting became a strenuous game. The forgotten, sleepy, pleasant parts of the town which lie toward the Capitol from the haunts of fashion were invaded. The lovely older city across the ravine was remembered, and "combing Georgetown for houses," as it was technically termed, became a leading outdoor sport—fashionable ladies hunted a home as in other days a fox. And some, touched with hysteria, even spoke of the possibility of living in those unexplored districts northeast and southeast of the Capitol.

Any one having a furnished house to let is strategically in a very strong position, and can demand things of prospective tenants which are not ordinarily considered in these dull transactions. Three young men from Chicago were last autumn taking an apartment from an agreeable woman, who said to them with a light, coquettish laugh, just as the lease was to be signed:

"Of course you understand that I'm to be hostess at all your dinner parties."

They, laughing too, took up the joke.

"Oh, of course," they answered. "Of course."

"But I mean it," she went on. "And it's been put in the lease."

And she did mean it, and they refused to sign and did not get the flat!

If the impression has been given that Washington now consists wholly of people who came there last week to live, this is exactly what is meant. The old Washington and the old Washingtonians now swim like the debris on a spring flood. Some, of course, having let their houses advantageously, have retired on a competence and are gone altogether. But though the others are here still they cannot in this tumult successfully put forth any claim to be aristocracy of the *vieille roche*, for to have had a residence in Washington as far back as May, 1917, is quite enough to give one this spring the feeling and character of an early settler.

The town has jumped in population like a bonanza mining-camp. Even now, though the pace is slackening a bit, the regular increase is five thousand a month. This makes a metropolis fast and provides a "floating population" beside which the famous "floaters" of New York almost sink into insignificance. Washington has never been thought a "theater-town." But this last winter, while the playhouses elsewhere have been sparsely patronized, those of the capital—one almost writes "the metropolis"—have been continuously and profitably filled. The audiences are cosmopolitan and competent. Will the day ever come when they "try it on the dog" in New York before they risk the Washingtonian verdict?

In other ways the capital has become agreeably metropolitan. Just as soon as she felt she could risk it, Washington began to tear up the streets—quite in the New York way. Inhabitants of that provincial seaport who had migrated to the banks of the Potomac may have flattered themselves that this was done so that they should not feel homesick, but it was merely another authentic note in the metropolitan picture. In such a place the housing problem is indeed no joke. There is talk of the Government's building, down by the Potomac, huge barracks to shelter, for

example, fifty thousand young lady stenographers. And equally monstrous accommodation will be required for every kind of helper in the
great governmental machine of war.

Just now Washington is swamped. Its inconveniences and inefficien-
cies are an endless tale. The telephone service is chaotic, sometimes
almost non-existent. The company does not exaggerate when, appealing
for operators by placards in the street-cars, it assures young women that
work in the exchange is a genuine patriotic service to one's country. The
street-cars, contrived with a cruel ingenuity for close-packing, are
crowded in a way that would do credit even to New York's rush hour in
the Subway. The express companies are distracted; goods confided to
them may be considered as put in safe-deposit rather than set in motion.
The battle for food in the hotel restaurants is bitter. The churches are
not absolutely congested yet, but they admit to having been considerably
"sped up" since the war began. Indeed, if proof were needed of the extra
works of righteousness entailed by this new influx, it need only be said
that the usual vast, low wooden tabernacle was put up by the railway station, and Mr. Billy Sunday tried to catch red-handed the vicious as they
arrived. There is no smallest vein or artery of the Washingtonian social
body which has not been stimulated by the arriving hordes. Even the
gentleman who has always wound the White House clocks and many of
the most fashionable clocks in the town says that the number of clocks in
Washington has increased so that his business threatens to overwhelm
him! But there is no need to go on with the list; there is, in Washington,
not enough of anything except incompetent people.

How far are we already from the day when a proud New York servant
in a registry office, besought by a frantic mistress to come to Washington
for the winter, replied, coldly: "I don't know, ma'am, as I should like the
life, not being what I'm used to. Could you tell me, ma'am, is Washington near any large city?"

If on your arrival at the station—that is to say, when you have been a
Washingtonian for not more than five minutes—you should be moved to
complain of the absence of Red-Caps and gray taxis, you will find that
you have said quite the wrong thing. You discover at once that inconveniences are rather a matter of pride in Washington; they prove how the
war has made of Washington a big city at last. You must not abuse the
poor telephone operator because she is the worst in the world—these are
war times and this is the nation's war capital and she is the nation's war
operator.

The deep thing behind this Washington pride in the town's confusion
is the fact that here at least the war is the only thing which is being talked
of, thought of, done. To this condition many of us believe the whole

country must and will come. But meanwhile, Washington is, as it has never been before, the nation's real interest incarnate, the real center, the real beating heart of us. The phrase on everybody's lips is that "America has a real capital at last." Some, who have known the old village of Washington, ask doubtingly whether it will go on being the capital when peace shall have come. But no one denies it that title now. . . .

The country's going to war has, almost paradoxically, accentuated the capital's Americanism. The sense that the country is at last definitely part of the great world has made everything that has to do with the country seem more worthwhile. Young men from the embassies are, of course, the fashion as always—but not all the fashion. Congressmen were never so well thought of, and indeed anyone from any department of the Government is in demand who can give one bit of information, add one line to the great picture of the land at war. Every one is caught in the rising wave of the new patriotism. How antiquated already seems the story of the sweet Philadelphia debutante of only a few years ago who studied French diligently all summer because her family were taking her to Washington for the coming winter and she imagined she "would speak so little English there"!

The passion for "inside information" which has always been Washington's, is now more robust than ever. If at an evening party you see the very silliest and most flirtatious lady present luring a member of the Upper House to some secluded and cozy nook you can be sure that it is only that she may, bending toward him with her very soul in her eyes, say, "Oh, dear Senator, do tell me an interesting secret about the war!"

The secrets that are bandied about every day are not very secret secrets, but they are interesting ones. To catalogue them, even to enumerate them, would be to write the history of the war. Various sorts of governmental activity have their vogue as the months go by. Food conservation was enormously the rage at first, some houses saving, others with a pretty humor attempting to see how many kinds of food could be piled upon one plate so that the three-course dinner could be as wasteful as the old seven-course. Then the housing problem came into fashion, interest in it being probably stimulated by the Government's threat of billeting stenographers and telephone girls upon the private residences of the town. Then for a while the scientific methods by which "defectives" are weeded out of the National Army occupied leisure hours. The examination questions were put of an evening to guests eager to test themselves. As to results—fortunately, no American hostess has ever dared run the risk of weeding defectives out of dinner parties.

To vary things there were, of course, spy stories, high officials found drugged near mysterious telephone wires over which, so the order was, any question on the most secret subject would receive from the War or Navy Departments an immediate and complete reply. From time to time, too, you would be solemnly assured at tea that So-and-so had been shot as a traitor, only to meet him that evening at dinner.

There would be trifling stories, too, of hints and suggestions sent in from people in every nook and corner of the land. Some one tried, for example, to get to the Surgeon-General's ear the interesting story of how a woman in Michigan froze both her ears, but by holding them in corn-meal mush for three days saved them! Not very useful to Pershing on the winter firing-line perhaps! And ludicrous; yet touching, too, when you think that by sending this information to Washington some one somewhere was trying to do his bit.

The gossip of the great enlisted and drafted army as it came in to the capital was endless. It made the picture of war preparations human, humorous, and pathetic by turns. It also gave to people gathered in a well-regulated, sophisticated town like Washington a new sense of the extent of their country and of how the new army was drawn from unknown or forgotten corners of the vast land. One boy from the Florida Everglades was reported to have supposed when he arrived at Norfolk in Virginia that he was already in France, and to have asked eagerly at once to be led against the Germans. Another, a mountain boy from one of those inaccessible valleys of Kentucky or Tennessee, was said to have lived in such remote Arcadian ignorance that when asked who was now the President of the country allowed it might most likely be Mr. Lincoln. It is perhaps permitted one to believe, *lèse majesté*, that a man might fight as well under the one leader as under the other. The boy knew he was American, and was ready for any fighting which that entailed. . . .

And Washington itself when, as winter came, it began to set its house in order, sounded a deep note of shame, abjuration, and a determination at last clear-eyed to be a worthy capital of an embattled nation. You caught again the sense that here by the Potomac, as of old, there throbbed the country's heart. You felt that Washington *was* the country, and was to be roused and brought fully into action as the whole vast land was roused. And you knew, somehow, that as the country slowly shook itself and swore by its memories of Washington and Lincoln and of all the line of great men whose ghosts might be watching their beloved Republic it would win victory against the evil thing that threatened the world, so Washington the city, white in shining coat of war, would lead the attack.

ELLEN MAURY SLAYDEN

The Capital at War

Washington Wife: Journal of Ellen Maury Slayden
from 1897–1919 (1963)

I like Mrs. Slayden very much. She not only seems to have been every-
where at once, but she intelligently and keenly observes everything. The
wife (for fifteen years already by the time they came to Washington) of
newly elected congressional representative James Luther Slayden, she
arrived in Washington in March 1897, from San Antonio, Texas. She
herself had been born in Virginia, which only partially explains her
constant criticism of fellow Virginian Woodrow Wilson—she thought
him "narrow-minded, too much of a Presbyterian, and too much of the
schoolteacher." For the next twenty-two years, the Slaydens divided
their time between Texas and Washington. They left only in March
1919, after Congressman Slayden, thought by Mrs. Slayden (and many
others) to be a victim of the "purge of Wilson of those opposing him,"
had withdrawn from the 1918 congressional race.

This is one of my very favorites of all the books I've looked at for this
project. I marked so much of it for inclusion that it could have taken up
fully a quarter of the chosen material. Luckily, only the last three years
of Ellen Maury Slayden's Washington tenure coincided with my start-
ing date of 1917. That helped me narrow my choices.

Here are a clutch of entries about the war that consumed Washington
during 1917 and 1918, and about the home front here. This should be
ample ammunition to send you to the library for more commentary from
this sensitive, honest, observant, and extraordinary Washington wife.

1917

Members' Gallery, February 3

This morning at breakfast J. asked me to give him a bite of lunch to
take with him—he gets so tired of the House restaurant—so I made him
three sandwiches, and now Stella Callaway and I are eating them while
we wait to hear the President address the joint houses on the German

situation. There is a mob around the doorkeepers and at the elevators, though they bear a placard "No admittance to galleries except by card."

Everybody is tense. This morning I called the Ainsworths to know what they had heard. The General had gone out for the papers, but Mrs. A's voice quivered with tears because the situation "meant war, and we are utterly unprepared, and we will just be annihilated." I had never thought of that, and I hate the idea of being annihilated, but I asked how the Germans would go about it. She said, "Why, just come over in their ships and submarines and do it." It sounds simple enough that way, but I still don't believe that our annihilation will be labeled "Made in Germany."

We have a long time to wait in the gallery, but we owe our good seats and escape from the crowd to J.'s alertness. As soon as he reached the Capitol and heard the news he telephoned that if I wanted to witness a great historic occasion I must "decide instantly"—his favorite phrase with me—and he would come for me in the electric. Of course he was ahead of time, and Stella C. was not ready and says she feels like a ragbag, her new dress covers such a collection of half-adjusted lingerie. It is a wild day, brilliantly clear, with a furious biting gale tearing at signs and shutters, just the weather to put people's nerves on edge.

Later

It was two o'clock before the Senate and the President came in, and I didn't know I was excited until I stood up for their entrance and felt pulses throbbing in all the fingers of my clenched hands. The President never made a better impression. He was almost modest, not dogmatic and schoolmasterish but like a normal man seeking advice and help of other men in a moment of awful responsibility.

But the most gratifying thing to an old observer like myself was the advance in dignity and restraint in the conduct of Congress in the nineteen years since the Spanish War. The quietness, even solemnity today compared with the spread-eagle stuff, the "frantic boast and foolish word" of that time, should fill us with pride and hope for our people. We are aging rapidly. No one looking on now could think that Congress wanted war unless driven to it to maintain our self-respect.

I joined J. on the House floor, and as we stood on the portico helplessly wondering how we could get our little car out of the crush of big machines, Attorney General Gregory and Solicitor General John Davis came up, and J. joyfully accepted their offer to take me home in what Representative Billy Kent calls a gov'ment hack. It was a handsome old-time coupé with two heavy elderly horses, and I enjoyed the clump-clumping of their hoofs, and at my door, the friendly courtesy of the old darky driver made me feel young again—even more than the pretty speeches of my two cavaliers.

J. had to go on to a luncheon at Congress Hall given for W. J. Bryan and expected him to talk about the war situation, but he said there was "something nearer his heart"—imagine it, today!—and held forth on prohibition. J. thinks he is hoping to ride into the presidency on that wave.

March 1

March came in like a lion, but a fluffy white one, with a coat of thick snow, too soft and lovely for the big black headlines of the *Post*—"German Plot to Conquer U.S. with Aid of Japan and Mexico Revealed." . . . We went to market and the prices looked as if we were already at war. Cabbage 12 cents a pound, onions 13 cents, and potatoes $4 a bushel.

The debate in the House on the President's being permitted to arm merchant ships, conduct a war by himself, and have a blank check for his expenses was very lively. The galleries were full, but compared to 1898 there was no excitement. A few speakers tried some warlike flights, but they gradually petered out, and asked to extend their remarks in the *Record*. That repository serves Congress as Hyde Park Corner serves the people of England—a place where they can ease their minds without boring others. Nearly every short speech began, "We do not want war."

History will record how Congress ended with a successful filibuster in the Senate, and I am not the only one glad the President was not given the power he asked for. . . .

The "twelve willful men," as he called the dissenting senators, have been excoriated by the press, burned in effigy in some places, and at a meeting of Navy League capitalists in New York, they cried out "Hang them." Will our people ever reawaken to the good old American belief that disagreeing with a President is not "treason"? Stratagems and spoils influence New York, I think. So much money lent to the Allies. . . .

March 25, 1917

. . . Flag waving becomes more frantic every day. Two years ago people were "just crazy about" the tango and the turkey trot, and now the same class has taken up patriotism. Much of the talk is the merest cant, more still the seething of small minds with the unaccustomed excitement of an idea. Worst of all is the inherited, almost conventional obligation to feel that every citizen of a country with which our country is in a dispute is an "enemy" whom you must traduce, abuse and imagine all manner of evil against.

The town is flaming with flags, very large ones generally on the outer walls of the houses of the "yellow rich" up in this fashionable district. They have spent their time and money largely in Europe and are enjoying the discovery of America just at this exciting crisis but are still not aware that it extends two hundred miles west of Newport.

The clergy, alas! are the worst. With very few exceptions they are war mad. According to them, our God has become tribal, a mere Lord of our far-flung battle line. Christ died only for us and the Entente Allies. The churches are bedizened with flags over the doors, in the vestibule, the chancel, and carried in the processional, and unctuous patriots bow as they pass. . . .

Sunday, April 1

Everyone, myself included, is so bad tempered. There are as many opinions on the war as there are individuals, and each one maintains that his view is the "righteous" one. . . . It was such a lovely morning, the earth appareled in celestial light, the little yellow-green buds making a sunny glow on the elm trees arched over New Hampshire Avenue. . . .

. . . I . . . cannot resist the Capitol when Congress convenes, and Miss Jeannette Rankin, the first Congresswoman, will be sworn in. Members have only one gallery card for these big days. . . .

April 2

Miss Rankin took her seat very prettily, but all other interests were obscured tonight when the President declared before the House and Senate that a state of war existed between us and Germany! I am such a foolish optimist; I never believe such hideous things can happen until I am stunned by the blow. . . .

The chief interest of the morning—even exceeding that in the election of a Speaker, as Clark was a foregone conclusion—was the new Congresswoman. Not more than a year ago men would say when arguing against woman suffrage, "Next thing you'll be wanting women in Congress," as if that was the reductio ad absurdum, and here she was coming in, escorted by an elderly colleague, looking like a mature bride rather than a strong-minded female, and the men were clapping and cheering in the friendliest way. She wore a well-made dark-blue silk and chiffon suit, with open neck, and wide white crepe collar and cuffs; her skirt was a modest walking length, and she walked well and unself-consciously. Her hair is a commonplace brown and arranged in a rather too spreading pompadour shadowing her face. She carried a bouquet of yellow and purple flowers, given her at the suffrage breakfast.

She didn't look to right or left until she reached her seat, far back on the Republican side, but before she could sit down she was surrounded by men shaking hands with her. I rejoiced to see that she met each one with a big-mouthed, frank smile and shook hands cordially and unaffectedly. It would have been sickening if she had smirked or giggled or been coquettish; worse still if she had been masculine and hail-fellowish. She was just a sensible young woman going about her business. When her name was called the House cheered and rose, so that she had to rise and bow twice, which she did with entire self-possession. J. was among the first to speak to her and later volunteered to say that she was not pretty but had an intellectual face and a nice manner.

The etiquette of her position is puzzling. Mrs. Kent and I got ourselves into a tangle of conjecture as to what her legal status would be if she should marry a congressman from another state: could she represent a Montana district, or would she become automatically a citizen of her husband's state?

April 3

... last night for the joint session ... a great crowd in the House, the Cabinet ladies in evening dress as if for a gala occasion, and a Congress earnest and attentive but not "wildly enthusiastic," as the *Post* reports today.

J. took Mrs. Butler, Mary Lloyd Andrews and me to the mass meeting for peace in that awful old barn Convention Hall. It was fine to hear men speak who were inspired by a great moral purpose and with no material or political gain in view. Dr. Jordan spoke without a suggestion of bitterness and made no reference to the mob that broke up his meeting in Baltimore the night before, led, shameful to say, by professors of Johns Hopkins and students of that and other Baltimore educational institutions. I asked him if it was true that John Latane led the mob, and he said in his big, kind way, "The papers said so, but I can't believe it. Why, John Latane is a gentleman and we are both teachers."

The "state of war" message was brought in and read from the platform to a depressing accompaniment of high wind shrieking through the ventilators and rattling the tin roof. When we came out the place was surrounded by soldiers to prevent a repetition of the disgraceful scenes in Baltimore.

When poor old Chaplain Couden began his prayer at the opening of Congress yesterday, we all felt serious and listened reverently until he dropped into politics. When he said, "O Lord, diplomacy has failed us," I said sotto voce to Mrs. Clark that I didn't remember the Lord's ever advising us to put our trust in it. Then we both laughed and missed the rest of the argument. I am constantly realizing the wisdom of Congress in employing blind chaplains who can't see how many are not present or not listening.

This morning there was an advertisement in the *Post* for a gold cigarette case lost by Mrs. Augustus P. Gardner in the gallery of the House yesterday. She is Senator Lodge's daughter, a leading antisuffragist, a violent antipacifist, and an incessant smoker. I believe I would rather have a man's right to vote than his privilege of smoking.

April 15

As usual when there is the most to tell there is the least time in which to tell it, so my notes on the war vote must be very sketchy. I was not present when the actual vote was taken. Mother was not well enough for me to leave, but I knew J. was going to vote in the affirmative. I had not asked him not to; perhaps I should have done it to ease my own conscience, but it would have been a departure from our usual custom and it would have pained him to refuse me. He had said for some time that voting for or against the war was unimportant; the war was an accomplished fact, the President had plunged us into it long ago, and the only thing we could do now was to work to finish it as decently and promptly as possible. Voting against it was a fine gesture but left a member helpless to do any good afterwards. But my antiwar sisters gave me some evil moments during the next few days. A few of the unmarried ones held me personally responsible for J.'s vote, not knowing, dear things, that husbands sometimes have opinions of their own with which a wise wife intermeddleth not. Emily Green Balch got so bitter in her expression of disappointment about J. that it would have been embarrassing if dear old Dr. Jordan, whose right hand always carries gentle peace, had not joined in with, "I was sorry, too, that Slayden didn't vote with us, but he could not afford to lose all his usefulness in Congress."

J. says the stories of Miss Rankin's weeping and hysterics when she cast her vote are almost entirely apocryphal. He was quite near her and spoke to her immediately afterwards—he likes her very much. He said there was a sob in her voice—there were many men quite as much moved—but she made none of the heroic or sentimental speeches attributed to her. She simply said, "I love my country, but I cannot vote for war; I vote No." It took a lot of courage and sincerity for her to vote as she did. Her brother and many political friends had been arguing with her for hours to make her vote the other way.

May 5

. . . Our excitement takes every form, but the latest is made logical by the government's frantic extravagance in the cause of war. Economy has become a raging fashion, and the richer you are the more you parade your thrift. We are invited almost daily to meetings at the biggest and most expensive hotels, with names of the biggest and most expensive women engraved on the cards, to discuss city gardening, conservation of food and household economics. Of course you are expected to join a club, send out more engraved cards to a still larger list of the humble poor and get the ball rolling by the time the expensive ladies go to their cottages in Newport and Lenox.

Josephus of the navy* says in his newspaper that Southern people ought to eat corn bread because we know how, and the flour can be sent to Europe. Mrs. Butler observes that it is an excellent time for the Europeans to learn how, and she will eat what she pleases.

Mrs. Charles Hamlin, whose house is one of the most elegant and interesting in town, was led into publishing the menu of a "simple little three-course dinner" to show the rest of us how it could be done without loss of self-respect. The fact that it was given to the Secretary of State was supposed to make it especially daring and impressive. The menu as published was: Cream of oyster soup, filet of beef, fresh asparagus, fresh peas, fresh mushrooms, ice cream and fresh strawberries.

Mrs. Charles Francis Adams told me that she was shown the menu before the dinner came off and suggested that champagne was rather an expensive wine for a "simple dinner," so the wine, whatever it was, was not mentioned.

Dr. Julia Harrison, a scientific housekeeper, very watchful of markets and prices, sends me the following estimate of actual cost of food for the company of eighteen:

> Creamed oysters 2.80
> Fresh peas 7.00
> Mushrooms 2.50
> Asparagus 5.25
> Filet of beef (not cold storage) 22.50
> Cream in form 10.00
> Cakes 2.40
> Strawberries 2.75
> Coffee, bread, and butter 15.00
> Flowers and relishes 70.20

---

*This is Josephus Daniels, Secretary of the Navy, under Wilson. For his own version of events, look at his two-volume *The Wilson Era*. Also not to be missed is his wife's *Recollections of a Cabinet Minister's Wife*.

Mrs. Porter tells me of a "very simple and informal luncheon" for twenty that she went to. There were three courses, all bad, and six men in livery between the front door and the drawing room.

May 12

. . . Another one of those preposterous appeals has come in, this time from the "Patriotic Economy League" urging me to simplify my manner of life to the end that we may have more money to give where money is needed, etc., and recommending "economy and simplicity in dress and a curtailment of purely social activities." They also ask me to sign three pledges to that effect, "for the duration of the war." The names of some of those sponsoring and signing this appeal are of women who, I have no doubt, spend more in a month than J.'s entire salary—Mrs. Medill McCormick, Mrs. William Corcoran Eustis, Mrs. Peter Goelet Genny, etc., etc.

I don't believe in pledges and would feel silly to see my name published in connection with these plutocrats, so I didn't go to the meeting. Of course it may be desirable for them to let their light so shine that other women may see their good works, but I can't imagine myself in such an arrogant role. Someone recalling J.'s magnificent salary of $7,500 a year might be moved to laughter.

July 27

The step from the sublime to the ridiculous is an everyday occurrence. The latest instance is the $6 billion war fund and Mr. Hoover's suggestions of economies to offset it.

When the President summoned Mr. Hoover to come and save his country as food dictator, he came as the conqueror comes. We all stood on tiptoe waiting for Congress to give him authority to announce his system of food conservation which was to revolutionize our housekeeping and make a helpful patriot of every housewife in America—Congress was reviled, because by the law's delay we were going on in wasteful ignorance. At last Mr. Hoover's sense of duty overcame him. He would not wait for authority; he would divulge his system at once, and lo! the mountain brought forth a mouse. We were solemnly admonished to eat more fruit and vegetables and less meat, to use stale bread for toast and sour milk for cooking, and "not to take the fourth meal"—as if any American west or south of the afternoon tea belt ever did take a fourth meal! There was much of "meatless and wheatless days," of not buttering your potatoes in the kitchen, and cutting your bread at the table. For pledging ourselves on cards to do all these things, we can, by sending 10 cents, get a card with the American shield in a wreath of wheat to hang in our windows and show the neighbors that we are patriots; 5 cents will get a button for our lapels, and 85 cents an entire costume to wear while we conserve. I am going to spend my dollar on food and go on wearing my blue apron.

The papers are indulging in such ribald wit as "Use quill pens and save steel for the Allies," "Save your combings to make mattresses for the Serbians," and "Use old envelopes for sanitary drinking cups."

November 26

. . . I have done a little Red Cross work, but can't put my heart in it. There is so much, or maybe I should say there seems so much affectation, waste and sentimentality about it. One morning six of us able-bodied women spent three hours ripping little red crosses from the fronts of coarse yellow cotton nightshirts and sewing them on the pockets six inches away. Then I helped another woman fold them with great care so that the crosses showed and was told that they were now ready for the laundry.

December 15

Sometimes we almost forget the horrors in contemplating the absurdities of war.

Yesterday Mrs. Porter, because of the importunity of friends, went to a fashionable Red Cross resort on Connecticut Avenue and helped to fill little muslin baby socks with 3 dates, 2 walnuts, 1 ginger snap, 6 peanuts, and some popcorn. Once she put in 7 peanuts, and the manager rebuked her. Twenty thousand of them were to be sent to make a happy Christmas for enlisted men in camp. . . .

December 30

The following verses lend themselves to endless variations and are getting as tiresome as a popular song:

> *My Tuesdays are meatless,*
> *My Wednesdays are wheatless,*
> *I'm getting more eatless each day.*
> *My coffee is sweetless,*
> *My bed it is sheetless,*
> *All sent to the Y.M.C.A.*
>
> *The barrooms are treatless,*
> *My home it is heatless,*
> *Each day I grow poorer and wiser.*
> *My socks they are feetless,*
> *My trousers are seatless,*
> *Oh—How I DO HATE THE KAISER.*

1918

January 23

There is no social life. An occasional dinner or debutante's tea only emphasizes the general dullness and gives the superpatriot something to criticize. Mrs. Porter gave one of her beautiful luncheons in December and her heartless extravagance is still commented upon. "But," they whisper, "you know she is pro-German, anyway." This reproach is hurled at anyone who doesn't parade some form of hatred or pray with that blasphemous mountebank, Billy Sunday, "God damn the Germans' stinking hide." I have pious and apparently reasonable friends who go with vast crowds to his tabernacle out near Union Station to hear him every day even in this bitter weather. My good friend Mrs. Lansing has taken the British Ambassador and his wife to hear him, and she set the seal of Administration approval by inviting a hundred people to meet him at her house. Plump Mrs. Daniels comes tumbling after with a morning meeting for him in her drawing room. One of his "prayers" published lately, and not contradicted, I copy to show what the war has brought us to. A congressman who went to the special meeting Sunday held for the U.S. Congress tells J. that it is practically word for word what he said, that he was applauded, and after some antics flopped down and said it over:

> O God, help the man on the ship who aims the cannon to send to hell a submarine every time one sticks its dirty stinking nose above the water. O God, damn Germany and Turkey and all that gang of thieves and cutthroats.
>
> O Lord, I don't want to bless them, and you can go ahead and damn them as soon as you get ready, as far as I am concerned; but, God, don't wait too long.

I wonder what posterity will think of us, calling ourselves "a Christian nation" so unctuously and applauding this sort of thing. And the regular clergy are almost as bad.

March 3

Mr. Wilson is not the only person who resents a difference of opinion on the war question. People I have known here for twenty years and counted as friends—not intimates, of course, but good, everyday friends—I find quite remote in manner; and one family with whom we have exchanged invitations every year I find had a large Christmas party and did not invite us because we were "pacifists." So stupid! They are pleasant people, and we have much in common, and I am vain enough to think they will miss us as much as we do them.

Today's paper announces the resignation of Professor Ellery Stowell from Columbia because Nicholas Murray Butler objects to his views on the international situation. He is the fifth to go for the same reason. Truly they are making our universities "safe for hypocrisy." Even the conservative old University of Virginia has driven a young man out with whips of scorpions for "unpatriotic (that is, pacifist) expressions" reported by the lady principal of a girl's school where he had been invited to make an address. In this line I believe "the female of the species is more deadly than the male." When they have sons at the front I can forgive them anything, but the spinster patriot—and she is ubiquitous—is intolerable.

April 12

This morning there are two inches of hard sleety snow on the ground, icicles on the tiny buds of the trees, and their brown branches outlined with ice. Snow fell yesterday afternoon as steadily as the wind would let it. . . . There will be no cherries, nor much other fruit, this summer. The peaches are killed in the Valley and the Piedmont country too, and I was planning a perfect riot of conservation! Brandy peaches will henceforth, I suppose, be only a tradition of the elders since the prohibitionists boast that they have gotten Washington "bone dry." . . .

April 29

. . . Truly this is a government of professors, by professors, for professors, but perhaps, with the war on, they may have a steadying effect on the purely military minded. . . .

June 2

. . . the social conditions that grow stranger every day have so detached me from the world that I am surprised when anyone calls or I have an invitation. The old arbitrary Washington custom of calling has lapsed entirely, and I lay a wreath on its grave without regret, but it leaves us rather at loose ends. We have evolved no system yet by which to carry on any social life, and it is awkward at times. Another curious thing, not altogether lamentable, is the disappearance of the ultrasmart and noisy rich set in their usual roles of freak dinners, hunt breakfasts, and suppers of which the particulars are told in whispers. It isn't good form for patriots to give parties, and while, no doubt, some are given by stealth, they must lack zest when they cannot be blazoned in the society columns.

The city was never so full of rich people. "Dollar-a-year men, earning fully 99 cts. of it," as the papers say, are everywhere. I am told, too, by a government official who has to sign vouchers, that many of them are drawing expense accounts larger than the incomes they had before they offered themselves to their country. But charity's the thing, and every entertainment must have the excuse of something to sell or to be subscribed to.

The becomingness of the Red Cross costume—which can be worn to all charity functions—as compared to the season's fashions easily explains its popularity. There are two extremes of it, the soft veiled kind, very womanly, and the ultramasculine, overseas cap, tweed coat and boots. I was invited to join some sort of "corps" and was told as a recommendation of it that they had adopted a charming little costume that cost only $85. Early one morning at Rigg's Market I waited at the dairy for a long time behind what seemed a "sort of a bloomin' hermaphrodite," a woman in a long-skirted and belted coat, khaki trousers, leather leggings, and boots planted wide apart. The cap of a Red Cross ambulance driver half covered a crisped coiffure dyed fiery red. When she finally stopped laying down the law to the poor meek old clerk, she turned toward me; her face was chalked and cheeks and lips painted like a clown's, the queerest combination of grenadier and courtesan.

July 3

We have a brand-new devotional exercise established by the clergy and that great spiritual institution, the Chamber of Commerce. It is called the "Noonday Angelus." When the clock strikes twelve everyone is to stop short for two minutes and pray for victory—for the Entente Allies, of course. But suppose some treacherous German or, worse still, "pro-German" seizes the opportunity to pray for the Central Powers. How it will mix things up, and what are we going to do about it? It is all very confusing. Can we pray by the alarm clock, or even by a notice so impressive as the blowing of a siren from the top of the Washington Monument which the Chamber of Commerce hopes to install? I remember a warning against those who "love to pray standing in the corners of the streets that they may be seen of men," but suppose the Angelus should catch you not even at the corner but in the middle of the street with automobiles and streetcars crowding around, and the drivers not stopping to pray? Neither my mind nor body is nimble enough to strike the right attitude and pray for victory under those circumstances.

I have not caught the effect in the street yet, but one day Mrs. Gregg and I were buying some curtains from a sallow, dejected old clerk at Woodward and Lothrop's when he suddenly raised one hand and dropped his head down on the other. We thought he was ill, and in our solicitude for him the two minutes were over before we knew that it was prayer and not vertigo.

The question of food is so absorbing now that market lists for "balanced" meals require as much attention as my engagement book used to. Meatless days have no terrors for me. My family smiles unreproachfully when they have macaroni a l'Italienne, cream of asparagus or black bean soup. This more restrained and sensible eating is the one thing for which I can really thank the war. We are constantly confronted with the poster "Food Will Win the War," so yesterday when I had made, labeled, paraffined and set in a row fifteen glasses of currant jelly, the Kaiser couldn't have felt prouder of the latest grandchild come to perpetuate the Hohenzollerns.

J. is down in Texas fighting for his political life. His opponent, a young man well within the draft age, is running on a platform of flaming patriotism, accusing J. of "disloyalty" and "pacifism." He reiterates, "Mr. Slayden voted reluctantly for the war"—as if any sane man would vote for a war any other way. . . .

July 11

. . . This afternoon I actually went to a tea party Mrs. Radcliffe gave at the Washington Club for a bevy of Michigan war brides and feel refreshed by the change after such long monotony. I told her I knew how Rip Van Winkle would have felt if someone had been good enough to wake him and invite him to a party, and she answered in her quick, pretty way, "But you are Rip van Twinkle and never need to be waked up."

August 22

Anyway the preachers and the Chamber of Commerce have got their siren going, and it is to sound every day at noon to remind us to pray for two minutes "against the Central Powers." Someday maybe we can spare a few minutes to pray against those older and more subtle enemies, pride, vainglory and hypocrisy, but almost at the beginning of the war we declared a moratorium on the Constitution and Christianity.

August 27

An awful thing seems to have happened yesterday. There were huge headlines on the front page of the *Herald*, "Baker Keeps President Waiting Though They Had an Appointment." The paper tells that "three minutes later the Secretary came down the corridor at double quick." Was it Louis XIV or some later autocrat who said to a courtier who arrived only a few minutes before his appointment, "Sir, you almost kept me waiting"? . . .

September 7

The air is fine and snappy today and the streets rather interesting with the sprinkling of foreign soldiers, English, French and Italian. They are picturesque but depressing, because so many are lame, or scarred, and all of them weary eyed. . . .

A great number of our boys have girls hanging onto their arms, tottering on the high, "hourglass" heels of their slippers, their ears elaborately concealed under round, snail-shell coils of hair, and their flesh-colored silk stockings elaborately displayed to the knee. They look so gay and pleased with themselves. Poor children! "Sing while ye may, another day will bring enough of sorrow." Still the President has spoken consolingly lately. He hopes the war will be over by 1920.

September 20

It was a sharp, cold day for the season, glaring sunlight alternating with stormy gray from big clouds rolled by a rough wind, but pouring down every path to the south portico were streams of women, overworked young geniuses that the government had given a holiday to help the Liberty Loan and welcome the foreign soldiers. En route they were practicing their welcome on everything in trousers.

There are said to be 30,000 of these department girls, drawn here from all over the country by McAdoo's advertisements in small papers. None of them, I understand, receives a salary of less than $1,100 but generally more, which must be out of all proportion to the value of their services. Two whom I happen to know were stock girls at my milliner's last year, sorting artificial flowers and delivering boxes at $10 a week. They are now drawing respectively $1,200 and $1,500. They all spend like drunken sailors, buying every sort of finery that the shops afford, a perfect orgy of extravagance. It is preparing a large class of women who, when the war ends and this inflation of wages collapses, will be as discontented as the taxpayers are now. Some church and Y.W. workers tell me that it has already led many of them into grave trouble. Village girls turned loose without guidance or responsibility are led into dangerous places and company every day. Notorious women from other cities have come here and opened "boardinghouses" with appalling results.

October 1

Spanish influenza, a brand-new variety, looms large in the foreign news. As the war tension relaxes, the papers need a new sensation, and everyone is talking about it and creating a mob psychology to help it to do its worst if it gets across the ocean. Of course it could not be as virulent here as in Europe where millions of people are undernourished and nervously exhausted, making them susceptible to any epidemic that comes along. . . .

October 11

It is tiresome to be a prophet without honor even from one's self. A few days ago I set down some sententious views on why Europe was more devastated by influenza than we could be even if it got here. The news day by day is giving me a taste of a tragedy as defined by Huxley— "A perfect theory bowled over by a fact." Since Saturday there have been 7,046 cases reported in the District and a daily average of 50 deaths. In the army already 889 deaths are reported, God knows how many more concealed. The local death list has an added touch of pathos by so many on it being young girl war workers. Poor things! without home or friends, foolishly dressed, and living on trash, inviting death from any illness. Eight, I hear, have been buried in the potter's field because no one knew where they belonged. Sweet little Madame Koo, wife of the Chinese Minister, died of it yesterday. The District Commissioners began their protective and preventive campaign by closing the schools, which are warm and well ventilated. The theaters are left open so the children flock to the movies, which are rarely ventilated and by their very nature can never let the blessed sunshine in. Then the churches were closed and at last, regardless of the President's evening pleasure, the vaudeville theaters. Now they have forbidden the rights of assembly even to passionate patriots longing to subscribe to the Liberty Loan in public.

The powers called a solemn assembly and asked for volunteers, "thousands of them," who would ring people's doorbells at ten o'clock on Sunday and plead the cause of the Loan. They rang ours at four, but J. told the rather swaggering youth that he would subscribe through his home bank and not otherwise.

Our homes are no longer our castles. If it isn't loans, it is housing war workers. No one (but the very rich or those with political influence) may keep an empty room. If you leave your house overnight you are likely to find it full of gum-chewing young women in the morning. The Porters have returned indignantly ten days ahead of their plans and their servants, because their agent wrote that he could not keep the house from being commandeered unless it was occupied. It is all such irritating nonsense and sensationalism, too. What they need is not more room but fewer idle, over-paid people in town.

October 21

My forecast of the epidemic becomes more and more inept. Conditions today might be copied from a history of the plague in the Middle Ages, an average of 1,500 new cases and 95 deaths a day. Nurses and doctors are broken down and dying of it, hospitals overflowing so that many buildings have had to be commandeered for hospital use. Soldiers by hundreds are detailed to dig graves, and the demand for coffins is so much greater than the supply that cemetery chapels are filled with bodies waiting for burial. The suffering and deaths in army camps are frightful.

Mrs. Radcliffe, whose courage and efficiency thrive on difficulty, organized a temporary nursing home for convalescent girls turned out of the overcrowded hospitals before it is safe for them to go back to work or to their horrible lodging houses. Mrs. Porter and I are helping two or three days in the week. It is a horrid job and place, in that unknown country south of the avenue, but gives rare opportunity for the study of war workers. Eight or ten girls at a time are dumped on us several times a day, all sorts and conditions, from illiterate little shop girls to graduates of Smith and Wellesley. A part of my duty is to help them to bed, get their names and home addresses, and, if possible, to induce them to return there. My methods cannot be very persuasive, as I have not yet found one with the least sense of duty to home or parents, nor assigning any reason for coming here, except that she chose to. "Momma 'n' Poppa didn't want me to come." Several have told me that "Momma works awful hard," but there is no response to my suggestion that she could serve her country by helping at home as well as spending $100 or more a month here entirely on herself. In packing their handsome bags I find almost invariably very much filmy silk and lace underwear. When I put a thick outing gown on them they protest, but soon fall asleep. We keep them from three to five days, and feed them on the fat of the land, largely contributed from the homes of Mrs. Radcliffe's friends, but not one of them has offered to give a penny toward the upkeep of the hospital and those who are well enough to be up take a cab to go to their lodging houses for their mail. What is to become of them when the war is over? They love money and have no sense of duty to God or man. . . .

November 7

This date will be marked with the biggest, whitest stone in all history's collection. I cannot realize yet that it means peace—peace to weary millions of men in trench and tent, to tens of millions of women and children all over the world borne down by sorrow and suffering. It is all too big and complicated to understand except that they ceased firing at nine o'clock this morning, they cannot kill any more. . . .

The morning paper said officers to sign the Armistice had left Berlin, but it meant little to me; papers say so many things. About one o'clock Rena and I were sitting in my room in a flood of sunshine. I was piecing up cuptowels from samples of Belgian linen sent to us in the fateful July of 1914. . . . Above the clatter of my sewing machine I heard a steam whistle, and then another, and another, unusual in this part of town. It was one o'clock and Annie came in to announce lunch. Her black face beamed as she asked, "Could they be peace whistles?" Just then the telephone rang, and it was Mrs. Gregg to tell us the news. She has one son in France, another waiting to go, and her voice was quivering. The *Post* had telephoned Mr. Gregg that the Germans had surrendered. Rena and I laughed and cried in a foolish way, and said, "Why aren't we more excited? Oughtn't we to feel differently?" Then the telephone again, and Mrs. James Brown Scott was there to tell us that the surrender was complete; the Germans had walked out into no man's land carrying a white flag and signed the Armistice unconditionally.

Annie was as puzzled as we were at our lack of expression, and asked, "Oughtn't we to put our heads out o' the window and holler, or do something?" Soon we saw people putting out flags, and the newsboys were calling "Extree—War's over" at the top of their voices. Mrs. Gregg came in from the Capitol with a bag of fresh chocolates, to celebrate, and said the people up there were wild, congressmen romping like boys, officers and privates embracing and slapping one another on the back, and the streets so full that the cars were blocked repeatedly. People were carrying flags, shouting and singing, and long lines of young women with hands joined winding in and out of the crowds. . . .

I wish Protestants could learn that lesson of quiet, a part of the peace that passeth understanding. I went into St. Andrew's, almost from a sense of duty, and found the vestibule covered with blood-curdling war posters and the chancel gay with flags. Coming home my old enemy, the crescent moon, peeped at me through the trees, and when I came in there was J. quietly reading the *Star*, which said the news of peace was all a mistake! All the same, I have had my hour of exaltation and am not disturbed because it was a few days ahead of time.

November 11

It has come at last! Since Thursday we have been like those who wait for the morning, and now there is news enough to satisfy the greediest. . . .

This afternoon there was a procession, a village performance with tawdry allegorical floats. We went to the Carnegie Peace Foundation (No. 2 Jackson Place) and had more fun getting through the crowd than in seeing the parade. I watched it from the shaky little balcony, and only the Y.M.C.A. and the Y.W. and the Salvation Army sections got much applause. The President reviewed it from the steps of the Executive Office, quite a new place.

In the balcony party Mrs. D., large, pretty, bland as a rule, said she was provoked with the President for asking us so promptly to begin saving food for our enemies and a friend of hers had said that she "wouldn't save one single lump of sugar for those damned Germans." It is funny how many women now seem pleased with themselves when they use that short and ugly word.

I didn't know when the President made the request until we saw the evening paper. He read the terms of the Armistice to the two Houses, "after his ancient fashion," as he would say, but sprang it on them too late for people to know it outside of the Capitol.

Members' Gallery, December 27

We are waiting to hear the President address the joint Houses before he sails away on his amazing trip to Europe, preparations for which exceed in grandeur those for the Field of the Cloth of Gold or the Queen of Sheba's visit to King Solomon. The apes and peacocks alone are lacking, and there are people unkind enough to say that even they will go along in one form or another. . . .

It is perhaps my last opportunity to be here for a great occasion while J. is still a member, so there is a bit of sentiment in it as well as the intrinsic interest, and I am glad to have my old seat in the front row to the left of the Speaker's section. The criticism of Wilson for going at all, for not informing or consulting the Senate, and for his insolent silence in general has been tremendous, but I feel sure that he will coin a phrase to catch the public taste and fool some more of the people some more of the time.

Later

He came in escorted by senators and representatives, some of whom I knew could have found more congenial tasks. He tripped lightly up the steps, reached over the desk and shook Clark's hand with a fine imitation of cordiality, then turned to the House showing his long teeth in that muscular contraction that passes for a smile.

House and galleries had risen respectfully when he entered, and a few noisy Democrats, like Heflin, added some whooping to the otherwise dignified applause, but we had hardly settled back in our seats before it was evident that something was happening, someone was being disciplined. He began with the war, the platitudes, and "sob stuff" of the last eighteen months, but he lacked his usual amazing grace of expression. Also, he was hoarse.

Some Democrats, not all by any means, seized the first excuse to applaud, and the next and the next, before I realized that the Republicans across the aisles were frozen in their seats. They did not move a finger until praise of our gallant and glorious army and navy compelled a politic approval. Then they stiffened again. It became really funny; their eyes were set in their heads, their bodies rigid. Iris Hawley sat next to me and I asked her, "Haven't you Republicans got any hands?" "Not for today," she said with a twinkle.

The President began to feel it. He stumbled a bit, coughed, hesitated, and even seemed in want of a word now and then. I made a mental note of "devastate" which I had not heard him use before. He spoke as usual of "disservice" but forgot the bland sweetness of "ancient counsel," generally used on these befooling occasions. Perhaps the icy stare of the Senate, with which he had failed to take either ancient or modern counsel, froze that pet phrase on his lips.

When with a slight change of voice he began with the phrase, "May I not"—which like Roosevelt's "dee-lighted" has become a joke—there was a faint ripple over the company and a look of expectancy. Everyone thought the time had come for him to tell why he was going abroad, but we were treated to more abstractions and even fewer facts. His presence was "ardently desired by all the Allied countries," though he didn't divulge the form of their importunities. He felt it his "duty" to go, and he felt sure of being "followed by the prayers and good wishes of a united country"; he would come home as soon as consistent with duty and with the demands being made for his counsel and the elucidation of his Fourteen Points "already accepted as the basis of peace settlements." It became almost a plea for sympathy as the coldness of the audience was made more manifest. At last he stopped. There was polite applause; he was escorted out, and everyone looked at his neighbor as if to say, "We know no more than we did before." There had been a rumor that he would be interrupted by some straight questions from "certain willful men," but no gathering of the legislators was ever conducted with more decency and order.

A Topsy-Turvy Capital

Presidents and Pies (1920)

Mrs. Anderson's book Presidents and Pies *deals essentially with life in Washington from 1897 to 1919, only a few years overlapping with those we're concerned with here—but how could I possibly leave out a book with this title? She says in her foreword that "twenty years in Washington, with its statesmen and diplomats, with its people from all over the world, with its wars and its crises, ought to furnish some underground spring [of material]. . . . I shall send the bucket down and see what is brought up." Her bucket came up full.*

Isabel Weld Perkins—Mrs. Larz Anderson—was the wife of a diplomat who had been chargé d'affaires in Rome, minister to Belgium, and ambassador to Japan. The Andersons spent the season—the winters, that is—here at their elaborate Florentine mansion of a home at 2118 Massachusetts Avenue, described variously as "the center of some of the Capital's most brilliant social gatherings," "the most sumptuous private residence south of New York," and "a veritable palace" (by no less an authority than Frances Parkinson Keyes).

Mrs. Anderson, however, was much more than a glamorous hostess. A biographical sketch, prepared by the Associated Press in 1930, characterized her life as "the kind that youth dreams about and which age so seldom achieves." She was an author who wrote more than twenty books, many of them for children, and she was referred to as the "Good Fairy of American Literature" because of the way she helped other writers. She was also one of the first Americans actively involved in war work, going to France as a nurse for the Red Cross, serving close to the front. She was awarded the Croix de Guerre by France and the Medal of Elizabeth by Belgium for her war service. George Washington University conferred an honorary degree on her in 1918—the first degree given to a woman by the university—both for her writing and her war services.

Here is a woman whose background and social status might have dictated an altogether different response to the public need in a time of crisis—the same woman who gave dinners described as dazzling, going bravely into homes infected by influenza, working at canteens, serving breakfasts and lunches to thousands of men passing through this capital city in the difficult days of wartime, a city that, as Mrs. Anderson wrote, would "never be quite the same again. . . . It makes one sick and dizzy to realize that the old distinguished, delightful Washington has disappeared, never to return."

WE RETURNED to Washington . . . and found that as time went on, conditions had become, if anything, worse. Houses were still full as beehives, with the war workers continuing to stream into town; girls of all sorts—some pretty and some ugly, some ladies and some toughs, some from town and some from country—a river of females that flowed from the offices at four-thirty, spread into every crevice of the city. Numbers of them had little to do but sit idly at desks all day and be paid by the Government; most of their money poured into their landladies' pockets, but what was left apparently went for silk stockings and high-heeled shoes.

Houses were commandeered, and lawsuits to get rid of tenants so that more profitable ones could be put in were an every-day occurrence. People rushed back to Washington from all corners of the earth to save their homes from being taken by the Government. During October you hardly dared leave for a moment, for while you were away a blue sign might be put up, saying that the house had been commandeered. A woman we knew gave her two servants a holiday and went out to luncheon; during her absence the key of her front door was procured and Government agents let themselves in, went all over the place, and put up the signs. Fortunately she could prove that she did war work and expected to have her bedrooms filled in a few days with others in service, so her house was given back to her.

It seemed as if the committee on housing "had it in" for the Northwest part of town, for there were a number of unoccupied dwellings in other sections. Investigators even went to small apartments. Owners returned and put their tenants out; sometimes the tenants refused to be put out. Such a time as there was here could not have been believed possible.

In the twinkling of an eye servants became as extinct as the dodo, and not even fossils remained. Most of them either became war workers or gave up working altogether. Wages for the few that remained, soared. Bolshevism began to appear.

Then there were spies, and stories of spies, to add to the excitement. It was discovered that a very prominent official in Washington employed a butler and his wife who were also in the employ of the German Government. The police went to the house to arrest them, but the mistress begged so hard that they might be allowed to stay through a dinner party she happened to be giving that her request was granted. As a result, of course, both of them escaped and were never found.

On another occasion the secret service men went to the opposite extreme and were overcautious. My husband entered a newspaper office one day with a friend who had charge of a Government department. Some stirring news had just come in and the editor with whom they talked told them all about it. When they came out, L. asked his friend if he wanted to stop and look at the bulletin board where the headlines were just being written down. Being in a hurry, Mr. X. answered rather emphatically, "No, I don't want to read it." When they reached the machine at the curb, two secret service men held him up and demanded what he meant by not wanting to read that news—did he disapprove of what the President had done? Before they would let him go, Mr. X. had to explain who he was, and why he did not want to stop to read the bulletin! . . .

On top of everything else the plague of influenza struck the city. Under ordinary circumstances it would have been bad enough, but with the crowded conditions here it was terrible beyond description.

I attended five funerals in a week, three military ones in a single day at Arlington. And such sad ones—a British army officer, an American naval officer, and a nurse. This last, a beautiful young girl of twenty-one, had been nursing at a camp, her father was fighting in France, and she was an only child. The British officer's funeral was quite pathetic—no family, few friends—buried in a lonely spot in a strange country. At the naval officer's funeral the weeping fiancée made it seem specially heartbreaking. From the cemetery gate the slow procession winding up the hill, with the autumn leaves rustling in the sunshine, the Potomac shining in the distance, and the smoke rising over the city, the tramp of the soldiers, the solemn military music, the black group at the grave, the bugler blowing taps, the firing of the last volley, the solemn words of the minister, the thud of the grave-diggers—and then only a patch of gay flowers left there on the hillside.

The army dispensary, I heard, was swamped with work, so I went down to see if I could help. It was crowded, chiefly by girls from the different Government departments who needed treatment. The woman at the desk wore a white mask. Doctors were examining people in the different rooms. I was asked to attend to the telephone. Messages poured in—"Jenny Andrews, ordnance department; has not been on duty for two days; please have her looked up, as she may be ill." "Daisy Irwin, very ill; quartermaster department; must have immediate attention."

Visiting nurses returned with reports: "Four girls turned out by their landlady, one off on a junket." "Seven girls in a room, each paying forty dollars a month rent; three in a bed, one with pneumonia, no attention." Hospitals all filled, few nurses, few doctors, drugstores mostly sold out; rumors that aspirin had been tampered with by the Germans; wild rumors—four doctors in camp found to be traitors, poisoned sweaters given to the army; poisoned socks I know to be absolutely a fact. So many people died they couldn't be buried; the bodies couldn't be shipped; the simplest funeral cost a fortune.

The dispensary became so crowded that the visiting nurses were transferred to a schoolhouse. Volunteers were called for. People offered their motors and were asked to investigate cases. Those who had had some experience did district nursing, so I offered my services. Such a variety of people and places as I was sent to!

Officer's family, for instance—three ill; the wife met me at the door, said her husband was better, but the two children were still very sick; however, they had been able to get a doctor and a nurse, so I gave them the telephone number in case another nurse was needed, and left.

The next house on my list was full of war workers, all more or less ill, and one girl dying. Two other girls were sleeping in the same room, as they had nowhere else to go. I made up her bed, bathed her, and combed her hair, got a hot-water bottle and the medicines, and went into the kitchen and warmed some milk for her. The doctor was there and said he would return later, and a fellow worker promised to stay with her. The landlady was kind and doing everything she could. I wrote down my report, "Nurse needed daily." They had not had one before, and begged me to stay, but unfortunately I could not.

My third address turned out to be a hovel, a colored shack in the slums of Washington, but there was crape on the door, so I went on, this time to a house in the fashionable quarter, but I did not stop there either, for the patient was a rich girl war worker who was well taken care of. Orders were not to stop unless absolutely necessary—the nurses had so many to visit, they were not even expected to clean up, but I always tried to do that.

Another address took me to the outskirts of the town—a small corner store behind which I found a filthy room with dirty linen all about, occupied by an emaciated woman who looked as if she had consumption. In the other room, the kitchen, her husband was ill in bed with double pneumonia. As usual, I took the pulse, temperature and respiration, then proceeded to clean up the two rooms, gathering up all the dirty linen and putting it on the porch, sweeping out the rooms and washing the dishes. There was only one clean sheet left in the house, and not enough bed-clothes. A sixteen-year-old girl, the daughter, who looked rather like a defective, came in, and a child with a bad cough; the family was apparently poor white trash. They were all too ill to think or talk very much, but had had a doctor, though no nurse. I cooked up something for them to eat, and went on.

My next card read "urgent." I ran into what might have been a boarding-house, near the Capitol. No one answered my ring, but that was not unusual. I called, but got no answer. The house seemed empty. Thinking I heard a sound inside, I opened the door and went in. Upstairs I found a sitting-room, very dirty, and filled with bottles, glasses, and cigar ashes. I wondered what kind of a place it could be. A bedroom opened from it, and in bed there lay a pretty young girl very ill with influenza. She told me that she had only been in town a couple of days, and that her landlady worked in a Government office, so that she was out. Like most of the newcomers, this girl was short of everything but flimsy lingerie and silk stockings. I thought the landlady was probably disreputable, and was getting quite excited about it, when she came in and to my surprise I found her a very nice Southern woman who promised to do everything for the girl. So I knew she was at least all right for the night. What the doctor decided next day I never heard. . . .

I was reporting at headquarters when a man came in and said two brothers, friends of his, were dangerously ill. The matron asked me to go at once with him to the house where they lived. I found one patient quite out of his head and the other dying. An old woman was taking care of them very inadequately. While I was there the doctor arrived and declared they would both die. It was too late to send them to a hospital, even if he could get them in, which was almost an impossibility. I bathed them and put clean sheets on the bed. The man who was delirious insisted on my showing him his new derby hat, which he never had a chance to wear, poor fellow. It was in this place that I first put on a mask, for they had the influenza very virulently.

Some of the cases, even in their desperation, had a grotesque side. A nurse on arriving at a lodging-house was greeted by the landlady, with a torrent of oaths. She said all the people there were sick, and no help of any kind could she get—why hadn't the nurse appeared before?

The girl tried to explain that there were so many ill that it had been impossible for her to arrive sooner, ending, "I have been extremely busy."

"Busy?" cried the woman, "busy?" She pointed through the window. "Do you see that funeral just leaving for the cemetery? Well, I am so busy I can't go to my own husband's funeral!"

WORLD WAR II

MARQUIS CHILDS

Washington Is a State of Mind

I Write from Washington (1942)

Mark Childs was a journalist who became a kind of expert on national politics. He worked first for the United Press and then became a feature writer for the St. Louis Post-Dispatch *in 1926, coming to Washington at the beginning of the Roosevelt era to work in the paper's capital bureau. Eventually, he started a column, "Washington Calling," which was also the title for a novel he wrote about the city. He received the Pulitzer Prize for distinguished commentary in 1970, the first ever given in that category.*

I also remember him as one of the first journalists to go on the lecture circuit, but he did seem to have something to say.

I think I first met Mark in the early 1940s, maybe in 1943, when he wrote a long article about my father, "Squire of Washington," for the Saturday Evening Post. *We got reacquainted later, when he married one of my friends from my college days, Jane Neylan McBaine.*

There are lots of inside stories in this book from a reporter who covered the New Deal and the transition to the war. It essentially focuses on the decade from about 1932 to 1942. Childs called himself an outlander, a Middle Westerner, with all of the attendant biases—"I have a deep suspicion of big government and big business. I have never been able to see how we could have a democracy if all the orders came from a few men in one city on the Eastern seaboard, whether that city was Washington or New York." Here is writing that could only have come from someone in the know.

THE LINE extended out into the street. These were girls reporting for work for the first time with their brand new Civil Service rating. Another line was the appointment line, run of the mine visitors. Around the desk marked "Congressional, Diplomatic, and Press" were men waiting to be identified before they could be given a badge, a pass, and an escort. The ceaseless milling of people back and forth goes on all day long every day, watched over by guards in uniform and enlisted men. This is the lobby of the Munitions building on Constitution Avenue where the tide of war flows strongest.

It is hard to believe it is the same place. Three years ago, two years ago, you stepped into a somnolent quiet, a deserted lobby with possibly an attendant who may have glanced up idly as you passed. You poked up the stairs past the portrait of Henry Stimson in his first tour as Secretary of War back in 1913; past other earlier secretaries in great, dusty gold frames. You strolled down the corridor and whether it was the head of G-2 or the secretary of war or the chief of staff you wanted to see, you usually found him in and willing enough to see you. That was peace, the long-disused apparatus of war that seemed as musty and as dim as the old secretaries looking down out of their faded gilt frames.

It has been the history of Washington from the beginning. The past is forever being caught up with by the violent present. Just when the capital is pleasantly arranged, as a monument, a museum, the theater of a debating society, then some cataclysmic event sweeps in with the force of a tornado and the pattern is forever upset. Each time it has happened, in each war.

The New Deal was some preparation for this upheaval. It was a kind of war. Thousands of new people, people utterly new to Washington, came in its wake. They began the crowding and the pushing, the bursting at the seams. Often they seemed, to the settled inhabitants, like noisy visitors who had suddenly burst into a shrine. They were irreverent, impatient, indifferent to the past.

Yet before the crisis of the war, the city had begun to absorb them. The crest of the wave had been spent. A process of crystallization had begun. This was to be no more than another tidal mark in the history of the capital. The flood would subside or, rather, it would become a part of the vast, subterranean stream of government.

In 1937 and 1938 the New Deal was being brushed and tidied up toward such a peaceful future. Physically, too, the loose ends were being snipped off and the place readied up. Across Constitution Avenue from the new Department of Labor building were the old green houses of the Department of Agriculture, a shambling line of untidy structures. They were an affront to the view from the tall windows of Madame Perkins's office, an affront to the dull and empty classicism of the new building. And, of course, they were an affront to the handsome plans of the National Capital Park and Planning Commission. Out they went, with not a trace left, and where they had been was a greensward so that the Secretary of Labor could look across an agreeable vista to the white stone temple of the Department of Agriculture.

Then the storm broke and before you could say Franklin Roosevelt a long line of gray Tempos—barracklike two-story buildings—had sprouted where the green houses had been. Plans were out for the duration. Tempos were built almost at the base of the Washington Monument. Great mountains of earth from the excavations were pushed back onto the Mall. This was war again and it had come before the ruins of the last conflict had been quite righted up.

Washington is a vacuum in which opposing pressure groups struggle for power. That struggle is charted, definable. In normal times it is the news out of Washington; a victory for one side, a defeat for the other side. . . .

There was never any fixed battleline. Nor was there any sharp demarcation, as between the forces of evil and the forces of virtue. Farmer, labor, industry, North, South, big business, little business, New Deal, Old Deal—the struggle is on a hundred shifting fronts. And in normal times it is possible to discern a kind of balance, precarious yet actual, that comes out of this conflict in the national arena. Franklin Roosevelt is a master at playing those forces one against the other.

In a time of crisis it is as though the stage lights were lowered. The struggle goes on but in an obscure and uncertain dusk. Something greater, more compelling, the unknown, the immeasurable, has dwarfed the contenders. How far it will go, where it will end, no one can say. Nor what will be the relative position of the opposed forces when the crisis is finally ended.

We who write from Washington day in and day out, the Washington correspondents, those of us who are not tied to any special beat but roam the town with considerable latitude, flatter ourselves that in a normal time we know pretty much what is going on all over the place. And within limits that is true. We have our own lines out here, there, and everywhere. We pool our information. Things rarely happen without some forewarning. We snatch at hints, we read meaning into cryptic intimations. Often we're fooled beyond belief.

But more often we sense the way the wind is shifting. It is a marvelous and fascinating game. Guessing, knowing, being right, you get a satisfaction out of all proportion to the event itself. There was once a correspondent in Washington called Joe Smith. You would tell Joe Smith something that was about to happen or that had just happened and his invariable reply would be, "Aw, I wrote that two weeks ago." Irreverently, behind his back, he was called "I-had-it-two-weeks-ago Joe Smith." He was a melancholy fellow whose only reward in life seemed to be that he did have it two weeks ago, if he did. And I could understand that. Most of us are more modest than Joe Smith, but we get the same compensation out of knowing a month, a week, a day or two, in advance which way the Washington weathervane is going to swing.

In a war there is no knowing, no guessing. The wind out of nowhere blows with overwhelming force. So much is happening that it is possible to know only fragments. Tremendous changes take place and are hardly reflected on the churned-up surface. We are all caught up in it, high and low. In a sense we are prisoners of this immeasurable force, prisoners with one degree of freedom or another.

It is the tenant of the White House who is most narrowly confined. At a little after nine-thirty each morning he is wheeled along the glass-enclosed walk from the house to the offices and from then on until five-thirty he is at the center of the vortex. Each word that he speaks is weighed and measured and its impact is reflected in circles that widen to the horizon's edge. And five-thirty is no release. This man, this President, is tied to telephones that are the nerve ends of a world-wide intelligence system. He must be there when they ring, for his is the final word.

Outwardly his manner is unchanged. To the world he still shows a blithe spirit; the smile, the cigarette holder cocked at an assured angle, the firm touch with doubters and dissenters. If the yoke that he labors under has galled, he does not allow outsiders to see it. His life is today far less public than it once was. This prisoner of war must be safeguarded as never before. The people who want to see him are filtered through a finer screen.

While the tenant is unchanged, the White House in his tenancy has undergone a transformation. It has lost the look of a leisurely country house deposited by some chance whim in the midst of a city. Under the burgeoning of the New Deal the cramped executive offices were expanded to sizable proportions with rooms for a fairly large staff. Now, on the opposite side, another and larger office building has been built.

It is the measure of a decade of extraordinary change. No longer is it a house that happens to have a small office attached to it. Rather, it has become a residence set down between two offices.

When you went there for parties in the past, you entered through the East carriage entrance, where the new offices now are. You went into a glass-enclosed area where there were rows upon rows of coat racks and then on into what is the basement. Here were vague rooms filled with odd, disused-looking furniture out of the President Hayes and the President Garfield eras. They had an attic quality, these rooms, stuffed with things that had a sentimental value and could not be thrown away, but

which nevertheless were no longer good enough for the formal apartments above-stairs. They summed up a great deal of Washington, those
rooms out of the conglomerate past; rooms full of crotchets of history
that had somehow escaped the auctioneer.

This new war is sweeping out many relics. Yet surviving each such
upheaval are strata out of the remote past. Washington is a vast geologi-
cal sink in which nothing ever wholly vanishes. Layer on layer these
strata are deposited—the monuments, the odd, irrelevant statesmen
immortalized in bronze or stone, yes, and the people and prejudices, too,
going a long way back into the past.

Even in the midst of this, the newest and greatest upheaval, you step
into a garden in Georgetown that is just as it has been for a hundred years
or more. The box hedges are higher but they give off in the heat of summer the same agreeable smell. The stones in the garden paths are worn a
little smoother. But essentially nothing is changed and that goes, often,
for the people in the gardens and the furniture of their minds; late Louis
Seize or, possibly, a tidy Biedemeier.

Likewise in government the geologic layers overlap. A boring, even a
superficial boring, will bring up bureaucrats and functionaries out of
other epochs who are going through their appointed rounds with a firm
determination to ignore the present. Fussy little men go on making
familiar motions, repeating rituals of government as though in so doing
they could exorcise the awful threat of change.

And in Washington you have, too, the same social strata that you have
in any other prosperous city of similar size. In large, comfortable houses
in Chevy Chase and Spring Valley are lawyers and lobbyists who have
cherished for Roosevelt the same hatred as their counterparts in Cleveland and Detroit and Los Angeles. They have grown richer on the New
Deal, unraveling new threads of government for wealthy clients; but
their conversation in club locker rooms is identical with the conversation
in all club locker rooms. And their wives say the same things over salad
luncheons, with, if anything, an extra dash of resentment that may come
out of inconveniences they have suffered in overcrowded Washington.

The surface of the city is hard, impervious. So much of the life that
flows through it is obscured by the sterile, classical face that is turned to
the world. Yet it is there, and close to the surface, with all the contrasts of
dark and light of an ordinary city.

In the spring and in the fall an old Negro woman sits on the steps of
the Riggs bank at the corner of Pennsylvania Avenue and Fifteenth
Street, a short block from the White House. Beside her she has some vio-
lets if it is spring, a few sprays of holly or some small tight bunches of
partridge berry in the fall. She never seems to make any effort to sell

these wares. It is as though she had brought them along for her own quiet enjoyment. She sits in the sun looking with peaceful indifference at the hard gray stone façade of the Treasury across the street while the furious world streams noisily past. I have come to look for her there with the change of the seasons and to think of her as the other face of the city; the dark noisome slums that are so well hidden you never see them unless you go looking for them; the people, patient and submissive or darkly resentful, who come out of these warrens.

Across from the White House is Lafayette Square which was once a pleasant, informal little park with crushed gravel paths, a pleasant overgrowth of shrubbery, and Andrew Jackson on a horse in the middle of it. The New Deal changed all that. Walks, boulevard wide, were run through and new trees set out in checkerboard patterns. Gone was the air of bosky quiet. Yet in the two years that have intervened the green has grown up again. The big horse chestnuts survived the cataclysm and so did the flocks of pigeons and so did a rumpled, stained, old man who sits on a bench and feeds the birds.

The city is unregenerate, chock full of reminders of other times in spite of the high wind that blows periodically down the avenue. So many reveilles have sounded, and now this one has shattered the heavy air of the Potomac basin, louder and more compelling than any in the past.

The Main Gate

Washington Broadcast (1944)

I'm not sure why I liked this book, but I think it had a lot to do with the author's—whoever the Man at the Microphone is—breezy approach to the serious business of Washington at war. For me, he sort of made it all immediate again. What he chose to comment on and describe was just what I was interested in remembering. In fact, the whole book reminded me vividly of what life was like here in the capital in World War II and in the weeks and months leading up to the war. Reading this made me remember the real thing.

I may also have liked the book because it's a real behind-the-scenes look at government offices and agencies and people we knew and with whom Phil worked, men who devoted their days to preparing for war and then fighting it—even if it was from behind desks in Washington.

I have no idea why this author chose to remain anonymous, but his account of the pace of events in wartime Washington and "its ever-shifting scene" are dramatic renderings of events in "Washington, D.C., the most important political radio date line in the world, the wartime capital and nerve center of the United States, the Western Hemisphere, and the United Nations."

WASHINGTON IS an idea. Like Time and Space in the lexicon of the mystic physicist, it changes constantly yet ever remains the same. It is all things to all people. You see it—and then you don't. Two weeks ago it was Franklin Delano Roosevelt. Four days ago it was Harold L. Ickes. Yesterday it was Clare Boothe Luce. Today at three in the afternoon it is a mixture of British, Dutch, Norwegian, and Turkish missions arguing postwar plans. Tomorrow it may be a scandal in the WAC or a dowager duchess in a night-club imbroglio.

Washington is an idea. Brilliant like a Fourth of July fete and colorless like Secretary of Agriculture Wickard. Liquid as a scotch and soda, solid as the monument on the Mall skirting the Potomac River. Lovely as the neighboring Shenandoah Valley, repugnant as the excrement of the star-lings that hover about the Treasury Department roof. Calm, forensic, wise, naïve: Washington is a little of this, a little of that, a little of any-thing else you might mention.

As an architect's city it has physical charm. As the celestial dream of L'Enfant it is several kinds of flop. The Frenchman gave it only the palace, the assembly rooms, and the locations where the idle can find diversion. More time is wasted in Washington than in any other city of the United States. More useless conversation helps to steam the always humid atmosphere of the capital than any statistician could possibly compute in figures. More money is spent, more careers are made and smashed, more lovely women are on the loose, more shortages are man-ufactured, more out-of-town men are in Washington every weekend when they are supposed to be in Detroit, Cleveland, and St. Louis, more crises are created and never amount to a damn! Washington is not only an idea, it is the great *more* idea! And the war has made it more so!

Wartime Washington is a bewildering bedlam with the palace in the dead center. It has its supergalaxy of stars, dazzling in the dark, and its minor firmament of pseudoglamorous starlets, presiding at the cosmic political canteens. The palace that M. L'Enfant envisioned is a sturdy white mansion facing the Potomac River, where Franklin Delano Roo-sevelt has lived in tumult and shouting since 1933. In this harrowing house, haunted by the ghosts of snorting Andrew Jackson and finicky John Tyler, he moves from one cavernous room to another waving his 12-inch cigarette holder as he thinks out—line by line and word by word—those amazing speeches, directives, executive orders, memos to his myrmidons, and occasional tributes to the American press; pausing, now and anon, to shuffle his ABC blocks and create a new kindergarten agency; turning anon to Harry Hopkins to hear the familiar words, "That's right, Chief," to which he has become accustomed since death cut off Louis McHenry Howe's equally familiar and oft-repeated com-ment, "No!" with the accent on the exclamation point.

Mr. Roosevelt, as President of the nation and Commander in Chief of its armed forces, is naturally our number-one man, and especially so among all those who reside in the sturdy white palace.

Mr. Roosevelt has charm—with a smiling, illuminated C. He has genius, but according to some it is with an out-of-focus G. Likewise, his arrogance is sometimes with a swaggering A, just as at times it would appear that he likes to get revenge with a grinning R. He effervesces, but he has temper and he is the thespian, both with a terrible T. He has ego, with the kind of an E that begins the word "election" and rhymes with "me."

Mr. Roosevelt has made so many public appearances during his longer-than-any-presidential-reign in the White House that by now his face, voice, and personality are familiar to every American—at home and abroad. He is indeed a remarkable man, one that Washington, the United States of America, the world at large, history, and the Lord Almighty may have difficulty in classifying. Therefore it is for us to pass hurriedly along and, before turning the lens on the assembly rooms noted by M. L'Enfant—those vast, impressive, and somewhat ornate chambers in either wing of the Capitol, wherein sit the two freely organized bodies that derive their powers directly from the people of the United States—proceed over the city itself for a brief long-shot before directing attention upon the personages of greater and lesser importance that it now contains.

Now for those places that attract the learned and entice the idle; they are adjacently situated to the Capitol in a relationship that frequently so confuses the public mind that Alabamans, Kansans, and Oregonians, upon arriving in the city for the first time, never can be quite sure which is which. Often, in ignorance and blinking dismay, these worthy visitors sit in the Mayflower Hotel lobby waiting for Speaker Sam Rayburn to mount the clerk's desk and summon the House to session at high noon. At other times they enter the Supreme Court Building expecting to engage a table or two and dance to the strains of Tommy Dorsey's schizophrenic rhythms. But M. L'Enfant cannot be compelled to stand ghostly trial for such innocent errors. The chaos that passes for decorum is at fault.

No city in the world has come to grips with cockeyed change so often in the last three decades as has Washington. It ballooned itself, in 1917, from a sleepy Southern municipality into a bureaucratic Pikes Peak. Between 1918 and 1932 it tried to hit a stride by walking on stilts. In 1933 it became volcanic, put on ponderous weight, lost much of its charm, abandoned the Pikes Peak stature for that of Mount Everest, and suffered invasion by an army of lotus-eaters.

Washington became a New Deal idea.

In the summer of 1943 Ringling Brothers–Barnum and Bailey's Circus played Washington for six days instead of the usual two days of previous years. It took that long for the famous traveling troupe to make its presence known in competition with what capital taxi drivers call "the greatest goddamn insane asylum of the universe."

Housing is a colossal headache. War workers pay exorbitant rents for shabby quarters, live as many as four in a cubicle, and wait as long as ten days to win the use of an antiquated boardinghouse bathroom. Transportation is a Poe-esque fantasy, reminding one of a maelstrom. The bus schedules are unrelated, and the rolling stock is so limited that the time losses are astronomical. Food prices go spiraling heavenward. Restaurants cannot service the crowds, and even the servicemen do battle for an egg. Laundry service is on a staggered basis, with most of the companies reserving dry-cleaning facilities for army and navy uniforms. Office space is ungettable except for the New Deal, whose expanding dynamics, like those of National Socialism, require an ever-increasing staff of clerical dawdlers who must be provided with thousands of square feet of floor space for conferring on policy, designing questionnaires, planning departmental tennis matches, wrecking typewriters, stuffing file cabinets with dead documents, and coming to herd each fortnight for a vicious grab at the Treasury's general fund.

No one can say with exactitude how many persons are attached to the Federal Government pay roll at any one time in wartime Washington, as the number changes daily. One week the War Department tells a House investigating committee that 100,000 employees are to be dropped; the following week the department announces that 200,000 will be hired. Merit or job aptitude apparently plays no part in the pay-roll-inflation tactics of the New Deal. It is something new every minute, and the Civil Service Commission is a dead duck.

The city is jammed with thousands of employees—clerical, stenographic, statistical, and legal—who do their shopping on Thursday night each week, swarm continuously into air-conditioned motion-picture theaters, stare and titter and get in the way in the hotel cocktail rooms at the Mayflower, Shoreham, Carlton, Statler, Willard, Raleigh, and Wardman Park hotels.

Most of them were born and lived their youth in small towns and carry with them a raucous naïveté that exposes them.

They are making more money in Washington than they've ever made before and are anxious to emphasize the fact to themselves.

They constantly talk about their jobs, deal in political and interdepartmental rumor and know-it-all war gossip, and always seem amazed at the total when the waiter presents the drinking check.

Paralleling the uncounted throng of civilian United States employees is the mixed crowd of Army, Navy, and Marine Corps officers, Waves, Wacs, Spars, and assorted sailors and soldiers. Of the latter two groups, dozens are constantly in the capital on leave, many of them seeing the "center of the whirlpool" for the first time. English, Canadian, Australian, French, Dutch, and Latin American military and naval officers add the appropriate foreign touch of decor, particularly in the swanky hotels and cafés.

The British Government has missions, commissions, and research and scientific groups permanently stationed in Washington with a mixed military and civilian personnel numbering over five thousand persons.

Against such a kaleidoscopic background the great world figures—who come unexpectedly and leave in the middle of the night—perform in company with the Great White Father and his palace janizaries in a city of nearly a million in population, fifty per cent of which lives under slum conditions.

All roads lead to Washington.

All planes stop over at its new airfield.

All confusion, conflict, contradictions, chaos, and crazy-quilt concoctions are created in this city on the Potomac.

M. L'Enfant's ghost, troubled probably with chronic indigestion, lurks in the shadows of the White House and wonders why he ever took the trouble to make a map.

Churchill Brightens
the First War Christmas

Washington at War (1970)

In light of the great success of David Brinkley's Washington Goes
to War, *few people probably remember any of the earlier books
that focused on Washington at war during World War II, including
Helen Lombard's* While They Fought, Behind the Scenes in
Washington, *1941–1946, published in 1947, and Scott Hart's*
Washington at War, *published in 1970. Hart's book, particularly,
is a well-written account that conveys the drama and intensity of
the time.*

A Washington Post *reporter at the time of Pearl Harbor, and a
longtime Washington resident, Scott Hart later went to work for* Time
*in its Washington bureau. He writes of the "special excitement that
gripped Washington" during the war, the "worries about sabotage of the
Washington Monument [that] forced its closure from 4 to 6 p.m. daily,"
the shutting off of the light in the Capitol dome that "troubled the
spirit" of Washingtonians, of women in war work, of the bedlam and
chaos of this madhouse of a place.*

*One of the loveliest chapters is an early one from which this excerpt
is taken, re-creating Churchill's long visit to Washington just after
Pearl Harbor. Churchill was one of Washington's most frequent wartime
visitors; in fact, Vera Bloom wrote that he "almost rates as a commuter
now." Churchill, of course, had come to Washington many times before
the war.*

*My mother had given a high-powered tea for Mrs. Winston
Churchill and her son, Randolph, in March 1931, according to
Mother's diary entry, Mrs. Churchill had "come to bring the boy home
as he ran away from college to give lectures over here." Among the guests
were four cabinet secretaries and several senators. This was at a time
when Mother wasn't impressed by Churchill himself, as evidenced in
her description of his wife as "very charming but looks harassed. Such*

a husband would worry a woman enough but to have the same kind of
a son is very trying for the staunchest woman."

But it was Churchill's wartime visits that were important. He came
to Washington and stayed always at the White House with his friend
Franklin Roosevelt, as though he were on a private visit and not com-
ing as head of state or prime minister. Alben Barkley wrote in his mem-
oir about what an "energetic guest" Churchill was, "bustling around
everywhere in his dressing gown, and bursting in on the President at
all hours." He wrote about calling the president one day during a
Churchill visit to ask if he "might borrow Mr. Churchill for a little lun-
cheon at the Capitol," to which the president responded with a "whoop
that practically shattered my eardrums, and said: 'For heaven's sakes,
do! Give him a glass of scotch and a good lunch, and, while you're
entertaining him, I will get rid of some desk work.'"

I N THE early afternoon of December 24, 1941—seventeen days after
Pearl Harbor—some 20,000 Washington men and women put aside
their last-minute Christmas shopping and little happinesses at home
to go to the White House for the twentieth lighting of the National
Christmas Tree. En route, they looked from streetcars, buses, and automobiles at store windows filled with fineries brightened by the colored
lights and tinsel. Those walking along the crowded streets saw the clear
sky and the sun slanting into the southwest and the Virginia uplands.

The people were edgy, and the kind of mood that bright sunshine
scarcely lifts and the white of snow deepens cut below the spell of Christmas. By now, that damnable but necessary war overshadowed everything.
They would see the tree (and the power of the Federal Government
would make it beautiful to the last green stem and colored bulb) and they
would see the President again and hear his familiar voice. He would talk,
as always, on the upbeat—if conditions had been bad, and if conditions
were worsening, all would yet be right in the end. He was a personality
cut to a pattern, and it was easy to guess what he would say. It would be
another Christmas Eve beside the tree—though this was the first time it
had been placed on the South Lawn of the White House. (In other years,
the tree had gleamed on the Ellipse south of the mansion grounds, or
even farther to the east in Sherman Square.)

But now, more compelling than Christmas and more powerful than
danger, deprivation, and death itself, was Winston Churchill, Britain's
Prime Minister, who seemed from his pictures like a bulldog in human
form, combat-ready, eager to confront the impossible, restive, tough, and

demanding that all of life be as unyielding as he. The people would see him and wonder whether such a personality could suddenly, by the mere motion of standing near a Christmas tree on a late afternoon, soften to the point of yielding to the power of a spiritual day.

(Around this time of day in Washington, night was down on the Kentish coast of England. The houses were dark. Children stood in the dark and sang carols, and some of them trembled when the German long-range artillery shells burst over the white cliffs of Dover. Far away from where the lonely voices trailed through the night the bells of Bethlehem rang.)

At 4:05 p.m., the southwest and southeast gates of the White House South Lawn were opened. Crisp commands of "No cameras, no packages" came incessantly to the visitors, eyed by the Secret Service, the White House police, and soldiers. The army had raised a long tent across the street on the grass as a package-checking station. But many people refused to go there and lose their place in line. Rather, they laid their Christmas bundles alongside the iron-picket fence. They jammed through the two gates at the rate of four a minute. Some veterans of the annual Easter Egg Rolling affrays (reputedly started during the Andrew Johnson Administration) pushed toward the Easter Egg Knoll, a vantage place near the portico.

The lawn filled quickly in the reddish glow of twilight. Nearly three thousand persons stood outside the fence. Low in the sky, a flight of birds passed silently within the roar of a passing airplane.

In the guest stand were Supreme Court Justices Jackson and Reed, and sharp-eyed Attorney General Francis Biddle. Massed choristers and the Marine Band stood nearby. The band struck up at 4:30 p.m., and the Christmas music faded into the traffic of the streets. A few moments after 5 p.m., the bandsmen stiffened, played "Hail to the Chief," and the fidgety crowd tightened.

The President and Winston Churchill came slowly upon the portico and faced the people. Through the music they could hear the echoes of the sunset gun at Fort Myer. Churchill's eyes roamed every part of the crowd, and then strained toward the Washington Monument, where a tiny red light shone in a window 550 feet above the ground.

Roosevelt pressed a button, and the tree lights glowed in the near dark. On the portico were Mrs. Roosevelt, Crown Prince Olaf and Crown Princess Martha of Norway, refugee friends of the Roosevelts, and their three children. And there stood Harry Hopkins, a household name but an elusive figure. Few looked at him; the eyes were on the man from England, whose face did not seem hard. He stood in the center of a long silence, close beside the President. Slowly, his eyes fastened upon the Christmas tree.

The Most Reverend Joseph Corrigan, rector of Catholic University, began the invocation with, "Hear a united people, girded for battle, dedicate themselves to the peace of Christmas, nor find strangeness in our words. All the material resources with which Thou hast blessed our native land we consecrate to the dread tasks of war." He prayed for "all who hold power over human life."

The crowd began almost visibly to become restless when the President started speaking. The change of mood appeared in little ways—the shuffling of feet, low-pitched conversations, and the gaze at Churchill. The question could be seen in many eyes: What would he say of the war and what, if anything, of Christmas? For some it didn't matter; they had seen Winston Churchill, and that was good for a week of conversation and something to remember and hand down to their children.

The President reminded them of his Proclamation of January 1 as a Day of Prayer, "of asking forgiveness for our shortcomings of the past, of consecration to the tasks of the present, of asking God's help in days to come." The soothing voice continued: "It is in the spirit of peace and good will, and with particular thoughtfulness of those, our sons and brothers, who serve in our armed forces on land and sea, near and far— those who serve for us and endure for us—that we light our Christmas candles now across this continent from one coast to the other on this Christmas evening."

The words went to all in the United States and by shortwave abroad. The President spoke of Churchill. The Prime Minister had arrived in deepest secrecy at an air base and was met by the President. Now Churchill wanted to speak to Washington and to the world. For a moment Churchill seemed to tighten within himself, and the crowd tensed with him. Then his voice came out:

I spend this anniversary and festival far from my country, far from my family, yet I cannot truthfully say that I feel far from home. Whether it be the ties of blood on my mother's side, or the friendships I have developed here over many years of active life, or the commanding sentiment of comradeship in the common cause of great peoples who speak the same language, who kneel at the same altars and, to a very large extent, pursue the same ideals, I cannot feel myself a stranger here in the centre and at the summit of the United States. I feel a sense of unity and fraternal association which, added to the kindliness of your welcome, convinces me that I have a right to sit at your firesides and share your Christmas joys.

This is a strange Christmas Eve. Almost the whole world is locked in deadly struggle, and, with the most terrible weapons which science can devise, the nations advance upon each other. Ill would it be for us this Christmastide if we were not sure that no greed for the land or wealth of any other people, no vulgar ambition, no morbid lust for material gain at the expense of others has led us to the field. Here, in the midst of war, raging and roaring over all the lands and seas, creeping nearer to our hearts and homes, here, amid all the tumult, we have tonight the peace of the spirit in each cottage home and in every generous heart. Therefore, we may cast aside for this night at least the cares and dangers which beset us, and make for the children an evening of happiness in a world of storm. Here, then, for one night only, each home throughout the English-speaking world should be a brightly-lighted island of happiness and peace.

Let the children have their night of fun and laughter. Let the gifts of Father Christmas delight their play. Let us grown-ups share to the full in their unstinted pleasures before we turn again to the stern task and the formidable years that lie before us, resolved that, by our sacrifice and daring, these same children shall not be robbed of their inheritance or denied their right to live in a free and decent world.

And so, in God's mercy, a happy Christmas to you all.

The gates drew open and the crowds pushed out upon the hundreds on the sidewalk where a man mumbled, "When I saw this mob I was just as glad that I didn't get inside." One who was inside said, "Now I know how a fellow feels to be let out of jail." But the crowd was more quiet than it had been upon its arrival. Walking in the crush became maddening; but overhead a crescent moon and one bold star lay peaceful in Roosevelt's and Churchill's and Washington's "world of storm."

DAVID BRINKLEY

Boom Town and the Strains
of the New

Washington Goes to War   (1988)

David Brinkley's book is probably as well known as any of the books chosen for inclusion here. I've read it more than once, and it can be opened and dipped into anywhere with gratifying results. Perhaps it's because this was my "era," so to speak, that I rabidly read Washington Goes to War. *In his preface, Brinkley calls his book "less a work of history than of personal reminiscence and reflection," and maybe it's the very fact that it is so personal that makes me respond to it so personally. This is real reporting based on firsthand experiences, and I was there, too, at the time and can testify that it rings the right bells.*

Brinkley writes, "The war transformed not just the government. It transformed Washington itself. A languid Southern town with a pace so slow that much of it simply closed down for the summer grew almost overnight into a crowded, harried, almost frantic metropolis struggling desperately to assume the mantle of global power, moving haltingly and haphazardly and only partially successfully to change itself into the capital of the free world." He goes on to paint a portrait "of the pain and struggle of a city and a government suddenly called upon to fight . . . a sort of Our Town *at war, the story of a city astonished and often confused to find itself at the center of a worldwide conflict." Here is one small part of what the subtitle calls "the extraordinary story of the transformation of a city and a nation."*

THERE was a joke that made the rounds of wartime Washington. A man crossing the Fourteenth Street bridge looked down into the Potomac and saw another man drowning. "What's your name and address?" he shouted to him and then ran off to see the drowning man's landlord. He asked to rent the now-vacant room and was told it was already taken. "But I just left him drowning in the river," he protested.

"That's right," the landlord replied, "but the man who pushed him in got here first."

Nothing was harder in Washington than finding a decent place to live. Even high-ranking government officials, heads of war agencies, members of Congress and cabinet members had to camp out in hotels. Harry Truman, for example, spent his first Washington years living in a small hotel room across the street from the Capitol while his wife and daughter stayed home in Independence. Jesse Jones, Leon Henderson and at least a dozen other ranking federal officials lived at the Shoreham Hotel near Rock Creek Park. And they were the lucky ones. Owners of private homes were pressured to rent out extra rooms and often charged exorbitantly for spaces little larger than broom closets, with bathroom privileges during certain hours only. Houseboat colonies sprang up along the Potomac, turning parts of the waterfront into a sea of shabby vessels with towels and socks and underwear hanging to dry from the masts.

The search for bed and board became an obsession, and at times an adventure. Young men and women new to town stood outside newspaper offices at press time to grab the first editions and thus the first look at the classified ads for rooms for rent. The next task was to decipher the cryptic descriptions of what space and amenities were offered. "Kit priv," of course, meant kitchen privileges. But what else did it mean? Access to the kitchen only at hours specified by the landlord? The use of only certain shelves in the refrigerator? One ad said, "Kit priv no cabbage garlic onions." What other rules would be announced after a homeless supplicant had paid the rent in advance and moved in?

Kenneth Banghart, an NBC radio announcer experienced in the sociology of Washington rentals and landlords, had these suggestions for newcomers: When you answer an ad and go to the house, look most carefully at the bathroom. Ask exactly how many people will be using it and ask about their work schedules. Then look around the bathroom for any little hand-written signs stuck on the wall such as "No clothes drying on the shower rod." Or "No reading in the bathroom," or "50-cent extra charge if light left on." Banghart's advice: "If you see any signs like that, leave. Because you know the landlord is a crabby son of a bitch. He'll pester you all the time. Every day he will announce some silly-ass new rule."

A woman near 35th and O streets in Georgetown advertised a basement apartment for seventy-five dollars. Applicants came by the dozens. She interviewed each one in embarrassing detail, inquiring about personal habits of every description—sexual, religious, social, dietary, working, sleeping. But since housing, any housing, was entirely a seller's market, applicants could refuse to answer her questions only at the risk of having to deal with another landlord even worse—or they could lie. Finally, behaving as if she were awarding the Nobel peace prize, she rented it to a young man named Walter Royen, who did do some lying. He promised to have no pets and no parties, to maintain a monastic silence, total sexual abstinence and complete sobriety, and to pay the rent promptly and in advance. He also agreed to keep her yard cleaned and mowed.

His troubles began when he discovered that the apartment, below ground and windowless, was so damp and airless his shoes mildewed, his typewriter rusted and the wallpaper slid downward off the walls into sticky coils on the floor. The end came when a young woman friend stopped by one morning on her way to work to have breakfast with him. The landlady, always spying, observed her leaving at 8 a.m., had not seen her arrive a half-hour earlier, and quickly concluded that unbridled licentiousness was occurring downstairs under her very feet. She ordered Royen out.

On Wisconsin Avenue at Hall Place, a middle-aged woman and her mother accepted a male roomer, not saying that he had to share the one bath with the two of them. They allowed no radios after 9 p.m., no pets, no use of the kitchen or the telephone and no smoking. When he sneaked cigarettes, they collected the butts and lined them up on a paper towel on his dresser along with threatening notes. In the bathroom the mother's spare set of dentures was always grinning at him from inside a glass of water, and every day her wet, dripping pink bloomers were festooned across clotheslines in the bathroom, making it resemble the inside of a sultan's tent. He had to climb through them to the mirror to shave. He left. . . .

THE HOUSING crisis was worst for blacks. Their community was growing at least as fast as that of whites, but the housing stock available to them was actually diminishing. One government committee entitled a report on the problem "Shrinking Negro Neighborhoods" and recounted in depressing detail how the federal government time and again appropriated land on which black homes stood when it needed space for some new structure. Two hundred black families were displaced from buildings that once stood on the site of the Pentagon. When Arlington National Cemetery was expanded in 1943, several hundred more families were forced to move. In Washington itself, black homes were demolished, the same report noted, to make way for "government buildings, highways, schools and recreational facilities; and no compensating housing has been built." Virtually all the new housing being constructed in Washington during the war was restricted to whites. The new neighborhoods, like the old ones, were governed by covenants forbidding owners to sell or rent to blacks. "In Washington," an official of the National Capital Housing Authority wrote in 1943, "the white population is very conscious of Negro expansion into areas formerly occupied by whites, but is scarcely aware of white expansion into areas formerly occupied by Negroes. . . . The net result is the loss of territory by Negroes."

One by one, former black neighborhoods disappeared. "The West End, known as Foggy Bottom, was once a good-sized Negro community," one housing authority wrote shortly after the war. "The Negro population has been steadily reduced. The land has been taken over piece by piece for white luxury apartment buildings, government buildings, among them the new State Department, additions to George Washington University, and most recently, the new George Washington University Hospital." Georgetown, once home to hundreds of black families, had by the late 1930s evolved into the fashionable community it remains today.

Housing for whites did expand, and expand rapidly, throughout the war, but never nearly fast enough to meet the demand. Private contractors tried their best to cash in on the need for housing, and new suburban developments began to spring up so fast that community services could not keep up with them. Arlington County, home of the Pentagon and thus of large numbers of defense workers, had the worst problems. "We live in Arlington," a Mrs. McGuire, mother of a nine-year-old girl, told a reporter for the *Washington Daily News* in 1943, "but the Arlington schools are too crowded—they won't take elementary school students." School officials were touchy. "It isn't any newspaper's business whether Arlington schools are too crowded," a spokesman for the superintendent snapped at the same reporter. "Why don't you stop snooping around?"

But it didn't take much snooping for the problems of the exploding Arlington suburbs to be obvious. The county's sewage system was obsolete even before Pearl Harbor, and local officials were pleading with Congress to help them pay the several million dollars needed to expand capacity. They got the money, but they could never keep up. In March 1943, county authorities had to evict families from a group of homes in the new Columbia Forest development because, the *Evening Star* reported, they had been "living since January without sewer service on a street pitted with yawning holes filled six feet or more deep with water." Complaints about such conditions even reached Capitol Hill. One representative rose in 1943 to ask, portentously, "Shall we members of Congress submit to such a program of inexcusable disregard of our health and die like flies by reason of infection and contagion? . . . Officers of the

Army and the Navy have come to tell me that they are more worried about losing their wives and children from disease . . . than they are about losing their own lives in the front lines of battle."

Even the most conscientious efforts seemed to flounder. Early in 1942, the Defense Homes Corporation—a New Deal–like agency set up to construct government-financed housing for war workers—began construction of an ambitious development: Fairlington, just south of the Pentagon. Acres of farm land were to be the site of Williamsburg-style red-brick garden apartments for 3500 families, a self-contained community with its own schools and services. By the summer of 1943, nearly 1000 families were already in residence, with another 150 moving in every month. They arrived to find no schools, no stores, few paved streets, inadequate garbage pickup and almost no public transportation. The promised sixteen-room school consisted only of a foundation. If all went well, residents were told, two rooms might be open by Christmas. The proposed shopping center was nowhere to be seen. Housewives had to walk up to three-quarters of a mile along unpaved streets and across muddy fields, children in tow, to the town's only bus stop, there to wait for one of the two buses a day that linked the community to downtown Alexandria; all that to buy even as little as a quart of milk. "No matter how you plan, you forget an item or two," one Fairlington resident complained. "I even bought a bike to ride back and forth to the store—but there isn't any store to ride to." Those who worked at the Pentagon or other government buildings had to tramp through the same muddy streets and fields and wait in long lines, sometimes for hours, for the same overcrowded buses; it took them up to two hours sometimes to travel the few miles to work.

Fairlington at least had sturdy, well-designed housing (most of it still standing today and now expensive townhouses and condominiums). Much government-financed war housing was shabby, makeshift and explicitly temporary—the residential equivalents of the dreary temporary buildings that now lined the Mall and surrounded the Washington Monument. All across the District, spilling into Maryland and Virginia, emergency housing developments were springing up—known in the trade as "demolishables," "demountables" and "T.D.U.s" (temporary dwelling units). "It would be difficult for anyone, whatever his architectural convictions and planning prejudices, to make the grand tour of Washington's housing without coming out sadder as well as wiser," *Architectural Forum* commented in early 1944.

Major Cannon R. Page of the 1st Army Corps sat in his office contemplating the new decision to allow young women to serve in uniform—Wacs in the army, and in the navy Waves. "What in hell are we supposed to do with them?" he complained. "Young girls away from home the first time and thrown in here with all these horny enlisted men? Does the army want to send a girl home to her mother with the clap? Or pregnant? It's going to be a goddamned mess!"

For the most part, it wasn't. The Wacs and the Waves proved valuable, even indispensable to the military and became a permanent part of the armed services, paving the way for their full integration in the 1970s and 1980s. But for them, too, Washington in wartime was a strange and at times difficult place.

The army and navy began an energetic program of building quarters ("duration residences," they were called) for their new women. On Nebraska Avenue, across from the Mount Vernon Seminary which the navy had seized, temporary plywood housing originally designed for male sailors was, at the last minute, reassigned to the Waves. Young women arrived from all over America to live in rows of cubicles, about sixty square feet each, with shelves, lockers for clothes, bunk beds and little else. The bathrooms were communal, designed for men, and were outfitted with rows of wall-hung urinals. In each urinal the Waves placed a potted geranium.

Many years later Vivian Ronca, a wartime Wave, recalled life in Quarters B on Nebraska Avenue. "The girls complained about being assigned to Washington because they thought there were no men here. But there were plenty, an abundance of young men. We'd go down to F Street, the shopping street, and wander around, and there were men all over. We'd just bump into them on the street. A lot of girls whose home towns were boring found Washington exciting. Many of them were married here. I was."

But it was not easy to arrange her wedding in wartime Washington. Her schedule was rigid—after one week at work she was allowed twenty-four hours off, after two weeks forty-eight hours, three weeks seventy-two hours.

"I was married on my seventy-two-hour weekend and then had to be back at work as usual. I had to get special permission to wear a bridal gown and special permission to go away in a white uniform. Always had orders on what we could wear, wedding day or any day.

"After a time our barracks were so crowded they allowed the married girls to move out and live elsewhere. Some of the girls married just to get out of the barracks.

"Some of them came into the navy expecting glamor and fun and games but found hard work and long hours and hated it, wanted to get out so badly. Some of those who wanted out tried to get pregnant and get a bad conduct discharge.

"People would come up to you in the street and say nice things to you. If you were on the street in uniform at 11:30 a.m. and had to be at work at noon, a dozen people would stop and offer you a ride to work. At bus stops, people always stopped their cars and offered rides. On the trolley cars they even wanted to give you their seats. Can you imagine that?"

One day, Eleanor Roosevelt rode out to Quarters B in the president's White House limousine, parked it in front, and invited the Waves to climb in, sit down for a moment, and climb out the other side and let another crawl in. "Write home," she said, "and tell your mothers you've sat in President Roosevelt's limousine."

She wanted to assure them that there was nothing wrong about a woman serving in uniform since, as Vivian Ronca recalled, "At that time there was a stigma in some places, not Washington, as if we were supposed to be prostitutes or something. Eleanor came to encourage us. She even took some of the girls over to the White House and gave them a private tour."

In these navy barracks on one long block of Nebraska Avenue were as many as two thousand young women, and so on summer evenings soldiers, sailors and marines stationed in the city, along with the few young male civilians who were still around, found their way there by the hundreds. They sat on the steps of the barracks, on the curbs or on the grass and leaned back against the trees in the still partly wooded neighborhood. They talked of home and jobs and the war and what they hoped to do when it was over if they survived and their lives were again their own. Then the men began bringing over small radios and long extension cords to run up through the barracks windows to the electric outlets inside. (The transistor had yet to be invented.) They sat on blankets on the grass and listened to the dance bands. Males were not allowed inside the buildings, and so in good weather it became a huge street-and-grass party with the men bringing blankets and paper sacks of fried chicken and potato salad—all patrolled by the navy. From this grassy, wooded area (oddly enough, the future site of the Japanese ambassador's residence) came the sounds of talk, laughter and a radio playing Artie Shaw's Gramercy Five. They were young and away from home and in these hours it was sweet.

"But all in all," Vivian Ronca remembered, "it was a lonely experience, so far removed from anyone you ever knew. Holidays were sad times. In the barracks you'd have Christmas and Thanksgiving dinner all by yourself. But we thought we were ever so much more comfortable than the boys overseas getting shot."

The first Wave commissioned officers came to Washington in late 1942 from navy training at Mount Holyoke College. One of them was Ellen Beckman, a former teacher, now a navy ensign. Years later she remembered, "We arrived just before Christmas and the navy had no place for us to stay. We were sent to the YWCA at Seventeenth and K, and they gave us five days to find another room."

On Christmas Day, the tireless Eleanor Roosevelt came to the YWCA and sat in the lounge and talked to the new officers. What was their most serious problem? Housing, of course. "I wish I could accommodate all of you in the White House," she told them, "but it's jammed with people and half of them I don't even know who they are. One of my sons came to Washington and we had to send him to a hotel."

Before her five-day deadline, Ensign Beckman found a room in a house "run by an old fuddy-duddy and his wife. As a patriotic gesture they kept turning off the heat. I was working in the navy code room all night, eleven at night until seven in the morning, and so I had to sleep during the day. The landlord didn't like it. So I moved.

"In the code room everything was so secret we could not let the janitors in at night and so we had to burn our own trash right there in the office.

"I rode the trolleys home and they kept getting new motormen brought in from out of town, they didn't know the streets and at the switching points at intersections they had to ask the passengers which way the car was supposed to go. We told them.

"The navy paid me thirty dollars a month for meals. It wasn't enough. I had to eat at People's Drug Stores lunch counters. So it helped to get invited out. There was a rule against officers dating enlisted men, but that broke down completely and nobody tried to enforce it. I think the admirals were kind of amused by the girls."

Lorraine Inman sat at a typewriter in the Army Exchange Service, headquarters for the PX's (post exchanges) on army bases around the world, and there, like thousands of other young women newly hired, she fought Washington's paper war, sometimes typing reports with twenty carbons and having to erase all twenty to correct every mistake. Fifty-four hours of this every week for twenty-eight dollars. Her immediate task was to issue tobacco allocation cards entitling officers to buy a set number of cigarettes a week, and to issue allocations for refrigerators for officers' housing and such other items as condoms and hair straightener. It was hard work at low pay in an expensive city, but she was luckier than most of the new women hired by a wartime government. She had always lived in Washington, had gone to work for the army when she graduated from Eastern High School in 1942, and so had escaped the fears and pains of all the women moving in from other places—principally the pain of finding decent housing.

Women in uniform had an advantage over civilians such as Lorraine Inman. The military housed their own—poorly and clumsily, perhaps, but they did it. The civilians usually had to fend for themselves. A government agency called the Defense Housing Registry tried to help. Women arrived at its offices just off the train or bus, walked up to the counter and said, "I want a suite with private bath within walking distance of the Munitions Building." They learned quickly. "NEWCOMERS DISCOVER PRIVATE BATHS WENT OUT WITH HITLER," the *Washington Post* reported. "Walking distance," it added, applied only to cross-country runners.

President Roosevelt—who managed still to fancy himself an architect even after looking out the White House windows at the hideous temporary buildings on the Mall he had helped design—tried his hand at devising a solution to the housing crisis for young women. He drew up plans for temporary residential buildings along the Mall, row after row of drab two-story dormitories as dreary as the office buildings they would adjoin. His designs called for a central hallway with ten small cubicles on each side. In each cubicle he sketched a cot, a dresser, a mirror and a curtained closet in a corner. At one end of the corridor he drew in a single bathroom for the twenty occupants and at the other end a lobby surrounded by alcoves, each just big enough to hold a bridge table and four players. Across the back, he drew in a cafeteria. These rooms, he said, could be rented for fifty cents a day. What did his housing experts think of it?

They thought it was terrible. For one thing, the partitions between the rooms stopped short of the ceiling. No one could play a radio without disturbing her neighbor and residents could not adjust the temperature to suit themselves. Roosevelt protested that when he was at Groton, expensive a private school as it was, the boys lived in cubicles with eight-foot partitions. The open space at the top had improved the circulation of air. Anyone who had to have the temperature adjusted so meticulously was some kind of sissy.

But this just wasn't up to modern housing standards, they told him. Each woman should have her own washbasin. Roosevelt replied that each woman could put on her lipstick in her own room. Thousands of students all over the country, even in the best schools, did not have separate bathrooms and washbowls. "I want a common washroom with about five showers, five toilets and with twenty tin basins and twenty tooth mugs in a row." The Hudson Valley squire, the Groton alumnus, the ultimate patrician. It was good for the soul—particularly other people's souls—to live simply, to suffer a little.

Roosevelt's housing plan was a failure. Nobody liked it. It would, he was told, be an eyesore out there on the grass among the trees and monuments. Roosevelt gave up, sighing over "these fancy people." Other and even more hideous temporary buildings for military offices were built on the Mall, but not his twenty-cubicle barracks. Instead young women had to live in even worse eyesores, some almost slums, in downtown Washington near the government offices.

District of Columbia housing officials inspected a typical rooming house for women and described their findings in a report Dickens would have understood. It was dark red brick with three stories and basement, nineteenth-century gas light fixtures still in place even though electricity had been installed. In its twelve rooms were two bathrooms, ancient toilets with the yellow oak water tanks mounted high on the walls and flushed with brass pull chains. All walls, floors, stairways painted in dark Victorian browns. The paint was peeling, the stairs sagged. In it lived nineteen government employees—fifteen women and four men—and uncounted rats and cockroaches. Two of the men were in two basement spaces separated by beaverboard from a coal furnace. Each had an iron cot, a table and a chair. Each man paid $17.50 a month. And from the basement to the third floor, every room except a small foyer was crammed with beds. In most, two women shared a room, and paid $21.50 a month each, three clean towels and one clean sheet a week included. The landlady was somewhat less greedy than most, since she allowed clothes to be washed in the bathrooms if one could ever be found unoccupied. She levied no additional charge for hot water. Handwritten signs in the bathroom were plentiful, but even with all its squalor, the house was always filled because the roomers could walk to their jobs.

Still the women came. The Army Service Forces combed the country, mainly in rural areas, recruiting young women to take clerical jobs in the military services, showing them enticing pictures of a bustling wartime city and talking about salaries of $1,440 that in the small towns seemed a fortune. In the town of Alma, Arkansas (population 776), one-fourth of the girls in the 1944 high school graduating class signed up to leave for Washington, and several of their teachers cast aside their low-paid jobs and went with them, all of them climbing aboard a Pullman car for their first train ride, looking for more excitement and money than they had any reasonable expectation of finding in Alma.

And so Washington became a city crowded with women. Sally Reston in the *New York Times* quoted a young typist working for the navy: "The men may have started this war but the women are running it." When the agencies shut down in the late afternoons, the streets looked like a women's college campus between classes. When the department stores finally realized that their women customers now worked all day and no longer had time to shop, they agreed to stay open late on Thursday nights and found this so successful they never stopped it.

But the story that had spread around the country—that in Washington women outnumbered men by ten to one—was always false. Young women did outnumber young civilian men, but at all times, day and night, the city was crowded with men in uniform as far from home as the women were and just as lonely. Many of them had military desk jobs in the city and were always available for dates, dances, and picnics. On slow news nights United Press reporter Douglass Wallop could look out the windows of the National Press Building and across Fourteenth Street into the windows of the Willard Hotel where couples lucky enough to find hotel rooms were too busy to lower the shades.

The Alleys of Washington

Journey Through Chaos (1944)

One of the things I admired about my mother was her crusading spirit. She had real values that were important to her, and she felt a responsibility for imparting them to her children and to the world. She believed in the importance of education, in justice and fair play, in equal rights and civil rights and civil liberties. For many years, from 1923 until 1941, she used her crusading spirit as chairman of the Recreation Commission in Westchester County, New York, defining recreation in the largest possible sense of helping people live happy lives in their spare time. Once my father had bought The Washington Post, *and it was clear that Washington was going to be their home, she turned her attention to the District.*

A northerner with European interests and instincts, Mother had a pro-underdog view. She had always been sympathetic to the plight of black people. She wrote in her autobiography that "My whole attitude toward the Negro race . . . arises from this instinctive sympathy for the victims of injustice." She couldn't bear the rampant injustices she saw in Washington. She felt strongly, and wrote that "If Americans could understand what a painful, searing experience it is when Negro children first begin to realize that the mere color of their skin is to be the source of a lifelong discrimination, it might do more to end our cruelty toward the Negro than all the preaching on justice and equality."

During 1943 and 1944, she visited twenty-six war centers throughout the United States to study the effect of the war on America's home front. She wrote many articles about this extended trip, all of which appeared initially in The Washington Post *and were later collected in a book that she titled* Journey Through Chaos. *(A decade later, when she published her autobiography, my father quipped that it was too bad she had already used what would have been the most appropriate title for the story of her life. Indeed.)*

In any case, in the part of the book excerpted here she outspokenly wrote about conditions in the District of Columbia, particularly Negro

*housing in the capital. She also wrote about the Negro in the army.
The Washington Urban League reprinted this piece and had it circulated throughout the city. There was a letter in Mother's papers at the
Library of Congress that someone sent her after the piece was published,
saying that she was told that my mother was "the only woman in Washington who could see that this filthy slum condition is cleared up." This
correspondent concluded, "I am told that you can perform miracles."*

*Well, Mother couldn't perform miracles, but she could continue cru-
sading, and she described part of what she was trying to do as "edu-
cat[ing] the white man to what the Negro is doing and has done with
the few facilities afforded him." She certainly influenced my father
throughout the 1940s to get the editorial page of* The Washington
Post *to write about health and education issues in the District. She felt
that if Washington was to be spared racial disturbances, it would be in
part because of the role of the "extraordinary liberal trend of editorials
in the* Post. *"*

She didn't stop focusing on the District. For the Post, *she wrote
about the great inequality in education in the Washington metropolitan area. She was the one who focused on "Horrible Hine" and "Shameful Shaw," two of the worst-performing schools. Nearly twenty years
after* Journey Through Chaos, *she had a piece in the* Atlantic *that
was titled "The Nation's Worst Slum: Washington, D.C.," the first line
of which was "Fear haunts the citizens of the nation's capital." But she
went on to offer constructive analysis and suggestions for the future.*

I N MY JOURNEY through the war centers I have visited the worst
possible housing. But not in the Negro slums of Detroit, not even in
the Southern cities, have I seen human beings subjected to such unal-
leviated wretchedness as in the alleys of our own city of Washington.

These alley dwellings and street slums must go! That is an old cry. At
this moment another congressional hearing on housing and slum-
clearance is in progress.

Statistics are again being piled up on the crime, delinquency, tuberculosis, and venereal disease that rise like a pestilential fume from these
overcrowded regions, for war-workers and lack of Negro housing have
congested these areas more than ever, have made slum areas of adjacent
properties and increased all the social and economic problems that even
in normal times determine the living conditions of the Negro in a large
city.

As usual in this city, a small group of public-spirited citizens is showing an active interest. But only an aroused and widespread public opinion will ever conquer the difficulties that surround any attempt at progress in a situation as old as the Civil War.

But surely the Washington housewives would rise in a solid phalanx and march upon Congress with demands for action if they could be made to realize that they live on the edge of a crater which constantly belches forth the most poisonous fumes.

For daily into their homes, to care for their children, wash their dishes and make their beds, come Negro servants, many of whom are obliged to live in these crime- and disease-ridden areas. If higher motives cannot be aroused, surely the primary instinct of self-protection should open the eyes of the least civic-minded person to the fact that no minority population can be continuously oppressed without direct repercussions upon society as a whole and that a sound social foundation cannot rest upon a submerged class.

General U. S. Grant, chairman of the National Park and Planning Commission, stated last week that 2,400 alley dwellings had from 11,000 to 12,000 inhabitants. Altogether there are more than 20,000 substandard houses in Washington having neither toilet nor bath and about 6,800 are without running water. Probably the alley houses are the worst because they are so old.

L'Enfant designed our city blocks around generous open spaces so that the citizens of the Capital could enjoy large gardens.

But when the flood of Negro refugees swept into Washington after the Civil War, real estate agents floated a project that made these back yards more profitable by constructing Negro shacks and barracks. Names like Foggy Bottom, Snows Court, Louse Alley, Shad Row and others go back to that era.

Pauperism then as now characterized the population, as Washington has never had enough work for unskilled labor, but the rents climbed whenever work on public buildings or a war put Negro housing at a premium. Today, due to overcrowding, the income from these properties is at a peak.

Here in Washington the same lack of good sense has been demonstrated that I found repeated over and over again in war centers. Negro housing for immigrant workers everywhere has been insufficient, and the already overcrowded Negro quarters had to squeeze in the newcomers. The results here must be seen to be believed. Not only houses have been subdivided, but small rooms, already too filthy for animal habitation, have been partitioned with cardboard to absorb more tenants.

In Burke's Court, 14 occupants have been stowed away in a single room; in Ninth Street, N.W., a small house held 19 persons, while a woman and three children lived in the basement.

Five or six persons to a room, occupying at times a single bed, is a commonplace. The outdoor toilets are frequently stopped up, so that several neighboring houses, as well as the passerby, use the nearest obtainable facilities.

In one row of houses the toilet and the well, where water is pumped by hand, are four feet apart. I remembered this pretty fact shamefacedly when I wrote of similar insanitary conditions at Willow Run, where temporary boom-town difficulties made them more excusable than in the Nation's Capital.

Here are some notes taken on the spot describing these slum dwellings—"4 rooms and bath, rotten kitchen floor, defective rain gutter, roof leaks, stopped-up toilet, hole in floor, rent, $17.50 per month" . . . "Holes in wall plaster, rats, defective door lets in rain, toilet won't flush, pipes leak, rotten window frames, rotten floor, split chimney wall, rent, $15.50 per month."

These are not exceptional reports. They repeat themselves monotonously. Many of the toilets have such defective doors that they afford no privacy. One row of houses below the street level and continually damp has such a long record of tuberculosis that it is popularly known as T.B. row.

How can such uncivilized things happen in Washington? Is there no inspection? Of course there is, by six different departments. But what can, for instance, our very competent Health Department do about it? The only thing it can do is put the tenants on the street because there is not, and has not been for six months, a single available Negro dwelling in Washington, except a few for immigrant war-workers.

Since 1897 the District law requires that no room should be used for sleeping purposes without at least 50 square feet of floor space per person. Last December the Commissioners had the bright idea of enforcing this regulation against overcrowding by penalizing "the person whose presence causes it" to the tune of $300. As long as there were a few rooms left in the National Capital Housing Authority projects, the sanitary inspectors could get results, but now it is a waste of time to go through the intricate proceedings of prosecuting landlords or tenants.

When the victims are expelled from one overcrowded place, they are taken in by relatives or friends whose rooms are still more congested.

Many families are broken up in this process, the parents and children scattering to any haven of refuge. It is futile and unjust for congressional investigators to blame our hard-pressed officials for such conditions. Bad as most of these slum pigsties may be, they cannot be condemned until there is some place for the Negro to go. He must have a roof over his head even if it leaks, and pushing these people around needlessly increases their resentment.

It would be much more to the point if the Health Department were praised by Congress for having achieved a marked improvement in the general health under such handicaps.

What aggravated a bad situation early in the war was the "bootleg" landlord who saw a chance to make a fortune out of other people's misery. One man bought every dilapidated shack he could find. These he "repaired" with refuse from the city dump, furnished with rusty iron beds and other junk he found there, and proceeded to rent rooms by the month, week, or night. In his heyday he had over a hundred such dives.

He collected his rent, club in hand, selling "numbers" as he went. Liquor, dope, and prostitution were little sidelines. When such creatures or their agents are caught operating without license and the city marshals clean out their illicit houses, the subtenants are put on the street without protection under any law, and must shift for themselves, though the Welfare Department does what it can.

Many tenants of these fly-by-night operators are constantly in an uproar because they are in jeopardy of eviction whenever the middleman fails to pay his rent on time.

Remodeling is another racket. One decent family with two children was suddenly evicted from a six-room house they had rented eight years, paying $40.50. The owner made $49.50 per room with the communal use of the bath out of his new "apartments" until the Rent Control Bureau caught up with him. But real rent control is impossible unless the victims of subletting make complaints. The only bright spot in the situation is the reputable real estate firms that charge reasonable rents and are patient with tenants who fall in arrears.

As Senator Capper has stated repeatedly at the present senatorial hearings on housing: "The chief reason why the alley slums have not been eliminated is because they are remunerative."

They always have been, even before the present boom. Many of them are so concealed that the average person never sees them. If these blighted areas were not hidden behind fronts, some of which, to be sure, are showing signs of decay, the indignation of the public would long ago have demanded concerted action for their removal.

Moreover, it is the shortage of housing for these very low income groups that makes them pay, and makes it unnecessary to keep them in decent repair. Landlords who are unwilling to keep up their property can only be forced to do so by a court order, which would almost invariably lead to condemnation of the building. This, again, would put the slum dwellers on the street with no place to go.

That is why the owners of these filthy, defective quarters are reaping a fortune. Their profits are as high as 25 per cent in normal times, and now many of the bootleg landlords as well as certain leeches who have always preyed upon these poor people are making fortunes.

The crowding in the slums of the District has also been intensified by the fact that not only housing but the areas formerly occupied by Negroes have decreased. Various developments such as public buildings, war housing projects for whites, and new roads have swept away many acres of ground heretofore open to Negro occupancy.

Within the District the construction of Federal buildings along the Mall displaced hundreds of Negro families; the improvement of the West End, or Foggy Bottom, area had the same effect. In Georgetown, only remnants of a long-established Negro population now remain, because so much of their property has been purchased and improved for white occupancy. Again, in the Southeast section of the District, a new military road to Camp Springs has destroyed more than a hundred old Negro homes, and so it goes.

Yet objections are raised against new sites for Negro housing within the District and our neighboring States of Maryland and Virginia do not welcome Negro housing across the District line, though they encourage white suburban developments.

Arlington County illustrates the most acute effects of displacement of Negroes by public condemnation unaccompanied by public responsibility for rehousing. The Pentagon, the Navy buildings and their road systems displaced 225 Negro families, some of whom had lived there since the Civil War. The only provisions made for them were trailers followed by 100 temporary houses, but no substitute was found for the land these people owned. Yet nearby thousands of permanent dwellings for whites were built with public funds.

Take one long slope for example: At the top, Fairlington, with 3,400 units and average rent of $75, an elaborate project constructed by the RFC; and in the hollow of the slope, the Green Valley trailers, rent $20, for dispossessed Negroes.

If all the outlying territory is closed to Negro suburban development, the time will come when the District Negro population, which has always remained in steady proportion to whites, about 28 per cent, will be forced upward, property values in the center of the city would be depressed and the economic burden upon the Nation's Capital increased.

What do these slums cost the city now? During the depression years 70 per cent of the relief cases were Negroes in these districts. One-quarter of the tuberculosis cases in 1940 came from that area, and more than half the patients at St. Elizabeth's.

The spread of tuberculosis in these congested, leaky dwellings can be easily understood, and the frequent mental breakdowns among Negroes would indicate that they are not quite as happy in poverty and degradation as is sometimes assumed.

Infant mortality is more than twice as high among District Negroes as among whites.

The slums have always been a focal point for the spread of venereal disease. The Negro is usually blamed for this, as the Negro's national rate is from five to seven times that of white people, according to statistics on the first two million selectees. But medical men have pointed out "that the most outstanding characteristic of areas of high prevalence for both Negro and white is a low economic status."

City officials and the United States Public Health Service have made a notable achievement in reducing the District rate, but the victory is and always will be temporary while living conditions in our slums remain what they are.

"Roamin' men," as a colored clergyman calls the floaters in the slums, are as much a source of infection as the more publicized "pick-up" girl. Recently four little Negro girls, aged twelve to fourteen, were infected by two temporary boarders in one house. Three of the girls had bad records, but one child, a first offender, was lured into the situation by her companions. The pattern of behavior long established in the alleys is impossible to resist except by the strongest characters.

The wonder is that so many of the slum families are decent, keep their houses clean, and preserve good moral standards.

The records of the Children's Court indicate that delinquency among Negro children has markedly improved since the war has increased the family income, and made it possible for more mothers of young children to remain at home. Whereas Negro delinquency used to represent 75 per cent of the total at the peak, it has now dropped to 58 per cent, but the increase of white delinquents accounts for some of the sharp comparative decrease. Twenty per cent of the delinquents committed to institutions or on probation before the war came from these slums, and 36 per cent of all the arrests were from these areas.

The total costs to the community of our 20,000 substandard houses, aside from health, delinquency and crime, namely, the endless court proceedings, the work of city officials, institutional care and other factors, is impossible to estimate, but, all told, the rest of the District inhabitants pay an enormous price for these slum conditions, economically, physically and morally.

To what extent would these burdens be alleviated, to what extent would the Negro in the lowest income group be benefitted by a better environment?

District officials for the past 10 years have conducted an experiment which sheds light on these questions. They set up, with consent and support of Congress, the Alley Dwelling Authority in 1934. This body was to receive regular appropriations and the program of alley rehabilitation was to be completed in 10 years.

Of the three million suggested for the first year's appropriation, the Alley Dwelling Authority received $865,000, as its total capital, with which 14 squares were reclaimed.

With additional loans from the USHA it built some 2,600 dwellings for Negro occupancy, some on slum sites, some on adjacent vacant properties. When the war came, all housing authorities, whether District or Federal, had to confine their efforts to providing for immigrant war workers.

It is significant that over 55,000 new housing units have been constructed for white tenants in the past four years in the metropolitan area and about 4,000—half of them temporary structures—for Negroes, although the Negro population was in greater need of space. This pitiful record is better than that of most war centers that I have visited.

In the early projects constructed by the Alley Dwelling Authority, now called the National Capital Housing Authority, several projects were necessarily for Negroes, as they are the majority of slum dwellers.

As some of these apartments have been in use for four years, the progress of the families is not of long duration, but already marked. In Hopkins Place, where the new development of NCHA doubled the population, there used to be three or four arrests per week. There was only one in the last year.

Not more than a quarter of the families in each new project can be relief cases, so that these new settlements will not be stigmatized as pauper homes. But all of the tenants were taken from the low-income brackets. At first all of the families were on graded rents, which means they could not afford to pay the economic rent, the difference being subsidized by the Government.

Today less than 30 per cent of these families are on graded rents, the others having earned enough income to pay the full cost rent.

Several of them have already graduated from public housing to private houses and home ownership, and many more are ready to buy homes if only they were available. In other words, the Negro will work if he gets a chance. The war salaries have, of course, stimulated this economic progress. The pity is that just as the Negro has enough income to move out of the slums as well as the housing projects, there is no place for him to go.

Better health, especially among children, is noticeable in the NCHA housing, due not only to improved sanitation, but to the fact that they now get more and better food because one or both parents have steady jobs. The quality of the clothing, and also the taste shown in selection, is very different. Gone are the zoot suits and vivid coloring, as well as the bare feet.

In one case the National Capital Housing Authority took the total population of a slum area, 116 families. They were grouped together, in two different projects. Not only was there no friction with neighbors, but now one type of family cannot be told from the other, so quickly did the slum-dwellers conform to the better manners and demeanor of the more fortunate group.

Yet there is no personal supervision in these housing units, no interference with private affairs and no rules other than a good neighbor policy.

It would be foolish to claim that housing is a Utopia where all ills are cured. The Negro needs, most of all, a continuation of what the war has offered so many of them—a chance to make a living. But it has already become clear through the NCHA's experiments that decent housing creates a superior neighborhood pattern of behavior to which the members of the community conform even when they are not conscious of a desire to do so.

Good housing is an education in itself, whereas in the slums all attempts at education of whatever nature must contend with low and long-established public mores.

The Negro in Washington has excellent schools. But the school environment and the home influences of the low income groups are in perpetual conflict. This was forcefully impressed upon me when I spoke to 700 young Negro girls on delinquency at Armstrong High School and the next day encountered a member of my audience, an undernourished, wizened youngster of sixteen, in a tumble-down, dirty, fetid, and overcrowded alley dwelling.

Against such odds, all welfare work, health programs and educational efforts, though more than necessary, are largely wasted.

The caption for this photo, which appeared on August 14, 1927, reads:
"A continual stream of visitors is seeking the top of the Washington
Monument these days for the view of the national capital from over 500
feet in the air. This photograph shows part of the usual daily crowd
in a queue around the base of the famous pile of granite awaiting
their turn in the elevators."

VISITORS TO WASHINGTON

Sooner or later, everyone comes to Washington.
—Marietta Minnigerode Andrews, *My Studio Window,*
Sketches of the Pageant of Washington Life

I'VE never understood why everyone doesn't want to come to Washington. I rarely wanted to leave it.

Since we lived here, my own touring was always somewhere else. I was lucky enough to have been a visitor to Berlin and Paris and Vienna and other exotic places in my childhood, and to New Delhi and Beirut and Cape Town, among other cities, later in my adulthood, but here in Washington I was a native, not a tourist. My friends and I ice-skated on the reflecting pool under the unblinking eyes of Abraham Lincoln from his perch at the top of the stairs on his memorial. We passed all the famous landmarks as we went about the city on our way to school and parties and dances and our fathers' offices. But everything surrounding us was mere backdrop, sights we took for granted, sort of everyday scenery.

One spring weekend, more than a dozen years ago now, I went sightseeing in the city with some of my grandchildren. Being children, they no doubt saw the sights quite differently from both what I saw and what I may have intended them to see. That's the beauty of visitors to Washington: everyone sees the place a little differently.

I know the locals often complain about the tourists—they clog up the city, they gawk, they walk too slowly—but I like them. I've always liked the idea of people coming to see what's here.

People continue to pour into Washington from around the country and around the world, coming to experience the beauty, the monuments, the magic. The famous and the unknown are visitors. Some send postcards home describing what they've seen, which are generally read only by their recipients. Others describe for a larger readership their own visits, or what they know about the visits of others. This section consists of a group of vignettes having to do with visitors to Washington. Let's see what they saw.

A Letter from a Self-Made Diplomat to His Constituents

The Saturday Evening Post   (1927)

Will Rogers spent a lot of time in Washington and no doubt gathered a great deal of his material here. After all, he was a political humorist first, and Washington was full of the kinds of people and stories and happenings that lent themselves to a humorist's touch. Cary Grayson, who was Woodrow Wilson's doctor and friend and who wrote a memoir of the president, said that Rogers was Wilson's favorite comedian—in fact, Wilson, known for going to the theater, hardly ever missed a show of Will's when he was in town. The feeling seems to have been mutual. Grayson wrote that whenever Rogers played in Washington he would visit the S Street house to which Wilson had moved from the White House and leave some message such as: "I am not asking to see him. Just tell him that I love him."

Rogers wrote of the president when he died, "The world lost a friend. The theatre lost its greatest supporter. And I lost the most distinguished person who has laughed at my little nonsensical jokes."

Here he writes about his visit to the White House under another president whom he may have liked less well but who seems to have provided him with even more material for his jokes.

M Y DEAR constituency: Having nothing but your welfare at heart, I feel that I should make a report to you personally on the matter that I have just investigated. All my other work has been carried on, as you know, practically private, for just the exclusive knowledge of President Coolidge, and naturally I wouldent blab any of that out to you. What I found out for him in Europe, and what I am to find out in America for him is none of your business. But what I found out about the President is some of your business. So, you see, while I am working for him I am also really taking care of your interests.

Now we only possess, with all of our wealth, one residence belonging exclusively to the complaining taxpayers and I thought it would be a good idea to let you know how it is, what shape it is in and what kind of a renter we got in there. You see, there has never been any detailed report on just how our lone residential asset was making out.

The United States owns outright 8,887,221 buildings, but the White House is the only one with a bed in it. The United States has some 30,000,000 employees—or people on salary, rather. But where they sleep is none of our concern. The Senate and the House of Representatives is the only help we have that we know where they sleep. We can read some of their bills and tell where they slept. But the President is the only help we furnish linen and silverware to. Rent is the one thing I can think of that the President don't have to worry about. Now you, as delinquent Taxpayers, have a right to want to know, Is the renter taking care of the place, and what kind of a man is in there?

Well, you see, the way it really is, the White House is supposed to belong to the Government. But the Republicans have it leased for an indefinite period, and they sublet it out to a family called Coolidge. I had just arrived back home from Europe with 350,000 other half-wits who think that a summer not spent among the decay and mortification of the Old World is a summer squandered. . . .

On landing I had to go down to Washington on the usual business, to see about the 1922 income tax—that's the year we all had trouble. . . .

So I wired Everett Sanders, Mr. Coolidge's very genial and likable secretary, that I was coming down to Washington the next day and I would like to drop in and say hello to our President. I had had a couple of very friendly chats with him before departing on this missionary work. But I had not heard from him all summer.

Well, sir, do you know that it wasent more than an hour before I got a wire back: "Let us know what train you arrive on. A White House car will meet you at the station, and you are to be the guest of Mr. and Mrs. Coolidge at the White House while here."

My Lord, I couldent believe it! I kept looking at it, and wondering what the catch was—if some one was kidding me or what. So I wired back to Mr. Sanders, as I was still leery about it: "I am stopping to have lunch with the editor of the *Post* tomorrow, and if you-all are kidding me about this White House visit, you better head me off in Philadelphia." I dident want to go dragging up to the White House with my old telescope and have two plainclothes men step out from behind those pillars and say, "Just a minute. Where are you headed for?"

Well, at lunch time in Philadelphia I dident get any word to turn back, so I told the editor of the *Post*, and he said, "Why, it may be on the level. I made it on the old Government Tug *Mayflower* myself once."

Well, that gave me encouragement when I heard the President was getting plain enough to recognize Editors. But I also knew that there was a lot of people that might get an invite on the Yacht that couldent come in through the kitchen to the White House. You see how that is. Mr. Coolidge is a pretty good Sailor—I guess about the best Sailor from Vermont—and, you know, it gets pretty rough down there off those Democratic states shores, even when election is not on. And they tell me Mr. Coolidge takes a kind of a fiendish pride in taking alleged friends down there and watching them hunt the rail. So you don't want to take the importance of a *Mayflower* invitation too serious.

I sent Mr. Sanders a wire telling him the hour of arrival and that I sure did feel proud to know that I was to sleep in the White House, even if they had to put a cot in the Blue Room. I put that little gag in there for a reason. I was afraid that after dinner they might send me out to some annex or dormitory or outbuilding to sleep, and I wanted them to know in advance that I wanted to be under the main roof, even if I dident sleep any.

Mr. Sanders met me at the train himself, and we drove in a White House limousine—name deleted by me myself, until same make car arrives at my home gratis, when due notice will be given publically. We got to the White House, and Mr. Sanders went on to his home and I went in, was met by Mr. Hoover—not the one that took our sugar away from us that time,* but an awful friendly kind of a bird that is equerry, or night-and-day club host to the White House. Well he took me in, and there sit Mr. and Mrs. Coolidge. My train was late. I knew I should have taken the other line.

Now there was the President of a Country a third as big as Russia and more than half as big as China. He and the Leading Lady of our land, waiting dinner on a Lowbrow Comedian. Now if any Nation can offer any more of a demonstration of Democracy than that, I would like to hear of it. It only shows that with all of our going Cuckoo over anything from abroad that is branded with an affliction of Royalty, why, we still have one home in America that is able to retain its democracy. It wasent because I happened to be the one. But I felt that the common people were being honored. I had heard so much in Politics about them going to

*Of course, Rogers is referring to Herbert Hoover's role in World War I as President Wilson's food administrator, responsible for production and conservation of supplies. Ellen Maury Slayden was among those who didn't look very positively on Hoover, saying that "When the president summoned Mr. Hoover to come and save his country as food dictator, he came as the conqueror comes."

do something for the common people and this was the first practical demonstration I had ever witnessed of it. Not only did I feel that he was paying a tribute to just a taxpayer but I felt that Illiteracy was finally coming into its own.

Mr. Coolidge met me very cordially. He was accompanied by another gentleman that I couldent see well enough to recognize. He was called "The White House Spokesman." Now if you don't know what one of those are I will tell you. Well he is some friend of the President's that Mr. Coolidge conceived the idea of sorter having around handy in case he wanted to say anything that was not for publication, why it's better to let it be said by the White House Spokesman. You see Mr. Coolidge don't say much anyway himself, and for publication he don't say anything. He brings in his double. . . .

Well, Mr. Coolidge, as I said before, when he walked up to me he held out his hand, opened his lips and as he did, "The White House Spokesman" said "Hello Will." Well for a minute I dident know which one of them was talking to me. I hadent met this spokesman and I dident see where he come in to be so familiar as to say "Hello Will" without an introduction: in fact, I wasent right sure it was him said it. Then I happened to think a minute and decided that I wanted to use the remark, "Hello Will" in my report back to the *Claremore Progress* [his hometown paper], so I knew it was the White House Double that had spoken to me. But I certainly appreciated Mr. Coolidge shaking hands with me so cordially, even if he dident say a word himself.

It was the spokesman and he said, "Well, Will, you made a typical American diplomat: you made us all laugh." Now beat that for real humor, either with or without a spokesman. I wish I had a spokesman that could think of as good and truthful things as that. I rate that about 99 percent among political humor.

Mr. Coolidge then introduced me to Mrs. Coolidge, whom I had never met. He did that himself without any double or spokesman at all. As I dident care to quote his introduction in a book or pamphlet, there was no use using up the spokesman more than we needed.

Now listen, Ladies, if you have never met Mrs. Coolidge, you certainly have missed a rare treat. We have been particularly blessed with the types of Ladies who have graced our Executive Mansion. But this one there now has the reputation, given her by everyone who has met her, of being the most friendly and having the most charming personality of any one of them all. She is chuck plumb full of magnetism, and you feel right at home from the minute you get near her. She has a great sense of humor, and is alive and right up and pleasant every minute, and Calvin is just setting there kinder sizing everything up.

Mind you, nothing is getting by him. He is taking in everything, but he ain't just what you would call bubbling over. A joke don't excite him any more than a Republican Senatorial defeat. He takes everything sorter docile. But with it all he is mighty friendly and nice, and talks a whole lot when he is with somebody that he feels can't tell him anything.

Now it was reported at the time through the papers that the night I stayed at the White House he went to sleep on me. Well, I dident deny it at the time, though it was a kind of slam against me. I had had some pretty good audiences go to sleep on me, and I knew it wouldn't do any harm to have him added to my list. But here is the joke of it, which I have never told before: Not only did he not go to sleep on me but I am the one that like to went to sleep on him. I had been asking him a lot of questions about various public things of interest, and naturally his answers would be rather technical or involved, and I would catch myself sorter blinking.

When I have the good fortune to be able to talk to some big man, I don't spent the whole time by spouting off a mess of my jokes. I am there to learn something from him. It's his ideas I want to get; not to try out any of my own on him.

We are sitting there at the table, just the three of us, chatting away about a little of everything, and here is something I want any of you children to know: If you have a dog and your mother won't let you feed it at the table, and says, "Don't feed that dog in here. What if company should come? Get him out of here." Say, go right on and feed your dog, Kids; it's being done in one of our best homes.

The Coolidges have a couple of flea hounds and they was handing out things to them all the time. One of them would come to Mr. Coolidge's place and one to hers, and they seemed to think an awful lot of those two dogs, and the dogs certainly were crazy about them. Well, they was feeding the dogs so much that at one time it looked to me like the dogs was getting more than I was.

Now I don't want this last remark to get out. I wouldent make it if I thought it would get around up in the Maple Sirup Belt. But at any rate the dogs were not as nervous about the quantity as I was. One old pup come around to me and I just looked at him and told him: "Listen, my rations won't permit me splitting with you. You are here every day. I am only here once." He went on back to the President. The colored Butler was so slow bringing in one course that I came pretty near getting down on my all fours and barking to see if business wouldn't pick up with me.

These mutts sure were pretty and fat. They are white Collies. But Lord, I would be fat and fairly pretty myself if I dident have anything to do but hang around that big Dining room and ride up and down on the elevator and lay on nice cushions and sofas. . . .

Now, you know, the Coolidges palling around with these dogs there like that, it showed a mighty human trait. It ain't everybody that a mutt will take up with. They can read character better than a Politician. It showed the plain side of the family. They fed their dogs up in Vermont and they feed these down here. The White House don't make any change in their life. . . .

We had fish that night for dinner. Well, I never paid much attention to the fish. I paid enough attention to it to eat it, but I never gave it any more thought. But the next day at lunch—get this! The next day at lunch—I was still there at lunch the next day! I suppose by all the laws of etiquette and the constitution of Emily Post, that I should have gone away the next morning, but I was still there. When the lunch bell rang I was the first one in to the table. I had been there so long by then that I knew my place: I knew just what chair to pull back.

Well, during the lunch the Butler come to Mr. Coolidge with a platter of something that resembled some kind of hash. The White House spokesman looked at it and asked, "Same old fish?" Well, that sure did sound homelike. I had forgot about the fish the night before, but he hadent. To hear the family discussing the rehash brought me right back among the mortals. I had eaten Turkey hash for generally about a week after holidays and Weddings. Chicken hash generally runs about two days. I had partaken of Beef hash, and I have eaten hash that nobody knows what the contents were. But when you get down to eating fish hash you are flirting with Economy. This old thing of saying he preaches economy but he don't practice any of it is the bunk. . . .

Mr. Coolidge asked me about being part Indian, and if I dident come from Oklahoma. I was telling him yes, and why I had to leave there, and was just on the verge of asking for Executive clemency, when he up and said, "I am part Indian, My Folks had Indian blood." Well, I commenced asking right away about the tribe, and where did they come from. He said he dident know the exact tribe, but he knew that away back his Ancestors had Indian blood.

I wanted to kinder drag him in with our Cherokees. I could see an appropriation for an Indian Hospital at Claremore, Oklahoma, the Home of the only water in the world that will cure you by smell only. Then he told me it was some tribe up in New England. Well, that let him out of our tribe. I knew it wasent the Cherokees.

Will Rogers out of His Element

Forty-two Years in the White House (1934)

Ike Hoover, a kind of legend in his time, at least in some circles, spent forty-two years in the White House—quite possibly a record. Certainly, in sheer numbers his forty-two years beat out Alonzo Fields's My 21 Years in the White House *and Lillian Rogers Parks's* My Thirty Years Backstairs at the White House, *and even Thomas Pendel's* Thirty-Six Years in the White House, *the last author having been doorkeeper from Lincoln to Teddy Roosevelt.*

It seems that at least one out of every two books about Washington that I've looked at mentions Ike Hoover, and no wonder. Even "wedding planner" was one of his job descriptions. Alice Longworth once wrote that "We have always said that I could never have gotten married without Hoover."

A native Washingtonian, Irwin Hood Hoover, always known as Ike, died on the job in 1933, only six months into his service for FDR, and just short of his sixty-second birthday. One senses that these two men would have liked each other.

Hoover is referred to by Marietta Andrews in My Studio Window *as the "time-honored major domo of the White House." A note at the beginning of his posthumously published book tells his simple story. When he was sent to the White House in 1891 to install electric lights for Benjamin Harrison, the powers that were at the time must have realized that someone was needed to deal with this new technology on a more regular basis, so Ike Hoover stayed on as electrician and moved up through the ranks in the ushers' office. He was appointed chief usher under Taft.*

There's something about the calm demeanor that is reflected in these excerpts from Hoover that makes me glad he spent his time at the White House, and especially glad that he wrote down some of his experiences. He's so unobtrusive on the page that one imagines him to have been equally so at the White House—quietly efficient, even indispensable, but not needing to call attention to himself. Hoover's reporting is in a measured tone. *You have to read closely to catch his criticisms and his witticisms, but they're there in abundance. Ike Hoover strikes me as both serious and high-minded. He may not have been that much fun at the office (or outside of it), but I'm sure he was a public servant in the very best sense.*

Part of Hoover's job as chief usher was to welcome guests, which he seems to have done with quiet aplomb. Here are some excerpts about several of the visitors to Washington and to the White House who were welcomed by Coolidge and some of the other presidents Hoover served—beginning with Ike Hoover's own take on Will Rogers's visit.

JANUARY 17, 1927. Reading in the *Saturday Evening Post* Will Rogers's story of his visit to the White House prompts me to record what really happened on this occasion.

Mr. Rogers had written the Secretary to the President of his intended visit to Washington and had asked permission to pay his respects to the President. When this request was placed before the President in the usual routine of such matters, he suggested that Mr. Rogers be invited to be his guest at the White House. This was done and the invitation was accepted.

On the day of his arrival, word had come from him that he would be here at six-twenty in the evening. He did, as suggested in his story, telegraph from Philadelphia to Secretary Sanders that he was on his way and that if there was a catch or a joke of any kind in the invitation, please to let him know and he would discontinue the journey. Word was sent back to him that the invitation was a genuine one and that a White House car would meet him upon his arrival at the station.

His train was late, on account of a railroad accident of some kind. At best he would have been just in time for dinner, which was always served at seven o'clock during the Coolidge Administration. When we learned that he would be late, we wondered whether he would have time to change and put on his dinner clothes. This was mentioned to the President, who remarked that if Mr. Rogers did not get there in time to change, he would not himself dress for dinner. However, as time went on, the President retired to his room and came forth arrayed in his dinner coat, having apparently changed his mind about not dressing.

The train arrived at six-fifty and at exactly seven o'clock the White House automobile drove up to the door. The President and Mrs. Coolidge had just come down in the elevator on their way to the dining-room and were told that Mr. Rogers was at the door. They made no effort to wait, but proceeded on to their places at the table.

We tried to hurry Mr. Rogers, but it took some little time to relieve him of his overcoat and hat and to take care of his suitcase. I also had to explain that the President and Mrs. Coolidge had just gone in to dinner and that it would be necessary for him to go direct to the dining-room, with no chance to change his clothes. He looked rather embarrassed when the matter of clothes was mentioned, but there was no time for discussion. So he was shown immediately into the dining-room, where the President and Mrs. Coolidge were already seated alone at the table. Mr. Rogers had on a blue double-breasted business suit and a soft collar.

Having been announced, he walked toward the President, remarking on the way, "This is what I call true democracy, the President and his wife waiting dinner on me, such as I am." Of course they had not waited at all, but the remark went over well, drew a smile from the President and something a little more than a smile from Mrs. Coolidge. The President half-arose, shook hands, and presented him to Mrs. Coolidge, who had not met him before. She invited him to be seated on her right.

The President took the lead in conversation by mentioning the train delay, the trip to Washington, and eventually the matter of Mr. Rogers's recent trip abroad. From then on Mr. Rogers held the stage; the President and Mrs. Coolidge just adding enough from time to time to keep the flame of his narrative alive. The remainder of the evening was spent in the west sitting-room. Some jigsaw picture puzzles were brought out and worked on for a while. Mrs. Coolidge did some knitting, the President smoked, and all retired at twenty-five minutes past ten. Mr. Rogers had been assigned to what is known as the pink guest suite, in the extreme northeast corner of the bedroom floor. It consists of a large room with a four-poster bed, a small dressing-room, which also has a single brass bed in it, and a private bath. He was escorted halfway down the hall by the President and his room pointed out to him. A doorman was summoned to have one last word with Mr. Rogers and learn if there was anything that could be done for him before he retired.

Upon entering the room, Mr. Rogers seemed rather hesitant about occupying the large four-poster bed that had been prepared for him. Turning to the doorman, he inquired if he had to sleep there. He was told of the small bed in the dressing-room and chose that in preference to the large one. The man turned down these covers and left Mr. Rogers with his own thoughts, to spend the night in the White House with all the thrills he afterwards described.

As was the custom during these times, Mr. Rogers had his breakfast in his room. After breakfast time rather dragged on his hands. He seemed to have no plans, except that he appeared anxious to get away as soon as possible. He really seemed uncomfortable. He did mention that he would like to go by aeroplane back to New York and inquiry for his benefit was made. He then sat around for quite a while in the Usher's Room adjacent to the main entrance. Here he met a number of people, principally those attached to the place. He engaged them in conversation, telling about some of his European experiences and mentioning also that he did not wish to be considered always as a humorist, but liked, at times, to be taken seriously. In fact he really tried to be serious during his White House visit. Referring to his late arrival the night before, and to the fact that he had been expected to dress for dinner, he said he had never owned a dinner coat in all his life.

He sat around for quite a while, and then at the suggestion of an official he decided to go over to the flying-field to arrange for his trip back in the afternoon. He went in a White House automobile and as he started out he said he was going to see Jimmy Davis, meaning the Secretary of Labor. This was about ten in the morning, and when he returned at twelve o'clock he apologized and explained that not only had he been to see Mr. Davis, but had also called on Alice Longworth and Mrs. McLean (Evalyn Walsh McLean).

He had lunch with the President and Mrs. Coolidge alone. He was then bidden good-bye and expected to be on his way. He was shown to his room, where he found his bag already packed, and immediately left in a White House automobile for the flying-field.

Thus ended Mr. Will Rogers's famous visit to the President and Mrs. Coolidge in the White House. It was just a plain everyday visit like hundreds of others. That he afterwards made so much of it, in amusing his audiences, is to his credit, for in reality his field was very limited. He seemed to interest Mrs. Coolidge just a little, and the President a great deal less. In fact, when someone remarked later to the President that it was hoped he got a good "kick" out of Mr. Rogers's visit, he replied casually, and without a smile, "Oh, Will! he is all right."

Will Rogers later offended Coolidge when he imitated him over the radio. He sent a letter apologizing, but never got back into the President's good graces. Coolidge especially disliked the nasal tone adopted in imitating him. He remarked that Rogers had been a guest in the house once, but, if he was to be again, some other President would have to do the inviting.

(Rogers also offended Harding with a sketch of a cabinet meeting, the President telephoning and talking golf all the while. Harding refused to go to see the show, after having promised to do so.)

The Young Hero from Colorado

Forty-two Years in the White House (1934)

Another visitor of whom Ike Hoover makes special mention is quite unlike Will Rogers and other famous visitors. Unknown prior to his visit to Washington and lost to history afterward, this "boy hero" seems nonetheless to have made quite an impression on the city at the time. Hoover describes his exploits matter-of-factly by relating that this boy from Towner, Colorado, had saved his classmates from a blizzard. As the newspapers from the time told the tale, Bryan Untiedt kept fifteen other children alive in a school bus. When the driver went to get help, Bryan took off his own clothes and spread them around to the other children. Also, according to Parks in her own account in My Thirty Years Backstairs at the White House, *Bryan "had saved them by keeping them moving—singing and dancing—until they were rescued after a day and a half."*

In recognition of his heroism and derring-do, the boy was invited by President Hoover to come to the White House. In fact, the invitation had come to Bryan while he was still in the hospital recovering from frostbite. Lillian Parks comments that Bryan "was the best thing that had happened to the White House in a long time, and backstairs, he was greatly applauded because he had treated the President in a thoroughly casual way. Too casual!"

APRIL 29, 1931. At the White House we knew about Bryan Untiedt, the boy hero of Colorado who had saved his schoolmates from death in a blizzard. We knew from the daily press that he had been invited to visit the President, but we did not know exactly when he was to come. Meanwhile, we were making extensive preparations for the arrival of the King and Queen of Siam, who were expected on the very same day that the son and daughter-in-law of the President were to return to the White House after a six months' sojourn in Asheville, North Carolina. These two events were quite enough to prepare for in any one day. So you can imagine how amazed I was when Mrs.

Hoover came back from the Executive Offices the day before the arrival of these two parties and told me that the Colorado boy would be here the next morning, at practically the same hour as the King and Queen. She was obviously much surprised herself. The arrangement had been made unknown to her or to anyone else who would have the responsibility of caring for the young guest.

She immediately called together several of the staff and laid the matter before us. We decided there would be lots to do on the morrow, with the three different parties all arriving at the same time. There would be a shortage of bedroom space and one of the lady guests was asked to double up with the other and give the boy her room. The two ladies were told to get their heads together and plan for Bryan's entertainment.

At eight the next day, the young Hoovers appeared, at nine the boy hero arrived, and at ten-fifteen the King and Queen drove up at the front door. This was a busy morning.

Young Bryan came unheralded and unannounced except that a White House car had been sent to the station with a secret service man to meet him. His arrival was uneventful. I was upstairs in conference with Mrs. Hoover about the reception of the King and Queen when he arrived, and I sent word to hold him in the Usher's Room for a few minutes.

Upon his entrance at the front door, he looked around inquiringly and walked to the room as he was directed. Several secret service men and employees immediately surrounded him, but he was quite composed in the midst of this audience. I took him in hand, introduced him to everyone, and tried to put him at his ease. I asked him how to pronounce his name and if he had enjoyed his trip East. The little fellow looked sad, yet composed. He had that unruffled calm that seems to city folks so characteristic of people from the country. His baggage consisted of a little paper suitcase, a flat pasteboard box tied with string—that had got quite crushed on the way—and a little Brownie camera, one of the kind that costs but a few dollars. What a contrast to the luggage of most visitors to the White House, which requires a baggage-wagon to fetch it from the station! This boy needed no baggage-wagon, and yet everyone was most interested in him. He was taken to the elevator and up to the second floor, where Mrs. Hoover awaited him. Introduced to her in formal fashion, he was unaffected enough to do nothing, and so acted his part well. Mrs. Hoover was lovely to him and took him to a hammock in the west palm room to sit beside her. Here she talked and laughed with him and made him comfortable and happy.

After a little while Bryan was shown to his room, where stood a big four-poster bed, large chairs, and other furniture. There was a private bath and a valet had been assigned to him. He was left alone for a few moments to get his bearings, although it hardly seemed necessary. Likewise he scarcely required a valet, but all the formality was gone through with. He had just enough clothes to get along, and no overcoat, though the weather was quite cool. He had two little caps, but very seldom wore them.

In a half-hour or so he was taken over to the Executive Offices to see the President. No royal prince or potentate was ever escorted with more courtesy. He joined the President in his private office and remained alone with him for some time.

Upon returning to the house, he was permitted to go to his room and await lunch. In the meantime, however, the two ladies of the household who had charge of him decided they would take him out for a ride. When the time came to leave, he could not be found. He had wandered out alone in the south grounds to take some pictures with his little camera. This showed his self-confidence, for only the man who was taking care of his clothes knew that he had gone.

Off for a ride he went to get a first view of the city before lunch. Upon his return, the photographers, who had learned in some way of his being out, waited around and nearly mobbed him and the lady with him.

Word had gone forth that he must not be subjected to being interviewed or photographed; in fact, that for his own sake he should not be given too much publicity. He was not permitted to see any of the daily papers that were carrying such big headlines about him during all the time of his stay in the White House.

At lunch there was quite a large gathering, although it contained no one outside the household. All came down to the Red Room, and when the President arrived they arose according to the custom. Not Bryan, however. Presidents coming into the room meant nothing in his young life, and he just watched from his seat on the big red sofa. It was amusing to see this little fellow, entirely composed, hold his chair when everyone else arose as if by magic. I walked over to him and with a soft word put the little fellow right. There was a smile on the faces of the President and Mrs. Hoover as the latter walked over to him and led him to the dining-room, seating him next to the President. It was a picture long to be remembered.

His innocence was beautiful, so different from anything that had ever been known at the White House before. No wonder the interest in him increased and multiplied as time went on! We originally thought that he was to spend only one night and wondered when he was to leave. It was up to the President to make the decision. The boy seemed indifferent. He had just placed himself in the hands of the President and he was quite contented.

During his stay, which lasted four days and nights, he was taken care of by everybody around the White House. He was made comfortable and looked after in every way. He was given no great amount of entertaining, but taken around to all the Government buildings, to Mount Vernon, to the parks, and got about as good a view of everything in Washington as could possibly be had in that length of time.

He always occupied the same room with all its big furniture and four-poster bed. He ate with the President and Mrs. Hoover when there was nothing special going on. When not with them, he ate with the secretaries or some of the ladies in the household. The papers had him eating and hobnobbing with the King and Queen of Siam, but of course this never happened. The chances are he never saw either of them unless he peeped out of the window of his room, which was just over the main entrance. This was exactly the sort of thing the President was particular to keep him away from.

To me the most interesting moments of his stay were when the President would take him off to his study all alone and talk to him, or rather listen to him talk. On one occasion I sat near-by and watched them for a full half-hour. The President said just enough to keep the boy going. The little fellow sat in a big armchair talking, telling the President all about his experience with an air of indifference and a calmness that was sublime. He would throw his leg over the chair, twist around calmly as he proceeded, pat the arm of the chair affectionately, and tell his story fluently.

During the stay the boy became fast friends with the little Hoover grandchildren. He seemed very happy in their company. They, the dogs, and his camera formed his principal amusements. He made several visits to the shopping district to buy souvenirs to take home to his family. Many were the interesting stories told of these exploits. His particular object was to get something for his mother. He thought perhaps it should be a dressing-gown, but she had told him that she did not want a very expensive one, for she had to have the kitchen painted.

During all his stay his wardrobe was being added to, so much so that when the time came to leave his little paper suitcase and pasteboard box would hold but a small portion of his belongings. A large leather suitcase, almost the size of a trunk, was purchased, and it managed to hold what he took back with him. This was in addition to two overcoats, a gun-case, and numerous other articles presented to him by the President and Mrs. Hoover. It is also probable that his pockets and the little pocketbook he carried contained more than they had ever been blessed with before. So he left, as he had come, in the company of one of the secret service men.

He departed in the early afternoon, the President having said an affectionate good-bye to him after lunch. Just before be left, Mrs. Hoover took him off to a room and they sat together on a couch. I went for him when it was time to go and heard Mrs. Hoover's last words to him. They were such words as only a mother could say to one in whom she was interested. They must have impressed this simple little boy, coming from one in her position. There were tears in her eyes when she advised him as to his future.

But he was stoical, solid, unconsciously understanding. He was appreciative, but not demonstrative. When he had gone, he left a beautiful atmosphere behind him. Everyone was sorry and had a kind and affectionate word for him. May all that is best in the world be his, for he has shown the quality that goes to make American manhood.

Lindbergh—the Perfect Guest

Forty-two Years in the White House (1934)

Lindbergh made a big splash in Washington in 1927, as he did around the world. He came here in June, just a few weeks after his most famous flight. Several books on Washington remarked on his visit. Lillian Parks was in the crowd waiting for his arrival. She noted that the young flyer's mother had arrived the day before and "watched timidly from a window the great ovation for her son," adding that "The President took second place to the great hero that day. But Coolidge didn't mind at all."

Four years after this visit, Lindbergh came again to Washington, and my mother had the privilege of being escorted into dinner by him at the home of her good friend Paul Claudel, who was then ambassador to the United States from France. She described it in her diary, with a zinger for Lindbergh's father-in-law, Dwight Morrow: "January 19, 1931: Went in to dinner at Clau's with Lindbergh. Very faithful of Clau to have arranged it. The boy has a peculiar independence and strength. He is much more of a personality than people as yet realize. I was charmed and impressed. Dwight Morrow on the other hand misses fire completely. He is a typical little man who is determined to show the world how great he is."

Mother's comments take us ahead of our story. Here is Hoover on the Lindbergh visit.

JUNE, 1927. Charles A. Lindbergh was returning to America as a conquering hero. He had accomplished the unbelievable feat of crossing the Atlantic in an airplane from New York to Paris. The whole world was sounding his praises; foreign nations had outdone themselves in an effort to recognize the greatness and the importance of his feat. It now remained for his own country to do him equal honor.

The officials at Washington were in a quandary, for they had no precedent to fall back on. To be sure, there had been plenty of celebrations for returning heroes, but nothing quite like this. They wondered how best to do justice to the occasion, and felt uncertain as to proper procedure. The subject was taken up in public and in private. The cabinet laid aside affairs of state to discuss what would be the most appropriate way to honor this youth who had, overnight, become the world's most popular figure. A committee of high officials, including cabinet members, were appointed to weigh the matter; out of this grew the large local reception committee. They got to work immediately, arranged for the arrival of the hero, the financing of the celebration, the order of ceremonies. The part the President should play remained in doubt.

The committee faced many perplexing questions. In what ship should Lindbergh come? Where should he stay in Washington? What part should his mother take in the program? Many papers were busy offering suggestions and announcing plans before they had been made. Still they accomplished something, for it was through their influence that a warship was sent to bring him back from France and that he was invited to be a guest of the President at the White House. But when it was announced in the press that Mrs. Lindbergh would also be a guest in the same household, there came a hitch. The young man had been invited, but, unfortunately, the mother had not. Still the papers continued to publish the fact that she would be, with the result that she finally was.

So at last all was settled. The U.S. Cruiser *Memphis*, on which the hero had sailed, was already at sea. No word came from Mrs. Lindbergh, however, as to her plans. A telegram had been sent asking her to let us know the time of her arrival, that she might be met by a White House car and conveyed to the temporary residence of the President on DuPont Circle. This message, however, did not reach her. As the time drew near for the arrival of the *Memphis*, the papers published the story that Mrs. Lindbergh had left Detroit on a certain train for Washington. No preparations had been made to meet her, for we had had no word from her. The next morning, again through newspapers, we learned at the White House that Mrs. Lindbergh had left the train on the outskirts of Baltimore, planning to go to the city by trolley car; that she had been recognized by some official and had accepted a motor ride to Baltimore. We telephoned several hotels and finally found her. We told her that the President and Mrs. Coolidge desired her to be their guest and that one of the White House automobiles was ready to go for her. She accepted the invitation. Accordingly the car, with driver, footman, and one of the President's junior aides, proceeded to Baltimore for the lady and returned with her to the temporary home of the President. This was late in the afternoon of Friday, June 10, the day previous to the scheduled arrival of her famous son.

Mrs. Lindbergh appeared to me a very agreeable person. She was self-possessed and seemingly unspoiled by the excitement her son was causing. She had a very pleasing personality and showed every evidence of a proper sense of proportion. She certainly made an excellent impression with everyone with whom she came in contact and conducted herself perfectly under most trying circumstances.

When Mrs. Lindbergh arrived there was a crowd assembled outside the house, the word somehow having leaked out that she was coming. A group of photographers had also collected and they promptly got busy as she alighted from the car. With grace and smiles she submitted to all their attentions. Upon entering the house she was shown to her room on the main bedroom floor, overlooking DuPont Circle, where the crowds had assembled. She was made to feel as comfortable as possible and permitted to rest before seeing the President and Mrs. Coolidge. Miss Randolph, the social secretary, joined her and explained what would be expected of her during the visit.

In due time Mrs. Lindbergh was taken to the President's study and formally presented to Mrs. Coolidge. The two engaged in conversation for fifteen or twenty minutes, until the arrival of the President from the Executive Offices. He joined them and remained for possibly another quarter of an hour, after which Mrs. Lindbergh was shown to her room again, where she remained until dinner-time. At this meal, in addition to the President, Mrs. Coolidge, and Mrs. Lindbergh was Mr. Dwight Morrow of New York. He had only by chance remained on until this time and it was fortunate for the Lindberghs that he did so, since he took a special interest in them and was of material help, both in Washington and later in New York. After dinner the party broke up, for the President and Mrs. Coolidge had to attend a government budget meeting. Mrs. Lindbergh was entertained awhile by Mr. Morrow and later retired to her own room to await the coming of her son in the morning.

There seemed to be some confusion as to the procedure on Colonel Lindbergh's arrival. Where and by whom should he be met? It was planned for the President and Mrs. Coolidge to go direct to the reviewing stand, but it was uncertain where he should first meet his mother. After considerable discussion it was decided that she should go to the Navy Yard and meet him at the boat. This she was willing to do, but she did not wish to have this first meeting between a mother and her son take the form of a public demonstration. At length it was arranged that, when the boat docked, Mrs. Lindbergh should be the first to go aboard and that she should be taken to a private room furnished by the Captain, where she could meet her son undisturbed by the public.

The ceremonies attending the arrival of Lindbergh in Washington— the parade up Pennsylvania Avenue to the reviewing stand, the exercises there, and the return to the temporary White House—formed one continuous ovation. In the first car came the President and Mrs. Coolidge and immediately behind, also in a White House car, rode Lindbergh and his mother. The cheers were for Lindbergh. For once the President and his wife were playing second fiddle.

Before going into the house the four people posed for pictures on the front steps. Once in the house, preparations were made to go to lunch; but the crowd outside was clamoring for Lindbergh, so lunch was delayed while the President and Mrs. Coolidge, Lindbergh and his mother went out on the veranda over the front entrance that the people might have another look at their hero. At his appearance they went into a frenzy of excitement. All through lunch they could be plainly heard calling for him. In fact there never seemed an hour while he was the guest of the President but what there were cries for him from the people assembled.

The lunch was very informal. When it was over, the young man was shown to his room, where, after greeting him and assuring him that I desired to be of service to him, I told him what was expected of him during his stay with the President and Mrs. Coolidge. All of this he calmly and graciously agreed to. He seemed especially pleased that someone should take the initiative in advising him. He was anxious to do "what's right," as he put it. So his entire stay was mapped out.

It was interesting to note his agreement with everything I suggested. He would reply "Check!" meaning "Yes!" I wondered how he came by this expression, but it was very characteristic of him. There were a lot of things to talk over with him; plans to be made for his visit and for the disposition of the mail and the gifts that were pouring in. His mail was arriving by the sackful. It would have been a physical impossibility for him to handle it personally and yet something had to be done with it. Among the gifts was about everything that could be imagined, some of it of real value, and much of it worthless. Every baker seemed to feel he must send him a cake; there was so much candy a store might have been started; there were fruits of all kinds, jewelry, art works, a number of flying-machine models, two suits of clothes, and so many cards and letters they almost filled a small room.

Alone with him in the quiet of his room it was easy to form an opinion of him. He was just a plain sweet character. He seemed rather bewildered, unable to realize what it was all about. When we had finished with these arrangements, he asked that his St. Louis friends be permitted to see him. He named Messrs. Knight, Bixby, Robertson, Blythe, and Mahoney. He did not have to wait long, for these very gentlemen were standing outside the door, hoping to be in at the first roll-call. So an appointment was made for them with the approval of the President and Mrs. Coolidge, as is customary in such cases. I suggested to him that some of these friends should be named to look out for his immediate affairs, especially to care for his mail, etc. This appealed to him, for he was anxious to see them, in his own words, "form some sort of an organization." They called him "Slim" and were glad of the privilege to serve him. When they left they took with them two taxicabs loaded with mail and presents.

Lindbergh seemed greatly relieved after this arrangement had been made. He could now turn his thoughts to the program that had been prepared for him. There was nothing scheduled for this first afternoon. He had opportunity to rest and he took advantage of it, pulling off his coat and stretching out full length on the bed. He spent some time alone with his mother and received a delegation of mail pilots who had come to Washington from all over the West to be here when he arrived. They all seemed to know him personally or so well by reputation that they addressed him as "Slim." No "Colonel" with these boys; he was just one of them.

When Lindbergh's baggage was delivered, it consisted of one lone suitcase. Fortunately he had a dress suit with him, since there was to be a formal dinner that evening. It was a very select affair, the guests few and strictly of the official set. . . . The dinner hour was set for seven o'clock, so that the evening program might be carried out. The guests were all prompt in arriving and shown to the main parlor on the second floor. There were the usual aides in attendance, in addition to the two chief aides who were dinner guests. The Marine Band Orchestra was stationed in the balcony. When everything was ready, Colonel Lindbergh and his mother were ushered in and, in true royal fashion, "made the circle" of the guests, being presented to each by one of the aides. Then, taking their places at the head of the line, they awaited the coming of the President and Mrs. Coolidge. After they had gone through the presentation ceremony, the President escorted Mrs. Lindbergh to the dining-room. Mrs. Coolidge was escorted by Colonel Lindbergh, who was seated on her right. The picture of this youth, but a short time ago an unknown mail pilot, taking precedence over all these officials actually sent a thrill through the old-timers like myself.

The Lindberghs, though they were the object of all eyes, seemed as composed as any of the others. Everyone seemed to feel that he was being especially honored at being permitted to be present.

At the conclusion of the meal the ladies retired to the library, the men to the large parlor where coffee and cigars were served. Lindbergh did not smoke, but he was, of course, the center of conversation and each one had an opportunity to say something to him. The immense throng that had assembled outside the house at his coming in the early afternoon had continued on, being reinforced from time to time. By evening it had become a multitude. As far as the eye could see from the windows there was a milling mass of people. They would yell and applaud at every possible provocation. "Lindy!" "Lindbergh!" "Colonel!" "Lone Eagle!" could be heard continuously above the din. "We want Lindy!" was begun in chorus and practiced until it became a perfect unison. When the men returned to the library from the parlor, they found the ladies of the party amusing themselves looking out of the windows at the people assembled on the street. Lindbergh walked over to one group, which included Mrs. Coolidge, and being immediately recognized there was a wild scramble outside by the people to get to that side of the house. It almost caused a panic and many accidents were narrowly averted by the prompt action of the police, who had been detailed in large numbers to hold the masses in check. The President and Mrs. Coolidge bade good-bye to their guests and retired to the private part of the house. But the guests made no attempt to leave until after Lindbergh had gone. Even the sage Secretary of State stayed on when he should have been the first to leave, not only because he was the ranking guest, but because he was to take part in the reception for Lindbergh by the Minnesota Society, to be held at the Willard Hotel. It was an interesting coincidence that the Secretary of State, Mr. Kellogg, had at some previous time directly opposed Lindbergh's father when both were candidates for the Senate. It seems that Mr. Kellogg won out, but that considerable feeling had remained even until now, to the possible embarrassment of both parties, in the light of the prominent part the Secretary of State had to play in welcoming his rival's son.

A White House automobile was placed at the disposal of the local committee and in this they took the Lindberghs to the reception of the Minnesota Society and also of the National Press Club in the Washington Auditorium. At both of these he received a wonderful ovation, so much so that upon his return to the home of the President at midnight he remarked that "they nearly mobbed me."

After a good night's rest, Lindbergh was clearly refreshed and ready for anything that might be on the cards. There were no definite plans for him in the forenoon, except that, if he was so inclined, he and his mother might accompany the President and Mrs. Coolidge to the eleven o'clock church service. When this was suggested to him he readily acquiesced. He had somewhere come into possession of a very light-colored suit of clothes and this he donned on Sunday morning instead of the traditional blue suit that had become associated with him. When the President noticed this, he inquired if it would not be better for Lindbergh to wear a dark suit. This was diplomatically communicated to him, but he did not readily see the necessity for it and it was only after considerable indirect persuasion that he agreed to make the change. Both on their way to church and on their return the Colonel and his mother were attended by the plaudits of the crowd.

Lunch was served soon after, having been moved forward to permit Lindbergh to fill the afternoon engagements planned by the local committee. At this lunch, in addition to the Lindberghs, there were Mr. and Mrs. Henry Cabot Lodge, whom the President invited at the very last minute.

After lunch the local committee took him in charge. Their plans included a visit to the tomb of the Unknown Soldier in Arlington Cemetery, a return to Washington through the Fort Myer Reservation, and a trip to the Walter Reed Hospital, which is many miles distant on the outskirts of the city, and Flag Day exercises at the Capitol. Between these engagements Lindbergh found time to go over to Bolling Field, to inspect the *Spirit of St. Louis*. After further ceremonies, the party returned through the heart of the city to the President's house, just in time to make ready for dinner. This was served very informally, there being no guests. . . .

The crowd assembled outside the President's house, seizing the opportunity to see him as he left for the station and as he returned. But this did not satisfy them and they remained long after he had retired, calling for him incessantly. A rainstorm came up during part of the time, but it did not seem to diminish the crowd. One girl sent in her card with this written on it: "Come on out, Lindy, it's raining!" Of course he did not see this, neither did he go out. Willing to the last to be obliging, he felt, however, that he had shown himself as often as he could with dignity.

Morning came and he was up bright and early. Arrangements had been made for his departure; the White House cars were ordered and a time set for his leaving. But everyone seemed nervous and when the committee arrived fifteen minutes early they persuaded him to go at once, thus for the first time breaking in on the scheduled plans. So, while he had arrived in the official White House automobile, he left in a hired car that was furnished by the committee on arrangements. He went to the Mayflower Hotel to attend a breakfast given by the National Aeronautical Association, and then on to Bolling Field, where after several attempts to start his own plane, he finally gave it up and proceeded in an Army plane on his journey to New York.

He left behind a splendid impression. He was always anxious to please and yet never pushed himself to the fore. There was no fault to be found with any part of his entire visit. His carriage and conduct were perfect.

The Greatest Man in the World

The Thurber Carnival　(1945)

The Lindbergh phenomenon was so big that it triggered our greatest twentieth-century humorist, James Thurber, into writing an irreverent piece taking off from it. It made me laugh when I first read it, and it makes me laugh now.

LOOKING back on it now, from the vantage point of 1950, one can only marvel that it hadn't happened long before it did. The United States of America had been, ever since Kitty Hawk, blindly constructing the elaborate petard by which, sooner or later, it must be hoist. It was inevitable that some day there would come roaring out of the skies a national hero of insufficient intelligence, background, and character successfully to endure the mounting orgies of glory prepared for aviators who stayed up a long time or flew a great distance. Both Lindbergh and Byrd, fortunately for national decorum and international amity, had been gentlemen; so had our other famous aviators. They wore their laurels gracefully, withstood the awful weather of publicity, married excellent women, usually of fine family, and quietly retired to private life and the enjoyment of their varying fortunes. No untoward incidents, on a world-wide scale, marred the perfection of their conduct on the perilous heights of fame. The exception to the rule was, however, bound to occur and it did, in July, 1937, when Jack ("Pal") Smurch, erstwhile mechanic's helper in a small garage in Westfield, Iowa, flew a second-hand, single-motored Bresthaven DragonFly III monoplane all the way around the world, without stopping.

Never before in the history of aviation had such a flight as Smurch's ever been dreamed of. No one had even taken seriously the weird floating auxiliary gas tanks, invention of the mad New Hampshire professor of astronomy, Dr. Charles Lewis Gresham, upon which Smurch placed full reliance. When the garage worker, a slightly built, surly, unprepossessing young man of twenty-two, appeared at Roosevelt Field in early July, 1937, slowly chewing a great quid of scrap tobacco, and announced, "Nobody ain't seen no flyin' yet," the newspapers touched briefly and satirically upon his projected twenty-five-thousand-mile flight. Aeronautical and automotive experts dismissed the idea curtly, implying that it was a hoax, a publicity stunt. The rusty, battered, second-hand plane wouldn't go. The Gresham auxiliary tanks wouldn't work. It was simply a cheap joke.

Smurch, however, after calling on a girl in Brooklyn who worked in the flap-folding department of a large paper-box factory, a girl whom he later described as his "sweet patootie," climbed nonchalantly into his ridiculous plane at dawn of the memorable seventh of July, 1937, spit a curve of tobacco juice into the still air, and took off, carrying with him only a gallon of bootleg gin and six pounds of salami.

When the garage boy thundered out over the ocean the papers were forced to record, in all seriousness, that a mad, unknown young man—his name was variously misspelled—had actually set out upon a preposterous attempt to span the world in a rickety, one-engined contraption, trusting to the long-distance refuelling device of a crazy schoolmaster. When, nine days later, without having stopped once, the tiny plane appeared above San Francisco Bay, headed for New York, spluttering and choking, to be sure, but still magnificently and miraculously aloft, the headlines, which long since had crowded everything else off the front page—even the shooting of the Governor of Illinois by the Vileti gang—swelled to unprecedented size, and the news stories began to run to twenty-five and thirty columns. It was noticeable, however, that the accounts of the epoch-making flight touched rather lightly upon the aviator himself. This was not because facts about the hero as a man were too meagre, but because they were too complete.

Reporters, who had been rushed out to Iowa when Smurch's plane was first sighted over the little French coast town of Serly-le-Mer, to dig up the story of the great man's life, had promptly discovered that the story of his life could not be printed. His mother, a sullen short-order cook in a shack restaurant on the edge of a tourists' camping ground near Westfield, met all inquiries as to her son with an angry "Ah, the hell with him; I hope he drowns." His father appeared to be in jail somewhere for stealing spotlights and laprobes from tourists' automobiles; his young brother, a weak-minded lad, had but recently escaped from the Preston, Iowa, Reformatory and was already wanted in several Western towns for the theft of money-order blanks from post offices. These alarming discoveries were still piling up at the very time that Pal Smurch, the greatest hero of the twentieth century, blear-eyed, dead for sleep, half-starved, was piloting his crazy junk-heap high above the region in which the lamentable story of his private life was being unearthed, headed for New York and a greater glory than any man of his time had ever known.

The necessity for printing some account in the papers of the young man's career and personality had led to a remarkable predicament. It was of course impossible to reveal the facts, for a tremendous popular feeling in favor of the young hero had sprung up, like a grass fire, when he was halfway across Europe on his flight around the globe. He was, therefore, described as a modest chap, taciturn, blond, popular with his friends, popular with girls. The only available snapshot of Smurch, taken at the wheel of a phony automobile in a cheap photo studio at an amusement park, was touched up so that the little vulgarian looked quite handsome. His twisted leer was smoothed into a pleasant smile. The truth was, in this way, kept from the youth's ecstatic compatriots; they did not dream that the Smurch family was despised and feared by its neighbors in the obscure Iowa town, nor that the hero himself, because of numerous unsavory exploits, had come to be regarded in Westfield as a nuisance and a menace. He had, the reporters discovered, once knifed the principal of his high school—not mortally, to be sure, but he had knifed him; and on another occasion, surprised in the act of stealing an altar-cloth from a church, he had bashed the sacristan over the head with a pot of Easter lilies; for each of these offences he had served a sentence in the reformatory.

Inwardly, the authorities, both in New York and in Washington, prayed that an understanding Providence might, however awful such a thing seemed, bring disaster to the rusty, battered plane and its illustrious pilot, whose unheard-of flight had aroused the civilized world to hosannas of hysterical praise. The authorities were convinced that the character of the renowned aviator was such that the limelight of adulation was bound to reveal him to all the world as a congenital hooligan mentally and morally unequipped to cope with his own prodigious fame. "I trust," said the Secretary of State, at one of many secret Cabinet meetings called to consider the national dilemma, "I trust that his mother's prayer will be answered," by which he referred to Mrs. Emma Smurch's wish that her son might be drowned. It was, however, too late for that—Smurch had leaped the Atlantic and then the Pacific as if they were millponds. At three minutes after two o'clock on the afternoon of July 17, 1937, the garage boy brought his idiotic plane into Roosevelt Field for a perfect three-point landing.

It had, of course, been out of the question to arrange a modest little reception for the greatest flier in the history of the world. He was received at Roosevelt Field with such elaborate and pretentious ceremonies as rocked the world. Fortunately, however, the worn and spent hero promptly swooned, had to be removed bodily from his plane, and was spirited from the field without having opened his mouth once. Thus he did not jeopardize the dignity of this first reception, a reception illumined by the presence of the Secretaries of War and the Navy, Mayor Michael J. Moriarity of New York, the Premier of Canada, Governors Fanniman, Groves, McFeely, and Critchfield and a brilliant array of European diplomats. Smurch did not, in fact, come to in time to take part in the gigantic hullabaloo arranged at City Hall for the next day. He was rushed to a secluded nursing home and confined to bed. It was nine days before he was able to get up, or to be more exact, before he was permitted to get up. Meanwhile the greatest minds in the country, in solemn assembly, had arranged a secret conference of city, state, and government officials, which Smurch was to attend for the purpose of being instructed in the ethics and behavior of heroism.

On the day that the little mechanic was finally allowed to get up and dress and, for the first time in two weeks, take a great chew of tobacco, he was permitted to receive the newspapermen—this by way of testing him out. Smurch did not wait for questions. "Youse guys," he said—and the *Times* man winced—"youse guys can tell the cock-eyed world dat I put it over on Lindbergh, see? Yeh—an' made an ass o' them two frogs." The "two frogs" was a reference to a pair of gallant French fliers who, in attempting a flight only halfway round the world, had, two weeks before, unhappily been lost at sea. The *Times* man was bold enough, at this point, to sketch out for Smurch the accepted formula for interviews in cases of this kind; he explained that there should be no arrogant statements belittling the achievements of other heroes, particularly heroes of foreign nations. "Ah, the hell with that," said Smurch. "I did it, see? I did it, an' I'm talkin' about it." And he did talk about it.

None of this extraordinary interview was, of course, printed. On the contrary, the newspapers, already under the disciplined direction of a secret directorate created for the occasion and composed of statesmen and editors, gave out to a panting and restless world that "Jacky," as he had been arbitrarily nicknamed, would consent to say only that he was very happy and that anyone could have done what he did. "My achievement has been, I fear, slightly exaggerated," the *Times* man's article had him protest, with a modest smile. These newspaper stories were kept from the hero, a restriction which did not serve to abate the rising malevolence of his temper. The situation was, indeed, extremely grave, for Pal Smurch was, as he kept insisting, "rarin' to go." He could not much longer be kept from a nation clamorous to lionize him. It was the most desperate crisis the United States of America had faced since the sinking of the *Lusitania*.

On the afternoon of the twenty-seventh of July, Smurch was spirited away to a conference-room in which were gathered mayors, governors, government officials, behaviorist psychologists, and editors. He gave them each a limp, moist paw and a brief unlovely grin. "Hah ya?" he said. When Smurch was seated, the Mayor of New York arose and, with obvious pessimism, attempted to explain what he must say and how he must act when presented to the world, ending his talk with a high tribute to the hero's courage and integrity. The Mayor was followed by Governor Fanniman of New York, who, after a touching declaration of faith, introduced Cameron Spottiswood, Second Secretary of the American Embassy in Paris, the gentleman selected to coach Smurch in the amenities of public ceremonies. Sitting in a chair, with a soiled yellow tie in his hand and his shirt open at the throat, unshaved, smoking a rolled cigarette, Jack Smurch listened with a leer on his lips. "I get ya, I get ya," he cut in, nastily. "Ya want me to ack like a softy, huh? Ya want me to ack like that baby-faced Lindbergh, huh? Well, nuts to that, see?" Everyone took in his breath sharply; it was a sigh and a hiss. "Mr. Lindbergh," began a United States Senator, purple with rage, "and Mr. Byrd—" Smurch, who was paring his nails with a jackknife, cut in again. "Byrd!" he exclaimed. "Aw fa God's sake, dat big—" Somebody shut off his blasphemies with a sharp word. A newcomer had entered the room. Everyone stood up, except Smurch, who, still busy with his nails, did not even glance up. "Mr. Smurch," said someone sternly, "the President of the United States!" It had been thought that the presence of the Chief Executive might have a chastening effect upon the young hero, and the former had been, thanks to the remarkable cooperation of the press, secretly brought to the obscure conference-room.

A great, painful silence fell. Smurch looked up, waved a hand at the President. "How ya comin'?" he asked, and began rolling a fresh cigarette. The silence deepened. Someone coughed in a strained way. "Geez, it's hot, ain't it?" said Smurch. He loosened two more shirt buttons, revealing a hairy chest and the tattooed word "Sadie" enclosed in a stencilled heart. The great and important men in the room, faced by the most serious crisis in recent American history, exchanged worried frowns. Nobody seemed to know how to proceed. "Come awn, come awn," said Smurch. "Let's get the hell out of here! When do I start cuttin' in on de parties, huh? And what's they goin' to be in it?" He rubbed a thumb and forefinger together meaningly. "Money!" exclaimed a state senator, shocked, pale. "Yeh, money," said Pal, flipping his cigarette out of a window. "An' big money." He began rolling a fresh cigarette. "Big money," he repeated, frowning over the rice paper. He tilted back in his chair, and leered at each gentleman, separately, the leer of an animal that knows its power, the leer of a leopard loose in a bird-and-dog shop. "Aw fa God's sake, let's get some place where it's cooler," he said. "I been cooped up plenty for three weeks!"

Smurch stood up and walked over to an open window, where he stood staring down into the street, nine floors below. The faint shouting of newsboys floated up to him. He made out his name. "Hot dog!" he cried, grinning, ecstatic. He leaned out over the sill. "You tell 'em, babies!" he shouted down. "Hot diggity dog!" In the tense little knot of men standing behind him, a quick, mad impulse flared up. An unspoken word of appeal, of command, seemed to ring through the room. Yet it was deadly silent. Charles K. L. Brand, secretary to the Mayor of New York City, happened to be standing nearest Smurch; he looked inquiringly at the President of the United States. The President, pale, grim, nodded shortly. Brand, a tall, powerfully built man, once a tackle at Rutgers, stepped forward, seized the greatest man in the world by his left shoulder and the seat of his pants, and pushed him out the window.

"My God, he's fallen out the window!" cried a quick-witted editor.

"Get me out of here!" cried the President. Several men sprang to his side and he was hurriedly escorted out of a door toward a side-entrance of the building. The editor of the Associated Press took charge, being used to such things. Crisply he ordered certain men to leave, others to stay; quickly he outlined a story which all the papers were to agree on, sent two men to the street to handle that end of the tragedy, commanded a Senator to sob and two Congressmen to go to pieces nervously. In a word, he skillfully set the stage for the gigantic task that was to follow, the task of breaking to a grief-stricken world the sad story of the untimely, accidental death of its most illustrious and spectacular figure.

The funeral was, as you know, the most elaborate, the finest, the solemnest, and the saddest ever held in the United States of America. The monument in Arlington Cemetery, with its clean white shaft of marble and the simple device of a tiny plane carved on its base, is a place for pilgrims, in deep reverence, to visit. The nations of the world paid lofty tributes to little Jacky Smurch, America's greatest hero. At a given hour there were two minutes of silence throughout the nation. Even the inhabitants of the small, bewildered town of Westfield, Iowa, observed this touching ceremony; agents of the Department of Justice saw to that. One of them was especially assigned to stand grimly in the doorway of a little shack restaurant on the edge of the tourists' camping ground just outside the town. There, under his stern scrutiny, Mrs. Emma Smurch bowed her head above two hamburger steaks sizzling on her grill—bowed her head and turned away, so that the Secret Service man could not see the twisted, strangely familiar, leer on her lips.

W. M. KIPLINGER

Tourists See the Sights

Washington Is Like That (1942)

As an indication of how much buzz this book received when it was published, it's interesting to note that two of its reviewers were Carl Sandburg and Malcolm Cowley. Both reviews were essentially very positive, and some of what each writer had to say about Kiplinger's book warrants repeating. At the time it was published, Sandburg was writing "once-a-week" pieces for the papers. His column of September 6, 1942, was a paean to Kiplinger:

> I read it all. Every page. W. M. Kiplinger wrote it. He writes crisp. Smooth. But crisp. Imagine he's a good talker. Talks long if he isn't stopped. But he breaks it up. Washington is like that.
>
> Good book still and all. Takes in a lot of territory. Covers more ground than you'd think. Better than a trip to Washington—if you've never been in Washington. Better than living in Washington—if you live there and don't know what's going on. . . .
>
> . . . a library of little books on Washington. . . . He shows off and shows up the national capital. He mocks at it and loves it. The city is human, the government human. Alive! Alive! Watch it. It breathes! It speaks! . . .
>
> Thanks, Kiplinger. You seen your duty and done it. Your book stands a good chance of rating as the best biography and portrait ever written of an American big city.

Cowley lauds Kiplinger by saying, "We needed a comprehensive book on Washington, and plainly Mr. Kiplinger was the man to write it. . . . His book contains more information about the national capital and the national government than any other single volume in existence—even the Writers' Project guide to Washington, the Congressional Directory or the United States Government Manual."

There are lots of guidebooks for visitors to Washington. Especially fun to read are the historic ones, the old ones. Kiplinger's book, how-

*ever, is much more than a guidebook. Indeed, separate chapters deal
with everything from "Money Shovelers" to "G-Men, T-Men, Sleuths."
Kiplinger used thirty-one men and women to spread out over the city
and help him dig up the facts.*

*W. M. Kiplinger, called "Kip," was a contemporary of my mother's.
He had come to Washington in 1916, a year before my parents, as a
reporter for the Associated Press, and not long after had begun a Washington newsletter for businessmen that continues today. Kiplinger has
become a Washington name. In fact, his son—my contemporary,
Austin—grew up here and was actively involved with Washington's
first mayor, Walter Washington, in spearheading the development of a
new museum that will send tourists into various neighborhoods of the
city to explore historic sites.*

*This section from Kiplinger focuses on the ordinary tourist; cer-
tainly not everyone who comes to Washington is a guest at the White
House. Kiplinger calls Washington the "greatest sight-seeing city in the
world," with which I quite agree—and at the least cost, I might add,
since so much of it is free, including the National Gallery of Art and
all the museums under the Smithsonian umbrella. This excerpt ends
with a nostalgic assessment of the city by an "elderly citizen from
Sacramento," who wonders what Washington would look like thirty
years from then. Unlike that man, this particular elderly citizen has
had the good fortune to see Washington thirty years from then, and
even thirty years after that!*

WASHINGTON is the greatest sight-seeing city in the world, the
rubbernecker's dream come true. In normal times, four million people come every year to the capital, the nation's history
factory since 1800. They find it jampacked with buildings where
occurred the events they read about at school. Cluttered with houses
where these days' men with headline names and newsreel faces brush
their teeth and growl about the toast. Bulging with big stone structures
which incase thousands of Uncle Sam's hired hands during working
hours. Splattered with embassies and studded with statues. Green grass
and trees grow all around. The city green and white.

All this puts a hankering to see Washington in the mind of anybody
who has a suitcase, a little spare time and enough loose change to make
the trip. The camera-lugging, guidebook-buying throng that rides into
Washington in each peacetime year outnumbers the capital's residents
four to one. It equals the combined populations of New Orleans, Min-

neapolis, Cincinnati, Newark, Indianapolis, Houston, Seattle, Rochester and Denver, with some thousands to boot.

This year, though the hankering to sight-see in the capital remains, it is harder to satisfy. Vacations are fewer and shorter, auto tires are scarce, the family car must be conserved, and hotel rooms in Washington are at premium. Nevertheless, hundreds of thousands still come to look at Washington's landmarks, and the capital still maintains its position as No. 1 sight-seeing city.

Peddling food, lodging, city transportation and gimcracks to the normal horde of 4,000,000 is one of Washington's "export businesses." The exports are the memories and impressions which tourists take back home. The business involves the money spent while those memories and impressions are being formed. Sight-seers spend, on an average, at least ten dollars each while in the capital. That mounts up to the total of at least $40,000,000 in a normal year.

The mass of four million tourists contains as many kinds of people as there are in the thousands of home towns from which they come. Overweight gents. Lads who peer twice at the price of a blue-plate lunch before ordering. Grand dames who have toured the world. Girls who are making their first trip away from home. Children and babes.

Twosomes (many of them honeymooners) and family groups are in the large majority. And there are high school students, under the chilling watch of chaperoning teachers. Assorted tourists bound together by the money-saving opportunities of the "everything-included tours." Newsboys, sent traveling by the youth-molding fancies of publishers. Workers who take to the joint vacation idea as a means of whittling costs. Unattached men and boys (a minority) who are going it alone. Unaccompanied women and girls (numerous) who are seeing the sights within the security of organized tours.

Those who get the least return for what they spend are the pompous folks who waddle up to desks in top-priced hotels. They hire limousines with uniformed chauffeur-guides. Setting themselves in the middle of dignity, they ride stiffly up Connecticut Avenue and the length of Pennsylvania Avenue. They do little looking—people might think they were looking.

Not so with the common herd. Arriving on the banks of the Potomac in family cars, as four-fifths of them do in the average year, they drive up and down the city, back and forth, gawking all the while, contributing to Washington's notorious traffic jams. Those who want nothing to do with aimless driving and traffic jams either pile on the rubberneck busses or hire the licensed guides who stand on street corners, waiting to sell their knowledge of the city.

Thousands come to Washington with no thought of driving their own cars on the streets, or riding busses, or hiring guides. They are those who fasten themselves upon friends or relatives residing in the capital. Result: Tired Washingtonians—trudging at the elbows of people they met casually in other cities, entertaining distant relatives and people whose names are at the tail-end of their Christmas card lists.

Apart from all that, most tourists who come to Washington have definite and fairly accurate ideas about what they are going to see. Credit this to the space Washington commands in papers and magazines and on the movie screen. No other city in the world is more photographed or more written about. Most sight-seers, therefore, are just soaking up details. Getting closely acquainted with things about which they have advance knowledge.

The man from Boise, sitting right behind the bus driver, sees that the Washington Monument looks just like he thought it would look. The Kansas City lady in the seat across the aisle had been seeing pictures of the Capitol Building ever since she was six, which was forty years ago.

The National Museum, under control of the Smithsonian Institution, attracts the most sight-seers. It normally draws at least 2,700,000 a year, according to the count kept by guards at the doors, with their clicking counting machines. Counts made at other buildings and memorials show the comparative popularity with tourists. Here are some recent annual totals: Lincoln Memorial, 1,600,000; Mount Vernon, 1,500,000; Congressional Library, 1,000,000; Washington Monument, 950,000; Bureau of Engraving and Printing, 425,000. No count is kept at the Capitol and, during the national emergency, the White House is not open to visitors in general. It should be noted, also, that the Washington Monument total is held down by the limitations of the elevators. And the Japanese cherry blossom crowds, who pour in every spring, are impossible to count. But anyone who has seen the cars packed bumper to bumper around the Tidal Basin and Speedway knows that the numbers run well into the hundreds of thousands in an average year.

A few tourists go up in the air and look down on the capital as though it were a giant picture spread out on the floor. The helium-filled blimp *Enterprise* (now taken over by the Navy) normally carries 6,000 passengers a year when operating commercially on its 20-minute sight-seeing trips. Another 18,000 do their aerial sight-seeing in airplanes.

Those people get a panorama of a metropolitan area of over 1,000,000 people, without a skyscraper, centered in a saucer between rolling hills, with the Potomac River a silver ribbon in the middle. Near the river are massive, squatty buildings spread for almost two miles between the Capitol and the Lincoln Memorial. With the exception of the two-story temporary war buildings, they are six-story structures, each covering about a city block. Most of them are on the river side of Pennsylvania Avenue. On the other side of "The Avenue" spreads the central business section. As the tourist looks northward he sees office buildings giving way to apartment houses, the area of fashionable residences, embassies, the suburban belt and, finally, the Maryland countryside. Net impression of Washington, seen from the air: It looks as though it had been plopped down in the middle of the woodland growth, with trees and grass showing through between the buildings. A flat city which sprawls over the ground, not rising toward the sky as does New York. A city with few factories and tall smoke stacks. A city dominated by one building—the Capitol.

If you look from the Capitol toward the north, south, east or west, you will see that it stands at the intersection of four thoroughfares which divide the city into four quadrants or sections, Northeast, Northwest, Southeast, Southwest. A set of numbered streets paralleling the north-south axis runs to the east from the Capitol and another to the west. Similarly, one set of streets designated by letters parallels the east-west axis on the north and another set parallels it on the south. This gives each of the four sections its own set of lettered and numbered streets. That is why Washington street addresses have to be written with N.E., N.W., S.E., or S.W. after the street names.

In the Northwest section are the main business sections, top-flight hotels, apartment houses, old mansions, government workers' boarding houses and above-the-average homes. The Northeast and Southeast quadrants are distinctly middle-class. The Southwest area is loaded with the big government structures, and railroad yards, and meat-packing warehouses, and that glamorous quarter, the fish wharf, where tony people go to smell the smells which are not tony. . . .

Tourists who do not get off the beaten tracks go away without seeing the incongruities which abound in the capital. Dingy and squalid buildings are only a traffic light away from some of the city's finest structures. Negro homes are within two blocks of the mansions of Dupont Circle. Solid blocks of homely shop buildings line both sides of Pennsylvania Avenue a block west of the White House. Beer joints, penny arcades, the home of the Gayety burlesque, and pool halls are just up the street from the magnificent building which houses the archives of the United States. Cheap hotels and rooming houses rim the pristine Supreme Court Building. Railroad trains clack along near some of the newer government buildings south of the Mall but have the good grace to dive into a tunnel just before they reach the Capitol.

Nor are such incongruities all that the tourists who "go by the book" or take only scheduled tours fail to see. Here are just a few of the things they miss: The old Georgetown water front to which eighteenth-century ships came from across the seas, now the abode of warehouses, coal yards, and gravel companies. Old forts which circle the capital, from one of which (Fort Stevens) President Lincoln watched a Civil War battle. The United States Naval Observatory, where the goings and comings of the stars and planets are observed "officially." Washington's little China-town on H Street. The great hall of the old Pension Office Building (now filled with desks and girl clerks) in which presidential inaugural balls were held between 1885 and 1909. The Octagon House which served as the executive mansion for President Madison and his wife Dolly while the White House was being restored after it was set afire by the British troops in 1814. The subway which hauls senators between the Capitol and their office building. Small stone gatehouses which were on the Capitol grounds until 1874, now in the Mall. Augustus Saint-Gaudens' famous statue over a grave in Rock Creek Cemetery, known as "Grief" because Mark Twain declared it represented all the woes of humankind. (Now a few Washingtonians visit it and call it "Hope.")

The efficient and most economical way to "do the city," unless a guid-ing friend or relative is at hand, is to ride the sight-seeing busses on tours which parade the capital's more obvious glories at from $2.00 to $3.25 per tour. The bus companies offer several tours, each requiring from two hours to four and a half hours. They are timed to enable tourists to cover two routes each day, one in the morning, one in the afternoon—or three, if an evening tour is taken. One company, handling approximately 50,000 passengers a year, signs up business at desks in hotel lobbies and calls at the hotels for its customers. Another specializes in providing chartered busses for groups attending conventions in Washington, parties orga-nized by travel bureaus in other cities and others who come to the capital "in the mass" to reduce expenses. Smaller bus lines, limousines in sight-seeing service, and taxicab drivers handle the rest.

Tourists waiting at a bus terminal for a tour to begin look like nothing else but what they are. They fidget. They tinker with adjustments on their cameras. They glance at bus company literature and then stuff it into purses and pockets. They do little talking, trying to hide their self-consciousness from passers-by, for ordinary men and women like to be tourists but don't like to seem to be tourists.

The bus pulls up. "This bus for the tour of government buildings," announces the starter. Like children bossed around by their parents, the ticket holders get into their seats. Ahead of them is a typical Washington tour (as it was before the war closed a number of public buildings to visi-tors): The ever-wagging tongue and ever-pointing forefinger of the lecturer. Miles of buildings sliding past the windows. Bus riding punctuated with stops at government structures. Stops which mean much walking down long corridors, around rooms, up and down stairs.

As the bus gets under way, the lecturer tilts his badge-fronted cap, braces himself. Then he begins his spiel by asking each passenger to speak up and tell the folks the name of his or her home state. In one bus-load there may be people from a dozen states. First comes the White House, living place of every President except Washington. Likenesses of them and their wives, done in oil. Rooms full of relics. High ceilings. Main attraction is the East Room, hall of state functions, weddings, funeral ceremonies ever since the days of John Adams.

On to the Bureau of Engraving and Printing, there to see sheets of blank paper become spending money. A snicker at the lecturer's stock gag: "Don't forget to bring me back a sample."

Then up the Mall toward the Capitol, stopping to go through the Smithsonian Institution buildings which house the National Museum exhibits. Everybody takes a gaze upward at Lindbergh's *Spirit of St. Louis* plane, slung from the ceiling. Women hasten to the large room where costumes of the Presidents' wives are displayed on wax figures. Men wander around areas devoted to machinery and transportation. Other exhibits, seen by the few who are not slaves to the bus schedule: Textiles, coins, naval and military history, firearms, medical and dental history, power, foods, wood industries and mineral technology.

Tiring legs and hot feet climb aboard the bus. The lecturer announces: "Next stop is the Capitol. One hour to go through the interior." The elderly couple from Louisiana take stock. She says her feet ache. He tells her his eyes are blurry. The lecturer prattles: "The Capitol is 750 feet long and half as wide. The corner stone was laid in the year 1793 and . . ." The voice begins to sound something like the motor— ceaseless, monotonous. The motor finally stops, but the voice continues. "We are now on the Capitol Plaza. You will enter the door at the head of the main steps in the center of the building. You will not be permitted to take pictures of the interior. Please stay with the guide assigned to your group."

Going up the Capitol steps, the comment is: "Here's where the Presidents are inaugurated." Inside, under the great dome, another voice, another pointing arm, more statistics, more details, more listening, walking—walking—walking—listening—paintings—statues—with stone-floored corridors in both directions.

The group jostles through a narrow door into the old Supreme Court Chamber. "We will next enter the chamber where the Senate is in session. We will remain five minutes." Twelve senators are at their desks.

Eighty-four are not. Disappointment. "Don't they ever do any work?" Outside again, and the guide takes pains to tell the tourists that senators and representatives work long hours in committee rooms and at their offices. "They really do most of their work there."

Then more looks at enormous paintings and statues of famous people. Dates, names, masses of information. Then a look at the House in session and the party returns to the bus.

Over to the Library of Congress, with the Declaration of Independence under protective yellow glass, the Constitution of the United States, the Gutenberg Bible and the Magna Charta (all taken off display until the war's end).

Tired feet plod out of the building. The bus again. The Californian wishes out loud that he was back in his hotel. "Hotel. Name your hotel," spouts the lecturer. "The tour is concluded and we will take you to where you are stopping. If you wish to purchase tickets for the grand double tour to Georgetown, Arlington National Cemetery, Alexandria and Mount Vernon, leaving at two o'clock this afternoon, I have them on sale."

The Mount Vernon tour attracts the most sight-seers. One company sells 500 tickets for it every week during a normal summer season. Running a close second is the tour of the government buildings. Others rank as follows:

Third: The general tour labeled "Seeing All of Washington Beautiful"—taking the tourist past the prime residences, the "fashionable shopping center" and the Lincoln Memorial.

Fourth: The religious tour of the Franciscan Monastery, the National Shrine of the Immaculate Conception at the Catholic University, and the National Episcopal Cathedral (with the Scottish Rite Temple and the Soldiers' Home thrown in).

Fifth: Short tour of Arlington National Cemetery, Fort Myer and Georgetown.

Sixth: "Washington at Night"—along the city's streets and avenues, around the Tidal Basin (famous for its cherry blossoms), along the river and ending at the gilded Library of Congress.

Seventh: The interiors of the new government buildings—including the Supreme Court Building, Folger Shakespeare Library, Department of Justice (with the FBI), the Archives Building and the new National Art Gallery (donated by Andrew Mellon).

In addition, out-of-town tours run to historic areas in Maryland and Virginia, all linked with the national capital by early nineteenth-century happenings and personages. Many of them have ties with the earliest of colonial history. . . .

One day I questioned several tourists who were resting their aching muscles in lobbies of three medium-priced hotels which cater to sight-seers about what they liked about Washington.

A grocer from Minneapolis was most interested in the homes of former Presidents and political notables.

A high school teacher from Pueblo, Colorado, "was just thrilled" at seeing the house near Twentieth and I Streets, N.W., where Peggy (O'Neale) Eaton lived as the glamour girl of Andrew Jackson's day when she played hob with national affairs.

A housewife from Wichita, Kansas, liked the interior furnishings of the Lee Mansion at Arlington and the Mansion House at Mount Vernon.

An oboe player from Boston was "intensely interested" in the Music Division in the Library of Congress.

A meter-reader from Pittsburgh remembered the Surratt House where conspirators laid plans for Lincoln's assassination (in the six hundred block of H Street, N.W., now the heart of Chinatown).

A 15-year-old girl from Litchfield, Illinois, liked the ride to the top of the Washington Monument, and the chance to see women members of Congress on the floor of the House.

A librarian from Oklahoma City was glad she had seen the house on M Street in Georgetown where Washington and L'Enfant did the work of planning the capital city.

A shoe dealer from Bridgeport remembered the houses noted for connection with men who were close to Presidents, such as the "Little Green House on K Street" (scene of goings on during the Harding administration), the Blair House (where Jackson's henchmen manipulated the "Kitchen Cabinet"), Tayloe House (residence of Senator Mark Hanna when he was the power behind the McKinley administration), and the "Red House on R Street" (where Tom Corcoran and Ben Cohen drafted much of the early New Deal legislation).

A retired merchant from Portland, Maine, told me he had a weakness for statistics and produced the evidence to prove it. He pulled out a notebook filled with figures, big and little, which he had collected from guidebooks and bus lectures. This is the sort of thing he had jotted down:

Pennsylvania Avenue is six miles long and 166 feet wide from building line to building line. The assessed value of the Capitol and improvements on its grounds: $37,500,000. Head-to-toe measurement of the Lincoln Statue in Lincoln Memorial: 19 feet. The bodies of 229 men who lost their lives in the sinking of the *Maine* are buried beneath the mast of their ship at Arlington National Cemetery. The Commerce Department Building is 1,050 feet long and occupies nearly eight acres. The top of the Capitol dome is 285 feet above ground level on the plaza side. The

Library of Congress contains six million books and pamphlets, 3,000,000 maps, charts and musical compositions. Washington has 700 parks, ranging in size from a few hundred square feet to Rock Creek Park (1,800 acres) and the Mall (one mile long and an eighth of a mile wide).

An elderly citizen from Sacramento looked as if he was sorry he had come. "Sure, Washington is a fine city and an interesting place. But it isn't the Washington I knew thirty years or so ago before I went out to the Coast. Everything's changed. There's a filling station at Connecticut and N Streets where the British Embassy used to be. A government building where Poli's Theatre stood. Old Center Market is gone and a Federal Triangle building covers the spot. Old Chinatown on Pennsylvania Avenue near the Capitol is torn down. Office buildings and apartment houses where fashionable people had their mansions. Restaurants, shoe stores and the like where there used to be saloons, musty and with sawdust on the floor, along the north side of Pennsylvania Avenue. Fancy steel and concrete stands out at the ball park instead of the wooden seats where real fans saw Walter Johnson and Ty Cobb when they were rookies. Office buildings in place of the fine old residences which once surrounded Lafayette Park opposite the White House. A noisy, overcrowded city instead of a place that was sleepy and quiet like a village. It's all a lot different than when I knew it. It's too dressed up. Wonder what it'll look like thirty years from now."

SIMONE DE BEAUVOIR

Washington

America Day by Day (1954)

Although Simone de Beauvoir, the French novelist and social essayist, is often utterly negative in describing the Washington she saw when she visited the United States on a four-month tour in 1947, I wish that she had stayed longer and written more. De Beauvoir was essentially traveling for pleasure around the United States, going from place to place and giving lectures along the way. While her book is presented in diary style, it was written retrospectively, and was meant to convey what revealed itself to her "day by day." She was here in Washington for only a few days and does seem to have viewed it more as a way station on her travels than as a true stopping-off place.

Elsewhere in her book, she says that New York and Chicago are "the most human, the most uplifting cities that I know." She certainly sees Washington differently. She calls herself a "conscientious tourist," and she takes great pains to give an honest view of the natural life of the city. Not everyone visiting Washington is a "conscientious tourist," nor should they be. Unlike de Beauvoir, I find none of Washington boring or depressing. But although I disagree with much of what she writes, her piece reminds me of how useful it is to see ourselves as others see us.

February 14

I took the night train for Washington, where I have another lecture to give. This is the first city in America that I'll see after New York. I don't know anyone here; I'll stay only a day and a half. Just when I was beginning to feel at home in America, I've become a tourist again.

My hotel is at the upper end of town, on the edge of a park vaster than the Bois de Boulogne. From my window I see tennis courts and a large garden. You'd think you were in a resort town. My room has the quiet, dull luxury of resort hotels. There's a radio you can listen to for two hours by sliding fifty cents into a slot. I don't really know what to do with myself. I know how to wander around a European city. But in America, it's another story . . .

I must take the plunge. I go downstairs. I take a taxi. These avenues lined with peaceful houses, elegant and discreet stores, are nothing like the streets in New York. All the houses are made of brick. There are few cars, few pedestrians. It's a provincial city. The taxi turns down a broad road lined with monuments as white as marble—perhaps they are marble. In any case, the style is Greco-Roman. In the distance stands the Capitol, which I've seen so often in movies. I stop. To gain time before leaping into the unknown, I've decided to go to the museum [the National Gallery]. It's also in the Greco-Roman style, with a huge, majestic staircase. The interior does not belie the facade. With its enormous marbled columns, its colonnades, its flagstones, and its green plants, this museum is a cross between a mausoleum and a Turkish bath. The richness of its collections stuns me. Yet there is something restful about finding yourself in the serene and international world of paintings: I could be at the Louvre, the Prado, or the Uffizi. The new world meets the old—there is only one past. When I emerge, I'm surprised to find myself in Washington again.

I am a conscientious tourist. I lunch in the commercial center of town—a glum and ugly area where geometry does not achieve grandeur but produces only tedium. And then I climb the Capitol's steps. Hundreds of Americans, coming from all corners of America, make this pilgrimage. As people do at all public monuments, they measure with their eyes the cupola's height and stop before the statues. The boldest ones climb to the top of the dome on a series of stone stairs and iron ladders. Everyone glances timidly at the great hall of Congress, half-empty at the beginning of this afternoon's session. Official guides explain the past and the present. I'm satisfied with a superficial glance. With its corridors, halls, underground passages, terraces, stairways, monuments, colonnades, and galleries, the Capitol is as boring as the Pantheon or the Chamber of Deputies. And the green esplanade that extends to the obelisk erected in memory of George Washington is more disheartening than the Champ-de-Mars. Despite the soft light and the freshness of the grass, it looks to me like a torrid desert—boredom burns. In the whiteness of their marble, the museums and embassies refract the dull heat of a relentless summer. I cross over to the left, fleeing these official splendors and going toward the docks that smell of fish and tar. The "Potomac"—it's a word to conjure with. Part of its poetry for me is no doubt owing to the beautiful red color of Cocteau's book [*La Fin du Potomak*] with its Mortimers and its Eugènes. And then there is the savage sound of old Indian names; this savagery is a surprise in Washington, which asserts that nature has been conquered by politics, diplomacy, and monuments to the dead. The Potomac is frozen. Boats, yachts, and ferries are caught in the ice. I'm at the water's edge. Children amuse themselves by throwing heavy stones onto the shining surface, which sometimes resists the shock and sometimes cracks. Large parks and green banks border the river, which curves out and extends into a lake. It's very large, and the wooded hills on the other bank seem far away. Down below, in an island of greenery, I glimpse the whiteness of marble colonnades—the Lincoln Memorial. A little farther, to my right, at the top of a ridiculous staircase, there's more marble whiteness at the Jefferson Memorial. Such ugliness is disconcerting in the land of noble skyscrapers. But if you sit on the staircase with your back turned to this city where History is petrified into boredom, you can contemplate a site worthy of the memories it evokes. The Potomac is a great northern river that shines with frozen brightness amid spring greenery under a blue southern sky. For the people of New York, Washington is already the South, and I feel the South in that unexpected warmth after leaving the snows of Central Park. It's marvelous to be sitting in the sun beside a frozen river under a bright sky. . . .

February 15

It seems futile to me to set out on foot this morning to see Washington; the dimensions of these American cities are discouraging. I want to take refuge in some corner with a book and pretend I'm not traveling. But this doesn't take into account the untiring kindness of Americans. Two old ladies telephone and offer to drive me around the city. Half an hour later we're already on our way. We drive down the hill and follow the bottom of a ravine. This park is a large swathe of unspoiled countryside, wooded, ever-changing, crossed by rivers bordered by huge rocks. It reminds me of Brittany near Huelgoat. In the middle of the woods stand the graves of an old cemetery. We reach a wealthy residential area. Once more, I'm completely astonished to encounter in reality what looked to me like a studio set in the movies. Along the deserted sidewalks I recognize those white gates opening onto flower gardens, and those white wooden houses, neat and monotonous. Suddenly, I'm surprised to find myself in the heart of an old Dutch town: the tidy, narrow streets are paved with cobblestones; the old houses are covered in a coat of red or white plaster through which you can glimpse the rectangular bricks beneath. This is Georgetown, the oldest section of Washington. Dates appear on the facades—1776, 1780. The small windows, pointed roofs, balconies, and wrought iron work remind me of the childlike houses of the villages of the Zuider Zee. A few miles away we're transported to an English village with its cottages of flowering geraniums, its broad, straw-colored roofs, its calm streets. I didn't at all expect to find the picturesque remnants of old Europe around Washington. I think joyfully that America still harbors plenty of unexpected pleasures.

We cross the Potomac and enter Arlington National Cemetery. This is a magnificent park where only highly honored officers are buried. There is no avoiding the dreadful monument* crowning the top of the hill, where the view of the Potomac and Washington is otherwise breathtaking. But nothing disfigures the green lawns and winding paths. The graves are vertically placed flat stones, bearing simply a name. No inscription, no crown, no flower. The trees and sky are enough to honor the dead. The stones are placed quite far apart, lost in the greenery: each dead man reigns over large subterranean spaces. And the general impression is that the placement of each grave was guided by personal considerations. There is no symmetry, no overall plan. Probably the shade of this tree suited this dead soldier, the open ground that one. . . .

On Broadway, despite the weighty affirmation of the skyscrapers, in Queens, despite the desolate uniformity of the working-class districts, in Arlington, despite the marble serenity of the Capitol, the cemeteries remind us that every existence is singular and that every man is in himself an absolute. They remind us that life is carnal, that even with air conditioning the air is breathed with real lungs. Returning to the earth, man gives proof that he is not a mechanical creature; he is flesh, and real blood runs in his veins. It's the graves in America that confirm with the greatest authority that man is still human. I don't know if Americans are aware of this reminder, if they feel more tenderness than they admit for the sleep that will give them respite from their breathless lives. The fact is, they don't bury their dead in rows, and their cemeteries have more personality than their towns. Among these stones half-sunk in the earth, one finally escapes the banality of daily life.

---

*We'll never know, but she may be referring to the Lee Mansion, which, of course, predated the cemetery, and which I (and most others, I imagine) find beautiful and imposing, hardly hideous.

DAVID McCULLOUGH

I Love Washington

Brave Companions (1991)

Here's a piece from someone who visits Washington often but not often enough, as he tells me. David McCullough's love of Washington is evident in this selection. This is a personal look at the city from another Washington-lover, made up of casual and human comments from a close and thoughtful observer. David is someone who sees with his historical eye how close the past is to us here. He talks of the "presence of history everywhere" and the "political fauna of Washington past," which sentiments tap into my own thinking about the oxymoronic omnipresence of the past here.

David likes much of Washington that I like, too—the scale of the place, the "slow shift of the seasons" (for me, not always slow but ever-changing), the long autumns, the winter evenings, the trees and skies of our civilized city. Although he settled elsewhere, David retains a particular and positive kind of Potomac fever. And I couldn't agree more with his observations about politicians often wanting to get away from the city when they could gain so much from being out and learning from its past and present.

What I like most about David's piece is how he makes the connection between the city itself and its personification of our values as a nation. As he writes, "It speaks of who we are, what we have accomplished, what we value."

I can't help commenting on the "colossal marble head" of Abraham Lincoln that he mentions toward the end of this piece. Coincidentally, this bust, sculpted by Gutzon Borglum, was a gift to the nation from my father in 1908, when he was only thirty-two. Having made money on Wall Street, he was pursuing his artistic interests, and had already begun collections of Dürer and Whistler etchings, as well as American literary manuscripts and autographed Lincoln papers. Dad had always felt that the best place for this superb head of Lincoln would be in a public building in Washington, to be enjoyed by everyone. He wanted to buy it and give it to the government, but Borglum told him that the government didn't accept gifts of art from private persons. Merlo

Pusey's biography of my father tells the story of how the head was displayed in the White House on Lincoln's birthday in 1908. Teddy Roosevelt, according to Pusey, "having lived with the solemn countenance of the Great Emancipator for a few weeks," thought it was such a remarkable work that he wondered what was to be done with it. When Borglum told him that a friend of his was ready to buy it and give it to the nation, Roosevelt said he thought it should go to the Capitol, and he asked Borglum to bring his friend to the White House. It was this first trip to Washington that reignited Dad's interest in public affairs.

THE ONLY one of our presidents who stayed on in Washington after leaving office was Woodrow Wilson, and for all his celebrated professorial background he certainly did it in style. Ten of his friends chipped in ten thousand dollars each to cover most of the cost of a house of twenty-two rooms on S Street, just off Embassy Row. S Street was quiet and sedate then and it remains so. But once, on Armistice Day 1923, twenty thousand people came to cheer Wilson. They filled the street for five blocks. I have seen the photographs. He came out finally, tentatively, for his last public appearance. He stood in the doorway while they cheered and sang, a pallid, frail old figure wrapped up in a heavy coat, Edith Bolling Wilson at his side, the vibrant, assertive second wife, who, many said, secretly ran the country after his stroke.

I think of her when I pass by. I wonder if, in fact, she was the first woman to be president. And I think about the crowds on that long-gone November day, in that incredibly different world of 1923. What was in their minds, I wonder, as they looked at their former commander in chief? What did they feel for that old man? Are some still alive who were there and remember?

"I am not one of those that have the least anxiety about the triumph of the principles I have stood for," Wilson said in a brief speech. A headline in the *New York Times* the same day was spread across three columns: HITLER FORCES RALLYING NEAR MUNICH.

I pass the Wilson house only now and then. The way to see Washington is on foot, and I like to vary my route. Early mornings are the best time, before the traffic takes over. The past seems closer then. The imagination roams freer. . . .

Washington is a wonderful city. The scale seems right, more humane than other places. I like all the white marble and green trees, the ideals celebrated by the great monuments and memorials. I like the climate, the slow shift of the seasons here. Spring, so Southern in feeling, comes early and the long, sweet autumns can last into December. Summers are murder, equatorial—no question; the compensation is that Congress adjourns, the city empties out, eases off. Winter evenings in Georgetown with the snow falling and the lights coming on are as beautiful as any I've known.

I like the elegant old landmark hotels—the Willard, now restored to its former glory, the Mayflower, with its long, glittering, palm-lined lobby, the Hay-Adams on Lafayette Square, overlooking the White House. And Massachusetts Avenue, as you drive down past the British Embassy and over Rock Creek Park, past the Mosque and around Sheridan Circle. This is an avenue in the grand tradition, befitting a world capital.

The presence of the National Gallery, it seems to me, would be reason enough in itself to wish to live here.

In many ways it is our most civilized city. It accommodates its river, accommodates trees and grass, makes room for nature as other cities don't. There are parks everywhere and two great, unspoiled, green corridors running beside the Potomac and out Rock Creek where Theodore Roosevelt liked to ride horseback or take his rough cross-country walks. There is no more beautiful entrance to any of our cities than the George Washington Parkway, which sweeps down the Virginia side of the Potomac. The views of the river gorge are hardly changed from Jefferson's time. Across the river, on the towpath of the old C&O Canal, you can start at Georgetown and walk for miles with never a sense of being in a city. You can walk right out of town, ten, twenty, fifty miles if you like, more, all the way to Harpers Ferry where you can pick up the Appalachian Trail going north or south.

Some mornings along the towpath it is as if you are walking through a Monet. Blue herons stalk the water. You see deer prints. Once, in Glover Park, in the heart of the city, a red fox stopped directly in front of me, not more than thirty feet down the path, and waited a count or two before vanishing into the woods, as if giving me time to look him over, as if he wanted me never to wonder whether my eyes had played tricks.

Even the famous National Zoo is a "zoological park," a place to walk, as specifically intended in the original plan by Frederick Law Olmsted.

It was Olmsted also who did the magnificent Capitol grounds and who had the nice idea of putting identifying tags on the trees, giving their places of origin and Latin names. I like particularly the tulip trees (*Liriodendron tulipifera*), one of the common trees of Washington, which line the main drive to the east front of the Capitol. There are red oak, white oak, silver linden, a tremendous spreading white ash, sugar maples, five kinds of American magnolias, a huge Japanese pagoda tree. A spectacular willow oak on the west side has a trunk three men couldn't put their arms around. In spring the dogwood in bloom all around the Capitol are enough to take your breath away.

There are trees and there is sky, the immense, overarching sky of the Mall. What American city has anything to compare to the Mall? At first light on a summer morning, before the rush hour, before the first jets come roaring out of National, the dominant sound is of crows and the crunch of your own feet along the gravel pathways. The air, still cool from the night, smells of trees and damp grass, like a country town. Floodlights are still on at the old red Smithsonian castle, bathing it in a soft theatrical glow, like the backdrop for some nineteenth-century gothic fantasy. The moon is up still, hanging in a pale sky beyond the Washington Monument, which for the moment is a very pale pink.

I AM ALWAYS moved by the Mall; by the Monument, our greatest work of abstract sculpture; by the Lincoln Memorial with its memories of Martin Luther King, Jr.; and by the Vietnam Memorial. I don't like the Hirshhorn Museum. It's ugly and out of place. And I don't like the ring of fifty American flags around the base of the Monument, because they seem so redundant. (How much more colorful and appropriate, not to say interesting, it would be to replace them with the fifty flags of the fifty states.) But I love the steady flow of life in every season, the crowds of tourists from every part of the country, all parts of the world. One Saturday morning I stopped to watch a high school class from Massachusetts pose for a group portrait in front of the colossal equestrian statue of Grant at the east end of the Mall, the Capitol dome in the background. They looked so scrubbed and expectant, so pleased to be who they were and where they were. . . .

Though I have lived in a number of other places, Washington has been the setting for some of the most important times of my life. I saw it first when I was about the age of those students from Massachusetts, traveling with a school friend and his family. I had seldom been away from home in Pittsburgh and could hardly believe my eyes, hardly see enough. We got about by streetcar. It was something like love at first sight for me. At the Capitol we were given passes to the Senate gallery and warned not to be disappointed if only a few senators were on the floor. There was almost no one on the floor and one man was reading a newspaper. No matter. I was overcome with a feeling I couldn't explain, just to be in that room. I would happily have stayed all afternoon.

The next visit was about five years later, while I was in college, only this time I was head over heels in love with a girl, who, fortunately, also wanted to see the sights. We stood in line for the White House tour, drove down along the Potomac to Mount Vernon. It was March, but felt more like May. The tulips were out at Mount Vernon, and the river, I remember, looked as blue as the ocean. That night, all dressed up, we had dinner at the old Occidental Restaurant, next door to the Willard.

In 1961, after Kennedy took office, still in our twenties, we came back again. I had a new job as an editor with the U.S. Information Agency, then under the direction of Edward R. Murrow. Only now we came with three small children. On summer evenings, my office day over, we would meet to walk around the Tidal Basin, the baby riding in a carriage. One Saturday afternoon at the Library of Congress, I found my vocation. . . .

NOT EVERYONE, I realize, cares for Washington as I do. "Neither Rome nor home," somebody once said. New Yorkers can be particularly critical, impatient with the pace, annoyed by the limits of the morning paper. Government buildings have a way of depressing many visitors, including some of my own family. I remember a woman from the *Boston Globe* who wrote at length about what a huge bore it all is. A one-industry town was her theme, which wasn't exactly new or true.

There is no local beer, no home baseball team. The tap water tastes pretty bad until you become accustomed to it. The cost of living is high, parking is a headache, the cab drivers may be the worst on earth.

And of course there is more than one Washington. There is lawyer-corporate Washington, in the sleek glass boxes along Connecticut Avenue, student Washington, journalist Washington, and black Washington, worlds I know little about. Violent crime has become a national issue. Its "inner city" ghetto, its slums, are a disgrace, like all slums, but here especially, "in view of the Capitol dome," as is said repeatedly.

What I'm drawn to and moved by is historical Washington, or rather the presence of history almost anywhere one turns. It is hard to imagine anyone with a sense of history not being moved. No city in the country keeps and commemorates history as this one does. Washington insists we remember, with statues and plaques and memorials and words carved in stone, with libraries, archives, museums, and numerous, magnificent old houses besides the one where Woodrow Wilson lived.

Blair House, catty-corner to the White House on Pennsylvania Avenue, is an example. The morning of April 18, 1861, in its small front parlor, Robert E. Lee sat with Francis P. Blair, Sr., who, speaking for Abraham Lincoln, offered Lee command of the Union Army. I never walk by without thinking of this—and of the historians who dismiss the role of personality in history, the reverberations of a single yes or no.

Blair House was built in 1824 and has been owned by the government since World War II, when, the story goes, Eleanor Roosevelt found Winston Churchill pacing the upstairs hall at the White House in his nightshirt. She decided the time had come for some other kind of accommodation for presidential guests. Later, the house served as quarters for the president himself, President Harry Truman, while the White House was being restored.

One autumn afternoon, right where you walk by Blair House, the Secret Service and the White House police shot it out with two Puerto Rican nationalists who tried to storm the front door and kill Truman. Truman, who was upstairs taking a nap in his underwear, ran to the window to see what the commotion was about. One assassin was dead on the front steps, a bullet through the brain. Private Leslie Coffelt of the White House police, who had been hit several times, died later. On the little iron fence in front of the house a plaque commemorates his heroism. . . .

On the high rise of R Street in Georgetown is a palatial red-brick house with white trim, large as a small hotel and all very Italianate, which was once a summer residence for Ulysses S. Grant and later owned by Rear Admiral Harry H. Rousseau, one of the builders of the Panama Canal. In the 1930s it was taken over as bachelor quarters by a band of exuberant young New Dealers known as the Brain Trust, with Tom ("Tommy the Cork") Corcoran as their leader. One of them remembers a night when a friend dropped by bringing his own grand piano. "A moving van arrived and three or four fellows got the piano up the stairs and into the living room. Tom and his friend played duets all evening. Then the boys packed up the piano and put it back into the moving van."

There is John Kennedy's house, also in Georgetown, at 3307 N Street, and the house on Massachusetts Avenue off Dupont Circle where for decades Alice Roosevelt Longworth held court. Across the street stands the monstrous, gabled brick pile that once belonged to Senator James G. Blaine, "Blaine of Maine," a brilliant rascal who nearly became president in 1884. It was a puzzle to many of his time how somebody with no more than a senator's wages could afford such a place.

The elegant headquarters of the National Trust for Historic Preservation, at 18th and Massachusetts, was once Washington's most sumptuous apartment house. Andrew Mellon, who served three presidents as secretary of the treasury and who gave the country the National Gallery, occupied the top floor. On G Street on Capitol Hill, near the old Marine barracks, you can find the little house where John Philip Sousa was born. On the crest of the hill at Arlington, across the Potomac where the sun goes down, stands the columned Custis-Lee Mansion. From its front porch you get the best of all panoramas of the city.

SOME OF the history that has happened here I have seen with my own eyes. When John Kennedy's funeral procession came up Connecticut Avenue, the foreign delegations led by Charles de Gaulle, I watched from an upstairs room at the Mayflower Hotel. It had been reserved as a vantage point by the *St. Louis Post-Dispatch*, so that Barbara Tuchman might describe the scene much as she did the funeral of Edward VII in the opening chapter of *The Guns of August*. Marquis Childs of the *Post-Dispatch*, a friend, had been kind enough to include me. So I shared a window with Mrs. Tuchman. "Look at de Gaulle, look at de Gaulle," she kept saying, as he came striding along in his simple khaki uniform, taller than anyone, his face a perfect mask.

On the afternoon when the Senate voted for the Panama Canal Treaties, I was watching from the gallery, and later that evening, as Washington was lashed by a regular Panama deluge, I was among the several hundred people who crowded into the State Dining Room at the White House to celebrate, to see Jimmy Carter enjoy one of the few happy moments of his administration.

Much of what I feel about the city comes from books I have loved. The story of the Brain Trusters and their piano, for example, is from a collection of reminiscences edited by Katie Louchheim called *The Making of the New Deal*. If the Wilson house stirs a chain of thoughts on my early morning ventures, it is mainly because of Gene Smith's *When the Cheering Stopped*.

I am never in the National Portrait Gallery, once the Patent Office building, that I don't think of Walt Whitman's account in *Specimen Days* of how the wounded and dying men from the battles of Bull Run and Fredericksburg were crowded among the glass display cases for the patent models. Passing the Capitol as a new day is about to begin I think of how, in *The Path to Power*, Robert A. Caro describes young Lyndon Johnson arriving for work:

> But when he turned the corner at the end of that street, suddenly before him, at the top of a long, gentle hill, would be not brick but marble, a great shadowy mass of marble—marble columns and marble arches and marble parapets, and a long marble balustrade high against the sky. Veering along a path to the left, he would come up on Capitol Hill and around the corner of the Capitol, and the marble of the eastern facade, already caught by the early morning sun, would be gleaming, brilliant, almost

dazzling. . . . And as Lyndon Johnson came up Capitol Hill in the morning, he would be running.

Like millions of readers, my view of the Senate and its protagonists has been forever colored by Allen Drury's *Advise and Consent*. Lafayette Square, for all its obvious charms, means even more because it is the setting for the Henry Adams novel *Democracy*.

Then to read Louis J. Halle, Jr.'s beautiful *Spring in Washington* is to have your eyes and spirit opened to a world that has nothing to do with government people or official transactions or anything much connected with the human hive of Washington. Written in the last year of World War II, when the city's sense of its own importance had reached a new high and the author himself was serving as an official at the State Department, the book is an informal, philosophical guide to the local natural history. It is a small classic still in print after forty years. "I undertook to be monitor of the Washington seasons, when the government was not looking," the author begins modestly.

Sometimes when I go looking for places that figure in favorite books, the effect has considerably more to do with what I have read than what remains to be seen, for, alas, much in the city has been destroyed, torn down in the name of progress. In *Specimen Days* Whitman writes of standing at Vermont Avenue and L Street on August mornings and seeing Lincoln ride by on his way in from Soldier's Home, his summer quarters. Lincoln, dressed in plain black "somewhat rusty and dusty," was on a "good-sized, easygoing gray horse" and looked "about as ordinary" as the commonest man. "I see very plainly Abraham Lincoln's dark brown face, with the deep-cut lines, the eyes, always to me with a deep latent sadness in the expression," writes Whitman. "We have got so that we exchange bows, and very cordial ones." A lieutenant with yellow straps was at Lincoln's side. The rest of the cavalry escort followed, two by two, thirty men in yellow-striped jackets, their sabers drawn, everyone moving at a slow trot.

Waiting for the light to change on the same corner, on a thoroughly present-day August morning, I look in vain for Whitman's Washington. The early traffic grinds by toward Lafayette Square. The buildings around, all recent and nondescript, include banks and offices and something called the Yummy Yogurt Feastery. Across the street, rearing above the tops of the cars, is a huge abstract sculpture made of steel. No signs of those other times. No sign of the man on the easygoing gray horse. . . . And yet, it happened *here*. This is no ordinary corner, never can be. "The sabers and the accoutrements clank," Whitman says, "and the entirely unornamental *cortège* as it trots toward Lafayette Square arouses no sensation, only some curious stranger stops and gazes." Maybe that's me now, the curious stranger.

The most engaging guide to the city's landmarks is *Washington Itself* by E. J. Applewhite, which is both well written and full of delightful, little-known facts. Thanks to Mr. Applewhite, a former official of the Central Intelligence Agency, I now know as I did not before that the statue of Winston Churchill in front of the British Embassy has one foot planted firmly in the extraterritoriality of the embassy's Crown property and the other over the boundary in U.S. territory, in tribute to Churchill's British-American parentage. I know that the Government Printing Office is the city's largest industrial employer; that the eight glorious columns inside the old Pension Building are the tallest ever built in the Roman style, taller even than those at Baalbek; that the Mayflower Hotel is by the same architectural firm, Warren and Wetmore, that did Grand Central Terminal in New York.

If asked to name my favorite book about the city, I would have to pick Margaret Leech's Pulitzer Prize–winning history, *Reveille in Washington*, first published in 1941, a book I have read and reread and pushed on friends for years.

It is Washington during the Civil War, a chronicle of all that was going on at every level of government and society. I read it initially in the 1960s, in those first years of living here, and it gave me not just a sense of that very different Washington of the 1860s, but of the possibilities for self-expression in writing narrative history. . . .

Any city that has the Library of Congress is my capital. Some of the best, most productive days of my life have been spent in its manuscript collection or working with its newspaper files. It is one of the wonders of the world. The statistics are staggering—twenty million books, of which less than a fourth are in English, nearly six million pieces of sheet music, more than one million recordings of music and the spoken word, the papers of twenty-three presidents, the papers of Clara Barton and James G. Blaine, the Wright brothers, Clare Boothe Luce, Margaret Mead, and J. Robert Oppenheimer, Sigmund Freud, Lillian Gish, and George Washington Goethals. Its Madison Building is the largest library building in the world. I prefer the old building, the Jefferson Building, as it is now known, with all its Beaux-Arts marble extravagance and beautiful workmanship. The domed Main Reading Room is one of the most spectacular interior spaces in America.

It was because he wanted to be near the Library of Congress that Woodrow Wilson chose to retire in Washington. Very understandable. . . .

·   ·   ·

OF NEARLY equal importance to the political historian or biographer, or anyone trying to understand the past, is what might be called the living model. People are the writer's real subject, after all, the mystery of human behavior, and a historian needs to observe people in real life, somewhat the way a paleontologist observes the living fauna to better interpret the fossil record.

This is very important. And all varieties of the old political fauna of Washington past are around today, alive and mostly thriving—the glad-handers and nostrum sellers, the doctrinaires, the moneybags, the small people in big jobs, the gossips, the courtesans and power-moths of every kind and gender, as well as the true patriot, the devoted public servant, the good, gray functionary down in the bureaucratic ranks, who, so often, is someone of solid ability.

Harry Truman used to talk of Potomac Fever, an endemic disorder the symptoms of which were a swelled head and a general decline of common sense. Were you only to read about such cases, and not see them with your own eyes, you might not appreciate what he meant.

Ambition, the old burning need for flattery, for power, fear of public humiliation, plain high-mindedness, a sense of duty, all that has moved men and women for so long in this capital city moves them still. The same show goes on, only the names and costumes are different.

It helps to remember how much good creative work has gone on here down the years in so many fields. Washington was the home of Alexander Graham Bell, Oliver Wendell Holmes, Jr., and the historian Frederic Bancroft, who also developed the American Beauty Rose. Bruce Catton wrote *A Stillness at Appomattox* here. Rachel Carson wrote *The Sea around Us* and *Silent Spring*.

Two further observations: First, I am struck more and more by the presence of Abraham Lincoln. He is all around. It is almost as though the city should be renamed for him. Most powerful, of course, is the effect of Daniel Chester French's majestic statue within the Memorial, our largest and, I suppose, our most beloved public sculpture. But there are three other Lincoln statues that I know of, one in Judiciary Square, another in Lincoln Park, a third in the Capitol Rotunda. Elsewhere in the Capitol are two Lincoln busts, five paintings of Lincoln, and down in the crypt a colossal marble head, an extraordinary work by Gutzon Borglum that deserves a better place where more people will see it. Lincoln is at the National Portrait Gallery—in spirit upstairs in the grand hall, scene of his first inaugural ball, and on canvas in a portrait by George P. A. Healy that dominates the hall of the presidents. There is Anderson Cottage at Soldiers' Home on North Capitol Street, Lincoln's summer White House, where, until the time was right, he kept the Emancipation

Proclamation locked in a desk drawer; and the so-called Lincoln Bedroom at the White House, where he never slept but where he signed the
Proclamation. A duplicate of the Healy portrait, Lincoln pensive, his
hand on his chin, hangs over the mantel in the State Dining Room. A
duplicate of the Lincoln bed in the Lincoln Bedroom is the bed
Woodrow Wilson died in at the house on S Street. Pew 54 at little St.
John's Episcopal Church on Lafayette Square, the Church of the Presidents, is marked with a silver plate as the Lincoln pew.

There is Ford's Theater with its flag-draped Lincoln box and, downstairs in the basement, a Lincoln museum, containing the clothes and
large black boots he was wearing the night of the assassination. Across
the street, in the Petersen House, is the room where he died the following morning. Maybe his presence is felt most of all in the rise and domi-
nance of the Capitol dome, which he insisted be completed during the
Civil War to show that the Union continued.

The second observation is really a question: Why do so many politicians feel obliged to get away from the city at every chance? They claim
a pressing need to get back to the real America. To win votes, many of
them like also to deride the city and mock its institutions. They run
against Washington, in the shabby spirit made fashionable in recent presidential campaigns. It is as if they find the city alien or feel that too close
an association with it might be somehow dishonorable. It is as if they
want to get away from history when clearly history is what they need,
they most of all, and now more than ever.

What if, instead of rushing off to wherever it is they come from, some
of them were to spend a morning at the Wilson House or on the Mall
with their fellow citizens touring the National Museum of American
History? Or what if they took time, say fifteen minutes, at the National
Gallery to enjoy and think about George Caleb Bingham's *The Jolly Flat-
boatmen*—that one painting? Might not that too be a way of reaching the
real America?

I have no sense that the people they represent fail to appreciate the
city or to feel its spell. They come in ever increasing numbers, by the tens
of millions. They climb the sweep of marble steps at the Supreme Court,
pose for a picture by the Grant statue. They move slowly, quietly past the
fifty-seven thousand names in the polished black stone wall of the Vietnam Memorial. They pour through the Air and Space Museum, the most
popular museum in the world, craning their necks at the technical mar-
vels of our rocket century. We all do. We all should. This is our capital. It
speaks of who we are, what we have accomplished, what we value.

WASHINGTON EVENTS

The march of events has been much too rapid.
                    —Agnes Ernst Meyer, from her diary

*November 11, 1921: A caisson bearing the casket of the Unknown Soldier
from World War I, preparing to leave the Capitol, where the body had
lain in state, for the solemn parade to Arlington National Cemetery,
the final resting place*

THINGS happen in Washington. In fact, big things happen here all the
time. Natural disasters can happen anywhere, but Washington is often
the locus of a different kind of major.event—political disasters at
times, but also political blessings. Some things are major events only in

Washington; others have ramifications for the rest of the nation or the world.

Major events that happen elsewhere—wars are an obvious example—have an impact on Washington that is often different from the impact on other places. Just as surely, all wars are events that affect Washington. From the Civil War to Vietnam, all had their transforming effects on the city. Because Washington is the seat of government and, therefore, the center out of which so much of our response as a nation flows, events take on immeasurable importance here.

The effect of any of these events on us—whether as residents of Washington or as those who merely visit—depends on many factors: our age, our temperament, the times, the nature of the event itself. We react differently to events depending on whether we experienced them directly or whether we were bystanders or observers from a distance.

The list of big and small events that have occurred in Washington during my lifetime seems endless. Local events—like the collapse of the roof of the Knickerbocker Theatre, great heat waves and blizzards, openings of exhibitions, memorable dinners—and events with more national ramifications—like the dedication of the Lincoln Memorial, Martin Luther King's "I Have a Dream" speech, the major marches on Washington in the 1960s, the protests during the Vietnam War—somehow take on more significance because of the nature of this place.

Sometimes we're overwhelmed by certain events; they become galvanizing moments in our lives or in the life of the nation. Others became major moments in my life alone, or in the life of any one of us individually. When someone of my generation focuses on days, times, or events that meant the most to us or were the most significant, several stand out. We were rendered stunned and speechless by Pearl Harbor, for example, and by President Kennedy's assassination. Neither, of course, happened here in Washington, but the effect on this city was electrifying.

Certain visitors who came to Washington became events in themselves. For example, Madame Chiang Kai-shek, who appeared formally before the House of Representatives and informally before the Senate, created quite a stir here during World War II. Vera Bloom wrote that "perhaps no wartime visitor has aroused the same pitch of interest and curiosity as . . . [this] almost legendary lady, symbol of a beloved and indomitable people, who came surrounded by suspense and pathos. No star ever had a more perfect entrance on the stage than Mme. Chiang on the Washington scene." The visit of the then future queen Elizabeth to see the Trumans also caused Washington to put on its best bib and tucker, although nothing like the protocol and program set up for the visit of her parents in 1939.

The pomp and circumstance of parades are part of the Washington tradition. From the Pershing parade in 1919 to the circus parades to the inaugural parades to the cherry blossom parades to demonstrations of every kind to Eisenhower's return to Washington from the European theater of operations in June 1945—a "hail-the-conquering-hero" parade—these events help define the place.

Other events are quintessential Washington—like Coxey's army descending on the city, or the Bonus Army, which Drew Pearson and Robert Allen called "an army of blind hope, lost hope . . . the Army of despair . . . they came in spontaneous pilgrimage toward the Mecca of their hopes."

There are also events that fade from memory. One such I only remembered when I reread a letter my father wrote to us "kids," as he addressed us, in January 1935. He sent along clippings and pictures about a flight my mother made with Eddie Rickenbacker and Mrs. Woodrow Wilson. They flew from Washington to New Orleans, returning the next day to Newark for lunch, and then had a "triumphant arrival in Washington at 3:30 the same afternoon," where they were met by a full contingent of reporters and newsreel people, society editors, and officials of the airline. As it happened, my father was a good friend of Eddie Rickenbacker, who, in his younger days, had been a driver for the old Maxwell Company, in which Dad was interested and had invested. Captain Rickenbacker had invited Dad to go on this promotional trip, and had come by his office at the *Post* to discuss it. On that same day, Mrs. Wilson had come to our house for lunch, and Dad had jokingly asked her if she would like to go along. To his astonishment, she said she would, and as Dad related, "she would not let me out of it now that I had invited her." Since Mrs. Wilson was going, my mother took Dad's place, and off they went, with Mother reporting on the flight for the *Post,* and Dad gloating over the fact that "all the newspapers and press associations had to carry it as news."

Sometimes historic events come at us with an incredible swiftness and in an abundance for which we are unprepared. Watergate was such a time. It was, of course, a major event in my lifetime in Washington—

a dramatic moment that came for a two-year stay. As Elizabeth Drew wrote, "And then came one stupefying event after another. The drama kept mounting, the story kept gathering momentum, until it seemed impossible that there could be any more. Yet there was more, and more." Drew also wrote, "It is harder to escape the events in Washington, to turn the conversation and the mind to other matters." And she put the significance of some of these events in proper perspective: "The close view we get of these events—in our newspapers, on our television screens, in our gossip—may seem to reduce their magnitude, but they remain the stuff of history."

July 28, 1932: The Capitol can be seen in the distance through the smoke of fires set by the United States Army to drive out the remnants of the Bonus Expeditionary Force, or the Bonus Army, as we came to know it.

Hope Tempers Sorrow of Whole People at Tomb of Humble Dead Soldier

The Washington Post   (November 12, 1921)

The Washington Post *for November 12, 1921, had a two-line banner headline: "Nation Reverently Lays Unknown American To Rest; President Prays For Peace As He Mourns War Dead." In fact, all the headlines on the stories "above the fold" on page one of that day's* Post *attested to the importance of the burial of the unknown soldier. Other headlines included: "Hope Tempers Sorrow of Whole People at Tomb of Humble Dead Soldier"; "End All War, Pleads Harding Over Tomb"; and "All America, Rich and Poor, Aged and Young, President and Commoner, Solemnly Bares Head to Unknown Hero."*

There was also a prominent headline—"Traffic Jam Blocks Roads to Arlington"—and an accompanying story about the traffic tie-up that forced Secretary of State Charles Evans Hughes to cross the Potomac River bridge "afoot" and that even stopped President Harding's car and forced it onto the grassy area of Potomac Park.

What was most striking about the front page of the paper that day, however, was a brief piece by George Rothwell Brown, a Post *journalist at the time. Far from being an objective news report of the event, his report was a ringing and poetic paean to this unknown boy who had died on foreign fields.*

Not everyone felt the way Brown made the dedication out to be. Mary Roberts Rinehart, in her memoir, My Story, *wrote that she came to Washington just in time for the burial of the Unknown Soldier. For her, rather than being a great and solemn spectacle, it was "stark hopeless tragedy." She wrote, "I wept dismally through it all, the beating of drums, the marching of feet, the whole panoply of war and death. What good was it all to that soldier, lying there under the flag, while the representatives of the nations came forward to lay on it their final tribute, their highest military decorations? What good?"*

But those in charge of the Arlington National Cemetery found Brown's version of events more resonant and his words memorable enough to be incorporated into their exhibits over the years.

W RAPPED in the brooding silences of eternity in the nation's Valhalla, where the white marble temple to its war gods on the wooded hills of Arlington stands guard above the Capitol, the well-loved son of the republic sleeps at last shrouded in his immortality.

A hundred millions of people have called him "son," and given to him a name that for all time to come in every heart shall be a synonym for sacrifice and loyalty.

In honoring him with solemn rite and ritual the mighty country for which he gladly gave his life touched a new and loftier height of majesty and dignity, as though the very government itself took on resplendent luster from the simple nobility of its humble dead.

A vibrant note of hope and joy ran like the music of a silver bell through all of yesterday's solemn services in the beautiful amphitheater of valor on the arbored crest of the radiant autumnal slopes, where the heads of his own and many foreign states, and a great multitude of his fellow countrymen, gathered to restore to earth the splendid product it had borne. The grief that filled each breast and dimmed each eye, the sorrow that bowed each head in tribute to the nameless soldier who had died for his flag, unknown, unsung, 3,000 miles away from home, was tempered by a promise which was exalting and uplifting. Never before perhaps did a hero have so wonderful a burial, so inspiring in its symbolism. Never had Americans found in such a symbolism such depths of spiritual meaning.

A tender beauty marked each passing moment of the day which saw the nation's final tribute to its unknown boy, home from the strife and hell of war, back in the arms of those who loved him dearly. The President of the United States walked through the silent streets of the hushed city, in the early morning haze, content to be a simple private citizen at the bier of the man who in his haunting mystery, typifies the spirit of America's dead.

The High Point

Our Capital on the Potomac (1924)

I was drawn to Nicolay's book for the richness of its language and because of her obvious love of this city. Nicolay wrote vividly about the dedication of the Tomb of the Unknown Soldier—she seems to me to create such a vivid picture that we can almost visualize the scene. My parents were also present at Arlington that day and my mother wrote in her unpublished journal:

> It was an imposing sight. The amphitheatre at Arlington glistened against the blue sky, the many colored autumn leaves softening what otherwise would have been too dazzling an effect. In the great circle of boxes were gathered gold-bedecked representatives of not only the allies, but every nation and province on earth except the central Empires. The effect was very military and we seemed the only really civil country among so many martial cohorts. Even the unknown soldier was not accompanied by a great show of military but was followed only by a handful of the lame and halt who had been singled out as a reward for their sufferings. It probably made a poor impression on nations like France and Japan but it was what every American citizen would have liked best.

I T WAS an ideal autumn day, with no wind, a cool air, and the sun shining through a thin film of cloud. Potomac Park, lying beside deserted pearly stretches of river, was very beautiful on the way out, and Arlington's many oaks were deep wine red. Against them as a background the sparse leaves on an occasional yellow tree shone like minted gold. The great amphitheater had been hung with garlands of laurel and banners and festoons of flowers.

Most of the great crowd saw it only from the outside, for huge as it is the amphitheater was too small to hold the officials, resident and foreign, who were bidden to the ceremony. It was said that even the Commandant of Fort Myer, who was in a way the host, was not allowed a ticket of admission. Arlington grounds were open, however, to all who chose to enter, though only the privileged could enter in their motors. The rest parked theirs in a wilderness of cars on the cavalry drill ground.

A space around the amphitheater had been reserved to insure plenty of room for the arrival of the procession and for its component parts after it disbanded. But the roping off had been cleverly done in a wavy line that almost doubled the possibility of securing front places, with their optical and mental advantages. People who had been crossing the bridges since early morning took their stand and waited contentedly for hours, watching and trying to identify the groups that went up the marble steps into the amphitheater.

There were civilian dignitaries of the Disarmament Conference, in high hats and frock coats, and foreign soldiers in strange uniforms—none of them more odd or picturesque than the French with their long capes of horizon blue, and as a token of official mourning, sweeping veils of crape hanging from their red caps. Most impressive of all were our own wounded boys from Walter Reed Hospital; especially the two who had to be carried into the amphitheater face downward on the backs of their comrades. Another group was made up of four Indians in white buckskin and gorgeous war-bonnets, who brought their tribute to lay on the tomb. It was not alone their regal dress and bearing that stirred the imagination, but the dramatic part their race had played as scouts in the war, swimming rivers with mud-concealed faces and in No Man's Land using their inherited skill, to aid the allies who had well nigh exterminated them.

An airplane circled about, photographing; a bird hung almost directly overhead, and far off there was a distant throb of drums, so faint as to resemble at first a feeling rather than a sound. Then it drew nearer and grew louder, and the eye caught the color of crape-enshrouded flags and a glint of bayonets winding among the trees. Finally the stately procession came into full view, with its groups of officers on beautiful horses, its men in varied uniforms, and true to the spirit of the century, women also, both those who had served overseas and war mothers who had made the richest sacrifice of all. These came wearing their gold stars over their hearts. Strictly according to scripture the last were first. The earliest soldiers to come into view were mere boys in years, though they carried a "Veterans'" banner. The few G.A.R. men in quaint Civil War caps looked incredibly old in comparison. The horses, keeping step to the music, seemed to realize as fully as their riders the solemn stateliness of the occasion. They were halted near the main entrance, while the caisson with its burden rumbled on to the spot where a vested choir waited to lead the way into the amphitheater. A few flowers lay upon the coffin, but not enough to dim the glory of the flag or hide the broad white ribbon Mrs. Harding had placed upon it at the Capitol.

When the services began, the chaplain's voice was plainly heard by all in the vast throng and, thanks to the radio, was followed in distant cities. The people standing among the graves at Arlington joined the President in repeating the Lord's Prayer, their response sounding like the sighing of the wind, for each one spoke low, and the many murmuring together made a noise that was like a summer breeze when it stirs and stops and begins again.

The impressive moment came when the shrill sweet note of the bugle called for the silent tribute, and a stillness settled over the great throng, broken only by soft inarticulate noises made by little children.

After two minutes the crowd stirred and woke to life again, but remained standing quietly as, one after another, the envoys from foreign countries stepped forward to make their citations and speak words of respectful praise. Then gradually the people dispersed and Arlington was left alone with its dead.

Era's End

Washington By-line (1949)

When Bess Furman's book appeared, the dust jacket trumpeted it as the "intimate, personal, behind-the-scenes account of a famous newspaperwoman's twenty busy years in Washington," with which I don't disagree. However, it went on to say that "Hers is a woman's view of Washington," with which I beg to differ. I think her book is an insider's view, offered by a hardworking reporter who keenly and closely observed the scene. Furman's book reads right—accurately and honestly.

This is a woman who loved Washington long before she got here in 1929. Called the "front-page girl of the 1920s," she went to work for the Washington bureau of the Associated Press; her main assignment in the 1930s was covering First Lady Eleanor Roosevelt. She later went to work for the New York Times, *as White House correspondent.*

Bess organized her book chronologically, focusing on the city in periods: "City of Confusion (1929–1932)," "Scintillating City (1933–1936)," "Synthetic City (1937–1940)," "City of World Strife (1941–1945)," and "City of Strange Survival (1945–1948)." She covers the people and events of two decades in this "city of a myriad madly whirling big and little wheels of Fortune. Washington, our great, gay, glittering, fey, embittering national capital."

CONGRESS hung on until mid-July of 1932 in a Washington filled with fear, sodden with depression. The ragged ex-soldiers of the bonus army were still in siege—eighteen thousand "regulars" under W. W. Waters, and a small contingent of "reds," which the Waters forces had ejected, under John Pace of Detroit.

Now and again Pace's men attempted marches on the White House which always were repulsed by cordons of police, a hundred strong, armed with night sticks and tear-gas bombs.

The last five days of the session a strange new element entered with the arrival of two or three hundred "California radicals" under Roy Robertson. For four days and five nights they staged a slow, silent, single-file, shuffling "death march," all around the Capitol and all around the clock. Whenever a man fell out of the long, long line that went up the House side of Capitol Hill, clear across the plaza, and down the Senate side, another man took his place. They called themselves the "Bonus March of Death," and never a wisecrack fell from their lips. The marching figures were a shadowy slow motion snake dance as the long night sessions ended.

Just before the close of Congress, the state of the nation was so low that President Hoover cut his own salary by twenty per cent, and Vice-President Curtis and all the Cabinet said they would return to the Treasury fifteen per cent of their annual pay—a total saving of $37,500. And Congress passed a RFC*-channeled two-billion-dollar relief bill that President Hoover was willing to sign.

Perhaps due to the presence there of the California men, the stern stay-off-Capitol-Hill discipline of the "regular" bonus army broke the morning of the last day of the session. By thousands, the Waters men came crashing through the thin line of the "death march," threatening to storm the Capitol. All the police in the city were called out to protect the Capitol and White House.

Mrs. Garner† and I stood at a front window and watched the moiling scene on the Capitol plaza. General Glassford himself, the police chief who was generally adored by the bonus army, lost control of the crowd when he had Waters, their leader, arrested and removed to the basement of the Capitol. It looked for a moment like stark riot ahead, but a quick-witted trained nurse who had been aiding bonus families, and therefore was known to the leaders, grabbed a megaphone and shouted: "Let's all sing 'America'!" They did—and under her leadership they sang a lot of other old familiar airs. They were all jolly again by the time they finished off with their favorite, "My Bonus Lies over the Ocean." Waters emerged, free. Speaker Garner further quieted matters by giving Waters a long audience. But all that day and into the night men milled around the plaza and filled the Capitol steps.

When the session ended shortly before midnight, Waters announced: "We are here to stay until 1945 if need be—we are going to eject every radical or red veteran from our ranks—and we will stay."

The California "death marchers" quit when Congress did. The rest of

---

*This was the Reconstruction Finance Corporation, on which my father served—and which caused him so much trouble, especially in 1932 and 1933, when he was doing double duty on the RFC and as governor of the Federal Reserve Board.

†Ettie Garner, or Mrs. John Nance Garner. Her husband was a U.S. representative from Texas, who served as Speaker of the House for the Seventy-second Congress and as FDR's vice president from 1933 to 1941.

388   BESS FURMAN

that night they stretched their exhausted bodies out on the Capitol lawn and slept unmolested. They had made their grand gesture; and they ceased to be a threat.

Before adjourning, Congress had granted the veterans transportation home—to be subtracted from their adjusted compensation certificates. The ex-servicemen had also been voted the right to borrow up to half the value of these certificates, and at lowered interest rates. Railroads had offered them reduced fares. The Red Cross would pay transportation for their families. Still they stayed on. One actual count showed 23,674 men, women, and children under Waters's command.

They were invited to leave, urged to leave, cajoled, given deadlines beyond which they would not be allowed to remain. They were at last served with eviction orders, scattered over their thirty-two ramshackle cantonments by airplane. These orders were then rescinded, but were supposed to hold firm for the lower Pennsylvania Avenue area. That must be cleared, and at once, authorities decreed.

Shacktown on the avenue was no hidden slum, but a festering boil right on the face of the body politic. The Capital beautification program, which had been interrupted when the first veterans moved in on Decoration Day, must go on.

One hot and heavy day in late July—the twenty-eighth—long-latent fear at last became force. A battle, by no means sham, broke out, a stone's throw down Pennsylvania Avenue from our Associated Press office. The old cliché, a stone's throw, really fitted here. That area abounded in bricks and stones, and they were flying fast. I was ordered to stay strictly out of it, but I hovered around the edges enough to see how things were going. And I got eyewitness statements hour by hour as tear-gassed fellow scribes emerged from the fray. One of them was my husband.

At ten o'clock that morning a government crew had come to demolish a Pennsylvania Avenue building occupied by veterans who would not leave peaceably. Police had to carry the occupants out one by one, and it took two hours to do it. By noon, feeling was as high as the hands of the clock. Authorities took that moment to announce a new and all-sweeping eviction order from the Attorney General of the United States, no less. Three veterans started back into the just-cleared building, and brickbats began competing with night sticks. Word of the fight grapevined fast, and from all the other bonus army camps reinforcements rushed in. One veteran was killed; men on both sides were injured.

President Hoover issued a statement again ordering eviction and calling on troops from Fort Myer to carry the order out. Secretary of War Patrick J. Hurley issued an order to General Douglas MacArthur, Chief of Staff of the Army, to "surround the affected area and clear it without delay." From the fort close to Arlington Cemetery, troops came into Washington. General MacArthur massed his forces on the ellipse back of the White House. That afternoon they clattered down Pennsylvania Avenue—the general and the cavalry at the head, then the tanks, machine guns, and infantry. Into the "troubled area" they swept. They beat back the bonus army, "inch by inch, foot by foot," one eyewitness said—the cavalrymen belaboring the evictees with the flat of the sabers; the infantry advancing with prods of fixed bayonets, the tanks ready as reserves on streets near by.

Thus the Pennsylvania Avenue area was cleared, and the bonus army shacks were set ablaze. MacArthur's men pressed on, made a second attack at the camps farther south. The soldiers tossed tear-gas bombs, which the slow-yielding veterans promptly tossed back, and with effect. Here, too, the shacks were fired, and all the downtown Washington bonus army was driven on to Anacostia. One reporter said that before the troops belaboring the veterans were out of sight, General MacArthur, with tears streaming down his face from gas bombs, remarked: "It is a good job, quickly done, with no one injured."

Apparently he thought at that moment Washington was all he had to clear. And indeed, General Glassford, who had himself been hit by a brick, did petition for a night's respite before proceeding with the rest of the eviction. But his request was denied, and as night came, the word was that Anacostia also would be cleared.

Bob [her husband] and I got into our car and followed the waves of excitement. In the Navy Yard section of southeast Washington, then still eerily lighted by gas and bumpily paved, by cobblestones, we watched the cavalry go by to Anacostia. It was more like watching a movie of days long past than anything remotely resembling reality. We fell in behind them, saw the first fires they started to show they meant business. Then we were ordered back across the river, and the drawbridge which spans the Anacostia River was raised in our faces—and kept up. We went on over to Hains Point, and from there watched until midnight a blaze so big it lighted the whole sky.

The families had been given thirty minutes' notice to move. Out into the open roads, in dilapidated autos or on foot, they were driven—a nightmare come to life. In war or peace, Washington has had no stranger chapter.

Women who had just had babies, or were going to have them, had been billeted for some time, with their husbands and other children, in a big old four-story condemned building just across from the Bureau of

Engraving and Printing. These families were left behind. As one would interview the rat left by the Pied Piper, I went there next day to see what they had to say.

To my astonishment and delight I found a cute little newspaper couple, so much like any other pair of footloose reporters that we were instantly on an easy footing. I shared a sketchy lunch with them. They had come from California but intended to claim Florida as their home since they had never seen Florida. Might as well get "sent back" there as anywhere, they argued. Washington was so anxious to get rid of all the veterans that nobody was asking to see any proofs of residence.

Out of jobs, this couple had joined the bonus army on the mistaken impression they could find a market for human-interest articles on its adventures, they said. They could prove they were reporters, too. See that old portable? Hadn't hocked it yet. No, he didn't mind talking to me—he knew the AP wouldn't send out a single word he said. None of the newspapers or the press associations would—one and all they had "played down" the bonus army, given it a reputation of being run by reds when it wasn't. That cockeyed MacArthur statement that another week of the bonus army in Washington would have meant the government was in peril—why didn't they give someone a chance to answer that? He turned to his wife: "You know, honey, how we always said that anything that had that little old AP over it was just as true as word sent down from heaven? Well, we don't believe it any more, do we, honey?"

I stood up for my outfit and went my way. But he had confirmed my own conviction that the Communistic threat, which held many close to President Hoover in a vise of fear, was really small, and could not have swept the bonus army into belligerent action. In the main, it was made up of run-of-the-mill, hard-luck Americans, forerunners of the Okies and the Arkies of later years.

Depression Days

Father Struck It Rich (1936)

I've always felt that Father Struck It Rich *was the perfect title for Evalyn Walsh McLean's memoir. I've read this book twice, parts of it more than that, and it never ceases to amaze me. Passion spills off the page. Initially serially published in the* Saturday Evening Post, *this book was read avidly everywhere, but especially in Washington, where people were fascinated to have a glimpse of the rich and famous—both of which she certainly was.*

Evalyn Walsh McLean was a true Washington character. Her father, Thomas F. Walsh, had struck it rich in the famous Camp Bird Mine in Colorado. He moved his family to Washington a few years before the turn of the twentieth century in part to protect his investments. Evalyn's mother had a complete gold service for sixty. Their home, at 2020 Massachusetts Avenue, was one of the truly great Washington houses.

In 1907, Evalyn married Ned McLean, son of John McLean, who "had power apart from money," as someone once said of him. The elder McLean's power stemmed from his ownership of the Cincinnati Enquirer *and was augmented when he purchased* The Washington Post *in 1905. It was soon after her marriage to Ned that Evalyn McLean bought the Hope diamond. In fact, her husband was reported to have said, according to* Boudoir Mirrors, *that she "bought her diamonds not by the stone but by the pound." She always said that the "curse" of the Hope diamond never worried her because of her faith in goodness and right working out in the end. The dramas in her life hardly warranted that conclusion.*

When my parents first moved to Washington, they went often to parties at Friendship, Evalyn and Ned's "country home" just north of Georgetown on Wisconsin Avenue on the then edge of the city. Mother wrote in her diary after one lunch, "The house enormous and uninteresting. The food too plentiful," but she seems to have been the only one who thought so. The McLeans were known for their parties. One Post *article was headlined, "Her Party Too Big, Mrs. McLean to Add Rooms for Dancers," and told of her ordering the front porch of her estate con-*

verted into two huge ballrooms for her annual New Year's ball that year.

Evalyn McLean really wanted good things for her children. She hoped that Ned, when he inherited the Post from his father, could use it as a base for power of his own. "I wanted him to have the admiration and acclaim that go to greatness. I wanted him to rule his father's fortune when the time should come, and above all else I wanted our sons to be fit to play and work with the leaders of the nation. They do not teach as plainly as they should, in any school I ever went to, that these things cannot be bought as swift horses, jewels, furs, and lawyers' services are bought."

It was during the Harding administration when she realized that power and greatness weren't going to accrue to her husband. The McLeans first met the Hardings at the home of Alice and Nick Longworth, where they had gone to play poker. Mrs. McLean wrote, the "one time in our life when I thought that Ned McLean was going to be saved from a disastrous end in dissipation was when he was going around with Warren Gamaliel Harding. . . . Yet what happened to us all was just about as tragic as if each one, instead of only I, had worn a talisman of evil. Some died, one probably was killed, one is blind, some went to jail; I suffered humiliation, and Ned lives on, a fancied fugitive, in an asylum where he pretends with characteristic slyness, that he is someone else who does not know McLean." A sad paragraph if ever there was one.

Ned drank himself into an insane asylum, having already driven the Post to the point of bankruptcy. Evalyn McLean tried to save the paper and was there on the day of the auction when my father, anonymously, bought it. I have always had a hard time imagining what it must have been like for her to be there in 1933, trying to save The Washington Post for her children. Hope diamond or not, she had a hard life.

Ultimately she did divorce Ned, writing at one point in this book that "I know now the best thing I ever did for myself and the children was to begin life over again like any average person." She learned that "with riches one inherits obligations," and she tried to teach her children to become useful members of society rather than "leisured playmates of society."

She worked hard to aid the poor in Washington, and was known in World War II for helping the amputees who had been brought to Washington for treatment. She was particularly moved when the Bonus Army came to Washington and made their camp.

*Mother and Dad were with President Hoover at Rapidan, his "camp"
in the Shenandoah Mountains that was the precursor for Camp David,
when the Bonus Army was in Washington. It was just one of the things
that Hoover was dealing with that weekend, but Mother's diary mentions a luncheon that was broken off when several officials had to leave
to telephone for help in handling the Bonus encampment. She wrote,
"Their idea is that this whole demonstration is a Communist thing but
I doubt it in spite of all their proofs. They forget how easily an epidemic
of this sort catches on in America. The men have no work, nothing to
occupy their time or their minds. Why not flock to Washington with a
prospect of food, excitement and possibly even a bonus?" Having heard
about how worried the president and other cabinet members were about
the Bonus marchers, when she returned to Washington she went to see
for herself "the encampment of these poor misguided people over at
Anacostia."*

*Her report in her diary reads, "The whole camp looked as those other
encampments must have looked when Americans were trekking westward. Rude sheds covered bags of hay which looked like fairly comfortable beds. As all of these people are unemployed, their situation is
probably better here where they are fed regularly than it is at home."*

*On another day, Mother wrote of leaving the Capitol and passing "a
group of bonus marchers lying in front of the Congressional Library
exhausted by their perpetual marching, ragged, filthy, eating some horrid smelling beans which were being cooked on the sidewalk in an army
range. For sheer ignorance in the Senate and in front of it the picture
was drab and discouraging beyond words. Of such materials is democracy compounded."*

*Evalyn Walsh McLean did something about the Bonus marchers. She
tried to help. The whole of her story is amazing. I was incredulous while
reading it, but it was all quite real. In the foreword to her book, Mrs.
McLean wrote that "The one outstanding lesson I have learned and the
one Father always taught me was, 'Think of the other fellow
first.' . . . Another thing I was taught is, 'Give part of yourself,' " and
she does seem to have done this all of her life.*

O N A DAY in June 1932 I saw a dusty automobile truck roll
slowly past my house. I saw the unshaven, tired faces of the men
who were riding in it standing up. A few were seated at the rear
with their legs dangling over the lowered tailboard. On the side of the

truck was an expanse of white cloth on which, crudely lettered in black, was a legend, "BONUS ARMY."

Other trucks followed in a straggling succession, and on the sidewalks of Massachusetts Avenue where stroll most of the diplomats and the other fashionables of Washington were some ragged hikers, wearing scraps of old uniforms. The sticks with which they strode along seemed less canes than cudgels. They were not a friendly-looking lot, and I learned they were hiking and riding into the Capital along each of its radial avenues; that they had come from every part of the continent. It was not lost on me that those men, passing any one of my big houses, would see in such rich shelters a kind of challenge—2020* was a mockery of their want.

I was burning, because I felt that crowd of men, women, and children never should have been permitted to swarm across the continent. But I could remember when those same men, with others, had been cheered as they marched down Pennsylvania Avenue. While I recalled those wartime parades, I was reading in the newspapers that the Bonus Army men were going hungry in Washington.

That night I woke up before I had been asleep an hour. I got to thinking about those poor devils, marching around the Capital. Then I decided that it should be a part of my son Jock's education to see and try to comprehend that marching. It was one o'clock, and the Capitol was beautifully lighted. I wished then for the power to turn off the lights and use the money thereby saved to feed the hungry.

When Jock and I rode among the bivouacked men I was horrified to see plain evidence of hunger in their faces; I heard them trying to cadge cigarettes from one another. Some were lying on the sidewalks, unkempt heads pillowed on their arms. A few clusters were shuffling around. I went up to one of them, a fellow with eyes deeply sunken in his head.

"Have you eaten?"

He shook his head.

Just then I saw General Glassford, superintendent of the Washington police. He said, "I'm going to get some coffee for them."

"All right," I said, "I am going to Childs'."

It was two o'clock when I walked into that white restaurant. A man came up to take my order. "Do you serve sandwiches? I want a thousand," I said. "And a thousand packages of cigarettes."

"But, lady—"

---

*The 2020 she refers to here is her house on Massachusetts Avenue, although it's difficult to describe any of the places she owned or lived in as mere "houses."

"I want them right away. I haven't got a nickel with me, but you can trust me. I am Mrs. McLean."

Well, he called the manager into the conference and before long they were slicing bread with a machine; and what with Glassford's coffee also (he was spending his own money) we two fed all the hungry ones who were in sight.

Next day I went to see judge John Barton Payne, head of the Red Cross, but I could not persuade him that the Bonus Army men were part of a national crisis that the Red Cross was bound to deal with. He did promise a little flour, and I was glad to accept it.

Then I tried the Salvation Army and found that their girls were doing all they could. I asked the officer in charge, a worried little man, if he would undertake to find out how I could help the men. With enthusiasm he said he would, and the next day he came to my house to tell me that what the Bonus Army leaders said they most needed was a big tent to serve as a headquarters, in which fresh arrivals could be registered. At once I ordered a tent sent over from Baltimore. After that I succeeded in getting Walter Waters to come to my house. He was trying to keep command of that big crowd of men. I talked to him and before long we were friends. I sent books and radios to the men. I went to the house in Pennsylvania that Glassford had provided for the women and children. There was not a thing in it. Scores of women and children were sleeping on its floors. So I went out and bought them army cots. Another day I took over some of my sons' clothing, likewise some of my own, and dresses of my daughter. One of the women held up one of little Evalyn's dresses and examined it on both sides. Then she said, "I guess my child can starve in a fifty-dollar dress as well as in her rags."

One day Waters, the so-called commander, came to my house and said: "I'm desperate. Unless these men are fed, I can't say what won't happen to this town." With him was his wife, a little ninety-three-pounder, dressed as a man, her legs and feet in shiny boots. Her yellow hair was freshly marceled.

"She's been on the road for days," said Waters, "and has just arrived by bus." I thought a bath would be a welcome change; so I took her upstairs to that guest bedroom my father had designed for King Leopold. I sent for my maid to draw a bath, and told the young woman to lie down.

"You get undressed," I said, "and while you sleep I'll have all your things cleaned and pressed."

"Oh, no," she said, "not me. I'm not giving these clothes up. I might never see them again."

Her lip was out, and so I did not argue. She threw herself down on the bed, boots and all, and I tiptoed out.

That night I telephoned to Vice-President Charlie Curtis. I told him I was speaking for Waters, who was standing by my chair. I said: "These men are in a desperate situation, and unless something is done for them, unless they are fed, there is bound to be a lot of trouble. They have no money, nor any food."

Charlie Curtis told me that he was calling a secret meeting of Senators, and would send a delegation of them to the House to urge immediate action on the Howell bill, providing money to send the Bonus Army members back to their homes.

Those were times when I often wished for the days of Warren Harding. Harding would have gone among those men and talked in such a manner as to make them cheer him and cheer their flag. If Hoover had done that, I think, not even troublemakers in the swarm could have caused any harm.

Nothing I had seen before in my whole life touched me as deeply as what I had seen in the faces of those men of the Bonus Army. Their way of righting things was wrong—oh, yes; but it is not the only wrong. I had talked with them and their women. Even when the million-dollar home my father built was serving as a sort of headquarters for their leader, I could feel and almost understand their discontent and their hatred of some of the things I have represented.

I was out in California when the United States army was used to drive them out of Washington. In a moving-picture show I saw, in a news reel, the tanks, the cavalry, and the gasbomb throwers running those wretched Americans out of our Capital. I was so raging mad I could have torn the theater down. They could not be allowed to stay, of course; but even so I felt myself one of them.

After that, I concluded it was high time the family of Tom Walsh went back to work.

HELEN LOMBARD

The Lion at Bay

Washington Waltz (1941)

In June 1939, I had been back in Washington for only a month or so, having just returned from my first working experience—as a labor reporter for the San Francisco News. *I was now working for the* Post, *getting used to the new city I had returned to and all of the contrasts with the old one I'd left behind when I'd gone off to college in 1934. I would turn twenty-two later that month. With all that was going on in the world, I was a bit surprised at the attention the upcoming royal visit was getting from every corner of Washington.*

Helen Lombard's book, Washington Waltz, *serves a purpose historically—provocatively discussing the role of diplomats in Washington. Although this piece tracks some of the same territory as the next two selections, it comes from a different perspective. From a diplomatic point of view, having the king and queen of the British empire visit the American head of state in June 1939 hardly gave the appearance of being neutral. Here are not just the reactions of social Washington to the royal visit, but political and diplomatic reactions as well—which, after all, is what makes a visit to Washington by a king and queen different from your or my visit to Walla Walla.*

THE SPIRIT of Munich was marching on. American papers were indulging in an orgy of Chamberlain jokes and cartoons, and British prestige reached a new low. The world was approaching another crisis—something had to be done to tighten the strings of the Empire, to mend Britain's diplomatic fences. Downing Street went into labor and produced an idea.

The young King and Queen were dispatched to Canada on a goodwill tour. They could hardly ignore Canada's powerful neighbor while they were on the North American continent, so a visit to Washington was included in the Royal itinerary.

At the news that Their Majesties would visit the Capital of the

U.S.A., Washington went into a state of social jitters that has not been equalled in generations, and Chamberlain's shortcomings were forgotten. British Royalty was coming to Town!

From November, 1938, through the spring of 1939, the King and Queen were the main topics of conversation in Washington drawing rooms. The speculations about the coming visit were endless. How long would they stay? Where would they sleep? Who would be asked to meet them? Would there be a large reception at the White House in their honor?

When it became known that the British Embassy would give a garden party for the King and Queen to which thirteen hundred people would be commanded, a state of semi-hysteria gripped nearly everyone in the Social Register, and a lot of people who were not in the Register, but who felt that they had other claims on Royalty. Ladies who pretended to Family Trees dating back to Norman times began to write in to the Embassy. Pasteboards were hurriedly left at the massive doors by numbers of tardy callers so that Lady Lindsay's secretary would not have the "she hasn't called this season" excuse for barring a name. The wives of United States legislators were not yet excited over the greatest social event that had ever been scheduled in the Capital. They were serenely certain that all of the "Hill" would be asked to meet England's rulers and were wondering whether it would be "American" to go. . . .

The excitement mounted in Washington when it finally leaked out that there were to be a great many out-of-town guests—that a painful process of elimination would have to be applied to local names. The British Embassy was up against a real problem—there was a definite limit beyond which the list could not be stretched. Convenience in handling the guests, the safety of the young monarchs had to be considered. . . . Official Washington alone exceeded, by thousands, the limit fixed. The culling process was not easy. Whom to choose? Whom to leave out? It was like walking on egg-shells.

Lady Lindsay and her well-meaning secretary, Miss Irene Boyle, did their conscientious best and succeeded beyond the wildest hopes of England's most fervent enemies. They managed, in one fell swoop, to insult half the Senate, three-fourths of the House, and all of the Washington press.

When it dawned upon congressional wives that a mere handful of them were going to be asked to meet the King and Queen, the controversy already raging in social Washington spread to the Hill, and the fears of the White House over the political repercussions of the visit began to be realized.

Few knew that Mr. Roosevelt had been dismayed at the news that the

King and Queen would probably include the Capital of the U.S.A. in their American tour.

Nobody understood better than the President that any sign of cooperation, in 1939, between the two great sea-powers would be hailed as "un-neutral" by large sections of Congress and the press.

Their Majesties could hardly be declared unwelcome, however, when with London's official notice to Washington of the Royal intention to visit Canada came an unofficial feeler about a possible trip to the United States. George and Elizabeth, were, of course, declared welcome and invited to stay at the White House.

That gesture of courtesy from the Head of one State to the rulers of another gave a fresh impetus to the speculations which were being bandied about in Senate corridors as to the real purpose of the trip to Washington. Isolationist members of the two Houses had already declared that it was a Roosevelt coup, designed to sell out American democracy to the British throne. The theories multiplied—Roosevelt would present the American fleet to His Majesty as a little souvenir of the visit, or he would pledge military support over the after-dinner coffee and cigars. The White House began to be worried at the increasing anti-British tone of certain elements in Congress.

President Roosevelt had set his heart on having the Arms Embargo lifted from the Neutrality Law. The Chief Executive was convinced that world war was not further off than the autumn of 1939. He thus warned House and Senate leaders.

The hubbub over the impending visit of British Royalty reached such alarming proportions that Administration strategists in Congress decided that there would be no hearings on the revision of the Neutrality Law until after the departure of England's King and Queen. Senator Guffey summed it up: "If hearings are going on while they are here, some very rude things will be said on the Floor about them and the reasons for their trip to America."

Social Washington, however, was engulfed in a wave of pro-British sentiment. From November to April, hostesses who possessed large houses worried themselves into a decline about where British Royalty would sleep. The ladies pointed out that the White House is a very modest dwelling designed for the Executive of a democracy and not for a King and Queen. It was known that etiquette required that the Royal Party spend one night in the White House. The rest of the visit was occupying the dream-life of the more ambitious of the wealthy ladies. Royalty had taken over private homes before. Here was a chance to make history—imagine being able to point out in years to come the very bed in which Queen Elizabeth had slept! There was a precedent—the Prince of

Wales had stayed in the Leiter mansion when he visited Washington in 1924. King Prajadhipok of Siam had occupied the Larz Anderson house in 1931.

Several matrons, despairing of drawing the Royal Pair, would have settled for a lady-in-waiting. The White House announced that the King and Queen would stay in the modest dwelling of the Executive of a democracy and that Queen Elizabeth would occupy Lincoln's bedroom. With that announcement, the excitement over the Royal Residence subsided.

In the meantime, the First Lady was having housekeeping worries over the impending visit—how to get the mice out of the upstairs closets. What to do with the mountains of luggage and the numerous ladies-in-waiting. The mice—economic royalists—had been living comfortably in the closets for generations and had resisted strenuous efforts to dislodge them. The need for closet space was urgent—experts were called in.

The White House could accommodate the Royal Retinue of ten persons, but there was no place for the retinue's retinue. It was decided that all of the Royal party would be quartered within the "British Empire." White House secretaries were busily contacting the British Embassy and the Legations of the Dominions. Finally, everyone was provided for. Some were given beds at the South African Legation, others at the Canadian.

Lady Marler, wife of the late Minister to Washington from Canada, took care of Canadian Premier Mackenzie King and his suite. Their Majesties' "plateman" was also quartered at the Canadian Legation. A "plateman" is a man who valets silver. He accompanied the royal knives and forks all the way from England to see that no profane hands touched Their Majesties' personal tableware. Royalty has travelled with its own silver and attendant "plateman" since the days of Queen Elizabeth. . . .

The Washington press, of course, was immersed in Royalty from dawn to dark. Every item connected with the visit of George and Elizabeth, every bit of information about the festivities in their honor, every detail that could be gleaned from the White House, the State Department, or the British Embassy, was "copy." The feminine press took possession of the Queen from her "hair do" to her slippers. Her wardrobe had been "released" by the Office of the Lord Chamberlain and was occupying columns of print. The Birmingham Chamber of Commerce, concerned about the "ferocious American mosquitoes," presented Queen Elizabeth with a dozen pairs of specially treated silk stockings guaranteed to repel the attack of the most carnivorous insects.

News leaked out that the White House had received a confidential communication from Buckingham Palace describing the sleeping habits of Their Majesties—the kind of sheets to which they were accustomed, and the color and weight of the down-comforter Her Majesty preferred for June nights. Buckingham Palace had evidently accepted the decree of the Foreign Office that Washington had become a temperate climate since 1930, when the diplomats' Hill allowance was discontinued. . . .

Shy Sir Ronald was caught right in the midst of a diplomatic nightmare—sixty strange pairs of ears [at a press conference] were waiting to turn whatever he might say into "journalese." He addressed them in about five hundred words. The first four hundred and eighty were a carefully prepared statement which boiled down to nothing. His last words—an afterthought—were full of dynamite. His Excellency, in referring to the already controversial garden party, said: "As for the garden party, it's just like heaven, some are chosen, some are not!"

When the list of those who had been bidden to "heaven" was definitely released, the buzzing reached epic proportions. The howls grew louder on every side as omissions began to register.

The Minority Leader of the Senate and Mrs. McNary had not received an invitation. Up until a few days before the party, veteran isolationist leader Hiram Johnson had not been asked. He was hopping mad and barked: "After all, the Senate is merely the treaty-making body of the United States and not the Social Register." Just why Johnson failed to get an invitation is a mystery. His name should have been automatically included as a member of the Senate Foreign Relations Committee which was supposed to be invited in toto.

The Chief of Naval Operations, now Ambassador to Vichy, and Mrs. Leahy were not on the original index. The list of omissions grew longer and longer. Sensible people were merely amused. Many more were resentful.

Lady Lindsay and her secretary had adopted a rule of thumb for official Washington. From the Hill, they had asked the Heads of Committees of both Houses, and all the members of each Foreign Relations Committee—with the exception of Hiram Johnson.

From the Diplomatic Corps, ambassadors, ministers and their counsellors were to don high hats and frock coats on that June afternoon. Certain officials from the State Department were included. The other guests were drawn from people who could have expected a presentation at Court if they had found themselves in London during the Season. They were socially prominent individuals from New York, Philadelphia, Baltimore and Washington.

The omitted congressional wives were in an uproar. Several wives of Representatives called the State Department and demanded to know why they hadn't been asked. They insisted that their constituents expected them to meet the Queen and that home-town papers had been asking for descriptions of their gowns. When the State Department replied that it had nothing to do with the British Embassy list, one angry lady made a dire threat. She announced that if an invitation were not forthcoming, she would be compelled to tell the folks back home that she had been asked and had refused on the ground that "to meet Royalty was un-American." . . .

Confident that the two legislative bodies were to be asked in toto to the party, the ladies had been debating whether a curtsey was undemocratic—whether a long dress would be appropriate. It had become quite an Issue.* Some of the congressional women were in a state of enraged pique when it became apparent that the Issue was purely academic as far as they were concerned. And as the ladies got mad their husbands' temperatures rose. The isolationists were sure they were being discriminated against socially because of their political opinions. The neglected interventionists were furious because they were being ignored by the Representatives of one of the countries they were trying to aid.

The furor reached such proportions that the harassed Lindsays did not know which way to turn.

An unexpected ally sprang to their side. Between huge, shy, conservative Scotsman, Ronald Lindsay, and minute, red-faced, conservative Texan, Jack Garner, there existed a real sympathy. The Vice President's political sense was offended at the threatened fiasco of the Visit. Garner knew all about pulling wires. To watch all the wrong ones being pulled and to hear the dissonant twang pained him. It pained him so much that the staunch isolationist called up his friend, the British Ambassador, and suggested that the Garden Party list be reopened—to include, at the very least, all of the Senators and their wives.

Sir Ronald followed the Vice President's suggestion and the omitted senatorial families got invitations to the garden fete just a few days before the event. There was no time to buy new frocks, to have white gloves cleaned, to decide the perplexing question: "To curtsey or not to curtsey?" Still it was better late than never—Garner was right; some of the uproar subsided. Hard-working, earnest Senator Claude Pepper breathed a sigh of relief. The Revision of the Neutrality Law was coming up soon—it was no time to take chances with that vexatious human trait—vanity. . . .

Thanks to Garner's intervention, the Senate wives calmed down but things didn't smooth out so easily as far as the House was concerned. It

---

*With this capitalizing of the word "Issue," Lombard seems to me to have made a point about Washington. In this town, issues quickly become Issues.

was too late to include hundreds of more people. Luther Johnson, veteran Texas legislator, who was doing rodeo-work for the Administration on the Neutrality Revision, was worried about the outcome.

The White House with an eye on the Arms Embargo was beginning to wish that Royal Garden Parties had never been invented. One of Mr. Roosevelt's Secretaries, after a hard day spent in trying to smooth out the ruffled feelings of the Solons who had no use for Royalty but who were furious at not being asked to meet the King and Queen, indulged in a rare moment of philosophizing: "The Garden Party will show up in the House vote on the Neutrality Law. People are the raw material of history—it's amazing how human human beings can be—little things do affect big issues."

Poor Sol Bloom, who had done his level best to smooth matters out in the House of Representatives, unwittingly made them worse. He and his family were automatically included in all the events connected with the Royal Visit. Chairman McReynolds of the Foreign Relations Committee was ill, and Bloom, second-in-line, replaced him officially. This and the fact that he failed to get his neglected colleagues invited to the Garden Party did not help in the spade work he was doing for the revision of the Neutrality Law and the lifting of the Arms Embargo.*

The Diplomatic Corps and Congress were seeing eye-to-eye for the first time in history. The Corps which had also been invited fractionally to the reception had its own indignant reaction to the whole affair. It was the plain duty of the President and Mrs. Roosevelt, the foreigners decreed, to invite everyone to an enormous "fete" in honor of the Royal visitors. They even picked out the scene for the Presidential reception—it should be held at Mt. Vernon where there was space enough to accommodate all who had any claim to an invitation to meet Their Majesties.

The White House could hardly explain that in 1939 too much fuss in Washington over George the Sixth and his Elizabeth would have immediately raised the cry of "Anglo-American collusion" throughout the country.

The Vice President was having a grand time. He had no responsibility for the Royal Visit and could forget his isolationist principles for the duration.

He fell a willing victim to the Queen's charm and grace. He declared himself as completely conquered by the lovely Scotch lassie and drank enthusiastically to the health of the Royal Pair.

*See the next selection for Vera Bloom's side of the story about her father's involvement in the Royal Visitor flaps.

On the night of the dinner at the British Embassy in honor of President and Mrs. Roosevelt, he found himself unable to attend. Their Majesties were hosts in their own Embassy and the dinner table had to be rearranged at the last minute. It was probably the first time in history that a Royal table had to be hastily reseated for anything less than a death or a major disaster. . . .

THE KING and Queen were approaching the Capital of the United States of America. Curious but undemonstrative crowds lined the streets as they rode up Pennsylvania Avenue. All the quills of a nation born in rebellion against a throne were standing up straight, but all the curiosity of a Republican country about a "real live" King and Queen was wide awake. The young Queen's beauty and charm were pulling hard against American suspicion of hereditary authority. The struggle was almost visible, but Elizabeth had what it takes. As she smiled and bowed, plain work-a-day Washington took her into its heart and the crowds began to wave as the young couple went by.

The weather smiled upon the garden party, perhaps too warmly, on that sunny June day. Lady Lindsay's famous rose trees were in full bloom. The terraced gardens stretched like huge green velvet steps down Massachusetts Avenue Hill. Refreshment tents of brightly striped awnings dotted the gardens. An enormous circus tent had been set up in the center of the beautiful lawn; Lady Lindsay was taking no chances with the Washington weather and had provided shelter for the lightly frocked ladies in case of unexpected rain.

Lyons, the famous English chain of restaurants, had sent sandwiches and cakes from London for the alfresco buffets of the famous event. There is an unwritten law in all British diplomatic missions abroad that Lyons must be their caterer for important occasions, whenever practicable. Edward, Duke of Windsor, had invested the major part of his personal fortune, left him by his grandmother, in Lyons stock. In addition to the Lyons delicacies, rushed over by fast boat, baskets of fresh strawberries, bowls of heavy yellow cream and huge quantities of punch were set out on the tables.

The ladies had settled the burning problem of what to wear to a Royal Reception by appearing in everything from long afternoon frocks and floppy hats to short dresses with bright accessories. Some of the men, who had visited England and who had attended the famous Ascot races in the Royal enclosure, had fished out of the mothbags their grey frockcoats and light "toppers." Others appeared in the conventional black cutaway, striped trousers and silk tubes. A few gentlemen from the "Hill," mindful of home-town reactions, braved the rigid British protocol and appeared in linens and panamas.

In strict keeping with Buckingham Palace ceremonial, the guests were already assembled before Their Majesties put in their appearance. Vice President and Mrs. Garner, the Cordell Hulls, the Morgenthaus, and a number of hand-picked American high officials were gathered on the stone terrace above the gardens. They were to be formally introduced to Their Majesties on British soil by Sir Ronald Lindsay. After chatting with this select company, the King and Queen went down into the garden and "were allowed to circulate freely," as Sir Ronald expressed it. The Ambassador accompanied the King and occasionally beckoned to some distinguished face in the crowd to approach and be introduced to His Majesty. The same procedure was adopted by Lady Lindsay in regard to the Queen.

Sir Ronald's many years of social experience on the Washington stage stood him in good stead. He had absorbed more information about Capital Society than one would have expected of an absent-minded man. He had evidently guessed what could happen to a "freely circulating" monarch. A number of attempts by garden party guests to turn a casual Royal greeting into a real conversation ("I had the honor of being presented to His Majesty, your late father, Sire." "I have been presented at Court, Sire!") were suppressed by the shy envoy with surprising firmness.

George and Elizabeth smiled through the heat and the crowds. They gave their best as standard bearers of the Empire and as Chamberlain's Special Ambassadors of goodwill to the New World. Little did the perspiring monarchs dream of the storm still raging among the wives of the neglected American politicians.

The revision of the Neutrality Law was passed in early July, 1939, but the Administration's effort to remove the Arms Embargo failed. The Amendment to maintain the ban on the sale of arms won out. The Administration lost by just two votes. . . .

The Garden Party had come and gone. The instrument to measure the effect of wounded vanity on world history has not yet been invented. That famous event would have been an interesting first experiment.

Royal Close-ups

There's No Place Like Washington (1944)

My first impulse on meeting up with Vera Bloom's book was to reprint the whole thing. First off, I couldn't agree more with the title. Also, from the beginning, the reader—or at least this reader—is hooked. For all her eccentricities, Vera Bloom has a way with words that makes you want to read on. She writes with gusto. Her book is witty, gossipy, and funny. Yet, for all that, it's also informative and illustrative of an interesting period in the history of this city, from the 1920s into the war years.

Vera came to Washington when her father, Sol Bloom, was elected to the House of Representatives in 1923 in a special election in New York City. He himself became an extraordinary Washington character and the ranking member of the House Foreign Affairs Committee. Abell and Gordon, in Let Them Eat Caviar, *wrote of him, "Sol is amazing. A short, stocky man, wearing pince-nez eyeglasses with a long black ribbon, he ambles about town jingling silver dollars in his pocket and talking interminably about George Washington." The reference to George Washington was due to his being the director of the commission set up to celebrate George Washington's two hundredth birthday, and he spent years planning the nation's tribute.*

Frances Parkinson Keyes also described the Blooms: "No one has ever said that they were born to the purple. In fact, it is obvious that they are unpretentious of origin, and they would tell you so themselves, good-naturedly. . . . The three Blooms are alike shrewd, intelligent, and kind-hearted. They know everyone and go everywhere, not only in Washington, but all over the world. . . . Occasionally Sol indulges in a bit of buffoonery which scandalizes the sedate, but Evelyn and Vera combine cordiality with effusiveness most expertly; their Tuesdays at home are crowded with the elite, which in turn hastens to invite them to their Thursdays and their Fridays." Vera, who remained single, adored her parents. When she died in 1959, at the age of sixty, the Post *reported that her will left money to Children's Hospital for parties to be thrown for the patients on the birth dates of her mother and father.*

There's No Place Like Washington made a huge splash when it arrived on the Washington scene in 1944. For weeks before its appearance, it was rumored to be "THE book on what goes on in the Capital." In talking about it, Marie McNair wrote in the Post *that Bloom "has woven in and around her stories a wealth of first-hand information on what's done in the Capital, how, and by whom and why." This particular section is excerpted from her account of what she calls "the outstanding social event in Capital history." I don't know whether, over the next sixty years, there has been an outstanding social event to outdo the visit of the British royals, but I do know that anyone who wrote about this period gave his or her own version of what happened to Washington in anticipation of the visit of King George and Queen Elizabeth in the summer of 1939. During the war, Washington hosted other royals, including Queen Wilhelmina of the Netherlands, King George of Greece, and King Peter of Yugoslavia, but the visit of the king and queen of England was what Vera Bloom called the "climax of climaxes." And here she describes Queen Elizabeth, who later became the Queen Mother, so that we can still see her, more than sixty years later, as she "smiled and made that slow, indescribably graceful gesture of her hand."*

There's still no place like Washington.

"THREE cheers for the King—and four for the Queen!" That was how one of the bewitched Washington newspapermen—with, I'm afraid, a faint flavor of lese majesty—saluted King George VI and Queen Elizabeth, as they left the Capital after those two June days that climaxed six solid months of preparation and excitement. For there was no doubt that, while the King looked on in smiling agreement, Washington had given the lovely little Queen of England the new title of Queen of Hearts.

Probably there never was such an avalanche of words about a happy happening: usually it takes battles, murder, or sudden death to make conquest of edition after edition of the newspapers and broadcast after broadcast of the radio chains. And yet I think the royal visit can bear another telling, from the viewpoint of someone who not only shared the general excitement in the city where naturally it was most intense, but who also watched and shared in the long preparation.

There were several reasons why we had a vantage spot in the wings while the stage was being set and the great scene being played. After nearly fifteen years on the Foreign Affairs Committee, Father was called on to be acting chairman—and within a month, chairman—during the most dramatic days the committee had known in years. For just as the struggle over his bill to revise the neutrality law reached its first great climax came the outstanding social event in Capital history. Since the chairmen of the Foreign Relations Committee of the Senate and of the Foreign Affairs Committee of the House automatically represent the Congress at all international state occasions, it was inevitable that Mother and Father would attend all official entertainment for the King and Queen. Also, because I was one of the few people in Washington who had been presented at Court, and because every Washington newspaperwoman was told to have a new and different story with a royal flavor every day for at least a month before the King and Queen arrived, it was only natural, I suppose, that they should think of me as a source of London lore. Day after day someone would telephone in desperation for a "new slant." Finally, after I had given almost my last crumb of Court procedure, someone was grateful just to know that the London papers speak of The King, in capitals, like that, even in the middle of a sentence.

From the moment the royal visit came in prospect, a storm raged over Washington that made the Dolly Gann–Alice Longworth feud look like a gentle breeze. The storm center was the garden party to be held at the British Embassy the day Their Majesties would arrive. There were three questions that almost shook the Washington Monument for weeks.

First, who was to be or not to be invited.

Second: to curtsey or not to curtsey. Far from being a poser only for the women concerned, this frightful issue not only agitated the whole country right down to its grass roots, but racked Washington's male officialdom nearly as much as its ladies. Father actually received a stern letter from a constituent containing a not very veiled threat of what would happen to him at the next election if he should send the wrong answer, and demanding that he return the letter with the one word Yes or No to the question: "Will you curtsey to the King and Queen?" Of course, since a man never curtseys, he was able to write a very large NO in red pencil, so his political career was saved.

One of the big news services telephoned Mother weeks before to ask her point-blank whether or not she would "bend the knee," since the garden party would take place on British soil. She seemed to make a very popular answer when she said that, though she followed the custom of the country and curtsied in England, she felt that the King and Queen would approve of Americans following their own custom, and would not expect a curtsey in America. As it happened, that was how the overwhelming majority of official wives decided the question.

The third burning question—although not so packed with political dynamite as the curtsey—was whether or not to wear a long, garden-party frock, that Washington usually ridicules even for the annual British Embassy garden party on the King's birthday. A long skirt seemed appropriate to the unprecedented great occasion; but many staunch democratic hearts trembled at the thought that this, too, might be looked on as "kowtowing" back home. A universal solution was not attained without some good old American log rolling. Eventually even the wildest Western Senators allowed their ladies to appear in long, frilly frocks, while they proclaimed their democracy by clinging to their ten-gallon hats.

The papers had a lot of fun when they discovered that the Capital's Court presentees—including me, under the No Daughters ban—had not been "commanded" to the royal garden party, although we would automatically have been on the list for the one at Buckingham Palace every year. They enjoyed themselves even more when they had figured out, by the next edition, that since Mrs. George Barnett, the Duchess of Windsor's cousin, was one of the few on the list, very likely we had all been "penalized" so that Their Britannic Majesties need not receive her. (Later, Mrs. Barnett remarked cheerfully that she thought she really might have rated a private audience, as the King and Queen owed so much to her family!) . . .

Meanwhile the battle for garden-party invitations still went merrily on. We even heard that one Washington official cabled to Lord Lothian, who had just been designated in London to succeed Sir Ronald Lindsay, soon to retire as British Ambassador, to beg him to "use his influence on Sir Ronald!"

And there was one group who exerted influence en masse. At first it had been decided that from Congress only the members of the two committees dealing with foreign affairs could be invited. At that such a wail went up from the Senate ladies (and the bill for neutrality revision hadn't yet passed the upper house, you should remember) that at the last minute the entire Senate received those precious pasteboards with the golden G.R.E. under the British crown.

All the while, the papers were keeping up a crescendo of excitement. It was like one of those old-fashioned band concert pieces where the finale goes on and on, when you think no composer could possibly think of any more endings. Society editors had sent out long printed questionnaires to everyone who might possibly be on the list for one of the great occasions, asking in detail what not only the ladies but the men would be wearing to each. Washington merchants had that same all's-well-with-the-world expression that the London merchants have at the height of the Season.

But all this was only the overture, after all. The symphony only really started when the Marine Band broke into "God Save the King" as Their

Britannic Majesties, accompanied by the Secretary of State and Mrs. Hull, who had gone to the Canadian border to greet them as they stepped on American soil, stepped from their train at Union Station at eleven o'clock the morning of June eighth, and walked down the broad blue carpet to the beautifully redecorated Presidential waiting room where, for the first time in history, a President of the United States was waiting to welcome a reigning British monarch to American soil.

Besides the Roosevelt family and the entire staffs of the British Embassy and the legations of the British Dominions, there were waiting, of course, the Garners, the Bankheads, all the Cabinet and their wives, the Pittmans, Mother and Father, and a few others, including the Undersecretary of State and Mrs. Welles, the nearly exhausted chief of protocol of the State Department, George T. Summerlin, and the chiefs of the armed forces, who were all presented to Their Majesties by the President with a few special, cordial words about each one. These were the official group who were to make up, with Mrs. Woodrow Wilson and a few additions, the guest list at the two state dinners—the first at the White House for the King and Queen, and the one at the British Embassy, the second evening, when the King and Queen were hosts to the President and Mrs. Roosevelt.

And with those moments at the station and the procession along crowded avenues to the White House, there began in earnest the Queen's complete conquest of America, already in its prologue on the journey from the border: a capture evident not only in the time of her presence but continuing long afterward as America paid her the supreme compliment of suddenly making soft femininity rather than brittle sophistication the fashion in women themselves as well as in their clothes.

We had had several good opportunities, in London, to see the Queen as Duchess of York, and we could appreciate the almost miraculous blossoming out of her personality since she had come to the throne. From a sweet and smiling but rather passive personality, the Queen, as she neared her fortieth birthday, had suddenly become a person completely enchanting. Her own qualities, plus the glory of the throne, and the complete and constant devotion of the King, had combined now to make her the very essence of a woman lovely, lovable, and beloved.

One thing that impressed Mother immediately, and to which one of the royal party agreed when she spoke to him of it at the White House dinner that night, was that Queen Elizabeth has the rare asset of being able to give her utter attention to the person who is with her at the moment—the highest form of flattery, they say, in any woman; much more in a queen.

As for the King, though he might lack that electric glamor his brother Edward had flashed as Prince of Wales, he showed himself to be extremely kind and keen, distinctly better looking, and so obviously and unselfishly delighted with the Queen's tremendous triumphs, that it warmed your heart to see it.

Not that anybody or anything needed warming! I cannot tell you why this great visit took place in a tropical Washington June, or whether the monarchs knew what they were likely to get into. One can only say that they suffered, and with unfailing grace. Before the long-awaited garden party, a storm came up, cleared just in time, and left the city hotter than ever. And Father, who after all had once demonstrably turned off the rain when he tested the loudspeakers for the President's speech at the Washington Monument, said to the Queen, "You see, Your Majesty, I stopped the rain for you!"

"Indeed you did," the Queen agreed. "But," she added laughingly, "didn't you forget to turn off the heat?"

From the Embassy garden party the King and Queen returned to the White House in time to rest a bit and change—the fourth time that day—for the dinner in the state dining room, at a table almost completely hidden by the thousands of white orchids that had been a gift to Mrs. Roosevelt for the occasion from one of the great orchid growers of the country. Everything that could possibly have been planned had been planned. No one could foresee that the air cooling system, so confidently installed in the White House not long before, would contribute nothing but nerve-racking noises to one of the rarest occasions in all White House history!

It was easy to see, Mother told me afterward, how the Queen must have been suffering, no matter how gallantly she carried on. In her wide crinoline gown of white and gold, her heavy ruby and diamond tiara, necklace, and earrings, and all her orders, and with the torture of a Washington sunburn on her fair, Scottish skin, it was no wonder that, as Mrs. Roosevelt disclosed later, the Queen had begged for a few minutes alone in the garden with the King after dinner, to revive her for the musicale which was to follow, and for which additional guests were beginning to arrive.

It was well they refreshed themselves, because—as nearly everyone who was there privately agrees—if ever there was a trial under the name of amusement, that was it.

For more years than anyone in Washington seems to remember, Steinway and Company have had charge of the musicales that invariably follow state dinners at the White House; and by an unwritten rule, none but great artists of world-wide reputation—a Paderewski, a Kreisler, or a

Tibbett—appeared on those programs, for which their only material rec-
ompense would be an autographed photograph of the President and the
First Lady, and an invitation to dinner.

With the second Roosevelt regime, however, all this began to change.
There was a New Deal in musicales, too. In Mrs. Roosevelt's opinion all
native American music belonged in the White House, and it soon
became a usual thing for the crystal chandeliers in the East Room to
shiver and shake to hillbilly bands, and to the stamping of backwoods
dancers in ginghams and overalls. And with the musicale for the King
and Queen of England came the climactic collision of the two schools of
thought.

To be sure, Lawrence Tibbett and Marian Anderson (then more than
ever famous because the D.A.R. were alleged to have forbade her appearing in Constitution Hall on grounds of color and not of art) were on the
program. But with them were to appear, beside Kate Smith, who as
radio's "Songbird of the South" stood somewhere midway of the artistic
scale, the most touchingly untamed and untrained groups of hillbillies
and revival-meeting singers that could probably be found in the entire
country. They would have been thrilling and stirring against their own
background, as, indeed, all folk music is throughout the world, but the
effect in the East Room was a trial for the audience that I think really
broke the heart of poor, old Mr. Junge of Steinway's, who had arranged
the White House musicales for all those years, and who had counted on
the one for King George and Queen Elizabeth to be the climax of his
career.

After the musicale (two solid pages long) the King and Queen had to
stand in line again to receive each and every one of the musicians, including the Marine Band; and upstairs in the private apartments, it is said, the
King and the President talked confidentially for an hour or more after
everything else. Yet both the King and Queen looked radiant and
refreshed the next morning when they arrived at the Capital at exactly
eleven o'clock, already having journeyed to the Embassy to receive all the
British subjects living in the Capital. . . .

The Embassy dinner, in contrast to the White House dinner the
night before, was really small: in fact only sixteen couples sat down that
night with the First Gentlemen and First Ladies of the two most powerful nations in the world, and only the Embassy staff was commanded to
come in after dinner.

As the guests arrived, it was Ambassador and Lady Lindsay who
received them; but when Their Majesties entered the drawing room, the
Lindsays stepped back and became merely guests, while the King and
Queen, naturally, became host and hostess on British soil. And it was fas-

cinating (as Mother and Father told afterwards) to see how the atmosphere immediately reflected their kind and charming personalities, just as every party, everywhere in the world, is made or marred by the host and hostess. Suddenly it seemed not a stiff state function, but like a friendly gathering.

The King chuckled as a man does over an old joke, when, making the "royal circle" among the guests, he came up to Father. "How many members of Congress did you say there were at the Capitol this morning? Don't you think some of them must have gone through twice?"

The Queen wore the most beautiful costume, undoubtedly, of all those created for her New World visit. It was one of the huge crinolines she revived so charmingly, with an off-the-shoulder bodice, of rose-pink tulle, embroidered all over as exquisitely as an eighteenth-century fan with Queen Alexandra roses of tiny rose-colored sequins outlined with gold and silver threads, and just here and there a touch of aquamarine blue stones, which matched her eyes. She wore marvelous jewels of diamonds and pearls, and the tiara with the straight rows of diamonds like icicles, that she wears on the coronation stamps, on her dark hair.

And she presented a rose-pink problem to Speaker Bankhead. For when he went to take his place at the Queen's left at the table, he saw that his chair had quite disappeared under the enchantment. Her Majesty's crinoline had acted as crinolines will, and, indeed, often did in olden days when it was not surprising for each lady of fashion to require three chairs for herself alone.

The Queen was already deep in an animated conversation with the President, who was, of course, seated at her right. So the Speaker stood and waited until she should turn around to him. When she did, she looked up at him in surprise, and he, with a gesture toward the chair, explained in his courtly Southern way, "Your Majesty, I am indeed at a loss to know what to do—" The Queen laughed, expertly handled the situation, and the Speaker took his place beside her. . . .

For Mother, the loveliest picture of that evening was when, after dinner—while the gentlemen, in the English fashion, stayed behind in the dining room where the port and cigars had been placed on the shining, doily-decked table before the King, who had moved around to the place beside the President—the Queen stepped out alone through the French doors from the drawing room onto the portico, and stood, in her wide, shimmering dress, in the doorway, with the dark garden as background.

After a moment the Queen went on down the garden steps to the lower terrace, while Lady Lindsay hastily instructed some of the footmen to follow with a sofa—the traditional "royal sofa"—and some chairs from the drawing room.

Miraculously, after those two dreadful days, the Embassy garden was cool.

Mrs. Roosevelt followed, and took her place beside the Queen on the sofa, and Lady Lindsay plied between the upper terrace and the garden, bringing one lady or two at a time with whom the Queen wished to chat for a few moments. The same procedure had been followed at the White House dinner the night before; and Mother said the Queen had been so helpful and spontaneous that, when her turn came, she hadn't even realized that in obedience to protocol she was only speaking when the Queen spoke to her.

After a while, probably when the King had suggested, "Shall we join the ladies?" the gentlemen came out onto the portico. The President, who is, of course, under the unwritten law that the occupants of the White House can never, in ordinary circumstances, visit an embassy, was enchanted with the beautiful setting.

The royal train was to leave Washington for New York and the homeward journey to England, over which war clouds were already beginning to gather, before midnight that night; and accordingly, the President and Mrs. Roosevelt departed early. Their Majesties made the circle again, with a personal word of thanks and good-by to everyone, and disappeared, and the guests left immediately after.

Everyone thought the Queen had probably gone upstairs to change for the train; but in a final endearing gesture, she had decided to go right on to the station as she was, only throwing a rose-colored feather cape around her shoulders, so that the thousands and thousands who lined the streets and crowded the huge station for a last glimpse of the King and Queen could remember her, too, "as a queen should look."

And I wonder if she and the King, riding by, did not feel a lump in their throats as group after group of good Americans, standing under the lamplit green arches of Washington's trees, spontaneously began singing "God Save the King."

The Royal Visitors

This I Remember (1949)

Eleanor Roosevelt essentially wrote two volumes of autobiography. The first, This Is My Story, *was published in 1937 and dealt with the first part of her life to just after World War I and FDR's return to politics after contracting polio. The second,* This I Remember, *appeared in 1949 and picked up the Roosevelt story from where the first volume left off, taking it through FDR's last term and death. Mrs. Roosevelt had modest goals for her first book: "I hope . . . my readers will find some reasons for kindly laughter and a little additional understanding of the human species as a whole." I think both books met those objectives.*

From the time the Roosevelts moved to Washington, in 1933, they dominated the city in a way that no president and first lady ever had previously. Mrs. Roosevelt was the official hostess for the United States for the visit of the British royals to Washington, so it is only appropriate that we read her version of the historic event.

THE ARRIVAL of the Swedish crown prince and princess in the United States in the summer of 1938 marked the beginning of a series of visits from members of Europe's royal families. It was evident that the people of Europe were deeply troubled by the general feeling of unrest and uncertainty on the continent, and were looking for friends in other parts of the world—hence their sudden interest in the United States. . . .

My husband welcomed these visits and I think encouraged everyone to come here whom he had any chance of persuading. Convinced that bad things were going to happen in Europe, he wanted to make contacts with those he hoped would preserve and adhere to democracy and prove to be allies against fascism when the conflict came.

That same spring the king and queen of England decided to visit the Dominion of Canada. It was quite evident that they too were preparing for the blow that might fall and knew well that they would need the devotion of every citizen in their dominions throughout the world. My husband invited them to come to Washington largely because, believing that we all might soon be engaged in a life and death struggle, in which Great Britain would be our first line of defense, he hoped that their visit would create a bond of friendship between the people of the two countries. He knew that though there is always in this country a certain amount of criticism and superficial ill feeling toward the British, in time of danger something deeper comes to the surface, and the British and we stand firmly together, with confidence in our common heritage and ideas. The visit of the king and queen, he hoped, would be a reminder of this deep bond. In many ways it proved even more successful than he had expected.

Their visit was prepared for very carefully, but Franklin always behaved as though we were simply going to have two very nice young people to stay with us. I think he gave some of the protocol people, both in the State Department and in the entourage of the king and queen, some difficult moments.

There was one person, however, who looked on the visit as a very serious affair—William Bullitt, then our ambassador to France. He sent me a secret memorandum, based on experience gained from the king and queen's visit to Paris the year before, in which all the smallest details were noted. I still keep that memorandum as one of my most amusing documents. Among other things, he listed the furniture which should be in the rooms used by the king and queen, told me what I should have in the bathrooms and even the way the comfortables [sic] on the beds should be folded! He admonished me to have a hot-water bottle in every bed, which I did, though the heat of Washington must have made them unbearable. One thing that was listed and that I was never able to find was a linen blanket for the queen's couch. Nobody I asked on this side of the ocean knew what it might be.

I always wanted to ask Mr. Bullitt whether, when he stayed in the White House, he had not found in the bathrooms some of the things he listed as essential, like soap, a glass, towels, and the like.

Mrs. Charles Hamlin presented to the White House some very lovely old English prints for the rooms to be used by the king and queen, and they still hang in there today.

One of the funny episodes of that visit arose from the concern of a firm which felt that the king and queen would not enjoy their tea unless it was made with the same kind of water that they used in London. The company had the London water analyzed and tried to reproduce it in this country, and sent me a number of bottles of it. The doctor insisted on analyzing it again, and I think it was finally decided that even if the tea did not taste so good to them it was safer for their majesties to use Potomac River water.

The Scotland Yard people had to stay in the house, of course, and outside the king's room and outside the queen's room was a chair where a messenger always sat. It seemed a little foolish to me, since their rooms were just across the hall from each other and their sitting room was down only a couple of steps. Not until 1942, when I spent two nights in Buckingham Palace and saw how large it was, did I understand the reason for the messengers. There they wait in the corridors to show guests where to go, and to carry any messages one wishes to send.

One day before the visit, I invited Lady Lindsay, wife of the British ambassador, to tea and asked her if she was being given any instructions which might be helpful to me. Lady Lindsay was an American whom I had known a long while, and we looked at things from more or less the same point of view. Her sense of humor was keen and she looked at me rather wickedly when she said: "Yes, Sir Alan Lascelles has been to stay with us and he has told us that the king must be served at meals thirty seconds ahead of the queen. He added that the king does not like capers or suet pudding. I told him we did not often have suet pudding in the United States and that I really had not expected the king to like capers. My husband sensed that I was saying something naughty and so I had to become serious and stop playing with words. I explained to Sir Alan that we rarely have boiled mutton and therefore capers were not much used in a sauce." I read her my memorandum from abroad, which amused her as much as it did me, and we parted with the promise that we would share any instructions we received in the hope that we would succeed in having everything as it should be.

In the White House there are in the dining room two special, high-backed armchairs, one for the president and one for his wife, and no one else ever sits in them at meals. They presented a great problem for the household on this occasion. Should only the king and the president have the armchairs? That did not seem respectful to the queen, but we could not take his chair away from the president. Finally Franklin solved the difficulty by inquiring quietly: "Why don't we buy two more armchairs identical with those we now have?" This was done and all was well.

I told Franklin that British protocol required that the head butler, Fields, stand with a stop watch in his hand and, thirty seconds after he and the king had been served, dispatch a butler to serve the queen and myself, and I inquired what was to happen about the White House rule that the president was always served first. He looked at me with firmness: "We will not require Fields to have a stop watch. The king and I will be served simultaneously and you and the queen will be served next."

Then came another serious question: Should the president sit with the king on his right and the queen on his left and me on the right of the king? Or should we follow our usual custom? This was a little more difficult, but Franklin finally decided we would follow the usual custom of the United States—the king would sit on my right and the queen at Franklin's right. The reason for this decision was that since the king and queen were going to see a good deal of us, it did not seem quite fair to box the king in between us when he had so little time in which to meet and talk with other people. Franklin later explained this to the king, who accepted every arrangement in the most charming and delightful manner.

THERE was much pageantry about their arrival and the procession to the White House. That was something my husband always enjoyed, for he liked to put on a show. I dreaded it. At the appointed time we went down to the station and, with the government officials who were members of the reception committee, stood waiting in the president's reception room for the train's arrival. Franklin had arranged for some of the members of our immediate staff at the White House to be in inconspicuous places where they could watch this reception and take part in the procession back to the White House.

After the presentations were over, my husband and I escorted the king and queen through the Guard of Honor, which was drawn up in front of the station. The British National Anthem and "The Star-Spangled Banner" were played, and there was a twenty-one-gun salute. Then the inevitable photographs were taken and finally my husband and the king, and the queen and I got into our respective cars and started with military escort on the slow drive to the White House. There were crowds all along the way and I was fascinated watching the queen. She had the most gracious manner and bowed right and left with interest, actually looking at people in the crowd so that I am sure many of them felt that her bow was really for them personally. . . .

She sat upon a cushion which I afterwards discovered had springs to make it easier for her to keep up the continual bowing. The same arrangements were made for the king. . . .

After lunch the king and my husband in one car and the queen and I in another drove about Washington. Our route was given out beforehand, so that people could have an opportunity to see their majesties. It meant, of course, that we had very little chance to talk except when we were driving where people could not line up on the sidewalks. At one point, the queen endeared herself to me by saying suddenly: "I saw in the paper that you were being attacked for having gone to a meeting of the

WPA workers. It surprises me that there should be any criticism, for it is so much better to allow people with grievances to air them; and it is particularly valuable if they can do so to someone in whom they feel a sense of sympathy and who may be able to reach the head of the government with their grievances."

We visited the Lincoln Memorial, the Cathedral Church of St. Peter and St. Paul, Rock Creek Park and other points of interest. We returned to the White House in time for the king and queen to dress, and at a quarter before five, they left the White House through a line of Boy and Girl Scouts drawn up on South Executive Place, to attend the garden party at the British embassy. While they were gone, my husband rested.

The garden party created much excitement among the newspaper women, all of whom wanted to be invited and some of whom were not. Like so many things that happen in Washington, this tempest in a teapot caused almost more comment than many much more important things.

While we were out some amusing things had happened at home. The housekeeper, Mrs. Nesbitt, was harassed and when she was harassed she usually went to Miss Thompson. The fact that the many servants quartered in our servants' rooms were requiring as much attention as she had expected to give to everyone combined, was in itself a burden she found difficult to handle; and Miss Thompson was her refuge. Even in this country, where people had shed their blood to be independent of a king, there is still an awe of and an interest in royalty and in the panoply which surrounds it. The first intimation of any real difficulty between our staff and the royal servants came when the housekeeper reported to Miss Thompson that the king's valet was making unreasonable demands from her point of view and did not like our food and drink. Miss Thompson has a certain decisiveness, besides a sense of humor, so when Mrs. Nesbitt said: "What shall I do?" Miss Thompson answered: "If you think you have done all you should do, just say so." Even the ushers were not having an easy time, in spite of all their experience, for they were not accustomed to having protocol hold good among the servants. As the queen's maid was walking down the middle of the second floor hall on her way from the queen's room to the elevator, one of the ushers asked her if she would tell the lady-in-waiting that the queen wanted her to come to her room. The maid drew herself up and said: "I am the queen's maid," and swept down the hall toward the elevator. The usher, who by this time was exhausted with the heat and the extra work, could think of nothing but a bit of good American slang and said: "Oh, you're a big shot, hey?" . . .

After the garden party the king and queen in some miraculous way managed to change and looked completely unhurried when the dinner hour arrived. I was fascinated by the queen, who never had a crease in her dress or a hair out of place. I do not see how it is possible to remain so perfectly in character all the time. My admiration for her grew every minute she spent with us.

The dinner and the party afterwards went very well, though there were a few harrowing moments. First of all, Marian Anderson was loath to sing Negro spirituals, but we discovered it in time to persuade her that people coming from England would want to hear the music that above all else we could call our own. Once we had to slow up the receiving line because the heat and the exertion of the day made the queen feel faint. Then Kate Smith thought she was going to be late for her broadcast, so we had to rearrange the program and let her sing first!

One of the young men who had been asked to sing some folk songs had been reported to the FBI as a communist or bolshevik and likely to do something dangerous. The charge was completely untrue and made by someone who wanted to be disagreeable, but when the FBI reported it to the secret service men they had to be true to their traditions and follow the tip through. When the young man came in after dinner he was "frisked" by our secret service men and then by the Scotland Yard people, and apparently was so frightened he could hardly sing. I hoped fervently he would not reach for his handkerchief during the performance, because I was sure both the secret service and Scotland Yard would jump on him.

When everyone finally got to bed that night, they must all, including the king and queen, have breathed sighs of relief.

Morning Means Another Day

Washington at War (1970)

Pearl Harbor was one of those historical events of such magnitude and impact that it causes people to remember exactly where they were when they heard the news. My generation remembers Pearl Harbor. I was with my parents that Sunday afternoon in Washington. Phil and Joe Rauh, our close friend and another Frankfurter law clerk, were at the Lend-Lease office at Twenty-second and Virginia Avenue, working to prepare a report to go up to the Hill the next day as was required every few months by the Lend-Lease legislation.

After getting the report to the Hill on Monday, they went straight out and tried to enlist in the air force. When Joe told me this story more than forty years later, he said that he was sure the air force recruiter was still laughing about the two of them. Trailers had been set up to facilitate recruitment. Phil and Joe were caught up in the moment and walked by one of these and decided to go in. They asked the sergeant what the requirements for enlisting in the air force were. Joe remembered that the guy found at least three things wrong with them that day—neither of them could see adequately, they both had wives, and Joe had children and Phil had a baby on the way. Even so, it wasn't long before they both were in the military and off to war.

Here, Hart gives us a snapshot of how that date that has lived in infamy played out in Washington, where the reaction to the event was both similar to but at the same time altogether different from the reaction in other cities around the country.

O N THE morning of December 7, 1941, Washington inhabitants awakened thanking God it was Sunday. For all but the Defense Program people who responded to their immediate supervisors' mandate that for six or seven days shalt thou labor, Sunday was a break in an ever-expanding chain of work days. The more fortunate people might turn over in bed and go back to sleep, or yawn and stare at the wall, engaging in various important introspections crushed out in the grind of weekdays.

There was much to consider seeing or ignoring in the course of a Sunday morning's drowsy deliberations. The Don Cossacks Chorus, with basses thundering from depths of ancient sorrows, would appear at Constitution Hall, home of the Daughters of the American Revolution. The Washington Redskins were sharpened for a game with the Philadelphia Eagles, the final game of the season in age-worn Griffith Stadium. Sammy Baugh would take to the air and the ball would speed like a bullet, in a display of a marksmanship brilliant enough to bring thousands to their feet. Later, Rosita Royce, the "Dove Girl," would flaunt herself at the Gayety Theatre on 9th Street, a hurly-burly thoroughfare of penny arcades and pawn shops, peopled with all manner of pitchmen and con men—a place, indeed, with everything that people of circumspection might secretly desire.

It was a Sunday like so many had been and should be, always. For Washington, compared to other cities, was not only a beautiful but a good town, or at least had been until 1933 when the New Deal brought in swarms of people, to be followed by those who had arrived eighteen months ago to handle the National Defense Program. This alone was enough to ponder while staring at the wall. And there was another matter to wonder on. Everybody knew that Hitler, a success at wallpapering, a failure at painting, now triumphantly bludgeoning Europe with lightning strokes, would eventually involve the United States. . . .

Thousands of these defense workers had come into Washington through the immensity of Union Station, and there was no single reason why they had come. Some may have been brought by the words chiseled high upon the southeast front of the Vermont granite building:

> LET ALL THE ENDS THOU AIMEST AT BE
> THY COUNTRY'S — THY GOD'S — AND TRUTH'S
> BE NOBLE AND THE NOBLENESS THAT
> LIES IN OTHER MEN — SLEEPING BUT
> NEVER DEAD — WILL RISE IN MAJESTY
> TO MEET THINE OWN.

In any case, Washington had spoken to them. A fool would know that much. But nobody knew just when the United States would be at war.

President Roosevelt knew it even while his personal bodyguard was taking the little scottie named Fala for his daily walk. Judge Samuel I. Rosenman, the President's stubby aide and speech writer, knew it as he entered the White House with scarcely more than a nod to the Secret Servicemen. Bernard Baruch, with the never-failing courtliness of his

South Carolina aristocratic heritage, knew it while sitting on a bench in Lafayette Park across Pennsylvania Avenue from the White House, raising his eyes in a sad and unobtrusive way at young servicemen striding past without any knowledge that this lonely-looking man who wore age so well could influence whether they lived or died.

Thousands had known of approaching war for eighteen months as the most powerful preparations for war in the nation's history were begun. But those of the innermost circles had not wanted to alarm the people, so they had not confided in them completely. The United States was arming itself for defense, went the official statement, but the words were ominous. From Warm Springs, Georgia, the "second White House," the President had remarked on November 29, 1941, "It is always possible that our boys in the Military and Naval Academies may be fighting for the defense of American institutions by next Thanksgiving." . . .

Proposals had flown for days between the United States and Japan, in anything but harmony. The President the day before had read an intercepted message between the Japanese architects of war and exclaimed, "This means war."

Indeed, if the late sleepers on December 7 had got to their newspapers they would have been informed by veteran reporter Mark Sullivan that "at the moment this is written we are extremely close to war with Japan." . . .

On the morning of December 7, the subdebutantes of the capital compiled the names of Christmas party guests which they had scribbled furtively in their notebooks when the teachers weren't looking. They were planning a big Christmas.

Downtown, far from the girls' Spring Valley and Chevy Chase homes, Secretary of State Cordell Hull, a tall gaunt man with misty eyes and a quiet deliberateness that he had brought with him to Washington from the Tennessee hills, a calm man but not one to be tampered with, met with Secretary of War Henry Stimson and Secretary Knox at the State Department. The two soon left, Stimson for his wood-crested residence, Woodley, and Knox for his Department. After their departure, Hull conferred with his Far Eastern experts. The telephone rang. The Japanese Embassy requested an appointment for Ambassador Admiral Kichisaburo Nomura and Special Envoy Saburo Kurusu with the Secretary at 2 p.m. He agreed to see them at 1:45 p.m.

EARLY that morning Chief of Staff General George C. Marshall looked at the day and readied himself for a recreational horseback ride. He was aware of the imminent danger of war but could not know exactly when it would explode upon the country. Perhaps he realized that the word "defense" was a politically adroit euphemism for war and that amid all the talk of "defense" he should think in terms of war and its demands on the treasury, the young manhood, and the spirit and capacity for endurance of the nation. He was all soldier. It had been stamped on his bulldog face during his youthful years at the Virginia Military Institute where he had engaged in athletics with a fury and endured painful hazing like a man. Everyone liked the young Pennsylvanian who had come down to be a cadet in "the West Point of the South." Marshall had distinguished himself in World War I, and thereafter when ordinary soldiers looked at him they saw a soldier, and when Roosevelt talked with him he found not only a soldier but a realist endowed with a brain. He did pose one problem: where could he best be used when the war began—as commander at the front or in Washington where it was evident, even with no war in progress, that a strong man must sit astride the War Department and oversee the continual building of fighting forces?

Marshall knew where he would want to be. But on this morning, with its indeterminate sky, he was interested in recreation. For years he had indulged a bent toward recreation at its proper time and place. He approved of the Department's policy of allowing officers to rejuvenate themselves periodically. For the General, an occasional morning horse-back ride was recreation and also work, because the quietude of the bridle paths gave him a chance to think. He had once observed that nobody could think after 2 p.m.

Outside General Marshall's quarters, a sergeant stood holding a bay horse. The General mounted and trotted away from the red brick buildings of Fort Myer spread widely along a crest across the Potomac from Washington. When he returned he could see in the rising day the Washington Monument piercing the sky and on the east the bronze statue called the Goddess of Freedom rising from her perch on the top of the Capitol dome. The symbolic goddess had been placed there in December 1863, while crowds below howled acclaim and the iron guns of 68 forts guarding the seat of government roared in salute. Now on this December morning the city lay sprawled in a Sunday calm. . . .

THE PEOPLE of Washington went about their usual affairs. On Meridian Place, N.W., between important 14th and 16th streets, a young married woman serving as a defense worker looked from her fourth-floor apartment to the fourth-floor windows across the courtyard and murmured, "It simply can't be true." Neighborhood gossips had related that during a recent party there the hostess had either fallen or been thrown from the opposite window and struck the grass without completely spilling a drink clutched in her hand.

The morning wore on. The people read the headlines "FDR Sends Note to Hirohito" . . . "Jap Convoys near Thailand." This was not good, but it was at least far away. And the weather was promising. From a December low of 31 degrees, the temperature had grown comfortable by midmorning, though the sky was intermittently overcast, and the mere ten-mile-an-hour wind didn't bite. Simply a good day to lounge at home and listen to one of the four radio networks. Or maybe to prepare for that promised brunch, a social ritual requiring the hostess to provide juice, ham and eggs, jam, and a brisk swig sometime around noon. . . .

The morning gave way to noon. On the 13th floor of the National Press Building, just north of Pennsylvania Avenue at 14th Street, scarcely anyone was about the Press Club bar or lounges. It was just as well, because the highballs that sold for 35 cents were prohibited on Sunday, and few would have wanted the available wine and beer. Club assistant manager Ernie Ball, whose entire metabolism was calibrated to the weekday crushes, reflected that "this is just another Sunday." From the windows of this tallest building in Washington the streets looked normal. There were a few strollers with no apparent destination. Ball looked at the switchboard beside the cigar counter and the bulbs were dark.

Outside, once more, the sky was unsure. The gray stone of the Washington Post Building, visible on E Street from one of the windows, seemed even darker than usual. Sunday required only a skeleton news staff, and most of those were at lunch.

A lanky reporter walked out of the newsroom into the sports department, throwing only a glance at the small marble bust of John Philip Sousa, placed there in honor of his "Washington Post March." The reporter began wondering what he could write; the city editor had made off, leaving no assignment. There was news, of course, on so-called cityside Sunday events, but it was unexciting. On the national side, Secretary Knox had issued a formal statement describing our Navy as second to none. And, earlier that week, the Third Supplemental National Defense Appropriation Bill, totaling some $38.5 billion, had passed the House by an overwhelming 309 to 5. Moreover, the nation was doing well in the air. National Aeronautics Association President John J. Jouett forecast that within twelve months annual airplane production would exceed 50,000.

It was a dull day, probably even dull for little Steve Vasilakos, the peanut vendor on Pennsylvania Avenue beside the White House, who was sometimes good for a story.

The lanky reporter sat at his desk, and after a while noticed that others had come in and they, too, appeared aimless. The Associated Press machines clattered behind a glass enclosure. Then the sound stopped for longer than usual, and resumed. A young reporter went to take a look and after a few moments called, "Somebody come back here. What's going on?"

The AP machines rang twelve bells, at that time the signal for a flash:

FLASH WHITE HOUSE SAYS JAPS ATTACK PEARL HARBOR.

This was followed immediately by the customary bulletin:

Washington, Dec. 7 (AP)—President Roosevelt said in a state-ment today that the Japanese had attacked Pearl Harbor, Hawaii, from the air.

The President's brief statement was read to reporters by Steven Early, Presidential Press Secretary. Sometime shortly after the first Flash (exactly when is not known) came a second Flash. It may have inter-rupted the Bulletin matter or have come after it. It was:

FLASH SECOND AIR ATTACK REPORTED BY ARMY AND
NAVY BASES IN MANILA.

The young man's face grew concerned, but then he relaxed and said that it was probably a war game in motion out there. The clock on the city room wall was somewhere around 2:35 p.m. Steve Early had origi-nated the message on orders from the President, and had told an aide to connect the three press associations on one line.

"All on?" he asked, and was told they were.

"This is Steve Early at the White House. At 7:35 a.m., Hawaiian time, the Japanese bombed Pearl Harbor. The attacks are continuing and . . . No, I don't know how many are dead."

In thousands of Washington homes radios choked off programs to announce the attack. Many people did not believe it, and newspaper switchboards became jammed with inquiring, frantic calls.

THE JAPANESE envoys had failed to appear until 2:05 p.m., twenty min-utes after the agreed-upon time. Secretary Hull chose to make them wait for fifteen minutes.

At about the same time, President Roosevelt, relaxed in a turtleneck sweater, was eating from a tray. He looked up occasionally for a word from his alter ego, Harry Hopkins, whose frail body never slowed his energies. The Navy Department had received a coded message, and it moved fast up the echelons to Knox, who telephoned the President. Pearl Harbor had been attacked. Roosevelt said one long-remembered word: "No." Then he recovered fast. He turned calm and telephoned Hull. He wanted, Roosevelt told him, the emissaries treated coolly.

But that was beyond the mountain code of the Tennessean. When he confronted the Japanese they received a burst of "mule-skinner" language. (There is a wide discrepancy in accounts of what he said.) . . .

Outside, a December wind was stiffening, and the sun fought a battle for the sky.

. . . ELSEWHERE in the White House that morning, thirty-nine men and women had entered the east entrance for luncheon with Mrs. Roosevelt in the upstairs Blue Parlor. These were government and service personalities to whom the First Lady owed a social obligation. At 2:45 p.m. Mrs. Roosevelt shook hands with them in parting, and the guests, stunned by the news, left quietly.

. . . AT THE White House there was little time for reflection—such as how the surprise had been so successfully sprung. There was much wondering how the nation's 132,000,000 people would react, inasmuch as there had been wide chasms of view concerning the conflict in Europe and the spread of violence in the East. . . . Politicians are frightened men; ever fearful for themselves, they distrust the people. So what would the people do now? If the politicians had read history they would have known that the people would pull together overwhelmingly. They had always come together. And the people now were the sons of the past.

By now, the switchboard lights at the National Press Club were twinkling, and Ernie Ball repeated monotonously, "Yes, it's true." The elevators climbed to the 13th floor and members spilled into the lobby, asking of no one in particular, "What is it now?" and the answer generally was, "It's bad." The members swarmed into the bar and hunched over glasses of beer and wine and then went on to the main lounge, asking questions almost totally unanswerable. They looked from windows upon the streets and at the automobiles moving more swiftly and at small groups of people standing about talking, but with little show of animation.

Behind the gray stone hulk of the *Washington Post*, Alexander F. "Casey" Jones, the superb and irascible managing editor, had arrived and lowered his tall figure into his chair at a desk behind a rail separating him from the newsroom. He looked at some copy piled on his desk and called for his news editors to budget an extra. Now more detailed information about the disaster at Pearl Harbor came in. It was clear that the sitting-duck fleet, the nation's Pacific first-line defense, was ruined. That there had been an appalling toll in deaths was obvious. Jones, World War I veteran, read the accounts and his eyes, ordinarily deep gray pits, reddened in anger and sorrow. (A night city editor had once said of Jones, "He comes storming out here raising hell, but dammit, it always brings out a better paper next morning.") Actually, he needed no one to budget the paper. He could put a paper together or a man in his place with his eyes alone. Pearl Harbor was the paper now, and his eyes settled on the calamity.

Jones looked up at a commotion beside his desk. Robert Tate Allan, the ebullient church editor, had leaped in to announce that he had a scoop: A Georgetown minister, he blurted, had, after long soul-searching, decided to leave town for a pastorate in another city. (There are conflicting accounts of what Jones screamed. Allan recalls that "Mr. Jones's face turned a deep purple.")

It was known by now that Hull had "cursed out" the Japanese envoys. But so many other things were vague. . . . The envoys in Washington appeared stunned. They went to the Japanese Embassy, a yellow and elongated building surrounded by gardens, a few blocks away from the British Embassy. The place had appeared quiet, befitting a Washington Sabbath. Then William Beal, a telegraph messenger, knocked on the door and a butler took the telegram. About this time of early afternoon, fifteen taxicabs stopped in fairly rapid succession at the high gate. In all, dozens of Japanese leaped out, some without hats, coats, or ties. Reporters, also, had arrived in taxicabs or in cars driven by photographers. They called to the Japanese, but the few replies came in the Japanese tongue. Two or three could speak enough English to say that they knew no English. The door of the Embassy opened narrowly, and when individuals or groups had slid in, the door closed and the lock snapped. The reporters speculated upon this sudden appearance of so many Japanese. Perhaps they had kept closely in touch with their Embassy, maybe by radio—a faster device than telephone.

A few Japanese reappeared from the Embassy. Within moments flashes brightened the gardens: the Japanese were burning their official documents. They brought these out to an iron grate in boxes with lighted fuses attached to each box. The boxes were metal and about twice the size of a workman's lunchbox. What appeared to be chunks of cement lay on the side of the containers, and inside the metal boxes were smaller wooden ones filled with papers. Vacant space was packed with excelsior. The Japanese talked shrilly in their language, as though to each other or to the orange flames.

One Japanese yelled to reporters who had entered through the carelessly unlocked gate, "Go away, go away. You must not come." The reporters didn't move. A photographer raised his camera, snapping three Japanese.

The Japanese seemed to be tiny men in the expanse of lawn. One appeared as from nowhere, carrying a wrapped object about the size of three telephone directories. He set the object afire. The glow brought an unearthly life to the backdrop of December's dying leaves on the trees.

A Japanese in a pin-striped suit told the reporters with a broad smile, "No, there is nothing for you here, gentlemen. Please go." . . .

A reporter asked the man in the pin-striped suit, "What were you burning?"

"Dear sir, those, of course, were my love letters. I hope you will not jump to the hasty conclusion that those were diplomatic documents." He paused, and in an even voice said, "Goodbye. I hope that we may meet under more pleasant circumstances the next time."

An aide was asked if the Embassy had taken extraordinary safety precautions. The reply came fast: "We do not expect to be molested. We have faith in the fairness of the American people." . . .

. . . Police Chief Edward J. Kelly had appeared in person at the Embassy and assigned a special detail to the site—an unexpected excursion into foreign affairs from his accustomed routine of pouncing upon brothels or raising hell about traffic snarls.

DOWNTOWN and in the residential sections the city lay like a coiled spring, and many wondered when it would snap open. There was some action: recruiting stations prepared for an onrush on a 24-hour basis, seven days a week. And the lines began forming. Meanwhile, the extent of the destruction at Pearl Harbor remained vague. The President, of course, had ordered the Army and Navy to fight back. They had already fought back at Pearl Harbor, but the instances of personal heroism were almost totally unknown. . . .

A late afternoon in mid-December brings a haunting melancholy as winter nears. In Lafayette Park, the five bronze statues of remembered soldiers fade into the night and the deeper hold of history. The street lights shine inadequately in the darkness of the spaced trees. Yet in the light, the young face of Lafayette glows like a cameo of an aristocratic youth. In the center of the park stands a statue memorializing Andrew Jackson, seventh President, cast from cannon captured at Pensacola during the War of 1812. In the late afternoon of December 7, around the once deadly metal, were fading flowers.

The crowd of men and women increased in the vicinity of the White House with approaching night. Some grabbed at the iron fence and pulled themselves up for a better view. White House police commanded by Secret Service Chief Edmund W. Starling, who walked with the studied jerk of a football player on a muddy field, kept repeating in monotone, "Move on, move on." And the crowd obeyed. But it moved only a little, shifting and weaving until the wide sidewalk seemed in sway. Mostly the crowd was silent, but occasionally a stranger spoke to a stranger in the way people do in crisis.

Automobiles moved slowly along Pennsylvania Avenue, and faces stared from the car windows at the crowd and at the lights of the White House, where Roosevelt was completing a first draft of the war declaration message. A larger crowd stood and swayed in West Executive Avenue, the narrow thoroughfare between the State Department and the White House. They jammed the double stairway of the Winder Building on 17th Street, a structure which had been the headquarters of Generals Winfield Scott and Ulysses S. Grant, but was more memorable for the visits Abraham Lincoln had paid to learn the turns of war. Along the curbs, a few people held children on their shoulders. Most of the faces were stunned, but a few were angry. Edward R. Andrews, a government employee, spoke quietly. "I was just standing here thinking that there's only one thing to do—get in there and beat the living hell out of them now. They've got it coming." Miss Dorothy Quine, of Boulder, Colorado, a visitor to Washington, appeared puzzled by the inscrutability of the White House lights. "I can't understand it, when Kurusu is here talking about peace," she exclaimed. . . .

About the White House, police began searching photographers' carrying-cases. The sound of "Move on, move on," was incessant. A mood of utter mistrust had taken hold of Washington. It affected the Chinese and Filipinos in the capital. They feared they might be mistaken for Japanese, and said so to the press. One of them, a reporter, wore a sign on his coat: Chinese Reporter—not Japanese.

During the early night, the sidewalk in front of the White House was blocked off with red lanterns and heavier police details. The Japanese Embassy, despite protection from thirty FBI agents and Chief Kelly's constabulary, additionally safeguarded itself by employing the Burns Detective Agency. The Munitions Building on Constitution Avenue, a "temporary" structure dating from World War I and now accommodating civilian and military forces, was guarded by Marines. Guards stood at all public utility installations, with 38 allotted to the Washington Aqueduct. . . .

THE DARK of December 7 was bright with lights. Behind the lighted windows of the White House, Roosevelt met with his Cabinet at 8:30 p.m. and with Congressional leaders at 9:00 p.m. in the second-floor Red Room Study. . . .

Embassy Row was illuminated. Late in the night, light shone in the windows of the cloister-office of Lord Halifax, and in the red-carpeted office of Soviet Ambassador Maxim Litvinoff. He had arrived in Washington only that morning after flying three-quarters of the way around the earth from Moscow. He had received the news by telephone during a luncheon at the residence of Joseph Davies, Presidential advisor on Far Eastern Affairs, a former Ambassador to Russia, and a top Washington socialite. The embassies and legations were cautious, saying, in essence, to reporters' inquiries, "We only know what we hear on the radio."

Lights glowed all night at the National Press Club, where everything is known in advance of the event. But now no one admitted to knowing everything. They did know one thing: this story was too vast, even locally, for the tremendous news-manpower of a city that, with the possible exception of New York, was the news center of the nation. Masses of detail already were overwhelming. These details—what might ordinarily be called trivia—helped make up a larger picture, and that picture promised to be a horrifying one.

No ONE entirely escaped the night. Mrs. Susan S. Long, part-time maid at the Japanese Embassy, finished her work at midnight. She was tired and there was a long way to go to her home at 1505 West Virginia Avenue, N.W., where her six children were asleep. When she passed through the servants' exit she was stopped by federal agents. They were polite to the extent of tipping their hats, but they were firm.

"You cannot leave, Madam," an agent said. Mrs. Long replied in a lilting Irish voice, "My husband must be at work at 5 a.m. He must heat the school for those children. What of my six little ones? They must go to church, and to school."

"We are only carrying out orders," she was told.

Mrs. Long stood quietly in the half-warmth of the doorway. She was noticeably weighing old indoctrinations. After a few moments she said, "May God bless these wicked people."

Inside the silent Embassy, the Japanese were unaware of her compassion.

COLBERT I. KING

The Parade of '53

The Washington Post (January 20, 2001)

Colby King is a native Washingtonian, a keen observer of the Washington scene, a friend, and an extraordinary jewel on the editorial page of The Washington Post. *Here he tells of an event that took place nearly half a century ago, but one that has been repeated every four or eight years throughout our nation's history. There may be different faces and names attached to the president and his family who parade before the people, but the expectations, the sense of history, and the hope for the future remain the same.*

EXACTLY 48 years ago today, I had the privilege of doing what President-elect Bush is scheduled to do this afternoon: travel from the U.S. Capitol to the White House straight down the middle of Pennsylvania Avenue with traffic blocked at every intersection along the way.

Of course, there were a few minor differences. I had to walk the entire route; Bush gets to ride in a shiny new 2001 Cadillac presidential limousine. When I reached the White House, I was required to keep hoofing another four or five blocks before calling it quits. When Bush arrives at 1600 Pennsylvania Ave. today, he'll be home. Two more points of contrast. Today is all George W. Bush's. In 1953, I shared the moment with 600 other Boy Scouts marching in mass formation with American flags in the first presidential inauguration of Dwight David Eisenhower. Second, beginning at noon today, Bush has four more years to go. On the other hand, my career as a fine upstanding Boy Scout ended shortly after the parade, at which time, in the words of Mae West, I drifted.

The former Texas governor's parents have every right to look upon their son with pride. But so did the parents of that 14-year-old King kid from the District's Liberty Baptist Church, who, nearly 50 years ago, was representing a Scout troop sponsored by the 19th Street Baptist Church (then located on 19th Street, N.W., as opposed to 16th Street, where 19th Street Baptist sits now . . . Don't ask).

It will be a challenge for today's parade to match the holiday mood of

1953. *The Washington Post* reported that Eisenhower's inaugural parade was the longest in three-quarters of a century if not in America's history.

The procession kicked off in the early afternoon, went on for four hours and 39 minutes, had more than 750,000 spectators, 25,000 marchers, 75 bands, 59 floats, cowboys, members of the armed forces, a 280mm cannon that was longer than the White House reviewing stand, herds of horses and elephants, and blimps hovering overhead.

For reasons I still can't fully appreciate to this day, we Scouts were ordered to assemble around 10 a.m. in a park near the Capitol, where we were left standing for the rest of the day under sunny skies and unseasonably warm weather that grew colder as the day went on.

How different the world looks through the eyes of an eighth-grader. Studying the news clips of that day, I'm amazed to see how times have changed.

Back then, the Secret Service had to spring into action against only a few enthusiastic spectators who managed to break from behind the police cordon at the intersection of Constitution and Louisiana avenues to run to Eisenhower's car. Agents simply shooed them back behind the ropes. Folks were easy in those days.

And then there was the cowboy who rode right up to the reviewing stand and lassoed the smiling president as the crowd roared with delight and the Secret Service had fits. That could not happen today.

Another difference:

Washington's mayor, Anthony Williams, will represent the city in today's parade. In '53, the District's standard-bearers were three presidentially appointed commissioners. How far have we come? Consider this inaugural parade item in the Wednesday Jan. 21, 1953 edition of the *Post:* "The District's Police Band got a rousing cheer with 'Dixie' as it passed before the President." How about them apples?

But some Inaugural Day '53 episodes are hardly distinguishable from events afoot today.

As in the case of three Trinity College students—Florence Sullivan, Mary Keefe and Mary Laforest—who used the Eisenhower inaugural parade to tell the world about the city's political plight. They held signs that read: "We Have No Vote but Much Taxation," "D.C. Scandal Rocks the Nation" and "District Suffrage." Forty-eight years ago.

You think only Bush Cabinet nominees face rough sailing? Less than an hour after taking the oath of office, Dwight Eisenhower's hope of having his Cabinet sworn in on his first day was dashed when maverick ex–Republican senator Wayne Morse of Oregon blocked a GOP unanimous consent request to confirm eight Cabinet members. Sound familiar?

But for us uniformed Boy Scouts waiting to do our good turn for the day in Eisenhower's colorful inauguration, politics never entered our minds. We just wanted our chance to march up Pennsylvania Avenue past the presidential reviewing stand. As the day gave way to twilight, however, fear set in that many in the crowd might be gone by the time we left the Capitol.

Finally our turn came. We stepped off in darkness. People were standing along the way, but not as many as when the presidential motorcade had passed by hours earlier. It was too dark to see the decorations along the Avenue or spectators in the platform seats.

But we kept on stepping.

When our formation turned onto 15th Street, we got none of the confetti or ticker tape that had fallen from buildings when Eisenhower went by. Band music could be heard in the distance, but the sounds were almost drowned out by the noise of 600 pairs of shoes scuffing the pavement. And then we made a left turn onto Pennsylvania Avenue and entered the final stretch that led in the direction of Washington Circle.

By luck, I was lined up on the left flank of the group, nearest the president's reviewing stand. The streets were dark, the moon was out, the crowds had thinned. As we drew abreast of the giant wooden structure, I was surprised to see a half-empty reviewing stand bathed in bright lights.

There, standing ramrod straight with his black homburg over his heart, was the president of the United States.

Ike had waited for us.

BEN GILBERT

and the Staff of *The Washington Post*

Thursday Night: First Sparks of Anger

Ten Blocks from the White House (1968)

The year 1968 was a seminal one in many ways in Washington and around the country. It was the year of two brutal assassinations, Robert Kennedy's and Martin Luther King's, of the Tet offensive in Vietnam, of the withdrawal of LBJ from the political race, of the ensuing Humphrey-Nixon-Wallace campaign, preceded by the Gene McCarthy and Kennedy primaries, and of the two political conventions with demonstrations and riots in Chicago.

To the citizens of Washington, the rioting that took place after the King assassination was a great shock. According to Ben Gilbert, then the Post's city editor, who, along with many staff members of the Post, put together an "anatomy" of the Washington riots, "one of the great shocks of the rioting . . . was that it was allowed to happen." Many people thought Washington was riot-proof. April 1968 proved otherwise.

As the reactions of blacks throughout the city to the news of the assassination began to be felt, riots broke out, especially in the area around Fourteenth Street, just a few blocks from the Post's plant and offices. I still vividly remember climbing out onto the roof of the building to look at the smoke rising from large fires that had been set around the city. National Guard troops were called out to assist the District police. Roadblocks were set up around the White House. Guards were posted everywhere, including at the bridge I crossed daily to get to my office from Georgetown. We deployed about one hundred reporters, photographers, and editors to work on the story.

Carl Bernstein, who was in his early days of reporting for the Post, was at Howard University, where the buildings had been taken over by students. Mayor Walter Washington later recalled that at one point Carl was arrested briefly. Apparently university officials and others were trying to liberate the buildings, and Carl was acting like one of the demonstrators.

I remember the atmosphere as being tense and truly scary for days, and I knew that people needed to hear and read authoritative information. Mayor Washington came on television at eleven that night to help calm the city. I sent word that I thought he should come on earlier, at six p.m., at least, and often.

Joe Califano, a Johnson aide at the time, was essentially living in the White House during this time of riots around the country. He is the one who told the president of a report that Stokely Carmichael was organizing a group to march on Georgetown and burn it down. Joe remembered giving President Johnson the report, and the president reading it and smiling, and then looking up to say, "Goddamn, I've waited thirty-five years for this day."

T HE INTERSECTION of 14th and U streets, N.W., was filling up with its customary nighttime crowd. It was a balmy Washington spring evening, but tension was in the air. The transistor radios many youths carried in their hands had announced at 7:16 p.m. that in Memphis, Tennessee, an assassin had shot the Reverend Dr. Martin Luther King, Jr., director of the Southern Christian Leadership Conference (SCLC) and America's most respected civil rights leader.

Homeward-bound black workers were thronging the 14th and U intersection, changing buses or stopping to shop in the drug and liquor stores, before moving on. Transients and other newcomers to Washington's "Harlem" often wound up here looking for action. This was a spot to pick up a woman, purchase narcotics, make a deal. It was also the unofficial nerve center of active black leadership groups—the place to go with a grievance.

Dr. King's SCLC Washington headquarters was on the northwest corner in an old, high-ceilinged converted bank building. Both the Student Nonviolent Coordinating Committee and the National Association for the Advancement of Colored People had offices not too far away.

Police considered this intersection the most volatile in the city's crowded Negro sections. Angry people had gathered here often in the past. Only two nights before, a crowd of several hundred youngsters and young adults had tossed bottles and stones at white policemen responding to a trouble call at the Peoples Drug Store outlet next to the SCLC office. Stokely Carmichael, former national chairman of the Student Nonviolent Coordinating Committee (SNCC), had told that crowd to "go home." Lieutenant Joseph Frye, a resourceful white plainclothesman who was on the scene, sensing that the presence of uniformed policemen was provocative, had sent them away. He had stayed alone to listen to the complaints of the crowd. Eventually, it dispersed. A fireman, using a hand hose to put out a small fire lit with lighter fluid in a nearby tree, was told, prophetically, by one of the youths: "Don't worry, motherfucker. We'll just light it again."

By 8:00 p.m. on Thursday, April 4, prostitutes, pimps, and female impersonators were lining the fronts of buildings between T and U streets, and the cafes had their doors open. Youths in their teens and twenties loitered in small groups on the corners, with the sidewalk in front of the SCLC office drawing the largest congregation.

At 8:19 p.m. came the news bulletin everyone had feared. Martin Luther King, the thirty-nine-year-old Nobel Peace Prize winner and apostle of nonviolent protest against poverty and racial discrimination, had died fourteen minutes earlier. Memphis police flashed a bulletin for a white man seen darting out of a flophouse near Dr. King's motel.

Hollie I. West, a reporter for the *Washington Post*, arrived at the 14th and U intersection just after word came that Dr. King was dead. The crowd was unusually large, even for this normally busy place; the atmosphere, unusually tense.

Betty Wolden, a reporter for NBC News, who appeared to be the only white woman in the predominantly black crowd, said to the black newsman that the sudden quiet in the area just then struck her as "ominous—like before a hurricane strikes."

She told West she thought she should leave the area. He agreed.

As Miss Wolden sought a taxicab, an elderly Negro woman said to her, "I hope no one picks you up."

The news of Dr. King's death spread rapidly along the 14th Street shopping strip and its narrow tributary streets. As minutes passed and the gathering crowd in the intersection of 14th and U swelled, expressions of shock at the tragedy in Memphis began to turn to hot words of anger.

"They did the wrong thing this time," was one comment.

West went inside the Peoples Drug Store, the third busiest in the prosperous area-wide chain, where a dozen persons were huddled around a transistor radio on the camera counter in the rear. They were listening to the muted voice of President Johnson speaking from the White House: "America is shocked and saddened by the brutal slaying tonight of Dr. Martin Luther King. I ask every citizen to reject the blind violence that has struck Dr. King, who lived by nonviolence."

On receiving the report of the events in Memphis, the President had canceled a scheduled appearance at a Democratic Party fund-raising dinner and postponed a trip to Honolulu, where he was to confer on Vietnam. His concern was evident in the tone of his words.

"I know every American of good will joins me in mourning the death of this outstanding leader and in praying for peace and understanding throughout this land," he said.

"We can achieve nothing by lawlessness and divisiveness among the American people," he went on. "Only by joining together and only by working together can we continue to move toward equality and fulfillment for all of our people."

The President's cautious phrases seemed to anger his listeners around the crowded counter.

"Honkie," said one.

"He's a murderer himself."

"This will mean one thousand Detroits."

Alive, Dr. King had been unable to avoid the eruption of violence in Memphis, where a protest march of garbage workers on March 28 had ended in looting and window-breaking and the fatal shooting by police of a sixteen-year-old looting suspect. A curfew had been imposed, and 4,000 National Guardsmen were summoned to restore order.

It was almost too much to hope that violence could be avoided after his death. Waves of disorder were to spread that night and during the weekend through the Negro sections of more than 120 American cities. And damage was to be heaviest in Washington.

At 14th and U that first night, the President's statement was still coming over the radio in the back of the Peoples Drug Store when a group of about thirty youths burst inside.

"Martin Luther King is dead," they shouted. "Close the store!"

In the group was a tall, slim twenty-six-year-old, with a startlingly handsome face—Stokely Carmichael, Trinidad-born, acknowledged revolutionary, and black activist, who had put together a "Black United Front" of Washington Negro organizations to provide a sounding board for black leadership. He sought out the manager.

"It's closed; it's closed," Carmichael excitedly told the white manager, G. N. Simirtzakis. As soon as he understood what was happening, Simirtzakis agreed.

Youths roaming store aisles told customers, "It's closed now, you can go," and steered them to the door. The fluorescent lights began to flicker off as Carmichael and his group left.

On the sidewalk outside, they joined more people, mostly young men in their twenties, and the growing crowd rushed diagonally across the busy intersection to Carter's liquor store, which had been about to shut, anyway, because the 9 p.m. usual closing hour was nearing. The crowd then began moving farther south on 14th Street.

When Carmichael first heard of the shooting of Dr. King, he had gone at once to the SCLC headquarters. There, sitting between two desks, with one foot on each, he had started making telephone calls to Memphis to find out what happened.

"Well," he was heard to state over the telephone, "if we must die, we better die fighting back."

Older men and women stepped inside the SCLC office to ask over and over again, "Is it true? Is it true?"

Off the telephone, Carmichael muttered: "Now that they've taken Dr. King off, it's time to end this nonviolence bullshit. We gotta get together."

He then went two blocks north to the 14th Street storefront Washington office of SNCC. In an inner office, Carmichael conferred with Lester McKinnie, Washington head of SNCC, and C. Sumner Stone, former editor of the Washington Afro-American newspaper and one-time aide to ousted New York Congressman Adam Clayton Powell. Eleven other men and four women, mainly SNCC members, were in an outer room, where a radio was tuned to Station WOL, popular "soul" outlet in Washington.

Bearded disk jockey Bob Terry, who usually works in an undershirt and sunglasses, tapping his feet and bobbing his head to the big beat and shouting, was talking calmly and quietly. There was organ music in the background.

"This is no time to hate," Terry was saying. "Hate won't get you anywhere.

"And let me tell you something, too, white man," he continued. "Tomorrow, before you get back in that car and go out to the suburban house, you better say something nice to that black man on the job beside you. You'd better stop hating, too."

McKinnie came out of the inner office to tell the others that he and Carmichael and Stone had considered calling a black strike and asking stores to close in tribute to Dr. King, but that he felt it might be better "if we took some time to react to this great tragedy."

But at that moment, Carmichael, wearing his familiar green fatigue jacket, burst out of the inner room, with Stone at his heels. Waving his hands, Carmichael shouted: "They took our leader off, so, out of respect, we're gonna ask all these stores to close down until Martin Luther King is laid to rest. If Kennedy had been killed, they'd have done it."

And then demanding, "So why not for Dr. King," he bolted out the front door. All but McKinnie and Stone followed him. By now, it was 8:45 p.m.

Heading south for the intersection, the group stopped first at Eaton's Barber Shop, where Johnny Jones, the only barber and a Negro, readily agreed. "The black man has just been pushed around too much," he later remembered thinking.

Next was the YanKee Restaurant, owned by How K. Chen. Chen nodded his head in acquiescence. "Solid," said Carmichael, and left.

Like a Pied Piper, Carmichael made his way toward the Peoples Drug Store at 14th and U, collecting a crowd as he went.

"Stokely, you're the one," a youth told him.

"Now that Dr. King's dead, we ain't got no way but Stokely's way," another said.

Mostly young men fell in with Carmichael. Many wore light jackets over flashy sports shirts or turtlenecks and slacks. Some had put on rain-coats against the on-and-off-again drizzle that had begun. Others were in workclothes or blue-collar uniforms. Although it was dark, some did not remove their sunglasses. Many of the men wore their hair in natural Afro style and had goateed beards. Dotted through the growing crowd walking with Stokely were past and present students of nearby Howard University. Tension rose as the crowds were swelled by more and more teen-aged youths and adults under thirty.

A short while earlier, the Reverend Walter Fauntroy, vice chairman of the Washington City Council and an official of Dr. King's Southern Christian Leadership Conference, had come to the SCLC Poor People's Campaign office immediately adjacent to the drugstore in response to a call that an angry crowd was gathering.

He found only a few persons outside the office when he arrived and went upstairs to meet with some of the SCLC staff. Looking out a window, he spotted Carmichael and his following, moving diagonally across the intersection from the drugstore. Fearing trouble, Fauntroy hurried downstairs and outside.

Carmichael and the crowd around him headed south on 14th Street for a time, crisscrossing the street, stopping at open stores, and asking them to close. (Berkeley Chaney, night manager of the Wings 'N' Things chicken carryout, remembered that the group was polite when it asked him to close, about 9:10 p.m.)

Catching up with Carmichael a block south of U Street and grabbing his arms, Fauntroy said, "This is not the way to do it, Stokely. Let's not get anyone hurt. Let's cool it."

Carmichael, a foot taller than Fauntroy, continued to walk, rocking back and forth to free himself.

"All we're asking them to do is close the stores," Carmichael said. "They killed Dr. King."

Convinced that Carmichael was finding a "useful channel of frustration," Fauntroy returned to the SCLC office, stopping to tell a plainclothesman in an unmarked car that he thought everything was going to be all right. He advised against bringing many uniformed policemen into the area, fearing such action might be provocative. By now, it was 9:25 p.m.

When Fauntroy again reached the second floor of the SCLC office, he heard glass breaking in the Peoples Drug Store window next door. It was the start.

Corners such as 14th and U streets in Washington's northwest Negro community exist in most large- and medium-sized cities in the nation. New Yorkers would recognize it as 125th Street and Lenox Avenue; Chicagoans would call it 63rd Street and Cottage Grove; San Franciscans, Fillmore and Ellis; Atlantans, Ashby and Hunter. In Cleveland, 55th and Hough or 105th and Euclid; in Memphis, Third and McLemore; in Minneapolis, Plymouth Avenue and Broadway; in Pittsburgh, Center and DeVilliers.

The report of the President's Commission on Civil Disorders says that such intersections, with a "relatively high concentration of pedestrian and automobile traffic," are places where riots are likely to start.

The 14th and U Street intersection is on the southern end of a twenty-block shopping strip bordering a congested and deteriorated area.

Among the more than 300 businesses on the twenty-block stretch of 14th Street and some of its side streets are clothing, specialty, five and dime, hardware, appliance, pawn, dry cleaning, and other shops that bring daytime crowds to the street. Some are branches of stores and national chains found in middle-class Negro and white neighborhoods; others are ghetto-oriented businesses selling on credit at high interest.

At night, this stretch of 14th Street turns on in neon. There are movie houses, bars, rock-and-roll palaces, other night spots, the rooming houses where the prostitutes take their clients, as well as the after-hours joints that open up after everything else but the carryout stores closes down.

The crowd with Carmichael had come back to 14th and U and turned east onto U Street, moving along the north sidewalk and passing the Jumbo Nut Shop, where Katina Mandes, a white woman and a co-owner of the shop, was working that night. She did not close when first asked. But, when the crowd passed her a second time a few minutes later, she was told this time that she had five minutes. She closed the store and hurried home.

As the crowd passed the Republic Theater, a block farther west on U Street, a stocky fifteen-year-old boy, wearing dungarees, a tan sweatshirt, and a sailor cap, suddenly punched his fist into one of the movie theater's glass doors. The glass shattered, and a younger boy slipped through the door frame into the theater and came back with a large bag of popcorn. The fifteen-year-old stood by the door, rubbing his fist, which was not cut, and smiled broadly.

"Way to go, kid," somebody called to him.

But Carmichael came up to the teenager and pulled him away from the front of the theater. "This is not the way," he shouted, so that others could hear him. Some SNCC members rushed over to the broken glass and told other youths in the crowd to stay out of the theater. The swirling crowd had grown large by now, and, on its eastern fringes, farther down U Street, a few twenty-year-olds went into the Lincoln Theater and told the manager and the customers that it was closed. They shouted at the people sitting in the dark theater, ordering them out onto the street. By now, it was 9:45 p.m.

Carmichael grew more and more concerned about what was happening. He turned around and headed back to 14th Street. Most of the crowd followed him. Reaching 14th and U, Carmichael turned north on 14th Street, walking along the sidewalk on the east side, across from the Peoples Drug Store.

After stopping at the Zanzibar Restaurant and asking owner Moy Hon Toon to close (he did), the crowd crossed to the west side of 14th Street, still heading north. The mob was so large now that it covered the entire block from U Street north to V Street. Those at the rear, in front of the Peoples Drug Store, began kicking in the rest of its broken plate-glass window. Some knocked over display cases before SNCC workers could get back to the store to stop them.

A middle-aged man walked up to the shattered drugstore window and aimed his foot at a piece of the glass that remained in place. There were tears in his eyes, and he was angry. He began shouting about the white man's evil. He picked up a city trash can off the sidewalk and threw it through the drugstore window. Still screaming, he went across the street and threw a bottle from the street gutter through the window of the National Liquor Store.

The mood of the entire crowd grew uglier.

"This is it baby," someone said. "The shit is going to hit the fan now. . . . We oughta burn this place down right now. Let's get some white motherfuckers. . . . Let's kill them all."

The cries became so loud that Carmichael stopped the crowd again and began arguing with a young man who had been among those suggesting that they should act to avenge Dr. King's death.

"You really ready to go out and kill?" Carmichael asked at the top of his voice. "How you gonna win? What you got? They've got guns . . . tanks. What you got? If you don't have your gun, go home. We're not ready. Let's wait until tomorrow. Just cool it. Go home, go home, go home."

There were echoes of his words in the crowd, probably repeated by SNCC workers.

"We're not ready," they said. "We'll be back. This ain't the way." Carmichael began telling the people to go home.

"Get off the streets. This is not the time, brothers," he shouted.

And Carmichael began walking north on 14th Street fast, the crowd still following him.

As they walked up the steep 14th Street hill, some of the teenagers began chanting: "Beep, beep, black power. Beep, beep, black power."

On a fringe of the crowd, a man ran into the street, went up to a D.C. Transit bus, and put his fist through the small window next to the driver. Others in the crowd ran out to grab him and pulled him away, as blood ran out of cuts in his hand.

From the SCLC office, Fauntroy could hear and see the trouble growing on 14th Street. With two of his nine brothers, Billy and Raymond, he drove to radio station WOL to broadcast an appeal for order. He was speaking as an SCLC leader and as vice chairman of the City Council. Then he got a police escort and rushed to all four major television stations and made brief appearances on the air, with the same plea for order. At each stop, there were tears in his eyes, sorrow in his voice.

Carmichael and the crowd passed the SNCC office on 14th Street and continued north. When they reached the corner of 14th and Belmont streets, five blocks north of 14th and U, a heavy-set woman in her thirties, wearing a raincoat, leaned against the window of the Belmont TV and Appliance Store and started bumping it with her broad backside. The window cracked and then fell in. The woman stepped away, smiling as the fifteen-year-old had smiled at the Republic Theater. A few young men in the vanguard of the crowd, mostly SNCC workers, rushed to the shattered window and stood in the way of anyone who might want to take the television sets that were left exposed, an arm's reach inside.

Carmichael, hearing the breaking glass, ran over and grabbed a youth who was trying to get past the SNCC workers and through the broken window. He took the teenager by the shoulder and shook him. Then, Carmichael produced a large, black revolver.

"If you mean business," he told the boy, "you should have a gun. You're not ready for the 'thing.' Go home. Go home."

The mob had turned south and was heading back toward 14th and U. Its size had shrunk and it seemed to be out of steam. As it passed the SNCC office, more people dropped off, some going inside SNCC, some appearing to start home. A light rain was falling steadily now.

But Carmichael could see that crowds were gathering again down the hill at 14th and U. He continued walking south, and some of the people around him followed. No uniformed policemen could be seen on 14th Street yet, although there were plainclothesmen in the milling crowd.

Just as Carmichael reached 14th and U, he heard what sounded like gunshots a block away. It was 10:24 p.m. At police headquarters, the sounds produced the first two trouble calls from 14th Street—windows breaking at Sam's Pawnbrokers and the Rhodes Five and Ten store, both a block south of U on 14th Street. This time, youths in the crowd made it to the stores before SNCC workers could intervene and began pouring through the display windows to grab watches, jewelry, radios, and television sets.

As Carmichael heard the two loud sounds, he saw a man in his twenties in the crowd brandishing a gun. Carmichael wrested it away from him, ending another argument about whether the crowd should act to avenge the assassination.

"Go home, go home, go home," Carmichael shouted. "None of this," he cried, waving the man's gun in the air. "None of this, we're not ready."

"But we've got no leader," a voice in the crowd called out. "We lost our leader. They killed him."

Carmichael answered: "You won't get one like this. You'll just get shot. Go home, go home."

Down the street, two SNCC workers, one a high-school youth who was wearing a Carmichael-style, green field jacket and had two binoculars around his neck, began pulling looters out of stores and display windows and telling them to "go home." The pair soon became discouraged. As soon as they cleared one store, rioters hopped into another to grab what they could.

A girl in her twenties, who had been in the SNCC office earlier, reached through one of the store windows. She came out with several transistor radios cradled in her right arm and a large cooking pot, which she rhythmically hit against her left hip.

"Got me something; got me something," she shouted to the thumping beat.

Youths with television sets, electrical appliances, clothing, shoes, and other items began streaming past Carmichael at 14th and U. Slipping away, he ducked into the doorway of the SCLC office, stood for a moment, and then dashed across 14th Street to get in a waiting Mustang and speed away. It was 10:40 p.m.

Carmichael knew his actions were being watched closely by federal authorities. He has since said he was determined to give them no cause to arrest him. Clearly, his decision to close the stores was an important factor in collecting the crowd. But he and his aides made strenuous efforts to check the mob when it grew unruly. He took his exit at the precise point of no return—as the memorial street demonstration exploded into riot.

By 11 p.m., windows were breaking on all sides of the intersection. Display dummies from the Federated Five and Dime on 14th Street were stripped and tossed on the sidewalk. Persons went by carrying suits on display hangers, cases of liquor, and expensive appliances. A man in a heavy jacket, work pants, and work shoes paused on the sidewalk to get a better grip on the portable television and three-piece portable stereo he was carrying.

"They got London, they got London," shouted excited teenagers, as they ran down the street.

Looters were coming out of the London Custom Shop just down U Street with shirts, slacks, suits, and hats. Trails of clothes were left behind. (Later that night, nineteen-year-old Carl McKinley Harris was arrested in front of London, carrying seven new hats. Just three hours earlier, at his grandmother's house a few blocks away, he had seen the television bulletin about Dr. King's shooting and he decided to go out to see "what would happen." He was charged with attempted burglary and released on $500 bail pending trial.)

The evening had started with a hostile, antiwhite tone. Now some of the hostility seemed to be forgotten in the carnival excitement produced by the looting.

The crowds continued to grow, as more and more persons poured out of the tenements on either side of the 14th Street strip to join the activity. They gathered along the twenty-block area in clusters.

Looting on 14th Street consisted mainly of hit-and-run attacks on display windows, the looters hurrying off to elude the police, who began to appear in force. By midnight, the police had effectively sealed off and occupied the 14th and U area. But farther north, where there was a concentration of larger clothing and specialty stores, more widespread looting occurred.

Six blocks above U Street, at the intersection with Clifton, youths stood in the middle of the street and tossed rocks and bottles at passing cars and buses. A teenager threw a bottle through the windshield of one of the first police cars on the scene, hitting the driver on the shoulder.

As police strength increased, the officers began arresting any looters they could pull away from the crowds. One of the first to be put in a paddy wagon was thirty-one-year-old Charles Herman, who was standing in front of the Belmont TV and Appliance store, where the plate glass had been broken ninety minutes earlier by the heavy-set woman in the raincoat. Herman, who lived nearby on Belmont Street, was carrying a brand-new portable phonograph. He was charged with burglary and jailed to await action of the U.S. Grand Jury.

Shortly after 11:30 p.m., the evening's intermittent light rain suddenly erupted into a heavy downpour. For a time, the rain helped break up bands of looters along the strip, but it ended only a few minutes after it began.

Up the 14th Street hill, a dozen blocks north of 14th and U, a crowd of about 100 youths grew quickly to 300, and then 500, as the rain ended. Singly and in groups of 6 to 20, they spread over a six-block area, between Girard Street and Park Road, smashing windows and looting dozens of the clothing and specialty shops there. The stores were in low structures built on what had been the lawns of six- and eight-story apartment buildings and old mansions, now overcrowded with large families. These buildings had been occupied by whites, mostly Irish and Italian Catholics, in the 1920's, when the first commercial incursions of the lawns began. Just before World War II, Negroes began pushing into the area from the 7th Street and Georgia Avenue neighborhoods to the east. Only a handful of white families remained immediately east of 14th Street.

The police were still badly outnumbered on upper 14th Street. They rushed at the massed crowds of looters, flailing nightsticks to break them into small groups that could then be isolated and arrested or chased away.

A group of touring city officials, including Mayor Washington, drove north on 14th Street from U just before midnight and saw the shadows of looters darting in and out of darkened storefronts. Police cars raced by, heading for the more serious trouble farther north. As the official party proceeded up the hill, looters were seen coming out of hardware stores, clothing shops, milk and ice cream stores, and package liquor stores, with loaded arms.

"Look at that stuff, will you," the Mayor commented as the car passed two teen-aged girls carrying dozens of dresses, coats, and skirts.

At 14th and Kenyon, the street was filled with frenzied blacks. An occasional rock or bottle sailed through the air. A policeman who stopped the car and recognized the Mayor advised, "You better get out of here."

The official party, which included Corporation Counsel Charles Duncan and Julian Dugas, Director of Licenses and Inspections, went on to the Thirteenth Precinct House near 16th and V streets, where a temporary command post had been set up. . . .

It was now past midnight and more than 500 policemen were on 14th Street, many on foot, equipped with tear gas and gas masks. They continued to try to break up the crowds. It became a game of hare and hounds. Youths would dart out from alleys and hit a store, to loot its merchandise or try to start a fire inside it, and then run when chased by police.

By 12:30 a.m., the mobs succeeded in starting the first full-scale fires of the riot in two neighborhood food markets on opposite corners of 14th and Fairmont streets. The first fire call actually had been received more than an hour and a half earlier, four blocks south at Belmont Street. Two Ford vehicles, a 1966 sedan and a light truck, had been set ablaze on the Barry-Pate and Addison used-car lot. These blazes were quickly extinguished, but they served to alert fire-alarm headquarters to the trouble ahead. At that time, Fire Chief Henry Galotta rushed to headquarters and put into effect an emergency plan doubling the men on duty at each firehouse during the next four hours.

At 14th and Fairmont, firemen were called to a blaze at the Central Market on the southeast corner. Five minutes later, flames broke out in the Pleasant Hill Market on the northwest corner behind them. This fire quickly spread to the adjacent Steelman's liquor store and threatened a four-story apartment building next to the liquor store. A small fire had already been started earlier downstairs in this building, in Judd's Pharmacy, by a man in his thirties who set burning newspapers inside the front door. But the rain had extinguished it.

When the firemen first arrived at 14th and Fairmont, a mixed crowd of youths and adults poured out of the apartments and the side streets to surround the firemen and pelt them with stones, bottles, and cans. Several dozen policemen converged on the intersection, and policemen and firemen donned gas masks. The police rolled and tossed more than 100 baseball-sized tear-gas canisters at the crowd—many from the windows and back door of a patrol wagon that was driven repeatedly into the midst of the crowd in an attempt to split it up. It was the first large-scale use of gas in the riot.

The smothering, eye-burning vapor drove the crowd back a block in all directions. Some people went home, but many continued to throw stones and bottles from a distance. As the firemen doused the flames at

14th and Fairmont, police answered the rock throwers with grenade launchers that sent gas shells in hissing arcs 20 and 30 feet into the air toward rioters as far as two blocks away.

At one point, a bottle, dropped from the roof of an apartment building, smashed to the street with a loud report that sounded like a gunshot. *Washington Post* reporter Robert Maynard had parked his radio car right by the spot where it fell. He radioed to the newspaper's city desk: "There are four policemen ducking for cover right beside my car. . . . They are down on one knee behind the hood and the trunk . . . with their guns drawn and cocked . . . aiming over the car at the roof above us.

"I'm now getting onto the floor under the dashboard as fast as I can. . . . Over and out."

Another policeman shouted that it was just a bottle. A tear-gas grenade was lofted onto the roof of the apartment building. The policemen holstered their guns. No shots had been fired, nor were there any other guns reported drawn by police that night. It was now nearly 2 a.m.

A group of youths, scattered by the tear-gas barrage, re-formed a block away, at Euclid, to attack another food store, the Empire Market. When they could not kick in the heavy front door, a short, husky youth wrenched a "No Parking" signpost out of the dirt. Half running, half dancing, he rammed it against the door, which gave way, and the youths rushed in.

In a fury of activity, the youths began pulling down lights, displays, and shelves and tossing foodstuffs at the windows, walls, and ceiling. When a group of twenty-five policemen arrived on the double, running downhill from Fairmont Street, the youths dived through windows and escaped to a parking lot across the street. A policeman fired a tear-gas grenade at them, but one boy picked it up and quickly tossed it back toward the police, who had taken off their gas masks. It exploded at their feet.

For forty-five minutes, the police jousted with the youths, who kept coming back determinedly to the store, trying to set it afire with matches and burning newspapers. Finally, a big fire was started and flames shot out the window openings and through the roof.

When the firemen arrived, the youths began to stone them. Police moved in quickly with more tear gas. This time, the gas dispersed the dwindling band of youths, and the firemen doused the flames. By now, it was 3:00 a.m., Friday, April 5, and the last large-scale confrontation on 14th Street had ended.

In about six hours, more than 200 stores had had windows broken; 150 of them had been looted. There had been 7 fires. More than 150 adults and nearly 50 juveniles had been arrested. There were 30 injured, including 5 policemen and 1 fireman. . . .

Most of the damage was on 14th Street, but stores at about a half-dozen locations outside the 14th Street police perimeter suffered broken windows and minor looting from roving bands of youths driving automobiles. The Hecht Company's main downtown department store, at 7th and F streets, N.W., had some windows broken. Also hit was D. J. Kaufman's, at 1005 Pennsylvania Avenue, N.W., an expensive, high-fashion men's shop, heavily patronized by blacks.

The downtown store was less than ten blocks from the White House and about the same distance from the Capitol along the historic Presidential inaugural route. Although the damage was not serious—a few pairs of shoes and some items of clothing were taken—the looting of Kaufman's suggested that the contagion could easily spread beyond the area the police had sealed off. Some of the looting occurred while employees, who had responded to the burglar alarm, were engaged in clearing the broken windows of merchandise.

At dawn Friday, with hundreds of policemen still lining the sidewalks, 14th Street was quiet. The rays of the rising sun glinted on those store windows that still contained unbroken glass. White foam, sprayed by street-cleaning crews, ran down the steep hill, carrying broken glass and debris along with it. Mayor Washington had ordered the crews out early and in force. Failure to clean the streets, it had been learned from the 1967 riots, invited more damage the next day.

Eye-stinging tear gas still hung in the air. Burglar alarms continued to jangle in an unsettling chorus. An early riser, viewing a ransacked clothing store for the first time, turned away, shaking his head.

"Oh, my God," was his only comment.

*October 3, 1961: Phil Graham looks on as President Kennedy speaks
at a special* Washington Post*–sponsored luncheon celebrating the
publication of the first four volumes of* The Adams Papers.

PRESIDENT WATCHING

The White House is two stories high but otherwise is one long story. You might call it the title-page to the drama of America.
      —Rufus Dart, *The Puppet Show on the Potomac*

PRESIDENT watching is a great spectator sport. People do it from all over the world, but in Washington we get to do it close up. Living in the same city as the president of the United States means that we can catch glimpses of him even if we're not among the invited guests to the White House. Beyond the glimpses, though, presidential activity is a local phenomenon here, so the media in Washington focus on this central citizen in a way that doesn't happen in other places.

If, indeed, as so many people have espoused and written through the years, Washington is a company town, then the president is the head of the company. Therefore, he has always been an important man in Washington, a big man around town. Those who surround him—wife as first lady, children and extended family (if any), staff, and various other appendages—are also important.

A president is at any given moment a panacea, a target, a butt of jokes, a politician, a boss, a son of a gun, an inspired leader. Herblock, in his book *Here and Now,* related a joke about everyone blaming FDR for all their ills. He wrote, "Back in the 30's there was a story about a man who went to the race track on his 55th birthday, traveled in car number 55, and found that his room in the hotel near the track was number 55. Knowing a red-hot hunch when he had one, he bet everything he had on the fifth horse in the fifth race, a steed named Five-By-Five. He watched his horse break in front, increase its lead at the quarter, and stay ahead until the stretch, where it was nosed out just under the wire. The hunch bettor stared darkly at the finish line as he tore up his tickets and muttered, 'Damn that man Roosevelt!' "

The job is so powerful that it immediately transforms people. There's a story my parents told about their once meeting Alice Roosevelt Longworth as she was coming out of the White House after seeing President Harding in his office. Mrs. Longworth was perfectly realistic about Harding, and didn't like him very well to begin with, but said, "Even that son of a bitch looks impressive in that getup."

As I noted before, unbelievably (even to me), I have been connected with more than a third of all the presidents. It strikes me that a walk past some of the presidents I have known may serve as an introduction to this section on president watching.

Since we Meyer children essentially stayed in New York during the Wilson administration, rather than moving to Washington with our parents, President Wilson was hardly a factor in the life of our family. Certainly he was my father's ultimate employer, but indirectly. My mother was often critical of Wilson, not just because he was a Democrat but because he was so much the "know-it-all," a quality that seems to have annoyed the public then, as it often does now when a president comes across as preaching and teaching.

As we have seen, Ellen Maury Slayden was another who actively criticized Wilson. She, in fact, disdained him, believing him to be narrow-minded, too much of a Presbyterian, and too much of the schoolteacher.

Probably my favorite censure of President Wilson from Ellen Slayden is her notation in her diary at the time Wilson's first grandchild was born: "Concerning the baby's name, there has been a ripple of fun since the pedagogue grandpapa announced (in the *Post*'s Society news) that to be truly effective, to come trippingly to the tongue of the masses, a man's name should be composed of two spondees and a dactyl. No one had risen to dispute it, perhaps because, like myself, the masses are not acquainted with either party."

Except for one occasion, I have no memory of Harding. I do recall, however, visiting the White House. I wrote my mother about it in May 1923, saying, in the true fashion of a not-quite-six-year-old who clearly was made to write a letter to Mother and who had yet to master punctuation: "We took a trip to the white house and I sat in the president's chair. While we were there I saw the Blue Room Red Room the Green Room and the West Room. Then we went to the Washington Monument. With love, Katharine."

What I didn't spell out in that letter, but which remains indelibly etched in my mind, is that when I sat in the chair, I somehow wrapped my Mary Janes around the legs of the chair and nearly tripped myself up.

My parents had a closer connection to Harding. They had met him from time to time in the few years they'd been in Washington. Mother, in fact, had been seated next to him at a dinner at the Belgian embassy in January 1920, and had not been all that impressed. She wrote in her diary that he was "one of our many Pretenders."

Mother made a formal visit to the White House to see Mrs. Harding in November 1921. She dealt with it fairly peremptorily in her diary: "My visit to Mrs. Harding was absurd. Her idea of seeing people alone was good, but her constant talk at the visitors instead of with them was simply stupid. She is either very nervous or very conceited for her realization of the other person is simply nil. She remembered meeting me at the Belgian Embassy and then she dashed headlong into personal talk of how she had been afraid to let her husband run for the presidency. Unfortunately I am not the only one who thinks she is making a fool of herself by such incessant chatter for the Brodericks said the same thing."

I don't remember ever meeting Calvin Coolidge, but I do remember seeing the Coolidges about town. Maybe they were more visible because they had to move out of the White House for eight months in 1927 while the mansion got a new roof. In my parents' day—and to some extent, still—an invitation to the White House was a command, however inconvenient. You had to cancel whatever else might have been on your calendar and hie thee to the White House. My sister Bis recalled once when Dad didn't heed the invite, however. They were out driving and happened on President Coolidge, walking along down the sidewalk, as he was accustomed to do. According to Bis, Dad had his driver, Al Phillips, pull over, and said, "How do you do, Mr. President?" After a brief—remember, it was Coolidge—exchange, the president asked Dad to come to dinner with him that very night, saying, "I'd be glad to have you." Bis recalled that Dad answered, "I'm sorry, Mr. President, but I'm having dinner with my family tonight." Then "Mr. Coolidge bowed and kept walking, and as we proceeded down the avenue Mother turned to Dad saying, 'Eugene, don't you know you never turn down an invitation by a president? Never.' Father looked perplexed. Then his face cleared and he said, 'Well, I just did.' "

All of us Meyer kids had met Herbert Hoover before he was president. When he was secretary of commerce, he visited us both at our house in Washington and in Mount Kisco. Bis, who was four and a half years older than I, remembered him especially. She remembered that

Hoover tried to join in with the kids and show off to the adults how well he got along with children. He even came down into the woods surrounding our house to our playground, and taught us how to build a trap for a bear. Bis recalled that "he went around crouched down, whispering as if a bear were around the corner." As children, of course, we had certain responsibilities in greeting our parents' guests. Bis wrote in her unpublished memoir, "We had to use proper decorum, but we were always a little bit unsure as to whom we were to kiss. When Herbert Hoover was Secretary of Commerce, I kissed him and Dad said, 'Oh, how nice. A kiss for Mr. Hoover.' I wasn't aware that Hoover was no pal of Dad's, and there was some degree of dislike."

In fact, despite that kiss, our parents' ambivalent attitude to Hoover seemed to have rubbed off on all of us children. I guess it was because Hoover had always caused Dad such difficulty that he was the logical recipient of family jokes. We had a framed picture of him holding the paws of our German shepherd, Pasha. A filing label was plastered across the glass, above his head, that read, "Even the dog is reluctant." On the other hand, who knows what Hoover must have thought of our family through the years? We were hardly a conventional group.

My mother seemed to have taken Hoover's measure quite early. He first appears in her diary on December 16, 1919, when she gave a dinner party for Lord Gray from England, and Hoover was one of the guests: "I disliked him enormously especially when he clinked his change during one of the Beethoven Quartets. Chance makes great men of some queer people, or rather I should say prominent men. One thing that Washington has clearly taught me is that prominent men are very rarely great men."

Hoover certainly had a tough presidency. He called the Great Depression "the nightmare of my White House years." Even twenty years after he left office, Hoover was still insisting that Franklin D. Roosevelt "overdramatized" the Depression.

However much Dad may not have liked Hoover, it was during the Hoover administration that he took on more demanding and more important government positions.

Of course, the Depression and its aftermath took its toll on anyone working on financial matters for the government and the nation. In June 1932, my father was called away from the dinner table to the phone. Soon, all we heard was yelling. He and the person on the other end of the phone were fighting. It turned out to be the president on the line. My parents talked at length about it when Dad came back to the table, clearly upset.

Mother, always protective of my father, went often to the White House to talk with Hoover, trying to get him to improve the situation for my overworked father. When she wasn't sending the president notes telling him how to deal with everyone from my father to the cabinet, she was going over to the White House to speak to him personally. Throughout his administration, her diary is peppered with entries in which she goes back and forth in her assessment of him. Mother felt that Hoover was "consumed with ambition," and that his "will-to-power is almost a mania." She went on:

> The idea of good works, of high achievement is strong in him but he is not interested in the good that must be accomplished through others or even with the help of others. Only what is done by Hoover, is of any meaning to him. He is a big man but he cannot bear rivalry of any sort. He is tortured by the fact that his vision is greater than his ability to execute. That is why he will compromise and does constantly compromise in any and every way, to achieve his purposes. For the first time I fully realized Eugene's difficulties with Hoover, and his with Eugene. Poor Eugene is trying to save the country, and the President is trying to save Hoover.

Her entry for July 19, 1932, reads, "If ever my children read this book I do not want them to think that the criticisms of Hoover noted here were ever spoken to anyone else. The President has his glaring weaknesses which are known only too well but nevertheless I believe in him and in his essential greatness. The very contradictions in his character and mind make him all the more fascinating to me. If he gets another term he will be one of the most effective executives the country has ever had."

But another term was not to be had. Once the election was over, Mother complained in her diary about Hoover repeatedly trying to get my father to leave office before March 4 and not even think about staying with FDR: "Perhaps like an Oriental widow he is expected to hurl himself upon his Master's funeral pyre. I think Hoover would like to go down to his political grave with all his retainers, household and even the pet dogs buried with him like the Iranian or Scythian chiefs. We parted after he had expressed a fear that all our social institutions would be irrevocably destroyed."

In the end, Hoover went out of office, as Mother wrote, "to the sound of crashing banks. Like the tragic end of a tragic story. . . . Even in the Presidency he never learned to turn his eyes away from himself. That is the secret of his tragedy."

My own limited view of Hoover is that he was a gracious man, gray-haired and attractive. I do recall that he wouldn't smile at people.

In any case, Hoover was gone and Franklin Roosevelt took Washington by storm. I went to FDR's first inaugural but remember much less than I would like to. Maybe, given that I was not yet sixteen, my age is my excuse. Like most young people, I was influenced in my views by my parents, including all the initial bad-mouthing (especially by my mother). My parents, of course, were Republicans—at least at that time. But FDR became my president and remained so for twelve years. FDR was the captain of the ship during the New Deal period, when the whole country was preoccupied with getting over the Depression.

George Abell and Evelyn Gordon wrote in *Let Them Eat Caviar,* "The advent of the new President changed everything. The Roosevelts transformed the White House as completely as the swift march of public thought and events had already changed the country. No longer did the Executive Mansion resemble a medieval castle besieged by the forces of progress. The drawbridges were figuratively let down, and the moats drained of their time-worn prejudices. The archers of reaction withdrew from the turrets, and the victorious New Deal army took over the battlements."

The years of FDR's administration that I spent in Washington (from 1939 until 1945) were full ones, and not ones in which I necessarily turned my attention to president watching. When Phil and I married, in 1940, I felt we were in the thick of things in Washington, and especially when he went to work for the Lend-Lease Administration we felt he was really working for FDR and, of course, for the country. In our circle of friends, nearly everyone was working for FDR, which became even more true once World War II came to the United States.

My only firsthand interaction with Harry Truman coincided with the first thing I did as a "civic wife." I was appointed in 1947 to the National Capital Sesquicentennial Commission, for which President

Truman was the honorary chairman. When Truman was elected in his own right in 1948, he returned to Washington from the campaign trail to a festive parade down Pennsylvania Avenue, with many *Post* people hanging out of the windows of our E Street building, along with the now-famous "Welcome Home from the Crow-Eaters" sign, reflecting how many newspapers, including the *Post,* had missed the story of Truman's ultimate win.

My father had long been interested in Eisenhower, and had even made a trip to Europe after the war to sound out Ike on his intentions and hopes for the future. In 1952, the *Post,* influenced no doubt by my father's opinions about the importance of Eisenhower's strength of character, threw out its independent stance when it came to primaries and supported Eisenhower over Taft. Phil even went so far as to campaign for the general, but although he had supported him, it wasn't long before he found a more like-minded man in Lyndon Baines Johnson.

Perhaps due to the advent of television, it seems that president watching became a more focused activity with the youthful John Fitzgerald Kennedy and his wife, Jacqueline. The dominant feeling for me when JFK was inaugurated president was a certain disbelief that there could actually be a president who was my age. I loved observing him, but for the most part I was always terrified of Jack Kennedy—certainly when he was president, and maybe even before. I remember one day going to the White House for dinner and, as always, I felt terribly awkward and was sure that I was going to bore him—which was, of course, the first way to bore him. I know that people were distressed at the idea of "twist" parties at the White House, but when you think that when the Kennedys got there, he was forty-three and she was not yet thirty-two, you can understand that they didn't want to live there the way their predecessors had.

In some ways, Lyndon Johnson was one of the presidents who didn't like Washington. Even Lady Bird writes about this in her *White House Diary.* She talks about Nixon having come to the White House to see President Johnson privately before the change of administration: "They discussed press relations in general, and I gathered they had a certain amount in common—particularly when I heard Mr. Nixon use the expression, 'Georgetown dinner parties,' with an inflection of voice reminiscent of Lyndon's."

My working relationship with Lyndon Johnson was affected by a number of factors, including that he had adored Phil Graham and that I was associated with a paper that I didn't "use" in a way the president would have preferred. LBJ did not like the press. He was always proud of Lady Bird, but he resented it when she got better press than he did.

Nancy Dickerson wrote that "The LBJ social style was something of a shock to the capital. Starting right at the White House, the Johnson way was different. . . . It's difficult to comprehend the LBJ style because even by Texas standards he had large impulses. When the Johnsons said, 'You-all come,' they meant it. Their lack of inhibition was new in Washington, a Southern city in the East. LBJ was a cowboy, and though that mythic figure is in the best American tradition, the Washington establishment, the press and the country were unaccustomed to a cowboy in the White House. The city shook its collective head." I believe that for months after Kennedy's assassination, it was incredibly difficult for Lyndon and Lady Bird Johnson to do anything much in Washington but lie low. However, the Johnsons gradually began to put their own mark on the city.

It's hard to know what to say about Richard Nixon, but certainly the president-watching population of Washington had a great time during his years in the city, especially when he was in the White House. He provided Herblock and all of the Washington columnists and commentators with endless material, and, from just a few months after the Watergate break-in, in June 1972, until his resignation, in August 1974, President Nixon kept us all buzzing and wondering and speculating. Needless to say, the beginning of Watergate was also the beginning of a period in my life when I was the most disconnected and cut off from the White House and the president, in every way.

I've always felt that it's difficult to get to know a new president if you didn't know him before he became president. That was true for me with Gerald Ford and Jimmy Carter, neither of whom I got to know well. I went to the White House in each of their administrations, but I was much more of an observer from a distance. On the other hand, as I've already written, Ronald Reagan was someone I knew before he was elected, so his coming to Washington as president was, for me, a chance to get reacquainted, which we happily did.

I never related much to George H. W. Bush as president—no doubt this was not helped by *Newsweek*'s publication of a cover story on "The Wimp Factor" during his 1988 campaign. Although I did go to the Clinton White House, his was the first presidency during which I felt that we were of very different generations, and that was a distance that I never was able to close.

If I seem to have focused more on certain presidencies than others, it doesn't mean that they're the more important ones; it's because certain presidencies are naturally richer in material, in anecdotes, in personality, in character—and in characters.

CARY T. GRAYSON

The Foremost Man of His Age

Woodrow Wilson, An Intimate Memoir (1960)

Admiral Cary Grayson was not only Woodrow Wilson's naval aide and personal physician from 1913 to 1924, but also his friend and confidant. At his side daily, he actually lived in the White House before his marriage. His memoir of Wilson was based on meticulous notes and a diary he kept and on recollections he wrote down in 1924, shortly after Wilson's death.

My father considered himself a very good friend of Admiral Grayson, and they discussed many issues and questions with each other. Dad said that Grayson was "perfectly willing to do so because he knew that I wasn't going to talk about them publicly. In confidence he told me many interesting things." He felt that Grayson's memoirs would be the most interesting of any on Wilson, since Grayson had obviously known him best and was closer to him than anyone but his wife. My father told an interviewer once that he understood that the memoirs' publication depended on the lifetime of Mrs. Wilson, which must have been the case, since this book wasn't published until 1960, long after Grayson's death in 1938. Even my father didn't live long enough to read it.

Grayson's close observations of President Wilson result in useful insights into Wilson's behavior. For example, Grayson writes that, in describing Wilson, "one cannot too often emphasize his preference for doing the same thing repeatedly" and doing only one thing at a time. He also points out that Wilson was frequently criticized for "exclusiveness" in the choice of those with whom he would play golf, "but the fact of the matter is that he did not want business mingled with his recreation, and he soon found that most men whom he invited to play with him insisted on introducing public business into the conversation." In referring to the practice of designating certain weeks for specific movements—such as "Be Kind to Animals Week"—Grayson writes that Wilson said "there should be a week designated for people to mind their own business."

This excerpt is clearly a case of "Washington Then." The kind of moments described here by Wilson's friend weren't long for this world.

Gone are these kinds of serendipitous meetings, bucolic walks, and leisurely presidential automobile rides through Rock Creek Park "to get cooled off before going to bed." Gone is the time when the president's car could be stopped by a bicycle policeman—a far cry from the motorcades now. But these stories take on life again in these intimate remembrances of a friend.

A MUSING incidents mingled with serious events. . . . One day while the President and I were returning . . . from . . . playing golf, a little boy about ten years of age stood in the middle of the road, and with the motions of a traffic cop, waved our automobile to a stop. It turned out that he had some oranges which he wanted to give the President. The President accepted the humble offering with thanks, asked the boy where he lived, told him to climb into the car, and drove the child to his home. The next day the President wrote him a nice letter of appreciation. A few days afterward while coming along this road the little boy waved us down again. He did not have a basket this time, but he told the President that he enjoyed the letter so much that he would like to have the President write him every week after he got back to Washington. The President was very much pleased over this little incident.

His interest in children was frequently manifested. My own little son, Gordon, was constantly in the companionship of the President during the months of his illness in the White House, and the President would hold Gordon's hand while being wheeled into the East Room to witness a motion picture.

Down in Pass Christian [Mississippi] we were returning another day from the golf course when he noticed smoke curling up from the roof of a residence. We ran to the door and knocked and were received by the lady of the house with flutterings of excitement. "Oh, Mr. President," she exclaimed, "it is so good of you to call on me. Won't you please walk into the parlor and sit down?" To which the President replied: "I haven't time to sit down—your house is on fire."

We formed a bucket brigade but the lady in her double excitement was so confused that she seized a pitcher without any water in it. Climbing through the garret to the roof we extinguished the fire and in recognition of our prowess both the President and I were elected members of the Pass Christian Fire Department.

. . . A SHORT time after the loss of his wife I was able to induce him to renew his automobile rides and his golf and go on an occasional *Mayflower* trip down the Potomac River.

He had keen powers of observation and was especially fond of striking out cross-country for a walk and chatting with farmers or workingmen he met along the road, always anxious to conceal his own identity. On one occasion a farmer said: "You favor the picture of President Wilson." And the President smilingly replied: "Yes, I have often been told that." He greatly preferred that people should not make a to-do over him.

An experience on a *Mayflower* trip illustrates this quality, and at the same time shows him in such a purely human aspect that I am tempted to relate it at length. One afternoon he and I eluded the secret service men by saying that we were going to take a little trip in the motor launch. When we landed at Yorktown we left the sailors in the boat and struck out alone through the streets of the old town, which had practically gone to sleep at three o'clock in the afternoon, and made our way to the Court House. In one of the rooms an old man was sitting at a table writing in a deed book with his coat off, his suspenders much in evidence, and sucking on a corncob pipe. The President asked him if he could see the courtroom, and the old gentleman kept writing, and said: "Yep, help yourself. Go right upstairs." The President said: "May I ask who is your Judge?" The reply was: "D. Gardner Tyler, son of the tenth President of the United States, brother of Lyon G. Tyler, President of William and Mary College, which is only twelve miles from here. And our Judge is a fine man too." All this talking was done without looking up. The fellow never realized the presence of his distinguished visitor. Upon entering the Clerk's Office we met Mr. Hudgins, who very politely acquiesced in the President's request to examine some old documents. Hanging on the wall was a large campaign poster of the President and I was rather surprised that Mr. Hudgins did not seem to recognize the visitor. There he was standing beside a large picture of himself. When we left the Clerk's Office I felt sure that the President had been unrecognized, but later I learned that Mr. Hudgins had realized who his visitor was and had made the statement: "The President did not introduce himself nor his friend and therefore I did not care to push myself forward by introducing myself." The President mightily appreciated this when he heard of it and said: "There was a true gentleman."

If he could have been received in the same way in the public offices in Washington he would have visited them all. But his continual complaint was that the moment he entered a public building all work stopped and everybody flocked about him. During his administration he promised himself that when he was what he called a free man again he was going to visit every public building in the city—a promise which he could not fulfill because of his illness.

We walked around Yorktown, went to the Post Office, bought some postcard pictures of the old Custom House and of Temple Farm, Washington's Headquarters, and of the Nelson House. The Postmaster, who was also the storekeeper, wanted to know if we did not want to buy some "pop" or ginger ale to cool us off on such a hot July day, assuring us that he would "sell it to us right." We did not take advantage of his offer. As we left the store the President noticed a group of citizens tilted back in their chairs against an old spreading tree, some half asleep, some exchanging random remarks, though no one recognized the fact that the President was passing. A group like this always interested him, because he felt that public opinion was made in just such environments; that the people in Washington did not really know public opinion because they did not associate with the vast masses, who, in country stores or outside of them, according to the seasonal conditions, really formed the opinions which settled elections.

As we walked up the street a bright-eyed little girl about twelve years old was the first person in Yorktown to give any evidence that she recognized the presence of the distinguished visitor. She paused and said: "Excuse me, sir, but you certainly do remind me of the pictures of President Wilson." The President smiled. Whereupon she said: "You are President Wilson, are you not, sir?"

The President replied: "Yes, I am guilty."

Then she said: "Won't you please wait and let me run and tell my mother. She will be so anxious to see you."

As we were almost at the front door of her mother's house, the mother in a moment was with us and said: "Won't you come up on the porch in the shade and have a glass of cold tea?"

We accepted the invitation, and while we were drinking our tea she brought out a communion service which proved to be that used in the old Jamestown Church, the first church in Virginia.

Presently the little girl in excitement said: "Look at the crowd coming up the street to see the President." I counted seven people. Among them was the Postmaster who inquired of the President if he might speak to him privately. The President told him to go ahead. He wanted to know if the President would not raise his salary as Postmaster, as he was only getting thirty dollars a month.

The little girl, Elizabeth Shields, to whom the President had taken a great fancy, acted as our guide to the Nelson House, which was next door, but said: "Mr. President, this was Cornwallis' Headquarters. The house you ought to see is the Temple Farm, which was George Washington's Headquarters." The President thanked her and said, "I will."

Accompanied by what the child called "the crowd," we visited the Yorktown Monument, and, leaving there, we got into the launch and proceeded down the river to Temple Farm where we were to see relics of the battlefield. There was no landing at this place and we could only get the boat within ten or fifteen yards of the bank of the river, so we pulled off our shoes, rolled up our trousers, and waded ashore. We scrambled up a steep embankment through the briars and the bees. In the field between us and the house we were attracted by a bull which was taking entirely too much notice of us. He began to paw the earth and bellow, and I, with a sense of responsibility, suggested to the President that we climb the fence and take a roundabout path to the farmhouse. After we got over the fence the President told the story of an Irishman who was chased by a bull and just as he got partly over the fence the bull hit him with his horns and knocked him completely on the other side. Then the bull began to paw and snort and the Irishman remarked: "You may bow and you may scrape as much as you please, but, be golly, if I don't think you meant it."

No man I have ever known was more quietly indifferent to danger than Mr. Wilson. He told me once that until he was over forty years of age he had the uncomfortable feeling that he did not know for a certainty whether or not he would be a coward in peril; but he was on a ship which went up on an iceberg, stove in her bow, and dropped back into the water seriously damaged, that none knew but what she might go down quickly, and that the perfect calmness which he felt on that occasion reassured him that he would never be a coward no matter what the physical peril.

He gave an example of his contempt for danger in 1914 when he led the funeral procession in New York of the Marines who had been killed at Vera Cruz. The secret service force unearthed a plot to assassinate him and begged him to review the parade from a stand. Mayor Mitchel of New York added his entreaties, saying: "The country cannot afford to have its President killed."

"The country cannot afford to have a coward for President," was Mr. Wilson's brief and conclusive answer.

ALICE ROOSEVELT LONGWORTH

Reminiscences of the Hardings

Crowded Hours (1933)

Mrs. Longworth didn't like the Hardings. She had many reasons not to, starting at least with the 1912 convention when her father was nominated for the presidency again, this time on the Progressive or Bull Moose ticket, by which time she had come to view Warren Harding as a crook. Of the Teapot Dome scandal that came to light later, she wrote, "The whole story that unfolded itself of the efforts to control the Oil lands was the record of about as corrupt and unsavory a performance as has ever taken place in this country. It was in no sense, as some people thought, part of the moral let-down which always seems to occur after a great war. It was merely the result of electing to the presidency a slack, good-natured man with an unfortunate disposition to surround himself with intimates of questionable character to whom he was unable to say no, friends who saw financial opportunities for personal power ripe for the picking and were unscrupulous in taking advantage of the weakness of character of the President."

Dad found Harding a friendly man but not a profound one—a man who would have liked to be a good president. Harding, however, faced many frustrations. He once was quoted as saying, "My God, this is a hell of a job! I can take care of my enemies all right. But my friends, my God-damn friends, they're the ones that keep me walking the floor nights!"

Marietta Andrews wrote in My Studio Window *that "I think there have never been a President and a President's wife in Washington who have made so transient an impression upon the life of the Capital, as Mr. and Mrs. Warren Gamaliel Harding." But Harding did have an effect on Washington. Here was the president who was supposed to bring about the "return to normalcy"—he had declared in a speech that "America needs not heroics but healing, not nostrums but normalcy, not revolutions but restorations, not surgery but serenity."*

Called the "apostle of normalcy," Harding threw open the White
House doors again after the Wilson years. The WPA guide to Washing-
ton reported the effect of Harding: "At once the atmosphere of Greek
tragedy dispersed in a radiant glow of jolly good fellowship. 'We are
just folks,' announced the President's wife; it was Old Home Week, after
a long exile. The Capital relaxed, yawned, became careless and open-
handed." In her history of the White House, White House Profile,
Bess Furman describes Harding as being "handsome, hail-fellow-well-
met," a man who provided a real and healthy contrast to the beaten
Wilson. One of his inauguration presents had been Laddie Boy, a dog,
who became a kind of "human-interest story" of the time, which the press
helped along by reporting on Harding practicing golf shots on the
White House grounds with Laddie Boy as retriever. Harding started
the year 1922 off positively by shaking hands with 6,576 people at
the White House New Year's Day reception.

Others who knew him—or at least reported on him—observe some
of the negatives in his few short years in the presidency. W. M. Kiplinger
singled him out as the only one of the presidents who didn't like the
job. James Watson, former senator from Indiana, wrote of Harding in
his memoirs, As I Knew Them, *and described him as "about as hand-*
some a man as I ever saw, and he had one of those affidavit faces whose
very appearance carries conviction, and withal he was a magnificent
figure. He just loved fellowship. He wanted to have a crowd around and
have a good time. . . . The truth about it is that he was altogether too
urbane, too good-natured, too generous-hearted, and too fond of hav-
ing a good time for his own good. The simple fact is that my dear old
friend just did not like to work."

I T IS ODD to have seen so much of people whom I never liked as I saw
of the Hardings. From the time he came to Washington as Senator in
1913, he and Mrs. Harding came to our house a great deal, chiefly to
play poker, a game to which he was devoted. Though Mrs. Harding did
not play, she always came too, and the job of the "Duchess," as she was
called, was to "tend bar." Harding and Nick and the others would say
when they wished another drink, "Duchess, you are lying down on your
job." And Mrs. Harding, who was watching the play of the hands, would
obediently get up and mix a whisky and soda for them.

I don't think that I held Harding's course in 1912 against him. Indeed,
I should have had few political associates if I had harbored the resentments that filled us during the Progressive campaign. Soon after he was

nominated in 1920, we talked of what he had said and done then, and agreed that we should both try to forget the details of that bitter year. When he came to Washington after his election, we saw him and discussed with him matters of policy and Cabinet prospects. I was put up to tell him how ill-advised many of his supporters felt it would be if he should give Harry Daugherty a Cabinet position. It was the wasted effort which we were pretty sure it would be. Their relationship, both personal and political, was too closely involved to permit any words of warning to take effect. The surmise and rumor about who would be in the Cabinet was that winter a national sport as it always is when there is a clean sweep—a change of administration accompanied by a change of party.

Inauguration was not the day of elation that it might have been. My joy at seeing the heels of the Democrats was keen, but Harding, and much of the set-up that was coming in with him, did not precisely inspire untempered confidence and enthusiasm. As we got to the top of Capitol Hill that morning on our way to the ceremonies in the Senate, there was the sound of a band and the click of trotting cavalry, and Harding, Wilson beside him, emaciated and mask-like, passed us. Wilson had discontinued the custom of holding an official inaugural ball, but Harding intended to revive it. However, there was a howl of economy in Congress that winter, and the inaugural ball, as a symbol of unnecessary expenditure, was not held. Instead, the Ned McLeans gave a dance at their enormous town house to which all Washington, visiting statesmen, the new Cabinet and other officials came in full force and revelled throughout the night.

The Hardings never liked me, and I can hardly blame them. One of their intimate friends once asked me if I realized that when I spoke to the President my manner was condescending, if not actually contemptuous. The fact was that though they came continuously to our house, I had never happened to go to theirs. Naturally when they came to the White House, whenever they asked me I had to go. I went there to call on Mrs. Harding with Ruth McCormick one afternoon, shortly after the inauguration.

She was a nervous, rather excitable woman whose voice easily became a little high-pitched, strident. That day in the course of conversation she told us, rolling an eye that never quite met ours, that she had a little red book which contained the names of the people who had not been civil to her and "Warren Harding" since they came to Washington. Those people were to realize that she was aware of their behavior. She usually spoke of Mr. Harding as "Warren Harding." It is impossible to convey her pronunciation of the letter R in print. Something like Wur-r-ren Ha-ar-r-ding.

Though violation of the Eighteenth Amendment was a matter of course in Washington, it was rather shocking to see the way Harding disregarded the Constitution he was sworn to uphold. Though nothing to drink was served downstairs, there were always, at least before the unofficial dinners, cocktails in the upstairs hall outside the President's room and guests were shown up there instead of waiting below for the President. While the big official receptions were going on, I don't think the people had any idea what was taking place in the rooms above. One evening while one was in progress, a friend of the Hardings asked me if I would like to go up to the study. I had heard rumors and was curious to see for myself what truth was in them. No rumor could have exceeded the reality; the study was filled with cronies, Daugherty, Jess Smith, Alec Moore, and others, the air heavy with tobacco smoke, trays with bottles containing every imaginable brand of whisky stood about, cards and poker chips ready at hand—a general atmosphere of waistcoat unbuttoned, feet on the desk, and the spittoon alongside.

I recollect that the first time we went to the White House after the Coolidges were there, the atmosphere was as different as a New England front parlor is from a back room in a speakeasy. Nick and I were abroad in 1923 at the time Harding died and we did not hear until we got back the rumors about the manner of his death. No matter what Harding's failings may have been, nothing more contemptible and distorted has ever been written than the gossip books that have been published about him. The assertions or implications that he was murdered, or killed himself, are of course without a vestige of foundation, though I think every one must feel that the brevity of his tenure of office was a mercy to him and to the country. Harding was not a bad man. He was just a slob. He had discovered what was going on around him, and that knowledge, the worry, the thought of the disclosures and shame that were bound to come, undoubtedly undermined his health—one might say actually killed him.

SAMUEL HOPKINS ADAMS

The Timely Death
of President Harding

Isabel Leighton, editor, *The Aspirin Age, 1919–1941*   (1949)

*Here is an extended profile of Harding. Written especially for
Leighton's brilliant anthology that was a big best-seller in its time,
Samuel Hopkins Adams's piece manages to encapsulate the whole of
Harding's life and anomalous career. Adams had spent years thinking
about Harding, having earlier (in 1939) published a long biography of
him,* Incredible Era, The Life and Times of Warren Gamaliel
Harding. *He had also written a novel,* Revelry, *even earlier (1926)
that had to do with the scandals of the Harding administration, a
novel that was also a bestseller and at one time was banned in Washington, in part because of its hints that Harding might have been
murdered.*

*Harding's was an extraordinary story. Even at the time of his death,
in 1923, at the age of fifty-eight, he was viewed so positively that
George Rothwell Brown could write in the* Post *about this man whose
"career, in many respects, was unparalleled in the history of American
politics. . . . [H]e was an American of the most splendid type this
country has produced."*

*Certainly not everyone felt so positively, as we've seen from Mrs.
Longworth. Even before his poker playing and womanizing became
publicly known and before the revelations of the Teapot Dome scandal
came to the public's attention, William Allen White, the famous liberal
Republican journalist from Kansas, had denounced the growing support for Senator Harding for the presidency, saying he hadn't had an
idea in thirty years and "he is against every advance made in this
country in a dozen years." White also claimed that "his public declaration is stupid where it is not crooked, sometimes both."*

*Here Adams shows why it was possible for people to feel both loving
toward and disdainful of Warren G. Harding, helping us understand
the tragedy of this president.*

A SIGH OF relief breathed from the nation on August 1, 1923. That beloved President, Warren Gamaliel Harding, the idol of the man in the street, the apotheosis of the Average American, the exemplar of the triumphant commonplace who lay, stricken, in a San Francisco hotel, was on the mend. The crisis was past, the prospects were favorable.

Thus officially spoke medical incompetence, through the sick man's personal doctor. Other physicians in attendance knew better. So did those close to the President. The public was fooled.

It may be doubted whether Harding wished to live. What was planned as a carefree junket had turned to a haunted pilgrimage. Private scandal and political disaster impended. Men do not die of broken hearts in the poetical sense. But unrelieved apprehension, the nerve strain of dread and disillusion and helpless wrath, can impair the central mechanism of life. Harding's heart had collapsed. The robust athlete who had entered the White House two years before was a wreck; he had nothing to look forward to but months of seclusion followed by semi-invalidism which would have disqualified him from fulfilling more than the simplest external demands of his great and rigorous office.

The threat to the President's good name was as little known to the people at large as the state of his health. So far as they knew, Harding's personal life was untainted; his Presidential incumbency, if undistinguished, free from scandal. To an extent matched by none since Lincoln, he was their President, simple, warm-hearted, human; the man whom they had chosen by a record majority, who had said that while he could not expect to be the best Chief Executive in history, he would like to be the best-loved. If hopes and prayers could preserve life, Harding would not have died.

Two days after the heartening and deceptive message was given out, a blood clot reached the President's brain. He died instantly and painlessly. So ended the distorted and misplaced career of an unambitious man, ruined by being dragooned into the nation's highest office against his better judgment.

His fellow countrymen mourned him with a sense of personal bereavement.

HIS IS a luck story; success achieved with little effort and less ambition under the impulsion of characters stronger than his own. Born to lowly circumstances, he came up the easy way. To draw a copybook moral from his career, one must reverse the formula. Inertia wins the prize.

An idle boy, son of a veterinary turned doctor through a term in a medical diploma-mill and of an industrious midwife, young Warren shirked the casual jobs of childhood in an Ohio hamlet, scamped an education in a local academy, and quit schoolteaching in midyear because it was too hard work. Drifting to the small city of Marion, he, with two associates, acquired a depreciated evening newspaper, "wholly destitute of either circulation or reputation" by contemporary report. The motivating idea seems to have been politics rather than journalism. At twenty-one he was playing first base on the ball team, alto horn in the Citizens' Cornet Band, and casual swain to the roller-skating girls. It may well have been at the rink that he met Florence Kling DeWolfe, daughter of the town mogul. So far apart were their social strata that she would have been unlikely to make his acquaintance in any less public place. She was five years older than he, a divorcée through no fault of her own, self-willed, hot-blooded, able, and unalluring.

Amos Kling did not approve of the association. . . . She married him anyway, and for fifteen years her father passed her on the streets of the city without speaking. For Harding it continued to the end an advantageous and unhappy marriage. . . .

Presumably he would have lived and died an unknown editor and small-town politician had a campaign speech of his not been heard by Harry M. Daugherty. Daugherty was a political fixer at the state capital, quietly useful to corporations. He could not promote himself; he was so repeatedly defeated for office that the *New York Times* likened him to a disillusioned boxer, punch-drunk from many knockouts, who wisely decides that his future lies in management. He picked Warren Harding for his champion on the strength of the young orator's flamboyant rhetoric and statesmanlike aspect. ("He looked like a President ought to look.") Daugherty became the second potent lever in Harding's rise. He and Florence Kling Harding ran the younger man's life for him thenceforth.

Harding slipped into the State Senate on a fluke. With his talent for ingratiation, he quickly became the most popular man there. He was re-elected, and sent back for a third term, this time as Lieutenant Governor. But when he ran for Governor with Harry Daugherty managing his campaign, he was badly beaten. Easily discouraged, he was ready to quit politics. Being editor of the *Star* and Marion's most popular citizen was good enough for him.

The Daugherty–Florence Kling Harding combination had other and more ambitious ideas. The United States Senatorship was open. Would Harding make the fight? He would not. To his natural inertia was now added the reluctance born of defeat. He ran away to Florida, whither

Daugherty, that inexorable promoter, "found him sunning himself like a turtle on a log and pushed him off into the water."

It was a happy push for him. Elected by a resounding majority, he joined "the most exclusive club in the world." That is precisely what it was to him. One of his secretaries made a shrewd distinction when he said that Harding "didn't like being a Senator; he liked being in the Senate." Harding himself put it this way to his fellow members:

"Mr. President: I like the fraternity of this body. I like to know that when the waters are muddy, I will be considered. I like to participate in the 'booster' proposition."

As a Senator he was negligent and negligible, almost null. Roll call found him present less than half the time. When he did appear, he refrained from voting on 35 per cent of the motions. Not one item of important legislation was presented by him. But he was having the time of his life! There was the jovial companionship of the more sportive Senators. There were golf and prize fights and baseball games; poker and drinking parties in his pleasant house and elsewhere. Thanks to his wife's vigorous management the *Star* was making money enough to support them in style.

Harding had also taken a mistress, a Marion girl who, robust and physically precocious at twelve years of age, had fallen in love with the handsome editor and at twenty had come East to capture him, a feat of no great difficulty. Nan Britton and the child she bore him were to complicate his life and tarnish his memory. His friend, Judge Gary, President of the United Steel Corporation, obligingly found a job for her in a handy office in New York City. She was pretty, vivacious, and intelligent. Harding's fellow sports in Washington knew of the liaison; the girl sometimes traveled with him as his niece. Whether Mrs. Harding also knew about her at this time is doubtful.

As preparation for the Presidency of the United States, Harding's record while Senator is something less than impressive. His one consistent policy was to get himself re-elected. . . .

The nomination of 1920 with its final act of "fifteen men in a smoke-filled room at two o'clock in the morning" has become a classic set piece of American politics. Wood and Lowden, swaying in long deadlock, had exhausted each other and the delegates. Compromise was the logical solution. The leaders compromised on a man who himself had risen by the arts of compromise. Oil, which was to besmirch the Harding record, had a hand. Through Jake Hamon, a millionaire Oklahoman who expected a government oil lease or a Cabinet position or both as his quid pro quo, it contributed twenty-five thousand dollars to Harding's headquarters expenses, and ten times that amount (according to Hamon) to background action.

To combat the rising threat of the dark horse, the opposition went to extreme lengths. Rumors of Harding's involvement with the Britton girl swelled from a whispering campaign to written "testimony." What purported to be signed statements about the illegitimate child were circulated, Nan Britton was in Chicago, employed at Republican headquarters, to the alarm and distress of the candidate's adherents. An older scandal connecting Harding with the wife of a department store owner in Marion was raked up. All this was known to the newspapermen; none of it could be printed. . . .

He was uproariously nominated on the tenth ballot.

"Harding is no world-beater," said Senator Brandegee, voicing the opinion of the inner circle, "but he's the best of the second-raters."

"I can see but one word written above his head if they make him President," cried Mrs. Harding, again in a slump of distrust, "and that word is Tragedy."

Harding's own gleeful comment was luminously in character. "I feel like a man who goes in on a pair of eights and comes out with aces full."

HARDING swept the nation by a record vote. War-weary, impatient of problems too weighty for the mind in the street, cynically intolerant of a half-wrecked world's troubles, avid to get back to the nation's business of making money, people accepted that spurious coinage, "normalcy," as the goal of existence. They chose as its spokesman a man of district-leader caliber whose spiritual and moral values were those of the drug-store corner: kindly, companionable, genuinely democratic, personally (and inexplicably when one considers his associations) free of graft, adroit in the minor manipulations of politics, handsome, and with a singularly winning personality. Of statesmanship he had not an iota, nor did he profess to have. He knew nothing of history, economics, or sociology. He was neither educated nor informed. His oratory, of which he was proud, had a certain gusto but lacked originality, logic, and sometimes grammar. Intellectually undervitalized, he shrank pathetically from problems which he knew to be beyond his powers.

Modestly acknowledging his limitations, he announced his intention of surrounding himself with the Best Minds. His Cabinet was far above the average, with men of the character and caliber of Hughes, Hoover, Mellon, Wallace, Hays, and Weeks. But it was Daugherty and Fall, not these greater men, who swayed and guided him. As for the Best Minds, they spoke a language incomprehensible to him. He wanted to understand; he wished ardently to live up to the expectations of the country which had given him so impressive an endorsement. But it was too much for him. He proved the most bewildered President in our history.

"We're in the Big League now," he told his subordinates, expecting them to accept the expanded responsibilities.

Grave issues impended: unemployment, national financing, taxation, tariff readjustments, the lawlessness attending prohibition, the peace treaties, and the League of Nations. Owing to the inertia of Congress, the machinery of government was all but stalled. "Never has any President come to the tremendous office with so much unfinished business and so many fresh problems of moment," warned one of Harding's influential newspaper supporters.

The President played poker. . . .

It would be unjust to say that Harding deliberately shirked his work. He was not lazy; he was not indifferent. It would not be far from the truth to say that he was daunted. Between nomination and election he had told friends that the office was too big for him and later had touchingly begged Bishop Anderson to "talk to God about me every day by name and ask him somehow to give me strength for my great task."

Had the strength been there, the equipment was lacking. Harding's dreary appreciation of this was part of his tragedy. He lamented that he was "a man of limited talents from a small town. . . . I don't seem to grasp that I am President."

To any interviewer he said with disarming humility, "I don't know anything about this European stuff. . . ."

As for finances: "I can't make a damn thing out of this tax problem," he complained. ". . . I know somewhere there is a book that will give me the truth; but hell! I couldn't read the book."

So he went back to the genial companionship of the Poker Cabinet, where everybody was so comfortable and no questions arose to put a strain on one's mind. He was on first-name terms with the whole bunch, though they maintained the external proprieties by addressing him as "Mr. President." There was that prince of good fellows, Charley Forbes—he loved Charley—and Ned McLean, maybe not very strong in the upper story but a millionaire and a society man and not a bit stuck up about it. There was "Doc" Sawyer, who might not be the most scientific guy in the world, having had only a couple of terms in a dubious medical school, but came from the Old Home Town, played a stiff hand of poker, and was good enough for Harding. And how Doc loved the trappings of a Brigadier General which went with his job as the President's personal physician! There was "Mort" Mortimer, a personal friend as well as a reliable bootlegger who knew where the best liquor was to be found and kept his pals well supplied—and to hell with the bluenoses who beefed about the evil example of illegal drinks in the White House! There were those prime Senatorial sports, Joe Frelinghuysen and Frank Brandegee. Harry Daugherty often dropped in for the semiweekly dinner followed by poker, with his henchman Jess Smith; so did Bert Lasker of the Shipping Board, Harry Sinclair, the big oil man, and Bill Wrigley of the chewing gum family, and Albert Fall was not too busy at his job as Secretary of the Interior to contribute his dry wit and frontier stories to the occasion. They were a grand bunch. The President was in his element.

So was the President's wife. Her fears and misgivings had been appeased. She had found a new seeress who descried a Star of Destiny burning upon her forehead. The star was to guide her and, through her, her illustrious husband to glory. She did not sit in at the poker but acted as amateur Ganymede, circulating with the liquor. Harry Daugherty called her "Ma." To Ned McLean she was "Boss."

This was play. Farther downtown business was going on, the undercover business of the Harding administration on a strictly cash basis. The Ohio Gang, a loose association of minor but favored politicians, had their headquarters in a little green house at 1625 K Street. There they dealt in liquor withdrawal permits, appointments to office, illegal concessions, immunity from prosecution, pardons and paroles for criminals, and various minor grafts. It was in its way a *maison de joie* as well as a commercial center. Senators, Congressmen, Cabinet members, and other officeholders—and the place was patronized by all these classes—could find drinks at any hour and be accommodated with feminine companions from a choice list of ladies-at-call. Gaston B. Means, the most notorious confidence man of his day, and an operative of the Department of Justice, made his headquarters in the Little Green House. Thomas W. Miller, Alien Property Custodian, and E. Mont Reilly, Governor of Puerto Rico, were regulars, as was Charley Forbes. Elias H. ("Mort") Mortimer conducted his bootlegging operations from there; trucks laden with cases delivered their goods in broad daylight.

Assurance of immunity was vested in Jesse W. Smith. He was the liaison between the Department of Justice and the Little Green House on K Street. A pulpy, spluttering, timorous, loose-lipped, dressy country sport, he loved to loll on the corners, greeting his hundreds of acquaintances with stale jokes and the stock query, "Whaddaya know?" His more cautious acquaintances were perturbed by his penchant for the contemporary song whose refrain he delivered in an untuneful and leathery voice: "Good God! how the money rolls in!"

One of the potent figures on the Washington scene, Jess operated in two worlds, the minor graft of the K Street house and the large-scale operations of his sponsor, Attorney General Harry M. Daugherty. He and Daugherty lived, rent-free, in a house of Ned McLean's on a fifty-thousand-dollar-a-year scale which appeared to later investigators as incommensurate with Daugherty's twelve-thousand-dollar-a-year salary. Although he held no official position, Jess had his office in the Department of Justice, franked his mail on the Attorney General's letterhead, traveled on a departmental pass, issued authoritative orders both in person and in writing, and was, in short, "the man to see" when one had ready cash to pay for an office or a favor. Washington called it the Department of Easy Virtue.

Daugherty had been appointed by Harding on purely personal grounds, over the protests of the Best Minds. He made the job pay from the first. When he took office he had less than ten thousand dollars, with liabilities of twenty-seven thousand dollars. Two years later he had deposited in his brother's bank more than seventy-five thousand dollars. Bonds to the value of forty thousand dollars, identified by a court decision as part of a graft deal, were found at the bank, listed as the property of Harry M. Daugherty. Two hundred shares of an aircraft company which had profited by three and a half million dollars' overpayment by the government found their way into Daugherty's possession. By a singular coincidence there vanished from the Department of Justice files the dossier upon which an action for recovery was to have been based. Pardons, inexplicable except on the assumption of value received, were engineered by the Department of Easy Virtue. When criminal charges impended, the Daugherty brothers burned the bank records.

Independently Charles R. Forbes was carrying on a highly profitable line of graft. He was another personal appointment, Harding having met him while on a Senatorial junket and been charmed with his bonhomie. Chiefly because he wanted his jovial playmate at hand, the President offered him several appointments, which he declined. There was nothing in them but the salary. Salaries did not interest the ambitious applicant; he was out for bigger money. He tried for the Shipping Board and settled for the Veterans Bureau. Nearly half a billion dollars a year was allotted to this agency. He got to work upon it. He chose as counsel for the Bureau Charles F. Cramer, a California lawyer.

Soon Charley Forbes became a notable figure in the capital's night life. Lavish entertainment was the order of the day; but the Forbes parties outdid anything else in that line. He did it all on a salary of ten thousand dollars a year. Nobody seems to have questioned it. Asking questions was not good form in the Harding regime.

Hospital sites were to be selected. Forbes went on a transcontinental tour, taking along White House Bootlegger Mortimer. It was an itinerant orgy, in which the main interest, money, was not forgotten. Forbes officially approved locations, upon which the price forthwith shot up to unprecedented heights. Building contracts were let on a percentage basis for the Director of the Veterans Bureau. His report so pleased the President that he narrowly escaped being made Assistant Secretary of War, where pickings would have been scanty and precarious.

Government storehouses near Washington were heavily stocked with supplies and equipment which hospitals all over the country desperately needed. Some of the goods were old or damaged; these could properly be sold on order from the Director. But there was little in the secondhand market for Forbes. So, at a time when disabled veterans were suffering from lack of bedding, bandages, drugs, pajamas, and other prime necessities, Charley Forbes was blithely chalking the x-mark of condemnation on freight-car loads of these very articles and selling them at absurd prices to chosen firms who paid him the agreed rake-off. Sheets in the original packages, bought at $1.37, were passed along by Forbes at 27 cents the pair. Oiled paper, at 60 cents a pound, went for 5. Brand-new gauze at $1.33 per roll suffered an 80 per cent discount. And so on, all to the profit of the Director and the crooked firms with which he dealt.*

General Sawyer—who, whatever his deficiencies, was an honest man—heard rumors, made a quiet investigation, and went to the President. So did Harding's sister, Mrs. Votaw, and Harry Daugherty, the one inspired by jealousy (she had been left out of the Forbes-Mortimer junket), the other by personal dislike. Blinded as always by his personal loyalty, the President termed the accusations "an abominable libel." Against testimony strong enough to convince any but a tight-closed mind, he clung to his faith in his friend Charley.

Looting on a grander scale was in progress in the Department of the Interior. Albert B. Fall, Senator from New Mexico, had long been a Harding crony. Harding would have liked to appoint him Secretary of State (Hughes was a second or third choice), which would hardly have fallen in with the New Mexican's calculations. He was "broke," and taxes on his run-down ranch were nine years overdue. He needed money badly and quickly. Oil meant money, and the Department of the Interior meant oil. But not oil enough to satisfy Fall's scheme. Some of the most valuable (and negotiable) properties in the country had been turned over to the Navy. As soon as Fall became Secretary of the Interior, he persuaded his

---

*Will Irwin in a series of articles on the Veterans Bureau estimated the government's loss on Forbes' operations at $200 million.

friend, Secretary of the Navy Denby, to turn control of the rich Teapot Dome and Elk Hills Fields over to him. Denby was not corrupt. He was simply and hopelessly stupid. High naval officers objected. But the President stood by his crony.

"I guess there will be hell to pay," he confided to a friend, "but those fellows seem to know what they're doing."

There was hell to pay—later. Fall was paid first.

Back taxes on his ranch were satisfied. The depleted property was put in prime condition and stocked with blooded cattle. Adjoining land was acquired at a cost of $125,000. The Falls were living high. All this on the $12,000 salary of a Cabinet officer.

Two generous friends, both oil magnates, were responsible. Edwin L. Doheny of the Pan-American Petroleum Company wanted Elk Hills, which, he estimated, should be worth $100,000,000 to him. So he sent $100,000, surely a modest percentage, to Secretary Fall in a black satchel.

Teapot Dome ought to be worth as much, by the calculations of Harry F. Sinclair. He and some associated oil men formed the Continental Trading Company, whose funds were partly invested in Liberty bonds. These bonds to the amount of about $233,000 found their way by devious routes into Fall's possession, shortly after the Teapot Dome lease delivering the oil over to Sinclair was signed. However devious the route, Liberty bonds are always traceable by numbered coupons. These particular coupons were cashed by Albert B. Fall. Their transfer, however, had been successfully concealed. When, after two years' incumbency, Fall resigned from the Cabinet to take open employment with Sinclair, his reputation was still untainted. Harding, of course, had full confidence in him.

THE YEAR 1923 opened inauspiciously for the harassed President. Congressional investigations threatened in several directions: oil, the Veterans Bureau, the Alien Property Custodian, the conduct of the Attorney General's office, the no-longer secret power of Jess Smith and the Ohio Gang, and abuses in minor departments of the administration. Unfair newspaper criticism (to the Harding type of mind any criticism is unfair) was getting under his skin.

Personal and family complications added to his distress. Mrs. Harding, if she did not know positively, suspected Nan Britton's side-door entry to the White House. There was an animated scene between husband and wife, and the mistress was packed off to Europe at Harding's expense. The Votaws were in trouble; Harding's sister Carolyn had married the Reverend Heber Votaw, who benefited by a nepotic and unfit appointment as Superintendent of Federal Prisons. Now the Department of Justice charged that the ex-missionary was protecting the dope-peddling ring which operated in the Atlanta Penitentiary. Forbes and Daugherty got into a row over that. There was jealousy and back-biting, tale-bearing and recriminations among the White House favorites.

The Harding genealogy popped up again. Professor Chancellor issued a book purporting to prove the President's Afro-American lineage. Without a shadow of legality the Department of Justice sent out a gang of operatives to confiscate the volume. They bullied and browbeat the purchasers into surrendering the book with such thoroughness that less than half a dozen specimens are known to survive.

The President's health was not good. He slept ill and rose unrefreshed. Finances worried him; he was $180,000 in debt to his brokers. How could a man do his job, beset by such vexations? He planned to get away, to take a long and restful trip somewhere. Alaska. That was it! He would see new countries, take a vacation from official troubles and problems. Of course he would have to make some speeches. He didn't mind that. In fact, he rather enjoyed it. "Bloviating" (his own term for his brand of oratory) came natural to him. All the rest would be jollity and junket in the company of such carefully selected friends as Ned McLean, Charley Forbes, Mort Mortimer, Frank Brandegee, and perhaps Harry Daugherty and Jess Smith if they could get away; good pals, all, who could be relied upon to divert his mind from the burdens insistently and irritantly imposed upon it by such solemn-minded associates as Hughes and Hoover, Weeks, Work, Wallace, and Mellon.

Le roi s'amuse. The President was going to have some fun. Invitations were sent out.

The first intimation of a break in the program came by letter from Europe. Colonel Charles R. Forbes, traveling for his health, resigned. It was an ominous note. Harding failed to recognize its import. He urged his old crony to reconsider; but Forbes knew now that he could never stand up to the threatened Senatorial investigation. He was through.

Resignations may be interpreted one way or another. A bullet is definitive. At dead of night in the house which he had bought from the President, Forbes' right-hand man, Cramer, shot himself. A Department of Justice agent was early on the spot. He hurried to the White House and got Harding out of bed.

"Mr. President: I have a letter for you."

"Who's it from?"

"Charles F. Cramer. Mr. Cramer is dead."

"Yes, I know." (How he knew is a matter for surmise. Cramer was alone in the house when he killed himself. Had he perhaps called up the President and given notice of his intention?)

"Here is the letter, sir. It was found in his room."

"Take it away. I don't want it."

The message was destroyed, unread, by Harry Daugherty, to whom the F.B.I. man delivered it.

Shortly after the tragedy Forbes returned from Europe. A chance visitor, misdirected in the White House, was horrified at breaking in upon a scene of violence. The President of the United States had a man by the throat, shaking him and gasping out: "You yellow rat! You double-crossing bastard!"

The victim was Charley Forbes.

It was the President's first positive disillusionment. Always a self-persuasive optimist, Harding might have been able to convince himself that Forbes' disloyalty was a sporadic instance, not symptomatic of a general condition of rottenness. But now disturbing reports that struck nearer home reached his ears, matters about which informed circles had been gossiping for months. Like the proverbial injured husband, the President of the United States is always the last to hear news affecting the honor of his house. Too many people are interested in keeping information from him.

Harding sent for Jess Smith.

Poor Jess was in eclipse. He had been evicted from his sanctum of power in the Department of Justice and banished to his native Ohio by Harry Daugherty, presumably because his loose-tongued bragging of easy money had become dangerous. Wretched in exile, he crept back to Washington. Possibly the first inkling of his error was when he was summoned to the White House.

The President had chosen his subject shrewdly. Under inquisition the pulpy grafter broke down and, in his slobbering, sputtery speech, told Harding what Washington's political underworld had successfully concealed from him for nearly two years. There is reason to believe that his revelations did not include his boss, Harry Daugherty, who was spending that very night under the White House roof.

"Go home," the President bade his visitor. "Tomorrow you will be arrested."

Jess returned to the hotel apartment that he shared with Daugherty and blew his brains out. Either before or, more probably, after the act, all his papers were conveniently burned.

The Smith disclosures shocked Harding not into political house-cleaning but into personal reform. The White House poker parties were abandoned. He told his intimates that he was "off" liquor. Nan Britton had already been banished to Europe. His nerve was shaken. He lost his taste for revelry. The plans for the Alaska trip were radically revised. Instead of an itinerant whoopee, it was now to be a serious political mission.

For the Poker Cabinet there was substituted a group of very different significance. The new Secretary of the Interior, Dr. Hubert Work, Speaker of the House Gillett, and Secretary of Agriculture Wallace were invited to go along, and Secretary of Commerce Hoover was requested by wire to join the tour at Tacoma. General Sawyer was included as guardian of the President's health, while Dr. (now Admiral) Joel T. Boone was to look after the other members of the party. There was to be a sprinkling of army and navy men, secretaries, and a number of wives. Mrs. Harding arranged to accompany the President. "Never let your husband travel without you" was one of her maxims for marital stability.

During the interval between Jess Smith's enforced exposures and the start of the journey, the President's mood was one of nerve-racked indecision. He sent for Nicholas Murray Butler to come from New York and, upon his arrival, chatted vaguely of such trivialities that the visitor never did discover why he had been summoned.

Early in the itinerary there was a touch of melodrama. A heavily veiled woman made her way into the President's suite at Kansas City and was closeted with him for nearly an hour. If the newspapers were aware of this, they practiced a discreet silence. The visitor was the wife of ex-secretary Albert B. Fall, who was already threatened with exposure. Whatever Mrs. Fall's errand, whether to impart information, give warning, consult upon measures of defense and concealment, or demand help, it left the President moody and fearful.

At Tacoma he had an important message to deliver. The surrender of the steel industry on the twelve-hour day and the eighty-four-hour week, and the reduction of this punishing schedule to an eight-hour day and forty-eight-hour week, had been brought about by Secretary Hoover after long negotiations. Mr. Hoover wrote the announcement into the President's address. But the Hoover style, which tends to a rather classical simplicity and directness, was an incongruous insertion in the midst of the Hardingesque sonorities, which once reminded H. L. Mencken of "a string of wet sponges." When he reached the interpolated passage the President paused, stumbled, and addressed his collaborator in an aside, half jocular, half annoyed: "Why can't you write English like I do?"

For the remainder of the speech he acquitted himself well enough.

From Tacoma on, the President was in a state of chronic jitters. He could not be quiet for five minutes on end. His one thought was to escape from thinking. To this end he organized a bridge game, with Secretaries Wallace, Work, and Hoover, Speaker Gillett and Admiral Rodman. The President played to exhaustion, twelve, fourteen, fifteen hours a day, with brief time out for luncheon and dinner. The game started immediately after breakfast and went on well into the next morning. Unlike the White House poker standards, the stakes were small; it was the escape from worries that Harding wanted. For the other players it was an endurance test. Being two more than the required number, they met it by cutting in and out for a respite of two or three hours each. The President played through every session.

By the time the West Coast was reached, his nervous demoralization was painfully apparent. It reached a pressure point at which he felt the need of relief. He sought out Secretary Hoover.

"Mr. Secretary," said he, "there's a bad scandal brewing in the administration."

The Secretary waited, but no details were forthcoming.

"What do you think I ought to do?" pursued the President. "Keep it under cover or open it up?"

It was not wholly news to Mr. Hoover. He had long distrusted and disliked Attorney General Daugherty; news of the Jess Smith suicide had reached him through the newspapers. He had not spent two years in Washington without hearing rumors of Charley Forbes' profligate expenditures on a small official salary.

"There is only one course for you, Mr. President," he replied, "Open it up completely and without delay."

Harding stared at him uncertainly, unhappily, and turned away. It was not what he had hoped to hear, though he could hardly have expected anything else from the Quaker conscience of Hoover. He never again brought up the matter. Though still slack with indecision, he did wire Harry Daugherty to come West and meet him when the tour should have returned from Alaska to Seattle.

On the Navy Transport *Henderson*, coming and going, on Alaska soil when he was not making speeches or receiving delegations, the President was indefatigably, interminably playing bridge. An airplane brought him a code message from Washington. After reading it he appeared melancholy; he shut himself away for a while. He was heard asking himself in an absent mutter what a fellow was to do when his own friends double-crossed him. Liquor being officially banned on the tour, a quart of choice bourbon was obtained from one of the correspondents for Harding's use. Doubtless he needed it. He went back to the solace of his bridge game. But his attention wavered at times; he was not up to his standard of play.

THE BEGINNING of the end was at Vancouver. It was a stifling day, the hottest in years. Harding spent the day going about in an open car, making speeches. He was listless, his delivery flat and dull. At Seattle he was in worse condition. Halfway through a long address he dropped his manuscript. Hoover, who sat behind him, gathered and arranged the scattered sheets, observing with concern as he handed them back the glassy eyes and vague expression of a man who was, in fighting parlance, out on his feet. The orator rallied and finished gamely.

It was here that Harry Daugherty rejoined him by command. They were closeted long together. When the President emerged from the colloquy his face was drawn and livid. Daugherty hurried away. He did not join the private train party, nor did he see the President again, though Mrs. Harding was urgent that he should go to the bedside in San Francisco.

The Daugherty interview broke Harding's waning resistance. Forbes, his old cronies of the Ohio Gang, Albert Fall, and now his mentor and intimate, Harry Daugherty—all had betrayed him. Whom could he trust? Where could he look for advice? He was supported to the train, quivering with nervousness. It was announced that he had suffered an attack of "acute indigestion" (General Sawyer's diagnosis) from crab meat (the same authority) which he had not eaten, though other members of the party had without any ill effects.

All engagements were canceled. The Presidential train set out for San Francisco. The next morning Dr. Boone, a physician of wide experience and high standing, declared himself dissatisfied with the Sawyer diagnosis.

"There's something far more serious," he told the inner circle. "I ought to have a look at him."

Officially he had no status. The President was Dr. Sawyer's patient. But there are occasions when the public interest transcends medical ethics. Another able physician was aboard, Dr. Hubert Work, then Secretary of the Interior. The two conferred and decided to visit Harding on their own authority. Their examination convinced them of the gravity of the case. The President was suffering from a coronary thrombosis, a major impairment of the heart, the symptoms of which, by their superficial resemblance to a sharp stomach upset, had led Dr. Sawyer into error.

Specialists in San Francisco were summoned to meet the train. Arrangements were made with a sanitarium in Santa Barbara to take the patient, should he be able to go there. Even if he survived—a matter of grave doubt—he must be sequestrated for at least six months.

Should the sick man be told of the seriousness of his condition? In view of his known physical courage, an affirmative decision was made. It was assumed that he would face the issue without alarm or weakening.

He did. But his first reaction was strange and, to those in the know, rather pathetic. He directed that the rooming arrangement at the Palace

Hotel be altered so that he would be between Secretaries Hoover and Work. It was as if, after the repeated treacheries which had broken him down, he craved the proximity of men whom he could trust. And he demanded fretfully to be allowed to return to Washington at the earliest possible moment. There were pressing matters there to which only he could attend. Mercifully, he had not been told of his impending invalidism.

Through the few succeeding days he was worse—he was better—pneumonia set in, the weakened heart being incompetent to pump enough blood to clear the lungs—it abated—the optimistic bulletin went forth while the specialists were profoundly concerned over their patient's increasing nervousness—the wandering blood clot struck into the brain like a bullet and the President died while his wife was soothing him with a eulogistic magazine article. The cortege across the country to Washington and thence to Ohio was everywhere held up by unparalleled throngs, mourning, weeping, praying, singing the dead man's favorite hymn. For that brief time Warren Gamaliel Harding was the well-loved President he had hoped to be.

I t   t o o k years to clean up the "debris of decency" which was the Harding administration's legacy to the nation. The public which had held its breath over the dying President now held its nose over the rising stench of scandal. The unfolding history of the aftermath reads like a combination of Greek tragedy and criminal court dossier. Few, indeed, of the dead man's intimate circle escaped unsullied.

Charles R. Forbes went to jail. Albert B. Fall went to jail. Alien Property Custodian Thomas W. Miller went to jail. Gaston B. Means went to jail after neatly swindling Edward B. McLean's wife out of one hundred thousand dollars. McLean, himself, went into a mad-house. Harry F. Sinclair went to jail first for refusing to answer questions on the stand and second for contempt of court in connection with jury-shadowing. Harry M. Daugherty escaped jail, thanks to two hung juries and his refusal to take the stand lest he incriminate himself. The Daugherty bank where his boodle was secreted—though insufficiently—crashed, bringing ruin to an Ohio countryside. His brother, Mally, convicted and sentenced, wriggled out on a technicality. The Attorney General was forced from office with not a shred of reputation left, but still able to boast that no charge against him was ever proven in court.

Two other members of the Harding Cabinet suffered in public esteem. Secretary of the Navy Denby resigned after revelations which proved no moral obloquy but almost unbelievable incompetence and ignorance of his job. Postmaster General Will H. Hays was shown to have acted as receiver of the Sinclair slush fund on behalf of the Republican National Committee, though his personal integrity was not impugned; none of the money stuck to his fingers.

The Ohio Gang, bereft of the advantages and privileges of Ohiohood, scattered and vanished into obscurity.

Rather than inflict the further scandal of a stock-gambling President upon the already overburdened record, Harding's personal brokers took a loss of $150,000 on the unsatisfied Presidential indebtedness and never said anything about it.

To the three previous tragedies of violence close to Harding— Hamon, Cramer, and Jess Smith—were now added two more. Elias H. Mortimer, charging that his wife was unfaithful to him with Charles Forbes, blew out his brains.

Frank Brandegee, involved in a discreditable bankruptcy, committed suicide in his Washington apartment.

Oil smeared the record. Because of participation in the Sinclair deals, a Standard Oil president (Indiana) was stripped of office by the higher authorities of the corporation. Two other oil company presidents fled beyond the reach of extradition and died in lugubrious exile. By a contradiction, not to say corruption, of the law's process, Fall was convicted of accepting a bribe from E. L. Doheny and Doheny was acquitted of giving that same bribe to Fall! But the hovering Harding tragedy descended upon him just the same. His son, who was bearer of the "little black satchel" containing Fall's hundred-thousand-dollar "loan," killed or was killed in a peculiar murder-and-suicide mystery involving him and his private secretary.

The dead President's personal record did not escape the afterwave of scandal. Nan Britton published her book, *The President's Daughter*, in 1927. In its main theme it is a convincing documentation of sordid intrigue, beginning with thirty dollars tucked into a stocking-top and ending with the White House as a place of assignation. It shamed and nauseated a nation which now asked nothing better than to forget Harding and all his works.

Though it enjoyed an equal *succès de scandale*, Gaston B. Means's volume, *The Strange Death of President Harding* (1930), bears every imprint of being a thoroughgoing fake as regards its basic thesis. Without making the charge in so many words, it advances the theory that Mrs. Harding poisoned her husband in a sort of "mercy killing," to save him from the impeachment which she foresaw. The absurdity of the allegation is sufficiently indicated by the fact that it presupposes criminal collusion after the fact by medical men of the character of Drs. Boone, Ray Lyman Wilbur, Charles Minor Cooper, and Surgeon General Sawyer (who, whatever his deficiencies, was an upright and honorable man), together with presumptive collaboration by Messrs. Hoover, Work, and others.

Unhappily, there were concomitant circumstances which could be twisted into a semblance of support for this theory. Mrs. Harding peremptorily refused to permit an autopsy. As soon as she reached Washington she collected all accessible letters and papers of the dead President, took them to Marion, and burned most of them. When Dr. Sawyer died in circumstances somewhat similar to those of Harding's death, the whisperers pointed out that Mrs. Harding was in his sanitarium at the time. The murder rumor spread widely and was accepted by a considerable part of the gossip-loving public and by a few serious (but in this case negligent) historians. Another report, equally baseless, attributed the President's death to suicide.

The anomaly of Warren Gamaliel Harding's career is that without wanting, knowing, or trying to do anything at all unusual, he became the figurehead for the most flagrantly corrupt regime in our history. It was less his fault than that of the country at large. Maneuvered by the politicians, the American people selected to represent them one whom they considered an average man. But the job they assigned to him is not an average job. When he proved incapable of meeting its requirements, they blamed him and not themselves.

That is the tragedy of Harding.

Coolidge Days

Starling of the White House (1946)

This is a wonderful book, and Starling of the White House was clearly a wonderful man, exactly the kind of man you want to have guarding the president, any president. And, indeed, Colonel Edmund Starling guarded five of our presidents—from Woodrow Wilson to FDR. He was the quintessential Secret Service man, whose total devotion was to duty. I lapped up his anecdotes about each president and personality and read this book as though I were a child reading a storybook. This is a real American book, as well as a book by a real American. Colonel Starling is marked by his old-fashioned sense of duty, his legendary work ethic, and his soft-spoken, nonjudgmental—and therefore compelling—on-the-spot observations of the presidents he served.

In his last pages, Starling writes about leaving the Secret Service detail, "after thirty years of uninterrupted service during which I did not lose a day through illness or for any other cause, and in the course of which I traveled approximately 1,200,000 miles." He summarized the quality of the job he did by writing, "I took with me the feeling that I had done my best with that which was entrusted to me, and memories that convinced me of my country's greatness and vigor and humanity. They were mixed, and they were largely inconsequential, but they proved, at least to me, that over the years democracy works, for the Presidents I knew were accurate reflections of the people who elected them."

Starling read the inscrutable "Silent Cal" Coolidge from the beginning and took the measure of the man and found him not wanting.

Coolidge became president after Harding's death, in 1923, when he took over in what likely was the simplest inaugural in American history. Olive Clapper introduced her chapter on Coolidge in Washington Tapestry *by writing, "Calvin Coolidge was never again as appealing and human as he was the night of August 2, 1923, when he was awakened in his father's farmhouse at Plymouth, Vermont." From then until Hoover's inauguration in 1929, Calvin Coolidge was an enigmatic president and person. Edward Lowry wrote of him: "The elections of 1920 imported into the City of Conversation, as one of its necessary consequences, perhaps the oddest and most singular apparition this vocal and articulate settlement has ever known. . . . A well of silence. A center of stillness."*

Known for his one-liners, Coolidge does seem to have been a quick-witted character with an odd, but ready, sense of humor. Coolidge jokes ran rampant around Washington. Once when he spotted Senator Borah horseback riding, he said, "Well, there is Senator Borah riding on a horse, and they are both going the same way!" On inaugural day in 1929, he commented, "It always rains on moving day." George Allen told the story in his memoir of someone proposing some "well-known captain of industry" for Coolidge's cabinet, to which an associate had objected, "But, Mr. President, that fellow's a son of a bitch." "Well," Coolidge replied, "don't you think they ought to be represented, too?"

Clapper related the story of the old lady clerk who carried to Coolidge his first paycheck and made a short speech about all the presidents from McKinley to Coolidge to whom she had brought such a check. The president listened without speaking, and when she was finished, he said, "Come again."

One of the stories Alben Barkley told in his memoir of Coolidge's "famous verbal impecuniosity" was of a dinner when Coolidge was seated next to a Washington society woman "who boldly said to him, 'Mr. President, someone has bet me that I would not be able to get you to say more than two words all evening.' Coolidge looked at her without a trace of expression, and opened his lips just wide enough to say, 'You lose.' "

W HEN WE left the cemetery at Marion, Jervis and I were, temporarily, free men. Our duty to President Harding had ended, our duty to President Coolidge had not begun. Other members of the Detail were watching him. On the ride back to Washington we relaxed, and when we arrived there I went to my room and slept the clock around. I was completely exhausted, and did not report for duty for another day. Then, at a quarter of six in the morning, I went to the Willard Hotel and waited outside the President's suite on the third floor. I had heard that he was an early riser. At a quarter after six the door opened and he stepped out, dressed to go for a walk. He recognized me and said: "Good morning, Colonel Starling, I've been wanting to see you. I want you to stay with me during my administration."

I had no hesitancy in answering him. He was a Congregationalist from the hills of Vermont; I was a Presbyterian from the hills of Kentucky. Though between such people there is a multitude of differences, the basis of their character is alike. This small but well-built man with reddish hair, soft brown eyes, and a determined chin was easy for me to read in general outline. He was honest, brave, religious, and stubborn. With such a man I could get along.

"I will be most happy to remain with you," I said. "I will consider it an honor to serve you in any way."

Instead of answering he walked to the stairway. I followed him. We descended three flights of stairs and went out to F Street, walking toward the Washington Hotel. A few newspaper photographers, already versed in the new President's habits, were waiting. He posed for them; then we continued, following the lines of the Washington Hotel around to Pennsylvania Avenue, turning into E Street and walking east to Twelfth, where we crossed and stopped in front of the Martha Washington candy shop. Here the President spoke for the first time since greeting me. I had presumed he was busy with deep thoughts and had not bothered him.

"Do they make good candy here?" he said.

Before I could pull myself together and reply he answered himself: "They must. My wife likes it."

We did some more window shopping, then walked back to the hotel. There was no further conversation. At the door of his suite I left him and went to get my breakfast. That afternoon we took another walk. Crossing Fourteenth and F Streets he yanked my coattail.

"Better be careful," he said. "That was a woman in a Ford, and that's a bad combination. One of them struck me in Northampton and bruised my hip."

Next morning we strolled again before breakfast, and I realized it was going to be habitual. At that time I was living at Thirteenth and Kenyon Streets, and in order to get to the Willard on time I found I would have to get up at four o'clock. While I was pondering what to do about such a predicament the President one day made a suggestion. We were in front of the Willard.

"You ought to move in here," he said. "It's a good place."

So I did, and remained there throughout his two terms of office, eventually getting a private telephone wire installed between my room and the White House. . . .

At the White House I waited outside each morning for President Coolidge, going into the lobby if the weather was bad. By a simple procedure, without saying a word, he showed that he had chosen me for his walking companion. When I was not on duty early in the morning he did not go out.

A few days after he moved into the White House we struck out at the usual early hour, just as a gang of laborers was going to work in front of the Executive Offices, where they were tearing up the street, a favorite occupation in Washington. The Irish foreman, seeing us, said to one of the Detail who was standing nearby: "What a fine looking man our new President is! So tall and straight! Who's the little fellow with him?"

He was told that the little fellow was the President.

"Glory be to God!" he said. "Now ain't it a grand country when a wee man like that can get to be the grandest of them all!"

From that time on President Coolidge was to us and all the members of the White House staff, the "little fellow."

I was distressed to find that he took no other exercise except walking. He did not play golf, ride horseback, fish, hunt, swim, bowl or even play billiards. He had no hobbies, not even stamp collecting. Moreover, he walked with his head thrust forward, his hands clasped behind him, his shoulders hunched, and his chest sagging. I finally got up enough courage to tell him that since he walked for a healthful purpose he should not defeat that purpose by his posture.

"It will do you so much more good," I said, "if you will keep your head up and your shoulders back, with your arms swinging. The important thing is to stimulate circulation in the chest."

He paid no attention to me, and for a week continued to walk as before. Then one day he suddenly struck out with his head stuck up in the air and his arms flailing, so that I had to walk at least three feet from him. I said nothing. After a while his arms fell into a normal swing. He never walked again with them behind him.

He liked to go to F Street and window shop. To get there we passed the Treasury building. The walk in front of it at that time was in wretched condition. The flagstones had lost their uniformity of level and formed pockets which filled with rain whenever there was a shower.

One day I noticed a young lady whose stockings were wet half way to her knees with water splashed from these puddles. I called the President's attention to her and commented on the state of the pavement.

"Yes," he said, "the Treasury Department ought to fix it. If they don't, some day my Secretary, ol' Andy Mellon, will come walking along here counting his coupons and stub his toe."

Everybody was "ol'" to him. I was "ol' Colonel Starling," Frank Stearns was "ol' man Stearns," Rudolph Forster was "ol' man Forster," and his Cabinet members were "ol' man Mellon," "ol' man Denby," etc. In the same way they were all "my": "my Secretary of the Treasury," "my

Secretary of the Navy," "my Secret Service man." All the material trappings of the Presidency were likewise "my": "my car," "my house," "my lawn," "my garden," etc.

This feeling of ownership was a part of his attitude which puzzled me. He was not particularly proud of being President; he hated arrogance and conceit in all their forms. It was as if he were a small boy whose daydream of being king had suddenly been made real by the stroke of a magic wand. He would almost tiptoe around, touching things and half smiling to himself. In his high shoes and his great galluses he was an odd sight in the White House corridors.

On awakening in the morning he would walk across the upstairs hallway to the Lincoln room in his long nightgown and slippers. There he would peek out the window to see whether I was on the lawn. I stood there each morning taking my setting up exercises while waiting for him. If he did not see me he would have Brooks telephone downstairs to ask if I were in the building.

When he was satisfied that I was waiting he would dress and come downstairs. Sometimes he would tell the elevator operator to take him to the basement. Then he would try to sneak out the East or the West entrance, just to fool me. Everyone on the staff cooperated with me and tipped me off, so I was always able to catch him. One day I turned the tables on him and hid in the police box on the East side. He came out of the engine room, up the East steps, and passed right by me. I fell into position behind him. When he reached the gate he turned around with a look of glee on his face, thinking he had at last eluded me.

"Good morning, Mr. President," I said.

He turned and headed for F Street without saying a word.

"Guess you wonder why I like to window shop," he said one day. "It takes me away from my work and rests my mind."

His appetite for pranks was insatiable. In the afternoon we sometimes left for our walk from the Executive Offices. If the mood suited him he would press the buzzer which notified everyone that he was on his way to the White House. Then, while ushers, policemen, doormen, and elevator operators were rushing about getting things ready and snapping to attention, we would stroll out West Executive Avenue and leave them. . . .

The serious side of his job he performed so ably that the staff in the Executive Offices soon relaxed. Rudolph Forster was able to lead a normal life again. He had been busy all through the Harding years, for Harding had trouble with details and paper work, and Rudolph had to work overtime.

"The little fellow wades into it like Wilson," he said. "He knows what he is doing and what he wants to do. He doesn't do anyone else's work either. He'll be all right at this job. He does a lot of thinking, and he looks a long way ahead."

It was true that he didn't do anyone else's job. One day his personal secretary, Ted Clark, came to the office and asked if he could show the President a file of papers which Secretary of Labor Davis wanted him to read.

"He would like to know whether you agree with his decision," Clark said.

"I am not going to read them," the President said. "You tell ol' man Davis I hired him as Secretary of Labor and if he can't do the job I'll get a new Secretary of Labor."

One evening as we came home at dusk I noticed a light burning in the office of the Secretary of Navy, Mr. Denby. I remarked that Denby was a hard worker, frequently staying in his office until late at night.

"He must be an excellent man for the job," I said.

"I wouldn't say that," the President replied. "I don't work at night. If a man can't finish his job in the day time he's not smart."

A few months later the newspapers were proclaiming that the only thing of which Denby was guilty in connection with the oil scandals was stupidity.

His uncanny judgment of people, and the things he knew about them, always amazed me. Once I described a certain man as stingy, and the President immediately reeled off a list of important contributions to charity which the man had made, and added that he had just sent a young fellow to Colorado for his health and was taking care of his family, which consisted of a wife and four small children.

He was so different from President Wilson that it was hard to realize the two were fundamentally alike. For both of them life was largely a mental experience, but whereas in Wilson this was obvious, in Coolidge it was not. I could never figure out, as we walked along silently, whether his mind was busy with great affairs of state or trivialities. In the end I decided that most of the time he let his worries drop back to the subconscious and enjoyed himself like a small town boy strolling down Main Street on Saturday night. The things he said to me might have been said in Northampton, Hopkinsville, or Lexington, Virginia. Passing a large department store one morning he said, "If you ever get married don't let your wife buy anything in there. My wife goes in there and it costs me a lot of money." . . .

Mrs. Coolidge had occasion now and then to visit Northampton. Her mother was ill, and she herself found the climate of Washington difficult to bear. She was bothered with sinus trouble, and the Capital weather seemed to make it worse. One morning when she was away the President said to me as we returned from our walk, "Want to have supper with me?"

"I would be delighted," I said, wondering what time dinner would be served.

"Come on then," he said, walking into the elevator.

We went upstairs and into his bedroom, where he telephoned for two breakfasts. He didn't ask me what I wanted; he just told the cook to make his order double. It was served in the room, and consisted of fruit, oatmeal, bacon and eggs, coffee, toast and marmalade. Every morning thereafter when Mrs. Coolidge was away I shared this "supper" with him (every meal to him, I discovered, was "supper").

Whenever a letter was expected from Mrs. Coolidge we ended our walk at the Executive Offices, where he cut the twine on the stacks of his personal mail and looked through it until he found an envelope addressed in her handwriting. He would stuff it into his pocket and walk quickly to the White House. I would go up with him on the elevator but remain outside his room until he sent for me. He would lock the door, and it was often as much as half an hour before he opened it again and asked me in.

He loved his wife deeply. He was, of course, a very sentimental man, and a very shy one. He loved a few people a great deal, and he was embarrassed about showing it. Gradually, as time went by, I found him to be so human and thoughtful that I came to the conclusion his outward reticence and aloofness were part of a protective shell.

On summer nights when Mrs. Coolidge was away we sat on the back porch together and smoked and talked—he made me smoke his big, black cigars and they nearly knocked me out. Often then he spoke at length of his boyhood in Plymouth, of his deep affection for his mother, of her fair-haired beauty, of her love for flowers, of her understanding of him, and of the help she gave him in the problems he faced from day to day. He seemed to remember every day he had spent with her. She died when he was young, and he nourished his memories so that now they were living things, as real to him as the days he now was living. He communed with her, talked with her, and took every problem to her.

"I wish I could really speak to her," he said one night. "I wish that often."

He clung to the habits of his boyhood as well as the memories. When we returned from our afternoon walks he would take me to the butler's pantry and make two sandwiches of Vermont cheese, one for himself and one for me. He cut the cheese carefully, measured the sandwiches one against the other, and if they were not equal would shave off a little more cheese to make the balance. Then he would give one to me and we would sit down and eat them. The cheese was as strong as a billygoat. One day he said to me, "I'll bet no other President of the United States ever made cheese sandwiches for you."

"No," I said. "It is a great honor."

He added gloomily: "I have to furnish the cheese too."

He would go upstairs to his bedroom and eat crackers covered with preserves. He always kept a supply in his room. He ate nuts and peanuts too, and the peanuts were unparched. It was amazing that he never got fat.

One day as we passed the stand of the White House peanut vendor he sniffed at the roasting chestnuts, stopped, and put his hand into his pocket. It came out empty and he turned to me.

"Colonel," he said, "can you lend me ten?"

"Ten dollars?" I said, reaching for my wallet.

"No," he said, "ten cents."

I gave him a dime and he bought the chestnuts. Some time after our return to the White House the elevator operator brought me an envelope. Inside it was a dime.

Later I became his banker on our walks, furnishing him with dimes and nickels for peanuts, magazines, and newspapers. I kept an account of my advances in my notebook, and every once in a while he gave me fifty cents to clear up the debt. When I was not on duty he took his afternoon walks with other members of the Detail. He took me up to his room one afternoon and while he changed his clothes I looked through the new *Collier's* we had just bought.

"I gave somebody a dime one afternoon to buy a *Collier's* and I didn't get my nickel back," he said.

"It wasn't I," I said.

"I don't know who it was," he said, "but somebody owes me a nickel."

"I don't owe you a nickel," I said.

"I didn't say you did," he said. "I don't know who he was, but he didn't give me back my nickel."

"Well," I said, "it wasn't I."

"Well," he said, "I'm not going to do anything about it. But he kept my nickel. He didn't give it back to me."

Not long after he entered the White House I saw evidence of his irascibility for the first time. He appeared one afternoon with a lock of sandy-colored hair showing from under his hat and the tip of his nose red. We walked rapidly toward Connecticut Avenue. At Jackson Place he said in a low, surly tone: "I'm not going."

I didn't say anything. A few blocks later he said: "I'm not going, and I'm not going to let that wife of mine go."

Some sort of comment was called for, I thought, so I said, "You certainly ought to follow your own judgment."

After a few more blocks he said: "When I lived at the Willard and was Vice President they didn't know I was in town. Now that I'm President they want to drag me up to their house for one of their suppers and show me off to a lot of people, and I'm not going."

I remembered the invitation now. It was from the current Washington social queen.

"I'm not going, and I'm not going to let that wife of mine go," he repeated.

He didn't, either.

In time I grew to expect anything of him, and he never failed me. . . .

One Sunday morning about a year after I had moved into the Willard, I was half way through shaving at six-thirty when the telephone rang. It was the night clerk. He was greatly excited. President Coolidge, he said, had just walked into the lobby on the Pennsylvania Avenue side and wanted to know if I could come down immediately.

I washed the lather off my face, leaving half of it unshaved, put on my shirt, tucked my coat and vest under my arm, and ran for the steps, knotting my tie as I fled down the hallway. I went down the steps three at a time to the main floor level on the F Street side of the building. As soon as I hit bottom I began wriggling into my coat and vest, when a voice just over my shoulder said: "I thought you'd come down this side."

He had walked through Peacock Alley to meet me, and was chuckling at his shrewdness in having correctly guessed which way I would descend.

While he watched I buttoned my vest and coat, straightened my tie, and set my hat straight on my head. Then we went out for our walk.

I WAS STILL not getting anywhere in my efforts to induce the President to take up some form of exercise other than walking. All his physical tendencies were toward inertia. . . .

My plan for a long time had been to rouse his interest in fishing and hunting. To do this I talked a great deal on our walks about the outdoors. He seemed to think he knew all there was to know about nature lore, and apparently was of the opinion that it was a boyhood fancy which men got over when they grew up. My project had tough sledding. One day he asked me the name of a certain tree and I told him it was a sycamore. I then recounted how as a boy I would climb out on a sycamore limb to get the eggs from an oriole's nest. He asked me what an oriole looked like. I told him it was a rather small bird, golden yellow and black in color.

"Oh yes," he said. "We have lots of them in Vermont. We call them bobolinks."

"That is not the same bird," I said.

"Yes, it is," he said.

So on our return I went to the dictionary and copied the definitions: oriole, golden yellow and black; bobolink, brown, sometimes called reed bird or rill bird. I then read the notes to him and he admitted that he was wrong. I was wearing him down, but it was slow work.

One day a friend sent me two rock bass, still alive, which he had caught on a fishing trip to Gunston Pass down the Potomac. I sent them up to the President by Brooks, thinking it would stir his interest. I expected him to send them to the kitchen to have them served for supper. The next morning he said to me: "I put my little fishes in my bathtub and they swam around all night. One of them hopped out while I was asleep and Mrs. Coolidge had to come and pick him up in a newspaper and put him back."

I was pretty sure that he was not asleep when the fish awakened Mrs. Coolidge with its flip-flopping. He probably opened the door between their rooms so she could hear it and then played possum.

I got some unexpected help in the matter of exercise when an electric horse was sent to the President. He knew nothing about it until he returned to his bedroom one day and found me riding it, while A. M. "Blondy" Thomas, chief electrician for the White House, pushed the buttons. He was fascinated, and laughed so hard he had to sit down when I imitated a cowboy on a bucking broncho. I made more racket than the White House had heard since the days of Teddy Roosevelt; so much so that Mrs. Coolidge came to see what was going on. The President insisted that I entertain her also, and he pushed the buttons.

He would not get on himself, but the next morning he tried it out secretly and that afternoon took me up to his bedroom to show me his prowess. He insisted on keeping his hat on. I told him to hold tight while I pressed some more of the buttons. I got a good grip on his coat then pushed the buttons. The horse jumped, the President lost his hat, and almost lost his seat. I stopped the horse and he got off and spent about ten minutes trying to find out what made the thing jump. After that we rode every day, playing cowboy like a couple of kids. . . .

He took me upstairs one afternoon to show me his new vibrator. He demonstrated it, in his underwear, and then made me try it. He noticed that I had a slightly inflamed eyelid and insisted that Doctor Coupal, who was also in the room, put some drops in it. While this was going on he said: "Colonel, seems to me that a man with your responsible position would be more careful of his drinking."

"What do you mean?" I asked.

"You can't get away with it," he said. "It makes your eyes all red and I have to get my doctor to take care of them."

With all this horseplay he ended up ten minutes late for dinner. But it made no difference to him. He would miss a meal anytime to play a joke.

He had what I call a sense of play—something different and apart from a sense of humor. I think he liked me because I responded to this part of him, and would follow him instantly from a serious discussion to something frivolous. It was make-believe, of course. We pretended all sorts of things, such as the fantastic notion that I was a great and secret drinker. I never pretended to dislike a drink of good Bourbon, but neither, for that matter, did he. Our joke was an effort to relieve the gloomy, depressing atmosphere which surrounded the subject of liquor during those days. The little fellow did not believe in prohibition any more than did the rest of the sensible citizens, but he observed it strictly while in the White House because he considered it his duty to do so. His opinion of it was simple and forthright.

"Any law which inspires disrespect for the other laws—the good laws—is a bad law," he said to me.

It was strange that he, the most popular man in the country, was the direct opposite in every way of what the public was taking for its model. He not only disliked the things that were going on, he feared the results of them. During that fall there was a lot of talk in favor of nominating the Secretary of Commerce, Herbert Hoover, at the Republican Convention the following June. One of Hoover's supporters dubbed him a "superman." As we strolled through the streets one afternoon the President said to me, after a long silence: "Well, they're going to elect that superman Hoover, and he's going to have some trouble. He's going to have to spend money. But he won't spend enough.

"Then the Democrats will come in and they'll spend money like water. But they don't know anything about money. Then they will want me to come back and save some money for them. But I won't do it."

He said "I won't do it" in his most stubborn manner, and I knew he meant it. I also knew, then, his practical reason for not running again. He saw economic disaster ahead. In the years that followed I was amazed at the absolute accuracy of his prediction. Truly, he was a long-headed thinker.

He had scotched all rumors that he might allow himself to be drafted for a third term in his address to Republican National Committeemen on December 6. The meeting was held in the East Room of the White

House. Just before leaving to attend it Everett Sanders and I were with him in his office.

"I want you two to go with me," he said. "They're going to try to get me to run again, and I won't do it." . . .

That spring I bought a brown suit. On the day I wore it for the first time I selected a green tie as a fitting accessory. I noticed the President looking at me sharply several times during our morning walk, but he said nothing. I thought he was appraising the cloth in my suit. I expected him to tell me how much it cost, or to ask me what I paid for it and tell me that I had been cheated.

The afternoon schedule called for a visit to a specialist, to have the President's sinuses examined. As he came out to get into the car he stopped, looked sharply at me again, then turned and went back into the White House. He got into the elevator and went upstairs. The staff began to whisper among themselves. Nobody knew what was wrong.

"He sure looks mad," John Mays said.

When he returned he was composed. In his hand he carried a small brown paper bag. He handed it to me.

"Here," he said. "Take this."

I put it in my pocket and we went on with the business of the afternoon. Only after we had returned to the White House and I was on my way to supper did I take the bag from my pocket and find out what was in it.

It was a brown tie. . . .

IT WAS January when we returned to the White House. Hoover had been elected in November and in a few months now the Coolidges would move out. I was to remain on the Detail until the little fellow was settled and ready for me. Then we were to take our fishing and hunting trip to the West Coast. I was as anxious for it as was he. Fifteen years in Washington had not succeeded in removing from me the constant yearning for a quiet, simple life, close to the outdoors.

During those last months of his administration the President consented to sit for a portrait which was to be hung in the famous Saddle and Sirloin Club of Chicago. The artist, who was commissioned by Arthur G. Leonard, President of the Chicago Union Stockyards and Transit Company, was Robert W. Grafton. He stayed at the Willard Hotel, and he told me his troubles. He made one attempt after another to get the President's likeness, to catch his personality, to divine his spirit. He failed utterly. The little fellow was too elusive. What he showed to the painter was not his real self. The intangible thing which formed his character would not come forth. Grafton was discouraged and nervous. He could not sleep at night. He became filled with despair. He was convinced that he could not execute the commission. He decided to make one last attempt and then give it up.

The sittings were being held in the northwest room on the second floor. It was a bright, clear, beautiful day when Grafton made his final effort. The President came in and went to the little dais on which his chair was set. He looked out the window at the sunshine and said to Grafton: "Good morning. It might rain."

Grafton was so shaken that he upset a can of turpentine. As he watched it spread over the beautiful rug covering the floor, despair completely engulfed him.

"Oh, Mr. President, I am so sorry!" he said. "Please have the rug sent to the cleaners and I will gladly pay the bill."

The President looked at him and a twinkle came into his eyes.

"Now, don't you worry about the old rug," he said. "I'm going to move out of here in a few days."

Grafton stared, then relaxed and smiled. Without a word he seized his brushes and began to paint. The spell was broken, the problem was solved. Grafton finished his work in a short time and did a grand job. He caught the little fellow exactly—half owl, half elf.

My own estimate of him is just that: he looked wise and solemn—yet he was full of mischief and laughter. The two were blended in him more completely than in most people. The average person's serious and humorous aspects are separate. In President Coolidge they were mixed, so that the one interpenetrated the other. To me it seemed a step forward in evolution, for the serious side of life needs to be looked at with the tolerance and understanding which a sense of humor provides and our laughter should be grounded in an understanding of the spiritual purpose of our existence. . . .

CALVIN COOLIDGE may or may not have been a great President. That is for history to decide. To me he was fundamentally and primarily something which I treasure above all the things of earth: he was a good man. He was thoughtful, he was intelligent, he was sentimental, he was wise. There were times when he was irascible; there were occasions when I was glad to be away from him. But I found him in the large and full portions of existence an admirable and a satisfying man, a peaceful and pleasing and loyal friend. His feelings, like his thoughts, ran deep and did not swerve. I liked him as a man; I loved him as a friend.

The First Christmas
with the Roosevelts

White House Diary   (1948)

Henrietta Nesbitt is the perfect example of someone who points up the limits of the power of the president. As Grace Tully tells us in her memoir, FDR, My Boss, *the president once said, "I want to be elected to a fourth term so I can fire Mrs. Nesbitt."*

But Mrs. Nesbitt knew no fear—or at least not after her arrival at the White House on the day of FDR's first inaugural, when she did admit to being "scared half to death" by the prospect of becoming housekeeper and cook in the biggest home she'd ever seen. In fact, this was her first visit to the White House, and to Washington. She had been a wife and mother in Hyde Park, known to the Roosevelts as a great baker of pies, when Mrs. Roosevelt asked her to come to Washington and take over housekeeping at the White House. She was already in her fifties when she took up the task.

For the next twelve years—through the Roosevelts and for one year with the Trumans—Mrs. Nesbitt ruled the roost, providing such dismal dishes that her reputation grew apace with FDR's aversion to her food. FDR was said to have spent so much time on the USS Potomac, *a kind of "floating White House," in part because it offered him a break from the cooking of his longtime nemesis. Her tyrannical ways did not go unreported at the time, and even Eleanor had to explain once that her husband was in a "tizzy-wizzy" over watery spinach. Blanche Wiesen Cook, in the second volume of her biography of Eleanor, devoted an entire chapter to Mrs. Nesbitt, which was titled, "Eleanor Roosevelt's Revenge."*

Despite her reputation for bland foods, Mrs. Nesbitt did manage to come up with a cookbook, which was published in 1951 and titled The Presidential Cookbook, Feeding the Roosevelts and Their Guests. *There is no mention of the rumors that some of these guests*

often ate beforehand when planning on attending a White House func-
tion where food was to be served.

D ECEMBER found me still up to my ears in fruitcake. The process
from chopping to packing is all joy to me, and part of Christmas.
I guess the White House favorite was the dark fruitcake that I
made for the household and their friends, and a big one, special, for the
President's birthday, every year. No matter how many cooks we had, the
cake was my work, and baking more than two hundred pounds of cake is
a long job. The kitchen help got the fruit ready.

Six pounds of cut dates. Six pounds of raisins. One and a half pounds
of almonds, blanched and sliced lengthwise. Two and a fourth pounds of
citron in long slivers. Three cups of orange peel also slivered.

I defy any woman to chop up fruits like these, all pungent and sugary,
and keep up any personal brooding. Fruitcake mixing can be heartily recommended as a cure-all for grouches and blues. For me, it always seems
romantic, and reminds me of lines in poetry. "Dates and figs of
Samarkand," and "lucent syrops, tinct with cinnamon."

I take my time with the fruit fixing, and enjoy it. Then I pour a pint of
brandy or rum over the mixed fruit and let it stand all night or longer.

The batter I mix like a pound cake:

One and a half pounds brown sugar. One and a half pounds butter.
One and a half pounds flour. Eighteen eggs.

To this mixture I add one and a half cups of honey, two grated lemon
rinds, one and a half teaspoons each of mace, nutmeg, and salt, a fourth
teaspoon of cloves, and three teaspoons of cinnamon.

Then I mix in the fruit, and bake it in lined pans at a low oven temperature with a pan of water in the oven to keep the cake moist. The
cooks did the baking and watching. The President wrote me a note once,
after I'd made one for his birthday. "Perfectly delicious! FDR."

All sorts of things come into my diary this December, along with the
accounts of the cakes. A note for December 14 says, "Cardozo and Chief
Justice Hughes to dinner." It makes me laugh, seeing this, and remembering how terrified I was, up till then, of Supreme Court Justice Cardozo. I had seen him on the bench, wearing the black gown, looking
serious and profound, but with his hair wild. I thought he was as frightening as Napoleon must have seemed in his day.

This evening I was in the corridor when he came trotting in on his
way to dinner, and recognized me and stopped to speak. I was so surprised I can't recall what he said. He was all prinked up, dapper and neat,
and with his hair combed so, it looked like a halo and made him appear as

innocent as an angel. Seeing him close, I realized those snapping eyes that looked so awful in court held a glint of the pixie.

I decided he was real human and after that I loved watching Justice Cardozo come in, always looking like a good little angel prinked up for the party.

Nobody seems awesome when you meet them face to face like that. Put a slice of good apple pie before any human, and he'll melt. Maybe that's why greatness doesn't awe me so much as it does some.

When Christmas came, all the five-ring-circus excitement of the past year seemed to gather to a point in the White House and explode in a lather of tinsel stars. I never saw so much excitement and so much affection shown. I never knew people that loved Christmas the way the Roosevelts did. And to think I'd survive a round dozen more with the Roosevelts, getting more exciting, and sweeping in wider circles—year after year! Even toward the last, Christmas was risen to, like a hymn, and no matter how busy Mrs. Roosevelt was, she remembered us all.

This was the day she had been fixing for all the year. It was her day. She never did think of herself. Maybe that was why.

I don't think she ever went on a trip or a shopping tour that she didn't bring home something. "That's for Christmas," she'd say, happy as a child. "Just put it away."

She'd sent big cartons down from New York filled with gifts to be kept in the storeroom. The last months of the year she sent in carloads of candy and toys, all to be packed and dressed in pretty ways for Christmas.

She bought specific gifts for specific people when she could. She liked handmade things, woven, or beaten out of metal, because she loved anything that people had joy in making. She tried to share her experiences so she did it with gifts, bringing back things from her trips to all of us, to let us know how other places were. She brought me a pin from Guatemala with silver fruits, a knitted suit from Canada, a set of hand-woven doilies from the Tennessee mountains. She always remembered the little things.

She tried to have something for everyone, because she had a place for everyone. She saw something in everybody that made them worthwhile—something of value, not to her, but to them. She tried to bring that out by giving them a feeling of self-respect and worth. She believed each person ought to stand alone, in his own right as a human being.

That was the spirit that came out strongest at Christmas-time. The President felt the same way, so everyone around the Roosevelts felt their happiness, and there never was a Christmas in the White House while they were there that wasn't joyous. Once Franklin was sick and away in school, and Mrs. Roosevelt went to see him, but she was back in time for the tree.

Everyone in America knew what went on in the White House at Christmastime, because the Roosevelts wanted everyone to know and share in it, but only those inside knew the work that led up to it.

Things started popping about a week before. By this time the store-rooms were stuffed, and the pressing room too. Gifts were on tables and shelves, and we set a big table upstairs, and Mrs. Roosevelt's secretaries and the maids would start wrapping, and she'd wrap, sometimes until two in the morning.

"The box is half the gift," she'd say, and she always did gifts beautifully, getting the prettiest boxes to be found, and tying them up with white tissue and the bright ribbons I bought from the five-and-ten. She wrote the messages herself, on their personal cards.

The Roosevelts' Christmas cards were pictures of the White House at various angles, or a photo of them both, or of the children, or maybe one of the dogs. The first Christmas card, in '33, was a scene of the South Portico. Tolly, the White House engraver, did the scenes by hand, and had them copied. He made the pretty shipping tags we used, too, with the steel engraving of the White House.

Meantime the rest of us were whooping it up downstairs. All those cakes and things had to be wrapped. First we worked on the boxes that were to go outside of Washington. There were the fruitcakes I'd mixed and supervised, and all sorts of jars of jams we'd been putting up in the different fruit seasons. We packed carloads of Christmas boxes in my office—a cake to a box, with some jams, jellies, nuts, Christmas cookies, and candies. Mrs. Roosevelt liked the fruitcake wrapped by itself in cellophane, with outer tissue and ribbons, and the other things tucked around, and a tray of candies and nuts on top. And this box might be just one of several we sent to a person.

Any friend of the Roosevelts was likely to get two boxes, one with things to eat and another with something pretty or useful.

Turkeys and fixings were sent out, too, as at Thanksgiving.

I had a long list of people to send boxes to each year. There were always a lot of older people she remembered. There was a vagrant she'd picked up in her car once, and got a job for, and his name was on her list of friends. There was Leo Casey, the New York State policeman who had been thrown from his motorcycle while guarding the President, and often came to see her in his wheel chair. Special boxes were made up for him Christmas and Thanksgiving, too, and I'd put in cheeses and fancy tidbits and ransack the storeroom for things he would like.

There were some names I would have given a lot to have scratched off the list. Even Christmas had its parasites. One man begged of her regularly, when he wasn't in need at all. Another Christmas recipient wrote

Mrs. Roosevelt that I had sent him a capon when he expected a turkey. He complained to her!

She didn't get cross, but I did.

Once Dad and I packed forty-seven cakes in one night, to get clear. Captain Lock came in and read us the riot act for overworking.

"You're here to direct, not work," he said. "Let the help do the packing."

But we were in full Christmas swing by this time and couldn't stop. Carloads of boxes were going out of the shipping room, and carloads more coming in.

It was all fun. Dad had two men checking lists, and was still way behind. My stenographer was making lists, and upstairs and downstairs secretaries were trotting around with long lists and mysterious expressions.

The children, of course, were in the usual Christmas dither. There wasn't a trick in old-fashioned Christmas feeling that wasn't poured out for the benefit of the Roosevelt babies.

I suppose world history was being made in the President's office, but I was too busy to think much about it.

Added to the general hullabaloo was the session of affairs that burst out this week before Christmas. December was the start of the winter social season, and there were dinners and luncheons, and one concert with an artists' supper at midnight that consisted of chicken, consommé, fillet of lamb, peas, romaine and grapefruit salad, orange blossom parfait, angel cake, and coffee.

Music seems to make people hungry. That day was solid party from dawn till night. The day before Christmas found us spinning. The trucks came around early to take the pretty boxes to those who lived in the city, and big pots of flaming poinsettia were sent from the greenhouse. The heads and help received one of these plants every Christmas, just as at Easter we were all remembered with Easter lilies. By this time Dad and I had the last of the big pound cakes wrapped and boxed, one hundred and fifty of them, one for each of the Treasury Police detailed to the White House.

These cakes I'd ordered from the outside, and we'd wrapped them in cellophane and pretty tissue, and they were in boxes tied with gay ribbon, and we piled them on our two house trucks and rolled them into the East Room.

The big tree was there, all dressed and lighted for the day. At three the policemen came with their children up to twelve years, and their wives, and the President and Mrs. Roosevelt came in and the policemen and their families passed in line. The President and the First Lady had a

Christmas greeting for each one that they managed to make sound special, and the cakes were passed out, and each child was given a paper cornucopia of candy and a toy Mrs. Roosevelt had chosen just for him—a doll or automobile perhaps, or a stuffed animal if he were a baby.

One Christmas my grandson Bobby was spending the day with me, and he wanted to see the Christmas tree so I took him in, and he helped Tommy hand out the candy to the little children, looking so serious and sweet. Mrs. Roosevelt thanked him gravely for his help, and at the very end pretended she had found a fuzzy Teddy bear just for him on the tree. He slept with it for years, and wore off all the fuzz.

After the police families the servants came, thirty or more, with their children, and went through the line before the glowing tree. There was Christmas money for the grown-ups and a toy Mrs. Roosevelt had selected for each little colored child.

She was having the time of her life. All day long she was racing from party to party, charity organizations, and community affairs, and extending the President's greetings as well as her own. There was a day-long in-between series of parties for children—children in need.

At one-fifteen she presided over one given in the White House by the Volunteers of America, and the minute this big staff affair was over she was off to another party for some very poor children in a dark alley.

The President's own big party was held in the morning in his office. The clerical staff came, and there was always some cute little trinket to commemorate our White House Christmas. I've treasured a White House paperweight and a pewter coin made at Val-Kil with the President's profile and a key ring with a little silver Scottie charm for the President's little dog Fala.

Five o'clock was sundown, Christmas Eve, 1933. I took Bobby by the hand and we went outdoors to the south lawn. All the presidential family was out there to see the President turn the lights on the big Christmas tree that was set on the lawn for all Washington to enjoy. There was a band and Christmas carol singing, and the President looked radiant and yet somehow sad with the lights of the big tree on his face.

I suppose he was thinking of other countries where lights were going out and people were living underground like scared rabbits. Dad and I looked at each other, and I know we were both glad that we had a grandson big enough to be there to see that Christmas tree shining on the kind face of a man who was head of the United States. It wouldn't be long until there were no more shining trees, not even in our country, and there would be none until our Bobby was tall.

The family dinner quieted down the day's excitement. They must have been tired by that time. Christmas Eve in the White House found all the Roosevelts together as a family and out of the public glare. Mrs. Roosevelt decorated their own tree on the family floor in white and silver, and late in the evening they'd all troop off to hang their stockings from the mantel in the President's bedroom.

They used big special Christmas stockings Mrs. Roosevelt's maid stitched up, and every one in the family had one, from Mrs. James down to the newest grandchild.

Festivities started early on the family floor on Christmas morning. The children opened their stockings on the President's bed, and there was a lot of shouting and whoops of surprise. Then breakfast, with sausage and tradition, and the family tree, where each Roosevelt had his own space under the tree, piled with gifts, and later a visit across the way to Christmas services in St. John's, and the President reading the abridged version of Charles Dickens's *Christmas Carol* to the family before the fire.

Christmas dinner was on Christmas night, with all the relations gathered around the table, Mrs. James Roosevelt, the President's mother, and Mrs. James R. Roosevelt, the President's half-brother's wife, and the children down to the littlest. On this first Christmas menu I see there were twenty-three to dinner and four trays, for nurses probably. Plain American it was, the way the Roosevelts wanted it:

1933 *Christmas Dinner*

Clam Cocktail	Cranberry Jelly
Saltines	Creamed Onions
Clear Soup	Green Beans
Beaten Biscuit	Candied Sweet Potatoes
Curled Celery	Grape and Rubyette Salad
Stuffed Olives	Cheese Straws
Filet of Fish	Plum Pudding
Sauce Maréchale	Hard Sauce
Sliced Cucumbers	Ice Cream
Rolls	Small Cakes
Roast Turkey	Cookies
Chestnut Dressing	Coffee
Deerfoot Sausages	Candy

Roast turkey and plum pudding were traditional, and the Roosevelts didn't want it any other way.

A lot of plum puddings were sent in as gifts, but they always wanted the two big ones I'd made, brought steaming in wreaths of holly, and blazing all over with brandy.

They were happy people. Apart from all they were trying to do for the world at large, they had given hundreds of individuals a joyous Christmas.

The day after Christmas was the Children's Party, with Sister and Buzzie as hosts, and not a guest over four. The Christmas tree was enjoyed all over again, and there were little gifts, and a collation of cereal and milk, scrambled eggs, brown bread and butter, peas, ice cream, cookies, and milk. I never missed a children's party, because the little ones were so cute and Mrs. Roosevelt so sweet with them. No matter what sort of party it was, there were always gifts and little favors, and nearly always a puppet show, and the babies' faces were wonderful to watch. Their mothers were served cake and tea in the Red Room. That was the only drawback to the children's parties. Sometimes we'd have as many as twenty-five children to fifty-five mamas!

This party and the Young Folks' Dance always came between Christmas and the new year. The latter was for Anna's set and the friends of the Roosevelt boys home from college. December 27 four hundred and fifty-six young people came to dance in the East Room and sit down to supper at midnight—creamed oysters on snowflake crackers, chicken salad, ice cream, candy, candied grapefruit peel, coffee, and punch.

Even the Roosevelt friends were traditional. Habitual guests came to share New Year's Eve—Mr. Endicott Peabody who had been the President's headmaster at Groton, and Bishop Atwood. They would have dinner, and a movie maybe, and then go into the President's study to wait the new year. The young folks came in just before midnight, in time to lift glasses of the eggnog that was also tradition.

White House eggnog has to be made a special way:

Twelve eggs. One pound sugar. Beat the egg yolks and sugar until yellow. Three quarts heavy cream. Coffee cream can be used. One half pint rum, a quart of bourbon whisky, brandy, and nutmeg to taste.

The President always gave the same toast.

"To the United States!"

So our first year in the White House was over, and if I had known the March before what it would be like, I doubt if I'd lived through it.

I hadn't had time to catch my breath.

But we had all come through, and, according to my diary, 1934 started out for us with a bang.

Life with Mamie

My Thirty Years Backstairs at the White House (1961)
(as told to Frances Spatz Leighton)

Lillian Rogers Parks wrote this book shortly after her retirement from the White House after thirty years as a maid and a seamstress. Her mother had been the head White House maid for thirty years, with ten of their years overlapping. This is Parks's fun-filled, anecdotal march through three decades backstairs at the White House, plus a couple more decades based on notes and stories from her mother. Frances Spatz Leighton, with whom Parks wrote this book, was a great collaborator. As the dust jacket described her, she is someone who "knows not only the inner workings of the White House but also that hectic and rumor-ridden milieu known as 'the Washington scene.' "

While Parks wasn't the first White House staffer to write a book about her experiences, she may have been the first to have got into hot water because of it. Traphes Bryant, author of Dog Days at the White House, *suggests that the furor over White House books began with the publication of* My Thirty Years Backstairs at the White House, *which, by the way, was an immediate bestseller. Bryant called Parks the "tell-all girl," and reported that when Jacqueline Kennedy read her book, "she added to the uproar and probably the book's sales as well by making everybody on the household staff sign an agreement that they wouldn't write about the White House after they got out. Nobody thought of me. I didn't sign any agreement. And even if I had, lawyers now say you can't make it stick. History will out."*

I would be hard pressed to pick my favorite stories and characterizations from this book. It's a very honest, no-holds-barred account of what Parks observed about the presidents and their families from her behind-the-scenes position. She tells of everything from Teddy Roosevelt as the loudest talker ever at the White House; to Coolidge's oversized underwear and giving his "protectors the most headaches, because he thought it was a good game to sneak out without them"; to Mrs.

Coolidge spending several years making a crocheted bedspread for the Lincoln bedroom; to President Hoover being so fierce about "invisible" servants (being neither seen nor heard) that everyone had to dodge and jump "like jack-in-the-boxes" into a closet so as not to be seen; to Harry Truman's response when asked how he thought his wife looked in her new hairdo (a poodle cut): "I think she looks just like she ought to look"; to Bess Truman, "who acted as if she had invented laughter"; to Mamie Eisenhower's being accused of being drunk because of her "disturbance of the inner ear that at times upset her equilibrium and made her footing uncertain." The stories, unfortunately, end long before we readers are ready.

I think Mrs. Parks's conclusion about what she learned remains true today. She wrote, "If there's anything I've learned, in my thirty years at the White House as a maid and seamstress, and from the stories my mother told me of her thirty years . . . it is to expect that things will never be placid, and that they are never as they appear to those on the outside."

W HEN MRS. EISENHOWER came to look over the White House before moving in, Mrs. Truman said to one of the maids, "Julia, by this time next month, you are going to have a fluffy White House."

We wondered what she meant. But we'd find out soon enough. We'd also find out the significance of the hat Mrs. Eisenhower wore on her visit.

Mrs. Eisenhower had looked very dignified when she visited and very conservatively dressed, but on her head was a cute pink hat. That color pink was the clue we weren't smart enough to see. But pink and fluffy were what we became at the White House. And fussy.

I've sewn a lot of things for a lot of exacting First Ladies, but I think the strangest or the fussiest items I've ever had to make at the White House were a cover for an inlaid hand mirror, whose beauty should have been enjoyed, and a cover for a lipstick holder, which was gem-encrusted. Both these items—I'm sure you have guessed it—were for Mrs. Eisenhower.

I also made a cover for the chandelier at Gettysburg. The work got so bad, that for the first time in my career at the White House, I even considered quitting before I was ready to retire. What stopped me was that Mama was bedridden, and needed nursing care round the clock. I was home nights, but since her pension was only $111.00 a month, I had to dip into savings for the nurses, both in the daytime and when I was working late for the White House entertainments, zipping zippers, and standing by in the powder room, with my SOS kit of needles and pins.

Mama had been living more and more in the past. But even so, her mind was sharp. When I would tell her about a President or First Lady, she would remember, and pick a name from the past. When I told her how fussy the new First Lady was, she said, "Mrs. Taft."

Mrs. Roosevelt's life had recalled to her the second Mrs. Wilson. Pepper-tongued President Truman had been "Calvin Coolidge." She would just whip out the name as if that explained everything.

I told her how everyone had expected President Eisenhower to be exceptionally friendly, because there had even been a slogan, "I Like Ike," and yet the President hardly knew we were there, and was definitely not friendly. She snapped, "Herbert Hoover."

She was right when I thought about it. And every Mamie Eisenhower assignment I would tell Mama about at home would always bring forth the same name, "Mrs. Taft."

I remembered the stories Mama had brought home about Mrs. Taft, and how she had striven to turn the White House into a palace. The two ladies were alike in many ways. Mrs. Eisenhower had also known the rigors of tropical life, and she often told me how she had been beset by every form of insect and reptile life, and every hazard of the elements.

She now showed great concern for public opinion, and I remembered that Mama had said that when the public complained because Taft played golf, instead of doing something for the people in order to get himself re-elected, the only thing Mrs. Taft worried about was that people might see her playing cards on the Sabbath. . . .

My first shocker in the work department was when Mrs. Eisenhower ordered me to make thirty-two pairs of curtains, because she didn't like the looks of the natural-color raw silk curtains on the second-floor living quarters. She wanted them made of "that white silk that is used for making parachutes" that you can "just swish out." Thirty-two pairs!

When I heard that I was to make enough for the whole second floor, I protested, "I don't see how I can do my regular work and make thirty-two pairs of curtains too," and said that for such big jobs we used outside help. Mrs. Eisenhower said, "My husband is in here to balance the budget, and we are going to do them ourselves."

So I sewed enough parachute material to float to the moon.

It took time, but Mrs. Eisenhower was always in a hurry. As I strained to please her, I remembered the new White House as we had moved in after leaving Blair House, and how the natural-color raw silk curtains were one of the things we particularly liked, because they took away from the "home show" look, and toned things down a little. Now the bright white of the parachute cloth would be more "home show" than ever.

And then, shades of pink! The order came for rose drapery and pink curtains. I was to make rose drapery for Mrs. "E"'s dressing room, and pink fiberglass curtains to replace the white ones in her bathroom and her mother's bathroom.

I remembered that when we were moving into the renovated White House, and there were still workmen around, we had to keep the doors locked, and Mrs. Walker had gone around with a big ring of keys around her waist. We maids kept borrowing the keys, and we would end up accidentally locking each other into rooms. I wished now I could tell Mrs. Walker to just lock me in, because I was losing my mind for sure.

The newest order of the First Lady had me really punchy. It was to make covers for the bottom of the rose drapery. I had to take old sheets and make a long case, open at one end. Every night, the maid would have to slip the bottom of the drapery into the sheets and tape them halfway up, to hold them, onto the drapery. This was to keep them clean while Mrs. "E" slept.

I was not the only one going out of my mind. The kitchen help reported that pink had crept onto the dining room table, and pink food was also the order of the day. Whatever wasn't peppermint-pink was mint-green.

Finally, the papers were making too much of the pink White House, or as we called it backstairs, "The Pink Palace," and so the table decorations became yellow, and yellow and gold were suddenly the only colors in demand.

I heard the head gardener say to the housekeeper, "I had to tell her this morning that if she didn't stop using so much yellow, the newspapers would be on her soon."

So we went back to "Mamie Pink," and a pink carnation was named for her.

It got so bad that on one occasion, pink candles were used at a luncheon. Some one passed me in a hurry and said, "Can you see candles on a table this time of day?"

The servants never fail to see every little detail and comment on it. After the luncheons, the ladies usually came to the ground floor to see a movie. I could leave the powder room and go to the theatre also. *Gigi* was shown five times, and the President saw it three times.

When Mrs. "E" had the annual luncheon for the "Senate Ladies"—

the wives of the Senators—she wanted pink tablecloths, so the house-keeper sent to a hotel for them. When I saw them, I asked her, "What are you going to do, use pink cloths and white napkins?"

She said, "We can't use the pink ones anyway, because they have the name of the hotel on them." I thought this was the best thing that had ever happened, because it turned out that the small tables with white cloths and "Mamie pink" flowers were just right.

Mrs. "E" would give favors to the ladies. Once they were little hat boxes with tiny hats inside. I remember having seen Mrs. John Kennedy at the Senate ladies' luncheon; she was the youngest person present, and the most simply dressed.

Mrs. Eisenhower broke with tradition in many ways in her entertainment, but, in the jive talk of the young folks today, of all the parties I have ever seen in the White House the Halloween party that Mrs. Eisenhower gave October 30, 1958, for the wives of the White House staff members, was really a "gasser." Even the old-timers backstairs could think of nothing to compare it with.

Some of the guests described it as "the most interesting" party they had ever seen at the White House, and I had a feeling they were simply at a loss for words. I guess it was "interesting" to come into the dignified White House and see scary-looking skeletons hanging in the ornate State Dining Room. Witches on broomsticks perched on the white table-cloth. Swinging from the elegant chandelier were black cats, witch heads, black owls, and goblins, mingled with fall foliage. Outside the room, brown corn stalks, huge real and fake pumpkins, and rosy-red, giant-sized apples clustered at the base of the corn stalks, and transformed the red-carpeted corridor into a harvest scene. Orange light bulbs were placed in the chandeliers in the marble corridor.

The worst part of it was that this spectacular was to be left over the week end for the sightseers to view. Most of them thought the children had had a party, the backstairs folks reported.

When another maid told me to please look and tell her if she were justified in shuddering at this sight in the White House, I looked, but I had just come through a one-and-a-half-day shock treatment of my own, and was beyond shuddering at anything. It had to do with the preparations for this same party.

Just two days before the party, Mrs. Walker came rushing into the linen room and said, "Put aside everything. Mrs. 'E' wants you to make pink flowered draperies to match the paper we are putting on the wall in the powder room off the library, and a skirt has to be made for the long dressing table."

The library on the ground floor is one of the choice rooms of the

House. The walls, lined with books, are made of the natural wood, nail holes and all, of the old White House before it was renovated. There is a dark red rug on the floor with an eagle in the center that was formerly in the Red Parlor. The black Baldwin piano, which President Truman ordered, is in this room. Well, when I was told to get out two pink rugs, for the bathroom and entry floors, I thought, "This is the last straw!"

They were salmon-pink, and whenever I opened the door to the powder room, something would hit me right in the face—Clash! Mrs. "E" thought the room looked fine, and on her way to the movie, she told me, "Lillian, the room looks very nice."

Frankly, I was too shell-shocked to shudder much for anyone else. Forty-nine guests sat at the E-shaped table, scattered with autumn leaves, ears of dried corn, autumn nuts, squash, and dried gourds, and backstairs, we hoped that none of the guests would make a mistake and eat some of them in the eerie light.

It wasn't just the fussy parties and the striving for perfection that was putting a strain on the folks backstairs. It was the effort to hurry so, and to be perfect even in what we said.

For example, Mrs. Eisenhower decreed that there would be no slang or nicknames. It began with her hearing the help call the houseman Enrique "Ricky." Everyone called him that. His full name was Enrique Aflague. She not only decreed no nicknames, but commented that she didn't like to hear her husband's name bandied about as "Ike."

Taking away nicknames was taking away the spice and fun of backstairs life. The handsome chief usher, James West, was called "Perry Como" because of a real resemblance. George Thompson, the likeable houseman, was "Jockey" because of his size. Head Electrician Johnson, who had operated the first movie projector under Hoover, was happily called "Short Circuit." Even Mrs. Walker, our housekeeper, was known backstairs as "The Tennessee Darling" because of her southern accent.

The White House is practically famous for its nicknames. I remember the time the carpenter's daughter came and asked for Mr. Benton. Not till she added, "He's known here as 'Tojo,' " did they snap to and find him.

And the irony of it all was that, while we had to use our dull, formal names, Mrs. Eisenhower still called her personal maid, Rose Wood, "Rosie," and her husband, "Ike."

By 1956, the First Family was spending a great deal of time at the farm. These trips got me down, because the White House linens had to be hauled back and forth. If I didn't send enough, Mrs. "E" would call for one dozen pillow cases to be sent eighty miles before she would use one of her own. The laundry in the basement was swamped at times, and so was I, because I had to keep a record of what went out and what came back.

I well remember May 24, 1956, because after handling over a hundred sheets, towels, and pillow cases that morning, I began to feel sick—all on my left side. I rested a few minutes, then took the elevator to pick up some clean washcloths from the laundry. When I got to the ground floor, I went straight to the housekeeper's office, because my left arm was becoming numb. It turned out that I was having a small heart attack.

What started out to be a few things turned into a mountain. For three months, I sewed slip covers, curtains, and other household items, and there was no letup. Each week end, when the family went to Gettysburg, Mrs. Eisenhower wanted to take as many things that were finished as possible, and if something weren't finished, she was very displeased about it. I disappointed her several times, but never let it worry me, because I could only do so much in the time that was allotted me.

In June of 1955, invitations were issued to a select group of the White House staff to attend a picnic at Gettysburg to celebrate the thirty-ninth wedding anniversary of "Ike and Mamie" and the completion of the President's house. Four years later, the oversight was corrected, and on June 6, 1959, a buffet supper was held for the entire staff.

Mrs. "E" stood on one of the three stone steps, and shook hands with each guest, making us feel very welcome. She wanted to know if I had bought my yellow flowered dress in California. I told her I had picked it up in a Washington store. Then she said, "It is a real California dress." I felt real proud of my $8.00 cotton dress, especially when Mrs. Robert Anderson, wife of the Secretary of the Treasury, said to me, "I ran over here to tell you how pretty your dress is."

My lifetime of making things over without a pattern had really been rewarded. Even the President got into the spirit of things, and posed happily for everyone who had brought a camera. Later, he graciously said he didn't remember when he had enjoyed himself as much.

Looking at Mrs. "E" as she drank a Coke and invited me to have one too, I couldn't help but think of how really likeable she is. She has an endearing quality that I am sure helped her husband get elected and re-elected. I suddenly thought, "Why, oh why, can't First Ladies be perfect?"

Well, they aren't, and they never were. And they are never as you think they will be from advance publicity. Since everyone parroted the slogan, "I Like Ike," I had thought that the President would have many friends, but he seemed to be clannish and to stick to just a few friends—all millionaires—whom he had known only since he had become an important General, and who were quickly nicknamed "The White

House Clan." The leader was George Allen, who also owns a Gettysburg estate.

Backstairs, we speculated that the man behind the "I Like Ike" slogan was really sort of an introvert, who liked to get away from people, and enjoyed painting because it was a solitary occupation. The real extrovert of the family was Mrs. Eisenhower, definitely.

The First Lady seemed never to stop talking, and you would hear her voice and laughter just as soon as she would reach the floor and get off the elevator. She wanted to be an outstanding First Lady, but her health was a great handicap. She had to spend much time in bed, and social gatherings usually turned into a torment with headaches, asthma, weakness, and the inner ear trouble, which made her feel dizzy, and which has thrown her step off balance more than once.

Mrs. "E" spent so much time in bed that, in spite of her feeling about nicknames, she was referred to in hushed tones as "Sleeping Beauty." Even with the servants, she wanted to maintain a gay, holiday air, and she was the first to order a birthday cake made for every member of the help. There were three cakes on my birthday, because I had to share honors with storekeeper Melvern Carter and messenger Shermont Brooks, also born on February first.

Usually Mrs. "E" kept close track of what was going on in the kitchens, by having the food brought to her for tasting, but on the birthday occasions, she would show up in the kitchens. The help said that she only saw the kitchens when she wanted to have her picture taken.

Never has a First Lady received more service, and that led to a housekeeping problem. In the past, there had been three housemen to do the cleaning of the two family floors, but when one houseman left and another retired, Mrs. "E" had three Guamian and Filipino housemen assigned to do nothing but wait on her. They took turns stationing themselves outside her door, to run errands and deliver messages. They also waited on her when she had her bridge friends in, and would go to Gettysburg to take care of her there. That left only one houseman, George Thompson, to do all the heavy cleaning of the second- and third-floor family quarters. And I used to smile when I would read that "Mamie is such a good housekeeper," because I knew that, though the rug might be swept clean of footprints, back in the corners the dust was collecting.

I wasn't surprised when I got the report, from good backstairs authority, that when Eisenhower returned from his last European trip in May, 1960, after the Summit Meeting fiasco, he took one look at the condition of the living quarters, and announced that he wanted the house cleaned up.

Of course, one houseman couldn't do the work of three. The

changeover had begun not many months after Mrs. Eisenhower had arrived at the White House. First, she brought in two men from the Navy—Enrique Aflague, a Guamian, and Francisco Lim, a Filipino. Then the third member was added, a Filipino named Jaunito Malapit. All of them had to wait on the First Lady exclusively, and travel to the farm. This arrangement left us short two men upstairs for the whole administration.

Mrs. Eisenhower never wanted anything sent to the cleaners, and prevented the housekeeper from sending things out to be cleaned. This was entirely her job to look after the upkeep of the mansion. She had to see that rugs, draperies, and all chair and sofa covers were cleaned, without first having to get permission from the First Lady.

But Mrs. Eisenhower wanted the feeling of really running her White House, and for the rest of us, permission had to be granted for every little thing. For some reason, if the rugs were brushed clean of footprints, she had a feeling that the house was sparkling clean. Much was made of the business of keeping Mrs. Eisenhower from seeing footprints on a rug before she appeared in any room; everyone became so rug-conscious, that even the police, Secret Service men, and ushers would step around the rugs.

This led to a vastly amusing but disastrous occasion. Mary Jane McCaffree, the social secretary, had become so rug-conscious that while showing some female newspaper reporters the table decor before a State dinner, she said quite sharply, "Please don't step on the carpet!"

Needless to say, the women were shocked. Of course, they didn't know that this was Mrs. Eisenhower's special idiosyncrasy. The witty George Dixon, who writes a column distributed by King Features Syndicate, related the comment of one of the angry newswomen. She had told Dixon, "What the blank did she think we were doing—wearing spikes?" . . .

We had thought that Mrs. Truman had shown a great interest in the running of the house, and was economy-minded, but that was only a prelude to Mrs. Eisenhower, who wanted to put to use her knowledge of budget-living, which she had acquired as a military wife.

She ordered that all leftovers be saved, and the help was afraid to throw away even a dab of something, because she might call for it again at any moment. Another economy measure was cutting down on electricity. When Mrs. Eisenhower first moved into the White House, and saw how dark the interior was, she ordered that all the lights must burn in the rooms, even in daytime, to keep the house from looking dreary. When, by chance, Mr. Crim told her how much the light bill was each month, the lights only burned when it was necessary.

Mrs. Eisenhower would hold daily morning bedside conferences on the running of the household. She would be sitting up in bed writing—here she would spend most of the mornings with her mail. Everyone would come to her—Mrs. Walker, who was really Mrs. Eli Ciarrochi (we simply added a "Mrs." to the Walker when she got married during the Truman administration, because the new name was too hard for us); Mr. West, the head usher; Charles, the butler; and, very occasionally, me.

I remember the day I saw Mrs. Walker carrying to the second floor a plate with four or five little squares of cake on it. I was horrified when I learned that cake mixes were to be used for the teas. Considering the amount we had left over from time to time, I judged that some of the guests didn't like them. The mixes were only used for sheet cake; other cookies and cakes were made by the cooks. I am certain that fewer meals were served during the Eisenhower administration than during any other I have known.

For months at a time, there would be no house guests—only the children in and out—and no parties for young people. All the parties seemed to circle round the older friends—Army buddies—and George Allen, who was like a member of the family.

For a time, Mrs. Eisenhower had a French chef, one of the most famous cooks and pastrymen in the field, François Rysavy, who had cooked for famous people all over the world, from ambassadors to Hollywood stars. But he only lasted at the White House about three years. He let it be known that cooking without onions and garlic was too hard on his nervous system.

The problem was that the President and First Lady did not share the same tastes for food. The President loved onions and garlic. Mrs. Eisenhower couldn't bear even the odor, and Rysavy was torn between their desires. He was ordered by the President to serve a little separate dish of onions on the side, but how could he do that without the odor? Mrs. Eisenhower would say, "I smell onions in my house."

Rysavy left, and we heard that he had returned to Hollywood to cook for David Selznick and his wife, Jennifer Jones.

Once I visited Mrs. Eisenhower in her room just after the second Inaugural Ball. . . .

Mrs. Eisenhower told me what a strain it had been for her to watch the parade, and how she'd worried about the President too, for fear he would become too fatigued. Then she said to me, "It is nice to have this chat. We seldom see each other."

After I walked out of her room that morning, January 22, 1957, nearly a year passed before I saw her again. I would hear her talking in the hall sometimes when the children were in the house, or she was on her way out, but I was so busy that I just never took time out to go to her room. When I finally did see her, she said, "Lillian, where have you been?" She was on her way to a movie for her luncheon guests. I told her, "Busy, and when I am not busy, you are."

I used to get very angry with her, and probably she with me. But we developed a warm feeling toward each other, and she gave me many little gifts that showed a personal touch, such as a lavender stole to go with my blue-tinted grey hair. And I reciprocated by trying to find something she wouldn't think of for herself—a candle snuffer for her home at Gettysburg. One year, I gave her a zipper zipper, to help when the zipper is in the back of the dress. I enclosed a note saying, "Maybe you won't need this because you have Rosie."

Back came the reply, "I can use this with or without Rosie."

I will never forget how kind she was when Mama died. In fact, everyone at the White House was most understanding. President and Mrs. Eisenhower sent a white cross made of carnations. There were flowers and a large donation from all the employees, some of whom had worked with my mother through the years.

I had been able to control myself pretty well until I learned one thing from the practical nurse who had cared for her those last years. Bertha Davis, who had also worked for Dr. Montgomery Blair of the Blair House family, told me how Mama had lived each day for the moment when I would return from work. She would look at the clock around 4:00 and 4:30 and say, "It's time for my little Hop-Skip to come home."

For all our talk and laughter about nicknames at the White House, I had never known that Mama had had a nickname for me all the time. And she had hidden it as effectively as the nicknames of Presidents and First Ladies are hidden at the White House.

JFK

A Good Life (1995)

Ben Bradlee came up with the perfect title for his memoir (with the help of his friend David Halberstam). His life has indeed been a good one, and continues to be. His book is full of his one-of-a-kind stories of "newspapering and other adventures."

A big part of a few years of his good life was his friendship with Jack Kennedy. Ben had first come to know then senator Kennedy and his wife when they became Georgetown neighbors in 1958. The relationship blossomed from there in large part because of like-mindedness and just plain attraction—each for the other.

Before he became ill, Phil, too, had a wonderful relationship with Jack Kennedy, one of mutual respect and admiration. While I certainly liked Kennedy, I felt terribly awkward whenever I was around him. I do remember at least one conversation with him quite vividly. We had been talking about something he had read, and I asked him if maybe he was reading too much and reacting too hard. His response was to tell me that being president was a "very cut off job" and his way of staying in touch was to read everything he could. Then he said, "And if you read, you're human and you react." I always remembered that; it was yet another sign of his own great humanity.

MANY OF the most important events of my life seem to have occurred by accident. Like not getting off *The Federal* at the Baltimore train station for a job interview at the *Baltimore Sun*, and instead staying on to Washington for a job interview at the *Washington Post*. And like buying a house in 1957 in Georgetown on the north side of the 3300 block of N Street, N.W., only months before the junior senator from Massachusetts and his wife bought a house on the north side of the 3300 block of N Street, N.W. Our first contact as couples beyond handshakes came on a sunny Sunday afternoon walking slowly through Georgetown, wheeling baby carriages. Their baby was Caroline, and ours was Dino, born just after Christmas in 1958. It was a warm

Sunday in early 1959, and we ended up in their back garden, looking each other over, while pretending to size up our respective children. Caroline was en route to becoming the world's most photographed child, and for good reason: she was irresistible. Dino wasn't bad, either. . . .

Living in Europe, I had missed Jack Kennedy's first flash across the American political firmament, when he wanted to be Adlai Stevenson's vice president in 1956, only to lose at the convention to Senator Estes Kefauver of Tennessee. I remember thinking how attractive he was, how gracefully he moved, despite his slight stoop. We discovered we were all going to the same dinner that night, a big bash given by the former Ambassador to Paris—and now Undersecretary of the Treasury—Douglas Dillon, and his wife Phyllis. In fact I sat next to Jackie, and Jack sat next to Tony. We came home together, and by the time we said good night, we were friends, comfortable together and looking forward to the next time.

My interest and involvement in domestic politics were slow in coming. I had never covered a presidential campaign, or any political campaign. I had missed the Eisenhower-Stevenson campaigns, and therefore knew none of the Stevensonian Democrats, and only a few people in Ike's administration. And so the choice political assignments went to reporters with more experience. But while covering the House, I had come to know a lot of people in Congress, and even more of their staff. When I got to know Kennedy, I kind of staked him out as part of my own territorial imperative, and as he prospered, so did I. Kennedy had decided privately right after he lost the vice presidency at the 1956 Chicago convention to go for Big Casino next time around. By the time I got to know him, he was writing magazine articles, making political speeches, barnstorming across the country, and spending little time in the Senate—especially after he was overwhelmingly reelected in 1958 by more than 850,000 votes, the largest total vote ever recorded by a Massachusetts politician. No politician anywhere running that year in a contested election ran up a bigger majority.

The earliest political trip I can remember taking was in 1959 with Kennedy, Jackie, and Tony in a small chartered plane. A short hop first from National Airport to some meeting of Maryland Democrats at an ocean resort, and then on to our first trip to Hyannis Port, where the Kennedy clan lived in a compound of summer homes. Jack plunged into the crowd, shaking a thousand hands, while Jackie stood frozen, staring resolutely straight ahead, daring anyone to make conversation with her.

The public signal that the Kennedy campaign was under way, the signal no one could deny, came in the fall of 1959 when the Kennedy family acquired the *Caroline*, a converted Convair, comfortably furnished with good chairs, desks, and a bedroom, and put it at the senator's disposition. More often than not, the passenger list on those early flights—generally to talk to small political gatherings—consisted of Kennedy and Ted Sorensen, or Kennedy and Larry O'Brien, his top political honcho, with no reporters. Sometimes one reporter (sometimes me), sometimes two, rarely more.

Little by little, it was accepted by the rest of the *Newsweek* Bureau and by New York that Kennedy was mine. If a quote was needed, I was asked to get it, and without really understanding what running for president entailed, or where it would all end, I was embarked on a brand-new journey. Nothing in my education or experience had led me to conceive of the possibility that someone I really knew would hold that exalted job. The field in front of him was filled with mines. His age—at forty-three, he would be the youngest man ever elected president, the first one born in the twentieth century. His religion—too much of America believed that a Catholic president would have to take orders from the pope in Rome. His health—he had been given the last rites several times, and had been referred to by India Edwards, chairman of the Citizens for Lyndon B. Johnson National Committee, as a "spavined little hunchback." His father—Joseph P. Kennedy's reputation was secure as a womanizing robber baron, who had been anti-war and seen as pro-German while he was Ambassador to Britain during World War II, and pro-McCarthy during the fifties.

Tony and I told Kennedy how strange it was for us that he should be a presidential candidate, and I asked him once if it didn't seem strange to him. "Yes," he replied, "until I stop and look around at the other people who are running for the job. And then I think I'm just as qualified as they are." And I remember asking him toward the end of 1959 if he really thought—way down deep—that he could pull it off. After an uncharacteristic pause he said, "Yes. If I don't make a single mistake, and if I don't get maneuvered into a position where there is no way out." That meant, he said, he could never finish second in a primary, never let himself get in a position where everything was riding on a single event—the way Harold Stassen had done in the Oregon primary against Thomas E. Dewey in 1948—and then blow it. Stassen had convinced himself and others that he could beat Dewey in Oregon, and that a Stassen victory in Oregon would stop Dewey cold.

I wasn't convinced. I was still new to politics, too new to trust my hunches, and the primaries were coming up soon enough to answer everyone's doubts. I trudged all through the snows of New

Hampshire. . . . Kennedy racked up a huge win there, even if he was running against the west wind, as my father used to say, in the neighboring
state of his own. In the next primary, Wisconsin, he expected to beat
Hubert Humphrey, a native of neighboring Minnesota and the personification of a midwestern Democratic leader, in nine of the ten districts,
and barely beat him, 6–4.

AFTER Wisconsin, *Newsweek* assigned me to cover Jack Kennedy full
time as he traveled the country in pursuit of the presidency. It is hard now
to re-create those early political trips, on the *Caroline*. I can still see Governor Abe Ribicoff of Connecticut, gray fedora in hand, alone on the
rainy tarmac greeting him, on an early trip to Hartford, Connecticut.
And Kennedy did not forget Ribicoff's early support. "Abe can have anything he wants," he said later.

Kennedy had decided to enter the West Virginia primary next to
prove he could win in a strongly Protestant state, against the advice of his
father ("It's a nothing state and they'll kill him over the Catholic thing").
The decision was taken at a family meeting in Palm Beach, when Jack
Kennedy said simply, "Well, we've heard from the Ambassador, but we're
going to go into West Virginia, and we're going to win." The Ambassador was aboard in a second.

We had been invited to sweat out the West Virginia vote with the
Kennedys in May 1960. To help pass the time, we decided to go to a
movie. Jack had selected something called *Suddenly Last Summer*, but the
film's publicity included a warning that no one would be admitted and no
one could leave after the film had started. So we went across 14th Street
to the Plaza Theater, which then specialized in porn films. Not the hard-
core stuff of later years, but a nasty thing called *Private Property*, starring
one Katie Manx as a horny housewife. (For the record, I later found out
that *Private Property* was on the Catholic Index of forbidden films. I never
reported anything about that particular night at the movies.)

When we got back to the Kennedys' house on N Street, the phone
was ringing. It was Bobby Kennedy, the campaign manager, and it was a
win. Big. After modest war whoops and a glass of champagne, Jack asked
if we would like to fly with them to Charleston on the *Caroline* for the
victory photo op. I knew it was the story of the political week, and I knew
that the whole night (minus the porn film) plus the flight down would
give me the personal detail and color that news magazine editors crave. I
got exactly what I bargained for, especially in Hugh Sidey's expression, as
my talented opposite number on *Time* watched me get off the plane at
the Charleston airport directly behind the candidate. . . .

The press generally protected Kennedy, as they protected all candidates from the excesses of their language, and from the sometimes outspokenly deprecatory characterizations of other politicians. This protection most definitely covered Richard Nixon, whose language "was worse than yours, Bradlee," according to Ken Clawson some years later, after he had quit the *Post* as a reporter to become a Nixon aide in the White House. When India Edwards called Jack Kennedy a "spavined little hunchback" in an effort to cast doubts on Kennedy's health, not a line appeared anywhere. Reporters tolerated then what they felt to be the excesses of partisan politics. That toleration has slowly disappeared with a new generation of reporters, and I am not sure who's the better for that. The rules changed about covering the private language and behavior of presidential candidates. And editors struggled to cope with them. (Gary Hart's campaign in 1987, for instance.) . . .

Finally. Election night was endless, as Kennedy stalled a few critical votes short of victory on Tuesday night. Illinois, California, Michigan, and Minnesota were still undecided, and it was well into Wednesday before his election was official. When Tony and I at last got back to the Yachtsman Motel in Hyannis Port, there was an invitation for supper that night with Jack and Jackie at the Kennedys' house in the Kennedy compound. It was just us plus Bill Walton, the charming former journalist (Time-Life, *New Republic*) turned artist turned Kennedy worker (he had run the Kennedy campaign in Arkansas).

We arrived early, Tony eight months pregnant, and were greeted by Jackie in the same condition. Kennedy came downstairs a few minutes later, and before anyone could say anything, he smiled and said, "Okay, girls. We won. You can take the pillows out now."

Over drinks, we talked nervously about what we should call him. "Mr. President" sounded awesome, and he was not yet president. He asked modestly, "What about 'Prez,' for now?" (Later when he was in fact president, we called him "Jack" only when we were alone together or with his closest friends, and "Mr. President" whenever anyone else was present.) Over dinner Kennedy talked about his sweating things out the night before. He said he had called Chicago's legendary mayor, Richard Daley, while Illinois was hanging in the balance, to ask how he was doing. "Mr. President," Kennedy quoted Daley as saying, "with a little bit of luck and the help of a few close friends, you're going to carry Illinois."

That quotation has haunted Kennedy's reputation. Since the dinner was explicitly off the record, I didn't publish it until I wrote *Conversations with Kennedy*, almost fourteen years later. And when I did, some Republicans chose to read it as confirmation of their belief that Daley had stolen

Illinois, and with it the election for Kennedy. They felt the quotation showed Daley promising Kennedy that he could, and would, produce enough votes—dead or alive—to guarantee victory. Me, I don't know what the hell Daley meant. If it was Irish humor, it seems peculiarly inappropriate, not to say dumb. . . .

The experience of having a friend run for President of the United States is unexpected, fascinating, and exciting for anyone. For a newspaperman it is all that, plus confusing: are you a friend, or are you a reporter? You have to redefine "friend" and redefine "reporter" over and over again, before reaching any kind of comfort level. And that takes time, before you get it right. If the friend is actually elected president, it gets worse before it gets better—a lot better.

I felt a particularly high discomfort level a few weeks after Kennedy had been elected. I'm not sure we had it right on the night of November 23, less than three weeks after Kennedy was elected, when Tony suddenly announced that Marina Bradlee was on her way into the world. According to past experience, we had less than twenty-five minutes before she would arrive, and we had no baby-sitter; our au pair was not due back from night school for another half an hour. I called Jackie to ask if her maid, Provie, whom my children knew, might be available for emergency help, but she had just left. I was really desperate when the newly elected president called to ask if one of his Secret Service agents would do, a man whose name I have unfortunately (or maybe fortunately for him) lost. He came over immediately. We left immediately. Marina arrived immediately. And when I got back to the house, everyone but Andy, aged twelve, was asleep, and Andy was watching transfixed as the Secret Service agent took his service revolver apart for the umpteenth time for Andy's entertainment.

With both our wives in hospitals after delivering children, Kennedy asked me if I would like to bring two-year-old Dino with him and three-year-old Caroline for a drive to Virginia and tea with his mother-in-law, the daunting Mrs. Hugh D. Auchincloss. Dino was named Dino because Tony and I like that nickname. His formal name was Dominic, only because the book we referred to while considering possible names said that Dominic and Ferdinand were the only names where Dino was an appropriate diminutive. The trouble was that I had to walk with Dino through the gauntlet of reporters and photographers guarding the entrance to the president-elect's house, and the trouble with that was that poor Dino looked like a war casualty. The day before, while ostensibly under my care, he had taken a swan dive from the top rung of the playground jungle gym to the cement. It had taken five or six stitches to stop the bleeding, and the only jacket I could find that afternoon was still covered with blood. I was stunned to see how excited the TV types and the photographers were by the photo op of the new president with a bloodied child.

Life changed for me when Tony came home with the new baby, especially at night, but down on N Street life went on, with the naming of the new cabinet and planning of the various inauguration festivities. After a fire in the boardinghouse across the street from us and, more important, from the Kennedys, Teddy Weintal and I had bought the burned-out building (with a down payment from each of us in the amount of $4,000). We rented the living room of this hulk to CBS—at an exorbitant price, even though there was no heat or water—for its round-the-clock surveillance of the goings and comings at the Kennedys'.

The inauguration festivities were marked by five Inaugural Balls for the first time, reminding someone of the Eisenhower Inaugural in 1953 when there was more than one Inaugural Ball for the first time. (CBS radio announcer Larry LeSueur sailed gloriously into the history books when he said, "And now we take you to Washington, where both presidential balls are in full swing," and broke into a guffaw before the engineers could cut him off.) I have frozen in my mind the sight of Hugh Gaitskell, leader of the British Labour Party, dancing in his overcoat and silk scarf with an aging actress, almost alone on the floor of the cavernous D.C. Armory, both sloshed.

History now will have us believe that once—or twice—Kennedy slipped away from an after-the-balls party hosted by columnist and friend Joe Alsop, ever so briefly with actress Angie Dickinson for God knows what reason. We never saw them that night, but I can believe it now more easily than I can understand it. I can see how it is physically possible, but the taste for risk and the belittling of women involved boggle the mind.

It is now accepted history that Kennedy jumped casually from bed to bed with a wide variety of women.

It was not accepted history then—during the five years that I knew him. I heard stories about how he had slept around in his bachelor days—unlike other red-blooded males. I heard people described as "one of Jack's girlfriends" from time to time. It was never Topic A among my reporter friends, while he was a candidate. Since most of the 125 conversations I had with him took place with Tony and Jackie present, extracurricular screwing was one of the few subjects that never came up, and in those days reporters did not feel compelled to conduct full FBI field investigations about a politician friend.

My friends have always had trouble believing my innocence of his activities, especially after it was revealed that Tony's sister, Mary Meyer, had been one of Kennedy's girlfriends. So be it. I can only repeat my ignorance of Kennedy's sex life, and state that I am appalled by the details that have emerged, appalled by the recklessness, by the subterfuge that must have been involved.

The inauguration itself took place on a day so cold, no one could have survived without special precautions. Cardinal Cushing's endless prayer warmed no one. And the cold froze Robert Frost's eyes shut as he started to read a new poem composed specially for the occasion. And then the inaugural address. Was Kennedy's voice really that high-pitched? I don't remember it that way.

Two days later, Kennedy's first Sunday as president, Tony and I were upstairs with the new baby, when Dino raced upstairs and seemed to be saying something about the president being downstairs. We had identified what seemed to be a little problem Dino was having with exaggeration, and so we paid no attention. Until a voice boomed up from downstairs, "Anyone home?" And there he was in the front hall (we didn't lock our front doors during daylight in those days) with some of his pals, walking back to the White House from mass at nearby Holy Trinity Church.

J. B. WEST

The Kennedys

Upstairs at the White House (1973)

As assistant to the chief usher at the White House from 1941 until 1957, and then as chief usher until 1969, J. B. West ran the president's house for six presidents and first ladies. Although he never gave an interview in all his years working in the White House, he wrote this book a few years after his retirement, relating stories that he had obviously stored up from his twenty-eight years of serving not any one president, but, as he writes, "the Presidency, and . . . the institution that is the White House."

In separate chapters on each of the families he worked for, from the Roosevelts to the Nixons, West focuses on his "life with the First Ladies." This selection clearly falls more into the first lady–watching category, since it was with them that West worked most closely, "these women [who] filled the most demanding volunteer job in America."

Here we see Jackie Kennedy from a "backstairs" at the White House perspective. Also, we see her both coming into the White House and going away——two very different moments for her and for all those upstairs and backstairs at the White House, in Washington, and in the country.

JACQUELINE KENNEDY whispered. Or so I thought, at first. Actually, she spoke so softly that one was forced to listen intently, forced to focus on her face and respond to her direct, compelling eyes. There was wonder in those eyes, determination, humor, and—sometimes—vulnerability.

When she looked around a crowded room as if searching for the nearest exit, people assumed that she was shy, uncertain. I don't think she was ever shy. It was merely her method of studying the situation: memorizing the room, or assessing the people in it. She spoke no small talk—no "I'm so very glad to meet you and what does your husband do?" She limited her conversation merely to what, in her opinion, mattered.

Her interests were wide, however, as was her knowledge, and she had a subtle, ingenious way of getting things accomplished.

I soon learned that Mrs. Kennedy's wish, murmured with a "Do you think . . ." or "Could you please . . ." was as much a command as Mrs. Eisenhower's "I want this done immediately." Mrs. Eisenhower had called me to her bedroom one morning several weeks after the 1960 election.

"I've invited Mrs. Kennedy for a tour of the house at noon on December 9," she said. "Please have the rooms in order, but no servants on the upstairs floors. And I plan to leave at one thirty, so have my car ready."

"Mrs. Kennedy's Secret Service agent phoned from the hospital this morning," I told the outgoing First Lady. "She asked that we have a wheelchair for her when she arrives."

At that moment, Mrs. Kennedy was still at Georgetown Hospital, recovering from her cesarean surgery of November 25, when John F. Kennedy, Jr., was born.

"Oh, dear," Mrs. Eisenhower frowned. "I wanted to take her around alone."

The thought of Mamie Eisenhower, the grandest of the First Ladies, pushing a wheelchair through the corridors of the White House—especially when the passenger had been a political enemy—was too much for me.

"I'll tell you what . . ." her carefully manicured fingernails drummed the night table. "We'll get a wheelchair, but put it behind a door somewhere, out of sight. It will be available if she asks for it," she said.

On the morning of December 9, the house was spruced up in its Christmas best, the wheelchair hidden in a closet beside the elevator, and I was waiting at the south entrance to meet the future First Lady.

Just before noon, the Secret Service agent who had been assigned to Mrs. Kennedy drove a dark blue station wagon into the circular driveway. She was sitting in the front seat, next to him.

Harriston, the silent, genial doorman, opened the door for her.

"Thank you," she smiled at him, and stepped out.

I was struck by how young she appeared. Dressed in a dark coat, wearing hat and gloves, she could have been a young Congressman's wife paying an obligatory call. She was taller than I had realized, as tall as I, even in her low heels. Very thin, it seemed to me, and quite pale.

"I'm Mr. West, the Chief Usher," I introduced myself.

"I'm Jacqueline Kennedy," she whispered. As if I didn't know.

She stepped, a bit hesitantly I thought, into the Diplomatic Reception

Room, looked around at the walls, sofas, and rug, and, without saying another word, walked with me through the green-carpeted hallway toward the elevator. Her wide, uncertain eyes took in everything around her, and I could tell she was somewhat ill-at-ease.

"Mrs. Eisenhower is waiting upstairs," I explained, as we entered the elevator.

She did not reply.

I thought suddenly of my daughter Kathy, who is always shy at first, and reveals nothing of herself until she is perfectly sure of her surroundings. Once sure, however, she takes over completely. Every time.

As the elevator door opened to the second floor, Jacqueline Kennedy took a deep, audible breath.

Mrs. Eisenhower stood in the center hall, a tiny figure under the high ceilings, surrounded by the beige expanse of hall. And very much in command.

"Mrs. Kennedy," I announced. Mrs. Eisenhower did not come forward.

As I escorted the young woman across the room to meet her formidable hostess, I was very much aware that neither lady had looked forward to this meeting.

"Hello, Mrs. Kennedy," Mrs. Eisenhower gave a nod and extended her hand in her most gracious meet-the-visitor pose. "I do hope you are feeling much better now. And how is the baby?"

I turned and left them, and waited in my office for a call for the wheelchair, a call that never came. At 1:30 on the dot, the two buzzers rang, indicating First Lady descending, and I dashed to the elevator.

The two women walked out the south entrance, where their cars were waiting. After the goodbyes and thank-yous, Mrs. Eisenhower stepped regally into the back seat of her Chrysler limousine and disappeared, off to her card game. Mrs. Kennedy walked slowly over to her three-year-old station wagon. As I caught up with her, to give her blueprints and photographs of the rooms, I saw pain darken her face.

"Could you please send them to Palm Beach for me?" she asked. "We're going there to rest until Inauguration Day."

Two months later, as we were tromping around the third floor, Mrs. Kennedy suddenly turned to me.

"Mr. West, did you know that my doctor ordered a wheelchair the day I first went around the White House?" she asked.

"Yes, I did," I answered.

She looked bewildered.

"Then why didn't you have it for me? I was so exhausted after marching around this house for two hours that I had to go back to bed for two whole weeks!"

She stared into my eyes, searching for an explanation.

"Well," I answered carefully, "it was certainly there, waiting for you. Right behind the closet door next to the elevator. We were waiting for you to request it."

To my surprise, she giggled. "I was too scared of Mrs. Eisenhower to ask," she whispered. From that moment, I never saw Jacqueline Kennedy uncertain again.

Mrs. Eisenhower's feelings about the young Mrs. Kennedy were never spoken, only intimated.

The morning after Mrs. Kennedy's arduous tour, Charles Ficklin, Mabel Walker, and I went up to the Eisenhowers' bedroom for our daily conference. As usual, the First Lady sat propped up against her pink headboard, with a bow in her hair, picking at the breakfast on her tray.

"See that the maids begin packing all my summer clothes first," she finished instructing the housekeeper, then dismissed her.

"Change the lamb stew to beef, and leave out the potatoes," she approved Charles' menu, dismissing him, too.

The President's wife took a bite of grapefruit, then looked at me.

"Well . . . ?" she asked, one eyebrow raised quizzically.

"The moving vans are scheduled to arrive on January 2 to take the first load to Gettysburg," I answered innocently.

"She's planning to redo every room in this house," Mrs. Eisenhower said. "You've got quite a project ahead of you." Then, in the voice she reserved for disapproval: "There certainly are going to be some changes made around here!"

Little did I realize how prophetic Mrs. Eisenhower's statement was. Throughout the next thirty-four months, not only would I become involved in coordinating the transformation of the mansion—from historic house to national monument—but also, I would have to adjust White House management from a regimented, stylized order-of-business to that of running an impromptu, informal household.

I would find myself dealing with Empire tables and rabbit cages; housing Maharajabs and ponies; steaming down the Potomac and wearing disguises; and thoroughly enjoying the most creative and challenging work to which the Chief Usher had ever been put.

The new First Lady turned the White House inside out, and she imprinted her own rarefied life style upon the mansion. But the greatest change in the White House was brought about by the presence of Jacqueline Bouvier Kennedy herself. She was thirty years younger than any of the First Ladies I had served, and, I was to discover, had the most

complex personality of them all. In public, she was elegant, aloof, dignified, and regal. In private, she was casual, impish, and irreverent. She had
a will of iron, with more determination than anyone I have ever met. Yet
she was so soft-spoken, so deft and subtle, that she could impose that will
upon people without their ever knowing it.

Her wit—teasing, exaggerating, poking fun at everything, including
herself—was a surprise and a daily delight. She was imaginative, inven-
tive, intelligent—and sometimes silly. Yet there were subjects that did not
amuse her one bit.

Relaxed and uninhibited, she was always popping up anywhere, wearing slacks, sitting on the floor, kicking off her shoes, her hair flying in
every direction. We all had fun along with her. Yet she also drew a line
against familiarity which could not be crossed.

It was only with the cameras grinding or guests coming in the front
door that the seriousness, the poise, the coolness that were also part of
her, began to appear.

She had a total mastery of detail—endless, endless detail—and she
was highly organized, yet rarely held herself to a schedule. For others,
she insisted upon order; for herself, she preferred spontaneity. She took
advice readily, but only when she asked for it, and she strongly resisted
being pushed.

The trick was to read her correctly, to accomplish everything she
wanted, and not to oppose her in anything. And it was a trick, because
sometimes she was so subtle she needed a translator.

I saw her move swiftly into three different roles: wife and mother to
her young children; commander-in-chief of the White House restoration; and chatelaine of the Great Hall.

THE CHANGES in the White House began on Inauguration Day, 1961.

"Please put me in the Queen's Room," Jacqueline Kennedy had told
me the week before, "and my husband will stay in the Lincoln bedroom.
We'll move into the family quarters as soon as they're done over. But I do
wish there were some way we could get the decorating finished before
the Inauguration!"

The morning of January 20, Mrs. Eisenhower read in the newspaper
that Jacqueline Kennedy would sleep in the Queen's Room.

At our breakfast meeting, she confronted me: "Who suggested that
sleeping arrangement? . . . You, I suppose!"

Mrs. Eisenhower kept the Queen's Room as a special guest room, and
you had to be a Queen to sleep there. She didn't think Mrs. Kennedy fit
that requirement.

Inauguration Day is easily the busiest day of the year for the entire

Executive Mansion staff. While the changing-of-the-guard takes place officially a mile away at the Capitol steps, it happens physically at the White House. Not only do we gear up for receiving important visitors from all over the country, sometimes with a formal reception after the Inaugural Parade, but we also must move the outgoing President's belongings out, and the incoming President's belongings in during the two hours of Inaugural activities at the Capitol. Every carpenter, plumber, electrician, engineer, doorman, butler is put to work.

The rule, of course, is that one Head of State occupies the mansion until his successor takes the oath of office. But White House tradition also has it that not one box, not one dressing table, not one book of the new President's must enter the mansion until he is duly sworn in. And we make it a point of pride to do all the moving, unpacking, hanging-up and putting-away, installing the new President in his home within those two hours of his Inaugural ceremony.

So, at noon on January 20, 1961, while President John F. Kennedy stood in front of the Capitol steps urging his fellow Americans to ". . . ask what you can do for your country . . . ," we were doing. Two sets of vans rolled down to the tradesman's entrance underneath the North Portico: One to carry what was left of the Eisenhowers' furniture to their Gettysburg farm; the other to bring in the Kennedys' clothing and personal effects.

Actually, very quietly and at the request of Mrs. Kennedy's social secretary, I had been receiving numerous boxes of toys and children's furniture from the Kennedy's Georgetown home during the two weeks prior to Inauguration. Lest anyone accuse me of breaking tradition, I stored them in the Usher's dressing room until noon, Inauguration Day, when a helicopter spirited away the last of Mamie Eisenhower's treasures, the portrait of her mother and a small electric organ.

When Mrs. Kennedy returned, exhausted, from the Inaugural Parade, I accompanied her up the stairs. Her tired eyes twinkled conspiratorially.

"I understand you and Tish Baldrige have been sneaking things into the White House under cover of night."

I laughed. "All those things now have been put in storage rooms on the third floor."

"Good. We'll bring them out as soon as the children's rooms are ready." She smiled as she stepped into the Queen's Room. "We've got a lot of work ahead, Mr. West. I want to make this into a grand house!"

To begin that work, Mrs. Henry Parish II, known to all as "Sister," arrived the very next day, with swatches of material, paint chips, closet designs. During the previous month, the New York interior designer and the new President's wife had pored over the color photographs I had sent via Secret Service to Palm Beach.

Mrs. Kennedy had done her homework well. By the time she moved in, she knew every inch of room space, every piece of furniture she would bring with her, every detail of where her family would live in the White House, and every penny of money in the federal budget to take care of the transformation.

Beginning on January 22, crews of White House painters, carpenters, and electricians worked simultaneously in the seven family rooms on the second floor of the White House. As the paint in each room dried, the same workmen hung pictures and rolled down rugs, unloaded furniture and arranged it according to the decorator's instructions.

The household staff stood awed by all the changes.

"I can't believe what they're doing," housekeeper Mabel Walker told me.

At every step, Mrs. Kennedy roamed the mansion, discovering "treasures" and removing "horrors." ("If there's anything I can't stand, it's Victorian mirrors—they're hideous. Off to the dungeons with them," she declared, laughing.)

Within the next two weeks, while the President and his wife reigned from the Queen's Room and the Lincoln suite, the "Mamie pink" of upstairs disappeared, the Grand Rapids furniture and heavy Victorian mirrors were packed away in storage. The carpenters and painters changed the dark walls to soft white, a background for the paintings, drawings, and prints from the Kennedys' private collection, and a new sophisticated blue dominated the President's living quarters.

The hotel-suite decor of Truman-renovation guest rooms made way for Caroline Kennedy's pink rosebuds, white-canopied bed and rocking horses. A wine-floral guest room became John-John's blue-and-white nursery, with white crib and playpen, and stuffed animals.

Between their bedrooms, we changed a dressing-room closet into a room for the nurse, Maude Shaw. ("She won't need much," Mrs. Kennedy whispered merrily. "Just find a wicker wastebasket for her banana peels and a little table for her false teeth at night.")

After a disastrous first-night dinner in the White House, when the Kennedys learned that the State Floor, even with its Family Dining Room, could not lend itself to the intimacy of their private entertaining, Mrs. Kennedy determined to install a dining room on the second floor.

"I want my children to be brought up in more personal surroundings, not in the State rooms," she told me. "That 'Family' Dining Room is just too cavernous." (Previous First Families had thought so, too, I told her.) Because of the location of the servants' elevator, I advised her to place the dining room across the hall from her bedroom, where she had originally wanted the nursery. In this arrangement, the children were down the hall, giving the President and his wife more privacy.

"We'll need a kitchen up here," she mused. "Do you think that could possibly be done?"

"Certainly," I said, looking at our shrinking budget. "Would you like to see some kitchen designers?"

"Heavens no," she laughed. "I couldn't care less about the kitchen! Just make it white and ask René what he wants in there."

René Verdon, the new French chef, Mrs. Parish and I designed a stainless-steel-and-white kitchen, with commercial-size ovens and refrigerators, which I ordered from a local wholesaler. Within two days it replaced the dusty-rose bedroom where President Eisenhower's mother-in-law had slept.

Hallmark of the new upstairs was Art: Gallery walls, filled with paintings and watercolors, original art in every corner: in the President's bedroom, in Mrs. Kennedy's bedroom, in the children's rooms, and in the halls.

From the Smithsonian, she "borrowed" twenty portraits of proud American Indians, painted by George Catlin. She selected the frames herself and displayed the paintings prominently on the walls of the wide center hall upstairs. And she set about to retrieve some magnificent Cézanne landscapes originally bequeathed to the White House, which President Truman had placed in the National Gallery of Art.

One morning during those first whirlwind days of redecorating, Mrs. Kennedy poked her head in my office. "Guess what?" she announced. "Mrs. Vincent Astor is presenting us with some fantastic wallpaper for the President's Dining Room, and . . ." She stopped in midsentence.

"Oh, Mr. West, you have a Grandma Moses!" she exclaimed, indicating the Fourth of July scene by the famous American painter, presented to the Trumans. President Eisenhower disliked the primitive oil painting so much that he banished it from sight, and it hung exiled on my wall.

"No, Mrs. Kennedy, you have a Grandma Moses," I replied. "It belongs to the White House."

"What a marvelous discovery—how I'd love it for Caroline's room," she said. "Would you mind terribly, Mr. West?"

We hung the colorful painting on Caroline's wall, across from another American primitive and a French Impressionist landscape.

The President's bedroom lost the murky green of the Eisenhower years, and acquired the canopied four-poster from the wine-floral guest room. For the old bed, Mrs. Kennedy ordered a special, extra-firm mattress to ease the President's back. She also ordered an identical, horsehair mattress for the President to take on trips, and another for one side of the queen-sized bed in her own bedroom.

In a note to me, she vetoed the first design for the First Lady's bedroom, the big room the Eisenhowers had shared. Although she realized the decorator was thinking of a room "severe enough for a man to share," she explained, "it is mainly my room and I do not want it too severe."

Her room was French in style, decorated in light blue chintz, accented with leopard-skin throws and good pictures—a boudoir fit to entertain a President. It was soft, relaxed, and elegant.

By the end of two weeks, we had used our entire $50,000 appropriation just to redecorate the family living quarters. Because the exterior of the mansion had been dressed in its four-year coat of white paint the previous summer, there was absolutely no money left to put grandeur into the State rooms.

"I know we're out of money, Mr. West," she said wistfully, "but never mind! We're going to find some way to get real antiques into this house."

During those first weeks, I had discovered two things about Mrs. John Fitzgerald Kennedy: her innate sense of organization and planning, and her irrepressible humor. Every day, she said something that was just plain funny.

Comic metaphors cropped up in all her notes to me, amusing me no end. She thought the bedroom curtains were "seasick green," their fringe like a "tired Christmas tree." The ground-floor hall was a "dentist's office bomb shelter," the East Room floor a "roller skating rink." Guests had to use "Pullman car ashtray stands," but the lobby, finally, was "just like De Gaulle's." When she despaired of ever being able to adjust the thermostats, she thought surely "the greatest brains of army engineering can figure out how to have this heated like a normal rattletrap house!"

For their first State function, a diplomatic reception on the afternoon of February 9, Mrs. Kennedy made three requests to liven up the State Rooms: no receiving lines, more "natural" flower arrangements, and fires in all the fireplaces.

For two days, black smoke poured from the chimneys as we checked out one fireplace after another, to test their first actual use in eight years. (Mrs. Eisenhower had installed gold-paper fans as fireplace screens, and never had fires lit in any of the rooms.) It took two days to get them all working properly. Or so we thought.

Meanwhile, Mrs. Parish and I prowled the State rooms, switching lamps, placing ashtrays, looking for likely flower bowls.

"She wants to put pictures of the children and pets around on the tables here to make it cozy," said Mrs. Parish, and laughed, as we went through the dull, imposing Green Room. We went searching—even to the National Botanical Gardens—for flowers that were not too "stilted."

Finally, the florist set out vases of tulips and wildflowers, the engineers lit the fires, and the diplomatic guests assembled in the Blue Room for cocktails and conversation.

All the ushers were dressed in formal day wear: club coat, striped trousers, gray cravats. I was determined to be excused from sight, because I had dislocated my shoulder sledding with my daughters. Just in case, though, I dressed in my "formals," and tied a black silk Navy regulation scarf around my neck for a sling. I was manning the Usher's office when a frantic call came from Bruce, a doorman on the first floor.

"Mr. West, come quick—the East Room. . . ."

I sailed down the hall to find the four East Room fireplaces belching smoke.

"Close all the doors to the room!" I ordered the doormen. "Open the windows, and bring up two big fans from the electrician's shop. Bruce, get a bucket and shovel to carry out the logs."

I stood at the fireplace, arm in black sling, directing the frantic traffic, and praying that the President and his guests would stay in the Blue Room and not call the fire department, when the door opened. Mrs. Kennedy and General Clifton, the President's military aide, stepped into the East Room. I braced myself as they walked over to the fireplace.

"Oh, Mr. West," Jacqueline Kennedy purred, "you look so glamorous—just like Zachary Taylor!" and making no mention of the commotion or smoke, she went back to her reception.

The next day I made a special trip into the Red Room to take a close look at the stern, military portrait of the twelfth President. I wondered how many fires he had put out. (Actually, I rather hoped Mrs. Kennedy meant John Tyler, the tenth President, who had posed for his portrait wearing a black scarf around his neck, and was, it seemed to me, a good bit better-looking than Zachary Taylor.) . . .

I DON'T know why she decided to go to Dallas. Politicking was certainly not something she enjoyed, and all of us were surprised that she'd step out of character and go. But then I remembered how closely she and the President had stuck together since her return from Greece—even to the point of canceling an invited houseguest to insure privacy on the second floor.

"To think that I very nearly didn't go!" she told me later. "Oh, Mr.

West, what if I'd been here—out riding at Wexford or somewhere. . . . Thank God I went with him!"

I ALWAYS seem to hear bad news via the radio. I was at home on November 22, attending to my own redecorating, when the bulletin was broadcast: The President had been shot. Within minutes, I was back in the office. By the time I arrived, he had died.

The White House staff was paralyzed. I summoned everybody, had the butlers prepare to serve coffee, had the maids prepare all the guest rooms, little meaningless gestures, but a signal that our work must go on, until the assassination was confirmed. I tried to remember what had been needed in the house for President Roosevelt's funeral, but I was numb. Then Bill Walton called.

"Mrs. Kennedy has asked me to take charge of the arrangements," he said, "and asked me to get in touch with you." I was so relieved to hear his voice. It told me that Mrs. Kennedy, even in her shock, knew what to do.

"She'd like the house to be just like it was when Lincoln lay in state," he continued.

We ran down to the Curator's office for a reference book, and Jim Ketchum found an old engraving of the East Room draped in black, and we worked from there. The President's brother-in-law Sargent Shriver came in, and helped make a list of what we needed. First of all, we had no black cloth at the White House.

I called Mr. Arata, who was doing some upholstery work for us at the time, to ask what kind of material we should use, and where could we get it at that time of night.

"I know just the thing," he said, and suggested webbing—the dark, thin material used underneath chairs to keep the springs from showing.

"But I don't have nearly enough," he said. So we phoned upholsterers until we found one who had enough material. The owner came back downtown, opened the doors, and gave us every bit of webbing in the shop.

Mr. Arata and his wife came back to the White House, and copying the 1865 engraving, they draped the webbing over the East Room chandeliers and windows. They worked all night.

Bill found the Lincoln catafalque at the Capitol, directed the florist to the magnolia tree Andrew Jackson had planted on the South Lawn, and set up the room. Two candelabra, large urns filled with magnolia leaves, and the catafalque waited starkly in the center of the East Room.

The priest also was waiting in the East Room when they arrived with the body, at about 4:30 in the morning. Nancy Tuckerman and I stood in the Blue Room, watching the military guard bring in the flag-draped coffin.

Mrs. Kennedy, with the Attorney General beside her, walked behind it. When Nancy and I saw her, still wearing her pink skirt with its vicious bloodstain, we stepped out of sight. We wanted to spare her the sight of two more grieving friends.

Robert Kennedy took the First Lady upstairs. He slept in the Lincoln Room that night, and Mr. and Mrs. Auchincloss slept in the room adjoining Mrs. Kennedy's, in the President's bed.

There was no sleeping at all for me. I took a shower, changed clothes, and went straight up to my office.

The priest arrived early, and, looking over the State floor, selected the Family Dining Room for the ten o'clock Mass. We removed the table and set up rows of straight-backed chairs for the guests. At ten, however, when Mrs. Kennedy came down, she looked into her most un-favorite of all the White House rooms, and saw her friends and family.

"Oh, no, I want it in the East Room, where Jack is," she whispered, and went back upstairs while we moved all the chairs into the East Room. She returned and the priest began intoning the Mass.

After the service, she came out to the elevator to go upstairs. I was standing in my office door.

She came over, put her arms around me, and said, "Poor Mr. West." I couldn't speak. It was all I could do to stand. I just held her for a moment.

"I want you to take me over to look at the President's office," she said.

"I'll come up for you whenever you're ready," I said.

"Oh no, I'll stop by your office," she whispered.

About twenty minutes later, she came down alone, and we walked over to the west wing. Down the same colonnade she had wanted to enclose so the President wouldn't catch cold. Past the swimming-pool door. Past the Cabinet Room.

But she never got to see the effect of the room she and Boudin had worked so carefully to perfect, for already President Kennedy's office was being dismantled. Movers were carting away books, packing up model ships, carrying out the rocking chair. The President's secretary, Evelyn Lincoln, stood bewildered in the middle of the room.

Without the soft brown wood of his furniture, the new crimson carpet seemed blatant.

"It must have been a grand office," she murmured.

"It was very nice," I managed to say.

As the moving men stood self-consciously by, Evelyn Lincoln said, "Oh, Mrs. Kennedy . . . ," and fled from the office.

"I think we're probably in the way," Mrs. Kennedy whispered, and she looked around uncertainly. Suddenly I remembered that first day she had come to the White House and, like today, how unprotected she had seemed.

Her eyes were like saucers, memorizing the Oval Office—the walls, the desk we had found in the basement, the small pictures of Caroline and John—then she walked out of John F. Kennedy's office for the last time.

We went into the Cabinet Room and sat down at the long mahogany table. She searched my face, as if she might find the truth there.

"My children," she said. "They're good children, aren't they, Mr. West?"

It was a question, not a declaration.

"They certainly are," I said.

We looked out over the sand-pile, the holly-encircled trampoline, the treehouse.

"They're not spoiled?"

"No, indeed."

She stared into my face.

"Mr. West, will you be my friend for life?" she whispered.

I could not make a sound. I only nodded.

ROBERT KENNEDY stayed in the Lincoln Room all that week, the Auchinclosses stayed only one night, and the Radziwills moved in with Mrs. Kennedy. Lee Radziwill slept in a bed in Jacqueline Kennedy's bedroom; her husband slept in the President's bed.

I slept on a couch in the Usher's office.

Sunday morning, the day the body was transferred to the Capitol, Mrs. Kennedy called down, "Mr. West, could you find me a mourning veil?"

"I thought Provy had found one for you," I replied. I knew that "veil" had been checked off my list.

"What she brought was a black lace mantilla, which is all right for today. But for the funeral tomorrow, I want a regular mourning veil like Mrs. Dulles wore."

I called every funeral parlor in town. "Very few people call for them any more," said one director in his apologetic, funereal voice.

Finally we had Lucinda make a black veil. It was, of course, correct.

On the morning of President Kennedy's funeral, Mrs. Kennedy called Jim Ketchum, the Curator, and asked him to perform a very special task. "While we are at the Capitol," she instructed him, "will you please get someone to help you, go up to the Yellow Oval Room, and remove the Cézannes from the wall. In their place, hang the Bennet and Cartwright prints [American aquatints, circa 1810]—and I'll tell you why. . . ."

He was astonished that she wanted the paintings removed—her "glorious" Cézannes, which she'd worked so hard to bring back into the White House, and which hung so prominently in her favorite room.

"This afternoon I'm going to be receiving President De Gaulle in this room," she explained to Jim, "and I want him to be aware of the heritage of the United States, and these are scenes from our own history." So Jim and Bonner Arrington, the carpenter, followed her wishes, and placed a strong stamp of America—prints of Washington, Baltimore and Philadelphia—in the room where the President's widow would receive.

When the procession came back in cars from the Capitol, we had lined up all the guests in the White House: All the visiting Heads of State were in the East Room; the Kennedy relatives in the Green Room; White House staff in the State Dining Room; and Congress in the Blue Room.

Mrs. Kennedy got out of the limousine at the White House, and all those waiting inside joined the procession behind her by order of rank, and walked behind the body to St. Matthew's Cathedral. After the ceremony at Arlington, she returned to the White House. Then she went upstairs to the Yellow Oval Room to receive, one at a time, President De Gaulle, Prince Philip of England, Emperor Haile Selassie of Ethiopia, and Ireland's President Eamon De Valera. Afterwards, she stood in the Red Room and received all the other visiting Heads of State.

Following this, exhausted, she turned to me with only one question.

"Mr. West, did you see whether President Johnson walked or not?"

"Yes, Ma'am," I said, "I saw both the President and Mrs. Johnson."

"The Secret Service didn't want them to," she smiled wanly.

ROBERT KENNEDY still stayed at the White House, as did I.

Every night until she moved out of the White House, Mrs. Kennedy and the Attorney General went to the President's graveside to pray.

On Wednesday, Mrs. Kennedy and the children flew to Hyannis for Thanksgiving, and I went home, for the first time in six days.

But I couldn't stay. We were fixing up the East Room for the month-long period of mourning, and although I had left instructions on how to do the room, I began worrying about it.

After dinner, I looked at Zella and, though I was about to drop, said, "I have to go back."

"I'm going with you," she said firmly.

As we walked into the East Room, Zella gasped, "Oh my God!"

Lying stretched out on the catafalque in the center of the room was Bonner Arrington, the carpenter. Wearing overalls, arms folded across his chest, eyes closed, he clasped a dead lily in his hand. At first, I was shaken with horror. Then I started laughing, and Zella started laughing, and the week of tension collapsed inside us, as tears of relief flooded my cheeks.

The White House would survive. . . .

WE MOVED Mrs. Kennedy into Averell Harriman's house in George-town (the Harrimans moved into a hotel), where she stayed until she bought the house across the street. The next week, she invited Nancy and me for dinner at the Harrimans'.

She met us at the door, and I kissed her.

"Oh, Mr. West, you never kissed me when I lived at the White House," she whispered. I started to laugh, and she stepped back, narrowing her eyes wickedly.

"Did you ever kiss Mamie?"

"All the time," I answered.

Mrs. Kennedy came back to Washington for the reburial of her husband, after his permanent gravesite had been finished. She stayed with Mrs. Mellon, who called to invite me to the service.

It was 7:00 a.m., and pouring rain, when I joined Mrs. Kennedy and her family at Arlington.

She greeted me warmly, then looked over her shoulder. "Oh, Mr. West, you'd better hide. Here comes President Johnson."

But, of course, I didn't have to hide. I was running the White House for the thirty-sixth President of the United States.

The Outrageous Memoirs of the Presidential Kennel Keeper

Dog Days at the White House   (1975)
(written with Frances Spatz Leighton)

This is not a typical Washington book—nor is it for everyone. It's not a picture of the glamorous life at the White House, but rather an irreverent, chatty, and "outrageous" (it's part of the subtitle, so I don't feel bad about using the word) behind-the-scenes book, this time from the perspective of the doghouse. Dogs appear in many books about Washington, but not usually as the leading characters.

Traphes Bryant went to work at the White House in 1951 as an electrician, but quite early on he was given extra duties looking out for the family pets. Over the next several years and administrations, he became the unofficial presidential kennel keeper, then the official one under the Kennedys. Mr. Bryant seems to have had not only dog lovers but "White House watchers" in mind as he wrote this book. He got help in the writing from that professional coauthor Frances Spatz Leighton, who helped write several Washington books, including Drunk Before Noon (The Behind-the-Scenes Story of the Washington Press Corps), *with Ken Hoyt, and, of course,* My Thirty Years Backstairs at the White House, *with Lillian Parks.*

Bryant's book is full of fun and at times has an almost naughty quality to it. However, it's also full of insight and perception, and tells us not a little about the presidents for whom Bryant worked, and their wives and families—again, the backstairs things. For example, of the Trumans he writes, "The Trumans were such a close family that they treated each other as pets." Bryant and Leighton also remark that the White House can be such a lonely place that "some presidential couples have given most of their affection to their pets," citing the Hardings as examples: "At times President Warren Harding showed much more affection toward his dog than he did toward his wife, with whom he was frequently feuding. That overindulged dog was Laddie Boy, an arrogant Airedale who had his own social calendar and his own chair to sit on at cabinet meetings." More personally, Bryant writes of one president who "almost took a poke at me because he thought I was getting too chummy with his wife. I was only getting chummy with his dog."

For someone without a dog of his own—he wrote that he was "still in the recovery room after years of taking care of presidential dogs . . . jumpers and bumpers and biters and kissers"—Bryant seems to have understood both dogs and presidents. He wrote that what the latter (from Kennedy to Johnson to Nixon) liked best "was the way I trained the dogs to meet the presidential helicopter, no matter what time of the day or night it arrived."

I well remember the last time I saw President Kennedy. Just before he went on that fateful Dallas trip in November 1963, he called to me as he was coming out of the White House gym, wearing a bathrobe. I was walking with Wolf, the Irish wolfhound. JFK told me that Charlie had snapped at Caroline in his office. He looked worried. That was the last time I heard his voice. Two days later he was dead.

I thought I could never feel emotion about a President again, never laugh with one, never feel close to one. Surely never feel any particular friendship. How wrong I was.

The days of transition from Kennedy to Johnson were as hard on me as they were on anyone else—harder. I was losing a dog and gaining a President I didn't know. Not only didn't I know him, I didn't think I wanted to know him.

He wasn't boyish or good-natured or quick-witted like Kennedy and I heard him cussing out the help when things weren't done fast enough. He was a perfectionist, and from the beginning lights were on at all hours in the presidential office.

At first everything reminded me of Kennedy. A month after the President's assassination, Frank Sinatra's son, Frank, Jr., was kidnapped from a gambling resort at Lake Tahoe, Nevada. The singer paid almost a quarter of a million dollars for his boy's release. Frank at one time had been a good friend of the Kennedys.

But as the weeks rolled by I began to realize that everything that had been associated with the Kennedys was now out. Sinatra and his "Rat Pack" clique of friends were out.

The New Frontier was out, the Great Society was in.

Terriers were out and beagles were in.

Jackie pink was out, Lady Bird yellow was in.

Chowder was out and chili was in.

The Georgetown crowd was out; Perle Mesta and Scooter Miller, an old friend of Lady Bird's, were in.

Toddlers were out and teenagers were in. Not only that, but collecting ordinary dolls, as Caroline had done, was out. Now you had to collect historic dolls; Lynda Bird had several that were a couple of hundred years old.

French was out and the Spanish language was in. So were all the Spanish-speaking embassies, especially Mexico's.

Johnson had a different set of showbiz buddies—Carol Channing and Hugh O'Brian were his favorites. Eventually, in about a year, we had a Hollywood character in on-and-off residence—the teenagers' idol, George Hamilton.

I was aware LBJ was less than thrilled about "Georgie boy," as he called him, and I liked the Prez for that. Hamilton was so slicked down and shiny he looked unreal. LBJ said it first, muttering to me one time as he saw George coming through the gates, "Christ, he looks like he was put together by a ladies' club committee."

It had taken me a while to discover that the President did have a sense of humor—a bit rough, but all his own. As he got used to me, more and more he seemed to relax by ribbing me. Here's a typical diary entry:

3/10/65 I washed Blanco and Him. Him chewed a six-inch length of rug in President's office. The Prez returned by helicopter at 9:15 p.m. The Prez said he would send me a bill for damage. I think he was kidding. The Prez took Him to the second floor for few minutes to keep him company on an errand. The Prez sure loves Him.

The President loved all dogs that wore his brand, even Blanco, that beautiful but dumb rare white collie who was so inbred, he hardly knew his paw from his tail.

A few days later I added another note in my diary:

3/14/65 Him chewed the same strip of President's rug. Now two feet.

The rug was getting ratty-looking. This time the President said, "Mr. Bryant, I'm starting to keep books on all this destruction. At the end of the year we're going to have to settle up." And again he took Him along with him to the second-floor family quarters just as if Him had been an angel and not a devil.

He said over his shoulder, "I'm getting you a set of weaving instructions."

It went on for days. I tried to avoid trouble by keeping the dogs away from their master, but according to my diary:

> 3/23/65 The President saw me in the West Lobby with the dogs. In a hurt voice, he wanted to know why I didn't bring them to his office. The dogs and I trailed along with the President. We went to Marvin Watson's office, then to the Press Information Office, then the President's Oval Office. He told me to bring a leash for Blanco and to get two bones from the White House kitchen. He gave the bones to the dogs. The dogs stayed in his office for two hours. I was called back to get them and the President told me to look at Him. He was almost asleep on the divan. The President started ribbing me and asked me about the rug that looked all chewed up. A TV reporter was with the President. I said it was probably done by the TV people during his telephone call to the two-man space ship. The President told me that I knew better than that. He obviously wanted the reporter to hear it from me. So I told the President Him had chewed on the rug—as if he didn't know.

I guess that's what started our friendship. Any man who felt about dogs the way he did would have won me over. And he didn't limit his enthusiasm just to dogs. When he drove around his ranch, an old buck deer he called George would sidle up to the car and he would feed him through the window. He'd carry goodies in his pockets for everyone— candy for kids, lapel pins for men, Unipets (flavored vitamin treats) for dogs, sugar cubes for horses, deer, and mules.

President Johnson was the greatest pet lover I have ever known—and possibly the greatest pet lover of all our Presidents. True, George Washington pampered his horses, President Jefferson trained a mockingbird to sit on his shoulder while he worked, and also to meow like a cat, and President Harding taught his dog to sit on a chair and attend Cabinet meetings.

But they were pikers compared with President Johnson. Animals for LBJ were a way of life, sometimes an exotic one. While he was Vice President, Lyndon had a dog named Old Beagle. When Old Beagle died, LBJ had him cremated and kept the ashes in a box over the refrigerator.

He felt so strongly about Old Beagle's passing, he couldn't bring himself just to throw the ashes out. Emotions were a familiar staple at the White House during his administration—everyone around him was entitled to express them, even the cook.

And so when Zephyr Wright, the family cook, found out what was in that small box on the shelf above the refrigerator, she blew a fuse. "Get that damn dog out of here," she said, and Old Beagle was laid to rest in a corner of the family burial plot at the ranch.

I don't think the President ever got over the death of any of his dogs. When Her died from eating a stone, I made a notation in my records: Her died after surgery—November 27, 1964.

As soon as the story hit the newspapers, more than three hundred offers of beagle dogs and puppies came rolling in. All were turned down with thanks. But one lonely beagle arrived anyway at National Airport, a cute brown and white female whose owner in Rushyule, Nebraska, hadn't gotten his rejection in time. Liz Carpenter thought the man was just making an offer, like everyone else, until she heard the dog was about to arrive at the airport and would be awaiting instructions.

So the pup got royal treatment, a ride in a White House chauffeur-driven limousine. But instead of bringing it to the White House where LBJ might have become emotionally involved, the chauffeur whisked it to Fort Myer where it was fed and pampered, then sent back from whence it came.

LBJ was touched and sent the man—E. D. Hollstein—a picture of himself holding Him and Her with the inscription "From one dog lover to another."

Some dog lovers will want to know exactly how a dog came to be eating stones at the White House.

What happened was that while I was away on vacation, usher Rex Scouten had the Capital Parks people put a small fenced runway area for dogs below the tennis courts on the South Lawn. They dumped some rocks and trash in there to keep the dogs' feet from getting muddy. If they had used fine gravel, a dog could have swallowed it, but these bigger stones were trouble for Her, who must have started playing with one out of curiosity or boredom.

Her was rushed to Fort Myer, which had good veterinary facilities. Dr. Ralph Chadwick operated and told me all about it. He said Her had survived the operation. After resting a bit, she had gotten up, walked a few steps, and fallen down. She died a short time later.

The news was almost more than LBJ could stand to hear. I felt miserable about it. Luci did too, and took to her bed with a cold, which I was sure was partially emotional—because Luci loved Her very much.

The President and I took Him, the surviving beagle, and Blanco to visit Luci. Him jumped on the bed and whimpered a little. LBJ, never one to keep things bottled up, came right out and asked Luci if she thought the dogs were suffering because they missed Her.

"Yes," Luci answered sadly, the tears starting to fill her eyes.

As the President and I walked back down the hall, trying to ease the pain, trying to lay the blame somewhere, anywhere, he burst out at me, "Damn it, why didn't you take better care of Her? Why did you let it happen?"

I was stunned. "Mr. President," I said, "I was on vacation when the dog died."

He went on as if he hadn't heard me. "You should have taken better care of Her!" I had to get away. I said, "Come on, Blanco! Come here, Him." I got into the elevator with the dogs, went down to the ground floor, and walked to the White House kennel, where I could control my emotions.

After that, I campaigned to have the dog facilities at the White House improved. I wanted the runway put elsewhere, near the President's office, and favored moving the dogs from the Bouquet Room to their own quarters. Eventually a proper doghouse was built with a Dutch door so the President could bring dignitaries around for a look, open the top gate, and reach in to pet the dogs without their getting loose.

Not everyone at the White House was as enthusiastic as the President and I were to see the dogs romping about. John Pustka, the man who took care of the dogs on the morning shift until I arrived after lunch, hated to chase dogs. He had diabetes and I think it made him a little bit cranky. Once the President asked John to let the dogs out, and then a few minutes later told him, "Go round them up and bring them back."

John glared at the President and snapped, "You turned them loose, you go get them yourself!" The President was so shocked he said nothing. Not at the time, nor later, or Pustka would have been transferred away from the White House immediately. The only way I found out myself was that Pustka told me.

As soon as I could, I casually mentioned to the President that John had diabetes. The President looked at me and just nodded.

President Johnson generously understood Mr. Pustka, but it is true that he could be vindictive over little things. Once without much notice he visited an air base at Harlingen, Texas. When his plane landed, he was met by a hearse instead of a limousine. Everything had happened so fast that the townspeople had not come up with a limousine in time. I can't myself believe they did it as a joke, but LBJ was so furious, according to the story that made the rounds, that he closed the air base, using a more acceptable reason for publication, of course—economy. Years later I visited Harlingen and it was still the talk of the town.

That was one of the other sides of the dog lover.

THE JOHNSONS arrived at the White House with just two dogs, the beagles Him and Her. Luci drove them over herself from The Elms, the vice presidential home that had once belonged to LBJ's friend Perle Mesta, the "hostess with the mostess."

The collie Blanco was soon added—a gift from a little girl in Illinois, as I recall. LBJ loved gifts, especially unusual gifts, as much as the next man. But he could see a problem coming up, because the sight of a President with two beagles gave everyone the idea of offering him still another pet.

So LBJ announced that his white collie would be symbolic of all the wonderful dogs he had been offered by Americans everywhere. All other dogs would be returned to their senders.

This was a statesmanlike decision, but the White House was always awash with dogs, anyway. The beagles had litters of puppies, for one thing, and even the ones that were given away tended to keep returning until they made the White House into a dog motel.

Lyndon made angry sounds about it but the truth was he loved them all. Even Blanco, the overbred collie who turned out to be practically a eunuch. But he didn't really love another dog as much as he'd loved Old Beagle until one afternoon toward the end of his days in the White House Luci brought a little mutt named Yuki into his life. Touchingly it was Yuki, not a human being, who was with him when he died.

I know Yuki, who is still in retirement at the ranch, commuting between there and Luci's home in Austin, must still be grieving for the President. They were inseparable at the White House, and afterward.

I remember President Johnson one time personally opening the door to the main ground-floor kitchen because Yuki wanted to go in. Frankie Blair, a clean-up man, didn't realize what was going on and chased Yuki out. President Johnson then went into the kitchen and asked Frankie, "Has Yuki eaten his dinner?"

Frankie said, "Yes, Mr. President."

President Johnson said, "Well, Yuki says he hasn't eaten. Are you trying to call my dog a liar?"

I HATED to see LBJ lose his popularity, going from cock of the walk to bottom of the barnyard well. Strangely enough, the decline had begun with his beagles, Him and Her, in an incident that ended the new President's honeymoon with the press and with a lot of the dog-loving public. He'd been hailed for his tax cuts, great new civil rights legislation, and countless other achievements. He'd even settled a railroad strike and gotten the Chamber of Commerce on his side.

And then in a flash everything changed. Or as one reporter—Mary McGrory—put it, "A yelp ended a winning streak."

The incident I'm talking about was the ear-pulling, and many people asked me about it. "You're the dog-keeper, why didn't you stop him?" they'd wonder. As long as I was at the White House, I kept still. I figured LBJ had $30,000-a-year advisors to tell him what he should or shouldn't do if he cared about his image.

But that's all over now—LBJ is gone, I'm retired, and I can finally say what I had the bad luck to see. Yes, I was there the day the President picked up his little beagle Him by the ears. I cringed to hear the dog yelping. It all happened April 27, 1964, at C-9 Post, right outside the President's office. He had been meeting there with some balance of payments experts, and as a relief from financial talk, he took them for a walk around the yard. A swarm of reporters and photographers followed, as usual.

What the President was trying to do was please the photographers by getting the dogs to do a trick. Lyndon Johnson was such a tall man he had to bend way over even to get near a beagle. So he was bending over and just took hold of Him by the most convenient handle, his ears, probably thinking of some Texas story about a farmer lifting his dog that way. Even when he heard the yelps, the President didn't seem to realize that anything was wrong. He just matter-of-factly explained that pulling their ears was good for the dogs, and that everyone who knew dogs liked to hear them yelp.

What the President didn't remember, or know, is that you can only try this lift-'em-by-the-ears trick with a puppy. Old-time farmers and hunters start to pick up a pup by the ears and if it yelps, they stop and pick up one that doesn't. Puppies are light, but grown dogs have more weight than their ears can comfortably support.

Even as the episode unfolded—with the dog yelping and the flash bulbs popping—I knew the fat was in the fire. Or to quote a favorite expression of Lyndon's, "the ox was in the ditch," and it was going to make news. I had just gotten some good stories in the papers about the presidential dogs, and now this! I felt sorry for both the President and the dog. . . .

After LBJ's goof, the White House was flooded with mail. Some defended the President; most condemned him. Reporters around the world were going to dog experts to poll their opinion on beagle ear-pulling. Veterinarians were anti-President on the matter. So were the National Beagle Club, the American Kennel Club, and the American Society for the Prevention of Cruelty to Animals.

But Bernard Workman, the chairman of the Canine Defense League in London, defended him. A clipping quoted him as saying, "I don't believe that a beagle comes to any harm by picking it up by the ears. Their ears are particularly strong."

When I showed it to the President he still didn't ask me, his dog-keeper, whether I thought he'd done right, which was a tipoff to me he really knew it had been a mistake. And since he didn't ask, I didn't volunteer. I just listened as he defended himself some more. "You know, Bryant, it's good for these dogs to bark. They have things too soft around here; they've got to exercise those lungs in case I take them hunting. Where else does a dog get such treatment as I give them? They lead a better life than I do. Hell, they even have their teeth cleaned for them."

I said, "Why don't you call a press conference and tell the reporters?"

"Oh, hell," he said, "I can't teach those guys anything. Half of them don't know their ass from their elbow. They're too ignorant. You can't teach anything to a shut mind. But I never thought a dog would do me in."

Then he got his second wind and decided to use the incident to his own advantage. "The only thing that saves my sanity is humor," he had told me. So I wasn't surprised that when he spoke to a group of Jewish clothing workers in New York City, he said, "I've been warned that you are mad at me because I pulled the ears of a bagel." He came back beaming and said, "They loved it. I went from beagle to bagel and let the bagel share the blame."

Now it can be told that the much-publicized April 27 ear-pulling wasn't the only time he pulled the dogs' ears. A few days later he went to the trouble of showing some tourists how he had lifted his dog by the ears, and again Him yelped. A tourist laughed and called out, "That was off the record." . . .

To the end of his term he still persisted in pulling the dogs' ears just to prove they really "liked it." The Prez hated to be wrong.

Never Send to Know for Whom the Wedding Bell Tolls

Ruffles and Flourishes (1970)

Liz Carpenter is one of the funniest people I know. She makes me laugh every time I'm with her. And she's not only funny, she's smart. This memoir of her years in the White House tells some part of her story. The book is subtitled "The warm and tender story of a simple girl who found adventure in the White House," and reading it is every bit like sitting down to a friendly chat with her.

Liz first came to Washington as a young cub reporter in 1942. It was, as she writes, "simply a matter of love at first sight." On her first arrival in the city, on the drive from the airport, she stopped the car by the Lincoln Memorial and raced up the steps: "The Lincoln Memorial is a temple, even more beautiful in the shadowed blue lights of the war. I defy anyone to stand there without a prayer."

While working for a news service in the early 1940s, she, along with all the other women, wore hats to Eleanor Roosevelt's press conferences and often carried white gloves. She got to know Lady Bird Johnson in those war years, because Liz had come from the congressional district in Texas represented by Lyndon Baines Johnson. Naturally, soon after her arrival here she called on her two senators and her congressman. Because Representative Johnson was then in the South Pacific, Lady Bird was running his office. Liz told me that that's when Lady Bird really came to respect the word "constituent."

In any case, Constituent Liz soon became friends with Lady Bird and therefore was known to Congressman and later Senator Johnson. When LBJ was selected by JFK as his running mate, Johnson called Liz right away and snapped her up. As Liz told me later, he said, "Lady Bird and I want you to take off and share the great adventure of our lives." So off she went.

So Liz then went to the White House as executive vice press secretary for Vice President Johnson, and then, when he became president, as press

secretary and staff director to the first lady. When people asked Liz to
clarify that title, she said, "I help her help him."

Liz loves Washington, and this book is evidence of that. She loved her
time at the White House, when she was living "with every wit chal-
lenged." I saw her in Texas soon after the Anita Hill / Clarence Thomas
hearings, and she told me, "I nearly died that I wasn't there sitting in
the front row. . . .That's when I miss Washington—when the conversa-
tion at the press table is fabulous and when one's heart is beating fast."

M ARRIAGES are not made in heaven. During my years at the
White House they were put together by a Social Secretary, a
Press Secretary, months of hard labor—and, as we discovered,
it best be Union labor!

The day Luci Baines Johnson married Patrick John Nugent of
Waukegan, Illinois—on August 6, 1966—and the day Lynda Bird Johnson married Captain Charles Spittal Robb of the U.S. Marine Corps—
on December 9, 1967—climaxed some of the most exhausting,
nerve-racking months of my life. I am glad they lived happily ever after. I
managed to live through them—but that is all I can say.

The problem of surviving was intensified because we still had business as usual on other East Wing activities, while trying to plan the wedding and satisfy the insatiable appetite of the press for wedding details.

There were still trips, receptions, State visits and correspondence.
During the week of Luci's wedding, the crescendo of activity was heightened by a State visit from the President of Israel. While the pastry chef,
Ferdinand Louvat, was putting the final touches on the five-foot wedding
cake, he was also making the strawberry bombe for the 186 guests at the
State dinner. And in the flower room, Elmer Young and James Nelson
were arranging facsimile bouquets for the rehearsal for twelve bridesmaids with one hand and with the other, eighteen centerpieces for the
State dinner.

The problem is—all the world does love a lover. And until Luci, then
a brunette sprite of nineteen, became engaged, there hadn't been a
White House bride for fifty years. Instantly every hard-bitten reporter
became a syrupy armchair cupid. Every would-be Washington hostess
wanted to entertain the bride. Every commercial firm wanted to supply
the necessary ingredients, from flowers to cake to blue satin garters.

There was, as I predicted shortly after the announcement, summertime rioting in the East Wing among five hundred news-hungry
reporters who wanted every morsel of information about the wedding,

which I kept trying to convince them was to be "a private family event." (I learned quickly not to say "affair.")

The world will remember the Johnson brides as two pretty girls walking down the aisle on the arm of their father, the President of the United States.

I remember the weddings as crises-on-crises. Once, Richard Nixon had campaigned on his experience—"The Six Crises of Richard Nixon." I always wondered how he could possibly feel he was qualified with only six. I had 6666 just working on weddings.

The reporters who came to cover the Nugent-Johnson wedding from the groom's hometown must have felt as I did. After the ceremony, they dispatched a wire to the "next" White House daughter, Lynda, saying, FOR GOD'S SAKE, DON'T MARRY A BOY FROM WAUKEGAN, ILLINOIS. Signed, SEVERAL WAUKEGAN REPORTERS. But we saw them again on the second round when Lynda's husband was from Milwaukee. She didn't marry a Waukegan boy, but she did pick one in the same greater Chicago circulation area.

My crises are the untold stories of the weddings. It is only now that I can laugh at them.

CRISIS NUMBER I: 'TWAS THE NIGHT BEFORE CHRISTMAS

The whole problem started with a call to my Washington home from Luci and her mother, who were at the ranch in Texas.

"Guess what?" said the breathless Luci. "Patrick has given me an engagement ring, and we want to announce it right away."

"Now?" I replied, looking at the clock which said 11:30 p.m., Christmas Eve.

"Well, we are going to Midnight Mass in Stonewall soon. There may be reporters there. I'm not going to take off my ring. And I don't want the story to leak. I want to announce it like any other girl."

This seemed like a reasonable request.

I concocted a brief announcement "like any other girl would have" whose father didn't happen to be President of the United States: "The President and Mrs. Lyndon Baines Johnson tonight announced the engagement of their daughter, Luci Baines, to Patrick John Nugent of Waukegan, Illinois. A late summer wedding is planned. Mr. Nugent's gift to Miss Johnson was a white gold engagement ring with three diamonds—a large center diamond and two smaller baguette diamonds on either side. Before placing the ring on Luci's finger, Mr. Nugent showed it to the President and received his approval to present it."

It was now nearing midnight and I knew that the White House press would be celebrating the Eve of this religious holiday in a non-religious manner. They operated out of a press room in Austin, Texas, during holidays when the LBJs went home to the ranch.

With announcement in hand, I telephoned Joe Laitin, an assistant to Bill Moyers, then the President's press secretary. Joe was dining with a large group of reporters, including Helen Thomas of LIPI, one of the most romantic-minded newswomen in the entire world. In fact, Helen had scored the beat on Luci's becoming a Catholic, and was determined she would have the story of Luci's engagement. She had written periodic rumor stories over the past weeks, much to the annoyance of LBJ who kept reading the news before Pat had even asked for his daughter's hand.

"I need to talk to you, Joe. Can you talk?" I asked.

Joe, an old-time Hollywood reporter who had gone straight—and into government—caught on immediately. "I'll phone you back."

With Helen Thomas eavesdropping, he decided it was best to find another phone. He went across the street, found a pay phone in an old deserted warehouse and called me.

I told him the big news, and Luci's desire for a midnight announcement, and asked him to call the press together then and inform them. This seemed to be the quickest way to get it done, and also the way to be fair to all reporters spending their holidays and their newspapers' money covering LBJ in Texas.

"Look, Liz," argued Joe who was totally unmoved by the glad tidings. "I wish this story could wait until morning. In the first place, it's going to be hard to lay our hands on all the reporters at this hour, particularly those being laid. For another thing, there are so many rumors going around about a cease-fire in Vietnam that a press call will make them think something is under way."

"Tell them it's a tryst, not a truce!" I demanded and continued to dictate the release. When I got to the "baguette" diamonds, I had to spell that word three times.

Suddenly both of us were convulsed with the humor of the situation.

Neither of us in all our days of journalism ever foresaw that our jobs would lead us to a Christmas Eve midnight announcement of the first White House wedding in fifty years. But the announcement was only the beginning, and Luci's story was page one on Christmas Day.

CRISIS NUMBER 2: BEWARE OF GIFTS

Soon after the announcement, it became apparent that we needed to set some rules to discourage gifts for the bride. Phone calls from foreign embassies wanting "advice" on what their Heads of State should give, letters from commercial firms wanting to bestow a whole electric kitchen on the bride and then advertise it, and an array of sweet hand-crocheted doilies—made by sweet little ladies with romantic hearts—began coming in by the dozens.

Bess Abell, the social secretary, and I were getting most of the heat in letters and phone calls; and we needed guidelines, what could be accepted and what couldn't. The press seemed to envision Kings and Queens arriving for the nuptials preceded by footmen bearing golden chalices and jewel-encrusted wedding plates. Part of the reason was the published reports of Alice Roosevelt's gifts when she married Nicholas Longworth in 1906.

I called Mrs. Longworth for advice. There was a credibility gap for you. "I only wish I'd gotten all those things they said I got," she said tartly.

We corralled Clark Clifford, prominent Washington attorney and a friend of the Johnson family, and went into a series of summit meetings that produced the guidelines which I was to discreetly leak to a "trustworthy source."

The Chief of Protocol was to discourage foreign governments from giving gifts and to advise their governments that it was a family, not a State, event. (There went that word "affair" again.) No gifts or visits were expected.

Gifts from strangers which had intrinsic value would be returned with a polite note. Gifts from close friends would be accepted. All gifts from commercial firms would be returned. The doilies and potholders made by little old ladies would be accepted and answered personally. (Mrs. Johnson had a weakness for not hurting any of the little ladies.)

Crisis Number 3: My War with *Women's Wear Daily*

Press interest began building to a crescendo! Hard as we tried to keep from saturating newspapers with advance stories, there was frenzy among wedding-minded reporters at the White House, long before the wedding date.

Magazines wanted layouts in January for their June bridal issues. Why couldn't Luci dash out, select her china and silver and wedding dress to suit their deadlines? This way they could carry the pictures of the bride in her gown in their June issues.

Even the *New York Times* chose to remind me of the important fashion news the wedding provided. Charlotte Curtis, women's editor, wrote me two months before the wedding: "I do hope you know we can hardly wait to report who designed all the clothes and what they will look like. This is a major fashion event, as well as a social event of the most historic sort."

Not to be outdone, I wrote her back a sarcastic note: "Isn't it funny?

All this time I've been thinking of Luci's wedding, not as a major fashion event, but a major romantic event. Oh well, it just goes to show how corny you can get here in the provinces."

Networks wanted to televise the whole thing. Even without consulting us, they made surveys of the National Shrine of the Immaculate Conception, the church Luci selected for the wedding, to check camera positions and lighting.

Reporters tried to interview bridesmaids, potential bridesmaids, groomsmen and the best man—and their families—and members of the clergy.

Speculation on all wedding clothes was the daily fare of the fashion houses in New York. And *Women's Wear Daily*, with its network of informants, both good and bad, could have given a few tips to the CIA.

Luci began to wonder whose wedding it was. While she had always been sympathetic to my problem of satisfying press needs, there were just some things a girl believes she should call her own. Being a traditionalist, young and the most sentimental of brides, she wanted to keep her wedding gown a secret from her groom. And I was determined to defend her right to observe the old admonition that a groom must not see his bride's gown until the wedding day.

Meanwhile the newspaper girls were demanding to know when they would know details.

Monsignor Thomas J. Grady, director of the National Shrine of the Immaculate Conception, called in amazement to say that Isabelle Shelton, one of the most able and knowledgeable reporters for the *Washington Star*, had invaded the Shrine, scene of the wedding, armed with a pad and pencil and hundreds of questions on the wedding plans.

"I think," the Monsignor said to me placidly, "you should design the wedding dress with a large hoop skirt so that Mrs. Shelton can run down the aisle under it making notes all the way." I adored the Monsignor—if that's permissible. He had the problems and the patience of Job. If we had let Isabelle run down the aisle as the Monsignor jokingly suggested, she might not have been alone. We also had a request from a German newspaper correspondent who wanted to interview the President during the wedding march. I wrote a memo to Bob Fleming, the President's assistant press secretary: "Gladly do I pass along this request. Now I have heard everything. He wants to interview him walking down the aisle." The request was not granted.

Obviously, order had to be brought into this free-for-all. Bess Abell was coordinating the bridal party's clothes, and so I worked out a press release schedule in conjunction with the clothes delivery dates. At the press's request, we put a penalty on anyone breaking the release date: no pass to the wedding area. This, the press said, would stop the bootleg reporting.

On June 20, I summoned the reporters together and put out the release schedule in an effort to say, "Relax girls, you're going to be treated fairly." It read in part as follows:

NOT FOR PUBLICATION
FOR GUIDELINE PURPOSES ONLY

In answer to inquiries and to accommodate your summer planning, the following dates are earmarked for stories in connection with the wedding of Luci Baines Johnson and Patrick John Nugent.

July 17, Sunday: Bridesmaids' dresses and flowers. (Sketches and detailed descriptions will be available on Wednesday, July 13 to accommodate Sunday layouts.) Any publication breaking the release date on either the sketch or the description will automatically be excluded from working press area and denied credentials for wedding coverage.

The action brought instant relief to my assistants who had been performing like switchboard operators on twenty-four-hour duty. It brought instant irritation to *Women's Wear Daily*. Most of the press were happy. They could begin to see the light at the end of the tunnel. And no one would be scooped in the interim.

Women's Wear Daily was off like a tiger in heat, stalking the clothing houses of the East Coast in search of the scoop on style, color, designer and price. They purposely skipped my July 13 press conference when I gave advance details of the bridesmaids' dresses for July 17 release—and, according to their code of ethics, thus freed themselves from my promise to ban any violators from the wedding. And possibly, guillotine them on the Mall!

That night several newswomen who were covering the story—and staying with the rules—phoned to tell me that they had been called by *Women's Wear Daily* to glean the details. Small surprise that *Women's Wear Daily* came out with a near description two days before the story was scheduled for release.

Hell hath no fury like a press secretary scorned! To my mind, a hold-for-release is a hold-for-release, whether or not the reporter is in attendance. I banned them from the wedding—publicly spanking them and stating there was no reason to throw chaos into Sunday newspaper layouts all over the country because of the "unethical behavior of one small publication."

The war had begun! The battle lines were drawn.

Women's Wear Daily editor Jim Brady, who must be descended from early shareholders in Western Union, started sending voluminous telegrams blasting me and the White House, and graciously made copies of his messages available to the wire service and networks.

Women's Wear Daily even quizzed the President about the decision to exclude their reporters.

Some newspapers, eagerly looking for copy to break the summertime pace, jumped on me. The *Washington Post* worried that I had "bridal jitters."

Bless the President, the First Lady and Luci! They never uttered one word to me, despite the furor, and simply left the matter to my judgment.

Much of the mail berated me for making such a fuss over a small thing "when our boys are fighting in Vietnam."

I have no regrets . . . only a few saddle sores from riding it out. Certainly nations weren't going to rise or fall over Luci's pink-pink bridesmaids' dresses.

I am not good at holding grudges, and my blood pressure no longer soars when *Women's Wear Daily* shows up. But this incident did introduce me to a new brand of mischief-making reporting—a brand I have seen reappear on some of the women's pages of major newspapers. I only hope it doesn't close the doors which have been opened by many hardworking newswomen throughout the years.

With all our energies and time devoted to the wedding, the bride's dress, and the pink-pink bridesmaids' gowns, Bess Abell and I had no time to think of what we would wear on that day.

"Don't even give it a thought," said Adele Simpson, the pint-sized, soft-spoken designer who was frequently in the White House planning Mrs. Johnson's dress.

Keeping her word, she appeared a few days before the wedding and while we had our ears on the phone, she pinned and fitted our wedding day dresses, hats and shoes. They were perfect.

CRISIS NUMBER 4: I WAS MARTYRED FOR ST. AGATHA

The closest I may ever get to Heaven are the two frantic weeks I spent in search of a saint. Not just any old saint! Luci, alas, selected an obscure saint, whom we ultimately established to be St. Agatha, the patron saint of nursing.

At the time of her engagement, Luci was studying nursing at Georgetown University. One of her teachers, who had a flair for public relations, suggested that it would be very nice if Luci left her bridal bouquet at the feet of the patron saint of nursing, instead of the Virgin Mary. To an old psalm-singing Methodist like me, the idea of a bouquet gift to a saint was an education anyway. In my church, brides take their bouquets with them and toss them to the most conspicuous old maid in the family. But Catholics, I learned, have a traditional moment when the bride and groom are departing the church. The bride leaves her bouquet at the foot of the nearest Virgin Mary and then departs with the groom. If she wants to toss another bouquet, she has a surplus bouquet handy for this purpose.

Luci's wish presented difficulties for a variety of reasons: establishing who was the patron saint of nursing, finding the replica, getting enough bouquets to satisfy both Luci and Dorothy Territo, the string-saver of LBJ papers and memorabilia. Mrs. Territo also had her eye on Luci's bouquet to preserve for the LBJ Library.

We ended up with several saints and three bouquets.

Searching for the patron saint of nursing was, if you'll forgive the expression, like looking for the Holy Grail. But I had as my ally Monsignor Grady.

"Monsignor," I said, for we were on very chummy terms by now, "how can we find out who is the patron saint of nursing?"

"That's no problem at all, Liz," he said. "I'll just look in my 'Who's Who of Saints'—I've got one in my library—and call you back."

In ten minutes, he was back on the phone. "Well, there is a slight problem," he said. "There are seven patron saints of nursing, four of whom are men."

"Pick a woman and tell me about her," I replied.

He did, and a more ghoulish biography I had never heard. In ancient Sicily, Agatha, a girl of noble birth who was sworn to chastity, refused to yield to a lecherous Roman official. So he had her tortured, using the Emperor's edict against Christianity as an excuse.

Even after being mutilated, Agatha refused to give in. To top it all off, she was rolled in hot coals, but she still would not die. Then, according to one version of the story, a well-timed earthquake put an end to these indignities, and eventually she went on to her reward.

I could see why she had become the patron saint of nursing, for if ever a girl needed a Band-Aid, she was it.

Bess Abell and I were both convinced that seventeen centuries later Agatha really deserved some attention, so we set about to find her statue for the big day.

I made phone calls to every church in town. Nowhere in Washington was St. Agatha to be found. I also enlisted the help of Monsignor Grady who had a lot more pipelines in this direction than I did. He finally gave up and asked me to come out to the Shrine and take a look at their craft shop, where they sold all sorts of saints.

"Most saints are really just symbolic," the Monsignor told me, waving toward the shelves of male and female statues with beatific expressions. "As a matter of fact, we have a lot of pretty nondescript saints here. Just pick one and we can place it on the altar."

I was shocked. "Why, Monsignor," I replied, "you are contributing to the credibility gap!"

The *Catholic Standard*'s reporter, Sheila Nelson, had located a rehabilitated St. Agatha at the Franciscan Monastery in Washington.

Their statue of St. Agatha had originally been St. Philomena, but had been repainted into Agatha when Philomena was stricken from the list of saints.

I could just imagine what would happen if we used this Agatha and the story leaked out. The headlines would be: "Saint Whitewashed for Wedding." So the search continued.

Meanwhile, back at the White House, the President's barber, Steve Martini, told me he had found St. Agatha in Brooklyn at a relative's church. "She stands five feet high and we can quietly borrow her if we can return her by Sunday," Martini said.

I started checking shipping charges on saints, and was secretly hoping this would work out because it would be the first time in history that a saint had been produced from a Martini.

Bess was much more practical in her search. She dismissed my Brooklyn Agatha "because she's the wrong size saint."

Meanwhile, she had given up locating an appropriate Agatha and simply decided to have one made to her own specifications.

Two sculpture artisans at the National Gallery of Art were busy shaping up two saints, one in bronze and one in plaster. In addition, the National Geographic had located a picture of St. Agatha which they were reproducing in beautiful color tints. The picture would be framed and Luci would choose between sculpture and painting.

In reproducing St. Agatha, her lurid past kept posing a problem. She is most frequently portrayed with pincers in her hand and two bosoms lying on a tray. Bess thought this highly inappropriate for a wedding; so she just left the pincers in hand and skipped the bosoms.

Luci finally selected the picture of St. Agatha for the altar but Bess found the new bronze replica so aesthetic she slipped it on the altar, too.

Some day in the Great Beyond, I hope I meet the real St. Agatha and tell her about our sacrifice.

CRISIS NUMBER 5: IN UNION THERE IS STRENGTH

Maybe Republicans in office don't have much trouble with their nuptials. But the Democratic Party, the workingman's friend, has so many ties of heart and tradition to organized labor that it is hard to turn your back on them.

Take Jacob Potofsky, the president of the Amalgamated Clothing Workers of America, and the only labor leader I know who looks like an ad for Colonel Sanders' Kentucky Fried Chicken.

Once, back in our Vice Presidential days, Mrs. Johnson was seated at dinner next to Mr. Potofsky. She found him absolutely delightful and was enchanted when he told her, "You have no idea how much you ladies in the news influence fashion and affect our economy."

He pointed out that it was—alas—a hatless era, that none of the Kennedy women were wearing hats, and it had a telling effect on jobs among the milliners.

Hats were out of fashion at the time due to the popular Jackie bouffant hairdos, but Mrs. Johnson never forgot Mr. Potofsky and about every third event, she would say, "I'll wear a hat today for Mr. Potofsky."

That was the thinking that lay behind our dilemma in the Great Luci Wedding Dress Crisis. Through Stanley Marcus of Dallas, we had obtained Priscilla of Boston to design and produce Luci's wedding dress. And, after looking over many designs, Luci picked the one. Now, to get it made!

Priscilla had been designing wedding dresses, I suspected, since John Alden and the original Priscilla. She is a pretty, prim New Englander— and was the match for the AFL-CIO organizer who started riding, like Paul Revere, all over Boston sounding the alarm: "Priscilla is a nonunion shop." The echoes reverberated through the trade press and clear back to the ears of David Dubinsky of International Ladies' Garment Workers Union fame, in New York. Mr. Dubinsky is an emotional man who literally wept over the phone when confronted with the thought that his good friend, the President of the United States, would let his daughter marry in a gown without a union label.

Poor President! Poor Luci! Poor nimble-fingered nonunion ladies who were sewing on pearls!

We leaned on the wise and able James Reynolds, Assistant Secretary of Labor. He welcomed this happy problem as an escape from the meat-cutters negotiations, now in the cleaver-for-cleaver stage.

One solution was a suggestion that Priscilla yield and join the Union. "Absolutely not," said Priscilla. "I pay higher than Union wages."

The next solution suggested was that we should choose another dress!

This put Bess Abell on the couch reaching for tranquilizers. She could not bear to think she would have to go through the long tedious selection process again. Besides, Luci liked the dress.

The third solution was to hang Stanley Marcus from the nearest tree for not warning us about this problem. But he was too likeable for that, and besides we all had handy charge accounts at his store.

So, we negotiated a compromise. Priscilla allowed the dress to be "assembled" at a nearby Union shop, and her own talented artisans did the beadwork which Union machines cannot do. This didn't please anyone completely, but Dave Dubinsky stopped crying, Priscilla kept her employees happy, Luci got a gown, and Bess and I survived.

We posted a poem of the week: The bride wore something borrowed, something blue—and a label from ILGWU.

This was not to be the end of the union problem.

August 6—the wedding day—loomed on the weatherman's calendar as a day when the Washington temperature would top 90 degrees. A sweltering Saturday was in store, and, as Marie Smith pointed out in the *Washington Post*, "There is no air conditioning in the Shrine."

Out of the blue, and in the middle of an airline strike, a United Airlines representative called to say, "We've read in the papers about the temperature problem at the church. We should be glad to help. Our blowers, which air-condition the planes on the ground, are just idling out there at the airport during the strike. We could turn the blowers into the doors of the Shrine the night before and have it nice and cool for the ceremony."

This sounded like a good offer, but I asked for time to check it out with our bridal consultant, Clark Clifford, to see if we could accept such assistance.

Clark thought the suggestion was acceptable, and I proceeded to map out the invasion of air-conditioning units to arrive at 6 p.m. Friday, August 5, the night before the wedding. At that hour the last Mass would be over. We would be moving telephone equipment into the crypt—our makeshift press room for the five hundred reporters covering the event. And the mobile blowers could be driven from United's hangars to the church and go to blowing.

Marcia Maddox, a member of my staff, headed for the Shrine, walkie-talkie in hand, to get these complicated operations under way. I was still answering queries and trying to go home and dress and get back to handle Luci's rehearsal dinner.

The phone rang and it was James Reynolds of the Labor Department. There was a note of alarm in his voice.

"I have a tip that United Airlines is lending you blowers to air-condition the church."

I confirmed this, and he—as politely as a man who has just left the meat-cutters for the airline negotiations could—let me know this was a terrible idea.

"I'm going to check with Bill Wirtz," I told him and promptly put in a call to his superior, the Secretary of Labor.

About this time my alarm button—three rings if it's the President—sounded, and You-Know-Who was on the phone.

The President asked me if the rumor about the blowers was true. "Yes," I replied. "Did it ever occur to you to check with someone?" His voice implied I was the dumbest woman in the world.

I confidently told him that I had checked with Clark Clifford.

"That's not enough, you should have checked with Bill Wirtz," he said.

"I'm trying," I replied. "But it's going to be hot in that church."

"Well, check it out," he said, "and if we have to sit there and sweat, that's just what we'll have to do."

I frantically tried again to reach Secretary Wirtz, who was still in his limousine en route home. Meanwhile I could visualize the airline trucks descending on the Shrine where TV cameras were already in place. I called on the Lord please not to let those cameras be hooked up or we would be all over the networks with our "struck" airline trucks showing.

When Secretary Wirtz and I finally got together, he was immovable.

"No! No! I know it's tough, but this strike affects 35,000 men. Feelings are high. Negotiations are difficult. All we need is a struck airline truck photographed at the President's daughter's wedding. Call them off!"

I let out a very unbride-like oath and grabbed a walkie-talkie. "Shrine, Shrine, come in Shrine," I yelled. "Do you read me Shrine?" I was calling my assistant, Marcia Maddox.

"This is Marcia at the Shrine," came the welcome voice. Marcia was in the crypt of the Shrine directing the electricians.

"Are the air-conditioning men there yet?" I asked.

"No, but they are on their way, somewhere in Rock Creek Park," she replied.

"You aren't going to believe what I am about to tell you, Marcia, but just don't ask any questions and follow instructions exactly," I said. "Get the Park Police and turn those trucks around and send them back to the airport."

"You've got to be kidding," she replied.

"Do it and don't argue—and then go to a phone and call me so we can talk privately," I said.

To her eternal credit she did just that. She countered the whole invasion of United trucks with Park Police, turned them around, and they never reached the Shrine. That girl will go to Heaven for sure!

Back at my office, I could just visualize how confused the drivers of the mobile blowers must have been to see the fleet of Park Service police cars converging on them.

I dictated a terse message to the President: "Mission accomplished. We'll just sit there and sweat."

Then, I headed for home, ankles swollen, nerves frayed, limp with the accumulation of eight months of pre-nuptial torture. I had grown to hate love. But I only had eighteen more hours to go until Luci walked down the aisle. I couldn't believe it when the car radio came on, "Is Springtime in car 17?" Springtime, bah! That was my Secret Service code name, but at this moment I felt like dead winter.

"Ask her to call the President's office on her arrival."

I did, and would you believe that this was the message: "Liz, the President says for you to find an airline that isn't struck that has blowers. Try to get them to air condition the Shrine."

Down with labor! Down with Presidents!

So I phoned Warren Woodward, our longtime friend and the American Airlines representative. "Look, Woody," I said, "you've always been known as a can-do man, and this is the test."

I outlined the problem.

"Liz," said Woody, as though he were talking to an idiot child. "We are not struck and we are using our blowers. Does that answer your question?"

Well, that's the way we didn't blow the wedding. . . .

One daughter down, one to go!

Peace at Last

White House Years (1979)

Henry Kissinger has been a president watcher for more than forty years. Interestingly, in 1957, my husband, Phil, sent then majority leader Lyndon Johnson a copy of Henry's book Nuclear Weapons and Foreign Policy. *Phil called it a "thick, ponderous book" but also a "must read," telling LBJ that "It is absolutely essential for you to dig through it. Neither this nor any other book has the answers. But this one does ask the right questions at the right time."*

Henry seems always able to ask the right questions. I first got to know him when Joe Alsop brought us together when he first came to Washington. We took to each other from the beginning, and have remained close friends for the last three decades.

Here is someone who watched President Nixon from close range, astutely and keenly. Although his observations in this piece are mostly about Nixon, his comments on LBJ are a kind of bonus. Additionally, this piece reminds us of the Vietnam War, not something any of us should ever forget. The simple sentence about the connection between LBJ's death and the end of the Vietnam War is profound and moving.

With his characteristically strong writing, Henry touches on Richard Nixon's second inauguration, in January 1973—just a little more than six months after the break-in at the Watergate complex— which Nixon hoped was a new beginning, as well as on Nixon's close relationship with crises and on his brooding nature. Although this piece also describes events that took place well outside of Washington, somehow everything has a Washington feel to it.

RICHARD NIXON's second Inaugural took place on a day much like his first, cold and clear and blustery. I sat on the platform behind the Cabinet with my eighty-six-year-old father. I was no longer surprised at being there, but I was somewhat stunned by the emotional events of the past months. The war would now soon be over and hope was pervasive. Senators and Congressmen came over to chat and to congratulate; my father, whose life's efforts had been destroyed when Nazism took over his native land, was beaming. He could not really believe what had happened; in a strange way all the anguish of his life seemed vindicated.

There was a blare of trumpets and Nixon appeared to the tune of "Hail to the Chief." He too seemed as if he could not really believe it had all happened; a term in office had not abated his sense of wonder at being there. And he seemed, if not really happy, indeed quite detached.

Triumph seemed to fill Nixon with a premonition of ephemerality. He was, as he never tired of repeating, at his best under pressure. Indeed, it was sometimes difficult to avoid the impression that he needed crises as a motivating force—and that success became not a goal but an obsession so that once achieved he would not know what to do with it. The festivities surrounding the Inauguration were large but not buoyant. Participants acted as if they had earned their presence rather than as if they shared in a new common purpose. Through it all Richard Nixon moved as if he were himself a spectator, not the principal. He had brought off spectacular successes. He had achieved the international goals he had set for the first term. He had before him a blank canvas, one of the rare times in history that a President could devote himself substantially to new and creative tasks of diplomacy. The legacies of the past were being overcome, the international environment was fluid, as happens at most once in a generation—waiting to be shaped. And yet there was about him this day a quality of remoteness, as if he could never quite bring himself to leave the inhospitable and hostile world that he inhabited, that he may have hated but at least had come to terms with. Perhaps it was simple shyness or fatalism; perhaps it was the consciousness of a looming catastrophe.

Two days later, January 22, I left for Paris for the final meeting with Le Duc Tho. It was to take place for the first time on neutral and ceremonial ground in a small conference room at Avenue Kléber, the scene of 174 futile plenary sessions since 1968. Even now it would be used for only a symbolic event. . . . In a final paranoiac gesture the North Vietnamese insisted that on completion each text be bound by string and the string sealed—I suppose to prevent us from deviously slipping in new pages overnight.

When I arrived in Paris, I learned that Lyndon Johnson had died that day. He was himself a casualty of the Vietnam war, which he had inherited and then expanded in striving to fulfill his conception of our nation's duty and of his obligation to his fallen predecessor. There was nothing he had wanted less than to be a war President, and this no doubt contributed to his inconclusive conduct of the struggle. In retirement he had behaved with dignity not untinged by melancholy, burdened with the terrible truth that the only pursuit he really cared about, that of public service, was now closed to him—like a surgeon who at the height of his prowess is barred forever from entering a hospital. Haldeman had phoned him on January 15 to tell him that the bombing would stop. (I had briefed him on Nixon's behalf many times in the past, but, now reduced to a "lower profile," I had been requested by Haldeman not to do so.) But I had sent him a copy of the peace agreement, with a warm note. It was symbolic that this hulking, imperious, vulnerable, expansive, aspiring man, so full of life, should die with the war that had broken his heart.

The meeting started at 9:35 a.m., Tuesday, January 23. Le Duc Tho managed even on this solemn occasion to make himself obnoxious by insisting on ironclad assurances of American economic aid to North Vietnam. I told him that this could not be discussed further until after the agreement was signed; it also depended on Congressional approval and on observance of the agreement. Finally, at a quarter to one, we initialed the various texts and improvised brief closing statements. . . .

America's Vietnam war was over.

POSTLUDE

On January 23, Washington was, as always before great events, consumed in technicalities. I arrived back in my office around 6:35 p.m. the same day, a few hours before Nixon was to announce the agreement and the cease-fire. For once I was not asked to brief the press until the next day. It was felt, correctly, that the President's speech would require no elaboration. The President briefed the Congressional leaders in the Cabinet Room, doing most of the explaining himself.

I sat alone in my office, waiting for Nixon's speech to the nation. It was the culmination of all we had endured and endeavored for four years. Over two million Americans had given parts of their lives to that distant land. Over forty-five thousand had laid down their lives for it; several hundred thousand had been wounded. They and their families could now take some pride that it had not all been in vain. Those who had opposed the effort in Indochina would, we could hope, close ranks now that their goal of peace had finally been achieved. And the peoples of South Vietnam, Laos, and Cambodia would perhaps attain at long last a future of tranquility, security, and progress, a future worthy of their sacrifices.

We stood, I fervently hoped, at the threshold of a period of national reconciliation that would be given impetus by the unique opportunity for creativity I saw ahead. Perhaps America had found the way to merge the idealism of the early Sixties with the sterner pragmatism of the recent past. China was now an important friend; we had built a new basis for stable relations with the Soviet Union through a Berlin agreement, the first strategic arms limitation treaty, and an agreed code of international conduct. The diplomatic revolution that had been brought about opened up an extraordinary opportunity for American diplomacy. This, in addition to the dispelling of our Vietnam trauma, was a reason for enormous hope. We had eased relations with adversaries; it was now time to turn to reinvigorating relations with friends, and to resolving unsolved problems. We had decided to make 1973 the Year of Europe, to reaffirm our Alliance ties with the Atlantic Community—and also Japan. We would show that these ties were stronger and deeper than the tentative new relations with Communist countries. On the basis of Alliance cohesion and vitality we would test the real opportunities for détente. We were at a moment of extraordinary opportunity in the Middle East; I was set to meet with President Sadat's national security adviser, Hafiz Is-mail, in February—my first step as a Middle East negotiator. Nixon entered his second term with an overwhelming public mandate, a strong executive at the height of his prestige.

Only rarely in history do statesmen find an environment in which all factors are so malleable; before us, I thought, was the chance to shape events, to build a new world, harnessing the energy and dreams of the American people, and mankind's hopes. Almost certainly I would not be able to take part in the whole enterprise over four years; after the peace was well established I would leave—perhaps toward the end of the year. I was grateful for the opportunity I had enjoyed to help prepare the ground.

Nixon spoke at 10:00 p.m. briefly and with conciliation. He paid tribute to Lyndon Johnson, who had yearned for that day, and he asked Americans to consecrate themselves to "make the peace we have achieved a peace that would last."

I called Nixon immediately afterward, as I had done after every major speech, to congratulate him. He seemed incapable of resting on any achievement. He was already worrying about the Congressional briefings that would start next day.

Mrs. Nixon took the phone to congratulate me. It took stout hearts to see it through, she said. What a gallant lady she had been. With pain and stoicism, she had suffered the calumny and hatred that seemed to follow her husband. Unlike the President, she was not capable of the fantasy life in which romantic imaginings embellished the often self-inflicted daily disappointments. She was totally without illusions and totally insistent on facing her trials in solitude. Her dignity never wavered. And if she seemed remote, who could know what fires had had to be banked in her stern existence. She made no claims on anyone; her fortitude had been awesome and not a little inspiring because one sensed that it had been wrested from an essential gentleness.

A few minutes later Nelson Rockefeller called. He had introduced me to public life and sustained me throughout. In a strange way he was both inarticulate and a bit shy, and yet enveloping in his warmth. One had to know him well to understand the tactile manner in which he communicated—the meanings of the little winks, nudges, and mumbles by which he conveyed that he cared, and conferred comfort and inward security. And he was quintessentially American in his unquenchable optimism. He could never imagine that a wrong could not be righted or that effort could not conquer obstacles in the way of honorable goals. He was always encouraging, supportive. He had been there matter-of-factly, unasked, through every crisis of those years. And in this spirit he spoke to me with pride of what his country had accomplished. He saw in America's strength a blessing conferring a duty—to defend the free, to give hope to the disadvantaged, and to walk truly in the paths of justice and mercy.

Around midnight, when I was at home, Nixon called from the Lincoln Sitting Room, where he was brooding alone. He was wondering whether the press would appreciate what had been done; probably not. But that was not what he really had on his mind. He knew that every success brings a terrific letdown, he said. I should not let it get to me. I should not be discouraged. There were many battles yet to fight; I should not weaken. In fact, I was neither discouraged nor did I feel let down. Listening to him, I could picture the scene: Nixon would be sitting solitary and withdrawn, deep in his brown stuffed chair with his legs on a settee in front of him, a small reading light breaking the darkness, and a wood fire throwing shadows on the wall of the room. The loudspeakers would be playing romantic classical music, probably Tchaikovsky. He was talking to me, but he was really addressing himself.

What extraordinary vehicles destiny selects to accomplish its design. This man, so lonely in his hour of triumph, so ungenerous in some of his motivations, had navigated our nation through one of the most anguishing periods in its history. Not by nature courageous, he had steeled himself to conspicuous acts of rare courage. Not normally outgoing, he had forced himself to rally his people to its challenge. He had striven for a revolution in American foreign policy so that it would overcome the disastrous oscillations between overcommitment and isolation. Despised by the Establishment, ambiguous in his human perceptions, he had yet held fast to a sense of national honor and responsibility, determined to prove that the strongest free country had no right to abdicate. What would have happened had the Establishment about which he was so ambivalent shown him some love? Would he have withdrawn deeper into the wilderness of his resentments, or would an act of grace have liberated him? By now it no longer mattered. Enveloped in an intractable solitude, at the end of a period of bitter division, he nevertheless saw before him a vista of promise to which few statesmen have been blessed to aspire. He could envisage a new international order that would reduce lingering enmities, strengthen friendships, and give new hope to emerging nations. It was a worthy goal for America and mankind. He was alone in his moment of triumph on a pinnacle that was soon to turn into a precipice. And yet with all his insecurities and flaws he had brought us by a tremendous act of will to an extraordinary moment when dreams and possibilities conjoined.

MICHAEL K. DEAVER

The Man
in the Emergency Room

Behind the Scenes (1987)

Mike Deaver was a president watcher from close up. He is one of those Washington hands whose loyalty to a higher-up knows no bounds—in the best sense of that phrase. Along with Jim Baker and Ed Meese, Mike was a member of the White House inner circle during the administration of Ronald Reagan. Those three formed a kind of triumvirate of advisers, seen often with their heads together—in fact, Hugh Sidey, of Time *magazine, wrote that Meese, Baker, and Deaver "sounded like an infield in the American league."*

Mike had known the Reagans for many years before they all arrived in Washington. He was a confidant, trusted adviser, and friend, especially close to Nancy Reagan. After Reagan's second election, there were a few months of frost between Nancy and me. The Post *had endorsed Mondale, and I hesitated to be the one to call her and resume relations. Nancy, I knew, was miffed, so I just decided that was that, and maybe it was the end of a beautiful friendship. After some months, it was Mike who asked me about it, very nicely saying, "You two can't keep this up for four years." It turned out that Nancy had understood the reality that I am not* The Washington Post, *but was offended because I hadn't called to congratulate her on the president's victory. Small incidents can get blown out of proportion, and I have always been grateful to Mike for helping us make peace. Such are the heightened sensitivities in Washington public and private life.*

Mike's book provides insight into a certain Washington experience, as he was first a White House insider and later a lobbyist. His book also reveals a great deal about the behind-the-scenes power struggles and the "body of power" that is Washington, D.C. Mike writes about "friendships in high places, and what happens to them when they go through the compactor of American politics." It was published before the end of Iran-Contra and the trials, before the end of the Reagan

presidency, before Ronald Reagan's brave and beautiful letter about his
Alzheimer's, so it was long before the end of the story.

But this is also a personal memoir, including a candid account of his
alcohol addiction and how he managed to keep it a secret for years, and
it's a portrait of a president and first lady whom he loved.

T HE MEMORIES of March 30, 1981, are still the hardest of my life
to think or talk about and, I suspect, always will be. Five of us
walked out of the Washington Hilton Hotel together, and four
were shot. I was the only one not wounded.

Men who return unscathed from combat, I am told, often carry with
them feelings of guilt for having been spared while friends and comrades
fell. This experience was mine as well.

We know it now as the day the president was shot. That he lived, that
he came back stronger than ever, makes it possible to look back with
relief at the larger drama. There were even moments of wit and humor,
most of them provided by Ronald Reagan.

In every respect the day had been routine. The president had entered
the Oval Office at his usual time, 8:45 a.m., to meet with his staff for the
first briefing. His calendar had been arranged, months in advance,
around a speech he was to make to thirty-five hundred AFL-CIO union
members convening at the Hilton. Two appointments, scheduled for
later that afternoon, would go unkept.

At 1:30 p.m., Raymond Donovan, the secretary of labor, appeared at
the White House to accompany Reagan to the convention. We traveled,
as we unavoidably did, in a caravan of five or six limousines. The president's car pulled up and was parked at the curb, twenty-five feet from the
hotel's VIP entrance, in order to avoid tying up the circular driveway in
front.

There were fifteen cars in the motorcade, a normal number for an
appearance within the city. On this day I rode in the control car, third in
line, the presidential limo being first. The Secret Service manned the
second, or follow-up car, code-named "Halfback." These three cars were
known, in security terms, as the "Package," and were not to be separated.
On foreign trips, I wound up in heated squabbles over whose vehicle
went where. We could not run the risk that some diplomat or general—
theirs or ours—might block the control car if the Secret Service suddenly
peeled off. The Package stayed intact.

The control car always includes a military aide who carries the so-
called Black Box, containing the codes that would enable the president to
activate a nuclear response. The box, actually a briefcase of standard size,

was known among the Reagan staff as "the football," an oblique reminder of the need not to drop it. The military aides, one from each branch of the service, working in shifts, keep the box within reach of the president twenty-four hours a day. They are an elite group.

Also in the control car were the White House physician, and the senior staff person, who would be responsible for making a decision at the civilian level, given the incapacity of the president.

Reagan's speech was short, general, not meant to make news. I checked my watch. We were on our way out at 2:25 p.m., less than an hour after we had left the White House. I had seen the reporters lined up behind a red velvet rope when we arrived. Now, as we made our exit, I instinctively grabbed Jim Brady, the press secretary, and nudged him through the door first to field their questions. I went next, turning left toward the staff car, with two security men and the president behind me.

I walked around Jim on my way to the other side of the car. I had reached the right rear fender when a reporter called out to the president. He did exactly what I had seen him do times beyond counting . . . he smiled and raised his left arm in a friendly wave, at once acknowledging the voice and rejecting the question.

Then I heard the first pop. Later, everyone would say what people often say of gunfire: It sounded like firecrackers going off. I knew differently. I got a quick whiff of sulfur and my reflexes took over. I ducked, the only one who did, and then, as more shots went off, I hit the pavement and stayed there.

Most of what happened next comes back to me in freeze frames. I suppose we are indebted to television for that piece of language. But what happened, happened in microseconds.

When the shots stopped I bolted to the other side of the president's car but could not get in. The special locks on the doors had clicked into place and my mind went blank. I had forgotten how to open them.

I can no longer separate what I actually saw at the time and what I observed later in constant television replays. But a picture of the president's face is absolutely branded on my mind's eye, as he stood with his arm in the air and the bullets began spraying. He did not realize he had been hit. But the smile was gone. His face froze. There was a moment of hesitation, a look of utter helplessness.

Then Jerry Parr, a veteran Secret Service agent, the head of the White House detail, virtually dived into the president, bent him over to make him less of a target, and threw him facedown onto the floor of the limousine. When they sped away from the curb, Parr's body was on top of his, shielding him.

I ran to the next car and jumped in. As we wheeled in behind them, I looked out the window and saw Jim Brady and two others lying on the bloody ground. They were Timothy McCarthy, an agent, and Thomas Delahanty, a Washington policeman.

As we raced down Connecticut Avenue, other cars now following ours, I had no time to collect my thoughts, or my breath. I had assumed we were returning to the White House. The next thing I knew, we swung into the driveway of the George Washington University Hospital. It was twelve blocks from the Hilton. We made it in five minutes.

Parr had radioed the Secret Service command post at the White House with the first report of the incident at the Hilton. His words were skeletal: Shots had been fired. "Rawhide"—the president's code name—was unhurt.

Actually, Ronald Reagan, who has a feeling that borders on hero worship for lawmen, for people who put their safety on the line, was mad as hell at Jerry Parr. He had been slammed so hard to the floor of the limo, he thought he had bruised or broken a rib. In complaining to Parr, I believe it is fair to say that he let out a curse word.

They had gone only a few blocks when the president coughed up blood. Parr could tell from the shade of red that it had come from the lungs. He instructed the driver to proceed to the hospital, and he radioed the command post of the change and asked them to alert the medical staff.

I leaped out of the backup car in time to see the president step out under his own power. He walked the fifteen yards to the emergency room, with agents on either side but not touching him. He moved through the door, out of public view, and then I saw him begin to sag. The agents caught him. His knees wobbled and his eyes rolled up. He was close to fainting, but still conscious. A paramedic lifted his feet and helped the agents, one under each arm, carry him into a private room off the lobby.

The hospital's trauma team was scrambling into place. As the door closed, I heard a doctor cry out, "Let's get some oxygen into him."

It is impossible to sort out all the emotions, all the confusion I felt at that instant. I was operating strictly on adrenaline. My first responsibility was to open a telephone line to the White House, and assure that a chain of authority existed.

At this point, it was still not clear that the president had been hit. The thought crossed several minds that he might have suffered a heart attack: His chest hurt. He was having difficulty breathing. He was a seventy-year-old man who had just suffered an attempt on his life.

In only the most disconnected way did the obvious questions run through my mind: Who, why, what? I had not seen a disturbed young dropout named John W. Hinckley, Jr., assume the police stance he had copied from television and click off six rounds in two seconds. From my vantage point, facedown on the cement, I had not seen the Secret Service men and hotel security guards, eight or nine of them, swarm all over him and take away the small revolver.

Struggling to stay calm, I got Ed Meese, the White House counselor, and Jim Baker, the chief of staff, on the phone and relayed what I knew: Brady and at least one agent had been hit. The president appeared to have a bruised rib. The doctors were examining him now.

Even as we talked, two ambulances arrived at the hospital almost simultaneously. They wheeled Jim Brady out of the first. McCarthy, shot in the chest, was in the second. The policeman, Delahanty, who had taken a bullet to the neck, had been delivered to the critical-care tower at another hospital.

While I waited for further news, keeping the line open, an intern in a green smock, holding a clipboard, approached me. He said, almost matter-of-factly, "Do you know who the patient is in the emergency room?"

I stared at him and saw that he was serious. I said, "Yes."

He said, "Would you give me his name, please?"

I said, "It's Reagan. R-E-A-G-A-N." I waited for a reaction.

"First name?" "Ron."

"Address?"

I said, "Sixteen hundred Pennsylvania."

His pencil stopped in mid-scratch. He finally looked up. "You mean . . . ?"

I said, "Yes. You have the president of the United States in there."

Baker and Meese, understandably, were anxious to reach the hospital. I asked them first to contact Mrs. Reagan and persuade her not to come. My relationship with Nancy was considered then, and is now, a special one. I did not believe the president to be in any danger. But people had been shot. There was a lot of blood. I felt it was not the right place for her to be, nor the right time.

But my message was too late. She had heard from the Secret Service that there had been a shooting, and she was on her way to the hospital.

With the phone line open, I ducked into the room where the president had been taken. They had literally undressed him in seconds. I was stunned by the sight of my president, my friend, stripped, not a stitch on him, being lifted onto an examining table. One of the doctors had already discovered the small bullet hole in his coat, under the left sleeve.

Fifteen minutes had passed since I first put the call through. I went back to the phone with new and depressing information to pass on. "It looks like the president has been nicked," I said. And I now knew that Brady's wound was to the brain. I repeated what I had learned of the condition of McCarthy and Delahanty.

Even as I talked, Brady was wheeled right by me on a stretcher. I believe that was the closest I have ever come to passing out. They had removed the first dressing from his wound. His head was wide open. I know my voice was hoarse and strained as I told the people at the other end of the line: "It doesn't look good for Jim."

Things were happening so fast, it was so kaleidoscopic, I can no longer be certain which message reached which person in what order. I had sent word on the open line to my secretary to please call my wife and mother and let them know I was okay.

The most pedestrian of daily chores collided with the scary reality of high human drama. My wife, Carolyn, had taken her sewing machine in to be fixed at a shop in Georgetown. She heard the news on a radio. It was two weeks later before she remembered to ask about her sewing machine. She had just left it on the counter, unticketed, and dashed out the door. When she walked into the house, she picked up the ringing phone and took a call from my secretary, Shirley Moore, who had been trying repeatedly to call to say I was all right. Two hours had passed since the shots were fired.

Next, Carolyn raced to Blair's school and pulled our six-year-old out of class. She brought him home and turned on the TV. The first thing Blair saw was a videotape of the shooting. He saw Jim Brady pitch forward in replay after replay, and thought it was me. He sat quietly, in a kind of shock. In the confusion, it did not dawn on Carolyn that Blair needed attention or reassuring.

Of course, Jim and I have the same hairline, and at the time, I was several pounds heavier. That night, when I walked into my home after 10:00 p.m., my son threw his arms around me and clung to my waist. Only then did we convince him that I was alive and uninjured. Meanwhile, five or six of our friends had been sitting up with Carolyn. They were all praying—for Brady, for the president, for the two officers.

When Nancy Reagan arrived at the hospital she was still unaware that her husband had been shot. Gently, the doctors told her he had taken a bullet, but was doing well. They did not know exactly where it had lodged and were preparing to operate.

I studied her closely. She was near hysterics when they wheeled her husband to the operating room, and his first words to her were: "Honey, I forgot to duck." She leaned over and kissed him. A little of the fear and tension went out of the room.

By now Baker and Meese had joined me, and the president spotted the three of us. "Who's minding the store?" he asked. We laughed, the kind of nervous laugh heightened by concern. And then the orderlies wheeled him into surgery.

I turned to Nancy and said, "You know, there is a little chapel upstairs. Why don't we go in there for a while?"

So we did. Then we were led to one of the doctor's offices to wait and watch the news coverage on television. It was there that we heard the first mistaken report that Jim Brady had died. My mind had been turned in so many ways by then it was hard to react. The report did not surprise me. I had seen Brady lying in the street, and again inches away when they rushed him into surgery. I did not see how he could live.

At that point, the confusion was simply out there where the meter does not register. I thought that this is what it must have been like on November 22, 1963, the day John Kennedy was brought into Parkland Memorial Hospital.

The double doors to the emergency area kept swinging open; patients on their aluminum carts were rolled in and out by teams of attendants moving briskly, holding the sides of the gurneys to keep them steady. Police were everywhere. Two or three times the Secret Service had to clear out the cops, just so the doctors could move through the halls.

Baker and Meese had found us, Nancy Reagan and me. We were still in the doctor's office on an upper floor, waiting for the outcome of the surgery. In the meantime, a matter of some importance had to be dealt with—running the country. I had put Baker on the line with Dr. Daniel Ruge, the president's personal physician, who described what was known about the wound: A small bullet had penetrated just under the armpit and Reagan had lost three or four pints of blood. Baker put down the phone and said his condition was "stable." The three of us looked at each other and nodded. The decision was made right there: not to invoke the Twenty-fifth Amendment, which would have transferred power to the vice-president, George Bush.

At the time of the shooting, Bush was in Fort Worth, Texas, speaking at a convention of cattlemen. He was to fly from there to Austin to address the state legislature. He was in the air when a coded Teletype message reached his plane, advising the pilot to refuel in Austin and continue on to Washington. The president had been shot.

The weight of those words humbled, and paralyzed, us. I pray to heaven we never hear them again. It begged the larger and once unthinkable question: Will the president die?

Finally, around 7:00 p.m., not quite five hours after the shooting, the president was delivered to the recovery room under an orange blanket.

Through part of the surgery, Nancy Reagan had sat with the wives of Jim Brady and Tim McCarthy in an office on the hospital's second floor.

I looked in on the president while he slept. I was shaken by how bad he looked. His skin was gray and drawn, his breathing labored. I would go home that night and tell Carolyn, "He will never be the same." In the first photographs taken of him, after surgery, he looked like a corpse. I really thought the doctors, with their encouraging reports, were putting on an act. I couldn't have been more wrong.

Of course, I said none of this to Nancy. The thoracic surgeon, Dr. Benjamin Aaron, came out of the operating room and said to her, "It took me forty minutes to get through that chest. I have never in my life seen a chest like that on a man his age." The words were meant to be reassuring, a compliment.

I remembered what the doctor who operated on John Kennedy said, when he was asked what went through his mind as he prepared to cut open the thirty-fifth president: "He is a bigger man than I thought."

Of course, bigness is not in size alone. The popularity of Ronald Reagan, the remarkable acceptance of at least the first six years of his presidency, began to take shape that day, driven by his grace and aplomb under circumstances hard to conceive.

He did not leave the recovery room until 6:15 the next morning. We walked in on him—Baker, Meese, and I—half an hour later. He had a tube in his throat and could not talk without discomfort. The nurses were still buzzing over the notes he had blitzed them with, writing on a pad of pink paper.

One read: "I'd like to do this scene again—starting at the hotel."

After he had slept, and was conscious again, he dashed off a question: "I'm still alive, aren't I?"

And then a more profound thought: "Winston Churchill said that there is no more exhilarating feeling than being shot at without result."

He just would not stop. He was like an old trouper who had found the world's most appreciative audience, which in a sense he had. Another note read: "Send me to L.A. where I can see the air I'm breathing."

Not until days later did we realize that three of the notes were missing. Threats had to be made before they were turned in—by the White House staff people who had lifted them. Nancy has them now. They will become an exhibit when a Ronald Reagan Library is built—priceless, historical quips, written in the dawn after a dark night.

One of his 14-karat-gold cuff links, in the shape of the California golden bear, disappeared from his nightstand and was never found.

The tube was removed from his throat at three in the morning, and, now able to talk, he wondered about the attempted assassination. He said he recalled hearing three or four rounds. He asked if anyone else had been hurt. No one gave him a direct answer. It had been decided not to say anything that might, at that point, impair his recovery.

He had been hit, it turned out, by a fragment of a bullet that ricocheted off the armored car door. The bullet had pierced below the armpit, traveled several inches down his left side, bounced off a rib, punctured his lung, and come to rest three inches from his heart.

The attempts by newsmen to explain the medical details resulted in more confusion, and in a way added to the growing Reagan legend. Reporters kept saying he had been shot in the chest. Chris Wallace of NBC announced that Reagan had undergone open-heart surgery. Of course, he had not. The doctors had opened his chest to locate and extract the bullet.

When the three of us walked into his room, he was sitting up in bed, brushing his teeth. "I should have known I wasn't going to avoid a staff meeting," he said. When I tried to assure him that everything was going smoothly in his absence at the White House, he retorted, "What makes you think I'd be happy to hear that?"

We had brought with us a bill for his signature, cutting back on federal price supports for dairy products. It was just a wee step on the president's road to reduce the size of government, but it represented our first real legislative victory.

I doubt that many people realize now that Reagan had been in office just seventy days when Hinckley made his assassination attempt.

We asked if he felt up to signing the bill. It was not really a matter of any urgency, but all of us felt a pressure to demonstrate that the government—meaning Ronald Reagan—was able to function. The system had not lost or sacrificed its continuity.

He grabbed the pen and signed the legislation on his breakfast tray. The signature was weak and wobbly, and if I had seen it under other circumstances, I might have called it a forgery. But it was his. And the significance of that fact was not lost on any of us.

The gesture was symbolic. The president meant it to show that he was on the job. (There are White House secretaries who are able to copy his signature, and of the hundreds of letters mailed each day from the Oval Office, most are signed by an automatic pen. The pen is not used on any official documents.)

Reagan had been sheltered from newspapers and broadcasts, but that afternoon it was decided that he needed to be informed of the other injuries. The job fell to Dr. Ruge, who described Brady's injury as a head wound. The president asked him the question Ruge hoped would go unasked: Did it go into the brain?

When the doctor nodded, tears filled the president's eyes. He was silent for a moment, and then he said: "My God, that means four bullets landed."

Hinckley had been firing at nearly point-blank range. The weapon was a .22-caliber handgun, a Röhm RG-14, small but designed for accuracy.

The doctors had predicted that the president would need a minimum of two weeks to heal. He warned them he was a fast healer. He was out of the hospital in twelve days but needed three weeks, not two, to return to his desk.

The entire White House staff, and officials of the administration and their families, some two hundred people in all, were waiting on the South Lawn in a drizzling spring rain on the day the president came home. He raised his left arm in an easy wave, as he had done so recently in front of the Hilton, and I found myself flinching when he did. But of all of us who were there, I have a hunch that he was the first to put behind him the terrible pictures.

How We Lived

My Turn (1989)

I know that my friendly relationship with Ronald and Nancy Reagan puzzled many people in Washington, but to me it was simple: they were friends of mine long before they came to Washington. Oddly, it was Tru-man Capote who first brought us together. Truman had got to know them somehow while doing research on capital punishment, after he had written In Cold Blood. *I was going to a governors' conference where they would be, and he encouraged me to meet them, saying I'd really like them. He was right. We hit it off from the start.*

The Washington Post *had endorsed Carter, albeit lukewarmly, and I had lukewarmly voted for him, but I wasn't at all displeased to be on the losing side. I thought change was needed, but I was worried about Reagan's conservatism. When Ron and Nancy came to Washing-ton after the election, I gave a dinner for them, although I hesitated at first. I felt that given the* Post's *position and my own politics, it might look as if I was trying to have it both ways. But they were my friends, so I proceeded. It was very exciting. Not since the Kennedy and Johnson years had I had the privilege of having a friendly dinner with a presi-dent and his wife. That night I had people from the incoming adminis-tration as well as from the outgoing one, members of Congress and press people, and longtime Washingtonian friends of mine.*

I remember that one thing we talked about was Reagan's hopes that the Democrats would work with him. I mentioned LBJ telling me that Republicans like Dirksen and Bridges had been extremely helpful and important to his legislative program, but Reagan responded that he didn't know of anyone who could do that now, that it took strong lead-ership to get the parties together. We also discussed the difficulties of presidents going out to dinner in Washington. I remarked that it seemed to be so difficult as to almost be prohibitive. He said, "Just ask me." We also talked about his age being a disadvantage, and I recall that he almost implied he didn't have a chance for a second term.

My friendship with Nancy grew stronger in the eight years the Rea-

gans were in Washington. We lunched together fairly regularly throughout that time—long, informal, gossipy lunches that definitely fell into the category of "ladies lunching" rather than involving any serious social or political agenda. The lunches were real conversations between friends.

I was very sympathetic to Nancy and annoyed at all the criticism she received. I certainly was sympathetic about the criticism she got as a mother. No one can see into the relationships of others, and I feel we shouldn't be so judgmental about things we know little about. I even weighed in to the Post's newsroom with my concerns, sending a memo to Ben Bradlee and Len Downie in the fall of 1988 that followed up on some earlier carping I had engaged in about Nancy's treatment by the press in general and by the Post in particular. Among other things, I wrote, "I'd like to know why Mrs. Reagan makes the front page (above the fold) about the borrowed dresses, and is covered in Style . . . when she's addressing an important issue, which in fact alters the U.S. position on the developing countries who produce and ship drugs. It has long been a sexist issue that if a woman makes a speech, or even if a government official makes an important talk to a women's group, it goes in Style. Should we change this ancient attitude?"

Nancy's memoir is another personal look at Washington. She writes about the emotion-filled years living in the glass house of the White House, what she describes as the "most difficult years of my life," and she writes about her lifelong love of her husband—a loving relationship that continues despite his terrible illness.

We witnessed a lot of change in the years that the Reagans were in Washington. From the time of the first dinner I gave for them, when they came to Washington in 1980, to the last one, as they were leaving in 1988, security had tightened to the point of madness. What had not changed was that Ronald Reagan still looked vigorous and young, and that we were still friends. I think one of the most interesting things he ever said to me is central to the sport of president watching. He said, "You know some people say 'How can an actor be president of the United States?' But I don't see how you can be president if you aren't an actor."

PEOPLE often ask me what it was like to live in the White House, and what routines we followed there. Our day normally began at seven-thirty, when a White House operator called on the telephone on my side of the bed and said, "Good morning, it's seven-thirty."

Sometimes I was still sleeping, but Ronnie was usually awake. I would push a button by the side of the bed, which rang a buzzer in the second-floor kitchen, and a minute later a White House butler would come into our room, pull open the curtains, and bring us the morning papers, which we read in bed.

Ronnie would start with *The Washington Post*, followed by the *New York Times*, and as for that persistent rumor that he turned first to the comics—it's true. Might as well begin the day on a light note. Later, at the office, he'd look through the *Wall Street Journal*. I usually began with *U.S.A. Today* and the *Washington Times* while waiting for Ronnie to finish the *Post* and the *New York Times*. Sometimes the butler would also bring the *New York Post* and the *Daily News*, and on Monday mornings they'd bring us *Time*, *Newsweek*, and *U.S. News*, all hot off the press.

While we read the papers, the television would be tuned to *Good Morning America*, in case Ron was on. All the morning news shows were taped by the White House, and if there was anything Ronnie's staff thought he should see, they'd show it to him at the office. The same was true with the print media: We both received a daily packet of press clips so we wouldn't miss an important story.

By the time the papers arrived we'd be sharing the bed with Rex, our brown-and-white King Charles spaniel, who was given to us by Bill and Pat Buckley. Rex slept just across the hall from our bedroom, in a basket in the kitchen. A few minutes later another butler would come in with the breakfast tray and lay it on the bed. The butlers worked in shifts, so it wasn't the same man every morning. But everybody who served us was from the White House staff. Apparently, we were one of the very few presidential families to arrive without any personal servants.

Breakfast was always the same: orange or grapefruit juice, cold bran cereal with milk (and sometimes cut fruit), and decaffeinated coffee. Ronnie would also have bran toast with honey, and once a week we'd each have an egg.

About a month after we came to the White House, I was surprised when the usher's office sent up a bill for our food. Nobody had told us that the president and his wife are charged for every meal, as well as for such incidentals as dry cleaning, toothpaste, and other toiletries. We paid for our guests' meals, too, unless they came on official business. Fortunately, state dinners were paid for by the State Department. I suspect people think everything is paid for by the White House, but that's not true.

At around eight forty-five, Ronnie would lean over the bed, kiss me goodbye, and leave for the office. On his way out, he took Rex back to the kitchen so that Dale Haney, one of the White House gardeners, could take him out for his morning walk. Then Ronnie went downstairs in the elevator, where he was met by Jim Kuhn, his personal assistant, and a Secret Service agent, who walked with him across the colonnade along the Rose Garden, and into the West Wing. He would pass the doctor's office, and John Hutton was always in the hallway to say hello. (Sometimes, on his way home, Ronnie would stop in for his allergy shot.) His first appointment of the morning was usually a nine o'clock meeting with his chief of staff and the vice president.

I almost never saw Ronnie during the day, and never for lunch. Sometimes he ate alone in the Oval Office study (which had been Mike Deaver's office during the first term), where a typical lunch consisted of a bowl of soup followed by half a grapefruit. Staying at the office, he could get more work done and continue to make calls. Every Thursday, Ronnie had lunch with George Bush.

When Ronnie left for work, I went into my dressing room, a soft, romantic room just behind the bedroom. I loved that room, with its peach-colored carpet and the peach-and-white floral draperies and upholstery. In there I had hung a wonderful nineteenth-century painting of a woman with her dog, a scene so peaceful it sometimes made me feel that I was born in the wrong century.

Outside the window was a magnolia tree that had been planted by Andrew Jackson. You could see the Rose Garden from that window, and if Ronnie was participating in an outdoor ceremony, I'd often perch up on the radiator and watch. Sometimes he'd wave to me, and the photographers would turn around and take my picture, too.

In addition to Pat Nixon's small beauty parlor, the first lady also has her own bathroom, a small one by today's standards. On the side of the washbasin I kept an inspirational text that a friend had sent me years ago, and I looked at it often during our years in the White House. It's called "One Night I Had a Dream," and the author is unknown:

I dreamed I was walking along the beach with the Lord, and across the sky flashed scenes from my life. For each scene, I noticed two sets of footprints in the sand; one belonged to me, and the other to the Lord. When the last scene of my life flashed before us, I looked back at the footprints in the sand. I noticed that many times along the path of my life there was only one set of footprints. I also noticed that it happened at the very lowest and the saddest times of my life.

I questioned the Lord about it. "Lord, you said that once I decided to follow You, You would walk with me all the way. But I've noticed that during the most troublesome times of my life, there is only one set of footprints. I don't understand why, in times when I needed You most, You would leave."

The Lord replied, "My precious child, I would never leave you during your times of trial and suffering. When you see only one set of footprints, it was then that I carried you."

I love that reading, and I've sent copies to many of my friends as they were going through difficult periods in their lives.

My FIRST stop of the day was down the hall in the exercise room, which had been an empty bedroom until we converted it after the shooting. Amy Carter used to sleep here, and before that, Tricia Nixon, Luci Johnson, and Caroline Kennedy. Now it served as a mini gym, with a treadmill, and a central unit with different stations for various exercises. I used to watch Cable News Network as I went through my morning routine.

Depending on my schedule, I might spend the rest of the morning working in my office, which was next to the exercise room and was once Lynda Bird Johnson's bedroom. I had a private line in my office, and my visitors were always amused by how often it rang with wrong numbers. Between these two rooms were closets, where I kept my clothes.

When I didn't go out to lunch, I usually had a light meal alone in the West Hall. Or, in nice weather, I sometimes ate on the Truman Balcony. In either case I sat by the phone, because by lunchtime in Washington I could start calling friends in California. To warm up the West Hall, I had moved in our two red floral-print couches from California, along with some lamps and tables, and two little needlepoint chairs that Colleen Moore had made for Patti and Ron. As Patti's godmother, Colleen had made her a chair showing a girl standing next to a grandfather clock. There was a mouse at the bottom of the clock (as in the nursery rhyme), and the hands of the clock showed 1:58, the exact time of Patti's birth. Six years later, when Ron was born, Colleen said, "His sister has one, so I'm going to make one for him, too." Ron's chair shows a little boy with his dog, sitting on a fence at a ranch. I'm sentimentally attached to these little chairs, because they remind me not only of my children but also of my mother and her friend Colleen.

The private living quarters are on the second and third floors of the original White House (that is, the original building, minus the West Wing, which was built in 1902, and the East Wing, which was completed in 1942). They're much smaller than you would expect. Ronnie and I certainly didn't need more room for ourselves, but there were times when extra bedrooms would have been useful, such as the two inaugurations, Christmas, and right after the shooting.

Although the White House is a state home, its scale is nothing like that of Buckingham Palace or Windsor Castle.

Mostly it was just Ronnie and I, with frequent visits from Maureen. Like the Carters and the Fords, Ronnie and I slept in what is sometimes called the First Lady's Bedroom, and I loved its beautiful airy shape and high ceilings. To warm it up, I covered the walls with wallpaper in an eighteenth-century Chinese print, with hand-painted yellow, green, and blue birds. The carpet was salmon-colored.

Maureen generally stayed down the hall in the Lincoln Bedroom, partly because Dennis, her husband, is very tall, and the bed in Lincoln's room is the longest one in the White House. Lincoln never actually slept in that room, although he did hold Cabinet meetings there. He slept in the same room we did.

But apparently his presence remains. Neither Ronnie nor I ever saw the legendary ghost of Lincoln, but one night Dennis woke up and saw a shadowy figure by the fireplace. Maureen just laughed at him when he told her about it—until she woke up one night and saw a man who seemed to be wearing a red coat. At first she thought it was Ronnie in his red bathrobe, but when she looked again she noticed that the figure was transparent! Maureen says he was staring out the window and then turned around to look at her before he vanished.

When Ronnie heard these stories, he just laughed them off. "If you see him again," he told Maureen, "why don't you send him down the hall? I've got a few questions I'd like to ask him."

But even Ronnie had second thoughts one night when Rex started barking and running toward the Lincoln Bedroom. Nobody was sleeping there at the time, but Rex wouldn't stop. Ronnie went in, looked around, and saw nothing, but Rex absolutely refused to enter that room.

I was in the Lincoln Bedroom one afternoon, and when I leaned over to straighten one of the pictures, the maid, who had come in to dust, said, "Oh, he's been here again." And when I asked one of the butlers if he had ever seen Lincoln's ghost, he told me that once, from the kitchen, he had heard the piano playing in the hall. When he walked out to see who was there, the music suddenly stopped. Most of the White House staff seemed to believe in Lincoln's ghost and they told stories of Eisenhower and Churchill both seeing him. Who's to say? But if he is there, I wish I could have seen him before we left.

WASHINGTON WOMEN

It was in Washington that the American Matron came into her own.
        —Helen Nicolay, *Our Capital on the Potomac*

Here I am (fourth from the left), in a fairly nondescript hat (certainly compared to my neighbor's on my left), at a prototypical 1950s ladies' luncheon. I have no memory of why I was there, or even where I was.

WASHINGTON is a tough town for women—and especially for wives. This is in large part because, since its inception, Washington has been and remains a man's town. For most of the decades of my Washington life, it was men who were in charge. The man and his position were what counted. Only in the last few decades have women in larger numbers come from behind the scenes to the fore.

It may seem odd or politically incorrect to have a separate section on Washington women, but women in Washington is a topic close to me. I wrote at some length about women in *Personal History,* but that was mostly about women in general. Women in Washington is a somewhat different matter. Women have long complained that life in Washington is especially hard. Married women feel they're judged by the identity and status of their husbands. I have friends who have confided to me that they've had men turn to them at dinner to say, "What does your husband think?"

Almost every Washington woman—whether single or married, old or young, long-ago or contemporary—who has written a book about her experiences here touches on, in one way or another, the difficulties she faces. Lindy Boggs wrote that she "discovered that the profession of congressional spouse is an extremely demanding and difficult one." Bess Furman wrote, "Many women in Washington say clever things, many more think them, but a wise diplomacy restrains the expression of them."

Comment on this phenomenon isn't limited to women. Even Dean Rusk wrote, in his memoir *As I Saw It,* that "Public life is tough on the wives and children of those whose names are in the headlines. The job of secretary of state often called for 15 and 16-hour days, including diplomatic dinners in the evening. Virginia and I ate at home with the family about once a month during my eight years as secretary of state, and the children essentially grew up on their own."

It's not just society that has changed, but women, too. Marietta Andrews, who wrote about women clear-sightedly and insightfully throughout her book, *My Studio Window,* was often called on to speak to women's groups on woman's work, because, "having failed, according to my own reckoning in four professions, art, matrimony, literature and philanthropy," she'd turned "to pageantry in which all fragmentary knowledge and general experience can be utilized!" She wrote,

Women themselves are changing. The World War awakened them from their dreams, and a thousand activities have opened to former society women, in business, art, politics, philanthropy. Character has changed, interests have changed, as much as dress has changed! There was a time when the business of life was to shove visiting cards into the hands of servants on "days at home," and mother and daughter of Bishop or Senator each in a separate carriage, each armed with a formidable list, took their separate ways, making calls from three o'clock to six every day except their own day. There was a time when luncheon and dinner invitations were issued so far in advance that your hostess might be dead and buried before the appointed date.

Women have certainly turned to other work than the business of calling and leaving cards. But the work they've taken up hasn't been easy either. When I took up my job at the *Post* in 1963, Clare Booth Luce told me, "What you should do is get dressed up and come into the office late after you come from your hairdresser. Come in, see people, go to lunch, and leave early. This way you won't irritate the men too much. You can't get too aggressive." I actually believed that at least part of that was good advice.

In an entry in *A White House Diary* dealing with the visit of the Nixons to look around the place before they moved in, Lady Bird wrote, "The men did most of the talking, and Pat and I were politely attentive." This strikes me as entirely typical of most of my time in Washington. Only in recent years have women ventured into being more than just politely attentive. In fact, even when we women were "allowed" to remain with the men instead of separating after dinner to take ourselves off to the hostess's bedroom or some other retreat for a ladies' chat, we mostly tuned into the men and what they had to say. Maybe we were feeling our way. Maybe we were scared and intimidated. Whatever caused the paralysis, it was evident, and that remained true for a long time. It's almost as though there had to be a transition. But at least we were there to hear what was being said.

IN MANY ways, Phil was a real equal-rights advocate. Shirley Potash, who later married Dick Clurman of *Time* magazine, was a friend of Phil's. She told me a story many years after he had died. She had gone to work at *Time* at twenty-three as assistant director of public relations, and in 1956, when Phil appeared on the cover of *Time,* she had been sent to Washington to see that the publication got some air time and advance publicity. She had called Phil to say that she'd send a copy over to him. He suggested that, instead, he go with her around to the networks and the stations to deliver it. Off they went to WTOP, which the Washington Post Company owned at the time, and where Shirley had an appointment with the head of the station. She told the secretary who she was and whom she was there to see. The secretary, recognizing Phil, said, "Oh, Mr. Graham, I'll tell him you're here." Phil immediately responded, "No, no. It's not my appointment. It's Miss Potash's appointment. Don't tell him. Just tell him that she's here." They were kept waiting for twenty minutes before the station manager appeared, and he immediately paled when he saw whom she was with. That was almost fifty years ago, but would it be a very different story today?

How women feel about themselves in Washington is affected by how men feel about them—from the president on down. President Hoover was known for treating women badly. George W. Bush is already being talked about for having women at the highest levels in the White House and around all the policymaking tables there. In an earlier era, male publishers and editors provided women's pages at all the Washington papers, but it was women who helped propel the pages away from complete absorption with society news and into another realm. Hope Ridings Miller, who was Society editor at the *Post* for a time, told me that she and others tried to see to it that the coverage of women and parties included who was where and why and what they said, not just what they wore, all of which helped change the tenor of social reporting.

There were certainly no women for many years in most of the rooms of Washington where the action occurred—the newsrooms, the congressional hearing rooms, the Supreme Court, the bankers' offices, the law firms. But women have always been there behind the scenes. Catherine Allgor's recent book, *Parlor Politics, In Which the Ladies of Washington Help Build a City and Government,* is great cultural history, but too early for our time period here. Her subtitle holds true even past the early nineteenth century, with which she deals.

Some comments about women in Washington over the years have the ring of familiarity. For example, the anonymous author of *Boudoir Mirrors* wrote, "Funny how virtuous and appealing domesticity appears in the eyes of male editors and press agents! During the Campaign, don't you remember how we had Mrs. Coolidge's blueberry pie and mincemeat and doughnut recipes, until I wondered if the poor girl was ever out of a bungalow apron." Isn't this all too reminiscent of Hillary Clinton and her home-baked cookies in at least one of Bill Clinton's campaigns? Even so, it's hard to imagine we will ever return to a time when the *Post* will once again sponsor a "Miss Civil Service" contest as well as a "Miss Beauty with Brains" competition.

From the government girls who swelled the population of the city in both world wars to the Little Sisters of the Rich (defined by Marietta Andrews as the "satellites of wealthier women and competitors of professional social secretaries") to secretaries to company presidents to housewives to suffragettes to maids to teachers, women have constantly held the interest of Washington watchers. Throughout the last eighty years, there have been countless women who have held Washington in thrall. Betty Beale, who was a society reporter for the *Post* and later the *Star,* and who wrote a column called "Top Hats and Tiaras," has a chapter in her book called "Belles of the Ball, Wonderful Women" that includes Lady Astor, Clare Booth Luce, Marjorie Merriweather Post, and Alice Roosevelt Longworth. Leila Pinchot, Mabel Boardman and her sister Florence Keep, Cissy Patterson, and my own mother are others. One of the most formidable, whom I very much liked and admired, was Mrs. J. Borden Harriman—"Daisy" to everyone. After making her mark in the war effort and the suffragette movement, she threw herself into Democratic Party politics.

In 1922, Daisy helped found the Women's National Democratic Club, and served as its longtime president. In the early years of its existence, she was known to have driven her own cook to the clubhouse on New Hampshire Avenue, just off Dupont Circle, to help with meals at the struggling new place. A VIP reception room is named for her there.

She also held many important positions in civic Washington, among them chairman of the Traffic Safety Council of the American Automobile Association, which was played up prominently in the papers in 1936 when she was caught speeding on Constitution Avenue—thirty-two in a twenty-two-mile-per-hour zone—and fined five dollars, two dollars of which she had to borrow from the arresting policeman to pay the fine.

Partly in recognition of her work for the Democratic Party, President Roosevelt appointed her in 1937 as only the second woman ever to become an ambassador. She was sent to Norway, where she not only showed great courage in the tension-filled prewar atmosphere and drove into exile with the king of Norway and his government, but also learned to ski at the age of sixty-seven, much to the delight of the natives.

What she became best known for in Washington were her Sunday-night suppers and soirees at her Washington home, Uplands, on Foxhall Road, which took the form of salons, and became a kind of Washington institution, once known as "Mrs. Harriman's teacup chancellery." Drew Pearson and Robert Allen, in one of their "Merry-Go-

Round" columns, wrote about her being "famous during the Harding, Coolidge, and Hoover administrations as a lone Democrat who lived only for the pleasure of baiting the reigning Republicans. She made them like it."

She certainly wielded power in Washington. She started discussions and arguments at her salons by throwing out provocative questions, or even deliberately reminding everyone that one senator disagreed with another—both of whom were present. Her ground rules for discussion were that "nobody gets angry, and nobody repeats elsewhere opinions heard in my dining room." She mixed up her guests, making sure to include those who would be on different sides of any issue. Once, when Winston Churchill was present at one of her dinners, she threw out the topic "Why don't the British pay their debts?"

By the time I knew her, I think she didn't have very much money, but she used it well by living modestly. Even when she was quite elderly, she kept up her interest in politics and in issues, especially relating to Washington. She became a kind of militant for home rule in the 1950s, serving as co-chairman of the Washington Home Rule Committee, attending hearings, stalking the halls of Congress, meeting with whoever would listen, leaving symbolic tea bags in strategic locations. She paid her federal income taxes under protest because of being voteless in the District, saying, "Taxation without representation is still tyranny in 1955." In April of that year, at the age of eighty-four, she marched with others to the Washington Monument to protest the "shame of a voteless capital," according to a Bess Furman article in the New York Times. The next year she was quoted in the Post as saying, "We're really going to get belligerent about home rule now."

She first voted when she was ninety years old, having experienced a lifetime without the vote, first because she was a woman and then because she lived in Washington, D.C. Called variously the "grande dame" and "godmother" of the Democratic Party, "Washington's No. 1 social citizen," and a crusader for equal rights, Daisy died in her sleep, a well-earned rest, at the age of ninety-seven, in 1967.

Her funeral was held at Washington's National Cathedral, with former secretary of state Dean Acheson offering the eulogy. Among the twenty honorary pallbearers were Averell Harriman, Supreme Court Justice Hugo Black, Senator Robert Kennedy, Stewart Udall, Clark Clifford, Ben Cohen, and James Roosevelt.

In 1963, President Kennedy had presented her with the first Citation of Merit, the nation's highest civilian honor for peacetime service. In a White House ceremony, she was cited for her "singular and lasting contributions to the cause of peace and freedom." At the time she was reported to have said, "I think nobody can deny that I have always had through sheer luck . . . a box seat at the America of my times." Indeed.

This is a personal (and highly selective) collection of pieces that focus either on groups of women or on specific women I've known and admired and who have had a major effect on this place.

Three Washington working women of the 1930s

On Women's Suffrage and a Notable Washington Woman

Washington Wife (1963)

Mrs. Slayden was a congressional wife with marked opinions of her own. These selections from her diary focus on the suffragists, with whom she was in basic agreement, and on Mrs. John B. Henderson, a noted Washington woman and character, whom I knew, and who, for me, is an example of how people reach back through the years and connect us with history.

I was quite amused to read Mrs. Slayden's reference to how old Mrs. Henderson seemed when she knew her. Mother in her diary from 1918 implied that she was quite old even then: "Mrs. Henderson, aged at least 105, was the sprightliest thing at the party." Obviously, she was ancient when I came to be her neighbor when my family moved in 1929 to Crescent Place, just off Sixteenth Street. She lived beside us in a landmark mansion, originally called "Boundary Castle" because of its location along Boundary Street (later Florida Avenue), which was then the boundary between the city of Washington and the District of Columbia.

Along with my grade-school chum Rose Hyde, I was once taken to task by my governess for trying to climb over the wall into Mrs. Henderson's castle. As children, we all worried about this old woman living next door, alone in this forbidding place. Although she would have been nearly ninety when we moved to Crescent Place, she still seemed quite formidable. Mrs. Henderson had wielded social and political power for decades, but neither my friends nor I knew about any of that.

It always amazed me that Mary Henderson, someone I had at least a passing acquaintance with, had been married to a man who was a friend of Abraham Lincoln's and the author of the antislavery amendment to the Constitution. John Brooks Henderson was a "dashing" U.S. senator from Missouri and an eligible bachelor when he first met Mary

Foote, *a very young and beautiful habitué of the ladies' gallery in the Senate, watching the events of the day. The Hendersons built Boundary Castle, which came to be called Henderson Castle, with its large stable for horses and four-car garage. Here they entertained presidents and diplomats over the next decades, and she gave tea dances in her ballroom on Monday afternoons.*

*Mary Henderson was also a writer and produced various political treatises (*Decadence of Nations, *among them), as well as books on food, including one titled* Dietetic Poisons, *where she laid out her ideas on the importance of eating vegetables and abstaining from alcohol. One writer suggested that Mrs. Henderson "collects that quaint and elementary form of social life, the United States Senator, whom she domesticates and feeds on vegetables." She cultivated the kind of eccentricity that Washington thrives on, being driven around the city in a purple Cadillac painted to match a Chinese vase she loved.*

Although people in Washington may not know her name, and though her castle, having been torn down in 1949, is known only in old photos now, Mrs. Henderson's legacy lives on in Meridian Park, which she helped develop and then sold to Congress. She was, as Mrs. Slayden's diary entry suggests, a Washington woman who was fully in command of her faculties.

January 2, 1918

Our militant sisters, whose methods I heartily disapprove, are bringing a lot of trouble to the suffragists. Last night on the street in front of the White House they brought on a riot by burning copies of the President's speeches, denouncing him as a "false prophet" and doing a lot of spectacular things that do nothing that I can see but alienate dignified people from our cause. Five of them were arrested and taken to detective headquarters but were soon released. They announce that they intend to keep watch-fires burning until the Senate passes the suffrage amendment.

January 23, 1918

Political sensations even outdo the weather. The President's flying leap—or was it a double back handspring?—into woman suffrage by federal amendment has brought laughter or tears according to your enthusiasm for "the Cause" or your respect for the Constitution. I made a bet with Mrs. Allender five weeks ago that he would do it—he has so often, "vowing he would ne'er consent, consented." She said he couldn't. He had refused even to see the suffrage committee, because the question of suffrage was not mentioned in his platform and that must settle it for his administration. But she doesn't know how many spurs there are for his single-track mind to run out on for political gain.

It is fun to see his thick-and-thin followers, who a few weeks ago opposed the suffrage even by permission of the states, trying to adjust their positions. I love to stir them up by casually remarking, "Evidently the pickets knew what they were about; they brought the President to terms." For months past women have stood like wooden Indians, one on either side of the two White House gates. They never spoke unless spoken to, their appearance was irreproachable—except in the bitterest weather when poor Billy Kent said his wife had dressed them in his fur coats until he had nothing to wear. Mrs. Kent also had her servants bring at regular hours a wheelbarrow of hot bricks and build new platforms for them to stand on. We used to drive down to see it done, the servants, the pickets, and their friends perfectly silent, only rank outsiders making ribald remarks. The public never complained, but somehow they got on the President's nerves, and he ordered their arrest for obstructing traffic, and five or six of them were hustled off to the workhouse at Occoquan. They were all refined, intelligent women, so our horror increased daily as we heard how they were being treated. They were denied the simplest toilet articles of their own, dressed in filthy prison clothes, given beds that were unspeakable, and seated at the table with the lowest drunkards and prostitutes, black and white, arrested on the streets of Washington. The conditions at the place are so outrageous that the publicity this affair gave it may save many a poor wretch in future.

The suffragists, of course, and many not interested before in the cause became more and more indignant so that we were all ready to meet them with a grand demonstration and parade the day their sentence was up. But the President took alarm and ordered their release one day sooner. I was at headquarters when our culprits came in and could hardly believe my eyes. They looked ten years older, unkempt, dirty and ill for want of the commonest conveniences and decencies of life.

All this makes the President's flop more absurd. Administration papers and friends have been calling the pickets "traitors" "pro-Germans" etc. Only a week before his change of heart, I heard Secretary [of Commerce] Redfield declaiming against them, saying they had "entered into a conspiracy to injure the honorable gentleman who kept the workhouse." His whiskers fairly shivered and shook as he declared that he "would not believe one of them on oath." And now the Fore-ordained is making common cause with them!

September 19, 1918

Sometimes I think I believe in suffrage for women in spite of the woman suffragists. Their ethics are so peculiar. J. tells me that the same committee of members' wives, who ought not to embarrass their husbands' colleagues, has been at his office three or four times to ask him to change his vote when the suffrage comes up again. I have never dared to ask him but once. He explained to them the first time that his vote was a matter of conscience, but they seemed to think that a trifle light as air. A senator tells me that Secretary Baker's wife has been lobbying through the Senate Office Building for some of her pet measures and greatly embarrassing the men. It is awkward to refuse the wife of a secretary— exactly what she counted on for her success, no doubt. Many women have lost their sense of proportion and dignity and are becoming pests. Pretty little Mrs. Jessie MacKaye (Percy MacKaye's sister-in-law) rushed up to me one night on the street, her face all lined with nervous strain, and told me with delight that she had been arrested three times last week. They go out from the headquarters on Jackson Place every night, make speeches and wave banners till they get themselves arrested, and march off to jail, handbags packed in advance with toothbrush and nightie, to revel in martyrdom. The next day there is a spectacular trial at the police court, conspiracies of silence, threats of hunger strikes, and irritated husbands pleading "Mother, come home." They say they are doing it "to influence the Senate." Now, as Adamson of Georgia remarked, "Having revised the tariff downward we are doing the same for the Senate." I can't believe it will succumb to such childish methods.

December 20, 1918

Never in my life have I felt such gross delight at being asked out to dinner. My Annie is sick and three weeks of my own cooking have almost persuaded me to join one of these nut-and-raw-carrot health schools. I jumped at the invitation to Mrs. John B. Henderson's last Sunday in spite of J.'s objection to peanut chops and cereal entrees, and what was our amusement when we arrived to find that the party was planned to celebrate the passing of the Prohibition Amendment, which J. has fought tooth and nail. Senator Morris Sheppard, the "Texarkana Titan," as the *Sun* calls him, was the *pièce de résistance* and so happy over the consummation of his dearest hopes that we all enjoyed ourselves in sympathy with him. Mrs. Henderson was not at her spiciest—a word she would no doubt resent, as spices are not in her lexicon.

I had Senator France of Maryland on one side of me and that ever youthful professional diner-out, Dr. Swisher, on the other. J. was opposite to me beside a grim female with a large hat secured by an elastic band under her chin in the fashion of the 6os. She had a wide mouth and sharp teeth that snapped when she talked. Obviously a woman with a mission.

Mrs. Henderson set the ball rolling by asking J. what he thought of the amendment, and he answered facetiously that it wouldn't do for him to express his opinion in such a select company. While the others gave the laugh his little witticism was entitled to, the lady beside him glared. In answer to a question of mine about her latest book of recipes, Mrs. Henderson said she was compelled to revise it, that now being rid of animal foods and alcohol she was opposed to salt, pepper and all the baking powders. The dinner was devised according to her latest prejudice, and a succession of dishes, beautiful to the eye, were apples of Sodom to the taste. At last we welcomed almost audibly a mold of ice cream knowing that its merits were not dependent upon either salt, pepper or baking powder, and one sip brought me a glow of delight—it was soaked with rum. A caterer had had his little joke. Shy looks of pleasure went around the table of twenty or more guests, and when I started to say something, Dr. Swisher laid his hand on my arm and said, "Oh, please don't tell her; she'll take it away from us." Nobody commented, and Mrs. H. and the Senator talked about proteins as they ate the last spoonful of their portions without knowing that they were destroying their efficiency and digging early graves for themselves.

After dinner, when the gentlemen went off to smoke, it came out that the lady with the elastic under her chin represented a Boston society for the suppression of the cultivation and use of tobacco. When everyone gets his or her favorite law to work how good we will be—or what hypocrites and lawbreakers.

January 31, 1919

Mrs. Henderson almost persuadeth me to be a vegetarian and a total abstainer! I might even forgo tea, coffee, salt, pepper and baking powder if I thought it would result in such radiant health and usefulness as hers at her age. They say she is eighty or more—she was called an old lady when I came here twenty-two years ago, but she still looks just the same. I sat by her at the Congressional Club last night and noticed how thick and soft her hair was, and her skin clear and rosy. She could never have been strictly pretty, but she is so pleasant to look upon. She does nothing to efface the marks of age, they just aren't there, and she talks as if she were playing a game with time, counting quite frankly every point she gains or loses. She said, "I like to sit in front, for I am getting a little deaf. I hate to lose any faculty, one oughtn't to."

ANONYMOUS
(Nelle Margaret Scanlan)

Alice Roosevelt Longworth: Defying Convention

Boudoir Mirrors of Washington (1923)

The introduction to Boudoir Mirrors *helps explain why the then anonymous author—Nelle Margaret Scanlan, as we now know her to be—turned her attention to the women of Washington:*

> A man goes down in history for the greatness of his courage in war, or prowess in politics. But when a woman keeps fifty hungry people from eating the decorations while the honor guest is found, sobered, and dressed for the dinner she wears no laurels for that achievement.
>
> While a man is pounding on the entrance door to the Inner Circle, his wife is quietly oiling the social key, which will gain admittance more surely. . . .
>
> The parry and thrust on the Senate floor is reported in the press, but there is less blood spilt here than in the flight of javelins across the tea tables. But this does not make a headliner—not yet. Just wait!

Every one of the portraits in Boudoir Mirrors *is worth reading, but one of the richest is that of Alice Roosevelt Longworth, that quintessential Washington woman. She came first to Washington in the late 1890s when her father, Teddy, was assistant secretary of the navy, and, of course, came back again when he was vice president and president. She married Congressman Nicholas Longworth in 1906 in a White House ceremony. He later became Speaker of the House from the beginning of Coolidge's elected term through Hoover's first two years, so it was then that the Longworths were, as she wrote, "very much part of all that goes on in political and office-holding life in Washington." Indeed, she was part of everything.*

Alice was a person of whom it could truly be said that she didn't suffer fools gladly. In fact, as Frances Parkinson Keyes said of her, "she did not possess the faculty for suffering them at all." Keyes was one of the few writers who didn't hesitate to be critical, however, and also wrote of Mrs. Longworth in 1937, "It is all the greater tribute to Mrs. L's fascination and prestige that in spite of her attitude of detachment the glamour of her personality is still undimmed and the pre-eminence of her position still undisputed. But it seems regrettable she should not have done more with the ten talents at her command when so many women have done much with only one."

Many other women have written about Alice Longworth. Nothing about her was sacred. Vera Bloom referred to seeing Alice at one social event, describing her as "without benefit of either coiffeur or cosmetics." Marietta Andrews prophesied that Mrs. L., "born to authority, schooled from her cradle to statesmanship," as she was, might become the first woman president of the United States of America. Betty Beale, in Power at Play, A Memoir of Parties, Politicians and the Presidents in My Bedroom, wrote that Mrs. L. once described herself as a "combination of Scarlett O'Hara and Whistler's mother."

What Alice Roosevelt Longworth did was to remain a kind of enfant terrible throughout her life. She was an acid-tongued, headstrong woman, incredibly witty and irreverent. Joe Alsop pointed out that she said of Dorothy Thompson, "Dear Dorothy is the only woman in history who ever got paid for having the menopause in public." He also recalled that when he once "foolishly" remarked that the movement for Willkie came from the grass roots, "Mrs. L gave a loud snort and said, 'Yes, from the grass roots of 10,000 country clubs.'" Her own father once said of her, "I can either run this country or take care of my daughter, Alice, but I cannot do both." She herself said that her "'publicity value' was, I fear, at times a trial to the family." Even when she was older, she admitted, "I am full of curiosity and overexuberance, and overexuberance is something I hate in the aged." She loved politicians and politics, calling the latter "a great game both to watch and be a part of." And she always set her own rules.

Alice Roosevelt Longworth died only twenty years ago, but it seems more like a hundred. She is still missed by many of us in Washington.

Take Alice Longworth—she's a singular character, that's what she is—singular. There was a time when she was considered wild, unconventional, daring. Perhaps she was. Yet I would rather call her singular.

As a child she was singularly shy. You would scarcely believe that, but she was. As a girl she was singularly impulsive. No one doubts that. As a woman she is still singular; she retains her individuality, those forceful characteristics inherited from her father, which set her a little apart.

Few women in America, outside the active workers in some public cause, have focused public interest to such an extent as Alice. The reflections of her *Boudoir Mirror* show—but you shall see them for yourself in a moment.

Poseur? Certainly not. What she does, unconventional though it may be, is not inspired by a desire to shock, so much as an expression of self-determination, a vigorous protest against irksome customs and restrictions. Her attitude is one of supreme indifference to public opinion.

Other people may model their modes and manners according to established precedents, but Alice Longworth will leap the social barrier with the same agility with which she performs athletic stunts, such as standing on her head. I must tell you about that.

One day a woman sat miserably talking about her health. She detailed her symptoms and their reactions, her sufferings and the heroic martyrdom which never permitted her pain to dim the happiness of her home. You know the sort of woman!

"Have you ever tried standing on your head?" asked Alice, leaning forward and betraying a sudden interest.

The woman looked at her for a moment, uncertain whether or not to take offense. But there was not a flicker of a smile on that Roosevelt face.

"It acts like a charm," she said. "Here, lend me a safety pin."

She secured the hem of her skirt between her knees, and taking a cushion, placed it on the floor.

The hypochondriac watched with bewildered interest.

Alice Longworth put her head on the cushion, and shot her legs aloft, where she remained poised perfectly. Standing on her head, and kicking at the chandeliers was a sort of daily exercise with her.

The woman gasped, and looked at the faces of the other guests. Oh, yes, there were quite a number present. They all knew Alice, and being deeply rooted in respectable orthodoxy, they envied the woman her daring, because she could do it and get away with it. No other woman in that room could have stood on her head and retained such perfect equilibrium of body or composure of mind.

"There, you try that every day, and you won't have lumbago or heart trouble," and she stood erect, returned the safety pin, and resumed her seat with leisurely ease.

All the world knows, of course, that Alice was one of the pioneers in smoking, and left a trail of ashes and smoldering disgust through conservative circles. The disapproval of the dames was to her like the ash, and she flicked it aside as meriting no more consideration. She was not deliberately rude, but rather delighted in the shocked look of her elders. She came and went like a merry flash, and skated skillfully over very thin ice. Alice Roosevelt had many of the privileges of a princess, without any of the restrictions.

One night Mrs. Leiter gave a party. It was a large and gorgeous affair, with diplomats and officials and titles there. Oh, this was some years ago, before the turkey trot and cigarettes had been accepted in the Best Society.

Few women were smoking then, and those who did, kept it dark. Madame Riano had acquired the art in Spain. She had been over with the ambassador, and had fallen into line with her adopted countrywomen.

In the middle of Mrs. Leiter's ball, Alice Longworth took it into her head to give an exhibition of the new dance, the turkey trot. But to add zest to the performance, she lit a cigarette first, and smoked while she danced.

She sailed down the middle of the room, puffing little jets of smoke at the ceiling, to the horror of the women. I forget who the man was who danced with her that night.

As one woman said, "Alice looked like a steam engine coming down a crimped track."

Society was shocked; unusually shocked. Even the press was shocked. Such behavior at a private ball! Not alone Washington papers beat the air in protest, but New York made this notorious young woman a headliner, and the episode was related in full, as a horrible example of modernism run riot.

"Now isn't that the cutest story you ever heard?" Alice said, laughing, when she read the shocking details of her conduct, tucked, frilled, and flounced, and set forth for the public.

I suppose most of you remember Count Cassini, who was Russian Ambassador during the Roosevelt régime. He appeared in Washington accompanied by a young and beautiful lady, known as "The Countess Cassini."

It soon became known that she wasn't a countess—that she wasn't any sort of Cassini. Old Washington, sedate, mid-Victorian Washington, put up its lorgnette and then dropped it. The alleged Countess became invisible to the naked eye. There was merely a hole in the air where she stood—nothing more.

Official Washington looked at each other behind its feather fans, and said: "Well, really, my dear— But one must draw the line somewhere!" So they drew it at the Countess.

The Countess, however, made a singular appeal to Alice Roosevelt. She's that sort. If she likes people, she doesn't ask for their birth certificate and demand their marriage lines.

Perhaps it was the adventurous spirit, the quest for big game, the sense of danger, but whatever the bond, the Countess Cassini and the Princess Alice became inseparable companions. "Princess Alice" was a familiar press title for the White House daughter during her father's régime. It wasn't her regal bearing, however, which induced reporters so to designate her, but rather her royal indifference.

What did these two do? Hus-s-s-sh! What didn't they do? you might ask.

Hurdle racing was one popular pastime. After dinner they would arrange the ottoman, chairs, and other suitable furniture at intervals round the room, and have a hurdle race.

If you backed Alice, you always backed a favorite, for she generally came in the winner. She didn't let skirts impede her progress by hanging down too long. A hitch or two, and away she went. Oh, they were gay times at the old Russian Embassy in those days! There is no doubt that Alice had a high old time, and if she missed anything, it was because she hadn't heard of it. . . .

ANY DAY you may see Alice Longworth come into the Senate. In winter a heavy beaver coat envelops a figure still slim and graceful. Her hat, no matter how becoming, is flung instantly aside, and shows her hair growing rather prettily around her forehead, and knotted at the back. It is the same in the few private homes where she visits. Off comes her hat the minute she is inside the door. She hasn't much hair, but it is pretty, and there is scarcely a gray streak in it.

Alice has big, dreamy eyes; at least they look dreamy until her interest is roused. Then they light up with vivid intelligence. Her skin is smooth and fair, and has no suggestion of the beauty parlor. In fact, she has no artifice of that kind, and her charm, though definite, is elusive.

Did you know that "Alice Blue" was named for her? She was always very partial to dull blues, and this shade became very popular during her residence at the White House. Since then, of course, we have had the Harding Blue and the Princess Mary Blue. Now we are getting a brand of Tutankhamen Blue. Well, every blue has its day!

When rubberneck tourists come chattering and clattering into the Senate chamber, and the barker points out the persons and places of interest, he has only to indicate the hatless woman leaning forward in the Senate gallery, listening intently.

"That is Mrs. Nicholas Longworth, daughter of Theodore Roosevelt," he says.

Interest in the Senate instantly wanes. All eyes turn to the Roosevelt daughter, and there is admiration, almost reverence at times, in the eager look from this mixed group.

In many ways she is like her father. Over and over again I have watched her, but she shows no embarrassment; in fact, she seems absolutely unconscious of this scrutiny.

Interest in politics has always been very real with Alice, and she has found it an absorbing topic. An interesting debate in the Senate was a lure she could not resist.

Not long after her marriage, I think it was, she was giving a big luncheon party. In the middle of it, some one called her up to say that an important issue had suddenly developed in the Senate.

Grabbing a hat, and hurling an abrupt apology at her guests, Alice left the astonished crowd to finish the party without a hostess.

Why, even last year, Alice went to New York for Christmas, with the intention of staying over New Year's Day. No sooner had the Economic Conference proposed by Senator Borah crowded the murders off the first page, than she came home. Politics comes first with her always. She sat in the gallery listening, her languid eyes alight.

"Hullo, I thought you were staying in New York until after New Year's Day," one woman said to her.

"Fancy staying in New York, with all this happening here," and she flung out a gesture indicating the Senate floor, where a wordy conflict was taking place.

Alice was only two days old when her mother died. Her grandmother, Mrs. Martha Roosevelt, you know, died the same day, and the double tragedy overshadowed the arrival of this vital little person. Her aunt, Anna Roosevelt, who was afterwards Mrs. Cowles, took charge of the baby until Theodore Roosevelt married Edith Carew in London. But Theodore Roosevelt was always particularly fond of Alice; she had a special corner in his heart, and there was a rare camaraderie between them.

I think it was back in the early seventies that some one divided the inhabitants of the United States into three groups—saints, sinners, and the Beecher family. A more recent version would have substituted the Roosevelt family, for presumably they have always been a law unto themselves. Yet not outlaws.

I remember a dinner at the White House one night. It was the first time I had been a guest of President Roosevelt. Alice wore a dress of her namesake blue, and long white kid gloves. I fairly gasped when I saw her eat asparagus with her fingers without removing her gloves! It may have been a bet or a dare, but it was probably just a perverse impulse, or perhaps there was present some one especially correct whom she wanted to shock! She was never in awe of the great, and parental discipline did not impose too rigid a regulation upon personal conduct.

ALICE ROOSEVELT was terribly disappointed when her father refused to let her go to London for the coronation of King Edward. But for consolation, she had that memorable Taft trip to the Philippines. That was about a year later, and oh, the wonderful stories we heard about that tour—stories in which the fair Alice was star actor.

These tales, well spiced, were the savory served at many a dinner table. They had percolated to America from the Far East, no doubt expanding in transit, and taking on a more lurid hue.

Nicholas Longworth was one of the Taft party, and the romance, which had been budding, blossomed fully on the voyage.

There is no doubt that Alice supplied conversation for many a dinner party by her activities in the Far East.

"My dear! Have you heard about Alice Roosevelt and the sacred elephant?" "Do you know what Alice did in a Chinese temple?"

That she was the theme of conversation in no way dimmed her ardor for adventure. If fellow travelers did relate how she had, when dared, dived fully dressed into the plunge bath, what did she care? And if there was nearly a war because she had ridden a sacred elephant outside a Chinese temple, while the pig-tailed officials prayed for vengeance—or was it an encore—why worry?

Goodness, how time passes! That is over seventeen years ago. I wonder how many remember the excitement there was about her engagement and wedding, and the maneuvering for invitations.

No one was surprised at the engagement, because the barometer had been "set fair" for some little time. After its announcement, Alice seemed supremely happy. Functions at the White House took on an added interest. Would Alice and her fiancé be there? The bride elect became the central figure, and so often after a brief appearance, she would quietly disappear—she and Nick.

All through the winter, I remember, each day Alice would accompany Nick to the Capitol. Even on her birthday, a few days before her marriage, she made her daily pilgrimage to the shrine of politics with her future spouse.

And the wedding! Washington will never quite forget that.

The President wished to make it a quiet affair, but that couldn't be done. Close relatives and important officials were the basis of the invitation list, but it grew until it held a thousand names.

Social America was on tiptoe, hoping for an invitation. The Has-Beens tried resuscitation, and the Never-Wasers resorted to novel tricks to break in. Many people, quite unknown to the Roosevelts, sent expensive presents, and then brazenly asked for invitations. Their gifts were promptly returned.

Strange, how some people seem to spend their lives courting snubs: never content with where they are. I could tell you a few who have—but that must wait till I get started on "breaking into society," and the best methods to use. Some jimmy the lock, and others creep in on the dumb waiter.

But to return to the presents. Exaggerated stories of the value of the gifts and jewels being showered upon the bride elect grew out of the President's reluctance to have the list published. Fed by imagination, they grew alarmingly. This brought a crowd of appeals. Some asked that Alice should give from her plenitude to various worthy causes. Others made personal requests for a silver teapot or a few spoons, where there had been duplication. They had caught the souvenir habit. A few anonymous epistles were sent with a hint of future peril, should she retain this abundance which had been thrust into her hands.

Nearly all the foreign royalty laid gifts at the feet of America's Princess Alice. We were so excited waiting to see what would come next. The Spanish King sent antique jewelry, Austria a diamond and pearl pendant. I forget what the King of England sent, but the jewelled bracelet from the Kaiser, I think, Alice afterwards gave to the Red Cross, during the War. I know the French gift was Gobelin tapestry, and the Italian King sent mosaic from Florence. So did Pope Pius IX. The Taft party, who had watched the romance grow and flourish, gave her a necklace of diamonds and aquamarines. Embroideries came from China and Japan, and I think Nick Longworth gave his bride a diamond necklace.

They were married on a Saturday, and Congress adjourned without avowing a reason, so as to avoid establishing a precedent. Not that the marriage of a President's daughter and a Congressman happens often. But you never know.

I remember Nellie Grant (Mrs. Algernon Sartons) was there. She had been married in the White House thirty-two years before.

In spite of all those jewels, Alice doesn't care a fig for personal ornaments. Jewelry makes no appeal to her. When earrings were not fashionable, she always wore them. Since the demand for earrings in the ten-cent stores has so definitely indicated the trend of fashion, she has ceased to dress her ears. A long platinum chain, studded with diamonds, is one of her favorite ornaments, and from this she suspends a gold turtle as big as a door stop. It is rather incongruous, but somehow it has a personal appeal to her, and that outweighs all fashion.

"Tiger! Tiger!" called Alice Longworth. I thought she was going to recite Blake's poem, but she was merely talking to the tiger skin, a souvenir of one of her father's hunting expeditions, spread in front of the open fireplace.

In every home there is a characteristic corner, some room more expressive of the owner than others. The Longworth drawing room is of the conventional type, but it is in the living room that you find the Roosevelt revealed.

The big tiger skin gives a definite note, a personal note. Alice worshiped her father, and would have fought like a tiger to defend him personally or politically. Photographs of Theodore Roosevelt, etchings and busts of him are there, with autographed pictures of famous men and women. There are also interesting cartoons reminiscent of past and present politicians and events.

It is a comfortable room, with an atmosphere of being lived in and loved. Not untidy, it has, however, the orderly disorder of books that are read, cushions that give comfort, pictures that please, and a faint odor of smoke. It is the home of people who prefer to live at home.

The Longworths are splendid pals. Each accords the other a generous freedom, differing without dispute, and meeting life's problems with understanding. Alice likes men and enjoys their company. Not as a vamp does she seek them, but for a pleasant interchange, a clash of wit, for deep reasoning, and good fellowship.

Next to her husband comes her brother Ted. She is very fond of Ted.

Her inanimate loves are politics and books, and they have, as I have told you, a real fascination for her. She is a great reader, and devours weighty volumes and frivolous nonsense. Far into the night she reads. I often think she prefers books to people. She certainly spends more time in their company.

Formal visiting is anathema to Mrs. Nicholas Longworth, I can assure you, and her Congressional calls are a huge, unpaid, social debt. Let no Congressman's wife feel personally aggrieved if her call remains unacknowledged. She treats them all alike.

"I hate calling; I just can't do it," she says, and there the matter usually ends.

Occasionally she applies a measure of self-discipline to herself, and sets out to pay off some social debts.

She started out one day with a Senator's wife—I think it was Mrs. Borah—with the fixed intention of paying calls.

When they arrived at the first house on the list, she hesitated.

"Oh! I don't think I'll go in here," she said. "I'll wait for you."

She waited, and Mrs. Borah went in. When the car stopped at the second place, she sat back contentedly.

"You go in—I'll wait." Again she shirked.

At the third place it was the same. When her social tour ended, her companion had left cards on ten women, but Alice had stuck to the car with amazing fidelity, and returned home with her indebtedness undischarged.

"I wasted the whole afternoon," she told me that night. "Absolute waste of time, I call it."

"And didn't you leave a card?" I asked.

"Not one," and she smiled a lazy smile, and sat back among the cushions.

If Nick Longworth were a different type of man, Alice might find plenty of activity in playing his particular game; but politically, do you think he will rise much higher? Frankly, do you?

What a sensation it would cause politically, if Alice decided to throw her hat into the ring! She could join the Lucy Stone League, and become a Roosevelt again. That would be worth thousands of votes. And what a Senator she would make!

I was out at a little tea party a few weeks ago, when some one suggested that Alice ought to run for the Senate. Instantly the room seemed riddled with ideas. Talk thickened. For ten minutes her assets and liabilities were tossed like leaves before the wind.

"She's a brilliant woman," said one.

"Look at her training in public life, her knowledge of politics. Why, she loves the game more than anything on earth, I imagine," said a second.

"She'd make a good Senator, but a rotten candidate," came in a Southern drawl. "She doesn't like people, and won't shake hands, and she has never been active in women's organizations."

"You mean that she doesn't 'suffer fools gladly,'" came from a redheaded woman.

"That's just it," said the hostess, as we gathered our coats and made for the elevator.

But just think what it would mean to have one electric, vivid, fearless, audacious young woman in that stuffy, stodgy assembly of fence-fixers, seed-senders, and afraid-of-their-mitten mediocrities! And what a daredevil campaign it would be! Can't you see sober traditions being broken, and precedents being carted away by the trash man! Why, the revelations of old Tutankhamen's tomb would pale before some of the stories that would develop in that battle.

And if she got in! Of course she wouldn't be spectacular all the time, but wouldn't those old partridges sit around, waiting, for fear they'd miss it when she was in action, making a six-cylinder speech.

Well, who knows what the future may hold, but I hope I am still alive to see it—if she should stand. I'd just hate to miss the fun.

Herald Angel

Cissy (1966)

Here is another woman about whom Washington remembers very little, but who had a big impact on the city. Eleanor Patterson came from a family of journalists, with interests in several Chicago papers; her brother, Joseph Medill Patterson, founded the New York Daily News, *the first successful tabloid in the United States. Cissy, as she was always known, inherited an interest in the* Chicago Tribune *and became editor of Hearst's* Washington Herald *in 1930. She added the* Washington Times *in 1937, leasing both papers at the time, but buying them two years later and merging them into the* Washington Times-Herald.

Cissy was among the first people Mother and Dad met when they came to Washington, although at that time she was still known as Countess Gizycka, having been separated from a Polish nobleman. She was incredibly glamorous, and my mother, although drawn to her from the first, was also wary. Mother wrote of her, "She has no great sensibilities and yet she appeals to my senses." Actually, the two had a great deal in common. For one thing, they both preferred men to women. In another entry in her diary, my mother compared Cissy with Alice Longworth, noting that Cissy had less energy than Alice, but finding whatever energy she had "equally misdirected," adding "But she is decent and likable." Cissy was someone with whom Mother gossiped, often "outrageously," as she herself admitted. One of the things they agreed on, Mother confided to her diary, was that in any affair, the woman "gets a rotten deal." Cissy actually was a bit awed by my mother. Luvie Pearson, who was a friend of both women, told me that on one occasion when she and Cissy were going to meet Mother, Cissy suddenly announced that she wasn't up to seeing her: "She's so good and does all these important things. I'm not up to it at all, dear. You'll have to go and manage."

Cissy clearly was looking for something other than a strictly social existence in Washington. When she took up, in 1930, the editorship of the Washington Herald, *against the odds and against the assump-*

tions of the Washington newspaper world, she set to work and pulled out all the stops, turning the paper around from a money-losing drain on Hearst's resources to the highest-circulation paper in his chain. There was something in the Herald *for everyone.*

Once my father bought the Post, *he and Cissy became rivals, while at the same time remaining friends of sorts—even through years-long lawsuits involving rights to print the comics. Cissy's exploits were legendary—she was even known to disguise herself as a homeless woman and go out at night to see what she could see on the streets.*

After Phil's death, Luvie Pearson thought she was strengthening my resolve when she suggested that I should go to work at the paper. She firmly told me, "Cissy did it; so can you." I was grateful for Luvie's support, but I remember thinking I could never be like Cissy.

Needless to say, Cissy's style as a newspaperwoman was hardly my style, but when it came to a threatened strike, she stood her ground. Reading the section relating to labor issues and the possibility of a strike, my stomach clenched in sympathetic understanding of what she was up against and what she must have felt. When she died of a heart attack at the age of sixty-three, in 1948, the whole city mourned.

ARTHUR BRISBANE WARNS THE EDITOR

Arthur Brisbane told me yesterday in New York that I've got to say something.

"Did you ever hear the story," he said, "of the parrot that spoke five languages? A man bought a prize parrot for his wife. Next day when he came home he found a parrot on the supper table, boiled, ready to serve. 'My God,' said the man, 'what have you done? Didn't you know the parrot spoke five languages?' 'Well,' answered his wife, 'why didn't he say something?' "

Now, Mr. Brisbane, I've said something.

(signed) Eleanor Patterson

THIS ITEM, boxed in black lines, appeared on the front page of the *Washington Herald* on August 1, 1930. When the staff members saw it, they were baffled and worried. Mrs. Eleanor Patterson was taking over that morning as their new editor and publisher. What did the zany manner in which she chose to introduce herself to *Herald* readers portend? It was bad enough that the new boss was a woman, and a society woman at that. She also apparently was addicted to expressing herself whimsically, if not enigmatically.

Late that morning the staff got its first physical view of Mrs. Patterson. Suddenly there she was, standing in the center of the city room. At her side was Frank Knox, general manager of all the Hearst newspapers, of which the *Herald* was one. She was tall and elegantly tailored, with red hair that glistened like copper, pulled straight back on her head, a snub nose, and a mouth set wide and straight in an oval face.

Knox introduced the glamorous stranger, and she spoke briefly, in a tone of quiet command. Her voice was throaty, like that of an actress, with a languidly imperious drawl.

"All right," she said, as the reporters and subeditors gathered around, "they say this is a stunt—a joke! Well, if that's their idea, let's show them—let's go to work and put it over!"

The men had begun to slip into their coats—reluctantly, for it was a torrid summer day. The new boss added with a smile: "And you don't have to wear your coats when I'm around either."

Then she turned and drifted from the room, trailing an exotic perfume. Most of the staff members shrugged and turned back to their desks. Others grinned at one another: Perhaps the hapless *Herald* had not, after all, seen everything yet.

Early in the afternoon there was another incident, but whether it was a good or bad omen remained to be seen. The new boss had been offered the plush office suite reserved for Hearst executives at the front of the *Herald* building and had turned it down. Instead she chose the relatively small space just off the city room which had been used by the sports department. A wall running only three quarters to the ceiling separated it from the bustle of the reporters, copyboys and editors.

"I intend to learn this business and run the paper," Mrs. Patterson explained to Knox. "And I want to know what's going on."

Knox kept his amusement to himself. He knew she wanted to be taken seriously as an editor. He had been rushed here from New York two days before to cope with possible hostility. Arthur Brisbane, the Grand Panjandrum of the Hearst organization, had dispatched him with this observation: While veteran Hearst men should long since have accustomed themselves to surprises, they might resent having to take orders from a woman. The appointment was to be regarded as an experiment. Never before had a female been editor of an American metropolitan daily. Knox had called together the top men of the *Herald* and implored them to be patient. After all, they had suffered through Hearstian innovations before.

"You know she won't be around long," Knox had said to them, puffing smugly on his cigar. "She won't last six months."

Six months was a good deal longer than some publishers had lasted at the *Herald*. In the paper's nearly three decades of existence, an average of almost one publisher a year had come and gone in an effort to rejuvenate the money-losing paper. Some of them had survived less than a week, and one had thrown up his hands after only one night and departed in disgust.

The *Herald* was one of the livelier papers in Washington, but it was undistinguished journalistically and considered not quite respectable. Now, in mid-1930, its circulation was down to an anemic 61,000, so who could argue that an offbeat editor and publisher was not worth trying?

But, ran the counterargument, granting that Mrs. Patterson was an offbeat choice, what was there about her that suggested she might bloom into a successful newspaper executive? When she was sized up, only the wildest of prophets could have foreseen that within a few years she would emerge as a hellcat who could stand the capital on its ear and command national attention. Or that in fifteen years her executive success would splash her into *Collier's* magazine as "the most powerful woman in America."

Who was Eleanor Patterson? To be sure, nothing about her was ordinary. She was a middle-aged millionairess, one of Washington's three so-called "whip-cracking hostesses"—whose parties were said to have an "Arabian Nights flavor." She was a true American aristocrat, authentic and dignified, whose lack of inhibitions provoked a restless, damn-the-torpedoes way of life.

This much was known to informed Washingtonians. Those who took the trouble to inquire further were rewarded, for her earlier past was sheer storybook melodrama. A belle in the *fin-de-siècle* European diplomatic set, she had married a Polish-Austrian count and had gone to live with him in a "castle" deep in Russian-held Poland. Within a few years she had fled from him with their baby girl over the midnight snows. The Count had pursued her, kidnapped the child and hidden her in a convent. Only through the intercession of President Taft with Czar Nicholas was the baby restored to her mother.

Divorced, and still known as "The Countess," she had married Elmer Schlesinger, a prominent lawyer, in 1925. When Schlesinger died in 1929, she had legally reclaimed her maiden name. Her close friends called her "Cissy," a family nickname dating from childhood.

To the *Herald* staff it was encouraging that the new boss was the offspring of a distinguished American newspaper dynasty. . . . [But she] herself was almost totally devoid of newspaper experience. Back in 1920 she had written some articles about the Republican National Convention and about her big-game hunting for the *Chicago Herald and Examiner.* Better known, and much more to her credit, were two novels she had written during the twenties. One, *Glass Houses,* was a cutting commentary on Washington's sociopolitical life. The other was *Fall Flight,* a fictionalized version of her own hair-raising life with the Count. Both books had been well received by the critics.

On one point there was unanimity: Cissy was no sissy. She had spirit and courage. She was a superb horsewoman, and there were people in Wyoming who claimed she was the best woman rifle shot ever seen in the state. As for conflict and controversy, the lifeblood of exciting newspapers, Cissy obviously thrived on it.

Gusto and imagination were what the *Herald* sorely needed. In 1930 there were five daily newspapers in Washington, and only one of them, the venerable *Evening Star,* was a financial success. And the outlook for an economic boom was nil. The country felt in its bones the economy was in a state of transition—but to what? The people were waiting impatiently for the promised end to the recession which had followed the stock market crash of the previous October. During the late winter and all spring, President Hoover and Secretary of the Treasury Andrew Mellon had soothingly forecast a business revival. But in midsummer it certainly was not in sight. . . .

If ever there was a time to hand over the fate of a newspaper in the national capital to a frivolous society hostess, perhaps this was it. The Hearst organization sought to capitalize on Mrs. Patterson's name value. Two days before she was to take over, Knox inserted a front-page, boxed announcement composed by Brisbane. Noting that she was the granddaughter of Joseph Medill, it stated: "The *Washington Herald* feels sure that Mrs. Patterson, who in accordance with Galton's Law, inherits the genius of her grandfather, and will be very successful and INTERESTING as editor of a Washington daily newspaper."

Privately, Brisbane had advised his protégé in New York that the way to be interesting in Washington was to attack a sacred cow. The notion appealed to Cissy; she had always enjoyed ridiculing sacred cows, and now she had a megaphone to do it with. In her third day on the job, she saw her chance. Sitting cross-legged on the third floor of her Washington mansion, she was scanning the other Washington newspapers when an item brought a gleam to her eye. It announced that Mrs. Alice Roosevelt Longworth would serve as "adviser and campaign manager" for Ruth Hanna McCormick in Mrs. McCormick's race for a United States Senate seat for Illinois.

Ruth was the widow of Cissy's first cousin, former United States Senator Medill McCormick, and the daughter of Mark Hanna, the shrewd

Republican boss who had engineered William McKinley's election to the Presidency. Alice Longworth, the celebrated "Princess Alice," was daughter of the late President Theodore Roosevelt and wife of Representative Nicholas Longworth, the Ohio Republican who was currently Speaker of the House. No one could wish for a cow more sacred than Alice.

Since nearly the turn of the century, Cissy and Alice had been friends—most of the time. Cissy liked to needle Alice, for Alice had the reputation of being one of the wittiest women in America. Like Dorothy Parker, her reputation was so great that she was sometimes credited with bons mots she had not coined. The description of President Calvin Coolidge as looking "as if he had been weaned on a pickle" was widely attributed to Alice; she admitted to having gleefully circulated the barb but disclaimed its authorship.

As a teen-ager in the White House, Alice had been America's hoydenish darling. She had shocked the post-Victorians by smoking cigarettes, betting on horse races, and diving into the ship's swimming pool, fully clothed, during a voyage to the Orient. Lovely, sparkling, photogenic, Alice had been simultaneously loved and criticized. . . . Now, as the Second Lady of the land, Alice was more dignified—in other words, a fine target for a Cissy shaft.

Alice later insisted to friends she "knew it was coming." Five years before, she had been unflatteringly fictionalized as a Washington hostess in Cissy's first novel, *Glass Houses*. When Cissy had a newspaper to play with she doubtless would strike again, if for no other purpose than to increase readership.

Sitting on the floor, Cissy pondered the item about Alice and Ruth McCormick's campaign, then looked around for note paper. Finding none, she tore a blank page from a book and began writing rapidly in pencil. Making some quick editing changes, she telephoned Mike Flynn, managing editor of the *Herald*. After dictating the item to Flynn, she said: "Put it on the first page, Mike. Mr. Hearst says people don't read anything anywhere else."

The "box" appearing the next day read:

INTERESTING BUT NOT TRUE

The news is that Mrs. Alice Longworth will not only be a confidential adviser to Mrs. Ruth Hanna McCormick, but that she will campaign publicly for her lifelong friend. Interesting but not true.

Mrs. McCormick takes no advice, political or otherwise, from Mrs. Longworth.

Mrs. Longworth gives no interviews to the press.

Mrs. Longworth cannot utter in public.

Her assistance will, therefore, resolve itself as usual into posing for photographs.

(signed) Eleanor Patterson

Washington bought the *Herald* as never before. The question was: What would Alice do?

The next morning Cissy looked at the *New York Times* and discovered that she was national news. The *Times* quoted the slap at Alice and reported that friends of Mrs. Longworth were "amused" by it. But from Alice herself came no comment.

Cissy continued to use her front page to titillate her readers. In October, she went after Alice again. Recalling that she had said previously that Alice had "no real gifts" to contribute to Mrs. McCormick's campaign, Cissy now observed in a box:

I was in error. I spoke hastily. In ignorance.

Senator Borah, another close friend of Alice Longworth's, has said that if Mrs. McCormick is elected he will vote to unseat her because of her excessive campaign expenditures. Mrs. Longworth may now present her real gifts. She may use her political influence, of which the country has for so long heard so much. She may soften the decision of the frugal gentleman from Idaho.

Senator Borah is also a close friend of Mrs. Ruth McCormick. They are all close friends.

But it is for Alice to come now bearing gifts.

Will she? Can she?

(signed) Eleanor Patterson

To those tuned in on Washington gossip, this was an inside joke. Like Alice, Borah had been the model for a protagonist in Cissy's *Glass Houses*—a western senator who attracted the predatory eye of both of the hostesses, thinly disguised as Alice and Cissy herself. The fictional triangle was based on fact.

Once again Cissy's public musings made the *New York Times*. It gave an account of the blast in its usual sober fashion but, in addition, its Washington correspondent, Arthur Krock, devoted a long paragraph to the item in his Sunday column. Noting that Cissy, Alice and Ruth had been chums since girlhood, Krock asked, with proper *Times* dignity, whether Editor Patterson's "cutting disparagement of Alice [between the two of whom he said there had been a sharp estrangement] represents a woman colleague's idea of what is of importance of comment." In time, Krock was to drop his disdain of Cissy Patterson's news judgments; he also became a good friend and married one of the *Herald*'s stable of society columnists. . . .

Mrs. Patterson's mercurial attitude toward her employees alone both flabbergasted and amused the capital. It ranged from an almost sadistic cruelty to outlandish kindness. Firings were frequent, impulsive, and sometimes bizarre. They were never dull, and a discharged editor could dine out for a week on his story of his last day at the *Herald*. By that time he was probably hired back.

Another conversation piece in Washington was Cissy's wardrobe. It hung from racks filling two rooms of the top floor of her mansion at Du Pont Circle—gowns, slippers, floppy hats, bathing suits and other items running into the hundreds. The ensembles were numbered, photographed and indexed in a catalogue. When Cissy was planning an evening out, she thumbed through the catalogue and gave her maid the number of her evening's choice.

Sartorially, if nothing else, she was the most startling newspaper editor in the country. She was likely to turn up at the *Herald* office at any hour of the day or night, and her "working clothes" varied with the hour. In the morning or early afternoon, she was usually in riding habit, and late at night, coming straight from a party, she would glide through the office wearing a dinner dress and dragging a mink coat. If she was wearing the coat, and it hung open, one could glimpse dazzling Oriental brocade pajamas, her favorite, and a daringly avant-garde, evening costume. The final touches of glamor were her long cigarette holder—longer even than FDR's—and red-painted toenails.

In the raffish city room of the *Herald*, Cissy was a shimmering vision. With it, however, came discordant sounds. Mrs. Patterson was always accompanied by a pack of French poodles. Before she entered the doorway, the poodles' commotion signaled the arrival. They yapped—drowning out her low, awe-inspiring remarks to the editors—and they nipped. Deskmen endured the attentions of the poodles, between silent curses, as occupational hazards. The dogs snooted the editors and reporters and were contemptuous of copyboys. They might tolerate a scratching of their ears for a time, but soon they stalked off, flaunting their snobbery.

To the men of the *Herald*, Mrs. Patterson was "The Lady," and to the women she was "Madame," a term of irony mixed with respect. On first meeting, no one was immune to her impact; it was remembered and discussed for a long time afterward. She had "presence" to such a degree that all eyes riveted on her when she made an entrance. This was not only because she was strikingly dressed. There was a confidence, a slowness, a deliberateness about her which suggested a tigress. Like a tigress, she had seldom-blinking eyes. When they fixed on you, they exercised a potency of will. Yet the strong will was cloaked in an outward femininity and charm that was irresistible.

Cissy's most envied physical characteristic was her carriage. Well into middle age, her figure retained the suppleness of an athlete. She was five feet, seven and a half inches tall, with a narrow waist and small, pretty feet—on which she was wearing ballet slippers years before they became the vogue, and she seemed to glide along like a ballet dancer. President and Mrs. Theodore Roosevelt were fascinated by the fluidity of her movement. They told their daughter Alice repeatedly: "Watch that Patterson girl when she walks—such grace, such beauty in motion!"

It was the grace of a feline animal. As one Washington columnist put it, "Cissy panthered across the room."

Cissy's glamor had nothing in common with the motion-picture-queen style of the twenties and thirties. Her face lacked classic lines and she did not indulge in lacquered makeup. Her turned-up nose, huge eyes and puglike contours carried more than a suggestion of Irish pugnacity—which she came by naturally. Yet the total effect was bewitching. One young Washington matron, blessed with more conventional good looks, complained enviously: "Cissy simply hypnotizes people into thinking she's a great beauty."

Cissy's voice had a cello-like richness. She spoke slowly and deliberately, every syllable articulated carefully. The pitch was low, and to some men the tone seemed caressing. Late in her life the tone became almost as husky as a man's. . . .

Cissy's incandescence glowed against a succession of glittering backdrops. She lived as the hoi polloi thinks rich aristocrats ought to live. In the early thirties, when the rich were just beginning to feel guilty, no American woman lived on a more independent or extravagant scale. Loving movement, she needed many places to alight, and over the years she acquired many. Her principal house was a marble mansion at 15 Du Pont Circle in Washington, D.C. Built by the famous architect Stanford White, it had thirty rooms and ten bathrooms and was manned by a staff of eighteen servants, including a green-liveried footman and a butler actually named Philpotts.

In nearby Marlboro, Maryland, Cissy kept an English-style house and country estate. In Sarasota, Florida, she maintained a winter residence on the Gulf, and at Port Washington, Long Island, she owned the estate formerly owned by Vincent Astor. In New York City she rented a year-round apartment at the plush Canton House. She had another place at Nassau. And at Jackson Hole, Wyoming, there was the ranch where she hunted elk and bear.

Between some of these residences—and to many other places—Cissy traveled with casual grandeur, like a maharani, in her private railroad car, "The Ranger," christened after one of her favorite horses. The fact that private railroad cars were already obsolescent luxuries in America did not bother her. Cissy was fond of hers. Mrs. Carolyn Hagner Shaw, her secretary at that time, was reminded of a French chateau when she entered the car. It was furnished daintily in chintz, had guests' bedrooms and baths, a cozy living room and a well-stocked kitchen.

Hooked onto the end of a regularly scheduled train and ready to roll across the country, "The Ranger" was a kind of barge-on-wheels for an American Cleopatra. The full complement included butler, chef, French maid, personal secretary, food, liquor, changes of slipcovers, and more than a dozen trunks just for Cissy. Sometimes she decided late at night to leave town on the car in the morning. The staff was immediately galvanized into furious activity to get everything ready to roll at dawn. Even the personal secretary did not always know the ultimate destination or how long they would be gone.

Once, Mrs. Shaw was told to ride the car to New York just to retrieve the poodles—who had unaccountably been left at the Port Washington house—and bring them back to Washington. Probably en route, the secretary speculated that she must be conducting the most extravagant canine escort service in history. Cissy played each of her roles for all it was worth. In the office, surrounded by editors who vied like courtiers for her favor, she reigned like Queen Elizabeth. On horseback, she rode as easily as a circus rider. At her Wyoming ranch she roughed it and shot like an elegant Annie Oakley. Skillfully guiding the conversation at one of her evening salons, she was Madame de Staël. Composing her thoughts for publication, she was George Sand. . . .

FOR THE first time in years, Cissy Patterson was dictating an open letter to her readers. It was January 30, 1939, and, journalistically, she was about to perform a marriage. She hoped the nuptials would carry her the last long distance toward her goal of becoming a true newspaper professional.

Pacing the floor, Cissy first reviewed in her mind the last year and a half, when she had for the first time functioned as an absolute boss. Confidently, she had started out to ride two horses—the *Times* and the *Herald*—at once, exulting in the new freedom to try out any idea that occurred to her or one of her editors. Circulation had risen, but nonetheless, both papers had remained deep in the red. It offended her pride as well as her pocketbook to operate two losing properties. In 1938 the total loss had come close to $1,000,000.

Washington obviously was overcrowded with five newspapers, and Cissy was advised by expert opinion in the publishing field to close the morning *Herald*, which was a bigger loser than the afternoon *Times*. She resisted this idea with all her force; the *Herald* was her first love, and she was tied to it with a passionate devotion. She had never liked or understood the *Times*. Some drastic new remedy had to be devised.

Now she was about to disclose what it was. Slowly she dictated the message which, signed and in boxed type, appeared on the front page of the next morning's *Herald* under the simple heading: "AN ANNOUNCE-MENT." It read:

I would like to make a statement to end all statements concerning the lease and sale of the *Washington Herald* (morning) and the *Washington Times* (evening).

On August 7, 1937, I leased both properties from Mr. William Randolph Hearst with an option to buy. On January 28, 1939, I exercised my option and purchased both properties and all their physical assets, with the intention of merging the two unnaturally divided papers into one.

I use the word "unnaturally" after considerable reflection and years of intensive experience of waste of time and talent, worry and ceaseless effort to keep those twin papers separate entities and apart.

Anyone who understands anything about the operation of newspapers knows the handicaps involved in such a divided setup. The duplication of expense alone, added to the enormous increase in cost of production since 1937, became finally a problem without any reasonable solution.

There has been, contrary to general opinion, a limited duplication of circulation between the *Times* and the *Herald*—only 17.3 percent of the whole. That is, 183,309 people are reading today either the *Herald* or the *Times*, and the reason for that is simple. Some of our readers want their paper with their morning coffee, while others prefer theirs around noon or when they get home at night.

So for sound editorial as well as business reasons, we have finally decided to pull up the sluice-gates which artificially divided these properties and let the two papers merge into one.

I will close without the usual quota of pompous promise and merely say we hope you will like the new *Times-Herald*—Washington's only around-the-clock newspaper—and that you, the people of Washington, will share with us in our success.

Only a very few round-the-clock newspapers have been tried in the United States, and their success has not been conspicuous. One of the main reasons Mrs. Patterson took the risky plunge was not mentioned in the open letter. For over a year she and her key staff members had held long conferences on the problem of attracting department-store advertising. To do this, the Patterson papers would somehow have to breach the bastion of the *Star*, which virtually dictated the advertising policies of the biggest advertisers in the capital. The *Star* was a fat old dowager whom nobody, seemingly, dared offend. But Cissy and her strategists felt that if they could offer the advertisers a package which would guarantee them more readers for the same rates they could not, as hardheaded businessmen, afford to pass up the extra business.

The shotgun wedding of the *Times* and the *Herald* united two of the city's oldest and most durable newspapers. The *Times*, started in 1893, had been bought in 1901 by the famous Frank Munsey, who in turn sold it to Arthur Brisbane, then chief editorial writer for the Hearst chain. Brisbane deeded it to Hearst in 1919.

The *Herald*, founded by a group of Washington businessmen in 1906, passed first to Clinton Brainerd of the McClure syndicate. In 1919, Brainerd sold it to a syndicate in which Herbert Hoover was a principal. Surprising as it may now seem, Hoover was interested in becoming the Democratic presidential nominee in 1920. After an unprofitable two years running the *Herald*, the syndicate sold it to Hearst.

Neither paper ever prospered under Hearst, but he was determined to maintain two windows in Washington at almost any cost. In 1924 he constructed a $1,500,000 four-story building at 1317 H Street N.W., and installed both the *Herald* and *Times* in it. The papers had separate offices but shared the same presses. It was this building that Mrs. Patterson acquired when she purchased the publications.

The new *Times-Herald* published ten editions over a 24-hour period—five editions from dusk to dawn, and five others through the day. The savings Cissy would achieve immediately were easy to see—the round-the-clock paper would carry the best features and comics of the *Times* and *Herald*, and the daytime editions also would offer full race results and jazzier headlines to lure street sales. Many costs would be cut in half.

But there was an immediate and significant casualty of the merger: jobs. Thirty-seven fewer staff members would be needed to put out the streamlined paper. Each of the thirty-seven was to be given the required Newspaper Guild severance pay for time served, plus a week's notice pay, plus two weeks' 1939 vacation pay—which was added over the protest of some of Cissy's financial advisers.

The vacation pay was more than was required under the Guild contract Mrs. Patterson had signed the previous summer with the *Times* and the *Herald* employees. Thus, she was surprised when she learned through the grapevine that the Guild was calling a strike meeting. But first there was to be a mass meeting to which all department heads and those who would remain on the staff were invited. Cissy herself was invited, and she went, feeling a little depressed and very tired.

When she walked into the room and faced the assembled employees, they were prepared to hear a plea or a pep talk. They got something much more dramatic, and much more in her own individual style. Cissy leaned against the table and told her story, simply, slowly, in a voice that broke only once. She said, first, that she could not understand the reason for the protest and the threatened strike; if she had taken professional advice and closed the *Herald*, hundreds of its people would have been left without jobs. She gave details of cost and duplication of running two papers, and said she could not afford to continue losing money at that rate. She thought she had found a way out: merger. She wanted to publish a good newspaper, and she knew they wanted one too. She had counted on their cooperation and loyalty. Then her voice dropped and she chose her words even more carefully.

"I want to save this paper," she said, "for you and for myself, because I think you love it as I do. If there is a strike, I will lock the doors and they will never be opened."

Then she turned and walked from the room.

Her audience, as hushed as a church congregation, included all sorts of people—newcomers, oldtimers, leaders of the strike movement, all of them imbued with the tradition that a newspaperman wears cynicism like armor. As Mrs. Patterson left, many of them were unashamedly blinking back tears.

The strike meeting was to go forward on schedule. The night before it, Cissy dined at Harvey's restaurant and seemed serene. The threatened strike had Washington buzzing, but she preferred to talk to her friends about a new type of mountain goat discovered in Idaho. When someone mentioned the Guild, she remarked quietly: "There will be no strike. If they picket, they'll picket against an empty building. There will never be a strike. I'll close the shop and lock the doors."

Later in the evening she went to a tiny office adjoining the roaring press room, where the first edition of the newly born *Times-Herald* was being spewed forth. It was a moment to be savored. She sat down at a desk and began to autograph the first editions for employees. She had, as usual, mislaid her spectacles and could scarcely see her own signature, but the name, Eleanor Patterson, in bold, feminine letters was unmistakable. Then, with a characteristic gesture, she swept off her large picture hat, pushed the heavy auburn hair from her forehead, and smiled contentedly around the room.

The next day no strike was called. Probably not a single staff member doubted for one moment that Mrs. Patterson had meant what she said.

Pioneer Woman
of the Twentieth Century

F.D.R., My Boss   (1949)

Probably no woman ever was more talked about and present in Washington than Eleanor Roosevelt. Although she came from and returned to New York, Mrs. Roosevelt was at the heart of many activities in Washington for the twelve years of her husband's presidency. She was also in the lead when it came to recognizing women and giving them opportunities to do good work. For example, she insisted on having only women cover her press conferences and activities. Scott Hart, in Washington at War, *reported that she did this for two reasons: one, so that she could talk about subjects of particular interest to women, and two, "by locking the conferences against men, to force the news media to hire women." Not a bad strategy. Every newswoman I knew from that period felt that Mrs. Roosevelt was awfully good to all of us.*

There was always much to admire about Eleanor Roosevelt—her openness, generosity, down-to-earth style, curiosity, and so many more estimable qualities, not to mention her energy, for which she was notorious (she was even referred to as "Public Energy Number One"). Vera Bloom wrote that "Mrs. Borah used to say that she would read Mrs. R's schedule for the day in the morning paper and promptly go back to bed, exhausted!" adding, "No one thought of trying to emulate her. Who could? She must be possessed of the most perfect health and stamina any woman ever had." At an annual Gridiron dinner, which as usual included skits poking fun at the president and administration officials, one skit ended with an appeal from a woman reporter: "Let's pray the prayer they say Franklin prays, 'Oh, God, please make her tired just one day!'"

Edith Helm, who worked for Mrs. Roosevelt directly as secretary, loved and admired her. She wrote of her, "If anyone were to ask me what I consider Eleanor Roosevelt's most characteristic gesture, I could answer instantly. I have never stepped into her study with even a casual mention of a pathetic case or a worthy cause but that she automatically reached for her checkbook. I had to learn to think carefully before making any comments which might inspire such sweeping generosity."

Certainly there were people who were critical of Eleanor Roosevelt—even some close to the president, including cabinet members, complained about her. Secretary of the Interior Harold Ickes wrote in his diary, "I wish Mrs. Roosevelt would stick to her knitting and keep out of affairs connected with my department."

Much of the criticism is similar to what one hears about any first lady—after all, Mrs. Lincoln, the second Mrs. Wilson, and, in our day, Mrs. Carter all attracted unfavorable comment. Reading about Eleanor Roosevelt is particularly parallel to what we read about Hillary Clinton during her husband's eight years in office; it all reflects the plight of the first lady as she tries to define her "job."

Grace Tully's book is highly personal, an informal book about her boss, filled with loving anecdotes about FDR. Tully herself was described by the Man at the Microphone, the anonymous author of Washington Broadcast, as "unknown to the average bus rider . . . the lady who knows today what Mr. Roosevelt is most likely to do tomorrow, the next day, or two months from now." As the president's secretary, she was able to observe Mrs. Roosevelt at close range. This is just one of the hundreds of books and articles written about Eleanor Roosevelt but, like (I hope) most of the selections here, it has an honest and accurate feel to it.

Eleanor Roosevelt's own words, from her memoir This I Remember, gave readers some insight into how she really felt throughout her Washington and White House years. She wrote, "I think I lived those years very impersonally. It was almost as though I had erected someone a little outside of myself who was the president's wife. I was lost somewhere deep down inside myself. That is the way I felt and worked until I left the White House."

I F THE overworked label "human dynamo" ever finds its most literally deserving personality it undoubtedly will be Mrs. Eleanor Roosevelt.

Never have I known a person, man or woman, with capacity equal to Mrs. Roosevelt's for work or play. To her, work is play and for more than twenty years now of my own close observation she has been racing through day after day and week after week of crowded activities with an effectiveness as devastating as General Patton's tanks. She is a fascinating and charming woman, in whom graciousness and generosity are as normal and as genuine as breathing. No person could command a more loyal friend than Mrs. Roosevelt, nor one quicker to translate that friendship from words into action.

But as in the case of F.D.R., Mrs. Roosevelt did not suddenly become an uninhibited human whirlwind simply because she moved into the White House in 1933. To my knowledge she had been the same since I first went to work for her in the Democratic National Committee headquarters in 1928 and she was then merely following the pace which has evidently been lifelong. Only the stage has changed—New York to Albany to Washington, Lake Success and Paris.

As a mother, a hostess or a boss, Mrs. Roosevelt is just about the most efficient person I have ever encountered. Her entire day, and every one of them, is planned in such a way as to permit no waste of time and to leave nothing undone that should be done. Her sense of organization is geared to a physical and intellectual energy and endurance quite equal to this formula of efficiency and it matters not whether she is dealing with domestic, diplomatic or political problems.

The impression she sometimes gives of breathless inattention is a complete illusion; nothing going on in her immediate vicinity either escapes her or diverts her from what she considers the business of the moment. Her memory is long and photographic.

Her instructions to her children, to a housekeeper, to a secretary or even to a President were precise and pointed. She remembered, when all of us forgot, either the first or the last item in a long list of things to be done. After having been caught without pencil or notebook in a few instances, I learned to tick off the number of her instructions on my fingers and then hope I could remember what each finger represented. If I couldn't, she always could—any number of hours later.

Mrs. Roosevelt's sense of charity was as genuine and as positive as all her other inclinations. I learned my lesson in that respect during the early Albany days when she handed to me a pathetic letter from a destitute young mother asking for help—not by any means an unusual type of appeal but one written with an arresting tone of deserving need. Dressed for travel, Mrs. Roosevelt was on her way to New York City when she stopped at my desk with the letter—and her instructions.

"I must leave, Tully. Please ask Whitehead (the major domo) to get some eggs and milk and a few other things and will you please take them over to this address. Here is a small check for her besides. I'll be back tomorrow."

This sounded to me like a generous but relatively simple manner of dispensing charity. I carried out the instructions and expected to hear no more about it. But not at all. When Mrs. Roosevelt returned from New

York the next day, one of her first inquiries was for a full report on the woman—how old was she, did she appear in good health, were the children clean and well clothed, what kind of a flat did they have, et cetera. The next thing I knew, Mrs. Roosevelt was over there herself and arrangements were made for the mother to come to Hyde Park for a few weeks. And while in Hyde Park, it was further arranged to have her instructed in seamstress work. When she returned to Albany, she was able to find work in the needle trade.

It was not simply because Mrs. Roosevelt was a President's wife that she became a journalist. She has an inquiring mind and a great facility for expressing it. Whether or not her opinions and conclusions find unanimous agreement is quite beside the point; I know of no other columnist who succeeds in being always right or universally popular.

Mrs. Roosevelt was an active and good reporter, a one-woman staff for the President. In her multiple engagements, social and business, and her pell-mell traveling around the country she picked up a lot of information. Most of it went directly to the Boss and it was not unusual to hear him predicate an entire line of reasoning upon a statement that "my Missus told me so and so." And by this I do not mean that Mrs. Roosevelt was "selling a bill of goods" or that the President was simply making snap judgments on the basis of womanly chatter. They debated many issues but all final decisions were his—not hers.

I was sitting with the Boss one afternoon during wartime when Mrs. Roosevelt burst into his study.

"Franklin, many people have suggested I should make a trip out to the Pacific. I get letters frequently about it. What do you think?"

"I think it would be a grand idea," he answered at once, "perfectly grand."

Both this trip and a previous one to London were criticized by those who criticized all Roosevelt actions but I know that her fresh and imaginative approach to what she saw and heard provided the Commander-in-Chief with new ideas and perhaps new ideals. All of the knowledge and best opinions scattered around the globe in wartime were not concentrated in the top military or diplomatic brass and Mrs. Roosevelt talked to many individuals of many nationalities who had provocative opinions to throw into the hopper.

Mrs. Roosevelt was most anxious to accompany the President to the Yalta Conference and asked him one day when just the three of us were lunching, "Franklin, darling, I'd like to go with you to Yalta. Is there any reason why I shouldn't?" The question, put up to him directly, was something of a poser and he hesitated as if studying the matter before making an answer.

"Darling, there won't be any other wives present," he replied in much the same manner as any husband might turn down a wife's request to go with him on a business trip. "I'm afraid I can't take you along." Mrs. Roosevelt accepted the decision calmly though I could see she was disappointed.

It was probably one of the few occasions on which Mrs. Roosevelt was treated as "any other wife" but the answer left her without any comeback. . . .

Despite all her other activities, Mrs. Roosevelt did not neglect the duties of a mother nor her wifely responsibility of supervising the housekeeping at 1600 Pennsylvania Avenue. She was almost always the one who had to administer any family discipline to the younger generation and I never heard the Boss scold one of the children or even speak critically of them in my presence. . . .

The Boss started their White House residence by giving Mrs. Roosevelt a $2,000 monthly allowance—his money, not the Government's—for normal household expenses. These included their food, that of the servants, numbering about thirty, and entertainment for thousands of people who did not come under the heading of officials.

That a President's salary is inadequate for the required standard of living in the Nation's Number One home is not disputed even by the political opposition. The Roosevelts found it so and F.D.R. frequently dipped into personal income to make the monthly finances come out right. . . .

So it was that on one occasion of frenzied figuring over the March tax catastrophe I asked him hesitantly if he thought he might reduce the monthly budget at the White House.

"I don't know," he laughed. "You try it—but I don't think you will get away with it."

With some timidity I then asked Malvina Thompson if she thought Mrs. Roosevelt would mind or if she could get by with less than the $2,000 monthly. Tommy's answer was: "I don't know either. Why not just try it?"

The next month the Boss forwarded a check for $1,500 to his "Missus." There was an immediate reply.

"Franklin: I can't quite make it on this."

But the ice was broken and a compromise figure of $1,800 resulted.

One of Mrs. Roosevelt's chores was to supervise the White House kitchen and the fare at the family table.

At Hyde Park, Mrs. Roosevelt had become acquainted with Mrs. Henrietta Nesbitt, a country neighbor who was active in the League of Women Voters and did some family cooking on the side. A practice developed of Mrs. Roosevelt asking Mrs. Nesbitt each year to make up some Christmas boxes and send them to relatives and friends of the Roosevelt family. When the Roosevelts came to Washington in 1933, Mrs. Roosevelt engaged the Nesbitts, installing Mr. Nesbitt in a job in the package room of the White House and making Mrs. Nesbitt the official house-keeper. Two cooks, Ida and Elizabeth, who had been with the family in Albany, were also brought down to work under Mrs. Nesbitt's direction.

When she was here, Mrs. Roosevelt used to go over the daily menus with Mrs. Nesbitt and even for short absences she would arrange to have several prepared in advance. No system, however, was quite equal to the housekeeper's conviction that the proper diet should be "plain foods, plainly prepared" and the President pretty much had to take it, like it or not. Mostly he didn't like it—and often he said so, with suggestions as to what should be done. Unfortunately, the suggestions didn't "take."

The most graphic disclosure of the Presidential attitude toward the "plain foods" came in the late summer of 1944 when I was chatting with him and his daughter Anna Boettiger.

"You know," the Boss suddenly remarked, "I really want to be elected to a fourth term."

It was a provocative remark and sounded like a momentous pronouncement.

"I want to be elected to a fourth term," he repeated, "so I can fire Mrs. Nesbitt."

Sometimes the President by himself was able to meet the challenge of the food served in the White House; sometimes the rest of the staff came to his aid. When the coffee brought to him had a consistently bitter taste, for instance, he met that trial by having a percolator placed at his bedside, and for the breakfast meal, at least, made his own coffee. Yet another time, when he was ill, I came into his bedroom and asked whether there was anything he wanted.

"Yes," he said, "I'd love some of that big white asparagus that comes in cans."

"Well," I said, "why don't you ask Mrs. Nesbitt to get you some?"

"I did ask her," he said, "but she said it was not to be found in Washington."

This seemed so much nonsense to me and I told him so, adding that within half an hour I could get him as much asparagus as he wanted. He expressed his wonder and gratitude, and I went out, put in a call to Toi Bachelder, who in turn went to the Woodward and Lothrop department store and returned with ten large cans of asparagus.

It may seem uncharitable to Mrs. Nesbitt to make a great issue out of so trivial an incident in the life of the historic figure she served. I do not mean to be uncharitable. I mean, instead, to point up the fact that the feeding problem inside a house that symbolizes the might and majesty of the United States, bears a democratic resemblance to what goes on in homes across the land. Of his own direct negotiations with the White House housekeeper Roosevelt again followed the pattern that prevails across the land. He planned his approach with all the care he gave to a major diplomatic move. During one breakfast, for instance, he suddenly exclaimed to me, "My God! Doesn't Mrs. Nesbitt know that there are breakfast foods besides oatmeal? It's been served to me morning in and morning out for months and months now, and I'm sick and tired of it!"

Later, during office hours, he called me in for dictation and returned to the same theme. He leaned back, and holding an advertisement before him which he had torn out of a newspaper, he went through it line by line. The dictation went something like this:

"Corn Flakes! 13 ounce package, 19 cents!

"Post Toasties! 13 ounce package, 19 cents!

"Cream of Wheat! Two for 27 cents!"

And on through rice crispies, wheaties and grapenut flakes.

"Now take this gentle reminder to Mrs. Nesbitt," he said when he finished.

"Oh, no, I don't!" I said, "—not until you sign your name to that memorandum and make it an official document. Even with your signature on it, it's going to have tough sledding, but without it you are sunk."

The President agreed. He signed his name and sighed, "Well, we'll wait and see." . . .

Roosevelt never did fire Mrs. Nesbitt because that was not within the area of his responsibility. But after Mrs. James Roosevelt died the Boss brought Mary Campbell down from the Hyde Park house and installed her as cook in the family kitchen on the top floor of the White House. Mary was devoted heart and soul to the Boss and warred with the rest of the White House management to see to it that he got what he wanted. She may have been persona non grata with others in the kitchen because of this, but Mary served her President well. From the time of her arrival the fare in the family kitchen, at least, took a decided turn for the better. Still later, in the last year of his life, the President lost all interest in food or how it was prepared. In this he came at last to view it in the same abstract way Mrs. Roosevelt always viewed what she ate.

Mrs. Roosevelt was blessed with good health and no amount of physical expenditure seemed to affect it adversely. In fact, with the idea that she needed even more exercise than her normal woman-killing schedule provided, she resumed a favorite earlier day pastime of horseback riding when she came to the White House. In order to fit it into the calendar of her day she had to be out on the bridle paths of Washington by 7 a.m. or earlier. She was then in her late forties.

She did have one affliction but in certain instances it worked more to her advantage than otherwise. Mrs. Roosevelt has been slightly deaf ever since I first met her and both Tommy and I made a practice of so advising some of her visitors who were not aware of the fact. For her part, Mrs. Roosevelt seemed to pretend in some cases that she had not heard some extraneous remarks by callers and by this device swept conversationally past much of the usual trivia to pin her visitors down closely to the exact business at hand.

It was a misfortune that the First Lady was such a poor subject before the camera and the results were consistently evident. In actuality, her face is possessed of such life and vitality that she is in person quite an attractive woman. For some reason, however, this vivacity and sparkle never seemed to register on film. If she cared, she never indicated it nor did she mind when the Boss used to twit her occasionally about some particular fantastic camera recording.

"Darling, what in heavens were you doing when this was taken?" he would ask.

"Oh, dear, it's just the usual," she would laugh. "Isn't it terrible?"

Her mannerisms of facial expression and tone of voice made her an easy mark for talented mimics and imitators. She knew about this Washington social practice and tried on several occasions to persuade some of these people to perform for her. It was reputed that Alice Roosevelt Longworth was one of the best but Cousin Eleanor was never able to entice Alice into a demonstration. Mary Eben, who is an amateur counterpart of Bea Lillie, was tops at the "Mrs. Roosevelt act" and was almost cornered on it at one of Mrs. Roosevelt's own parties for the Gridiron Widows at the White House.

"Mary, dear," Mrs. Roosevelt called from in front of the group, "I understand you do a perfectly wonderful imitation of me dictating my column to Tommy. Won't you come right up here now and do it for us?"

The Private Lives
of Government Girls

Washington Holiday (1955)

Eleanor Early was a well-known feature writer in the 1950s who also specialized in travel books, particularly of New England. Her Washington Holiday *is a charming guide to the capital city. Some of it is standard fare, but I liked this part from the chapter on "the private lives of government girls." In many ways this material is trapped in its time period, but it strikes me as a fairly accurate picture of a certain group of women who spent their lives working in Washington and loved it.*

Iₙ 1800, when the government moved from Philadelphia to the Federal City, the 130 officials and clerks got to Washington as best they could. The journey (now two hours by train) took two days. They traveled by crowded stagecoach, which was drawn by four horses, and seated twelve persons. Everyone carried his lunch and, when it grew dark, they stopped at a tavern for the night. At dawn they resumed their journey and when they reached Washington, they started room-hunting. Among the clerks were two "female employees" who, presumably, had plenty of beaux. There were numbers of boarding houses then, with room for everybody. And the cost of living was extraordinarily low.

Moreau de St. Méry, a refugee from the French Revolution, arriving in Washington at about the same time, was astonished at the way hotels put strangers together in double beds. Bedbugs, he declared, were plentiful, and summer flies stung painfully. Girls in Washington, observed Monsieur de St. Méry, were pretty much like the girls he had met in New York and Philadelphia: charming at fifteen, faded at twenty-three, and old at thirty-five. American women were fussy and cold, he said, did not bathe enough, and had bad teeth and unattractive hair. They were crazy for dancing, "continuously tripped the light fantastic," ate too much, and generally started the day with a thick slice of pork, or salt fish.

Now everything is different. A hundred thousand girls hold jobs that were undreamed of in 1800. In the battle of the sexes, the odds have been reversed, and estimates of the ratio of women to men in Washington vary all the way from five girls to a man to ten-to-one. Few of the men are eligible; most of the girls are lonely; and living is costly. Hotels never put strangers together in double beds. Bedbugs are scarce and flies don't sting. American women are perennially youthful and addicted to bathing. Girls in Washington have beautiful teeth and shining hair, but little opportunity to dance. And they never have pork or salt fish for breakfast.

The average Government Girl is a stenographer, typist, telephone girl, receptionist, filing clerk, or duplicating machine operator. She is between eighteen and thirty-five, unmarried, and likely to remain unmarried. She took a high-school business course and went into civil service because she wanted romance and/or security . . . and on romance, she was sold short.

As for security—if she sticks out a six-month probationary period, it is practically impossible for a Government Girl to get fired. She has a short day and a long vacation. She gets sick leave and assorted benefits. Eventually, she will get a pension. But most girls want to get married, and Washington is not a place to find a husband. On the other hand, neither is a small town; and the majority of girls in the capital come from small towns.

A new typist assigned to the stenographic pool in the Pentagon blinked when she saw thousands of able-bodied men, all employed under one roof. "Back home," she said, "I worked in an office where there were three men. One was sixty, one had T.B., and the other had fits." Although there are thousands of men in Washington, four out of five Government Girls are destined to be old maids. And neurotic spinsters often end up in Saint Elizabeth's (federal institution for the mentally ill).

If the Government Girl marries at all, it will be later than most girls, usually to a man who is her male mate in government. She will continue to work, and carry twice the burden of the average small-town wife. Her husband will become dissatisfied and restless—middle-aged government employees lose ambition and feel frustrated. They will save money and buy a car, live in suburban Virginia or Maryland, and drive to work mornings. This is the best she can hope for, and the chances of achieving it are only one in five.

Secretaries have been known to marry the boss and live happily ever after. One of them married the Secretary of the Interior, moved in exalted circles, and had handsome children; when her husband died, he left her a fortune. But such cases are rare.

Faced with the facts of life and love in government, thousands of young women walk out on their jobs. There was, for example, Mildred

Forbes, twenty-three, of Saint Louis, who worked in the Pentagon, the biggest office building in the world. In the Pentagon there are more admirals than ensigns, more generals than lieutenants. Mildred chucked her job. "The top brass is old," she explained. "Every officer I met was married. And every girl I knew took herself to the movies."

A capital haberdashery advertised for a salesgirl, with a guarantee to "provide cocktails at 5 p.m. and a husband within six months." Mildred took the job. But she didn't get a husband and, pretty soon, she went back to Saint Louis. . . .

There are many departments and bureaus in Washington where a girl may work. The Pentagon, probably because it is dramatically huge and imposing, is considered particularly desirable. Built for the wartime army at a cost of $83,000,000, it houses the Defense Department. It covers 34 acres, a plot three times as big as Bedloe's Island where the Statue of Liberty stands; and has five sides and five stories, which is why it is called the Pentagon. It is so big that carpenters pedal from job to job, girls have to get their shoes reheeled every two weeks, and new employees get lost on their way to the lavatories.

There is a story about a very pregnant girl who nervously implored a guard to show her the way out. The corridors are 17½ miles long and she obviously had no time to waste. "Lady," he said, "you shouldn't have come here in that condition." "But I wasn't when I came in," she wailed.

There are two hospitals in the Pentagon; a TV-radio Studio; and an Officers' Club with five handball courts, four bowling alleys, and a Turkish bath. Its cafeterias comprise the biggest restaurant project under one roof in the world. Sixty thousand meals are served every day—that's calling such snacks as doughnuts and coffee a meal. There are ten snack bars, twenty-eight cafeterias, and two private dining rooms for the brass. In warm weather, tables and bright umbrellas are set up in the courtyard and trays brought outdoors. The last time I ate in the Pentagon, I had meat with two vegetables, bread and butter, coffee and dessert for forty-five cents.

In the concourse are shops where employees can buy all manner of things. A girl actually bought the following one day during her lunch hour: a bra and a frying pan, a formal and an apple pie. Once a guide told General Charles de Gaulle that a Pentagon girl could buy both a wedding ring and a baby carriage within its walls. The Frenchman asked, "Which does she buy first?"

As a matter of fact, girls who work for Uncle Sam lead a sort of boarding-school existence in which sex is largely vicarious. They go to movies, visit art galleries, play golf on public courses, swim, bowl, and play tennis. And on Saturdays, a great many of them visit cocktail bars, but not with men. The Mayflower lounge, known as the Snake Pit, is a favorite rendezvous, especially in the wintertime. The girls drink dry martinis and loathsome pink ladies. They sit around all afternoon, watching the door for celebrities. And afterward they take themselves to dinner, thereby acquiring neither wedding rings nor baby carriages.

There are gay and wonderful parties every night, but Government Girls don't get to them. To many outsiders, the girls may seem to represent Washington. Actually they move in a little world of their own that is not even on the fringe of social excitement.

Next to government, society is Washington's biggest business. Its annual expenditures run to tens of millions of dollars. Its hostesses are famous and their parties fabulous. Government Girls devour the gossip columns about the dinners and the dances and the wonderful clothes, the champagne and the orchids. Society works awfully hard to have a good time. But if it did not make its own fun, it would have nothing to do at night and no place to go, for there is no distinguished night-life in Washington. . . .

To save money, girls often rent an apartment together, and take turns at housekeeping, shopping, and cooking. When they first come to town, they usually go to one of Washington's 439 rooming houses. But after a week or two, they are likely to move, to be with a new girl friend, to try a house with men in it or, perhaps, to go further out where rents are cheaper. They read the classified ads, which are in a sort of code. Here, for example, is one from the *Star:*

> *3rd fl lrg com f rom, 4 bds, nx*
> *ba, unl phn, 4 win, slg m prf*

Room-seekers quickly decipher: Third floor, large comfortable front room, four beds, next to bath, unlimited telephone service, four windows, single men preferred.

Lonely girls often advertise for a companion:

> *Rfnd joly wm wshs yg bus*
> *wm shr conv rm sep b*

A refined jolly woman wishes a young business woman to share her convenient room with separate beds.

Some landladies won't take Government Girls. The landladies say that the girls do their laundry in the bathroom. But that isn't the worst of it. It's how long it takes them to have a bath. And the way they stay in nights, using up electricity. It's because they get lipstick on the towels and cold cream on the sheets . . . and because they are always using the telephone.

During an acute housing shortage, numbers of girls counted themselves lucky to get a bed in a room filled with strangers. "How many share your bath, Madam?" an inspector asked a landlady. "Sir," she said, "people take their baths separately in this house!"

Five girls once rented a room, and when they went to bed they made so much noise that the landlord put them out in the middle of the night. The girls took the man to court, and the judge ordered him to pay them seven hundred dollars each.

There was another landlord who had six girl roomers, and one of them spent an hour each morning taking a bath. The other girls stormed and raved, until the landlord took off the bathroom door. The indignant bather complained to the rent administrator, who ordered the door put back and the plaintiff to take quicker baths. One young woman, when rooms were at a premium, advertised for a corner in a basement, promised to put up a partition and buy her own bed.

During the wartime housing shortage the Scott brothers, Ralph and Harry, who owned fifty-odd boarding houses, decided to build a hotel for women; they conducted a poll among the roomers to find out what Government Girls would like in a hotel. In Scotts' rooming houses, two girls usually shared a room and seemed to enjoy it. But the poll showed that when a young woman gets to be thirty, she wants a room of her own. Girls prefer showers to tubs. They like old-fashioned bureaus better than dressing tables. A private telephone (if a girl must choose) is more to be desired than a private bath. They asked for easy chairs, good reading lights, desks with straight-backed chairs, adequate closets, and utility cabinets—"somewhere to keep things like aspirin and bobby pins."

When the requests were tabulated and estimates made, the Scotts borrowed half a million dollars from the RFC and built their answer to the maidens' prayer—a six-story, brick building on O Street, more like a club than a hotel, surrounded by trees and green lawns, and within walking distance of many Departments. Scotts' two hundred fifty rooms are all singles. Each room has a telephone, and four girls share a shower.

The Scotts added a few ideas of their own: laundry facilities, a sewing machine and a hair dryer on each floor, a row of "beau parlors" in the lobby, and sun decks on four roofs. Each six-by-eight beau parlor has a small love seat, discreetly shaded lamp, and curtains that don't quite close. To make the point, names of famous lovers are inscribed over the entrance of each alcove: Antony and Cleopatra, Dante and Beatrice, Romeo and Juliet—and You and Me. On one of the roofs is a fireplace for barbecue parties, another has a polished brick floor for moonlight dancing. No men are admitted above the lobby until 8 p.m., when they are whisked to the roof by express elevators.

For girls who like communal living, it is cheaper—and in some ways, it is pleasanter—to rent an apartment. For about eighty dollars a month, four girls can rent a furnished, two-room flat, with twin beds in the bedroom and a double studio couch in the living room. Girls who share an apartment usually have breakfast and dinner at home. On Saturdays, two of them clean house and the other two go shopping. They take turns preparing meals and washing dishes, and split bills four ways. If they knew one another before they team up, it usually works out pretty well.

Co-operative living makes it possible for Government Girls to live better, wear prettier clothes, and learn more in Washington than they could back home in West Overshoe or Punkapoag. It takes some planning, but a smart girl, bent on culture or a career, can usually get what she wants. Evening schools offer 142 courses that include such a variety of subjects that a girl can study virtually everything from broadcasting to flower-arranging, including conversation and comptometry.

There are art classes at the Corcoran Art Gallery; Arthur Murray has a dancing school; and a woman called Clara Lane has something called a Friendship Center (that smells like a matrimonial agency) where a girl can meet a "lovely man" for $150.

I went around to see Mrs. Lane who guaranteed to turn up a "perfect gentleman" for me—for $75 down—and she would trust me for the balance.

"Just your type, dear," she promised. Fay Thompson, who preceded Mrs. Lane in the Washington date business, advertises that her studio is "the place to meet friends." I telephoned her for details. Miss Thompson declared that she has "many nice gentlemen from eighteen to seventy," and would be delighted to arrange a "private date" for me. Both women claim to do business with Government Girls and to have promoted many romances. . . .

One of the things that Government Girls like to do on their days off is to visit the National Airport, three and a half miles from downtown Washington on the Mount Vernon Highway. Buses go out from 12th Street and Pennsylvania Avenue. The airport was built to encourage sight-seeing and is patterned after the European rather than the American idea of a busy air terminal. Ships take off and land in eight directions. Flying facilities are said to be better than those of any other city in the world. The girls sit in the spectators' promenade and sometimes eat in the airport restaurant.

On Wednesdays and Saturdays, many of them go to Sloan's auction room. The capital is a great town for girls with auction fever, and there are many auction rooms in town. Most of them have honest sales and authentic bargains. But Sloan's on 13th Street is top-notch, the oldest of them all, and the most famous. Sloan's ask that articles to be sold have an aggregate appraisal value of $20, but never refuse to sell anything; they have been known to knock down to the highest bidder such amazing things as a tombstone and a coffin, a little French poodle and a moth-eaten mule.

Uncatalogued sales take place twice a week, and seven times a year there are catalogued sales at which real treasures are sold. Then social leaders, diplomats, and Cabinet members rub elbows with Government Girls and their landladies, curio hunters, antique collectors, and tourists. There was a piece about Sloan's in the *Saturday Evening Post* which said that Mrs. Sigourney Thayer bought most of the furniture for her lovely Georgetown home at Sloan's, and that she didn't pay over $35 for any one piece.

Painted on a beam across the ceiling it says: "The Trash of One Generation Becomes the Treasures of Another." And there was never a day when someone didn't exclaim, "Look at that! My grandmother had one of those things, and we gave it to the Salvation Army."

One Saturday morning five Government Girls piled out of a taxi and trooped into the auction room. They had rented an apartment and planned to furnish it between Sloan's and the Five-and-Ten. A few hours later, they owned two studio couches, a rug, a card table, six Windsor chairs, a loveseat and a bolt of flowered chintz; and were en route to the Five-and-Ten for kitchen equipment and china.

Girls who were never in a taxi before they came to Washington take cabs frequently because fares are cheap; taxis swarm the downtown streets. In the District there is one cab for every 140 citizens—the capital leads the nation. About sixty of the taxi drivers are women. One of them was formerly a bacteriologist with the FBI, another was an opera singer at the Metropolitan. A few of the women own their own cabs, but most of them rent for a fixed fee of from five to seven dollars a day. They have the cabs for twenty-four hours a day, and some of them work double shifts.

One of the wonderful things about living in Washington for Government Girls is that they can do everything that distinguished visitors do, even V.I.P.'s who are entertained by the President and the First Lady. Take Queen Elizabeth, for instance. Of course, most girls can't stop at Blair House, dine at the White House, or wear a diamond tiara for dinner at the British Embassy. But outside of where Elizabeth slept and what she wore, she didn't rate anything in Washington that every Government Girl can't have. Moreover, Elizabeth didn't climb the Monument, or go canoeing on the Potomac. She didn't meet her date at Wardman Park or have a fish dinner with him at Hogate's. As a matter of fact, Elizabeth and Philip didn't do half the things that you and I have done. They visited the

Capitol, the Supreme Court, and the Smithsonian. They took a sight-seeing trip around town, stopped at the National Gallery, and laid a wreath at the Tomb of the Unknown Soldier. And that is all they did.

Government Girls know the V.I.P. itinerary like the back of their hands, and they have been everywhere (well, nearly everywhere) that royalty goes. It may be true that there is more loneliness to the square block in Washington than in New York, Chicago, Paris, London, or Cairo—or so I have heard. But there are many things to make life rich and beautiful (everything but men!). The sole business of the capital is government and politics. Government has created a city which is like no other—the hub of the nation, capital of the free world, and one of the most beautiful cities on earth. The pleasures of this unique capital are plentiful, generally free and, mostly, good for a girl. And if there is more loneliness, there is probably less disillusionment. Which is the way it is in New York, Chicago, Paris, London—and Cairo too, I guess.

Political Wife

Private Faces/Public Places (1972)

Abigail McCarthy's book is personal, yet it has public and political ramifications. This short selection from a much larger section of her book dealing with the difficulties and opportunities presented by being a political wife depicts only one particular type of woman in Washington. And it's important to caution against generalizing. As Marvella Bayh (another senatorial wife) pointed out, "There is no such thing as a 'typical' political wife. We in this sorority are as different from each other as are the political precepts in which we believe, as are the divergent regions of this country in which we grew up, as are our own talents and interests. We are individuals in our own right, and many are beginning to speak out candidly about the psychological pressures of being submerged in a husband's career."

I suppose the political wife exists anywhere there's a politician—a local mayor, a town selectman, a governor—but political wives in Washington are a demographic unto themselves. Most of the 535 members of Congress are men, and most of the men have wives. Abigail (Mrs. Eugene) McCarthy, as Ellen Maury Slayden did long before her, and Marvella Bayh and Lindy Boggs and Lady Bird Johnson and many others also have, writes of women at the center of government, just one step removed.

My mother's take on most official wives was that they "get nothing out of their positions because they cannot learn to look upon their activities as a job which is in its way as important as that of the men if they make it important regardless of whether it happens to be amusing or not. They are unable to share their husband's work and unwilling to develop their own functions. The resulting frustration and unhappiness are none the less real."

GENE'S IDEAS about the vocation of politics were part of an important area of discussion in the 1940s and 1950s, a rediscovery of the fact that laymen are part of the Church. At the same time there was a resurgence of interest in the theology of marriage. . . . Inevitably, perhaps, the conclusion often was that if the priesthood was a vocation, then marriage was also a vocation. If a man's vocation was to marriage and family life, then his work in the world took on secondary importance, although he could of course take into account his interests, talents, opportunities. But all this was subordinated to the care and education of his family. Gene had rejected this idea for himself early. . . .

If his vocation was to politics and marriage was not a vocation, what was my vocation? The whole question of woman was then latent in our lives. Laying aside any theological considerations, it was taken for granted that to be the wife of a man in politics and the mother of his children was not only a full-time occupation but a worthy calling in itself. Lady Bird Johnson had given voice to this for all of us when she said in a speech to congressional wives, "I am sure that we would say the life of any congressional wife revolves around three things: husband, children, and home . . . as wives of busy men whose daily business is the nation's business, our best chance to find the significant is to help our husbands achieve their own legislative aims." She had asked Lyndon what he felt were the three most significant things in his career and he had said that helping push and extend the draft act in August of 1941 when it passed only by one vote was one of them; the Civil Rights Act of 1957 was another; the Space Act of 1967 was the third. "I recommend," she said, "that you ask that same question at home. It is well to be reminded that all of the fragmentation of self—as Anne Lindbergh describes the daily living of today's homemakers—adds up to something."

I think we all agreed to that even as late as 1963 when Lady Bird said it. It was part of the American political tradition that in one sense a man and his wife were both "elected." We need only recall the days when Ohio voters welcomed the Tafts on his first Senate election with a huge sign saying "Congratulations, Bob and Martha." Those few wives who led independent lives with independent careers were for the most part wives of the very rich congressmen or senators to whom politics might be a vocation but not a living. Running a business which added to the family's fortune, as many wives did including Lady Bird with her television station, Betty Talmadge with her meat business and Emily Malino Scheuer with her decorating, was not thought contrary to the pattern. In 1968 I voiced the same point of view when I said in an interview, "Honors, writing—they're by-products of the mainstream of my life which has been to be the wife of an involved man with four involved children." It was in 1970 that a congressional wife thought to question this attitude publicly, when Arvonne Fraser of Minnesota told a New York reporter, "A lot are unhappy here. They have no life of their own and wonder, who am I? Am I just somebody's wife? Or is there something more?"

We worked very hard at what we thought was our vocation, we political wives. We held campaign schools at the Democratic Wives Forum and at the Congressional Club, trading campaign experiences, learning how to dress for platform appearances, learning how to use television, radio, and how to deal with the press. . . .

Very few of us thought in the terms Marvella Bayh expressed so frankly in an interview in 1971: "I've always longed for a career of my own because I never really did have one. Some women don't have a need for it, but I was an only child and I was always made to feel that I could have a career and could contribute. I live completely through him. . . . But I suppose it would be a rude awakening if something happened to him. Not only would I lose a husband, a best friend and a breadwinner, but my own career."

I was struck, reading this, at how completely accurate it is as a description of the situation of the political wife. The political side of her life is a career in itself. She works in the field of public relations; her job is to interpret, reflect, and round out the image of the public man. Besides that, she is often confidential adviser, behind-the-scenes organizer, and sometimes speech writer. She often represents him, if not always at public functions, then at benefits and semisocial occasions like official receptions. . . .

I did not want a career of my own. I had come to marriage with a modest reputation as a college teacher, lecturer, and reviewer and with ten years of work experience behind me. It was taken for granted that I could always teach again if I had to; Gene often scandalized eager insurance agents in those early days by saying that my M.A. was my insurance and that he didn't need to take out any more than he already had. None of the things I could do harmonized very well with the circumstances of the political life except writing and there was very little of the requisite energy left for that. I was perfectly happy to help Gene as I could. I used to help with speeches and articles, not so much with the text itself—Gene's own style was so distinctive—impersonal, compressed skeletal, and Latinate—that only he could write it—but in outlining ideas, finding references, calling his attention to background books and articles. And the traditional American wife's role of keeping in touch with relatives and friends expanded to take in our expanding political family and friends. We felt strongly that the Christmas card should not be a political tool, for example, but the personal list grew and grew.

Inevitably, inexorably, unless the wife becomes her husband's actual office aide or confidential secretary (and many do), the congressional husband and wife begin to live separate lives. To some wives this change comes with shocking suddenness before the life has developed any compensating factors for her. "I cried for three months," admitted a congressional wife, interviewed recently in the *New York Times*. In the beginning her husband was out most of the time meeting people, being seen, learning the ropes, and most of his invitations did not include her. "I was alone, I didn't know anyone, and had no one to talk to," she said. "When he did come home, and I was dying for conversation, he would ask, 'Would you mind if I take a nap?' "

"You develop interests in things you can do without him," said Jane Muskie to me when we were talking about this one day, "—or you go mad!"

Even at first Gene never felt that these multitudinous engagements were so important, and he early began dropping into the pre-dinner reception to greet everyone necessary and then coming home to have dinner with me and the children. When he thought the dinner important enough, we went together. Our concept of Christian family life was still precious to us; we said evening prayers with the children and he helped put them to bed. From the beginning we had mutual friends who shared our ideas and ideals, and I never felt isolated. Gene's natural love of home gave me a feeling of great security and I was entirely untroubled when Mrs. Edward Thye, wife of our senior Minnesota senator, said, "I never see you with your husband. It doesn't look right, you know." I knew it was more important to be with the children and, in any case, I didn't care to be at the Chamber of Commerce dinner, the Fire Insurance Underwriters' dinner, the Savings and Loan Association dinner, the hundred and one lobby receptions where congressmen were more demeaned than honored. It bothered me to see Gene subjected to the "You'd-better-listen-we're-the-taxpayers" approach. I was content to attend the official congressional and White House affairs and we went to small dinners together. It was at these that we really came to know people well.

But the legislative life is demanding in itself, and keeping in touch with the constituency often means that a husband must be in his home district more often than his wife—or that he must be back in Washington when she is at home. The husband and wife cease to be a team working together; they begin to play complementary roles. In my own mind I came to terms with this as a normal expansion of the marriage roles we had talked of so solemnly when we planned our married life. In public life the roles expanded beyond the boundaries of home and work, but the goal was the same. There are some things one wife can do to help her husband, others that another can do. The wife's role remains supportive yet responsible as in the adaptation of the Benedictine rule for oblates:

"The husband is the abbot; the wife, the cellarer—both with great responsibilities for the community." Sometimes the complementary role is so subtle and all-pervasive in a political life that it is not recognized until it surfaces dramatically in a time of great need or stress: one remembers Lady Bird Johnson's anticipating Lyndon Johnson's first public statement after his aide and long-time friend Walter Jenkins was trapped in a morals offense. The tone of understanding and compassion was irrevocably set; the public attention focused on the suffering family. There was also her statement when they emerged from the plane which carried the body of John F. Kennedy from Dallas. It is the statement and her demeanor of sad dignity which one remembers from that moment so impossible for both her and her husband. Who has become President under more difficult circumstances? Jacqueline Kennedy's theatrical grace and courage at the same time made one realize how much of the unique mystique of Camelot was hers—the mystique which convinced the whole world that we were in a time of new beginnings. And I think of Muriel Humphrey's post-1968 statement, "He is not what he was; he is not what he will be"—a masterly concentrated message of reality and hope about her husband's situation and future which, for me, at least, and surely for other readers, lifted him out of a morass and carried him forward.

The complementary role of a wife was most visible in the case of Mrs. Roosevelt, but it is necessary to recall the opprobrium she suffered for it, exactly because it was overt and visible. The cruel jokes, the naked hatred she evoked certainly served to intimidate lesser women. No one of us Minnesota DFL [Democratic-Farmer-Labor Party] wives would have affirmed for ourselves in the 1950s what Senator Birch Bayh so cheerfully ascribed to wives in the interview I have quoted: he freely said that his wife was his best political confidante and adviser. "In public life you are surrounded by admirers. They are worshipful and it's easy to get carried away. But there is a sense of security to have someone who loves you and helps you keep your feet on the ground."

It was more or less true in each of our cases, but our husbands belonged to a party whose chief strength lay in farmers and union men, who would have felt such a confession a sign of weakness, and our husbands, college men or not, would have felt their position weakened by such a statement. Yet we were fortunate in that we were expected to take active roles, to campaign, and to participate in party politics. . . .

Generally, however, we recognized that columnist David Broder's dictum held true: a woman's role in politics is rough, especially if her forte is organization. My own flair for organization, discovered in Gene's first campaign, seemed best used behind the scenes, and then best used in the volunteer efforts which were always part of his campaigns and kept him somewhat free and independent of the state and county party organizations. I liked it that way. From the first I was terrified by the clashing drives and open confrontations which seemed part of the work in the party. Although we recognized the moral obligation to work in and with the party, it always seemed to me that working with the women and volunteer organizations was a way to promote civility, objectivity, and issue-orientation. It was also clear to me that people from these groups usually ended up with a personal loyalty to Gene. It did not occur to me then that there was something ultimately corrupting about a wife's hidden role like this because of its essential falseness.

In those years I was never comfortable with the official wife role, either. After every interview I lay awake in a black nightmare of anxiety, fearful that I had said something which would do Gene irreparable harm. A phrase or a statement which I deemed unfortunate would literally rise out of my consciousness to strike me with a paralyzing fear and sense of inadequacy. . . .

Between 1947 when Gene first thought of running for Congress and 1957 when he began to talk of running for the Senate I had had four babies and participated more or less actively in five campaigns. It seemed to me that I was always physically tired. Despite our part-time help I did a great deal of the housework—almost all of the cooking, for example—and I was always and forever feeding those monsters which are supposed to take the place of help—the dishwasher and the washing machine—and piling up ironing.

Eleanor Roosevelt writes that in those years in her life when her children were small, she made mistakes out of timidity because she was unsure of herself and dominated by the children's nurses and her relatives. I made the same kinds of mistakes in trying to live up to impossible ideals and irreconcilable ones.

Women and Children

Washington (2001)

Meg Greenfield was called a credit to her sex. Of course, like all women praised for their expertise and abilities and insight, she was a credit to any sex. I wrote about Meg in the foreword to her book, so there's not much to add about her here, except to repeat that she was the consummate observer of the Washington scene. She had a particular talent for seeing people in ways that they didn't see themselves.

Part of what Meg conveys in her book is the unique background she had that helped her as a woman do the traditional man's job that she did. Meg wrote, "I had been brought along in my first years in journalism in NewYork by a famously good and even more famously autocratic male editor, Max Ascoli of the Reporter, *an equal-opportunity oppressor who believed that all of us on the staff—men and women alike—could do anything he suggested, and damned well better." She confessed that Ascoli threw copy on the floor when he didn't like it, but added, "My contribution to his taming was to be the one person who wouldn't pick it up."*

I've chosen this piece on women from Meg's book because she's clearly the right person to help us understand more about how women see Washington. Elsewhere in the book, Meg wrote about a representative Washington wife giving off a "feeling that she had taken out just one load of sodden garbage too many on a chilly night, while the overburdened one was off participating in a symposium on Section Eight housing policy at a tropical resort somewhere." She believed that women's attitudes and approaches to life and work in Washington were shaped by the "ever-dwindling but still considerable peculiarities of man's-town Washington, the only context in which the woman's changing role can be understood." I believe that that last sentence is the essence of the challenge women face in Washington.

WASHINGTON in the Kennedy era, when I first saw it, was still home to a kind of demeaning, grown-up little-girl culture. Coming to it, as I did, from an independent, somewhat raunchy postcollege life in the Village in New York, this culture stunned and amused me, struck me, in fact, as encompassing everything I had left my conventional life at home to escape.

In my youthful self-assurance, I was right about the culture but dead wrong in supposing, as I did, that it took a committed nonconformer to its rules such as myself to see what was ridiculous about it. Only slowly and as a result of acquaintanceship with some of the women involved, did I come to realize the different truth. It was that the premises on which the wife culture was based were already being quietly, often sardonically questioned by many women who felt politically compelled to go along with it publicly, and that it had begun to be rejected outright by a handful of audacious others.

The world itself was one of flossy, party-favor luncheons (a lobbyist's gift of French perfume or pretty scarves or costume jewelry at every place setting), where pointless gab was expected. The occasional, quick stop-by of the hostess's public-personage husband would produce the requisite waves of appreciative tittering when he said something like: "Well, it looks to me like you ladies are really having a good time. I sure wish I could stay here with you instead of going back to the office. But then all your husbands would get jealous!"

The underlying premise was pretty clear. It was that these were mindless dollies with nothing much to occupy their afternoons except airhead chatter and tiny, glutinous mounds of chicken à la king, whereas their menfolk—the daddies—were busy and had important things to do at the office.

In this unperceptive reading of them, the only serious contributions such women could make to their husbands' professional lives were as hostesses (often laboring unthanked at full-time, semiofficial duties that went with the husband's post) or as attractive but prim adornment-adjuncts to their husbands' careers. They served as stage props, meant to be seen and not heard at certain office and social functions and to grace the platform at the departmental swearing-in or the late-night campaign rally.

The reward for their uncomplaining attendance at untold numbers of these events, forever beaming and wordless, would be an acknowledgment from the podium by their husbands, with the traditional chuckle about how they had married "above" themselves. "My wife is too good for me," these guys used to love to say, tribute to the durable, Washington set-piece notion of the wife as better-born guardian of the family's table manners and enforcer of its occasional, recalcitrant forays into culture.

The single transcendentally important thing to be said about all these stilted tableaux is that they were based on false assumptions about the women involved and the lives they really led—even then, back before Gloria and Betty and Simone and Germaine had been heard from. Of course, there were always some who seemed to enjoy the baby-doll aura and were happy to busy themselves with what were essentially time-killer activities. And it is true that thirty years ago far fewer of these women were working at paying jobs outside the home than now.

But the number of real enthusiasts for the patronizing conception of themselves embodied in that grown-up little-girl social life was always pretty small, in my observation. And the affront to the rest had nothing to do with the irrelevancy of whether they worked at paying jobs or not. The affront was to the dignity, seriousness, and value of what they were doing as intelligent women, wise wives, conscientious parents, and very often tireless contributors to the well-being of the communities they lived in.

The prevailing contempt for them was summed up in the much-repeated *bon mot* of the Washington wit Alice Roosevelt Longworth that Washington was "a town of successful men and the women they married before they were successful." (Paradoxically, the same contempt for women who were fulfilling a conventional role in the family and the community was also strongly implied in the rhetoric of some who regarded themselves as true feminists, especially in the early days of the contemporary women's movement.) On the whole, Washington's wives put up with the put-down, but they neither deserved it nor especially relished the social and ceremonial obligations it imposed on them.

"Put up with" is the key phrase. On my fitful excursions as a reporter into the prevailing wife culture of those years—once for a fairly good stretch of time while I was doing a long magazine piece about the off-stage political role of Lady Bird Johnson, and sometimes while covering campaigns on the road—I was repeatedly struck by how many of these women were actually working around or against that culture, which sought to segregate and trivialize them as a species. I will get around in a moment to the circumscribed, rule-ridden world of the exceptions—those women who successfully functioned politically and professionally in the capital under the prevailing inhibitions, doing what was still tacitly assumed by practically all to be "men's work."

What numerous of those wives were doing was far tougher, in my view, than what the rare professional woman had to bring off. I think of certain cabinet wives, congressional wives, wives of men who worked on the White House staff who over the years dutifully went along with the party-favor-lunch thing as bored good sports yet managed to keep their sanity and self-respect and to live lives of independence and influence.

Lady Bird Johnson would be a good example; it was what I found so interesting about her. So would Lindy Boggs, the savvy wife of Representative Hale Boggs of Louisiana (and mother of ABC and NPR correspondent Cokie Roberts), who before her husband's death and her own election to his seat was a model congressional missus who doubled as one of the smartest women in town.

Another was Barbara Laird, the late first wife of Melvin Laird of Wisconsin, who was a Republican congressman and Nixon defense secretary. Although Laird's protracted career as a Washington big hitter may have made his wife the champ participant in these command-performance events, she always exuded a seriousness, wisdom, and sly wit (including about some of the policies he was promoting) that made it plain that Barbara Laird was miscast as a mainstay of the ladies-luncheon circuit.

The same was self-evidently true of Pauline Gore, wife of a senator and mother of a vice-president, whose family I knew when we both lived in Washington's Fairfax Hotel. Gore, a lawyer by training at a time when female lawyers were rare, and a truly bright woman who had an enormous impact on the careers of both her husband and her son, was also a faithful, publicly uncomplaining attendee at the time-devouring, mind-numbing social ceremonies of wifedom.

Such women were just a few of the many who, though they might quietly confide their own impatience with these ceremonies, were at pains to give no offense and commit no heresy—starting with the major heresy of not turning up—that would call unfavorable attention to themselves and by extension do some damage to their husbands' standing in the political/governmental community.

The conventions were the conventions, and they were controlling. If you think this sort of thing went out with the bundling board and the bed warmer and Ye Olde Antique Shoppe, you need to know that in the mid-1960s, after Robert Kennedy had been elected senator from New York, it was considered a very big deal in circles where the protocol lingered whether Ethel Kennedy would participate in the weekly sessions, mandated by ladies-auxiliary-type custom, wherein the Senate wives got together and rolled bandages for the Red Cross in the old-fashioned, World War II way.

This they were doing years after modern medical science and industry had rendered their handiwork obsolete, so the more or less compulsory bandage-rolling bees were ridiculous, and the answer was that at first she didn't turn up. But in time, under pressure she did—even Ethel Kennedy, touch-football and practical-joke-playing, famously modernist, I'll-do-it-my-way Ethel Kennedy. That was the force of the prevailing myth. Women were always having to recertify that they were who the long outgrown culture said they were, even when they knew it was not true and when they were living lives that daily refuted it.

The same held true until fairly recently for professional women in Washington; whether wives or not, they made comparable concessions to the unwritten rules. There had always been a few women in the picture, of course, who were simply too big or smart or willful or well connected or unflagging in what they did to be ignored, let alone put in their place, wherever that was. I'm thinking of women as unalike in most other respects as publishing powers Agnes Meyer and Cissy Patterson; cabinet officials Frances Perkins and Oveta Culp Hobby; Maine senator Margaret Chase Smith; and a handful of others.

Each of these was much too much of an independent power to be called a "token." They weren't chosen by anyone to "represent" women. All became, in different ways, forces to be reckoned with in the capital's affairs. Not quite in their class, yet still a kind of outsized exception to the rule in her time was the durable, dogged journalist May Craig, correspondent for a number of papers in Maine and one of the relatively few women in journalism, in my early days in Washington, who were not writing for what were then known as either the "women's" or "society" pages. Her split-screen public persona nearly perfectly illustrates the ambivalence people still had well into the 1960s and 1970s about women's working in traditionally male jobs, as well as the concessions such women reflexively made and the snickering they routinely accepted as part of the deal.

On one half of the screen was the May Craig who was famous for her tea-party-style hats, who seemed not to mind being habitually made fun of and treated as a harmless crank whenever she got journalistically as tough as the guys did. She was a woman who appeared easily to countenance being regarded as a somewhat comic, freaky phenomenon precisely because she was (by then) an elder female in what was thought of as a wisecracking, middle-aged guy's job.

On the other half of the screen, this woman, who went along with the dotty-old-lady gag and sometimes seemed even to play to it, was a hard-driving reporter who frequently turned up on the TV interview shows of the day and was known for her obduracy in asking hard questions. (She used to pull her chair up until she was right under the nose of Everett Dirksen at his crowded, nontelevised weekly Q-and-A sessions in the Senate Press Gallery, and she would never release him from her fixed, accusing stare, except when she took notes. "Does that answer your question, May dear?" Dirksen invariably asked, with mock solicitude, at the end of his remarks, to which, with a disgusted shake of her hat, she would just as invariably reply, "No.")

Craig is actually credited by many with getting language into the 1964 Civil Rights Act that extends its coverage in certain key areas to women. Her campaign to enlarge that law's scope was much guffawed about at the time, as Craig made a sort of holy mission of it at press conferences and elsewhere. The relevant proviso was (and still is) sometimes referred to as the "May Craig Amendment." Some believe it was adopted only with the help of anti-civil-rights legislators who thought it so preposterous that it would help them kill the whole bill.

But if that's true, the joke's on them. The point is that May Craig embodied the yes and no of women's role as professionals in Washington at that time. Like so many others—wives at home as well as women with daily jobs—she worked with, through, and around the reigning beliefs about the limited capacities and the proper pastimes of women and seemed sometimes to defy them, sometimes craftily to exploit them for her journalistic purposes, and sometimes even to believe them herself.

This was more or less what all of us did. Although I might have fancied myself some kind of daring rebel, it is clear to me, surveying those times from the vantage point of the 1990s, that I still knew my place and that I abided by most of the rules. These rules were about much more than what was suitable and perhaps even required for the wives of important officials to do in their spare time. They also covered mixed social events I would attend, when all the women were dispatched as a group from the dinner table after dessert and sent to powder their noses and wait while the gents stayed on in the dining room to engage in the only good political conversation likely to go on that evening—exchanges it was presumably felt the women would not have much interest in and would divert or otherwise wreck by their presence anyway.

When the now fairly famous uprising against this custom finally came in the 1970s, I was expected to be among the women who declined to evacuate to the parlor so the fellows could chat. I played my expected part but was always kind of uncomfortable about it. This was not because of any grief I might be causing the men on whose sanctuary I was encroaching but because so long as most of the other, nonprofessional women did go off and gather, I thought it looked as if I thought I was too good to be with them. An overly tortured consideration, maybe, but it did bother me.

More important, the man/woman rules also covered—and inhibited in different ways—our actual ability to do our jobs. Clubs routinely excluded females, for example, and not just social, old-geezer clubs either, but clubs that were nearer to being professional associations from which exclusion could carry a price for a woman in that line of work.

I had such an experience as a brand-new Washington correspondent for the *Reporter* in 1961. I was taken upstairs from the offices of the magazine's bureau in the National Press Building to the top-floor National Press Club, there to be shown where the wire-service ticker was. I would need to consult it to keep abreast of late-breaking news as our publication neared its closing deadline every two weeks. This was a normal, safety-net practice followed by our bureau and dozens of others and was one of the principal services the ticker was there to provide.

I was taken there by Douglass Cater, the man I had been sent to town to replace while he took a brief leave from his job as the magazine's Washington editor. But the club official on duty, seeing me there in the hallway with Doug, looked shocked and at once informed him that I could not set foot in the place for any purpose that did not come under the strict rules that provided for "ladies' presence" at certain social events—and then only in certain prescribed areas of the club. Women were not permitted to be members (they are now), and, contrary to Doug's expectation, a woman subbing for a bureau chief would not be allowed to walk the ten or so feet of sacred club ground from the door to the ticker to check the late news for five minutes on her magazine's closing day. Period. Doug, incensed, argued, but to no avail.

I do not regard this episode as one of the great human rights violations of our time, nor myself as some pitiable victim. Nor, when I reconsider it, do I even try to figure out how on earth such silly rules could still have been in force in our trade at that late date. They simply reflected the regressive professional and social ambience of the city as a whole.

What I do find startling all these years later is my own wimpish "que será, será" reaction at the time. For it was Doug, not I, who did the only complaining either then or later. Sore as I felt to have to accept this exclusion, it did not even cross my mind that I could or should do anything to try to get the rule reversed. I felt only that I needed to make up for it by getting access to another wire in some less handy place, regarding the outcome as just one more unreasonable inconvenience that called for extra effort on my part, not an inequity that I needed to challenge and fix. And so I set about finding out how I could get a last-minute check on the news some other way, not even remembering to feel annoyed about the circumstance for long.

It is plain to me in retrospect that in this and countless other small questions of conduct and privilege, I had become, like most of my female counterparts working in Washington at that time, highly adept at the fine art of mixed maneuvering that I could spot, with some amusement, in the redoubtable, quirky, period-piece May. I may have thought of myself as quite different from her in generation, outlook, and practically everything else. Hey, I was a modern, serious, no-hat reporter, wasn't I?

Yet each of the elements apparent in her approach to her professional circumstances was, in slightly different form, apparent in mine: defiance of the rules of who should be in this particular workplace to begin with, combined with exploitation of the female stereotype for my own purposes and—yes—tacit acceptance of the legitimacy of limitations imposed on the way I, as a young woman, might go about my business. This triple-headed way of operating wasn't something I even thought about much or can remember thinking up at all. It was just something I did.

The defiance had nothing to do with boycotts or bills of particulars or political organization or anything like that. It lay solely in the nature of the work I had chosen to do. That was the defiance. There was at that time a thriving journalistic subculture of females, always described as "women reporters," who were hired to cover, in a gushy way not allowed on page one, what was accounted strictly women's business. They gave much attention to what they called the "doings" of the wifely lunch bunch, of which their own group was a kind of journalistic offshoot.

Some among them were pretty tough and skillful, not to say ruthless, reporters who could wring real political news out of a half dozen indiscreet remarks that might have been dropped along the way by the wife of this big shot or that by the time the chestnut parfait was served; others were an embarrassment to their press cards. But all were essentially ghettoized.

Whether they got nuggets of political news or not and whether they brought a subversive, satiric eye to the proceedings or not, their product appeared amid the recipes and bulletins on fall hemline lengths out of Paris. That was the law. It was seen almost as natural law in the old medieval sense, a way of behaving that had been ordained and instilled in the human breast by divine will. Women reporters wrote women stories about women and household or fashion, the only things women could be counted on really to read about anyway. It was the way life was meant to be. Not to abide by this law was to challenge the God-given order of things.

*A cartoon my great friend Herblock drew for my seventieth birthday
in 1987, depicting my father calling out to Mother about my early
interest in* The Washington Post

WASHINGTON HUMOR

*Washington people have always been blessed with the ability to laugh—
at themselves if possible, at others when possible.*
                                    —Bill Adler, editor of *The Washington Wits*

THERE'S not enough laughter in Washington—at least not publicly.
This tends to be a serious place. But it's odd, because for all the drama
of Washington, what I most remember is how much we all used to
laugh.

It's hard to re-create that atmosphere now, and whenever I try to
relate some incident or retell some anecdote, I end up saying something to the effect of "It must have been a you-had-to-be-there kind of
scene." Maybe it was.

The humorless here in Washington—of whom there are many—
inevitably become fodder for the humorists. Certainly that's how it's
worked with most of the funny people who have turned their attention to this place. And I've been lucky to have met up with some very
funny ones in my day, people with humor to spare, and, happily, who
shared it.

Many of my colleagues on the *Post* also kept me laughing through
the years. In the days when it was routine to work on Saturdays, at
least for part of the day, a group of us would frequently take time out
for lunch together at some close-by watering hole, where we would
end up talking for hours about all the great issues of the day. I remember nothing but the laughing. Ben Bradlee, the *Post*'s executive editor,
was, of course, one of the ringleaders. Howard Simons, who was the
Post's inimitable managing editor throughout the 1970s and early
1980s, used to send me memos with the caveat "Eat after reading." I
had only to encounter him on the paper's fifth floor, the newsroom
floor, to find myself guffawing over one thing or another. There probably was never a time when Meg Greenfield and I were together that we
didn't laugh, even under the most trying of circumstances, as during
the pressman's strike at the paper. For me, some of the laughter left
when she died.

The Attic in My Edifice: Some Random Notes

That Reminds Me   (1954)

Alben Barkley was a regular guy. Maybe that's one of the reasons he was so funny—he didn't take himself and others too seriously. He was certainly not caught up in being a Washington big shot. He first came here in 1913, having been elected as a U.S. representative from Kentucky in the election of 1912. In 1926, he was elected to the Senate, where he served (including as majority leader) until his resignation, on January 19, 1949, having been elected vice president on the Democratic ticket with President Truman in 1948. He again was elected to the Senate after his vice presidency, and this time served from January 1955 until his death, in April 1956.

*   That Reminds Me is Barkley's memoir of his life, forty-seven years of which were spent in public service. The book includes a few stories about his father, who had been a farmer, came to Washington soon after Barkley was first elected to Congress, and served as a doorkeeper in the House of Representatives, which Barkley said was "the adventure of his life," and which lasted only through the Democratic Wilson administration. Barkley wrote that "strangers visiting in the House gallery sometimes were startled when Father would tap them on the shoulder, point down to where I was sitting, and say, 'That's my son.' "*

*   George Allen devoted an entire chapter, "One Enchanted Political Career," in his book* Presidents Who Have Known Me, *to talking about Barkley. It begins: "I like to think of Alben Barkley as the very model of a modern American politician," and focuses on his "humorous intelligence, rugged integrity, and durable ingenuity," noting that "Even the Vice-Presidency hasn't submerged him. Any Vice-President who can make the country remember his name and face well enough to keep his identity from becoming a catch question in the radio quiz programs a few weeks after election day is no ordinary man."*

Barkley, who was wedged in as vice president between the vice presidencies of Harry Truman and Richard Nixon, tells many anecdotes about being "the veep" and about people's perceptions of the office. He quotes Charles Dawes, Coolidge's VP, who growled, "This is a helluva job! I can only do two things: One is to sit up here and listen to you birds talk, without the privilege of being able to answer you back. The other is to look at the newspapers every morning to see how the President's health is!"

Barkley made the most of his vice presidency, as he did with everything he turned his attention to on behalf of the public. And he did it all with humor, as we can see from the following speech that he gave at the National Press Club's reception for freshmen members of the House and Senate in 1945.

I HAVE BEEN asked to give you Baby Senators some good, sound, wholesome advice, and I hope you will take it with the degree of seriousness and solemnity with which I give it.

Do not entertain on anything approaching a lavish scale. I am sure most, if not all, of you have rented, furnished, decorated, embellished, contracted for, purchased, mortgaged or otherwise mismanaged some stately mansion, or other form of baronial estate here in Washington, with a view of unseemly, if not vulgar, entertainment. Let me dissuade you from this. You cannot afford to entertain one senator unless you entertain all senators, because, being prima donnas, they are very jealous of one another. Furthermore, do not get it into your heads that you can advance your senatorial, vice presidential or presidential ambitions, or your judicial aspirations, by entertaining all the members of the House of Representatives. They have no influence in conventions. Neither have senators, regardless of the length of their tenures. I know!

Moreover and furthermore, do not make the mistake of beginning the ordeal of feeding the members of the Press. It is in this field where habit-forming is most frequent and most persistent. If you feed one member of the Press, you will have to feed them all, and they are more "prima donnical" even than senators. If you ever feed all of them once, you are sunk, for it is a continuous performance. And they are all healthy and usually hungry.

Another thing. Never give a newspaperman a drink. . . . Not only will your beneficiary, or victim, as the case may be, return himself for another, or others, but, as a rolling stone gathers moss, especially when subjected to the dampness of *spiritus frumenti*, he will return with a pal or pals, depending somewhat, but not always, on the brand of the case under consideration.

This is important. Avoid all publicity. What you do or what you think, or what you think you think, if you think, or if you think you think, is your business. . . . There is one exception to this particular instruction: If you can find a newspaperman who is foolish or idle enough to listen to you, talk hell out of him, with the understanding that he is not to report back to your constituents what you think, and especially what you say.

Never act as a judge at a beauty contest or a baby contest. It is impossible to be impartial. If it is a beauty contest, you may have designs on the beauty. If it is a baby contest, the chances are that the unsuccessful babies will become voters before you quit running for office, and you will have built up a bloc of opposition which may prove disastrous.

Accept no gratuities of any kind—unless you need them. Accept no stock market tips, unless you know you are going to win, and, if you make investments under these circumstances, make up your mind that you will be happy as a loser.

Do not ride in any Government-owned or operated car . . . unless you are willing to seal your lips against the practice on the part of others, which you do not intend to do.

Forget that you have the franking privilege. Forget that you have a mileage allowance for every trip you make to and from Washington, especially if you come from the Far West.

Follow this advice and you will be different—yes, sir, you will be damned queer!

When giving constituents your Washington address, do not fail to spell out in full "Senate Office Building." If you give him the abbreviation—S.O.B.—he will not know whether you are calling him one, or expect him to call you one.

If, on official trips, you put bay rum on your expense account, then put it on your hair. Otherwise, it is petty graft.

Do not permit yourself to go on junkets. It is a waste of time and it costs money that comes from the taxpayers. Avoid all such excursions, unless your remaining in Washington in the usual performance of your duties would involve greater waste of time and the people's money.

When in the Capitol or the Senate Office Building, walk up and down the stairs or ride in the public elevators. Pay no attention to elevators marked "Senators Only," and never ring the buzzer three times, which is the senatorial password for "haste." If you get into this habit, you will find yourself doing it in hotels and office buildings wherever you are. When doing it around the Capitol, some constituent is liable to see you at it and accuse you of enjoying special privileges not accorded to others—and, whether a Republican or Democrat, you will be guilty.

Never agree or disagree with a constituent who writes you his views on pending legislation. Always tell him there is something in what he says, which you will be glad to consider, if and when and under whatever circumstances the pending measure may ever come up.

This is confidential among us senators. If you think one of your colleagues is stupid in debate, which you will think if you are here long, refer to him as "the able, learned and distinguished senator." If you know he is stupid, which you probably will, refer to him as "the very able, learned and distinguished senator." This form of address conceals a multitude of shortcomings.

Do not worry too much, if at all, about preparing your speeches. The one you prepare is never the one you make; and the one you make, everybody knows you did not prepare, and it bears no resemblance to the one you prepared, the one you made, or the one you wish you had made. It is the one your friendly and partial newspaper friend sends hot over the wires to his newspaper or his news association as the one you prepared and delivered amidst the enthusiasm of your colleagues, though he knows all the time he is lying in your behalf.

RUSSELL BAKER

The Natives: Their Work and Curious Temperament

An American in Washington (1961)

Here's Russell Baker again. Part of the explanation for this perfect title for a book on Washington is a story he tells about Eisenhower on the campaign trail in 1954:

> *Campaigning in the West . . . he told audience after audience that, by golly, it was good to get out of Washington and see "Americans" again. This not only left his audiences feeling superior but, by suggesting that Americans were not to be seen in Washington, warmed them to Eisenhower as a man willing to put down among aliens in order to champion the American way. Here, they were invited to believe, was a rare and noble creature, an American in Washington.*

"What are they like, these Washingtonians?" Baker asks, and he answers his own question most memorably. Here he is on the "natives," among whom I am delighted to count myself.

WHAT ARE they like, these Washingtonians? Very much as you and I would be if we found ourselves in the curious jobs that Washingtonians perform. Which is to say, cocksure and uncertain, devious and naïve, ebullient and melancholy, pompous and frivolous, bored, hard-working, shiftless, wide-eyed and tired of it all, full of dreams and schemes, and, without quite realizing it, a little absurd, for they are mostly common men distinguished largely by possession of uncommon jobs.

Let us try to catch the city in action and, through a montage of events, to capture the essence of the Washingtonian at his daily routine. Here, with all incidents based on fact or sound probability, is the chronology of a fairly representative Washington day out of the recent past:

Between 6 and 7 a.m.

Alarm clocks ring beside four senators running for the presidency. In the moment between rising and shaving, each yields to the dawn's awful intimation of mortality and asks himself: "Is it really worth it?"

At the White House the President of the United States rises, accidentally kicking to the floor the cowboy story with which he had read himself to sleep last night. Yawning at the dark silhouette of the Washington Monument visible from his bedroom window, he remembers that he must attend a "prayer breakfast" at the Mayflower Hotel with a prominent evangelist and twenty-three congressmen and then lunch with an asthmatic tyrant from the Middle East. Retrieving the cowboy story, he fleetingly recalls his boyhood dream of horseback living under prairie stars and asks himself:

"What am I doing here?"

In a network television studio a television correspondent famous in eighty million living rooms edits the questions he will ask an equally famous labor leader who has been accusing the President of callousness to human suffering. The correspondent, who must do his stuff for breakfasting America, is in a suppressed rage, having just been advised by his New York office that the time allotted the interview has been cut from five to three minutes. The network producer believes that five minutes of the labor leader will kill the audience and has decided to lighten the show with a two-minute act by that new comic from the Coast who does funny monologues with a telephone.

The twenty-three congressmen who are to breakfast with the President rise. Five have hangovers. Three require their wives to read aloud from the *Congressional Record* speeches that they delivered yesterday in the House of Representatives. These treat, respectively, of pornography in the mails, the depletion of oyster beds in the Chesapeake Bay, and Communist influences on African nationalism.

The Secretary of Defense ignores his alarm clock. This afternoon he must start on a flight to Asia to mollify the South Koreans and the Chinese Nationalists. This, he tells himself, entitles him to an unbudgeted thirty minutes of sleep.

The second assistant to the deputy to the Assistant Secretary of State for Inter-American Affairs scolds his wife. Later today he is to receive a medal for completing forty years of faultless service to the government. The ceremony will be conducted in the office of the deputy to the Assistant Secretary, and the second assistant must wear his frayed sports coat and slacks. His wife forgot to collect his suit last night from the cleaner's.

Between 7 and 8 a.m.

Two hundred thousand government workers eat breakfast. Most of them laugh discreetly at Herblock's cartoon in the *Washington Post*, which depicts the President in chaps and spurs astride Old Paint and galloping for the hills to escape the responsibility of the White House.

The Secretary of State gloats to his wife about his success in having foisted off the Asian tour upon the Secretary of Defense and decides to scare the French with an ambiguous statement at his news conference this afternoon. It never really works with the French, but then it never really hurts either.

At the Mayflower Hotel the President bows his head while the evangelist prays over the sausages. The President is thinking that perhaps he has been too tough lately toward the French and that he will say something pleasant about them at his news conference tomorrow.

At households throughout the city 40,000 men pause, before setting off to work, to inspect roses, azaleas, rhododendrons, forsythias, and brown spots in the lawn.

Two hoodlums subpoenaed to appear before a House investigating committee at 10 a.m. are rehearsed by lawyers over coffee in the proper form for refusing to testify under the Fifth Amendment.

In a Pentagon cafeteria two officers exchange greetings in the coffee line. "Heard about the security-conscious secretary who left her Pentagon job to take a job with a bishop?" asks one. "She filed all his correspondence under two headings—Sacred and Top Sacred."

Between 8 and 9 a.m.

In thousands of government offices millions of pieces of paper are put manually into transit between desk baskets.

At the White House the news teletype in the Press Secretary's office taps out a report that the head of a small African state has died on the Scandinavian leg of his world peace tour. The Press Secretary composes a message of condolence and orders it mimeographed for later issuance under the President's name.

The Senate Majority Leader tells his secretary to set up appointments with two aging senators about to retire. He will need their votes to arrange a tie vote on an important labor bill. The Vice-President, who hopes to become President, will have to vote to break the tie, thus infuriating either organized labor or organized business and, in either case, making the Majority Leader a very happy man.

The Vice-President, in his office just across the hall, is being photographed accepting a citation from the Society for a Wetter West. The

Vice-President, the citation declares, "has ever been a fighter in the cause of a more fully irrigated West."

Between 9 and 10 a.m.

Approximately 100,000 government workers begin approximately 20,000 staff conferences that will last until lunch.

Two congressmen returning from the prayer breakfast are asked how the President looked. "Bad," says one. "Never better," says another.

"Let's have some coffee," suggest 125,000 people, more or less simultaneously.

The chairman of the House Appropriations Committee decides to deny an Air Force request for $248,000,000 for spare parts for obsolescent aircraft.

In Spring Valley a popular hostess who last month contributed $5,000 to the Republican National Committee inspects a poll showing a rise in the popularity of the Democrats and writes a check for $5,000 payable to the Democratic National Committee.

Between 10 and 11 a.m.

Fourteen reporters telephoning officers of the State Department are told that the men they want are in conference.

At the White House the Press Secretary calls in reporters to announce that the President, upon learning of the African head of state's tragic and untimely death in Scandinavia, has just cabled a message of condolence.

Two hoodlums subpoenaed before a House investigating committee refuse to testify, claiming their privilege against self-incrimination under the Fifth Amendment, and issue mimeographed statements accusing the committee of abusing human dignity and flouting the Constitution.

The senior senator from Mississippi, deciding that he is overdue for a speech denouncing the newest civil rights proposals, buzzes his secretary. "Get me my white-supremacy expert," he instructs her.

At the Burning Tree Club a three-star general and a senator step out of the shower. "I know how the Budget Bureau feels," the general argues, "but when you come right down to it, what the hell is another billion dollars more or less?"

Between 11 a.m. and Noon

On the Senate floor the Majority Leader talks to reporters about the labor bill. "I never tell anyone how to vote," he is explaining. "On this one, every man will vote his conscience. We're going to be constructive. We're going to be positive. We're going to be responsible. We're going to do what's right for the country."

Between Noon and 1 p.m.

The Secretary of the Treasury, lunching with the chairman of the Senate Appropriations Committee, explains that while he is an Administration team man 100 per cent, the Secretary of State's new international banking proposal smacks strongly to him of fiscal irresponsibility.

At the National Press Club bar an oil lobbyist meets the information officer of the Egyptian Embassy and asks: "Have you heard about the security-conscious secretary who left her Pentagon job to take a job with a bishop? She filed all his correspondence under two headings. . . ."

Between 1 and 2 p.m.

The senior senator from Wisconsin interrupts the debate on the labor bill to read "An Ode to the Old Dray-Horse," by a ten-year-old constituent.

A famous newspaper columnist meets secretly with the Majority Leader to learn what the Senate will do on the labor bill. The Majority Leader assumes his most confidential look. "We're going to be constructive," he confides.

Two governors arriving on the same flight at National Airport blame unemployment in their states upon the President.

Between 2 and 3 p.m.

The State Department correspondent for a weekly news magazine wins six dollars at poker in the Department's pressroom.

The President, while debating whether to retire a three-star general who has been going over his head to influential senators at the Burning Tree Club, receives a telephone call from the Vice-President. The Vice-President is worried. He suspects that the Senate Majority Leader is maneuvering him into a position where he will be forced to cast the tie-breaking vote on the labor bill. Perhaps, he suggests, this awkwardness could be avoided if the Budget Bureau would change its mind and agree to reactivate that old Air Force base in the Majority Leader's home state.

Between 3 and 4 p.m.

One hundred thousand government workers have a last cup of coffee to sharpen their wits for the rush-hour traffic.

The Senate debate on the labor bill is interrupted for the introduction of a delegation from a small Southeast Asian republic which is making a world peace tour.

Between 4 and 5 p.m.

At his news conference the Secretary of State makes an ambiguous statement calculated to scare the French. The first news-agency bulletins misinterpret it to mean that the President is considering a break in diplomatic relations with India.

The Director of the Budget Bureau, calling upon the Secretary of the Treasury, voices the thought that has long been hanging unspoken between them: "Suppose—just suppose, mind you—that the President had the political courage just to abolish the Army altogether. . . ."

Between 5 and 6 p.m.

The State Department press office calls a news conference to announce that, contrary to some interpretations, there is no consideration being given to breaking diplomatic relations with New Delhi.

The Senate debate on the labor bill is interrupted for a speech against the newest civil rights proposals by the senior senator from Mississippi.

Evening cocktail parties begin in all hotels, fifty-five embassies, and hundreds of private homes and apartments.

Between 6 and 7 p.m.

Watching the early-evening news show on television, the President is flabbergasted by a film clip of the Secretary of State's ambiguous news-conference remarks about France. The President misconstrues them to mean that the Secretary is having an interdepartmental study made on the possibility of ceding Hawaii to Japan. A moment later the Secretary explains over the telephone that this is not the case at all.

The Senate debate on the labor bill is interrupted for a discussion of the relative merits of the rose and the marigold as the national floral emblem of the United States.

The President suggests to his wife that after Congress adjourns they vacation in Hawaii.

Between 7 and 8 p.m.

The Vice-President and the Senate Majority Leader are photographed in friendly embrace at a cocktail party. "Say," asks the Vice-President, "have you heard about the security-conscious secretary who left her Pentagon job to take a job with a bishop?"

The second assistant to the deputy to the Assistant Secretary of State for Inter-American Affairs arrives home with his medal. "How did it go?" asks his wife. "The Assistant Secretary was there personally to make the presentation," he says. "He mispronounced my name."

The Senate debate on the labor bill is interrupted while Administration critics take the floor to denounce the Secretary of State's news conference statement, which they interpret as a hint that the government is about to recognize Communist China.

Between 8 p.m. and 2 a.m.

A great Washington correspondent slips out of a cocktail party after talking to three officers of the State Department. He wires his paper an exclusive report on "the inside story behind the Secretary's news-conference gaffe today." What the Secretary's remarks really foreshadow, he reports, is nothing less than the dissolution of the North Atlantic Treaty Organization.

After reading a Central Intelligence Agency report on new missile installations in the Soviet Union, the President plays a game of cribbage with his wife and retires with a cowboy story.

The Senate, unable to muster a quorum, adjourns for the day.

Four senators running for the presidency sit up with their wives until all television stations go off for the night and there is no more chance of seeing themselves on the screen. Dropping off to sleep, each thinks: "I know I'm the man for the job."

Between 2 and 6 a.m.

The city sleeps, and each among its thousands of dreamers dreams of how brilliantly the country would be led if only he were the man in the White House.

The man in the White House dreams of six-guns and bunkhouses and of horseback living under prairie stars.

Four Funny Columns

I Chose Capitol Punishment (1963)

I've always thought Art Buchwald is one of the funniest men alive. He wrote his first column for the European edition of the Herald Tribune *in 1949, and went on writing for it for seventeen years, many of them spent in Paris, before bringing his "Capitol Punishment" column to the* Post *in 1966. I certainly had read Art's column for many years, but I don't think I ever met him before he moved to Washington.*

In the early 1980s, a former Post *writer and a friend of mine, David Lawrence, who was then wearing two hats—one as editor of the* Detroit Free Press *and another as editor of the* Bulletin *for the American Society of Newspaper Editors—wrote me that he had a sense that "a classic and continuing newspaper weakness is a lack of humor on our pages." He had just seen a video presentation at* Newsweek's *fiftieth-anniversary celebration that included Art Buchwald making some of his trademark funny comments, and he asked whether I might induce Art to write a piece for the* Bulletin *on the need for more humor.*

I passed David's letter on to Art, noting only that I felt David was right. Art did write something and sent it off to David with a cover note saying, "When Katharine speaks, even I tremble." Typically, he took the tongue-in-cheek approach in offering his reasons for the lack of humor in newspapers:

> It is no accident that there are very few syndicated humor columns for editors to choose from. Russell Baker, Erma Bombeck, Art Hoppe, Andy Rooney, and I have a humor OPEC organization, and we have discouraged all young people from going into the business. . . . In this way, we can keep the price of our humor columns high and we won't glut the market with a lot of aspiring journalists who would love to push us out of the business, or the window.

Typical of Art's humor are the connections to reality that make his columns so compelling. In saying that their cartel had been helped by

*newspaper editors themselves, "most of whom don't have much humor,"
he may not have been far off the mark. And he added that "Another
reason for the lack of humor is that most of the stories now appearing
in newspapers are so funny in themselves that it is hard to top them."
I think Art is right in this. Sometimes stories emanating from Washington need no humorous spin to them. They make us laugh out loud as
they are.*

In 1973, when he sent me his book I Never Danced at the White
House, *Art sent along a signed sticker to paste inside the book, with a
note: "That way you can't sell it." I didn't sell it. I've kept every one of
Art's books, especially his "Washington" books, like* Laid Back in
Washington, The Buchwald Stops Here, Washington Is Leak-
ing, Getting High in Government Circles, *and* The Establishment Is Alive & Well in Washington. *It's hard to choose from
among the thousands of pieces Art has written, but here are a few of my
favorites.*

OUR TOWN (WITH APOLOGIES TO MY GOOD FRIEND, THORNTON WILDER)

STAGE MANAGER: The name of the town is Washington, D.C.—just
across the Maryland State line. It's a nice town, y'know what I mean?
Nobody remarkable ever come out of it s'far as we know. We're just
plain, simple folk here, and we can't claim to be nothing more than
just another town along Route No. 1.

I better show you around a bit. That large white house over there
is the home of the Kennedy family. They rented it for four years,
with an option for another four. Not that they couldn't afford to buy,
but the owners wouldn't sell. The Kennedys are kind of important
around here, since they're the only family in town that owns a pony.
Hello there, Macaroni!

Over there on the hill is what folks in our town call the Capitol.
Not too much been happening there recently. You can hear a lot of
yelling and screaming from the Hill, though people are apt not to
pay too much attention to it.

Well, as I said, it's just about morning and people are starting to
go to work. There's Lyndon, just got back from a trip. Hi, Lyndon.
How did Ladybird like Turkey?

LYNDON: Jus' fine, jus' fine.

STAGE MANAGER: As you can see, there's nothing uppity about the
people in our town. Look, there's a light on over there in the Penta-

gon. Let's wander over and see what's going on. Hi, General. What's new?

GENERAL: Nothing much. Just moving some troops around Asia, planting some missile sites in Alaska, and keeping tabs on armored cars in Berlin.

STAGE MANAGER: Well, have fun, General. Things are starting to buzz over at the State Department factory about this time. There's Dean. I see you got some mail, Dean.

DEAN: Same old stuff. Notes on disarmament, South Vietnam, North Korea, Communist China, Argentina, Laos, Algeria, and de Gaulle. Nothing ever changes around here.

STAGE MANAGER: That's what I've been telling the folks. People 'round here have the same problems as people everywhere. Well, let's skip a few hours and go over and see one of our Senators at lunch. Senator, what's on the docket for today?

SENATOR: I have it on reliable information that the Russians sent five aircraft carriers and two Sputniks to Cuba last week. I'd like to say that I think this is the most dangerous—

STAGE MANAGER: Thanks, Senator, we have to be moving along. I see Billie Sol over by the grain elevator. Billie Sol don't live in our town, but he's a frequent visitor here. Hello, Billie, you planting any cotton this year?

BILLIE SOL: Shucks, no. Bad year for cotton planting. Think I'll just lay off for a spell and take it easy.

STAGE MANAGER: Good idea, Billie. No sense killing yourself with taxes what they are.

We got a few foreigners in our town, too. There's Serge Orlov, a Russian fellow. Lives out there in the embassy section. Hello, Serge. What are you doing today?

SERGE: Spying.

STAGE MANAGER: Serge's a real quiet fellow. Nothing uppity about him, either. Here comes our public prosecutor. Hello, Bobby. What's new down at the courthouse?

BOBBY: Nothing much. Antitrust suits, integration problems, Jimmy Hoffa, kidnappings, bank holdups, gambling cases, espionage, and my kid brother Teddy's election. Hardly enough to keep me busy. Might take a trip around the world.

STAGE MANAGER: There's one of our nine judges. Hello, Earl. Anybody want to impeach you today?

EARL: Haven't picked up my mail yet. I've been over at the public school praying with the kids.

STAGE MANAGER: Well, it's getting on to bedtime. There's a party going on over there at the French Embassy, the Shrivers are having a cookout for the Peace Corps, and the Kennedys are having Leonard Bernstein and the Philharmonic Orchestra in for a quiet evening at home. Outside of that, most people in our town are tucked in for the night after another uneventful day.

Hmmm. It's eleven o'clock. Good night, all.

WASHINGTON PARTIES ARE VERY REVEALING

Ever since I moved to Washington I've been reading the society pages with interest. The Washington society pages are different from any others in the world and most people turn to them before they read the front pages. The reason for this is that the hard news about world events is oftentimes buried in paragraphs devoted to embassy receptions, official dinners, and New Frontier cocktail parties.

This is how a typical Washington society-page story might sound:

"The Russians threw a wonderful party at their embassy last night to celebrate the arrival of the Bolshoi Ballet. In the receiving line was First Secretary Karnonsky, who with his lovely wife, Zina, greeted the guests. Zina told me she was sorry the Ambassador couldn't be there, but he had been called over to the White House for important conferences with the President. When I asked Zina where the Ambassador's wife was, she replied, 'She's packing the Ambassador's bag for a trip to Cuba.'

"I was very disappointed, as I enjoy talking to the Ambassador so much. But despite their absence, the table was loaded with caviar and smoked sturgeon and there was a lovely centerpiece of flowers which were arranged to look like an ICBM missile. Zina can do wonders with flowers.

"In the main salon I met General Werick Jablonsky, the handsome Polish military attaché, and his beautiful wife, Minka. Werick was telling some funny stories about Berlin and when I asked him if he thought Russia would sign a pact with East Germany, he handed me a glass of champagne and said, 'It's quite possible.' Minka was wearing a stunning blue dress and a blue hat with a veil to match. She always seems to have a nice word for everybody.

"I met Mrs. Nganda Ula, wife of the Congolese Minister for Economic Affairs, who said her husband could not be there as he was being held prisoner by the Katangans. Mrs. Ula was wearing an Indian sari of gold threads interwoven with pink and she looked striking.

"I was about to ask her how she was doing with her house-hunting when Colonel Singh of the Indian Military Mission and his wife greeted me. I hadn't seen them since Jackie Kennedy's visit to New Delhi. The

Singhs made me promise to come to a dinner party they were giving for Prime Minister Nehru, who was coming on a secret mission to see President Kennedy.

"General and Mrs. Birch of the British Embassy told me it looked as though Britain would soon join the Cuban embargo. But what I really wanted to know was where Mrs. Birch got her beautiful beaded bag. 'That,' she said, 'is a military secret.'

"Charley Graham, of the Bureau of Standards, told me about a new drug which would cure the common cold, but I only listened with half an ear as I was so taken with Flora Graham's latest hair-do. It was a bouffant behind the ears with a daring flip. When Flora is with Charley, no one pays any attention to what he has to say.

"Major Hang Po, of Nationalist China, told me an amusing story about Quemoy and Matsu. He also revealed he was being relieved to take over a squadron of F-104s and I was sorry to hear it as Major Po is so well liked in Washington circles and supports all the charities in town.

"It was a wonderful party and would probably have gone on all night if someone hadn't shot the Bengonian Chargé d'Affaires. I had to go off to the Swedish Embassy for a candlelight dinner, so I never did find out who did it.'"

Getting the News Is Always a Battle

There has been a lot of talk about news management in the Government these days, but if you go through history you can find that every presidential administration tried to manage the press in one way or another. I found an old transcript the other day of a press briefing between Abraham Lincoln's press secretary and White House reporters, which shows that even in those days attempts were made to bottle up vital news of interest to the public.

Here are excerpts from it:

QUESTION: Mr. Nicolay, yesterday the President gave a speech at Gettysburg, and he started it out by saying, "Fourscore and seven years ago our fathers brought forth on this continent a new nation." Sir, would you mind telling us the names of the fathers he was referring to?

SECRETARY: I'm sorry, gentlemen. I can't reveal the names at this time.

QUESTION: The *Saturday Evening Post*, which is published in Philadelphia, said he was referring to Washington, Jefferson, and Franklin. Is that true?

SECRETARY: That's just conjecture. The President is not responsible for everything written by his friends.

QUESTION: The President said yesterday in the same speech that the country was engaged in a great civil war, testing whether that nation or any nation so conceived and so dedicated can long endure. He didn't say how he intended to win the war. Does this mean he has a no-win policy?

SECRETARY: The President in his speech was only concerned with the Battle of Gettysburg, which incidentally we won. The Department of War will give you full details on other battles.

QUESTION: The Department refuses to give us any information. We don't know how many troops were used at Gettysburg, who commanded them, or how many casualties there were. All we were given were some lousy photos of Confederate gun emplacements. How can we be sure the Confederates still don't have artillery hidden in the hills around Gettysburg?

SECRETARY: We have constant surveillance of the hills. To the best of our knowledge all Southern artillery pieces have been removed.

QUESTION: What about Confederate troops? There are an estimated seventeen thousand in the area.

SECRETARY: We have the South's promise they will be removed in due course.

QUESTION: Mr. Secretary, why didn't Mrs. Lincoln go with the President to Gettysburg?

SECRETARY: Mrs. Lincoln feels that her place is at home with her children. But she did send a telegram.

QUESTION: In talking about the government of the people, by the people, and for the people, did the President have any particular group in mind?

SECRETARY: Not to my knowledge, gentlemen. But I'll check it out just to make sure.

QUESTION: Mr. Secretary, didn't the President in his speech yesterday indicate he intended to manage the news?

SECRETARY: In what way?

QUESTION: He said, "The world will little note, nor long remember, what we say here." It seems to me in this phrase he was intimidating the newspapermen who were there.

SECRETARY: I don't think you have to interpret the speech in that manner. The President's remarks, written on an envelope, were off the cuff, and he felt there was no reason to be quoted. An official version of his speech will be made available to the press in due time, as soon as the President has a chance to go over it again.

Dream Interview with Richard Nixon

Every once in a while, late at night when I'm tucked in bed, I shut my eyes and have a dream interview with some leading statesman or world figure who would not be available to me otherwise. One night I dreamed I interviewed former Vice-President Richard M. Nixon, who had just lost out in the gubernatorial race in California.

Mr. Nixon never looked better, and he was in wonderful spirits. He said, "I'm delighted to be able to talk to you, as I have the highest admiration for people in your profession."

"Then you're not upset about losing the election?"

"Heavens, no! In American politics it isn't who wins or loses but how we play the game that counts. I admire the way Governor Brown ran his campaign and I think he deserved to win."

"But don't you think he made some vicious charges against you and your family?"

"That's just politics. I never took the charges seriously. In this business you've got to have a sense of humor. I'm proud to say I never lost my temper once during the campaign and even in defeat I've been the first one to laugh."

"Sir, there have been rumors that you felt the press was unfair to you during the campaign and that they didn't report what you said accurately."

"Now where would a rumor like that ever start? Some of my best friends are newspapermen, and I think everyone leaned over backward to report my campaign without fear or prejudice. Without exception I have admired everything they have written about me, and I think my campaign was made so much more pleasant by having them with me during these difficult months."

"Do you feel that Governor Brown accused you of lack of patriotism or lack of heart during the contest?"

"What a ridiculous question! The one thing I admired about Governor Brown was that he never made any personal attacks on me, and I in turn never made any on him. The issues were quite clear from the start and they boiled down to one thing. 'Who was the best man for the job?' The people of California thought he was, and I would be a sore loser if I said that he questioned my patriotism during the campaign. Do you think I'm a sore loser?"

"Heck, no. Not in this dream anyway," I replied.

"Well, that's the kind of guy I am. I wouldn't want people to think otherwise."

"Do you think Governor Brown spent more money on his campaign than you did?"

"Maybe, but what difference does that make? I don't think money played an important part in this campaign. It was Cuba that probably caused all the difficulty. I was for the President's taking a strong stand in Cuba, but I didn't think he'd take it while I was running for office. The Communist threat was in California, not in Cuba, but people forgot about it out here. If the Russians had set up their missiles in Los Angeles, I think I would have won."

"Back to the press, sir. Someone quoted you as saying after you lost that the press wouldn't have Nixon to kick around any more. Would you like to elaborate on that?"

"I was misquoted," he replied. "I said 'stick around.' I was sorry the press wouldn't have Nixon to stick around any more."

"What are your plans now?" I asked him.

"Well, I might run for congressman, and if I lose, I might then run for State assemblyman, and if I lose that, I think I would make a good city councilor. I enjoy the give and take of politics, and besides it's the best way I can keep in touch with all my friends of the fourth estate."

P. J. O'ROURKE

The Winners
Go to Washington, D.C.

Parliament of Whores (1991)

This is a different generation's humorous take on Washington—and an incredibly funny one. O'Rourke is a political humorist of the first order.

Perhaps his early writing and editing at National Lampoon *set him on the road to political satire. What he does in* Parliament of Whores *is delineated in the subtitle: "A Lone Humorist Attempts to Explain the Entire U.S. Government." O'Rourke goes after a lot of sacred cows, including some good friends of mine, but in Washington we're all potential targets for humor, and that's probably good for democracy. He certainly doesn't spare himself. At one point he acknowledges: "Washington journalists are seduced by their proximity to power, and that was me. Power had my lipstick smeared and was toying with my corset hooks before I even got off the Trump Shuttle."*

WASHINGTON is a fine place for journalists to live as well as to brown-nose. It has plenty of the only kind of people who can stand journalists—other journalists—and plenty of the only kind of people journalists get any real information from—other journalists. It is, like most journalists themselves, not very big (Washington is smaller than Memphis, Tennessee) and not as sophisticated as it thinks. And it's pretty. Washington has lots of those Greek- and Roman-style buildings that practically make you feel like a senator just walking up the steps of them. Senators, in particular, are fond of this feeling, and this is one reason official Washington escaped the worst effects of modern architecture. Also, steel and glass skyscrapers are relatively cheap to build, and cost effectiveness is not a concept here. As Article One, Section 9, paragraph 7 of the U.S. Constitution says, "No money shall be drawn from the Treasury, but in consequence of appropriations made by law. . . ." So it's obvious what the whole point of lawmaking is.

But Washington, though it costs taxpayers a fortune, is itself inexpensive—at least compared with New York or Los Angeles. In Washington journalists can afford to live almost as well as people who work for a living. Those stories about crack wars and the "murder capital of America" are nonsense, of course—as long as you stay in the part of Washington that concerns itself with real wars and being the regular capital. This is the part that extends northwest along Connecticut, Massachusetts and Wisconsin avenues from the tourist attractions on the Mall to the Maryland suburbs—the "white pipeline." People do occasionally venture outside this zone, people who come in to do your cleaning or mow the lawn.

Numerous demonstrations, marches, PR stunts and other staged events are held in Washington to give journalists an excuse for not covering real events, which are much harder to explain. Barely a weekend passes without some group of people parading in the capital to protest the piteous condition of those inevitable victims of injustice, themselves.

One Saturday it's opponents of abortion dragging little children along to show they hadn't been killed. The next Saturday it's advocates of abortion dragging little children along to show they'd been born on purpose. The homeless come and make themselves at home around the Washington Monument. The Vietnam veterans are veteran gatherers at the Vietnam Veterans Memorial. Earth Day organizers litter the streets with posters and pamphlets calling for trash to be recycled. The AIDS Memorial Quilt is unfolded, and the Cancer Sampler and Car-Wreck Duvet are probably coming soon.

FOR THE people in government, rather than the people who pester it, Washington is an early-rising, hard-working city. It is a popular delusion that the government wastes vast amounts of money through inefficiency and sloth. Enormous effort and elaborate planning are required to waste this much money. At 10:30 on weekday nights Washington bars and restaurants are as empty as synagogues in Iraq. I have never gotten up so early in Washington—or stayed up so late, for that matter—that somebody wasn't already awake and jogging by beneath my apartment window. On my first full day in Washington I saw an astonishingly beautiful young woman, slim, doe-eyed and still dewy from a hinterland childhood, the kind of girl who would be streaking like a Tomahawk cruise missile through the New York fashion-model and dance-club world. She was reading "Defense News" on the Metro at 7:45 a.m.

People in government jobs, especially political appointees and high-level bureaucrats, are customarily at their desks by eight in the morning and still there at six at night. They return calls, are courteous over the phone, prompt in their appointments and helpful to the point of obsequiousness.

Government people work so hard for the curious reason that their output can't be measured. There are plenty of ways to determine bad government, but good government is hard to quantify. How can streets be too clean or crime rates too low? A poverty threshold is easy to establish, but nobody's ever too rich. The casualties of war are simpler to count than the augmentations of peace. And that's why government employees work so hard—since output can't be measured, input has to be.

People in government are also a cheerful and indefatigably optimistic bunch. At first I was mystified. Government work would seem to be a run in a hamster wheel. Government can do nothing, at least nothing right. For instance, the deficit is terrible, but lower spending will hurt the poor and higher taxes will lead to a recession causing more people to become poor and get hurt by the lower spending needed to bring taxes down to end the recession, and so on. But since government rarely succeeds, it hardly ever fails. And government programs aren't necessarily designed to go anywhere. Like the joggers beneath my window, who are the people who run those programs, they just go. The results—sweat, ruined knees, America as a second-rate world power—don't matter. It's the effort that makes the action worthy. Frank Lavin, who was the director of the Office of Political Affairs in the Reagan White House (notice my access), told me, "People who believe in government regulation and intervention in life—for them government is a church." And people who are truly committed to government exhibit the same dull self-satisfaction and slightly vapid peace of mind as do devout churchgoers. They also know their business is never going to be bought by Sony.

WASHINGTON'S optimistic enthusiasm, dreadfully wholesome energy and overabundance of media types is never more evident than when a fresh batch of optimistic enthusiasts and wholesomely energetic dreadfuls is sucked into town by a new presidential administration and all the media types rush there to meet them.

This was particularly true in the case of George Bush. Usually journalists suffer a brief, syrupy infatuation with an incoming chief executive. But everybody had such a crush on George that you began to wonder if the *New York Times* editorial board wasn't maybe driving by George's house in the middle of the night and pining out the car window or sneaking into the Kennebunkport Yacht Club to leave anonymous poems in his locker.

First the jerk disappeared—the tall schmo with the voice up his nose, the one who was running for president but nobody could figure out why because he kept getting his tongue in a clove hitch and calling every whatchamajigger a "thing." He vanished without a trace. You'll remember that until the beginning of January 1989 George Bush was a skinny, inconsequential doofus, an intellectual smurf and moral no-show who'd wound up in the White House by default. Then one day I saw in the newspapers that the president-elect was a seasoned Washington professional, a man who knew where all the levers and pedals and remote-control channel changers of government were located, plus he was a symbol of unity and strength reaching out to Americans of every hue, stripe and polka-dot pattern and gathering us together in an immense bipartisan hug, cuddle and smooch.

Next George was applauded like an Academy Award–winning actor with cancer for his proposed cabinet appointments. (This being before the U.S. Senate decided that former senator John Tower was too drunk and silly to be secretary of defense but not quite drunk and silly enough to be a senator again.) In fact, only two of Bush's nominees were other than mundane. There was William Bennett, who had been so much fun as Reagan's secretary of education. You had to love a man who'd made that many schoolteachers mad. Bennett always seemed about to say, "Anybody who doesn't know what's wrong with America's schools never screwed an el-ed major." However, now Bennett was to be "drug czar." Would his scholastic background help? Would he make dead crack addicts stay after life and write, "I will not be killed by rival gangs of drug dealers" one hundred times on the blackboard? Then there was Jack Kemp, the proposed secretary of Housing and Urban Development. But was it a bold stroke or a mean prank to make the only real conservative in the crowd go down to the ghetto and explain the Laffer curve?

Anyway, for the moment, the media was treating Bush's cabinet picks as if they were the nine worthies, the three wise men and two surefire ways to lose weight without dieting. And this was nothing compared with what had happened to Barbara Bush: apotheosis. Now, Barbara Bush was reputed, on good authority, to be a nice woman, warmhearted, funny, sensible and all the things we usually say about our mothers when they're listening. But it wasn't as though she'd actually done anything or even said much. Barbara Bush, it seemed, was elevated to secular sainthood strictly on the basis of gray hair and a plump figure. And such is the remarkable speed of fashion in Washington that, within hours of the swearing in, snowy bouffants and comfortable tummies appeared everywhere among the politically chic. A few extra pounds were spilling over the waistband of my own boxer shorts, in fact.

Even the Dan Quayle market was—very temporarily—up. This is the fellow who was supposed to answer the question once and for all "Can a person be too dumb for government?" But in February 1989 columnists and commentators were mumbling about what a hard-working senator Dan had always been. The *Wall Street Journal* went so far as to call him "an avid reader . . . not just of newspaper clips or an occasional magazine piece, but of real live books." Quick to note a vogue in toadying, the *New Republic* offered a Quayle Revisionism Award, only to have readers write in suggesting the prize be given to the *New Republic*'s own senior editor, Morton Kondracke, for saying Dan Quayle was "well-informed, intelligent, candid and engaging."

There was a giddiness in the District of Columbia during inauguration week, and not just among Republicans dizzy from victory and cheap, warm domestic Inaugural Ball champagne. Liberals were sidling up to each other and confessing profound relief that Puckermug Micky was back in Boston with a huge, poorly balanced Massachusetts state budget about to fall on his head. Garry Trudeau had run out of punchlines for his *Doonesbury* comic strip and was stuck with an "invisible George" joke about a president so hopelessly visible that he seemed to show up everyplace except *The Oprah Winfrey Show*. Jesse Jackson and George Bush looked to be on the verge of starting their own two-man Operation PUSH chapter. Jackson said Bush's inaugural speech "set exactly the right tone." And the *Tehran Times*—this is true—welcomed George Bush to the White House and opined that he'd "acted wisely" at the onset of his administration.

On inauguration day anti-Bush demonstrators were thin on the ground. A smattering of ERA signs were held aloft along the parade route. A few devoted peace buffs were camped across from the White House in an antinuke vigil that they'd vowed to continue until the world didn't blow up. The homeless were nowhere to be seen. I suppose the police had told them to go home. The *Washington Post* devoted only fifteen column inches to "alternative" celebrations in its special Saturday inauguration section. And I saw just one protester outside an Inaugural Ball, a lonely flake in pigtail and knapsack with a message about the Super Bowl hand-lettered on notebook paper: "If Joe Montana Passes Like Dan Quayle Speaks, the Bengals Will Win." (They didn't.) The liberal liberals, the serious hemorrhaging valentines, the real giveaway-and-guilt bunch, had disappeared into the same black hole as the jokes about Barbara looking like George's mother. Alas, the pinkos—they'd lost to the guy who lost to George. They weren't even ranked anymore.

Of course, in those bastions of GOPery, where you'd expect the welkin to ring, there were rung welkins all over the place. At a Republican National Committee staff party at the Grand Hyatt, the crowd was young, integrated, drunk, loud and seemed to have lost its copy of the "How to Act like a Republican" manual. A large can of men's hair-styling gel had been discovered in the hotel suite's bathroom, and people were being tackled at random. "Mousse him! Mousse him!" went the cry. Someone would go down in a pile-on and emerge with improbable hair spikes projecting above pin-striped suit jacket.

A clean-cut person in his middle fifties with very good posture walked in. "It's the general!" yelled the RNC staff. "Hey, General! Hi ya doin', General?! MOUSSE HIM!!!" He came out looking pretty good, too. Later I remember somebody, possibly me, weaving down the hotel hall with a large cigar in one hand and a larger drink in the other, shouting, "We had all the money! Then we won all the votes! Now we've got all the fun!" while his wife kicked him and threatened to call security.

IT HAD been a long while since there was this much good cheer and auld lang syne at a presidential inauguration. You'd have to go back to 1961, when Jackie was a tomato and Jack was giving the world a nudge and a wink, and the New Frontier stretched before us full of challenge, potential and shoving people into swimming pools. (Although it's instructive to remember what happened in the late sixties and early seventies when we reached the unexplored regions of that New Frontier—war, drugs, STDs, disco music and about a billion ruined marriages.)

George Bush looked like he'd be a cozy president, old shoe, gemutlichkeit. This wasn't the same as having a smug little wiseacre or a big Hollywood movie star in the White House. The first word of George Bush's inaugural address was hey. (That is, of course, after he'd said "Thank you, ladies and gentlemen," because this is a president who minds his manners.) "Hey, Jack, Danny," said George, looking around at Congressmen Jack Brooks and Dan Rostenkowski as though he'd just stepped up to the podium at a Monday Rotary lunch. "Mr. Chief Justice, Mr. President, Vice President Quayle, Senator Mitchell," George continued, "Speaker Wright, Senator Dole, Congressman Michel, fellow citizens, neighbors, friends . . ." For a moment it seemed as though the president might just keep on greeting people for hours, like a little kid trying to include everybody in the God-bless section of his bedtime prayers: ". . . colleagues, compatriots, associates, acquaintances, distant cousins, people who graduated from high school about the same time I did . . ." But he stopped himself, gave the world a goofy smile and delivered a speech we'd all heard a hundred times before but never from a president of the United States. It was a speech we'd all heard a hundred times from our dads:

... This country has a meaning beyond what we can see ... our strength is a force for good. ...

We are not the sum of our possessions. They are not the measure of our lives. ...

We have more will than wallet; but will is what we need ...

The final lesson of Vietnam is that no great nation can long afford to be sundered by a memory. ...

A president is neither prince nor pope, and I do not seek "a window on men's souls." In fact I yearn for a greater tolerance, an easygoingness about each other's attitudes and way of life. ...

Most dads don't have Peggy Noonan speech writing for them, so their phrases aren't so orotund and rhetorically balanced, but it's the same lecture in the den:

You should thank your lucky stars you were born in the United States of America.

Money isn't everything.

Hard work never killed anybody.

Family is family so quit picking on your little brother. ...

I can't follow you around for the rest of your life keeping you out of trouble, so use your common sense and don't do anything stupid; it would break your mother's heart.

Then the Reagans blew out of town. The herds of anchorfolk covering this on TV did their best to make the departure damp-eyed, but you could practically hear the nationwide sigh of relief. They are really lovely, lovely people, the Reagans, and we enjoyed their stay, we really did, but, well, you know. ... They have been here quite a while, and they're frankly not getting any younger. And they're a bit—let's be truthful—la-di-da, especially her. When you come right down to it, it's great to have them out of the way so we can spend Sundays padding around in our bathrobes with the funny papers all over the place and can leave the TV on during dinner if we want.

Which is apparently what the Bushes were doing. Twenty-eight members of the Bush family spent the first night of the Bush presidency at the White House. "You kids cut that out! Go to sleep this minute! No pillow fighting in the Green Room, you'll break the gosh-darned antiques!"

During the inaugural parade Bush kept darting in and out of his limousine, and the crowd reacted as if he were the early Beatles. These popouts were much better received than the Jimmy Carter business of walking the whole parade route. We Americans like our populism in small doses and preferably from an elitist. A Democrat populist might mean what he says and take our new Toro away because a family down the street can't afford the self-starting kind with the de-thatching attachment. A Republican populist is only going to indulge in the popular types of populism and will then get back in his Cadillac and behave.

Dan Quayle stayed in his Cadillac entirely and broadcast cheery greetings to the parade viewers over the car's built-in PA system: "Section A . . . stand 21, how are you? Hello, Section B." (These are actual quotes.)

IT WAS worth going to the Inaugural Balls on Friday night just to see hundreds of newspaper reporters in bad tuxedos and mortal pain from rented dress shoes. I went to two of the things, which is about all a non-elected human being can bear. Ball procedure consists of standing around chatting amicably in itchy clothes if you're a man, or, if you're a woman, standing around chatting amicably in clothes that parts of you are about to squeeze out of. You can't drink because the bar is two hundred fifty thousand Republicans away from where you are. And you can't dance because the music is being played by marines on sousaphones. This must be what entertainment was like in the nineteenth century, before fun was invented.

The Young Americans Ball at the J. W. Marriott Hotel was particularly crowded, and the Young Americans were horribly well behaved. I'd bet most of them weren't even on drugs. This may be just as well. What kind of hallucinations would these clean-cut juveniles have? "Oh, man, I was staring at these clouds, and they looked just like falling bond yields." Though I'm a conservative myself, I worry about the larval Republicans. They should act up now and get it over with, otherwise misbehavior may come upon them suddenly in middle age, the way it came upon the protagonist of Thomas Mann's *Death in Venice* and, also, Gary Hart.

The Maine and Indiana Ball at Union Station was better, full of the most reassuring kind of grown-ups, who looked like grown-ups used to look thirty years ago—happy, prosperous, solid, sensible, a little boring and not about to turn up in a Bret Easton Ellis novel. It was worth hundreds of hours of transactional analysis and a prescription for Valium just to walk around among their merry, placid faces and ample cummerbunds.

Dan Quayle arrived at Union Station about 10:30 wearing a smile that said—as only an open, honest, corn-fed midwestern smile can say— "Fuck you." Who can blame him? There was terrific press bias against Quayle during the election because most journalists worked harder at college than Dan did and all it got them was jobs as journalists. Marilyn

Quayle was there, too, looking—it was indeed a strange week in Washington—great. She had her hair done up in something my wife said was a chignon, and whatever it was, it made Marilyn look considerably less like a Cape buffalo than usual. Though actually I admired the Cape buffalo look. I have an idea that—like the Cape buffalo—if Marilyn Quayle gets furious and charges, you've got only one shot at the skull. You wouldn't want to just wound her.

The next night the president's campaign manager, the supposedly cold-blooded Lee Atwater, staged an immense rhythm-and-blues concert at the Washington Convention Center auditorium. This was more or less Atwater's first official act as the new Republican National Committee chairman—inviting Sam Moore, Percy Sledge, Bo Diddley, Albert Collins, Joe Cocker, Ron Wood, Willie Dixon, Etta James, Dr. John, Stevie Ray Vaughan, Delbert McClinton, Billy Preston and about a dozen other blues musicians to entertain, of all things, the GOP faithful.

I'd like to travel back in time to January 1969, when Richard Nixon was being inaugurated, and Pigasus, the four-footed Yippie candidate, was being inaugurated, too, and the country was a mess, and so was my off-campus apartment. And I'd like to tell the self that I was then: "Twenty years from today you will watch the chairman of the Republican National Committee boogie down on electric guitar. And he's going to duck walk and do the splits and flip over backward and sing 'High Heel Sneakers' at the top of his lungs. And when he gets finished, the president of the United States—a Republican president—is going to be pulled up on stage by Sam Moore of Sam and Dave and presented with another electric guitar with THE PREZ painted on the front. And the president of the United States and the chairman of the RNC are going to trade blues licks in front of a crowd of eighty-five hundred Americans very similar to yourself, who are going to go wild with politically motivated glee."

I'd like to know what I would have thought, that is, after I got over the shock of seeing myself come back in time so jowly and with an ROTC haircut.

Anyway, the concert sounded like Jesse Jackson had been elected, except the music was better. Jackson would have felt compelled to have boring Sting there and some Suzanne Vega and Tracy Chapman depressive types and dreary Rainbow Coalition stuff, too, probably featuring "Hava Negilah" played by a marimba band. The Republicans were under no such constraints.

When President Bush entered the auditorium, no one played "Hail to the Chief." Instead, the 1967 Bar-Keys instrumental "Soul Finger" had been chosen as the presidential theme. Bush walked, as he'd have to for at least the next four years, inside a hollow square of stiff-necked fellows with long-distance looks and pistols in their armpits. But within the Secret Service phalanx you could see one bright, white head swaying and nodding to the beat. Barbara Bush didn't sit down all night.

Atwater, whose health problems were still a year away, proved to be an excellent guitar player and a, well, very enthusiastic vocalist. The evening's master of ceremonies, the president's son Marvin, bellowed into a microphone: "They call Frank Sinatra the chairman of the board, but they call Lee Atwater THE CHAIRMAN OF THE REPUBLICAN NATIONAL COMMITTEE!!!" The audience went crazy. Sam Moore tugged on the president, got him up on the stage. "I taught Lee everything he knows about that kind of dancing," said George Bush. The crowd went crazier. "I know when to shut up and when to say something," continued Bush, "and this is a time to shut up." Though he didn't quite. He wanted to talk about how he'd thrown the White House—the "People's House" he insisted on calling it—open to the public that morning and how, even after these people had been waiting outside in the cold for what must have seemed like forever, they didn't complain. They looked around in awe "just like me and Barbara."

"We've got a little present for you," said Sam Moore.

"Dancing lessons, I hope," said the president half under his breath. And there was a smile of real pleasure when he saw the guitar. It almost looked as though "the prez" knew how to play it.

And when the music began again, something was shaking in the GOP. All across the auditorium thousands of honkies were coming out of their tuxedo jackets. The convention center was wall-to-wall in a pattern of jiggling suspenders over soaking-wet dress shirts, like a huge attack of extra Y chromosomes. Did they have rhythm? No. But this is America. You can achieve anything in America. Republicans might even achieve sympathy and a little soul.

WE'D HAD eight years of talk about patriotism and family values from a man who saw less combat in the service than I saw as a hippie and whose children spent his whole administration exiled to the *Good Morning, America* gulag. Now there was an actual household in the White House, one where Dad really was a war hero (if not exactly an ace pilot).

Our country was all smiles and handshakes with the USSR. The first faint blush of political freedom was visible in Eastern Europe. Wars were petering out in Afghanistan and Angola. Central America was idling in neutral. The economy was OK. It seemed to be a genuinely promising moment in the history of the nation, a moment for—as Dr. Johnson said about second marriages—"the triumph of hope over experience."

How Washington Works

The mystery of government is not how Washington works but how to make it stop.

—P. J. O'Rourke, *Parliament of Whores*

The caption for this photo, which appeared on April 19, 1963, reads: "Here's how news gets around: And what more fitting place for a demonstration of same than the annual Stunt Party dinner given last night at the Statler-Hilton for members of the American Society of Newspaper Editors and wives. This, to be specific, is the pre-dinner reception where everything first started to tick."

IT'S NOT easy to get a handle on Washington. Everyone has a different angle on the Washington experience, depending, of course, on his own experience. Certainly Washington is many cities in one—it's a city of paradox and bewilderment. George Abell and Evelyn Gordon, in *Let Them Eat Caviar,* wrote, "It is the Wonderland of a hundred Alices, the despair of diplomats, the blurred hope of the proletariat."

Washington as the nation's capital and Washington as a local city where real people live are two different places. The city is full of contradictions, which many people feel is really part of the charm of the place—part of its genius loci. The city seems to be one thing and then another. It's a place people look to for leadership, yet at the same time they feel free to criticize whatever leadership is attempted.

Washington is a power center—full of intrigue and maneuvering and private plotting and personal scheming, as well as of planning and policymaking and positive impulses and public service. It's also a hometown, where people serve on juries and need their garbage picked up and their roads cleared of snow, and deserve good schools and sensitive social services. Sure, there are people here whose motives can and should be questioned, schemers who pursue every avenue for personal advancement, but there are also dreamers here, and hard workers and caring professionals and ordinary citizens for whom politics and power are remote concepts.

Certainly, this is a political place—political is perhaps the main defining characteristic of Washington, at least for those outside looking in, for those "beyond the Beltway." Clearly, political people are drawn to a town where policy gets made. Jim Hoagland, intrepid *Post* reporter, insightful columnist, and my friend, once wrote of Meg Greenfield's sure hand at the *Post*'s editorial helm that "she would slide the *Post*'s editorial bias from center left to center right and then back again as new presidents and Congresses changed the capital's sense of political gravity." That was certainly true of Meg, and it is also true that the center of political gravity in Washington changes depending on the president, the Congress, the people. What is significant and central is that the main pendulum on which the city swings is a political one.

Some people think that Washington is only about power, and there's no question that power is important here. Stewart Alsop wrote that "Power is what Washington is all about. Power is what attracts able men into government and politics, and keeps them working ten hours or more a day, and enduring ulcer-inducing pressures, year after year, for far less money than they could make elsewhere." But power in Washington is a complicated phenomenon. Here, there's not necessarily a correlation between wealth and power. Power in Washington is more apt to be a mixture of position and personality.

Edward Lowry wrote something in *Washington Close-Ups* that gave me pause: "In Washington there is nothing quite as perishable as prestige." But I think it's easier to think of people who've kept their prestige, or their reputation, if you will, of which the current most prominent one is Henry Kissinger. Heads of state from foreign lands come to two places when they come to the United States: the White House and Henry Kissinger's office. There's no question about his prestige. I think that if the people are inconsequential to begin with, they revert to being inconsequential and fade. A lot of people have more than one life in Washington; they reappear. Dick Cheney and Donald Rumsfeld are two examples. Secretary Colin Powell enhanced his prestige in Washington. George Shultz kept his and remains highly regarded.

People here are often defined by what they do. Russell Baker wrote in *An American in Washington*, "If you want to get anything done in Washington, you must be in. In the know. In the swim. In the chips. In on the ground floor. In at the finish. In up to your ears. People who are not in are worse than out. They are nobody. And when you are nobody in Washington, you do nobody any good."

And what do we do here? My friend Ward Just wrote in his novel *Echo House:* " 'That's what we do in Washington,' Harold said with sudden emotion. 'We fix things up. We compromise; that's the essence of our society. We give a little and get a little and out of the chaos comes an order that we can live with. It isn't perfect. But it's what we do.' "

Where people and personalities, with all their humanity, are involved, there is bound to be drama. Washington has more than its share of Sturm und Drang. Public scandals here get elevated immediately to the national level. Scandals usually make the big time in Washington—whether it's Congressman Wilbur Mills chasing after Fanne Fox the Firecracker, or President Richard Nixon chasing after a spotless legacy.

Well beyond the social realm, there are unwritten rules for behavior in this city. People are always offering advice and tips for survival in Washington. Among Russell Baker's ten simple rules for avoiding trouble in Washington, number seven is: "Be careful about seduction. This is not Hollywood, and anyone caught exhibiting more interest in the libido than the ego is apt to be dismissed as a trifle ordinary." Even my mother had some advice on this front. She wrote in her diary, "If one wishes to flirt in Washington, it can take place only in the sanctity of one's own home."

What is the truth about people here? Clearly, it's risky to generalize. As Stewart Alsop wrote, "It is possible to be factual about Washington . . . but it is not really possible to be 'objective' about Washington, for the word suggests that there are immutable truths about the place, and there are none."

What I think I know is that people love to talk in Washington. Some, although not enough, love to listen. Talk is big; conversation provides a focus, a center, a diversion, an activity that counts as legitimate. Everyone comments on Washington as the "City of Conversation." Marquis Childs wrote about the "whispering gallery that is Washington." Elizabeth Drew remarked on the constant "Babel of voices" in the city. Sally Quinn wrote that "The whole idea of conversation as entertainment is especially true in Washington." Abell and Gore wrote that "Everyone chatters incessantly—about anything. Naturally none of them wants to leave Washington, because Washington is the queen city of gossip."

Indeed, gossip is a big part of social and political Washington. I love the gossip in my mother's diary, whether she's reporting on what she believed to be the "authentic version" of Coolidge's famous "I do not choose to run" statement; or on some woman flirting with my father, whom she comments on as feeling "the injustice of this world when men like Eugene are wasted on women like me"; or commenting on noted Washington figures behaving like spoiled children; or even her comments on the "ignorance and pettiness" of the Senate at one point, behaving "like a group of savages who find a watch upon the beach."

People's thinking about how Washington works has certainly been affected by the media. Perceptions about this city are also affected by fiction—from Henry Adams's *Democracy* to Cissy Patterson's *Glass Houses* to Gore Vidal's *Washington, D.C.* Many of Allen Drury's lines in *Advise and Consent* stayed with the readers long after the last page was turned. One particularly memorable bit was: "Of course, that was the thing about Washington, really; you didn't have to be born to anything, you could just buy your way in. 'Any bitch with a million bucks, a nice house, a good caterer, and the nerve of a grand larcenist can become a social success in Washington,' people said cattily, and indeed it was entirely true."

In many ways this is a strange (but wonderful) place. It's the last place in America where the citizens are subjected to completely un-American taxation without representation. It is a city, as Arthur

Schlesinger once said, "where the most serious purpose lurks behind the greatest frivolity." Adlai Stevenson described Washington as a sedate town that ran on "alcohol, protocol, and Geritol."

I believe Washington is an open place, more egalitarian than many, perhaps most, other cities. Sure, Washington has "headliners"—some of whom deserve the headlines and some who don't. Something Mother wrote in her diary I think holds true still: "The odd part about Washington is that for a little space of time it always accepts a man at his own valuation. If thereupon he does a fairly good job and equally good advertising, he is made, but if he slips, the vengeance taken by Washington is in proportion to his strut."

Define it however you will; I think Washington works and works well. It functions as the nation's capital, and it functions as home to hundreds of thousands of people and to millions more in the metropolitan area. It is where we live and work, and it works for us.

Mrs. Boggs Gets Seated

Washington Through a Purple Veil   (1994)

Lindy Boggs is a friend and contemporary. Certainly this would have predisposed me to read her book, but all that she chose to touch on about Washington compelled me to read on. What she captures is the energy and interest of the times—people filling the halls of Congress to listen to hearings, watching from the galleries at Senate and House debates, the fear that Washington might be bombed during the war, the friendly, leisurely town she found on her arrival, when there was no parking on the streets between four and six p.m. because those were the "calling hours."

Lindy first came to live here in 1941 when her husband, Hale Boggs, was elected to Congress. It was just a year or so after the movie Mr. Smith Goes to Washington, *and Hale even used as his slogan "Mr. Boggs Goes to Washington." Lindy had arrived on the train with her children just in time for FDR's third inaugural, and they had moved into a little rented apartment on the top floor of a small Capitol Hill hotel, where she "could hang diapers on the roof." She writes of the Lend-Lease hearings as being the "most popular events in the capital" at the time, and it was true. I was impressed by her story of being late to an event at the White House because her child was cutting a tooth—to which Eleanor Roosevelt said, "I'm glad someone has her priorities straight."*

While I had lived here nearly my whole life, Lindy was new to Washington and saw everything in a new light. Of the Capitol, she writes,

> I fell in love with the Capitol dome. It was the beacon leading me to pick Hale up in the evenings before I figured out Washington's peculiar traffic system. I was always pulling over and stopping, sometimes getting out of the car to look at it in different lights, pink as a wedding cake at sunset or shimmering bright white against a cobalt sky. Someone was standing next to me outside the Capitol one evening as I gazed at it.
>
> "Isn't that the most beautiful sight in the world?" he asked.

*I turned and saw that it was "Mister Sam" Rayburn, the
Speaker of the House. Whenever he was frustrated or fatigued,
he'd go out to look at the dome and be reinspired.*

*We share the fact that we have both continued to be inspired by the
Capitol—and by Washington—through all of our lives here.*

I FIRST went to Washington to live in 1941 when my husband, Hale
Boggs, was elected to Congress. We had been active in New Orleans
in a reform movement to break the grip of the scandal-ridden incumbent political machine, and Hale was swept into office on a wave of public support. At twenty-six he was the youngest member of Congress. I
was a twenty-four-year-old wife and mother in love with my tall, handsome husband and in awe of his innate political skills, which had brought
us to official Washington so early in our careers. He was my brilliant
mentor in the world of public service. If I had not been married to him, I
would have nonetheless been his enthusiastic supporter anyway.

The Speaker of the House of Representatives was Sam Rayburn, a
shrewd Texan and strong leader known for recognizing leadership qualities in young, untested congressmen. Assessing Hale's political and intellectual abilities, he assigned him to the prestigious Banking and
Currency Committee just as the committee began its debate and public
hearings on Lend-Lease.

Newly empowered by his third-term election victory, President
Franklin D. Roosevelt was pushing Congress to authorize sending millions of dollars' worth of war supplies and food to Great Britain and
China through direct sales, as a loan, or by lease arrangements. German
air raids had the British fighting for their lives, while the Chinese battled
a Japanese invasion. Although the president likened the aid to lending a
neighbor your garden hose to put out a fire, the opponents of the Lend-Lease Bill saw it as an irrevocable step into another world war.

The prevailing mood of the country was one of isolationism, with
which Hale and I and most of our friends, the children of the World
War I generation, agreed. We were reluctant to be associated with other
countries' wars, as we had noisily demonstrated while we were in college.

The Lend-Lease hearings were the most popular events in the capital. Everyone seemed to have a strong opinion one way or the other on
sending supplies to our allies. As soon as the doors of the hearing room
were opened each day, people streamed in to take every seat and listen to
the arguments. There was always a long line of those hoping to get in,
standing for hours in the hall.

Hale called me at our apartment one morning and asked me to come and listen. He felt I wouldn't understand the serious nature of the arguments in favor of the necessity for the Lend-Lease Act unless I heard the testimony. The international situation was more complex and threatening to democracy than we had recognized, he said.

I threw a jacket over my sweater and skirt, and made up my face, brushed my hair and put on high heels. I left little Barbara, who was nineteen months old, and baby Tommy with Lucy Boutwell, the nurse who helped me, and rushed down to the Capitol.

We had no specific Congressional identification cards in those days, no picture on a driver's license, no credit cards. I walked past the line of people waiting and went directly to a young clerk who stood at the closed door of the hearing room.

"My husband is a member of the committee," I said, "and he has asked me to come down to the hearing. May I go in, please?"

"Oh, sure, honey," he said, looking away. He totally disbelieved me.

It was imperative that I get into the hearing room. Hale was expecting me. I suddenly thought of Mrs. Dugas, a beautiful New Orleans socialite who had told me, when I was leaving for Washington, that the most sophisticated and becoming thing a woman could wear was a purple veil.

I dashed back to the apartment and changed into my best outfit—a black Davidow suit, a pretty silk blouse with my pearl circle pin, a little black velour hat, and kid gloves. At the Palais Royal, a store near the Capitol where on our very first day in Washington I had opened a charge account in order to purchase a baby bed for Tommy, I hurried to the veil and scarf counter and had the saleslady drape a purple veil on my hat.

When I returned to the hearing room, the same clerk was guarding the door. I took off one glove and then the other with as much authority as I could muster. In my sweetest Southern accent, I said, "I'm Mrs. Boggs. I'd like to be seated, please."

"Oh, yes ma'am. Come right in." He opened the door and led the way. That day I became a true believer in Mrs. Dugas's purple veil theory.

During the next fifty years I often thought of the lesson I received from the purple veil story. I recognized that you played the Washington game with confidence and authority and graciousness, and so I was prepared to accept the challenges, the triumphs, and the heartaches of life in the shadow of the Capitol dome.

JACK ANDERSON

Washington's
Curious Caste System

Washington Exposé (1967)

Jack Anderson is in the liberal tradition of the investigative reporter. He came to prominence as Drew Pearson's partner—after Robert S. Allen—for his syndicated column, "Washington Merry-Go-Round," by then written for The Washington Post *and which featured exposés of government figures and facts. Anderson started with Pearson in 1947 and took over the column when Pearson died, in 1969. He won the Pulitzer Prize for national reporting in 1972, just a few years after this book came out. Anderson has written a number of other books about Washington, including his autobiography,* Confessions of a Muckraker, *and* The Washington Money-Go-Round. *Here he writes about the "hidden side of Washington, the side the public is seldom shown," acknowledging that "Washington has a magic of its own."*

PERIODICALLY, a new device is tried out in Washington to shoo the starlings from the eaves of government buildings. The startled birds rise fluttering and twittering, then settle back after the alarm has passed. Much the same effect is produced on the bureaucrats, bigwigs, and brass hats every time a new President moves into the White House. He may barge about his new domain, switching off the lights, moving around the furniture, and otherwise creating the impression that changes will be made. Customarily, he sounds a solemn warning to the vast federal bureaucracy that he expects renewed vigor from them. But like the starlings, the officials flap and flutter a little, then invariably return to roost among their status symbols.

Such symbols are held sacred by the stuffed shirts who, as evidence perhaps that hot air rises, often ascend to high office. Their VIP standing is determined in exacting detail by their office acreage, rug plushness, furniture array, and limousine service. They are known, too, by their dining, parking, washroom, and elevator privileges. Whether they sip water from a silver decanter, brown plastic jug, or water fountain in the corridor is another sign of their status. The protocol extends even to dog tags, the lower numbers going to the pooches of the prominent.

A bureaucrat's immediate domain, his office, provides the real clues to his importance. Is it large enough, say, for football scrimmage? Is there a trim of woodwork around the walls? What color is the rug, and how deep do you sink in it? Does the office contain a king-size desk? a flag stand? a sofa suitable for taking naps? These are the things to watch for. For sheer size and splendor, few grand ballrooms can compare with a cabinet member's office. Secretary of State Dean Rusk's sumptuous suite, for instance, not only could accommodate a United Nations session; it could provide the delegates with built-in television, meals from an electric range, and washroom-shower facilities. Many a sub–cabinet officer, too, has room on his rug for a public event.

The biggest status scramble in each department is for office space near the Secretary's suite. It's who's up front that counts. This sometimes can be expensive for the taxpayers. During the construction of the new, $35 million State Department building, for instance, the builders were obliged to keep juggling the plans to satisfy everyone. Final formula: the Secretary and Undersecretaries got 684 square feet apiece, Assistant Secretaries 450 square feet, Deputy Assistants 350 square feet, office directors 270 square feet. Not only do the officials with the biggest worries have the most floor space, but Secretary Rusk and his two Undersecretaries stride back and forth on beige carpets of luxurious thickness. Deputy Undersecretaries pace on brown and black rugs. Assistant Secretaries have green rugs, their deputies common grey. It takes at least an Assistant Secretary to rate foam rubber padding underneath.

In all government bureaus, of course, the plushest furniture goes to the biggest bosses. Most coveted item: a sofa. To get one, a bureaucrat must be at least in the top three civil service grades. But only presidential appointees are allowed to display the American and departmental flags in their offices. Then there is the protocol of the water jugs. Presidential appointees are entitled to chromium-plated jugs which are kept filled by messenger boys. Lesser government bosses get plain plastic jugs, usually brown, and are obliged to send their secretaries out for water.

In the Pentagon, status works outward from the interior "A" ring of the five-sided colossus. An individual's advancement is measured by his progress toward the outer "E" ring which the top brass inhabit. The civilian chiefs (Assistant Secretaries and above) are entitled to a fresh paint job and new, wall-to-wall carpeting when they move in. But the real yardstick is a three-foot trim of woodwork around the walls. Enter a Pentagon office with this executive paneling, and you are dealing with a man of consequence. Also, only the highest ranks ride the Pentagon elevators; all others must use the stairs or escalators. In the downtown departments across the Potomac, elevator privileges are also a measure of a man's importance. Most cabinet officers have private elevators, running in some cases from office to limousine. In figuring status at the State Department, possession of a key to the Secretary's elevator is akin to being able to unlock the Pearly Gates.

Who's who in our bureaucracy can also be calculated by the sleekness of their limousines. The Cadillacs, Lincolns and Chrysler Imperials carry the top brass; the Chevrolets, Fords and Plymouths transport the lesser officials. The line-up of glossy government cars at any big Washington function is enough to take a taxpayer's breath away. Cabinet officers are permitted to use their glory wagons for private as well as business purposes, and their wives often are driven to the supermarket in sumptuous style. This is a sore point with Senators and Supreme Court Justices who have no standing at the government motor pool. Only the Chief Justice and Senate-House leaders are entitled to limousine service. The others, though they outrank the chauffeur-driven Assistant Secretaries, pilot their own cars and console themselves by displaying low-number license plates.

Next to a limousine, a parking sticker is the most prized badge of distinction. The State Department provides only one parking space for every eight employees. The situation is even worse surrounding other government buildings. The Commerce Department, for example, has 140 parking spaces for more than 3,000 employees.

The worst sticklers for protocol, as might be suspected, are the brass hats. There is a constant stir, for example, over who should be allowed to embellish their hats with scrambled-egg designs. It used to be that no one below Navy captain or Army–Air Force colonel could wear this golden scroll. Then the Navy opened the privilege to commanders, and the Army responded by authorizing scrambled-egg hats for majors. Now the status seekers in the Air Force are demanding equal hat privileges.

But the most coveted symbol of Army status is tenancy in one of the cavernous, barn-like houses along "Brass Row" at Fort Myer, Virginia. Senior Admirals are scattered around town in Navy homes, but they have had their status troubles, too. When Arthur Radford became the first Admiral to head the Joint Chiefs, there arose the prickliest of protocol problems. The Navy chief traditionally lives in a rambling old house at the Naval Observatory. Admiral and Mrs. Robert Carney were ensconced there. But since Radford outranked Carney, the question was: could the Carneys be evicted? This became a battle of the wives. Mrs. Carney egged her husband into getting a ruling from the Navy's legal department that the Observatory house was the official residence of the Navy chief. Thus she outmaneuvered Mrs. Radford who threatened to pull her husband's rank but ended up in a three-story, eight-bedroom house formerly occupied by a mere Rear Admiral.

Despite the urgent manpower needs in Viet Nam, the brass hats always seem able to spare enough men from the war to wait on tables, mow their lawns, and perform other menial chores. When some heretic suggested that the Generals should adopt the communist practice of taking occasional turns at KP duty in order to maintain "comradeship" between officers and men, the idea was regarded with horror.

The Pentagon's civilian chiefs, once initiated to the privileges of rank, sometimes become even more protocol-minded than the brass hats. When Assistant Secretary Arthur Sylvester learned that he was entitled to fly a five-star flag on his auto fender, he not only insisted upon displaying the flag at one base but stopped the car to unfurl it when it became wrapped around the staff.

The top man on the protocol pole, of course, is the President. Lyndon Johnson has too much Texan in him to be impressed with striped-pants formality. Yet he clearly enjoys the accouterments of office, takes satisfaction from the scurry of subordinates. His favorite song is "Hail to the Chief." When he was a mere Vice President, he delighted in lunching at a table that rose like a giant lily out of his swimming pool. Barefoot servants with pantlegs rolled high splashed in and out of the pool to wait on him. LBJ still likes to be pampered.

Vice President Hubert Humphrey hasn't yet been spoiled. He discouraged efforts to uproot him from his modest, eight-room suburban home and ensconce him in an official mansion. He settled finally for a fashionable downtown apartment that reportedly cost about $85,000. He hasn't forgotten his college days when he and his bride lived in an attic. In case of fire, their fire escape was a rope which they kept handy to heave out the window. His wife Muriel still sews her own clothes, though she splurged and bought an expensive blue gown for the 1965 Inauguration. "I hope you wear it every day," said the Vice President when he saw the bill. "It's the only way we'll get our money's worth out of it."

Like No Other City

The Good New Days (1963)

*One of the things that Merriman Smith helps demonstrate is how
Washington works differently under one president than another. Smith
was a longtime Washington journalist who in this book attempted "a
not entirely reverent study of native habits and customs in modern
Washington." A White House correspondent for United Press International beginning in 1941, Smith wrote several books on specific presidents and on the presidency in general. Liz Carpenter called him the
"self-crowned king of the White House press room," the one who had
covered five presidents and who, in her tenure at the White House, was
the senior correspondent who concluded the press conferences by saying,
"Thank you, Mr. President."*

*I think this book is especially good on change in Washington, of
which we've all witnessed so much. Smith writes, "Washington once was
a town you could count on, but no more. Normally significant social
and economic signposts, known among eager eclectics as status symbols,
have become about as mixed up as District of Columbia traffic lights."
He attributes this change in signposts largely to the advent of the "New
People" of the Kennedy era. I particularly like a phrase from the last
sentence in his first chapter—"there is no better spectator sport in
America than watching Washington." I couldn't agree more.*

THERE always have been periods of crisis in Washington, but earlier in this century people of the capital could endure sweaty
excitement that gripped the city for days because they knew these
things had a way of subsiding. District of Columbia inhabitants, for
example, could count on October. The general weather picture has not
changed, but other factors have come to bear.

It still is warm during October daytime, but nights bring in faint
traces of forest smoke from Maryland and Virginia, and capital residents
may sleep again in something approaching comfort.

October once was a blessed time of year with the town quieter and essentially ours, people who live and labor here. No hordes of West Ashton school children gibbering before the White House gates in garish carnival hats with Betty or Buddy stitched on the brims; few if any bewildered out-of-state drivers athwart motor lanes trying to decipher Washington's schizoid traffic signs.

There was a season when even halls of Congress were silent while members talked taxes and tariff to Rotary Clubs back home. And it was a time when society leaders rushed back to the capital from Europe to lay party lines for the season ahead. In short, this once was an uncomplicated and peaceful part of the year for Washington.

But no more. No such seasons exist. Surcease and relaxation have departed the banks of the Potomac for what may be an interminable period. Or for as long as men and nations speak of wars and weapons that cannot bring victory, but only endless valleys and plains of cindery stillness, twisted and broken places where people once dwelled, and greasy seas where fish float with white bellies upward.

It would be inaccurate, however, to charge the changes in Washington to Russia and atomic scientists. They're only part of the Good New Days. Chiefly responsible for a vastly new capital way of life are the New People. They're like the Golden Age, a rough classification.

The New People, hot-eyed, curious but unconcerned with protocol, and yeasty with shocking ideas, began swarming into town with F.D.R. when he first was elected President. Some came in shirt-sleeves with tweedy, straight-haired wives who leaped at problems of the nation beside their husbands with time out for such sidelines as progressive education and social acceptance of reform-school hoydens.

Others came from campuses, pipe-sucking and a bit bewildered at first, but later strong-voiced, activists, and organizers of long walks beside the smelly old Potomac barge canal.

Given enough time, and this they had with Roosevelt's four terms, even New People will stabilize as their mores and customs cease to stir up amazement. This happened with F.D.R.'s people. As stabilization set in, Southern Senators and senior ambassadors resumed positions of importance, proper young men from the State Department began swimming again in Miss Anne Archbold's ancient pool, and one heard less of Corcoran and Cohen.

Then came World War II when Washington, like other world capitals, was unsettled by the presence of thousands of strangers who came with khaki credentials instead of political license. Customary values and behavior patterns became hopelessly confused, altered or forgotten. Second lieutenants roomed in basements of good families. Diana Hopkins wanly attempted to grow radishes in the South grounds of the White

House and Roosevelt spent long hours motoring the upper Hudson Valley searching out respectable housing for refugee royalty. From 1940 to 1945, capital habits and customs lost their distinctive pattern except for the talking and drinking. The same sort of jumble took place in London, Paris and elsewhere. People who had counted were hard to count. With Roosevelt's death and then war's end, the high tide of New People resumed as Harry S. Truman and his followers continued alterations to Washington begun by the New Dealers.

Professional Washingtonians and permanent residents who remained in town regardless of political climate began to see and hear of such people as Bull Canfield, the federal marshal in Kansas City; of Major General Harry Vaughan, who, in spite of his closeness to the new President, spurned invitations to the Right Places and went instead to hot-dog suppers of a men's Bible class at a small Presbyterian church in Alexandria.

To the undying appreciation of those who are uncomfortable with less than three forks at dinner, the arrival of President Dwight D. Eisenhower and his followers in 1953 quickly dislodged most of the New People who had come to town under Truman.

Ike and Mamie, although they were definitely Army, brought a great degree of social satisfaction to the permanent colony on the Potomac. For one thing, people in their government tended to be more like the Old People of the pre-Roosevelt era.

Many Eisenhower people were of first generation wealth, but they had been in funds for sufficient time to develop a sheen of financial and social security with taste by Abercrombie and Fitch. Their people were New Newport, but still Newport. They played golf and shot quail and watered in Southern California more than in Florida. They had private planes and new $2,500 shotguns by Purdy. Money did not matter as long as one had it. The frayed-collar idealists went underground or worked with belligerent futility for Adlai Stevenson and Planned Parenthood.

It became fashionable and indicated to read *Nation's Business* instead of the *New Republic*. Walter Lippmann was a respected island, but David Lawrence a better indicator of what the government would do. Wednesday afternoon at the Burning Tree Club became about as reliable a mark of standing in the community as having a Cabinet member to dinner. Mamie was a cute dresser for some of the older, conservative ladies who had stuck it out in their Massachusetts and Connecticut Avenue cliffs after the twenties, but she did entertain people who could be found in Dun and Bradstreet instead of some of the Grant Wood types favored by the Trumans.

There were a few nonconformists within the Eisenhower perimeter, but they were individuals of particular or peculiar talent and their presence derived from political and professional origins. Their influence did not extend into the drawing rooms, although effect of their actions did bob up occasionally in board rooms of corporate America.

While Mrs. Eisenhower may have had a penchant for pink and her husband preferred friends of the golf course, bridge table and hunting fields, they were undisputed society leaders. Any President is society; he is status and a cultural guidepost by the mere counting of votes every fourth November. And each new President, with thousands of followers he brings or attracts to Washington, expectedly produces noticeable changes in the life, and even appearance, of the capital.

Untold man- and woman-hours go into taking down old pictures and putting up new ones. This sometimes leads to removing name plates from certain post offices, even changing names of dams, as happened when the Eisenhowers relieved the Trumans.

When Truman took over for the late F.D.R., people who fancied the lavish display of photographs of those in power were up against it. There's so much wall space in an office of a lawyer or lobbyist. The question was how to fit pictures of the New People in with those of New Dealers. Some were reluctant to take down pictures of F.D.R. and Henry Wallace right away lest it seem blatantly fickle. The war was still on and patriotism also had to be considered. But after a few months of getting acquainted, lawyers and lobbyists began shifting New Deal pictures to less prominent locations and putting up fresh portraits of Harry Vaughan, John Snyder and Howard McGrath.

After the 1952 elections, the problem was easier. There was no reason to pick and choose. Down came Truman photographs and up went impressive new pictures of Eisenhower and his crowd.

Easy at the start, the problem of pictures became complicated when it turned out that Eisenhower was a painter. At Christmas, 1953, he and Mamie gave out hundreds of lithographs of his portrait of Lincoln. Picture framers worked far into the night catching up with a flood of new orders, and Eisenhower art work—a bit short, say, of Gainsborough in portrait technique—shone from virtually every respectable wall in Washington, save that of the Americans for Democratic Action.

With exception of one holiday when they distributed photographs of themselves, Ike and Mamie gave a D.D.E. color lithograph each Christmas. One recipient of the entire series complained just after Christmas, 1960, "My den now looks like the courthouse sidewalk during Art Fair week at Stroudsburg, Pa."

The next great picture-pulling came with the arrival of President Kennedy, Jacqueline, Caroline, and platoons of their kinfolk in 1961. Nothing since Harry Hopkins and Hugh Johnson did as much to upset and change Washington as New People of the Kennedy Administration. Towering figures of old Washington simply did not tower any more. A couple known to relatively few Washingtonians entertained the President-elect on the eve of his inauguration. And after taking office, the new President darted around at night to homes of friends for dinner, something almost unheard of in a town where frumpy old dowagers liked to believe they had entertained for virtually everyone of any importance except, of course, a President who was supposed to stay put in the White House.

It was true that John F. Kennedy had been around Washington for fourteen years as a Congressman and Senator before moving into the White House, but his impact on the town was not particularly noticeable. This is no reflection on Kennedy, because all rules of the game change quickly when one is elevated to the Presidency. Prior to the White House, his force and personality were felt largely on Capitol Hill and in certain union circles due to his Senate curiosity about labor racketeering. But because he and his family were new, attractive and interesting, they became a national fad after the votes were counted. Georgetown real estate prices zoomed upward even though the Kennedys were moving to Pennsylvania Avenue. The town filled with energetic men and women slavering to set the country free after what they regarded as eight years of Eisenhower bondage.

As might have been anticipated, the New People approached Washington virtually as something of their own creation. This is far-fetched, but truly, they wanted little contact with or reference to the past, even Democratic past.

Learning from experience with its necessary transferral of wisdom had been one of man's problems even before Jim Farley. It is a matter of no less vitality today than it was when Archimedes was trying to tell people about the lever.

The New People, circa Truman as well as J.F.K., came to Washington with a certain inbred distrust and often vocal dislike of the past. Roosevelt had not been overly consultative with Truman even when the remarkable gentleman from Missouri was Vice President. Consequently, when F.D.R. died suddenly and Truman was propelled into the driver's seat, people riding with H.S.T. looked almost with suspicion on some of the Roosevelt followers. General Vaughan, for example, worried for days about when Mrs. Roosevelt would move out of the White House and what she would take with her.

When the New People of 1961 arrived over the prostrate forms of the Old People, their chief rallying point or nearly common denominator was youth or a reasonable facsimile thereof. This banner of tennis shoes with small sailing craft rampant produced not only social problems, but some fairly knotty involvements of government.

Young men have an aversion to advice, particularly after titanic accomplishment of the magnitude of national political victory, when so many had said it couldn't be done. They will accept knowledge and teaching of a much older man, but not from one just a bit older. A thirty-year-old will listen with respect to sage rumblings of a seventy-year-old, but God deliver him from advice of a forty-year-old. This goes beyond acceptance of advice and into basic human emotions.

The New People literally hated Richard M. Nixon, who was not much older than Kennedy; but they merely disliked Eisenhower, who could well have cost them the election if he'd come out swinging for the Republicans a bit earlier in the fall of 1960. Former President Hoover became kindly old Herb to New People and they accepted the stainless reputation of Bernard M. Baruch, whose brilliant economic consistency was matched only by his pronounced preference for virtually all American Presidents since Taft.

Suddenly, it didn't matter what most hitherto and slightly mossy oracles thought. The New People had their own habits, customs and oracles. No longer did crowds shove to the steps of National Presbyterian Church on Sunday mornings for a glimpse of Ike and Mamie. They shifted to Holy Trinity in Georgetown, sometimes standing outside through several Masses before the Kennedys arrived. Hair became quite popular. Great masses of it. Crew-cut boulevardiers began to let it grow. Government secretaries spent long hours in beauty parlors where twitchy little men studied photographs of the First Lady and tried to puff up the locks of their customers to a state of luxuriant top-heaviness.

The Kennedy New People, in more ways than hair styles and church preference, wrought vast changes. In their dithering push forward, by hurling themselves at future history and rushing in their brown loafers over sputtering sachems of the past, New People of 1961 mashed into the very skin of the town ways of life first imported in smaller volume by New People of 1933.

Washington continues to be a pleasant place in which to live—no industries to soot the air, wide streets and pleasant parks, good shops and restaurants, advanced public schools. All of which is amazing when one considers that much of the population is relatively transient. There is, of course, a basic population which feeds to a large extent off the floaters. There also are some oddballs with enough money to permit their looking without participating. These are fortunate if sometimes annoying people, for there is no better spectator sport in America than watching Washington.

EUGENE ROBINSON

A New Black Dilemma

The Washington Post Magazine (1986)

Gene Robinson has been at the Post *reporting and editing for more than twenty years. He knows a lot about this city, having worked as an editor on the city desk and currently as assistant managing editor for Style. He writes here of a Washington dilemma that is true for every other city as well—the problems that arise when not everyone shares in the wealth and prosperity of a place. And he touches on one of our newer phenomena, our incredible ethnic diversity, given the large Hispanic, Asian, Islamic, and other populations that have so changed the face of the city.*

THE EVIDENCE: plush living rooms in North Portal Estates, with African wall hangings and smoked-glass coffee tables; crowds of impeccably dressed young professionals comparing BMW keys and tax shelters over happy-hour spritzers along the Southwest waterfront; quiet, stolid, gracefully aging neighborhoods in Northeast, where family and church are more than words on a kitchen cross-stitch; the downtown power-lunch restaurants where a new group of sharp-eyed players convenes to carve up the vast sphere of power and money that has come to center on the District Building.

You can see more on any downtown street, where kids in $75 blue jeans and $50 red-and-black Air Jordan sneakers bustle past businessmen wearing outfits whose labels add up to a short course in Italian; where proud, stylish women sport hundreds of dollars' worth of hairdo, facial and manicure work as they browse through exclusive boutiques; where all around are the sights and sounds of a booming black consumer market that spends freely, buys quality and pays with American Express.

For a big, bold visible part of black Washington, the evidence proclaims, life has never been better.

The problem is that although many have shared in the prosperity, not everyone has. While some blacks in Washington were realizing the American dream, another group—call it the aspiring black middle class, the Toyota crowd as opposed to the Volvo set—found it necessary to move away to find jobs, decent housing, better schools and safer streets that had become so frightfully expensive inside the city's borders.

And the rest of black Washington, perhaps as much as a third of it, simply went to hell.

For along with the visible evidence of new black power and affluence in Washington, there are other sights—harder to spot, perhaps, and certainly more painful to notice—of slow death.

Sights like the boarded-up storefronts along U Street, once the heart of a thriving black community. Like the chimerical crowds of junkies at 14th and U, a twilight zone where one minute the corner is deserted, and then another minute scores of sullen men and women somehow appear, slinking out of alleyways and apartments and parked cars for the ritual police call "feeding time."

Like the slabs of apartments that hug the hills of far Southeast, dreary places where children struggle—against almost prohibitive odds—to raise children of their own.

And like the spectacle of nine young men and one young woman, all of them really nothing more than kids, sitting in a D.C. courtroom last year charged with the unspeakable murder of a 99-pound, 48-year-old woman who was bludgeoned to death in a Northeast alley while a crowd cheered on her assailants.

These are sights of Washington's "underclass." The term is one to be resisted, because of the hopelessness it implies, but one that seems increasingly appropriate. The situation of these people is getting worse, not better, and no one seems to have any answers.

It was never accurate to talk of black Washington as a single entity. This city was one of the first in the nation to develop a viable black middle class, and there have always been the relatively affluent and the relatively poor here. But 25 years ago it seemed more accurate to call black Washington a community, diverse but with a shared dream.

The dream was of freedom and full equality for all black Americans, and it was a powerful unifier. Now, although no one pretends the dream is fully realized, its sway is undeniably diminished.

Black Washington has fractured into the haves and the have-nots; or perhaps a split more ominous: the already-haves and the never-will-haves. All indications are that the fault line is widening, driven by forces more powerful than all the world's good intentions and racial solidarity—both of which black Washingtonians have in ample supply. There are no real villains here, just a set of winners and a set of victims.

BLACKS in Washington now have a range of options that once were out of the question, from selecting a career to deciding where to eat lunch.

The achievement of some self-government is alone a bold achievement, although home rule probably has a lot more to do with how people feel about their city than whether their garbage is picked up on time.

Remember, until a decade ago residents of the nation's capital had no mayor, no city council, no elected school board; until 1964, they couldn't even vote for president. Now there is a rapidly maturing political apparatus, headed by a former street activist who has long since shed his dashikis for three-piece worsteds by Yves Saint Laurent. The disenfranchised have become the establishment. Washingtonians still don't have complete authority over their government, but they've come far enough to feel immense pride.

Even more significant is that 25 years ago, no black in Washington could escape the simple fact of segregation.

Louis Martin, now a Howard University official, came to Washington in 1960 and stayed to become a kind of black political godfather, or at least a consigliere, offering sage advice over the years in countless floor fights, court battles and political campaigns touching on the issue of civil rights.

"I came in with the Kennedy-Johnson campaign," Martin says. "Washington then was a small southern town, that's the way it struck me, coming from Chicago. The segregation struck us all. Opportunities were just dismal for blacks then. You couldn't really enjoy your own city."

Martin recalls urging President Kennedy, shortly after he took office, to make a big push toward integrating the federal bureaucracy.

"I never will forget that one day, Kennedy and some of his aides toured several federal buildings," Martin says. "We went to this one building—don't recall just which one—and on the first floor, we saw a few blacks. On the second floor, there were fewer. On the third floor, fewer still. Finally when we got to the top, there were no blacks anywhere.

"Kennedy turns to me and says, 'They get whiter the higher they get.'"

The upper reaches of the federal bureaucracy hereabouts still remain mostly white, but Washington's largest employer did become substantially integrated at lower levels, and as federal salaries rose, the well-being of black Washington improved.

Washington's good-ol'-boy business community has been much slower to integrate. Just a decade ago, the Board of Trade had no meaningful black membership; more recently, the entertainment at the Board's annual dinner one year consisted of what looked and sounded to some blacks in the audience like an old-fashioned minstrel show. Attending a board function nowadays, and watching the red carpet rolled out for

Mayor Marion Barry, must be sweet irony for those who remember the days when the white establishment considered him perhaps the city's most dangerous militant activist.

The Board of Trade has seen the light. It now has lots of black members, and it skillfully plays ball with the black political establishment. The city government, meanwhile, has taken great pains to foster black economic development in the city and has had some success.

Meanwhile, just as the black baseball league began to wither when blacks were allowed into the major leagues, so has Washington's old black business infrastructure weakened and become less important. The D.C. Chamber of Commerce used to be of great importance to black businessmen in Washington, serving the same purpose for blacks that the Board of Trade served for whites. Now, with the Board of Trade open to blacks, the chamber is no longer at the center of things. It still has a lot of members, but basically they are the owners of small businesses. The big black-owned businesses, the ones that would increase the chamber's clout and influence, now can afford to pay the board's dues, and to send their own representatives to lobby the City Council and the mayor.

The two biggest black economic forces in the city remain institutional: the city government itself, and Howard University, which spends $300 million a year and employs 8,000 people.

The barriers that used to keep blacks out of some neighborhoods have come down, but basic housing patterns have not changed, except that once-black neighborhoods like Capitol Hill and Shaw have become whiter through the process called gentrification. One examination of census data showed that during the 1960s, the city's housing patterns actually became more segregated. The part of the city west of Rock Creek Park remains overwhelmingly white; the Northeast and Southeast quadrants remain overwhelmingly black.

These patterns are reflected in the city's public schools, which are now, by all accounts, on the rebound. The school system went through a kind of cultural revolution during the 1970s, as administrators sought to make them relevant to the black urban experience—at the expense, many felt, of making them good schools.

First whites fled the school system, then middle-class blacks fled. Finally, the school system began a concerted effort to improve itself and took the position that retaining some of these fleeing students was crucial. Now, as test scores rise under a new back-to-basics curriculum, administrators take unabashed pains to keep white and middle-class black students.

The creation of a new "model" high school, Banneker, reminds some of the days when schools were segregated and the black community had its own superior school, Dunbar. In a sense, the schools have come full circle.

Blacks in Washington are doing very well compared with blacks elsewhere in America. A recent comparison showed more black Washingtonians in high-income groups and fewer in poverty than among blacks in any of a half-dozen cities of comparable size. Income and educational levels here have skyrocketed. In other cities, like Chicago, blacks are striving for political power; here the effort is to consolidate that power and use it for economic development. The confidence of a black Washington is such that recently it helped elect a white City Council chairman without undue concern about losing power.

The gains are tangible and real. The losses, less tangible, but no less real, derive in part from the gains. They come with the turf.

Wealth and power bring complications. Howard University offers an example. For many years Howard has been the nation's premier black intellectual center, but in the past two decades it has grown immensely, its annual budget increasing tenfold. Howard has even substantially bucked the trend afflicting other historically black colleges, still attracting good students and professors despite the lure of bigger, white institutions.

But last year, Howard, the crucible of civil rights law, found itself fighting a "reverse discrimination" lawsuit and arguing in court that it had an effective right to ensure with its hiring policies that it remained a black-oriented institution. The campus community was divided over the issue. Years ago, few white academics were interested in working at Howard; today more are, and the school must deal with the price of its success.

The breakdown of segregation in housing has made it impossible to rebuild the commercial strips like U Street and H Street that were dealt a death blow by the riots. These areas, in the days of segregation, had been vibrant, economically integrated communities, places where blacks of all income levels went to eat and be entertained. As blacks began to be welcomed elsewhere, the businesses along these strips began to decline; as middle-class blacks moved out, only the poor were left. After the riots, there was no longer a reason to rebuild. The pattern of blacks patronizing black-owned establishments had broken down.

The phenomenon can be seen all over town, as mom-and-pop corner grocery stores, many of them formerly owned by blacks, are bought by Asian immigrants who use them as stepping-stones to the middle class. The process brings complications: Is it racist to object to the trend? Perhaps. Is it racist to wish that blacks were reaping the benefits of these little stores? Is there anything that can, or should, be done?

And finally there is the growing isolation and desperation of the black underclass, a group for which the lights seem to dim with each passing year.

In 1960, one of every five black households in Washington was headed by a woman. Today, one in two is female-headed. Many of these families include teen-age mothers. A third of all black children in Washington live below the poverty line. The gap between poor blacks and others is increasing—while one group of blacks gets better educated and more affluent, another group stays poor and uneducated, and has less and less chance of escape.

Gentrification makes fewer neighborhoods affordable for the poor. Government tries to intervene, but for many of the poor there is less and less meaningful contact with the more affluent. Horizons are shrinking, not expanding; and the black family is in crisis.

Washington is far from being the "crime capital" of America, as President Nixon once called it; and crime has been dropping steadily over the past decade. But Washington keeps more of its citizens incarcerated than any other jurisdiction. Washington has a problem of heroin addiction said to be the worst, per capita, in the nation. Cocaine is sold openly on the streets in quantities small enough for non-yuppies to afford, and it has found a new market—and an extensive sales force—among poor black youths. PCP, an even more insidious and debilitating drug, has taken hold among the city's teens; you can pick the heavy PCP users out of a crowd because they're the ones drooling.

How do you change these people's lives? How do you even reach them? How can a private sector that increasingly needs workers with technical skills do anything for the uneducated? How can a city government, even one with the noblest of intentions, worry about maintaining a tax base and creating a favorable business climate and still wage a determined, lonely, necessarily costly war against poverty?

No one knows the answers. Small-scale successes abound—a group of teen-age girls is taken in for counseling against getting pregnant; a youngster from Anacostia is accepted at Ellington, the high school for the performing arts, and turns out to be a prodigy; a youth parlays a summer job into a career, but the problem has been growing, not shrinking.

Three decades ago, Constance M. Green wrote a book about black Washington called *Secret City*. Today, most of black Washington has emerged into the light. But there is a new invisible Washington, and the good life that most of us share has passed it by. The years have been good, not kind.

Life Inside the Beltway

The Power Game (1988)

Here, Hedrick Smith, longtime chief Washington correspondent for the New York Times, reports on Washington almost as if he is writing a contemporary biography of a city. This is the quintessential "how Washington works" volume, focusing on power and "the players and the playing field" in the 1980s. One of the things we learn from reading Hedrick Smith is why Washington doesn't work better.

W HEN A brand-new member of Congress comes to Washington, he is fresh from the heady experience of winning public acclaim for his politics and victory for himself. Then suddenly, the newcomer is a naked freshman in a world of veterans, a stranger in the political home he has won for himself. Instinct tells him immediately that no individual politician can operate as an atom. He must make his way to clusters of comrades, to small survival groups, to networks of power to which he can attach. He must come to know the folkways of the power city.

Up close, just as from afar, Washington can seem a foreign place, even though its Capitol dome, White House lawn, and Washington Monument are familiar symbols. But to freshly minted political victors, it is suddenly a strange universe. Near the end of 1980, on the very night that Michael Deaver arrived with his family from California to begin work in the Reagan White House, his five-year-old son, Blair, asked in his innocence a question that must silently sit on many adult tongues: "Daddy, is Washington part of this world?"

Eighteen months earlier, at the depths of his political despair in the summer of 1979, President Carter had given his own angry, frustrated answer to that question. Carter openly derided Washington as an island "isolated from the mainstream of our nation's life."

In an era of Washington bashing, this is a theme that many people voice and many politicians exploit: this theme that Washington is disconnected from the country. But it is a misleading notion.

Washington is different, yes; but it is not isolated. With high-speed jets and round-the-clock television news, the capital is closer to being on the same political wavelength as the rest of the country than at any previous time in our history. Congress works a short week in Washington (Monday afternoon to Friday morning), to give members more time with constituents; members are constantly dashing home to maintain the umbilical connection with their voters. In their obsession to keep track of grass-roots sentiment, politicians are forever putting up wet fingers to test the wind, To keep in touch, they have become compulsive consumers of opinion surveys.

More to the point, Washington is surprisingly open to newcomers, even to those it initially intimidates. Practically everyone in political Washington has come from somewhere else. Each new political tide brings in waves of newcomers. In presidential election years, especially when the White House changes hands, the influx is wholesale. The new crowd from Georgia or California take over literally thousands of the choicest jobs in town. Even in midterm elections, one or two dozen new congressmen and senators arrive with fresh messages from the country for the old hands. The Washington political community is "almost absurdly permeable" to outside influence, suggested Nelson Polsby, a keen academic observer of American politics.

"What other community in America," Polsby asked, "regularly accords automatic, immediate, unshakable top status to someone from out of town, even if that someone's public conversation consists mainly of unpleasant statements about the community and attacks on its oldest inhabitants?"

Indeed, Washington regularly takes in newcomers, absorbs them and makes them its own. Those who arrive to serve in Congress learn to live in two worlds—in their hometowns and states, and in the special world of the capital. The longer they stay in Washington, the more they become Washingtonians, buying homes, raising children, worrying about parking places and street crime, some even rooting for the Washington Redskins football team against their home-state teams.

Newcomers arrive full of idealism and energy only to discover what a tiny fragment of power they grasp. To expand that fragment, they make alliances, join groups, get appointed to committees, make contacts with the press, find friends in the administration. Before they know it, they become caught up in Washington's internal politics, involved in the rivalries of Congress and administration, consumed by their committee work, their personal specialties, their Washington careers—the clout they develop in Washington and the amount of attention they can command in the Washington power game.

In short, people who come here to serve in the executive branch or Congress catch "Potomac fever"—the incurable addiction of wielding political power or feeling at the political center. When their president leaves office or they lose their congressional seats, very few politicians go home to retire or make money. Most stay in Washington and become lawyers, lobbyists, or consultants, because they've grown accustomed to Washington's ways and to thinking of themselves as movers and shakers, and no other place has quite the same excitement and allure.

Power, of course, is the aphrodisiac—the special brand of federal power that is Washington's monopoly. New York and Los Angeles have enormous financial muscle. Houston, Chicago, Pittsburgh, and Detroit have industrial and commercial might. Silicon Valley outside San Francisco is at the leading edge of high-tech science and electronics. Hollywood and Broadway create stardom. But Washington is where the nation's destiny is set. The incomparable titillation for politicians and government officials is doing the public's business and feeling that the nation is paying close attention.

Political Washington is a special community with a culture all its own, its own established rituals and folkways, its tokens of status and influence, its rules and conventions, its tribal rivalries and personal animosities. Its stage is large, but its habits are small-town. Members of Congress have Pickwickian enthusiasm for clubs, groups, and personal and regional networks to insure their survival and to advance their causes. They love the clubbiness of the member's dining rooms and such Capitol Hill watering holes as the Monocle or the Democratic Club. And downtown, politicians, lobbyists and journalists like to rub shoulders and swap stories at Duke Zeibert's, Mel Krupin's, or Joe and Mo's, where the movers and shakers have regular tables.

Political parties have a social impact; most politicians fraternize mainly with colleagues from within their own party. But when I first came to the city, I did not realize how personal relationships often cut across party and ideological lines, so that conservative lions and liberal leopards who roar at each other in congressional debates play tennis on the weekends or joke together in the Capitol cloakrooms. And yet, for all their backslapping gregariousness, politicians strike me as a lonely crowd, making very few deep friendships because almost every relationship is tainted by the calculus of power: How will this help me?

Above all, Washington is a state of mind. I'm not talking about the 3–5 million people who live in the Washington metropolitan area: the hospital administrators, shopkeepers, schoolteachers, and the people who inhabit the middle-class city of Washington and its Virginia and Maryland suburbs; rather, I'm referring to the hundred thousand or so whose life revolves around government, especially the few thousand at the peak who live and breathe politics. To the people of that world, this is the hub, the center, the focus of what Henry Adams once called "the action of primary forces." The conceit of this Washington is not all that different from the conceit of Paris or Moscow.

Example: The city and its suburbs are encircled by a sixty-four-mile freeway loop known as the beltway (U.S. 495). The political community of Washington talks as if that beltway formed a moat separating the capital from the country. "Inside the beltway," political Washington's favorite nickname for itself, is a metaphor for the core of government. Hardly a dinner or a meeting goes by without someone observing that the mood inside the beltway on Iran or a new Soviet-American summit or on protectionist measures is running ahead of the country, or that the president, any president, is in trouble inside the beltway but not "out there," with a wave of the hand toward the boondocks.

The distance between Washington and the rest of the country is partly a matter of language. Jargon is a vital element of the Washington game. Washington jargon is impenetrable and often deliberately so, to exclude all but the initiated.

For starters: Unless you're President Reagan, you can't be a major player in budget politics unless you know the difference between constant dollars and current dollars, between outlays and obligations, between the baseline and the out-years; you can't enter the arena of arms control without some grasp of launchers, throwweight, and RVs. If you're an insider, you will have mastered such trivia as knowing that the shorthand for the Department of Housing and Urban Development is pronounced "HUD," but that the nickname for the Department of Transportation is pronounced "D-O-T" and never "dot." You will also know that bogeys are the spending targets the secretary of Defense gives the armed services and that beam-splitters are the nearly invisible TelePrompTers that flash the text of a speech to the president as he turns his head from side to side.

The split between capital and country also reflects a different awareness of how Washington really works. The veterans know that the important, knock-down, drag-out battles in Congress usually come on amendments to a piece of legislation, not on final passage of the bill. They understand that when some member rises on the floor of the House or Senate and says that a piece of legislation is a "good bill" and that he wants "to offer a perfecting amendment," he is really getting ready to gut the legislation. Sometimes an amendment is a complete substitute bill with quite different impact and meaning, known in the trade as a "killer amendment." That's the way the legislative game is played. . . .

WHAT REALLY sets Washington apart, of course, is the heady brew of power and prominence. Washington combines the clout of the corporate boardroom and military command with the glamour of Hollywood celebrities and Super Bowl stars. That magnetism and the stakes of the battle are what draw armies of politicians, lobbyists, lawyers, experts, consultants, and journalists to Washington. It is a self-selected group, ambitious and aggressive, marked by collective immodesty. Politicians love to be noticed, and they take their notices very seriously, assuming their own importance and grasping for daily confirmation in the attention of the press and television.

Many people treat the word "politician" as a synonym for hypocrisy, but I believe most politicians come to Washington largely motivated by a sense of public service, and usually with a deeper interest in policy issues than is felt by people back home. Most politicians really want to contribute to the public weal, as protectors of their home districts or exponents of some cause; their early motivation is the ideal of better government. Most people who make a career of government could earn a good deal more money in other walks of life. And they toss into the bargain the loss of personal privacy for themselves and for their families. Not all politicians are that self-sacrificing, but I believe a majority are; only a small minority seem charlatans. Their agendas differ greatly, but if one urge unites them all—and really makes Washington tick—it is the urge for that warm feeling of importance.

That ache for applause and recognition shows in the weighty tread of senators moving onto the floor and glancing upward for some sign of recognition from the galleries. It shows in the awkward jostling for position as a group of congressmen approach the television cameras and microphones outside a hearing room, or after a White House session with the president. I have marveled at it in the purgatorial patience of politicians with endless handshakes, speeches, receptions. I have sensed it, too, in the flattered eagerness of corporate executives arriving at a White House dinner in their limousines. And I have felt it in the smug satisfaction of a select group of columnists and commentators called to a special briefing from the president in the family theater of the White House. None of us is completely immune to that siren song of being made to feel important.

"Washington is really, when you come right down to it, a city of cocker spaniels," Elliott Richardson once remarked. Richardson, a

Republican Brahmin from Boston, held four cabinet positions in the Nixon and Ford administrations and after a few years out of the limelight felt the ache for attention badly enough to make an unsuccessful try for the Senate.

"It's a city of people who are more interested in being petted and admired than in rendering the exercise of power," Richardson contended. "The very tendency of the cocker spaniel to want to be petted and loved can in turn mean that to be shunned and ignored is painful, and there is a tendency in Washington to turn to the people who are in the spotlight and holding positions of visibility at a given time."

In their collective vanity, the power players are willing to endure long hours of boredom to bathe in the roar of the crowd. Talking with me in his Senate study one rainy afternoon about the vanity of the political breed, Senator Charles McC. Mathias, the Maryland Republican, recalled an incident at an American Legion dinner in Washington years ago. As Mathias arrived, he saw two fellow Republican warhorses—Leverett Saltonstall of Massachusetts with his arm in a sling and Everett Dirksen hobbling on crutches.

"It was one of those many functions which you attend but where your absence might not even be noted," Mathias observed. "Saltonstall and Dirksen had valid excuses [to stay away], but they came anyway. And I thought: Is there never surcease from this demand and this compulsion to get out to these things? But of course, they would be put at the head table and introduced, and the spotlight would fall upon them, and the people from Massachusetts and Illinois would wave their napkins in the air when their names were mentioned, and the band would play their state anthems. It is all utterly meaningless, and yet those two wanted to be part of the act, too."

"Narcissism" is not too strong a label for the Washington syndrome. Political Washington is consumed with its own doings: Who's up, who's down, did you hear what the president said over an open mike, how's the tax bill doing, should we have bombed Libya, what's next? Surely ranchers in Texas, car makers in Detroit, textile executives in South Carolina, or doctors and lawyers anywhere are equally self-absorbed. But Washington, rivaled perhaps by Hollywood, allows itself the collective vanity of assuming that people elsewhere are fascinated with its doings.

"The capital, with its curious mixture of high ideals and hard work and base ambition and blind vanity, becomes the universe: If I am so famous that the [*Washington*] *Post* is writing about me, then, of course, the whole world is reading it," observed former Secretary of State Alexander Haig, with the wry detachment of hindsight, once he was out of office.

"Going into the White House every day to work, seeing the iron gates open and then the iron gates shut, you're in an almost-unreal world," Carter White House aide Stuart Eizenstat commented. "There is something almost unnatural about the way in which people treat you. There's a certain unnatural deference. You have microphones thrust in your face and cameras watching you when you make a speech. You begin to think, perhaps, you're more important than you thought you were when you came into the job. All of these things have the potential, if you're not careful, to make you again feel that you have the kind of unbridled influence to do that which you will, that somehow you're a voice of wisdom. And I think that one has to fight against that feeling."

Washington is a city mercurial in its moods, short in its attention span, and given to fetishes. Events flash and disappear like episodes in a soap opera, intensely important for a brief period and then quickly forgotten. Like a teenager, the political community lurches from one passion to the next, seized for a season by the Gramm-Rudman budget-balancing act, later consumed by a battle with Japan over trade sanctions, or gossiping madly over the millionaire antics of White House officials turned lobbyists.

But whatever the twist and turns, the themes are invariably political. People visiting from New York or Los Angeles complain that Washington is a guild town with just one industry and one preoccupation. New York has the intensely self-preoccupied worlds of Wall Street, Broadway, publishing, and advertising, and Chicago with its corporate headquarters, grain trade, steel industry, and distribution centers. Each city has variety, while Washington, in spite of its growing world of art, theaters, opera and symphony, has only one passion.

"It's a one-subject town," lamented Austin Ranney, a political scientist from California who spent a decade at the American Enterprise Institute in Washington. "I don't know how many dozens or hundreds of dinner parties I went to, largely as an outsider, an observer, and yet I almost never had a conversation about music, about novels, or very briefly about anything except the weather. It was always politics, politics, politics, of the insider variety."

Hugh Newell Jacobson, a prominent Washington architect, protested to Barbara Gamarekian, a *New York Times* colleague of mine, "This is the only city where you can go to a black-tie dinner [in a private home], and there at the foot of the table is a television set up to catch a press conference!"

In Washington, people take their own importance so much for granted that their first instinct with a new book is to turn immediately, not to the first page, but to the index to see whether they are mentioned. Yet very few politicians will admit in print how much they hunger for public recognition. Paradoxically, one who did was Paul Tsongas, a Massachusetts Democrat, who had impressed me during his ten years in the House and Senate as less driven by vanity than most. Tsongas had voluntarily retired for family and health reasons. But after retirement, he confessed to me what "heady stuff" it was to win the title of U.S. Senator. His mind flashed back to the moment on election night 1978 when over the radio in his car came the first word that he was the likely winner, and a campaign aide blurted out, "The goddamned senator!"

"It was so overwhelming to have that word next to my name," Tsongas said, a bit of wonder in his quiet voice even years later. "It just seemed so unlikely to everybody in the car, and yet from that moment on, that title attaches. And the respect accorded to that title, irrespective of person, is enormous, and you begin to think of yourself in those terms. To a lot of senators that title is life. I've seen people who have been defeated and who basically never got over having lost the title."

In a very different vein, Newt Gingrich, a voluble, publicity-prone junior Republican from Georgia, admits to the exultation of making it to Washington. "There are very few games as fun as being a congressman," he gushed one evening over a Chinese dinner. "Talk to guys who spent Christmas break traveling the world. Talk to people who landed on an aircraft carrier or went to see the space shuttle launched or had dinner at the White House or got to talk to people from the *New York Times*. There's a sense of being at the center of things. This is the great game!"

MEG GREENFIELD

Mavericks and Image-Makers

Washington (2001)

What Meg's book makes clear is that she knew Washington inside and out. She was one of the most astute and incisive observers of the Washington scene I've ever known. In part because she was always willing to listen and learn, she was able to step back and see behind the facade and below the surface to what was really going on. She could penetrate through anyone's false front, which made her especially important in Washington (and to the Post*). Felicity Barringer, in Meg's obituary for the New York Times, wrote, "as an editorialist, she was both a judge and a connoisseur of the foibles of the city's political and intellectual elites." She illuminated issues with her special kind of insight—among the things she does so well in this book is to explore why so many people dislike Washington.*

With Washington, *she gave us a book that is almost a primer of our city today. George Will wrote of her, "She knew that much of what Washington, in its incorrigible self-importance, thinks is important isn't. She also knew what was important, and why." Every line of her book reveals some lesson about how Washington works.*

THERE'S not a one of us who has lived for a long stretch of time in the capital, I believe, who has not experienced that awful moment of realization that a friend or acquaintance with some public responsibility is losing the gift of normal discourse. He will have begun to address us over a casual drink or at the supermarket as if he were orating at the United Nations. One of the most frequently uttered prescriptions one hears for a politically prosperous life in Washington is, "I never say anything I wouldn't want to see in the papers tomorrow morning." Think of it: self-installed monitors continually at work in the brain. What a way to live!

We journalists, of course, bear much of the responsibility for this phenomenon. Modern technology makes us an ever-present, all-seeing eye on public life. There is not a precinct beyond instant camera range anymore or the text of a craven statement, flipping away from a previously sworn-to flop, that we can't access on our laptops or PalmPilots as soon as it is uttered. Once the flip-flopping politician was safe from our depredations while gassing off out in Podunk. Now there is no place to hide.

Just as important, the rules of journalistic engagement have changed. Much that we once considered off-limits because it was private, unofficial, or irrelevant is now routinely reported. Winston Churchill, at his 1943 Casablanca conference with FDR, ran into the traveling press corps one morning, clad only in his red dressing gown and black slippers. When photographers raised their cameras, he cried, "You can't do this to me!" They didn't.

Some two decades after that, the same principle still was in force in Washington. I remember sitting in the Senate Press Gallery with a bunch of colleagues from big newspapers in the mid-1960s and observing the raving drunk Senate floor manager of the bill under consideration having to be helped out of the chamber by another senator and an aide. He wasn't exactly carried, but he sure as hell wasn't walking either. Each of the two helpers had an arm under one of his arms, raising his feet a couple of inches off the floor and whisking him up the aisle and through the exit. None of us wrote about it except indirectly, with coy hints like "high-spirited."

What we consider private, unofficial, and irrelevant has clearly changed. The drunken-senator episode would be fully covered in the media today, as I think it should be. But Churchill's undignified, bathrobe photo would be there too, blown up on the front pages of the tabs, zoomed in on for television, everywhere. We say we judge material by the standard of whether it is relevant to the conduct of public business by the figure in question. And we do. But somehow, under this standard, we are always able to fit some juicy item into our papers or onto our screens.

The point is that public personages in Washington—a category that has come to include more and more people in and out of government who have acquired modest celebrity—now understand that there is practically nothing so intimate, unofficial, or even trivial in their daily lives that it may not turn up, to their mortification, in the news. Add this emerging worry about round-the-clock surveillance to (1) the basic, built-in, traditional anxieties of competitive Washington life and (2) the new compulsion to strike poses and take positions that satisfy the non-negotiable demands of an all-powerful but hopelessly mercurial public opinion god, and you get the dimension of the problem.

People in Washington react in a few classic ways to the challenge all this presents. They may defy the challenge, they may try to play it out with two separate personalities (one for show and one for real), or they may surrender to it unconditionally and permit themselves to be transformed into something else. Each of these general approaches to the contradictory demands of Washington life existed long before those demands became as acute and frightening for people as they are now. Each represents a timeworn response to pressures to go along with political phony-baloney people neither believe in nor especially like but that in some irreducible amount is deemed necessary for their own or their organization's survival.

The defiers are rare and admirable people who, most of the time and where it counts, just say no. These folks are the class of Washington. I don't mean the lone wolves or the people who strike holier-than-thou poses. I mean the civil servants and legislators and administration appointees who manage to be effective at what they do for a living in Washington while retaining the natural identity they brought to town.

They may turn up at any point on the left-to-right political spectrum. I don't say they are perfect or that the true identity they brought to town is in every case appetizing. Nor are they virginal strangers to politics. They are, after all, political people. I say simply that they are people of unusual temperament and decency who know where the lines have to be drawn and who have remained unassuming and untempted by the eternally beckoning trapdoors of political life. . . .

Here is my test for identifying such people: Take some shameless, demagogic political speech you have heard, and see if you can imagine a particular public figure giving it. You will be surprised how many of those you really admire could plausibly deliver the awful thing (and afterward explain why they had to do it and how it will really help the right cause in the end because it will enable them to be more effective in other fights).

The kind of people I am talking about should not be confused with what Washington calls "mavericks." "Maverick," like "whiz kid," is one of those terms meant here as part compliment, part put-down. It is more often something people are called or call themselves than something anyone really is. As a put-down it is a word an irritated leader will use to disparage a legislator, agency head, or cabinet head who has just refused to go along with his policy: "Well, you know Margaret. She's always been something of a maverick." Margaret's action is thereby reduced from one of principle to one of idiosyncrasy. The policy is fine, the leader is saying, but Margaret is a nut.

When used as a compliment, the term refers to those who habitually think for themselves. Usually mavericks seem impossible to predict, except to say that they cannot be taken for granted as safe votes for their party or as silent observers when someone is doing something they really dislike. The late Oregon senator Wayne Morse—Republican, then Democrat and, as Democrat, early absolute nemesis of Lyndon Johnson on Vietnam—was the nearest thing to a pure, lifelong maverick in my time.

But there aren't that many real ones. Often the term "maverick" is applied to people who defy their party on a single hobbyhorse issue, while going along with tomfoolery on almost everything else. For some it is just another impersonation, one of many Washington affectations of cranky, down-home candor by people who are really something else. "I'm just an ole cracker-barrel country judge," their manner says, or maybe a "plainspoken cowboy" from the West, "and I just tell the truth as I see it. Cain't help it, I s'pose." We always have a supply of these. Odds are that like Tennessee senator Estes Kefauver in his coonskin cap, they have a degree from Yale Law School.

These impersonators belong to a different species and a far larger one: Washington people who try to handle the pressures of the place by constantly slipping in and out of dual selves. The public, blah-blah-blah-I'm-glad-you-asked-that-question person lives in the same skin with the other one, who acknowledges in a hundred different ways to a multiplicity of large and small Washington audiences every day what a crock he knows the blah-blah-blah to be.

I am not talking about a handful of unusually jaded pols here. Far from it. This kind of two-track existence has been a hallmark of Washington life as long as I can remember. It is actually celebrated in some of our most famous tribal rituals, such as the annual Gridiron Club dinner in March. At this white-tie event, about fifteen hundred people, including the president, vice president, cabinet members, chairman of the joint chiefs, a couple of Supreme Court justices, the congressional leadership, and hundreds more from government, business, the military, and the press watch some of their leaders and representatives deliver speeches or participate in skits that mildly incinerate what they have been doing and saying all year for the public record.

The feeling of inside-the-Beltway solidarity this betrays is bolstered by the idea (naturally, not very successfully enforced) that the mammoth gathering is "off the record." The proceedings, which can sometimes be hilarious, are meant, in other words, as a fun secret to be shared and kept by the throng present who truly understand the two-track life because, in truth, we all live it. The very term "off the record," when you think about it (along with "off the record's" kin, such as "background," "deep background," and "not for attribution"), is evidence of an institutionalized way of life in which we have one gear for speaking what we think and another for speaking what we really think. The most frequently used phrase with which sentences begin in political/governmental Washington is probably: "Don't quote me on this, but ..."

Many people outside Washington are repelled by the custom. Within the place, however, it has become so automatic and effortless that it can even be managed by fall-down drunks. When I first came to Washington, I was astounded when a TV correspondent friend told me that legislators came to the press gallery for scheduled broadcast interviews who were absolutely slobbery incoherent with booze.

But, he said, the problem didn't alarm him as much as it had the first time. Again and again, he had seen these fellows jerk into simulated sobriety when the little red on-the-air light flashed, vent the well-articulated gravities they wished to share with the American people, and then, when the light went out again, sink back into slurred nonsense and stagger out the gallery doors.

I should not have been so surprised. The two-track conversation is as close as the capital comes to having its own language. In time and with daily immersion, as with any language, you become adept in its subtleties. In most of the rooms where Washington people spend their working and relaxing time, its rules are understood. From time to time there will be an uprising. A newspaper or other media organization will declare that it will no longer take off-the-record or unattributable comments. But in time it relents because it decides it cannot function competitively while using only the disingenuous boilerplate dished up by official spokespeople.

Likewise, anti-Washington administrations that come to town determined to keep their distance from the compromised capital types who talk and live this way almost immediately backtrack. They increasingly yearn to tell the journalist who is covering them or the congressman who controls their spending what they really intend but feel they cannot quite yet own up to publicly. Before they know it, they are up to their eyes in the twofold way of doing business. . . .

I once sat in Dirksen's office getting his unvarnished, disgusted reaction to Republican senator Barry Goldwater's opposition to the Civil Rights Act of 1964. Dirksen had cooperated with the Democrats on the landmark bill and regarded its enactment in some part as his own personal achievement, not to mention a ticket to hosannas from history.

As the 1964 Republican convention approached, Goldwater, the certain nominee, was taking an ever harder anti-civil-rights line. The furious Dirksen denounced Goldwater to me. The interview was interrupted when his assistant, Glee Gomien, came in and announced that a Girl Scout troop from Urbana, Illinois, had arrived.

Dirksen kept fulminating about Goldwater as we headed toward the big double doors that led from his office. When they were opened and the little girls in their green uniforms appeared, a whole new self dropped over him. Glower gone, Dirksen adopted the quasi-silly look he favored for such occasions and the famously syrupy public voice, so unlike the one in which he had been speaking only moments before: "Welcome, my pretties! What lovely little ladies you are!" Naturally this made them giggle, as intended. Even then, I remember thinking that I had caught a rare snapshot of the Washington political molt as it happened. . . .

What people find out in time is that the false self they are inhabiting isn't much of a friend after all. Nor is it any great shakes as a refuge or consolation. They begin to live lives of pantomime, in which gesture is all. They spend more and more time attending social functions with "friends" they don't much like, smiling when they want to frown or yell or tell someone off.

But life inside the image doesn't leave all that much time for real pals, in any event, because the image requires continuous care, feeding, and, above all, protection. That is the worst of it. Merely contemplate having to pretend twenty-four hours a day that you are a single-minded, perfectly comported, morally unimpeachable, endlessly motivated toiler for the public good. It's like never being able to get undressed. People who take this course will become increasingly lifeless.

And although they may believe they are acting to protect themselves, they are not. For it soon will have become the phony "self" that urgently needs the protecting—first as a means of staying in office or in favor with public opinion and shortly thereafter so as not to be found out as a fraud, as a figure far different from the paragon one has been pretending to be. Each new imposture, each new deception along the way has carried with it a new burden to be seen ever after as living up to it, however nonsensical or implausible the claim might be.

Finally all else will be made to yield to the urgency of preserving the false picture. The family and personal life that were once a haven for the beleaguered public figure have been shoved onstage too, and turned into something different. In truth, those who fall into the image-as-reality trap develop a kind of deadening Midas touch. It turns everything not to gold but to the equally lifeless cardboard of public presentation.

The spouse, the kids, religious belief and practice, and the lifestyle— right down to the allegedly favored recipes and spectator sports—get dolled up, revised, cheapened. They reappear in newly idealized and totally unrecognizable public form. We in journalism, I fear, go along with the gag. We used to call our rare dips into these people's domestic lives "color," meaning the odd item about workshop-type hobbies and tastes in breakfast food. Such touches were meant to make an article more readable and its subject more humanly understandable but were usually stilted caricatures, no truer than the rest of the person's public presentation. And this is still the case, even though we are writing less apologetically now about the so-called private side of public persons.

I say "so-called" because it is so often hoked-up private life and, as such, no more convincing than the professional self-presentation it is meant to complement. We don't really, deep down believe them, of course, but we nonetheless hold them to the standards they have so recklessly adopted for themselves. It is our schtick. We are, as a profession, ever less willing to let them get away with doing one thing and saying another—at least in our presence. We have become much more skittish about letting them function in the old, cozy, two-track way.

Thus our reporting on them appears to assume that, contrary to all human history, these people in public life can actually be expected to function as the bloodless, thoroughly consistent incarnations of political ideas and principles they profess to be. Then, when they fail, we let them have it. But until that moment of exposure when they are caught out, we behave as if we really thought that through their waking days and dreaming nights they could be first, last, and only, let us say, practicing neoconservatives or Christian populists or moderate liberals or pro-choice activists or some two-word tag like that—full-time, human captions.

The growing tendency of people in public life to take refuge in such pretense is what has gotten so many of them into big trouble. Real life won't be thwarted forever. So they become, in different degrees, sneaky indulgers of lusts, ambitions, and tastes they have renounced before the world. They take backstage actions they are not proud of to make the tableau on stage come out looking right.

It is by now a commonplace that practically all scandal these days, of which there is such a plenitude, is cover-up—less about what someone did in the first place than about the frantic, insane steps he took to preserve Mr. Image. But once things have taken a bad turn, there is nothing in the tinselly value system he has made his own that can save him. The bolstering vanities and affectations collapse, the hard-bought and much-treasured perks of power are taken away. Most important, the phony friends and supposed allies and fickle worshipers are out the door. The hapless, once-proud public figure, stripped of his false covering and of any residual dignity as well, stands before us, naked and discarded.

This humiliating moment often evokes a cry of pain from the real person. But one of the monstrous ironies of the situation is that the rest of us in Washington, still mercifully unhusked and wrapped in our own images and conceits, are unable or unwilling to recognize it as true pain.

Our Washington receptors can only discern more sham, more posturing, more artful dodging, because we are still living happily in the pretend world and find it hard even to imagine the other life anymore, let alone to credit it when it appears.

I thought I saw something like this the morning of Nixon's resignation from the presidency in August 1974, when the disgraced leader delivered that long, rambling meditation on his mother and father and what they had dreamt for him. I speak as one who will likely be the last unreconstructed Nixon critic on earth. But to me it seemed most natural that at a moment of such unendurable shame, one's thoughts would go back to one's parents, to one's anxieties about how they would view the spectacle, to indirect pleas for their forbearance and love. Anyway, that's how I reacted as I listened on my car radio.

But I live in the other Washington. So I was only mildly surprised, on getting to the office, to find that no one else I knew was willing to entertain the thought or even quite grasped what I was getting at. Live by the image, die by the image. They saw Nixon's speech merely as evidence of further faking: "Did you hear that performance? Would you believe he's still trying that stuff? Yecch!"

I thought this reaction said something not about Nixon, but about us.

SALLY QUINN

Why Do They Hate Washington?

The Washington Post (April 12, 2001)

Of course the headline that accompanied this article caught my atten-
tion. It's a question I've been asking myself for decades. The answer is
something I feel very strongly about. I tend to take attacks on Washing-
ton personally. Joe Alsop wrote about the time in the early 1950s, soon
into the Eisenhower administration, when Phil was seated at a dinner
next to Mrs. George Humphrey, the wife of the new secretary of the trea-
sury. Mrs. Humphrey began to go on about what a sacrifice her husband
had made in giving up his corporate job in Cleveland and coming to
Washington. Phil listened at some length to her complaints about
Washington before responding to the effect that "We happen to think
that that kind of remark here in Washington is like belching in Shaker
Heights. We believe that serving the United States is a privilege, not a
sacrifice." I'm not sure that Mrs. Humphrey was able to speak for the
rest of the dinner—or that she ever spoke to Phil again—but he was
right to call her on her complaining.

I, too, consider it a privilege to serve my country and am always dis-
mayed by the negative reaction of so many to Washington. Exaggerated
misconceptions about the city actually make me angry. I have always
disliked hearing candidates for jobs in Washington—from the Con-
gress to the presidency—talk as though they're running against Wash-
ington and that their only reason for wanting to be here is to clean it
up and make it safe for the rest of the country.

I was happy to read Sally's piece when it appeared in the Post
because it expresses what I feel. I do take all of this personally. It's not
easy—and has grown more difficult over the years—to be a public ser-
vant in Washington, but there are good people here, working hard.
Some people might say that I'm overly sensitive about my town, but I
think there's every reason to come to its defense. Washington doesn't
always work the way we want it to, but I believe that there's a great deal
that's noble about it.

"MY ZIP CODE is 78701. That's Austin, Texas. It's not Washington, D.C. If you were to call me on the telephone, it would be area code 512, not 202.

"I'm not of the Washington scene. . . . I'm not a chairman of a powerful committee like the Commerce Committee. I come from outside Washington, D.C."

That was George W. Bush, mid-campaign, January of 2000.

Today his Zip code is 20500. His area code is 202.

And here's what he had to say about Washington in February of 2001:

"No one can speak in this Capitol and not be awed by its history. . . . And when we walk through Statuary Hall, and see those men and women of marble, we're reminded of their courage and achievement. . . . If we work together, we can prove that public service is noble."

Though this was George W. Bush speaking, it could have been Andrew Jackson or Ronald Reagan, Jimmy Carter or Bill Clinton.

To hear them tell it when they're running, Washington, D.C., is the *real* evil empire, it is Sodom and Gomorrah, the source of corruption and scandal and big money and elitism and everything that is wrong with our country.

And yet—they will spend two years of their lives and hundreds of millions of dollars to get here. Why? So they can change Washington, of course. They can tame the beast. They can make it kinder, gentler, more civil, more bipartisan, more productive, more compassionate, more fair, nobler. End result: In most cases, they become part of the very culture they have been excoriating.

In 1994, Republican George Nethercutt of Washington State defeated the Speaker of the House, Tom Foley, who had served thirty years in Congress. Nethercutt's campaign theme was that Foley had lost contact with the real people. "We don't need a Speaker, we need a listener," was his slogan. It worked.

Foley understands why. He remembers listening to a constituent, an ironworker, discuss his views on the life of a congressman in Washington at a focus group in 1994. Asked what he thought dinner would be like at the home of a congressman, he responded that he would be picked up by an enormous limousine, taken to a huge mansion in Georgetown, seated at a fancy table laid with silverware he didn't know how to use and served food he didn't know how to eat.

"All I could think of," chuckles Foley, "was the humble basement apartment I lived in while I was flying back and forth to my district every weekend."

At the time, Nethercutt was in favor of term limits. During his campaign, he promised to serve no more than three.

You know the rest. Nethercutt realized after six years that he wanted to stay. When he ran (successfully) for a fourth term, he was vilified for going back on his word.

What happened?

"After the second term I felt like I knew what I was doing," he says. "I began to have the knowledge and the experience." Leaving at that point "limits your effectiveness to your district." Learning how slowly government works is frustrating for those who "want to serve a short term and have a deep impact," he concedes. "It takes time and patience to get experience."

As for Washingtonians, he says, "it was a pleasant surprise that there are fine people here, good human beings who have the best interests of the country at heart." He was also surprised "by the friendly nature of the city" and he does not feel at all corrupted living here.

So now it's Nethercutt on the receiving end of criticism. He is constantly surprised, he says, by the anger he sees when the police block Independence Avenue so that he and other members of Congress can get to the Capitol during the fifteen minutes they have to vote. Drivers honk their horns in exasperation. "It's symbolic of the perception that there is an elitism for those of us who serve," he says. "All we're trying to do is vote. We're trying to do our job and we hope to help the people sitting in those cars."

The mere phrase "inside the Beltway" makes people hyperventilate. "K Street," the symbolic home of the lobbyists, is anathema; "the Hill" conjures up images of corrupt congressmen taking paper bags full of money; "Georgetown" is the impenetrable bastion of the elitists, and now even "the White House" is synonymous with scandal and vulgarity. Enter at your own risk; fail to turn your back on it when you leave and you turn into a pillar of salt.

Stand on a hill in Arlington National Cemetery and look down across the Potomac to the Lincoln and Jefferson Memorials, the Washington Monument and the Capitol, symbols of all that is noble in Washington. Look past the graves of those who have sacrificed so much to protect these very institutions that so many now revile. Has Washington changed so much from those first idealistic and ebullient days when those who founded the city had such great hopes for it?

Apparently most Americans think so. In a 1998 *Washington Post* poll only 33 percent of Americans said they trusted their government.

"People dismiss Washington," says Ari Fleischer, President Bush's press secretary. "To the American psyche there's the real world and there's Washington."

Four or five years ago, Fleischer was out at Bull Run watching a Civil

War reenactment. In the re-creation, people had come over from Washington to see the fighting. When a congressman was taken prisoner, he says, the spectators started clapping.

Fleischer says that the president "hopes to change the manner in which we comport ourselves. If we tone it down it makes it easier for others to tone it down." The president's campaign, he says, "reflected the need to change the tone in Washington, which is why people applauded at Bull Run."

Foley thinks that Hollywood's portrayal of Washington reflects the popular view. In the movie *Mr. Smith Goes to Washington* the elegant Cosmos Club was used for the senator's father's house and everyone was in white tie with footmen carrying silver trays.

"The notion is," he says, "that when you get here you get captured by the mindset of the city with its disregard for ordinary values and ordinary people. . . . You become estranged from the fundamental decent instincts of the people. You become preoccupied with seeking power and rendering influence with lobbyists and pressure groups. If you're not corrupted in the traditional sense by the city you are corrupted by its attitudes."

That image is dead wrong, says Foley. But it wasn't any better in a more recent movie, *The Distinguished Gentleman*, starring Eddie Murphy. Foley says he was asked by Disney, when he was Speaker, to sponsor a screening of the film to coincide with the opening of Congress. He had a private screening before he agreed and was stunned to see how the lawmakers were portrayed. "It was a modern-day *Mr. Smith Goes to Washington*," he says. "Every kind of canard and slander, and people thought it was funny. There were only one or two decent members of Congress. The rest were powerful, evil, brilliant and manipulating."

Today, *The West Wing*, which portrays an honorable president and his equally noble-minded staff, is one of the biggest hits on television. Does this reflect a change in the public perception?

Probably not, says Gerald Rafshoon, Hollywood producer and former Carter administration communications director. "It's an idealized version of what people would like to see. And a president they wish they had. These programs happen because people are disenchanted."

All the things Americans think are bad, says Mayor Anthony Williams, "they think are manifold in Washington. And the local part gets maligned, too." Unfairly, he says. The proof? "More people are coming to Washington than are leaving."

Why do candidates feel they have to run against Washington?

"Because it works," says former Nebraska senator Bob Kerrey, now president of the New School University in New York. "The dogs eat the food. It's been going on since democracy began."

He finds it deplorable. "[Ralph] Nader says everybody is on the take. Nader is such a liar. People aren't running around taking cash. Washington is cleaner now than it's been in twenty-five years. People complain that we're working in back rooms until midnight but if we went home early they'd say we weren't working."

Kerrey acknowledges that government can do stupid things. "I do stupid things, too," he says. "But not because I live inside the Beltway." He tells of his old colleague, the late senator Ed Zorinsky from Nebraska. "Ed was the master of persuading people that he hated Washington. But he said to me, 'Man, this is the greatest job I've ever had in my life.'" Zorinsky died in office.

Running against Washington, observes commentator Mark Shields, is what he calls the Br'er Rabbit approach to politics. "Don't throw me in that Briar Patch!" As former senator Claiborne Pell once observed, "There are only two ways people leave Washington. By the ballot box or the undertaker's box."

That is because, concludes Shields, "Washington is not a bad place."

Former senator Alan Simpson, whose father was a senator, too, understands the compulsion to run against Washington.

"You run against the State Department," he says, "and you say all those guys do is sit around and drink tea and eat cookies. And then you get here and you learn.

"If you get elected and then crawl into a hole and say, 'I never go to parties, they're not going to corrupt me,' you get bitter. You don't learn. If you keep running against Washington once you're here, you're not effective. . . . You don't get pollination. I learned more from those parties than anything. Sitting next to some diplomat's wife, you can learn a lot."

Some superficial things—language, clothing—can turn constituents off. That's why Frank Luntz, a Republican pollster, counsels his candidates against looking, sounding, and acting like Washington. "I've done presentations with Washington politicians where they look like cadavers and morticians. Washington politicians will wear a dark suit and a red tie to a pig roast."

And Kerrey remembers that during his '94 campaign his children forbade him to use the expression "with all due respect" ever again.

Fair enough. But Kerrey was irritated by the constituents who would tell him, "You don't live in the real world like I do."

"That's baloney," he says. "What's the real world? Or they will say, 'Nobody seems to be speaking to young people anymore.' And most politicians will give obsequious answers instead of saying, 'Hey, buddy, you know who runs the offices in the Congress and the Senate? Young people under thirty run this place.'"

Ken Duberstein, who used to be Ronald Reagan's chief of staff, points out that the people who migrate to Washington are "the cream of the crop. You don't get elected class president unless you're good. You don't get elected to Congress unless you've been through the wars, or get into the Senate or the Cabinet or the presidency unless you've got good things going for you. There are nothing but high achievers here."

Sure, the stereotype is the "quick buck, the campaign payoff, the yelling and shouting at one another, the nasty sound bite. But when they get here they realize that it ain't so bad. . . .

"Everybody's in love with the monuments," he says. "But when you get here you also fall in love with the Longworth Building."

It's a time-honored American tradition to distrust the distant government.

That's why senators are rarely elected president, says Democratic campaign consultant Bill Knapp. "It's much more likely for a governor. People are suspicious of Washington. It's seen as an island removed from the rest of the country. It's seen as a place of evil."

"When candidates run for the presidency they have historically associated themselves with their humble origins," says historian Michael Beschloss. "In 1840 William Henry Harrison ran on the slogan 'log cabin and hard cider' even though his father had been governor of Virginia and had signed the Declaration of Independence. Estes Kefauver wore a coonskin cap even though he had graduated from Yale Law School. And you would never guess from the rhetoric of George W. Bush who his father and grandfather were."

Newt Gingrich, former Speaker of the House, points out that the United States grew out of opposition to centralized power, what he calls the "Whig-Jeffersonian distrust of authority coupled with the Jacksonian anger. . . . Somewhere there's 'them'—people who do bad things compounded by authority."

Gingrich deliberately resisted the establishment. He says he is in the Reagan tradition. "We were both visitors," he says. "There's a big psychological difference from those who see themselves as part of the establishment looking out. Reagan never actually lived here. Andrew Jackson was a visitor." George W. Bush, he says, "will always be the guy who goes back to the ranch."

And he asks rhetorically which is better—"running the establishment and wishing the American people weren't dumb or wishing the establishment weren't dumb and working for the American people?"

According to Chris Matthews, host of MSNBC's *Hardball*, hostility toward the capital traces its roots to Europe, where the people in the countryside were suspicious of city folk. Matthews cites that as one of the reasons Americans decided to move the capital away from a major city. "Americans have always rebelled against government," he says.

During times of crisis, that attitude may change as people rally around a cause. During and after World War II, he points out, "everyone in government was popular. The Cabinet members were all heroes. The generals and the commanders were heroes. We won."

After Vietnam, though, "just as victory was shared, defeat was shared. There was no love affair with anybody. Today defeat is always shared in this city. Today it's always, 'God, they screwed that up.' "

Columnist and political commentator Mark Shields also traces the turning point to Vietnam—and Watergate. That's when people began to run against "the ethical eunuchs and moral lepers" in Washington, he says. Members of Congress opened up offices all over their districts and held endless town meetings. "Implicit in this," he says, "is that this was the real America. Back there in Washington is corrupt. I get my batteries recharged at the Junior Chamber of Commerce Car Wash."

And Michael Deaver, Ronald Reagan's adviser, sees the dynamic going one step further as the media turned distrustful. "You can track the cynicism of the press and cynicism of the public," he says.

Cultures need culprits. For most of the seventeenth and eighteenth centuries people blamed the Devil for society's ills. In the nineteenth century the Devil was Wall Street, big business and banks. In the latter part of the twentieth century, it became Washington.

Campaign consultants know this, and capitalize on it. NBC anchor Tom Brokaw regards the consultants as the "principal villains" in Washington's demonization. "They're the hired guns riding into town. They set up a billboard of Washington and shoot holes in it and ride out of town again. . . . They have turned it into the evil empire."

"It's the stereotype," says Bill Knapp, who was Al Gore's campaign consultant. "Bureaucracy, waste and fraud, taxes used for ridiculous purposes. And over the years there has been an increased focus on scandals. Amorality rules. That's the image they see. High-paid lawyers, the Gucci scene."

Congress, the White House, the Supreme Court—they've all been sullied in the public's eye. "None of the revered institutions are revered anymore," Knapp says. Of course, the tourists keep coming, but that doesn't mean they love their government. "Their problems are not with the buildings," he says. "They're with the people."

Still, Washington is "a great place to live," he says cheerily. "The stereotype is not fair, but we're saddled with it." And, he says mischievously, "I keep using it." . . .

In some respects, the hostility to Washington may be inevitable. "As government has become larger," says Jody Powell, who used to be Jimmy Carter's press secretary, "inevitably you build up the number of people who are upset about something.

"Actually, government has gotten better," he says, "even as the resentment of it has gotten worse. . . . I believe that the vast majority of people in the government want to do the right thing, not because they think they'll get rich afterwards, although some do, but because they are motivated by the desire to make the government do the right thing."

George Stephanopoulos, a first-term Clinton adviser, also sees a certain unavoidable negative response to the federal government. "Washington means whatever people are bothered by at that moment. It's about power and privilege and the way things are."

So politicians naturally run "against the status quo. . . . If it doesn't have to be changed, the challengers can't win."

David Gergen, a counselor for presidents Nixon, Ford, Reagan and Clinton, concurs: "Washington has become the boogeyman, the hidden force under the bed and in the closet. When you don't want to be precise about what you're running against you say Washington because it covers a multitude of sins." But he thinks Washington deserves much of its bad reputation. "Bill Clinton was a polarizing figure and things are much more polarized than ever before," he says. "There is so much more emphasis now on winning rather than doing good. What has almost vanished is the feeling that one belongs to a large community dedicated to the public good as opposed to being in a warrior class trying to defeat others."

No longer, he says, is there "a sense of having a common sacrifice and a common purpose that crossed party lines and party boundaries."

One of the most popular segments on *NBC Nightly News with Tom Brokaw* is called "The Fleecing of America." It depicts how the government wastes taxpayers' money.

"The money thing has gotten worse," Brokaw says. "It's dialing for dollars. The perception is that people are not coming as representatives but to enrich themselves in some fashion."

The press, too, has played a role, he feels. "All these cable shows are organized around being cynical about Washington." The irony, says Brokaw, is that "Washington is the first place people go when they need help."

Mary Matalin, who once worked for the elder George Bush and now is an adviser to Vice President Cheney, points out that "it's an easier story to write negative about Washington. People know the more they attack Washington the more likely they are to get covered, and the more coverage there is the more entrenched the metaphor becomes. It's less about what goes on here than the way it's covered."

"I like Washington," says Fox talk show host and best-selling author Bill O'Reilly. What outsiders dislike, he said, is the sensibility rather than the city. "It's the idea of the cocktail party circuit and the arrogance of power. Regular folks don't want to be looked down upon by the effete, elite, corrupt Washington, or Hollywood or New York."

O'Reilly says that most of the population in the United States feels powerless. "They are at the mercy of every outside force," he says, "so you can understand the resentment over people who do have power." O'Reilly feels that Bill Clinton abused his power as did Richard Nixon. "But those who didn't," he says—Ronald Reagan and Jimmy Carter, for example—"are now revered."

Brian Lamb, the founder and chairman of C-SPAN, remembers when he was asked to come to a senator's office. The senator, unhappy with the way the network was showing empty seats during quorum calls, lamented that people were watching this on television.

"He said to me, 'People think we're not doing anything.' " Lamb explained that "it's not my job" to shape what unfolds in front of the cameras.

"This place is both good and bad," says Lamb. "There's a lot more money being chased here than even twenty years ago. You send folks off to Washington and they never come home. They just move to K Street and triple their salaries. The public becomes cynical."

According to Beschloss, this reaction is not a bad thing.

"In a way," he says, "the criticism of Washington is extremely healthy. Because the idea of Thomas Jefferson was that to make the system work, Americans always had to be in a state of semi-revolution against the government. He would have been terrified to think that in 2001 Americans might be uncritical of Washington and let it steal their liberties."

Tom Foley tells about a North Carolina congressman who would come to Washington only to vote.

"He didn't want anything to do with the city," Foley says. "He had a sense of contagion, that this was a pesthole of bad values and evil interests. If he left town he was less likely to catch this terrible plague, to be brought down by the atmosphere, that he was less likely to end up in a huge mansion in Georgetown offering his constituents food they didn't know how to eat."

BEGINNINGS AND ENDINGS

Washington is a place of continuous farewells. I have seen so many even in our short stay and always I have seen people go with the consciousness that others would take their place who would be equally nice and equally interesting.

—Agnes Ernst Meyer, from her diary, 1920

Chief Justice Charles Evans Hughes swears in Franklin D. Roosevelt at the President's third inauguration, January 20, 1941. Eleanor Roosevelt is at the extreme left, next to Speaker of the House Sam Rayburn.

In Washington, one person's beginning is often another person's ending. I've had a lot of beginnings here in Washington—from the time my father bought the *Post,* to when I returned from San Francisco and went to work on the paper, to when Phil came back after the war and started work on the *Post,* to after Phil died and I went back to the *Post* in an entirely changed capacity. Certainly there was a new beginning when I turned over the job of publisher (a job I loved) to my son Don—already twenty-two years ago—and later when I retired as chairman of the company. All of these beginnings took place in Washington. It's interesting that I've described them all as beginnings, when they could be seen as endings as well. I guess it's all in the way one looks at things.

These were personal beginning and endings, but Washington has more than its share of public ones. In so many ways there were too many endings in these years—FDR's death, John Kennedy's, Martin Luther King's, Robert Kennedy's.

Among the most notable ending and beginning in my memory was Richard Nixon flying off from the White House lawn on that strange August day in 1974, and the appearance of President Gerald Ford proclaiming that our long national nightmare was over. At the time, I didn't think of this as an ending or a beginning, just a relief, a lifting of pressure.

Washington has many formal and informal occasions to mark beginnings and endings. It used to be customary to bid farewell to cabinet officers by seeing them off at the station. Marietta Andrews wrote of Washington's Union Station filling with "well-wishers as an outgoing Secretary and his family pass from Washington's official life: their last memory is of this double or treble cordon through which they pass, as hundreds of their friends and countrymen are lined up to bid them God-speed." I like this picture of departing Washington officials being ceremonially piped out of town, and I am sorry it's a habit that fell by the wayside.

Inaugurations, moments of high drama in Washington, are another example of a beginning and an ending at once. Josephus Daniels wrote poignantly about an important one, Woodrow Wilson's last "official" appearance as president, on March 4, 1921, when Daniels sat with Wilson in the president's room in the Senate wing of the Capitol. He described the scene as the outgoing president sat talking with members of his cabinet for the last time:

Lodge entered the room just before the time set for Harding's inauguration. The Senator, with a cold look as hard as the ice on the White Mountains in December, and in frigid tones said: "Mr. President, we have come as a Committee of the Senate to notify you that the Senate and House are about to adjourn and await your pleasure."

With studied politeness and the suggestion of a smile on his drawn mouth Wilson, whose speech had been impaired by illness, said, some thought icily: "Senator Lodge, I have no further recommendations to make. I thank you. Good morning."

The New Freedom went out of the door as Harding and Teapot Dome came in through the window in the spirit of, "The King is dead. Long live the King."

I love this view of a moment just prior to the passing of the presidential baton.

There is a great deal of grand and inspired writing about the highly public beginnings and endings in Washington. Here is some of it.

The Wilsons
Leave the White House

My Memoir (1939)

The ending for Woodrow Wilson came well before the end of his second term. There have been scores of books written about Woodrow Wilson, but probably none so poignant as this memoir by his second wife, Edith Bolling Wilson. Interestingly, her dedication in the book appears at the end: "To my husband Woodrow Wilson, who helped me build from the broken timbers of my life a temple wherein are enshrined memories of his great spirit which was dedicated to the service of his God and Humanity."

From the first sign of the president's illness in 1919—initially diagnosed as "nervous exhaustion"—worries arose about when he would be able to resume his duties as president, if ever. Even more uneasiness was aroused in Washington and the country when Wilson's wife began to protect her husband from the outside world by filtering his contacts. Edith was called the "first woman president," although she adamantly denied she was shaping policy. With the White House isolated, all of Washington was affected. Edward Lowry wrote of the atmosphere at the time, "It all made for bleakness and bitterness and a general sense of frustration and unhappiness."

It was not a pretty picture. Edna Colman, in her book White House Gossip, *described the scene when Woodrow Wilson appeared at Harding's inaugural: "Feeble, worn, white, and thin, his helpless hands and wavering feet were placed for him when he took his seat beside Warren Harding for the ride to the Capitol. . . . Ex-President Wilson did not remain for all of the ceremony, but returned to his home, which became a mecca for pilgrimages of his followers until his death."*

It is significant that after they left the White House, the Wilsons chose to stay in Washington. Mrs. Wilson describes in her book their hectic and stressful last month in the White House, and worrying about

the renovations that were being made to their new home on S Street,
which is where they retreated to on that inaugural day in 1921.

At Wilson's death, in 1924—six months after the death of the
seemingly hardy Harding—silent, reverent crowds gathered outside of
that house, some kneeling in the street to pray while bells tolled
throughout the city. Wilson is one of the few presidents to be buried in
Washington. Also significant is that Mrs. Wilson chose the National
Cathedral for Wilson's burial place. Cary Grayson explained it this
way: "Because his greatest work had been done in Washington and
because he had selected the Capital City as his home, it seemed to Mrs.
Wilson fitting that he should rest here."

L EARNING that President-Elect and Mrs. Harding were in Washington visiting Mr. and Mrs. Edward B. McLean, I asked Mrs. Harding to come to tea, suggesting the housekeeper could take her through the House so that she could know conditions and be able with that knowledge to make her plans. I sent the invitation by note to the McLeans' house early in the morning, and was starting downstairs to lunch when I met the usher with a reply saying that Mrs. Harding would be glad to accept and if agreeable to me would bring Mrs. McLean with her.

I sat down at the writing table in the hall and sent a second note suggesting that, since she was coming to go over the house and discuss personal plans with Mrs. Jaffray, the housekeeper, she should come alone. To this Mrs. Harding replied that she had not understood my first note, and that, of course, she would come alone.

She arrived on time, wearing a dark dress, a hat with blue feathers, and her cheeks highly rouged. Her manner was so effusive, so voluble, that after a half-hour over the tea cups I could hardly stem the torrent of words to suggest I send for the housekeeper so she could talk over her desires as to the house. I told her Mrs. Jaffray was very good in her position and that she had been first employed by Mrs. Taft. I said Mrs. Jaffray would take her through the house, except the President's own room where he was resting. Otherwise I hoped she would feel free to look at everything. The housekeeper, I added, would point out to her the things that were our personal belongings.

I rang for Mrs. Jaffray. The new mistress of the White House did not shake hands with the housekeeper, but gazed at her through eyeglasses which she put on over a black mesh veil fastened tightly about her face.

I said goodbye, explaining it was time for an appointment which would take me out of the house and so they would have the place to themselves.

I did not get in again until seven-thirty, and when I was going up in the elevator I heard a voice far down in the kitchen. It was Mrs. Harding talking to the cook. She remained until after eight o'clock.

I did not see her again until March 3rd when we asked that she and the President-Elect come to tea with us. My husband was already downstairs to join me in greeting them, and we had tea in the Red Room. As I recall it she wore the same hat as before but another dress. We tried to make things go, but they both seemed ill at ease and did not stay long. Mr. Harding sat in an armchair with one leg thrown over the arm.

That, of course, was a very crowded day. My maid and the President's valet packed our belongings and put them in place in the S Street house. I. H. Hoover, who had done all he could to assist us, came to me to beg that we leave everything in Mr. Wilson's room undisturbed until March 4th. When we left for the Capitol he said he would personally see that each article was carried and put in its accustomed setting in Mr. Wilson's room in the new house. In this way my husband would at once feel at home and would not be inconvenienced on his last night in the White House by the deprivation of the small things that make for the comfort of an invalid. This tender thought on Hoover's part touched me deeply. I was a little loath to adopt it, wishing to leave everything in perfect condition for Mr. and Mrs. Harding. But faithful Wilkins, the houseman, added his pledge to see that all should be in shape there while Hoover went to the new house; so I gave my permission.

I had been so busy at the White House I had not been able to go to S Street since the night of March 2nd. At that time only the bedrooms were in order. Our new servants were already installed; but on account of delay in getting all the inside work finished, particularly the elevator, dirt and rubbish covered the lower floors, no rugs were down or pictures hung.

For a week or more previous to this my habit had been to stay with my husband until he got to his room at night and then, about ten-thirty, go to the new house, where my brothers and the servants would be at work. I would help until two or three o'clock in the morning. Mr. Wilson's books had been catalogued before leaving the White House by Mr. W. T. Marshall who had rendered the same service for every President since Grover Cleveland; and this same kindly person came also at night to help unpack and place them on the shelves.

So the 4th of March dawned. We were up early, and by nine o'clock the house was filled with aides, Senators, Cabinet officers and their wives;

and everything ready awaiting the arrival of the incoming President and Mrs. Harding, and the new Vice President and Mrs. Coolidge.

I was anxious about the effect of so much excitement on my husband. But I knew that, cost what it would, he would pay every respect to his successor, and go through the physical suffering without flinching. All the White House employees had been remembered, and we said good-bye to them with genuine appreciation of what they had done for us.

The cars were at the door, and I went up to tell my husband. I found him ready, dressed in morning coat and grey trousers. His room was in order with all his personal belongings around him as though he might return in a few moments. Brooks, the valet, held his high hat and gloves and gave him the cane which, alas, he could not walk without, and which he whimsically called his "third leg."

Slowly he walked with me to the elevator, where Hoover was waiting with the door open. We went straight to the Blue Room, reaching it just as the Hardings arrived. Greetings soon over, we moved towards the entrance door where the camera and moving picture men held full sway. The car stood under the porte-cochère and the President and President-Elect, accompanied by Senator Knox and former Speaker Cannon as escort, entered. Thus the man who had brought our country through war to victory and peace and had given his all in strength and health to make the peace permanent left the White House forever.

Mrs. Harding and I followed in another car. As we passed down the familiar drive she called out in hearty tones first on one side, then the other, greeting the newspaper reporters whom, she explained to me, she called "her boys." Our progress was slow as crowds cheered the car in which were the President and President-Elect.

At the Capitol the accustomed procedure was for the incoming and outgoing Presidents to drive to the front of the building and walk up the steps together. As this would have been too much for my husband's strength, he explained to Mr. Harding he would have to take the lower entrance out of sight of the crowd and use the elevator, and that arrangements had been made to this end. The Chairman of the Inaugural Committee had told us that he was sure Mr. Harding would accompany the President in the elevator. However, Mr. Harding alighted from the car and, smiling and waving his hat, ascended the steps, thoughtlessly leaving my husband to drive on alone.

Our car followed quickly and Mrs. Harding fairly raced up the steps. How I longed to follow the lonely figure just then making his painful way through the lower entrance! But I knew he would want me to play the game. With a heart hot within me, I followed Mrs. Harding, until I joined my husband in the room reserved for the President. At the close of each session of Congress it is the custom for the President to come to this room to sign the bills just passed, and when this is done a joint committee of both Houses notifies the Executive that the Congress has completed the business before it and now stands ready to adjourn unless the President has any further message to communicate. The spokesman of this committee is generally the Chairman of the Senate Foreign Relations Committee, an office at this time held by Senator Henry Cabot Lodge. . . .

This over we extended our congratulations to the new President and Vice President and departed. With Dr. Grayson, Mr. Tumulty and two Secret Service men we took the elevator and left the building.

Driving to our new home I expressed my indignation at the performance at the Capitol, saying just what I thought of it. My husband laughed at my fury. Where I was bitter, he was tolerant; where I resented, he was amused; and by the time we reached the corner of Massachusetts Avenue where we turned into S Street we were both happy and felt a great burden had been lifted from our shoulders and that we could return to our own affairs in a home of peace and serenity.

PHILIP HAMBURGER

"We Have Nothing to Fear . . ."

The New Yorker (1983)

Philip Hamburger has written for The New Yorker *for more than six decades. He enchants with the richness of his writing, in part because he creates pictures that allow us to really know what something was like—how some event unfolded, how people looked, what they were feeling, the buzz in a room. He is a great guide, and over the years, although living in New York with only a short stint in Washington during the war, he has written often about the Washington scene.*

Here he describes a scene that I saw for myself—FDR's first inaugural. I was fifteen years old, and as unknowing as any teenager is ever likely to be. Although I lived in Washington and had watched public figures come and go at our house throughout my childhood, I took it all for granted. The very idea that I was there at the beginning of FDR's presidency awes me. It's hard, at close to seventy years' distance, to remember in any unadulterated way, but here is what my mother recorded in her diary about that March day in 1933:

> *Took Kay to Inauguration Ceremony. Vast crowd very alarming. It was all we could do to arrive at the reserved seats. Ominous cold grey sky, long wait for the dignitaries because crowd was so dense in Capitol that even the President could not break through. Bad management made poor impression. The radio announcement was so vulgar as to rob the ceremony of all dignity. The oath of office, a great and solemn moment, completely ruined because announcer held it up to talk trivialities. When Roosevelt came out Hoover for first time heard "Hail to the Chief" played for another.*
>
> *In Senate he sat next to Roosevelt grim, silent and the radio man made the most of this contrast to R's smiling triumphant manner.*
>
> *The inauguration speech was bold but colorless and empty, I thought. I heard every word through Hoover's ears and felt that*

Roosevelt might have avoided the references to the "inaction" of the past years. It wasn't tactful to say the least but he was completely oblivious of Hoover's feelings. There is small love between those two.

Leave it to Mother to blame bad management on the Democrats and to view FDR's first inaugural speech as colorless and empty—but also leave it to her to acknowledge what amusing places the world, and Washington, are.

FIFTY years ago, on March 4, 1933, Franklin Delano Roosevelt was inaugurated president of the United States for the first time, and I was there, in the crowd. (This was the last of the March 4 Inaugurations; ever since, they have taken place on January 20.) I was eighteen, and I drove from college in Baltimore to Washington in a battered Ford owned by a classmate; the mere fact that he owned a four-wheeled vehicle gave him the appearance of being exceedingly rich. The times were desperate. Thirteen million Americans were out of work (including my own father); thousands of families were living in makeshift shacks in our greatest cities; farmers were rioting to prevent foreclosure of their land and homes; hunger was commonplace; and every bank in the nation was about to be closed. I was lucky: I had a scholarship that credited so many hours of work in the library against so much tuition. I was young and healthy and had my share of dreams.

The day was ominously overcast, and became more so as we approached Washington, forty miles south. Thick dark clouds hung over us; I was certain it would rain, and rain heavily. We had no tickets or credentials. The idea was to get as close as possible to the Capitol's East Front, within sight of the Inaugural stand, and find a citizen's perch for the ceremonies. My friend at the wheel knew nothing of the complexities of Washington traffic, and we drove around the city's circles and broad boulevards trying to find a place to park. Soldiers and policemen were everywhere; flags and bunting hung from every lamppost. But there was no hint of festivity in the air. Small knots of people had begun to line the sidewalks (it was late morning), but for the most part they appeared dispirited and sullen. We parked not very far from the Capitol, on a quiet, tree-lined street with neat, clean row houses with white stoops. It was a poor, black neighborhood. I was dressed for the day in the clothes of the time: a dark-blue vested suit (no jeans, of course), a long dark winter overcoat, and a snappy gray fedora with a huge brim. (The suit, as I recall, was a hideous shade of blue, and had come with

two pairs of pants, for thirty-two dollars.) In my pocket I carried binoculars.

We worked our way fairly close to the Capitol before being stopped
by a Marine guard. With extreme amiability, he asked for our tickets. He
then gave us a friendly wink and pointed at a nearby icicle-laden, leafless
tree. My friend and I scrambled into the tree and surveyed the special
nexus of the nation that spread out before us. The white dome of the
Capitol was gray, partly obscured by wisps of fog. The official grandstand
was filling up with top-hatted dignitaries, all bundled up against the
expected downpour. There must have been a hundred thousand people
spread out over the vast Capitol grounds. For the first time, I examined
my neighbors in our particular tree, each on a separate bare limb: an
elderly gentleman in rumpled and ancient green tweeds, with patches; a
beautiful redheaded young woman wrapped in a skimpy coat of rabbit, or
of some other unfortunate domestic animal; a woman of indeterminate
age who can best be described as dressed in rags, and whose face was
lined with worry and pain. For the moment, at least, we were precariously snug in our tree house, waiting for a president to be inaugurated.
President or no president, I had a hard time taking my eyes off the redhead; we subsequently became close friends.

The ceremonies were scheduled to start at noon. Noon came and
went. The crowd was strangely silent. One could sense the unease.
Rumors began to spread through the crowed, called up to the tree people
by the less fortunate groundlings. Rumor: A mob somewhere along
Pennsylvania Avenue had broken through police lines and surrounded
the car containing President Hoover and President-elect Roosevelt.
Rumor: Machine guns had been spotted along the route of the cavalcade
from the White House to the Capitol. Rumor: Roosevelt had been
wounded by an assassin's bullet, perhaps fatally. The lady in rags prayed
quietly in the tree: "No more trouble, please, God. No more trouble."
The man in the patched tweeds said that he had known all along that
something terrible was going to happen on this day, and that one man's
leaving office and another man's taking over would have no effect: only
revolution would turn things right side up, once and for all. Nonsense,
said the redhead; have a little faith, and don't fall out of the tree. Suddenly, there was a stirring in the crowd. The red-coated Marine band
directly in front of the grandstand began to play. I pulled out my binoculars and focused straight ahead. President Hoover, glum and downcast,
appeared and took a seat in a leather armchair to the left of the rostrum.
A sound like the rustling of otherworldly leaves went through the crowd.
Far away, through the giant center doors of the Capitol, appeared the

president-elect. He was totally without color. He made his way, painfully and slowly, along the ramp leading to the rostrum, leaning heavily on the arm of his son James. He seemed to be drawing on bottomless reservoirs of physical and mental strength to make the short journey to the rostrum and the presidency. The crowd held its collective breath. I doubt whether anybody at that moment, knew that he was carrying ten pounds of heavy steel around his crippled and wasted legs.

I spotted the white-bearded chief justice, Charles Evans Hughes. He was wearing an odd black skullcap. As he delivered the oath of office, Roosevelt repeated every word of it in frightening solemn tones. Once power had passed into his hands, he seized it kinetically, with a vigor and force that stunned the throng. Both hands firmly gripped the rostrum. "This is preeminently the time to speak the truth, the whole truth, frankly and boldly," he said, in a clear and unforgettable voice. "This great Nation will endure as it has endured, will revive and will prosper. So, first of all, let me assert my firm belief that the only thing we have to fear is fear itself—nameless, unreasoning, unjustified terror which paralyzes needed efforts to convert retreat into advance. In every dark hour of our national life a leadership of frankness and vigor has met with that understanding and support of the people themselves which is essential to victory. . . . Yet our distress comes from no failure of substance. We are stricken by no plague of locusts. . . . Plenty is at our doorstep, but a generous use of it languishes in the very sight of the supply. Primarily this is because rulers of the exchange of mankind's goods have failed through their own stubbornness and their own incompetence, have admitted their failure, and have abdicated. . . . The money changers have fled from their high seats in the temple of our civilization. We may now restore that temple to the ancient truths. . . . Happiness lies not in the mere possession of money; it lies in the joy of achievement, in the thrill of creative effort. . . . Restoration calls, however, not for changes in ethics alone. This Nation asks for action, and action now. Our greatest primary task is to put people to work. This is no unsolvable problem if we face it wisely and courageously. . . . We do not distrust the future of essential democracy. The people of the United States have not failed. . . . They have asked for discipline and direction under leadership. They have made me the present instrument of their wishes. In the spirit of the gift, I take it."

The crowd had come to life. It shouted approval. Roosevelt, still holding tightly to the rostrum, gave no sign of satisfaction. His expression was as grim as when he had started to speak. The ceremony was over. "I think we'll live," said the redhead as we climbed down from the tree. The man in tweeds burst into tears. "You know something?" said my college friend. "It never rained."

For many years, I have kept a tattered bulletin board in the kitchen, every inch covered with tacked-up addresses, memos, cards from loved ones, stray quotations from Shakespeare and Yeats (life-sustaining forces). Among them is an old, pockmarked newspaper photograph of F.D.R. leaning on a cane and listening intently to two ragged men who appear to have stopped him somewhere. I have no idea where the picture came from, but it is one of my priceless treasures. One of the men is small and scrappy-looking. His hands are in his pockets, and he is leaning into Roosevelt's face. The other man, larger and older, is wearing an ancient greatcoat, and is unshaved. Roosevelt's gray hat is somewhat smashed. He is being attentive to every word that is being said to him. The caption reads, "He knew how to listen."

Since that far-off Inauguration, I have learned that the family Bible on which Franklin Roosevelt took the oath of office lay open to the thirteenth chapter of I Corinthians—to "And now abideth faith, hope, charity, these three; but the greatest of these is charity."

Scintillating City

Washington By-Line (1949)

*Here is another view of that March day in 1933. Four years after Bess
Furman's own arrival in Washington, the New Deal made its entrance.
Furman wrote that "dizzying, dazzling, Washington . . . waltzed me
around, didn't let my feet touch the ground, for four exciting years."
Certainly a new energy filled the city with the beginning of the New
Deal and its alphabetic agencies and its magical promise.*

THE NEW DEAL rolled into Washington spectacularly. It came
on a special train from New York the night of March 2, 1933.
Bob and I watched the train arrive at the lower level of Union
Station, saw the rear-platform photographs taken by flashlights that cut
through drizzle. In one group stood the President-elect and Mrs. Roosevelt and their oldest son, James. Off to one side were their prep-school
sons (Groton of course), Franklin, Jr. and John. Their daughter, Anna
Roosevelt Dall, and her two small children, Anna Eleanor and Curtis,
called Sistie and Buzzie, were already in Washington. Their other son,
Elliott, and his wife would arrive next day.

On the special train also was the President's aged and aristocratic
mother, Sara Delano Roosevelt, and his pretty daughter-in-law Mrs.
James Roosevelt. In came his secretariat and men named to the Cabinet
and their wives. In came the President-elect's closest friends, members of
his brain trust, and a covey of the New York press.

Everybody piled into autos and rode out past cheering crowds to the
Mayflower Hotel. Bob, with his genius for short-cuts, got us there well in
advance of the Roosevelt party. We watched them unload at the apartment entrance on De Sales Street, under the eagle eyes of Secret Service
men determined to have no repetition of what happened in Florida—a
shot fired at Roosevelt by a madman had fatally wounded Mayor Cermak
of Chicago.

There was no gala arrival spirit here. Roosevelt went right into the hotel to hold conferences on the crisis. Mrs. Roosevelt stayed outside, taking a brisk walk along the block through the drizzle that streaked outside the lighted entrance canopy. She was having, I thought, one last long breath of freedom. On a leash was her little black Scottie, Meggie, her constant companion during her earliest days in the White House.

When we women reporters started to question her, she invited us to go up with her to her room. There she outlined her inauguration program, in which, she said, she was reducing her social appearances to a minimum, due to the sudden death of Senator Tom Walsh, who had been chairman of the Chicago convention, and had just been appointed Attorney General by Roosevelt. Senator Walsh had died on the train, on his wedding trip, en route back from Havana, Cuba, where, to the amazement of his closest friends, he had married Señora Nieves Perez Chaumont de Truffin, widow of a Cuban sugar magnate.

I had scarcely left Mrs. Roosevelt when a telephone conversation with the AP office sent me dashing off to the apartment house where Mrs. Walsh would be arriving at midnight with the Senator's body. There was no difficulty in identifying the black-veiled figure who entered the foyer. I had expected her to send me packing, but with dignity and pride surmounting grief, she talked to me. Later I learned that she and Senator Walsh had met at a New York dinner party, had dined together frequently thereafter both in New York and Washington.

"I came with my heart full of hopes and love to help the man with whom I left my Havana home," she poetically explained. "For two years he has been writing me every day. In Cuba I was living the life of Washington. Our wedding was postponed because my son lay very ill. The convention that nominated your President—I was all through that. By radio I listened to him presiding as I bent over my son."

So Mrs. Walsh and her husband's state funeral were a part of the great inaugural scene, already much too far advanced for any festivities to be cancelled for official mourning in honor of a not-yet-official Cabinet officer. People were here from forty-eight states—the show must go on. She was content to have it so. She postponed the Senate services for a week.

I finished that day's work at two o'clock the next morning, only to arise four hours later to meet a carload of Roosevelt's fellow poliomyelitis patients from Warm Springs. The Georgia editor who had written the first Roosevelt-for-President editorial six years before, and the local sheriff who had organized this expedition, were the only fully ablebodied persons on the car, so our office had been informed by the AP in Atlanta.

Left to my own ingenuity, I would have canvassed the railroad yards in vain for the car of "polios," but Bob suddenly found them, hidden away in a deep railroad cut. It could be reached only by two long, steep, open, newly built flights of steps leading to a viaduct. By what special brand of stupidity a carload of cripples was shunted into such a place, I never had the time to find out. Had there been a telephone within walking distance, I certainly should have called up all and sundry to see if something couldn't have been done about it. I looked at the crutches, and looked at the wheel chairs, and said that these brave people couldn't possibly get up those stairs. But they did—pushing and pulling each other, laughing and joking and having a wonderful time. They were by all odds the most cheerful group I saw during the whole inauguration season. I figured they had the same mind-over-matter determination that took crippled Franklin D. Roosevelt to the top.

We went on to the Capitol and had breakfast, stopping to see Mrs. Garner, who was putting in a few more licks of hard work at her old hideout. Mrs. Roosevelt that morning paid an early secret visit to a shrine she considered the most beautiful in Washington—that of the St. Gaudens statue of a seated woman in Rock Creek Cemetery. Lorena Hickok went with her in a taxi. She told the rest of us about it at a noon press conference. That afternoon we followed Mrs. Roosevelt here, there, and everywhere—to the Walsh apartment, where she and the President-elect made a long call; to the Congressional Club, filled with official wives; to the Democratic Club, where women who had been vigorous campaigners clustered around Mary W. Dewson, the feminine patronage dispenser of the New Deal. They had the theory, correct for once, that there might be more feminine plums in the basket since it was certain now that there'd be a woman Secretary of Labor, Frances Perkins.

Inauguration day was cold and gray and cheerless—all day. It took all the color that all the Roosevelts and their entire entourage had, to bring that day up out of the doldrums and make it a high point of history. Banks in forty-seven states either were under a moratorium or their deposit withdrawals were limited to between five and fifteen per cent.

Everybody knew that this was to be the last of the March 4 inaugurations. The Norris Lame Duck Amendment now was law, and from here on, the incoming Presidents would be inaugurated in January instead of March. An inauguration committee, headed by genial Cary T. Grayson, physician to the late President Woodrow Wilson, had rallied governors galore to make it momentous. Even Al Smith, drawn back into active Democratic ranks during the campaign by a secret visit from Jack Garner, was in Washington to strut again in the Tammany section of the inaugural parade.

But people's minds were on their banks. Many a governor already had argued to many a hotel management that his check couldn't possibly be suspect—only to read the name of his bank on the lengthening list of those whose doors had been closed.

My route on inauguration day took me first to the Senate gallery, for Vice-President John Nance Garner's swearing-in, there to describe a radiant Mrs. Garner with her son Tully; Ann, her "daughter-in-love" she always called her; and her granddaughter Genevieve. I knew them all well, though I had never seen them. With much detail I also described the Roosevelt family, the Hoover family, the outgoing and incoming Cabinet officers and their families. Then I went out of doors to the jam-packed Plaza for the inauguration ceremony, which took place on a bewreathed stand at the top of the central front steps of the Capitol. I sat in the press box, but Bob, who was supposed to sit there too, was all over the place taking miniature movies to show the folks in Nebraska.

The scene was so shivery, and the plight of the nation so dishearten-ing, that when an ambulance siren shrieked close by, it exactly expressed my tense feelings. When Roosevelt said he was going to ask for the equivalent of wartime powers to fight the depression, I watched Mrs. Woodrow Wilson, sitting beside tall, silk-hatted Bernard Baruch. I thought of what she and her husband had gone through. I figured that perhaps it wasn't much stiffer than what Roosevelt and his wife would see. My spirits had not even lifted when the new President early in his speech had interpolated the theme "we have nothing to fear but fear itself." This thought, suddenly made fine and free, did not get through to me. I still had in mind an earlier version in which this sentence had been buried in a paragraph on aiding the needy.

But hope did rise within me when, to the familiar strains of "Hail to the Chief"—a new Chief—Roosevelt slowly, gallantly walked down a long, long ramp on the arm of his son James, to the cheers of crowds fast dispersing to get places for the parade, and to the throbbing drone of air-planes formation-flying overhead. The professional movie men were not allowed to take this picture of Roosevelt, but Bob took a long shot so that we could prove to our people in the Midwest that here was a cripple who was not a cripple. Here was a man who had conquered fear.

Here too, was an all-American family, four generations, typed as for a play from dowager great-grandmother on down to fairy-pretty Sistie Dall with her long, flaxen hair falling below her waistline. Sistie got caught in the crush on the ramp, and her father tossed her to his shoulder and carried her on down. Behind the Roosevelts came game Dolly Gann, waving and smiling, able to adjust to any circumstances. Republican Dolly also was a part of indomitable America.

I saw the inaugural parade in snatches, making my way back to the AP office through side streets. There I found wires cleared for copyright matter—Lorena A. Hickok's interview with Mrs. Roosevelt the moment she became mistress of the White House, indeed as she drew off her gloves on her return from the Capitol. It was a journalistic accomplishment, revealing and prophetic, a notable addition to the scanty accurate records on the wives of Presidents. Mrs. Roosevelt had gazed soberly out of White House upper windows toward the Virginia hills, and had said to Miss Hickok:

It was very, very solemn and a little terrifying.

The crowds were so tremendous, and you felt that they would do anything, if only someone told them what to do.

No one at all close to people in public life today can fail to realize that we are all of us facing extremely critical times.

No woman entering the White House, if she accepts the fact that it belongs to the people and therefore must be representative of whatever conditions the people are facing, can light-heartedly take up residence here.

One has a feeling of going it blindly because we're in a tremendous stream and none of us know where we're going to land.

The important thing, it seems to me, is our attitude toward whatever may happen. It must be willingness to accept and share with others whatever may come and to meet the future courageously, with a cheerful spirit.

There was much more to the interview, family matters, household matters. Mrs. Roosevelt told Hick, too, of how she hoped while in the White House to serve as much as possible as eyes and ears for her husband, seeing as much as possible of the people and telling him what they were saying and thinking. The long-range program that she outlined— far longer range than she dreamed of—she followed to the letter, day after day down the long, long years, serving as "eyes and ears." . . .

Three thousand people were served at tea that afternoon. Mrs. Long, the Hoovers' housekeeper, who had stayed over to help Mrs. Henrietta Nesbitt, the Roosevelts' housekeeper, get started, told me they had to send out again and again for more sandwiches, more little cakes. The tea guests, including my big-eyed self, were still hanging on when the dinner guests started to arrive. Dinner was for seventy-five Roosevelt relatives, among them representatives of the Republican clan, Alice Roosevelt Longworth, Mr. and Mrs. Archie Roosevelt, and Mrs. Kermit Roosevelt.

The inaugural ball that night was bedlam. I never came so near getting completely crushed in all my life. A girl fainted at my feet as I tried to get out of one spot that proved to be a bottleneck with a cork in it. The emergency-meeters who always come forward at such a time managed somehow to get her into a little side office, and then they couldn't get water to her.

Sigrid Arne and I, who were supposed to be covering the story together, parted at the entrance of the big hall with an agreement to meet at the far end. We never once managed to battle across the room to each other the whole long evening through. We communicated by leaving telephone messages with the girl at the Associated Press switchboard, such as: "Don't look for Dolly Gann, I've found her having a whee of a time," and: "You check the Roosevelt box, I'll never make it." I wouldn't have known how far along we were on the program if Bob hadn't been tall enough to see the crossed sabers under which the governors were marching. When we at last emerged into the midnight air, my evening wrap was torn beyond repair, and the old pumps that I had had sense enough to wear were ready to be junked.

I went home to a nice long sleep, but such was not the lot of the President and Mrs. Roosevelt. At the White House that night a mass swearing-in of all the Cabinet was held. Within twenty-four hours after President Roosevelt had taken the oath of office, he had ordered a national banking holiday, declared a gold embargo, and called a special session of Congress.

After that, things happened so fast that skepticism ceased to be the sword and buckler of the A.P. I remember a day when one of our desk men stood over a ticker that was bringing into our office the news from Senate and House.

"Just a minute," he said. "I am waiting for a flash that the world has come to an end, and I want to beat the rest of them out with it."

And I am sure that if such a flash had come down from Capitol Hill, it would have gone to the wires without anyone's batting an eyelash.

For the first hundred days and nights of the New Deal, and often thereafter, the Washington Monument served the city as an appropriate exclamation mark.

JONATHAN DANIELS

Death of the President

Frontier on the Potomac   (1946)

FDR's death was an ending that few of us could imagine, a terribly sad ending, coming way too soon and stunning everyone, because, except for those closest to him (and maybe not even they), few people had known the president was ill. Only in retrospect do we look at photos from the period and see the deterioration and the effects of the war on his face. And, of course, after twelve years as the leader in Washington, the country, and now the world, none of us could imagine him not at the helm.

At the time of FDR's death, Harry Truman was an unknown—at least outside of Washington and Kansas City, Missouri. Not only had the nation lost its beloved wartime president, but it had to go on fighting a war with an untested commander-in-chief. I described it in Personal History *as being "as though we had suddenly lost a father figure in whom we had the greatest confidence and were confronted by an unknown, relatively inexperienced, and seemingly uninspiring Midwestern former senator," who, by the way, just the day before had been quoted as saying that all he had ever wanted to be in Washington was a senator. The future loomed more threatening after Roosevelt died.*

FDR had exuded confidence always—even when he was unwell, as he must have been for months before his death. What he had done for the country was too enormous to comprehend. From the difficult days after his election in 1932 to the moment of his death, Franklin Roosevelt had worked to give the American people what Francis Biddle wrote was a "vision of what their country could be, of what their government could mean to them."

When told of the president's death, Eleanor Roosevelt was reported to have said, "I am more sorry for the people of the country and the world than I am for us." Indeed, a generation mourned when FDR died. Here Jonathan Daniels writes about the death of Roosevelt in terms of its effect on Harry Truman, who had to immediately step into the presidency and who would eventually come into his own in it.

SEEN AT its worst, the Government of America is worth seeing. What I report is only one man's view of a government which deserves all men's eyes.

As big as it is, that government is not easy to see all in one place at one time. But I think I saw it clearest and best for myself and for the inrushing pattern of the American future the night that Harry Truman, as the clock under the portrait of Woodrow Wilson in the Cabinet Room passed 7:09, suddenly ceased to be "Harry" and became "Mr. President." Then within the time it takes for the clicking of cameras, he was the almost superstitiously honored man-symbol of America who can still, after our pattern of reverence, be described in the native argument in the American language as one angry truck driver would describe another.

Just fifteen minutes before sunset that evening they had found him in the pleasant hide-out office of bald-headed Sam Rayburn, Speaker of the House, on one of the maze of hardly used corridors in the Capitol. The Vice-President, dry after presiding over hours of Senatorial debate on a water treaty, had come to join the Speaker and other convivial officials and friends in late afternoon relaxation. "Harry" smiled through his thick lenses as he came in eager for the Speaker's bourbon. He got the telephone call instead.

It was nearly dark when he drove into the White House grounds. And behind him, swiftly in the deepening twilight of a hot April, the Government of the United States began racing through the guarded gate. Then the people came to mass themselves against the great iron fence: A mass, that grew through the evening, of patient and pathetic people, curious citizens and spectators before history. Ed Stettinius, beautiful, rich young man, ran across Executive Avenue from the State Department where before him Cordell Hull had talked to Jap diplomats in the language which in Cordell Hull's Tennessee youth had been reserved for United States Revenue officers. All the Cabinet came, except Postmaster General Frank Walker, who had been caught by the news in Lynchburg, Virginia. Sam Rayburn, his bald head gleaming above his grim face, led Democratic Congressional leaders through the newspapermen who swarmed around the big mahogany table in the lobby of the Executive Offices. Minority Leader Joe Martin, a Republican partisan as implacable as any of the Democrats, hurried across Lafayette Square from his apartment in the hotel built where that other Massachusetts man, pessimistic old Henry Adams, had watched democracy with an erudite fastidiousness. Senators arrived. The Chief Justice of the United States came, and Bob Hannegan, the moon-faced Irishman who had risen from the precincts of St. Louis to national chairmanship of the party in power. Harry Truman walked slowly along the covered back gallery by the rose garden from the White House residence to its offices to meet them. In the long Cabinet Room he looked like a little man as he sat waiting in a huge leather chair. Mrs. Truman was late in arriving.

The government waited, for the government had come in the personages described by the Constitution, in its human pieces and checks and balances and powers—as human as the men in Philadelphia who had designed their functions. They were the men of Lincoln's central imperative preposition—the "by" people of democracy.

Chief Justice Stone wore no robe of judicial sanctity. He was an aging, kind-eyed man in a blue serge suit—the sort of suit professors get chalk on and which scholars wear bright at the elbows and the seat. Somehow, Truman waiting was still "Harry," whose room on the seventeenth floor at the Stevens in Chicago the summer before had been so full of sweaty well-wishers. He wore his solemnity and his affability together. All around the room, the Congress of the United States was a collection of people, shocked, puzzled, a little wary, and as precise as well-trained children in the proprieties of the hour. The Executive Branch stood about the room or sat in the big chairs as the men most hurt and most uncertain in change. There was an uneasy feeling of an era ending and of careers interrupted. There was an eager feeling present, too, concealed but tangible. The clock under Woodrow Wilson was speaking of the future.

Here was change. No American feared any tumult such as might elsewhere attend such change. But in it men wore masks as solemn as the Constitution itself. The heartbroken were self-contained. So were those whose hearts quickened. The masks were worn—but the masks were off, too. There was time for the proprieties but not for prolonged pretenses. Men moved in unconscious nakedness which showed in the tone of voice they used in speaking to the little man who was to be Bigness so soon. A certain sleekness slipped into the words addressed to him by attendants and some statesmen. There was real grief, there was also patriotism, shrewdness, understanding of power and a wonder about its directions. There was order and dignity. Here, also, was the whole human struggle of a nation. Here were States' Rights, the division of powers, the hope and push of the Right and the Left. Here were the insistent contending American regions, the conflict of minority rights and majority rule, little ambitions and big questions, privilege and politics. Around the little man in the chair were the same forces that have been shaping America around the written document from the beginning.

Mrs. Truman came in, sad and a little frightened. The Government of the United States arrayed itself in an arc of faces across the end of the room. Before it the Chief Justice repeated the great oath. In his flat Missouri voice the President responded from a little sheet of paper. America spoke its greatest man-pledge under the glare of lights and the clicking of cameras. There were more newspapermen and photographers than officials there. They sprawled over the Cabinet table. They quarreled almost automatically among themselves. And the President took the oath a second time, not for greater certainty but for more pictures.

He was not Harry Truman any longer; he never would be again. The prison of the Presidency dropped around him. The Secret Service scurried beside him as he moved. The personages shook his hand and fell away. The President of the United States walked down the hall to the big lobby past the wide mahogany table. His car had turned into a procession which roared him out to his Connecticut Avenue apartment where he ate a roast beef sandwich in a neighbor's flat. Behind him the big reception clerk spoke an old day's-end speech above the noises of the lobby: "The President has left his office."

He spoke transition.

It was not easy then to see what transition was. There had been no such transition in America in great crisis since Lincoln died and Andrew Johnson took the oath in the parlors of Kirkwood's Hotel. In an April, too, Johnson swore to defend the Constitution in a future which was to be filled with the furies of the American struggle through anger and aspiration, corruption and partisanship toward the American destiny. Nobody could count the similarities and differences between the futures beyond 1865 and 1945. Times, not men, had changed: Johnson was a tailor until he was thirty-four; Truman was a haberdasher when he was thirty-eight. Haberdasher and tailor together could perhaps have counted the change in costume and appearance. There was not a beard in the Cabinet Room when Truman took his oath. But the same tempestuous, teeming, determined America was around it.

It was the same oath. Chief Justice Stone repeated it in the lobby to the swarm of newspapermen.

He smiled: "It is a good one if you live up to it."

And it is a good Constitution. It is no mere document. It is certainly not the mere body of the determinations of men in the past. It is the strange informal and inflexible, solemn and irreverent, ruthless and sentimental system by which we live as a people together. We know that our politicians are the damnedest set of men on earth—and that together they make the greatest government in the world. Much of it the Founding Fathers would not recognize. Some citizens and foreign visitors do not like it—and may get a false notion that many of us don't like it either. We ourselves cuss it, cherish it, cheat it, and argue about it. We shall probably do so eternally and certainly as long as we do we shall be what men have always meant when—hesitating, in observation, between dismay and admiration—they have called us Americans.

The people standing quiet in the street before the White House that April night understood that. The President was dead, and they stood in sorrow; the President drove past them into the night, and they saluted him in loyalty. They waited in grief, without fear. There was nothing strange about the future; they had faced it before. It would be America; they are it.

SCOTT HART

There Is No Armor Against Fate

Washington at War (1970)

Maybe it's the reportorial instinct in me, but I do like to read about the w's—the who, what, when, where, and why of it. For me, there is a great deal of historical value in reading some piece of journalism that just gives us information we want and need, whether it's about a time that mattered, a place where something happened, or a person who counted.

I especially like this piece of reporting about a day that I remember with great sadness. It was all too incredible that the president could be dead. I was one of the throng who had gone downtown to see the funeral procession that brought the president's casket from the train to the White House. I was nearly nine months' pregnant at the time, and my husband was in the Philippines, fighting a Pacific war that promised to go on no matter what happened in Europe. Like everyone who surrounded me, I was full of emotion, standing there watching the casket pass. My son Don was born eight days later.

THERE was nothing normal about Washington on the morning of April 14 except the first gropings of the flowers and the pale featherings of the trees in a bright but humid day. Stores, showplaces, and government offices were closed. Twenty-six hotels announced through their Association that dancing and other diversions would be discontinued until Monday. Church and synagogue doors were open and people came in to pray and meditate. The National Theater canceled two performances of the Maurice Schwartz play *Three Generations*. A reminder hung upon the day: On another April 14, President Lincoln—the first of three great war Presidents—had been fatally struck down. The capital suddenly now was without song or love or laughter.

The people stood five deep on the sidewalks between Union Station and the White House. There was a brief flurry when a woman fainted in the crush or under the worst part of it all—the nerve-wracking silence.

The special train arrived at Union Station at 9:50 a.m. As the mile-long procession moved westward from the station the crowds turned, staring. But the soldiers lining the avenue with bayoneted rifles didn't flinch. A faint breeze came from nowhere and rippled the flags at half-staff on the buildings. The world seemed in motion again, whirled along in the furious roar from the skies of Flying Fortresses and Liberator bombers. The Marine Band played, and to a *Washington Star* reporter, the music "was almost unbearable in its solemn tones." The roar of the planes faded into the distance, but the sounds of sobbing could be heard, near and sometimes loud. There was an almost uniform gesture along the line as the people passed: people put their hands to their faces, pressed their faces for a moment, and then released their hands.

The band played Teckham's "Our Fallen Heroes," the "Marche Pathétique," and "Our Illustrious Dead." Behind it marched in dress uniform 680 midshipmen of the 3rd Battalion of the United States Naval Academy. The beating of drums was heard, and the pounding of feet. Reconnaissance cars moved four abreast, each bearing eight helmeted soldiers. Armored cars passed, and machine guns poked upward.

The flag-draped coffin on the black caisson moved slowly behind the six white horses, flanked by an honor guard. The crowd tried to move with it. The procession went on. The Navy Band led four companies of marines, four companies of sailors, and companies of WAACs, WAVES, and the women of the other services. The automobiles bearing the family and President Truman and Cabinet and diplomatic officials passed by. Far along, the Washington Monument reached high into the April blue, but nobody looked at it.

The procession turned toward 15th Street within sight of the White House, and there the crowd was dense and quiet. For a full half hour two British army officers had stood beside the Treasury Building without saying a word to each other. When the caisson rolled by they stiffened in salute. Their eyes followed the caisson for a while and their hands snapped down. Without a word they moved along with the crowd.

The crowd of mourners—estimated at 400,000—was densest in the vicinity of Lafayette Park. They were men and women and servicemen and servicewomen and infants held on people's shoulders. Some looked for a while at an old Negro woman sitting on the sidewalk and crying, "Oh. He's gone. He's gone forever. I loved him so. He's never coming back."

The caisson made a crackling sound when it rolled into the White House drive. The coffin was carried in. The white horses and the caisson stood before the door, and the crowd peered from the park. The day was so quiet now that the smallest birds could be heard. The sun had become hot, but its heat was overlooked in the hour of drums and death.

IN THE East Room, the casket was centered upon a small Oriental rug. A wall of flowers brightened the gun-metal gray bronze coffin. The scent of the flowers was heavy in the room and the lighting from the three chandeliers was dim. But the lighting illuminated the gold of two hundred straight-back gold-colored chairs. In front of these and in the center were a dozen chairs upholstered in green brocade. These were for the family.

Mrs. Roosevelt entered the room and everyone stood; President Truman entered and everyone kept his seat. (Observers of this action did not believe that any discourtesy was intended; the mourners were preoccupied.) Harry Hopkins, who had arrived from the Mayo Clinic in Minnesota, was as pale as death himself. The service, conducted by Bishop Angus Dun of the Episcopal Diocese of Washington, was simple and lasted 23 minutes. At the start the mourners stood and sang "The Eternal Father," the Navy hymn. At the close they sang "Faith of Our Fathers." The diplomats and the others left to go about their business affairs, to be conducted now under an untried man. But the Washington people kept their vigil across the Avenue.

The people meant to honor Roosevelt to the last. That night when the body was conveyed back to Union Station, a crowd of some 200,000 packed 15th Street and Constitution Avenue, and the Station Plaza. While the Army Air Force Band played "The Star Spangled Banner," the casket was placed at 9:47 p.m. aboard the last car of the seventeen-car train. A short while later, a light, warm rain began falling. Charles Harrison, forty-nine, the porter on the car that bore the body to Hyde Park, said, after a moment of thought: "This is the greatest honor of my life, although it's a very sad thing."

"FDR (and Me)"

Margaret Truman, editor, *Where the Buck Stops* (1989)

Here is Truman himself—plain speaking, as it were—telling about Roosevelt's end and his own beginning in the presidency. This piece reinforces the idea that it wasn't just the rest of us who were worried about this unknown man. In many ways, Truman himself was worried—in fact, just plain scared. It was widely reported that he told journalists the very day after he became president: "Last night the weight of the moon and stars fell upon me. If you fellows ever pray, pray for me."

AND THEN all at once, on that terrible spring day in 1945, Franklin Roosevelt wasn't with us any longer. He was in Warm Springs, Georgia, planning to remain there for a three-week vacation, and the day was particularly relaxed. Franklin was working on a speech, an artist named Elizabeth Shoumatoff was looking over at him and working on his portrait, and his cousin Margaret Suckley was sitting and crocheting. Then suddenly the President said, "I have a terrific headache," and lapsed into unconsciousness, and at 4:35 p.m. he was dead of a cerebral hemorrhage. The words he'd written before that were both memorable and typical of his thinking: "The only limit to our realization of tomorrow will be our doubts of today. Let us move forward, with strong and active faith." It was a simple restatement of his famous philosophy: "The only thing we have to fear is fear itself."

And then, just as suddenly, I was president of the United States.

Sam Rayburn, the Speaker of the House, had asked me to come over to his Capitol office that afternoon and discuss some bills on which the Senate and the House weren't seeing eye to eye, and when I got there, Sam was sitting and talking with two other men, Jim Barnes, a White House legislative assistant, and Lew Deschler, the House parliamentarian. Sam started to mix us some drinks, and then mentioned, almost as an afterthought, that Steve Early, the President's press secretary, had called and asked that I call him as soon as I got there. Sam obviously didn't think it was anything important, and neither did I, but I returned the call, of course. And Steve told me, "Please come over here"—to the White House, that is—"as quickly and quietly as you can."

I went over immediately, stopping only to get my hat and tell one of my secretaries where I was going, and I walked out to my car and driver so quickly that the Secret Service didn't know where I was and spent some frenzied minutes catching up with me. But I still didn't have the faintest guess of what had happened. And I wrote to my mother and to my sister, Mary, a few days later, "I thought that the President had come to Washington to attend the funeral of the Episcopal Bishop Atwood, for whom he was an honorary pallbearer, and who was his good friend. I thought that possibly he wanted me to do some special liaison work with the Congress. . . ." Then I was taken up to Eleanor Roosevelt's study on the second floor of the White House, where she was with Steve Early, her daughter Anna, and Anna's husband, John Boettiger. And then I knew, from the look on their faces, what had happened even before Eleanor put her hand on my shoulder and said, "Harry, the President is dead." And when I asked her, "Is there anything I can do for you?" her answer was, "Is there anything we can do for you? You're the one in trouble now."

Just the day before, I'd joked about being the vice president when I addressed a group of newspapermen covering the Senate. One of them called me Mr. Vice President and I said, "Smile when you say that," and I told them that the Senate was the greatest place in the world and that I wished I was still a senator. "I was getting along fine," I said, "until I stuck my neck out too far and got too famous. And then they made me VP and now I can't do anything." But now I wasn't the vice president any longer, and there was plenty to do.

I won't deny that, at first, I felt plenty of fear myself at the added and overwhelming responsibilities that had come to me so suddenly. I tried to deal with it lightly, telling Mrs. Truman that I thought I'd make a good president because Abraham Lincoln and I had so much in common. And when she looked hard at me, probably wondering if I was turning pompous in my old age, I told her that I wasn't comparing myself to Lincoln in terms of intelligence or administrative ability or anything really significant like that. But at least, I said, Lincoln and I had three other things in common.

First of all, I said, Lincoln and I were alike in that we both didn't like to hunt and didn't like to fish. He didn't like to kill anything, and I didn't like to kill anything, either. Second, I said, I think Lincoln and I both had a sense of humor; and, I told Mrs. Truman, a sense of humor is a tremendous help to any man in a position of authority. Because when a stuffed shirt tries to tell a man in a place of responsibility what he ought to do, the best way to settle the argument with him is to stick a pin in him and let the wind out—and if you have a sense of humor, you'll have a good time doing it. And third, Lincoln and I both went broke in business. Lincoln's partner went broke in business, and Lincoln ended up owing eleven hundred dollars. Lincoln also didn't mind the store because he was always lying behind the notions counter reading newspapers and books to keep himself informed. Well, my old partner, Eddie Jacobson, says that when our business was going broke, customers would come in all right but I was always in a corner reading about Andrew Jackson. I'll admit that I've probably read more about Jackson than anyone else in the country. It took us a long time to pay off our creditors too. It was 1935 before they were all settled and taken care of. . . .

. . . So now there I was, at 7:09 p.m. on the evening of April 12, 1945, as Chief Justice Harlan Fiske Stone swore me in as president of the United States in the Cabinet Room at the White House, underneath a portrait of Woodrow Wilson. And as I've already admitted, I was plenty scared. But scared or not, and prepared or not, I promised myself one thing that evening, and in the days and nights that followed: that I'd work damn hard and try damn hard to be a good president.

I think most people will give me that much: that I tried hard to be a good president. And I hope that some people, at least, will feel that I succeeded.

EMMET JOHN HUGHES

A Word of Introduction

The Ordeal of Power: A Political Memoir of the Eisenhower Years (1963)

Emmet Hughes was a friend of ours. I think Phil and I first got to know him on more than a passing basis early in 1962, and by the end of that year, Phil had hired him as an "editorial adviser," to help with The Washington Post–Los Angeles Times News Service, which had just taken wing, and to write a weekly column for Newsweek. *In those first years after Phil's death, Emmet helped me enormously, especially in crafting speeches that I felt paralyzed about making.*

Emmet had been a journalist and certainly was one of the New Deal generation, fired by, as he wrote, "the lasting force of the memory of Franklin Roosevelt," as well as having been affected by the issues of the 1930s that had so churned up passions in politics. Like Phil, he had been of a Democratic mind until 1952 but had turned to Dwight Eisenhower as the best candidate for the presidency that year. Certainly, Phil and my father had both backed Eisenhower, Phil putting the force of the Post *behind the general to such an extent that he had a real conflict with Herblock and had his cartoons dropped from the paper for the last weeks of the campaign.*

Hughes first met Eisenhower in September 1952, just before his election, when he went to work for Eisenhower's campaign staff, writing speeches and papers. He then went with him to the White House, to help with getting things started. From time to time throughout the first seven years of the Eisenhower administration, he went back to help out in one way or another. Only when a book Hughes wrote, America the Vincible, *appeared in 1959, criticizing the drift of the nation's foreign policy, did they fall out.*

The Ordeal of Power is in itself a kind of period piece, a look at the 1950s and the man who dominated most of the decade. I liked it long ago when I first read it, and I liked rereading it. I was moved when I opened my copy of the book and was reminded of a whole era with Emmet's inscription in the front: "For Phil—a friend of courage, a seeker of truth, and a comrade in the arena."

To BEGIN at the end . . .

The end came in Washington, D.C., in the numbing cold of late morning, on Inauguration Day, Friday, January 20, 1961. Just before eleven-thirty, President Dwight David Eisenhower and President-elect John Fitzgerald Kennedy strode down the broad front steps of the White House, climbed into the black limousine awaiting them, and began their ceremonial journey together along Pennsylvania Avenue to Capitol Hill. Vice Presidents, wives, and Secret Service followed in solemn, poised attendance. Tens of thousands along the route shivered in the icy wind, but they warmly waved and breathed great gray puffs of cheer into the frosty air. And yet, as the two men sat back and stretched their legs—the older man seated on the honored right for the last time—they both were, seriously and inescapably, quite alone in the world. Probably, each was alone with his own sober thoughts and tense emotions. Certainly, both were alone in their silently shared knowledge of the awesome power and the poignant isolation—the matchless hopes and hazards—of the office that would pass in a few moments from the one to the other.

The scene and the encounter were arresting. Beside the President who, at the age of seventy, had become the oldest Chief Executive in American history, there sat the man who, at forty-three, was the youngest ever elected to the office. He was the first, too, born of his particular religious faith, as well as the first born in this particularly tempestuous century. The lives of both were renowned—their words and acts, their countenances and gestures, already long familiar to millions. In the sight and thought of the nation, therefore, they were logically, almost intimately linked. Yet they were not at all known to each other. Until a few weeks before, they had barely met or spoken.

Behind this meeting, of course, lay an encounter of quite a different kind: the conflict of ideas and of parties that had been the 1960 National Election. The younger man had accused the older one, by sharp word or broad insinuation, of many lacks and failures—above all, of letting the political conscience of his country slumber, leaving the people to blink and gape at the surge of crisis in all the world of free men. The older man, drawn into a fray he would have shunned, had turned scorn on the young critic, chastising him for a poverty of experience and a wealth of misinformation. For all its stridence, the clatter of words occasionally had given true sign of their serious clash of views upon the standing of the nation and the state of the world, the role of government and the duty of a President, the strength of American arms and the force of American convictions. And back of this conflict lay the eight years of the older man's regime, with all those years' historic events and symbols:

Camp David and Little Rock, riots in Berlin in 1953 and riots in Tokyo in 1960, summits and Sputniks, Korea and Lebanon, Cuba and the Congo, "open skies" and offshore islands, hope at Geneva in 1955 and humiliation at Paris in 1960, spectacular presidential missions to distant lands and faltering missile-flights to outer space, the cheering millions of the Far East, the sneering mobs of Lath America, the whine of British bombers over Egypt, the crash of an American plane on a mission of espionage deep within Soviet frontiers.

Did the two men speak of such things this day, as they rode slowly toward the Capitol? No. It was a more quiet, resigned time. Bracing for the cold, they had just sipped coffee together at the White House. The President had decided to honor the occasion by the precedent of donning a top hat, and the young President-elect had laughed appreciatively when Mrs. Eisenhower had said gaily to her husband: "Till seeing you in that, I never noticed how much an Irishman you look!" Now—alone— they chatted easily, and the older man set the subject. He groped back beyond memories of the days when he twice had taken his own oath of office, back to the past beyond all his life in the presidency. He returned, in thought and speech, to the time of World War II, when he had been Commander of all Allied armies in Europe, while his youthful companion had been a courageous but obscure PT-boat officer in the distant arena of the Pacific waters. Their political views of the world of today seemed almost as remote from each other as then were their military assignments. And as their limousine rolled on, the President murmured his reminiscences of the Allied invasion of Normandy in 1944. The historic amphibious operation across the English Channel, he recalled, had been greatly aided by an element of surprise that had turned on so seemingly minor a matter as accuracy of weather forecast: the Allied prognosticator had caught glimpses of a little spell of calm weather, benignly moving in from the Atlantic, that had wholly eluded the German watcher of the winds.

A rapt eavesdropper might well have wondered: was it suggestive or significant that the man should fill these particular moments, near the instant of surrendering the presidency, with remembrances of so distant and so different a scene? Were these memories more consoling or more assuring than those of years more recent? Perhaps all the talk meant no more than an agreeable wish to find bland conversational matter to fill the void of this ceremonial hour. Or—could it have been prompted by some vague but troubling awareness that the tricks of human fortune, ruling lives and decreeing history, had lately been much less kind than the Atlantic winds and the Channel water of that unforgotten late spring day? . . .

Only a few moments later, President Kennedy, his oath of office taken, delivered a stirring Inaugural Address. All the while, ex-President Eisenhower watched and listened. He seemed grave, attentive, and approving. Quite clearly, he liked the words: "Let every nation know, whether it wishes us well or ill, that we shall pay any price, bear any burden, meet any hardship, support any friend, oppose any foe to assure the survival and success of liberty." He may have noted, even pondering somewhat the worth of words, that he himself had said much the same thing on precisely the same occasion in 1956—and earlier too, in 1952, a full eight years past. But now, with this Inauguration: "Let the word go forth from this time and place, to friend and foe alike, that the torch has been passed to a new generation of Americans."

But the young man, through the august ceremonies, had been watching the older man, too. For he found something at which to marvel a little. He explained the matter, late that night, when all the rituals of Inauguration were done, and he found himself sitting quietly with a few friends, recalling what had so forcibly struck him. "The vitality of the man!" he exclaimed. "It stood out so strongly, there at the Inauguration. There was Chris Herter, looking old and ashen. There was Allen Dulles, gray and tired. There was Bob Anderson, with his collar seeming two sizes too large on a shrunken neck. And there was the oldest of them all, Ike—as healthy and ruddy and as vital as ever. Fantastic!" . . .

The young President voiced his wonder, at day's end, in the living room of a gracious house in Georgetown. The hour had been past 2 a.m. when he had startled his friends by knocking on the door and entering, as naturally as a neighbor, to find relaxation in some amiable, aimless conversation to close his unforgettable day. Trim and buoyant and festive in his tuxedo, still a little excited in voice, he sat slowly sipping a glass of champagne, his left ankle casually thrown over his right knee but moving restlessly and rhythmically—the only physical sign of the inner tension he hoped to ease a bit, far from official throng and duty, before retiring for his first night of sleep in the White House. But his reminiscences did not go back beyond the recent political campaign. All the stir of Inauguration itself had done nothing to upset the cool detachment of his view of that contest—or of his own political self. Candidly, he assessed his election as "a miracle." Professionally, he marveled at the seeming folly of his Republican antagonists. With uncompromising realism, the man who had become President of the United States less than fifteen hours earlier calmly insisted that he could have been routed by a stronger opponent.

He had more to say of Eisenhower, however, and the subject plainly fascinated him. He acknowledged having been impressed by the older man, more than he had expected, in their few talks between Election and

Inauguration: "He was better than I had been prepared for. . . . Takes a simplified view of most things, but . . . better than I had thought." Yet what deeply excited his attention was the personal drama of his predecessor's so sudden departure, now, to private life. "What a transformation, what an adjustment it must be! Just to go off like that by himself . . . President this morning—and now . . ." Thrice he came back to this reflection, as if it nagged and troubled him. And suddenly one sensed the obvious: the young President was thinking less of Eisenhower on this day than of himself, on the same day four years or eight years hence, facing the extraordinary experience of becoming a former President—at the age of forty-seven or fifty-one.

The older man, by this hour of this night, was far from the official scene. The Inaugural formalities completed, he had attended the modest retirement ceremony of a luncheon with his Vice President and some of their close colleagues and wives. Then he had left Washington by car. There had been no grand official cavalcade. He had been escorted only by his family and a token Secret Service detail, soon to leave him altogether and abruptly to his privacy. And in the frosty, fading sunlight of this late January afternoon, he had reached his farm at Gettysburg.

There, for as long as he lived, he would be listening with interest—with a sharply questioning glint in the bright blue eyes, a serious set to the strong mouth, a deep grimace or a swift smile—as various voices swelled the slow-rising chorus that, some day, would speak the judgment of history upon what he had done and what he had left undone.

PHILIP HAMBURGER

White Tie

The New Yorker (1961)

There really was nothing like it. The Kennedy inaugural dazzled in ways unexperienced before. Phil and I had been planning a huge reception, to which both President-elect Kennedy and Vice President–elect Johnson were to come, but the paralyzing icy blizzard that hit Washington that day prevented them and most of the six hundred invited guests from getting to our house. It was terribly disappointing, but the two hundred or so who did manage to get through, mostly by walking, ended up staying for hours—not what we had in mind, but full of fun of a different sort.

Despite the snowstorm, these inaugural days in January 1961 had a glamour all their own. Our friend Bill Walton, who was a longtime friend of the Kennedys and had been intensely involved with planning the inaugural activities, was scheduled to be with Jack and Jackie Kennedy on the evening of the galas, the night before the inauguration. The Secret Service called him at about eight p.m. to say that they would not be able to come by for him, but that they would wait if he could make his way to the Kennedys' N Street house. Bill was in his evening clothes but put on a pair of boots and raced over there on foot from his own Georgetown house.

When he arrived, the Kennedys were just coming out, so Bill threw off his boots and hopped into the limousine for the ride to the DAR building for a concert, to which most of the musicians were late or never arrived. When the soon-to-be-presidential party left there, they were driven across the Mall to the next gala event. Bill recalled the scene for me many years later: "We were driving through the snow-covered streets, and I think it was the most beautiful thing I've ever seen. The snow was coming down in ribbons that you could see in the lights of the Washington Monument. People whose cars had been stuck were out and had made bonfires all up and down. It was the most dramatic and beautiful scene."

And then Jack Kennedy turned and looked at Jackie in her tiara and white satin dress, and said to Bill, "Oh, look, look at her. She looks so beautiful. Let's turn the lights on so at least they can see her." And the lights of the soon-to-be president's limousine were turned on so that the people standing along the roadways could see inside the car.

Bill also told me that as they drove along with the car lit up, Kennedy started reading the program that had been on their seats at the previous gala, which included Thomas Jefferson's inaugural address. He got to the end, turned to Jackie and Bill and said, "So much better than mine."

O UR MAN Stanley blew into the office the other day wearing a rented topper and the cool, detached expression of a man who has seen history in the making. "Jacqueline is yummy," he said cryptically, and deposited the following dispatch:

"Have been to Inaugural Ball, in Washington. 'Ben-Hur' intimate, cozy affair by comparison. Was house guest of friends in Georgetown, block or so from President's former home, mile or so from President's new home. Heart of things. Earlier, had spent several frigid, numbing hours on snow-swept Capitol Hill, watching swearing-in ceremonies. Moving, impressive beyond measure, but lost contact with seven toes. Returned to Georgetown, lay down under heavy blanket, concentrated on reestablishing liaison with missing toes. When all ten toes present and accounted for, rose and dressed for small private dinner with host and hostess, several guests, and my companion, a rose-beige job with close-fitting bodice and velvet trim. Ran into snag with wing collar. Wing collar a little devil. At dinnertime, entered drawing room wearing tailcoat. Ladies in party glittering in sequins and satins, gloves drawn up to shoulder blades; men elegant, distinguished, filled with muted national gaiety. Small talk. 'Remarkable speech,' 'New national purpose,' 'Rededication,' 'Don't forget your tickets,' and so on. Gobbled dinner, donned overcoat and white silk scarf, patted topper into position, and climbed into limousine for long drive to National Guard Armory. Armory miles away, on other side of town, through glazed streets. Passed Lincoln Memorial, ablaze; Washington Monument, ablaze; White House whiter than white, ablaze; and bright dome of Capitol, ablaze. Snow piled everywhere. Skiddy, brilliant night.

"Armory ablaze, too, from huge spotlights. Long parallel lines of cars drawing up to green canopies stretching from Armory to street. Arrived as Russian Ambassador stepped out of his. Moment of peaceful coexistence. 'Slushy, I said, 'but probably more like a spring night to you, with your long winters.' Ambassador noncommittal. Trained diplomat. Smiled, said nothing. Too soon to begin negotiations anyway. Handed ticket to man at door, walked onto vast Armory floor—stunning orange-and-tan drapes hanging from ceiling, floor sanded, great golden bandstand along one side, long box on other side embellished with royal-blue drapes and with seal of the President and the Vice-President. Handed ticket stub to Ruritanian general, who summoned West Point cadet—from long line of cadets and midshipmen—who graciously stepped forward, offered arm to my companion, escorted her to box. I walked alone. Box a sort of stall, containing camp chairs, tray with empty glasses, and empty ice container wrapped in silver foil. Shook off cadet and asked companion for a twirl. Still room to twirl. Meyer Davis orchestra playing. We twirled, exchanging discreet national gaieties. Presidential box still empty, except for Senator Dirksen, alone in rear seat, wearing ruminative smile. I headed, with companion, for frigid refreshment tent at east end of Armory. Refreshment tent offering domestic champagne in paper cups, various colas, orange pop, slices of fruitcake. Ate slice of fruitcake, hurried back to warmth of Armory. Armory now taking on aspect of mob scene. Meyer Davis, on revolving bandstand, revolved. Count Basie orchestra swung into view. Basie in full swing. Raised temperature in Armory fifteen degrees. Not much room to dance. Estimated fifteen thousand now in Armory. Passed block-long confectioner's display, surmounted by cake of White House. White House cake almost as big as White House, decorated along side of base with red sugar roses. 'Please don't nibble the cake!' short man standing alongside cake cried out. 'We want to keep it looking beautiful for when the President arrives.' Man said that Local 51 of Cake Bakers Union had baked cake and made twenty-five thousand slices in addition, for this and the four other Inaugural Balls that were going on simultaneously. Struggled over to post beneath Presidential box. Boxes on each side filling up—friends of the President, aides-de-camp, admirals, generals, politicians, cousins. Swish of taffeta almost drowned out Count Basie. Flurry of excitement in presidential box. Mr. and Mrs. Joseph P. Kennedy arrived, headed for seats in front row center. Mrs. Kennedy in sequined white. 'Molyneux,' whispered my companion. Joseph Kennedy removed overcoat. Also inadvertently removed tailcoat. For few moments, President's father, high in box, in shirtsleeves. Instantly rescued by Mrs. Kennedy, other ladies, restored to paternal elegance. Several regiments of uniformed men cleared center aisle between bandstand and Presidential box, pushing throngs on each side behind white ropes. Count Basie disappeared, Meyer Davis reappeared.

"Crush overwhelming. Now impossible to twirl. Pretty lady in front of me fainted dead away, was carried off by two sailors. Future admirals, those chaps, friendly, quick to perform duty. Mounting excitement in Presidential box. Vice-President and Mrs. Johnson arrived with Lynda Bird (in white), Lucy Baines (in blue). Lady Bird in pink. Greeted crowds warmly. Mrs. Johnson spotted friends, gave short, fluttering greetings, tugged at Vice-President's sleeve. Nice family. Suddenly, fanfare from band, intake of breath from crowd. Into box stepped First Lady, a vision, poised, regal, with melting, restrained smile. 'Sheath of *peau d'ange*,' whispered my companion. 'Overblouse of white chiffon. Silver-embroidered bodice. Long white gloves. Hair bouffant, but not too bouffant.' 'Golly Ned,' I said. Band played 'Hail to the Chief.' The Chief arrived, tanned, confident, controlled, swift-moving, happy. Bet he had no trouble with his collar! Box suddenly filled with Kennedys—sisters, brothers, brothers-in-law, sisters-in-law. Vigorous, athletic faces aglow. President and Mrs. Kennedy stared at packed mass below, packed mass below stared at the Kennedys. Inaugural Ball had now become Inaugural Viewing. Crowd cheered and cheered again, fluttered handkerchiefs. President and his wife smiled, waved. Dignified smiles, dignified waves. President on top of world, but his waves were Presidential waves, restrained, powerful. Great musical fanfare as Cabinet, led by Mr. and Mrs. Stanley Woodward (Mr. Woodward co-chairman of Ball), walked in brisk line down center aisle and passed in review under Presidential box and out into the night. Orchestra played new, specially written song entitled 'Jacqueline' ('Jacqueline, Jacqueline, Jacqueline, she is charming, she is sweet') and one entitled 'Lady Bird' ('I keep my eyes on the skies with my dreams about Lady Bird'). Jacqueline and Lady Bird smiled politely. President got up, moved around restlessly, and shook hands all over box. Mr. and Mrs. Joseph Kennedy sat down beside Jacqueline and chatted with her. Medley of Texas songs brought Johnsons to their feet, waving; medley of Irish songs revealed gleaming teeth of Kennedy family. Couldn't take my eyes off Jacqueline. Couldn't move even if I had wanted to. She chatted with Johnsons, smiled her detached smile. She looked around once or twice at President, who was still in motion. I spied Hugh Gaitskell, Hubert Humphrey, man from Local 51. More flour-ishes, and Presidential party suddenly departed—heading for more balls, and White House, and the long big years. Hail to the Chief!"

ARTHUR M. SCHLESINGER, JR.

The Drums of Washington

A Thousand Days (1965)

All too soon it was over. The thousand days of the Kennedy presidency passed too quickly. This was yet another ending for which none of us was prepared. Again, it was an ending that didn't happen in Washington—only the pageantry that followed in the next few days took place here. We were all so stricken that there was among our circle of friends a sense of paralysis.

This was just over three months after Phil's death, and I felt traumatized again and numbed in a different way. I wondered how it would ever be possible to find the right words to say to Jackie. At the time of Phil's death she had written me a letter that I still hold dear and that was such a comfort to me at the time. I could not imagine how she would begin to deal with her new life.

I've always been moved by Arthur's rendering of these sad days. As he wrote, and as I remember so well, "It all ended, as it began, in the cold."

O N FRIDAY morning I had flown to New York with Katharine Graham, whose husband Philip had died three months before, for a luncheon with the editors of her magazine *Newsweek*. Kenneth Galbraith had come down from Cambridge for the occasion. We were still sipping drinks before luncheon in an amiable mood of Friday-before-the-Harvard-Yale game relaxation when a young man in shirtsleeves entered the room and said, a little tentatively, "I am sorry to break in, but I think you should know that the President has been shot in the head in Texas." For a flash one thought this was some sort of ghastly office joke. Then we knew it could not be and huddled desperately around the nearest television. Everything was confused and appalling. The minutes dragged along. Incomprehensible bulletins came from the hospital. Suddenly an insane surge of conviction flowed through me: I felt that the man who had survived the Solomon Islands and so much illness and agony, who so loved life, embodied it, enhanced it, could not possibly die now. He would escape the shadow as he had before. Almost immediately we received the irrevocable word.

In a few moments Galbraith and I were on Katharine Graham's plane bound for Washington. It was the saddest journey of one's life. Bitterness, shame, anguish, disbelief, emptiness mingled inextricably in one's mind. When I stumbled, almost blindly, into the East Wing, the first person I encountered was Franklin D. Roosevelt, Jr. In a short time I went with my White House colleagues to Andrews Field to await the return of *Air Force One* from Texas. A small crowd was waiting in the dusk, McNamara, stunned and silent, Harriman, haggard and suddenly looking very old, desolation everywhere. We watched incredulously as the casket was carefully lifted out of the plane and taken to the Naval Hospital at Bethesda. Later I went to my house in Georgetown. My weeping daughter Christina said, "Daddy, what has happened to our country? If this is the kind of country we have, I don't want to live here any more." The older children were already on their way back from college to Washington.

Still later I went back to the White House to await the last return. Around four in the morning the casket, wrapped in a flag, was brought from the Naval Hospital and placed on a stand in the East Room. Tapers were lit around the bier, and a priest said a few words. Then Jacqueline approached the bier, knelt for a moment and buried her head in the flag. Soon she walked away. The rest of us waited for a little while in the great hall. We were beyond consolation, but we clung to the comradeship he had given us. Finally, just before daybreak, we bleakly dispersed into the mild night.

We did not grieve alone. Though in Dallas school children applauded the news and in Peking the *Daily Worker* ran a savage cartoon entitled "Kennedy Biting the Dust" showing the dead President lying in a pool of blood, his necktie marked with dollar signs, sorrow engulfed America and the world. At Harvard Yard the bells tolled in Memorial Church, a girl wept hysterically in Widener Library, a student slammed a tree, again and again, with his fist. Negroes mourned, and A. Philip Randolph said that his "place in history will be next to Abraham Lincoln." Pablo Casals mused that he had seen many great and terrible events in his lifetime—the Dreyfus case, the assassination of Gandhi—"but in recent history—and I am thinking of my own lifetime—there has never been a tragedy that has brought so much sadness and grief to as many people as this." "For a time we felt the country was ours," said Norman Mailer. "Now it's theirs again." Many were surprised by the intensity of the loss. Alistair Cooke spoke of "this sudden discovery that he was more familiar than we knew." "Is there some principle of nature," asked Richard Hofstadter, "which requires that we never know the quality of what we have had until it is gone?" Around the land people sat desperately in front of television sets watching the bitter drama of the next four days. In Washington Daniel Patrick Moynihan, the Assistant Secretary of Labor, said, "I don't think there's any point in being Irish if you don't know that the world is going to break your heart eventually. I guess that we thought we had a little more time. . . . Mary McGrory said to me that we'll never laugh again. And I said, 'Heavens, Mary. We'll laugh again. It's just that we'll never be young again.' " . . .

In Washington grief was an agony. Somehow the long hours passed, as the new President took over with firmness and strength but the roll of the drums, when we walked to St. Matthew's Cathedral on the frosty Monday, will sound forever in my ears, and the wildly twittering birds during the interment at Arlington while the statesmen of the world looked on. It was all so grotesque and so incredible. One remembered Stephen Spender's poem:

> *I think continually of those who were truly great. . . .*
> *The names of those who in their lives fought for life,*
> *Who wore at their hearts the fire's center.*
> *Born of the sun they traveled a short while towards the sun,*
> *And left the vivid air signed with their honour.*

It was all gone now—the life-affirming, life-enhancing zest, the brilliance, the wit, the cool commitment, the steady purpose. Richard Neustadt has suggested that two years are the period of presidential initiation. He had had so little time: it was as if Jackson had died before the nullification controversy and the Bank War, as if Lincoln had been killed six months after Gettysburg or Franklin Roosevelt at the end of 1935 or Truman before the Marshall Plan.

Yet he had accomplished so much: the new hope for peace on earth, the elimination of nuclear testing in the atmosphere and the abolition of nuclear diplomacy, the new policies toward Latin America and the third world, the reordering of American defense, the emancipation of the American Negro, the revolution in national economic policy, the concern for poverty, the stimulus to the arts, the fight for reason against extremism and mythology. Lifting us beyond our capacities, he gave his country back to its best self, wiping away the world's impression of an old nation of old men, weary, played out, fearful of ideas, change and the future; he taught mankind that the process of rediscovering America was not over. He re-established the republic as the first generation of our leaders saw it—young, brave, civilized, rational, gay, tough, questing, exultant in the excitement and potentiality of history. He transformed the American spirit—and the response of his people to his murder, the absence of intolerance and hatred, was a monument to his memory. The energies he released, the standards he set, the purposes he inspired, the goals he established would guide the land he loved for years to come. Above all he gave the world for an imperishable moment the vision of a leader who greatly understood the terror and the hope, the diversity and the possibility, of life on this planet and who made people look beyond nation and race to the future of humanity. So the people of the world grieved as if they had terribly lost their own leader, friend, brother.

On December 22, a month after his death, fire from the flame burning at his grave in Arlington was carried at dusk to the Lincoln Memorial. It was fiercely cold. Thousands stood, candles in their hands; then, as the flame spread among us, one candle lighting the next, the crowd gently moved away, the torches flaring and flickering, into the darkness. The next day it snowed—almost as deep a snow as the inaugural blizzard. I went to the White House. It was lovely, ghostly and strange.

It all ended, as it began, in the cold.

The Beginning

A Very Human President (1976)

In some ways, Jack Valenti probably knows this town as well as anyone. He was with Vice President Johnson in Dallas when LBJ became president. He flew into Washington on Air Force One in one of the most dramatic flights in history on that November day in 1963. At LBJ's request, he moved in with the Johnsons for the eleven days they stayed at their home, the Elms, while Jackie Kennedy remained in the White House. He then moved with them to the White House and lived on the third floor for another month before he was able to find a home in Washington for his wife of just one year, Mary Margaret, who had been Lyndon Johnson's assistant for nine years before their marriage.

In what is one of the most intimate memoirs of Lyndon Johnson and his presidency, Jack gives an insider's kind of personal and political picture of the man whom he served so faithfully. It was indeed a "strange turn of fate" that had brought him to this point, and that had, as he wrote, "tilted a nation, set into avalanche a train of events which no seer could have foretold. Just a few feet away a new president was in his bed, getting ready for his first day as the nation's leader. This was the beginning, and I was eager to join the morning as fast as it could come."

"GET IN the second chopper and come to my office as soon as you land. Understand?" Lyndon Johnson, just a few hours into his presidency, the thirty-sixth in a line that began with George Washington, cupped his hands against my ear to shield his words from the deafening roar of two presidential helicopters whirring impatiently in the night air of Andrews Air Force Base outside Washington, D.C.

Air Force One bearing the new president, and the body of the slain John F. Kennedy, had just landed after a flight from Dallas. It was a few minutes after 6:00 p.m., EST, Friday, November 22, 1963.

The trip of eighteen miles by chopper from Andrews to the White House took seven minutes. The memory of that first of many journeys from Andrews to the White House and back is still vivid in my mind. We skimmed low across a flickering chasm of illuminated homes and darting headlights ribboning their ways in dismantled design across Washington. I could have almost reached out and touched the slim tower of the Washington Monument as we passed. Then I saw the ground coming up to meet us. Across the Ellipse, we dropped quickly and then floated, suspended in the air, as the pilot maneuvered to touch the grassy opening at the South Grounds. (The helicopter landing pad at the White House is but a few short feet from the entrance to the Diplomatic Reception Room, the prime entering area of the south side of the White House.)

This was my first visit to the White House.

I had over the preceding years driven around the White House when I visited Washington. The line of tourists waiting to visit the public rooms was always so long I was never tempted to try it myself. One day, I thought, I will see if I can arrange some kind of special tour without waiting that interminable length of time. But I never got around to it.

Now I was truly going to get a special tour. . . .

The vice-presidential office was a three-room suite and within minutes it was crowded. The president ensconced himself in the large, high-ceilinged, fireplaced room, comfortably but not luxuriously furnished.

Shortly before 7:00 p.m., I escorted Senator J. William Fulbright, chairman of the Senate Foreign Relations Committee, and Ambassador Averell Harriman into the office.

I fidgeted outside, in the middle of what would have appeared to an objective onlooker to be a melange of confusion. No one of the Johnson aides—Marie Fehmer, his secretary; the late Cliff Carter, his chief political agent; Bill Moyers, nor any of the rest—was quite certain of what lay ahead. We were all busy on the phone and trying to assemble what measure of office discipline we could construct. Supervising it all was Walter Jenkins, the number one assistant to the president, a privileged post no one in the Johnson entourage contested, nor chose to. Jenkins, a mild and scholarly man, generous to his colleagues, full of integrity, endlessly at work, sat in the background and, as usual, was on the phone constantly with his notebook in front of him, transcribing conversations as he talked in that swift Gregg shorthand he knew so well.

A bit after 7:00 p.m., the president talked with former President Harry Truman, and at 7:10 he conversed over the phone with former President Dwight Eisenhower. Some moments later he was on the phone to Sargent Shriver, the slain president's brother-in-law.

At about 7:40 the congressional leadership came to call. They were ushered in. I sat quietly inside near the wall of the office, listening to the president importuning them for their help and their counsel.

Some moments after 8:00 p.m., LBJ sat at his desk to have some soup. It was his first food since his morning breakfast in Fort Worth.

At 9:27 p.m., the president came out of his office followed by Walter Jenkins and Cliff Carter. He smiled at Marie Fehmer and then he motioned for me to come to him. He put his arm around me and said, "Drive home with me, Jack. You can stay at my house tonight and then we will have a chance to do some talking. Are you ready to leave now?" Well, I thought, I suppose I am ready in view of the fact I was not quite sure precisely why I was even here in the first place.

I fell in beside the president and with Cliff Carter we marched down the hall of the Executive Office Building flanked in front and rear by Secret Service agents. We emerged onto the street separating the West Wing from the EOB and climbed into the big black limousine waiting for us, two Secret Service men in the front seat. The rest of the agents piled into another car in back and we headed toward the Elms, the large dwelling the Johnsons had purchased from Mrs. Perle Mesta.

When we arrived at the circular driveway at the entrance to the home it had all the appearance of a small convention. A security post had been set up at the driveway approach and a legion of agents was literally surrounding the house. When we stopped, agent Rufus Youngblood, the soft-talking southerner who had so courageously flung his body over LBJ's to protect him from whatever might be assaulting him, spoke: "Mr. President, we have not had time to really arrange phone communications here. For the time being, we are operating over your residence phones."

Youngblood also vouchsafed the totally unnecessary information that the phones were taking a helluva beating from the incoming calls. An emergency phone had been put in to take care of the Secret Service communications net and it would be several hours before the presidential communication system could be set up at the Elms. The president nodded, and climbed the step to his front door. He had left this home as one man and he was returning as very much another.

Mrs. Johnson embraced him warmly, kissing him and hugging him. The president said, "Bird, I would like a bite to eat and could you fix something for the rest?" Mrs. Johnson opened her arms as if to collectively embrace us. "Darling, we have food in the dining room. Come sit down and relax."

First, though, the president wanted to sit in the library. Mrs. Johnson brought him a large glass, chocked with ice and orange juice and the president sprawled in the massive black chair in the library. He sipped his orange juice and then abruptly, though easily and without apparent thought, lifted his glass to a picture of the late Speaker, Sam Rayburn, on the wall, the grim bulldog visage staring at us, the bald pate looming above the stern countenance.

"I salute you, Mr. Speaker, and how I wish you were here now, when I need you." The words were spoken softly. The president was obviously moved by the spark of that moment.

By this time the house was beginning to fill with Johnson people who came to see the new president. Horace Busby, the scholarly Texan who for years was the chief wordsmith for the president, gripped the edge of the president's chair and began to talk to him in low tones. Shortly, the president and all of us moved to the dining room where we ate the first full meal most of us had had in a long time.

The time sped by. About midnight, the president decided to go to bed. He beckoned to Cliff Carter, Moyers, and me and we climbed the stairs to the second-story bedrooms. "Bill," he said to Moyers and Carter, "you and Cliff find a bedroom on the third floor. Put your things up there and then come on down so we can talk." They headed to the third floor and the president took me by the arm. "You stay in this bedroom, Jack," he said. We went inside the bedroom. He sat down on a chair near the doorway.

"I suggest you call Mary Margaret and get some clothes sent up here for you. I also think you ought to get your affairs in order in Houston so you can dispose of your business. I want you to be on my staff at the White House. You can live with me here and at the White House when we finally move there. Meanwhile, you can look for a house so that Mary Margaret and Courtenay can join you." (Indeed, I did live at the White House, occupying a two-room suite on the third floor of the mansion from December 7, 1963, until February 15, 1964, when my family arrived to take up residence in Georgetown. The Johnsons waited fourteen days before moving into the presidential living quarters at the White House.)

That was the way it was. I hesitated a bare moment. I was not certain how to respond. In truth, I had no response. The president had clearly thought this through and he was not giving me any alternative, even if I chose to explore one.

The president rose and I followed him to his bedroom at the end of the hall. He got into his pajamas and lay on the vast bed, triggering the television set into life by remote control. He sat half-upright on the left side of the bed and motioned me to a chair at his side. We watched now the unfolding drama on the TV set, the endlessly probing eye of the camera and narrator's voice recounting just who Lyndon Johnson was, his background, his career, and there were speculative accounts by various commentators on how fit a president he would be.

By this time Moyers and Carter had come in, Carter sitting at the foot of the bed and Moyers sitting on the right side. We watched in silence for some time.

I had picked up a notepad and was doodling when the president began to speak, almost as if he were talking to himself. He mused about what he ought to do and began to tick off people he needed to see and meetings he should construct in the next several days. I scribbled down the essence of what he was saying so I would have a clear view of what he wanted, so it could be done without fret or delay. Within an hour I had scrawled over thirty pages of that notebook. It became my direction-finder the next several days as all that the president had described was put into concrete action.

That night the president had what might be called his first staff meeting. Bill Moyers, Cliff Carter, and I listened more than we talked.

The president seemed relaxed, stretched out on the bed, watching the bright glow of the TV set. He was surrounded by men whom he trusted, and in whose persons he fully knew reposed love and respect and enduring loyalty to him. Here in this bedroom was the man the whole world was inspecting via television, and whose measure was being taken in every chancellery in every capital in every country on all continents. He had spent over thirty years in the political arena. He knew all the tremors and soft spots and the unknowns that infested every cranny of the political jungle. He could catalogue a thousand good and bad qualities, achievements, as well as errors made visible by those national leaders whom he knew.

He was mindful of what lay ahead of him, this was evident. There was not what one would call eagerness to greet the next day, but there was studied appraisal of the weights and scales into which a hundred swift decisions must be fitted and he gave no outward sign that he was anxious or worried or hesitant.

It was early morning when finally he signalled he was ready to get some few hours of sleep. Moyers, Carter, and I, still gripped with an inflexible tension (at least I was), said our goodnights and each took to our beds. I wandered to my bedroom and for an hour I lay awake, trying to assess the capricious wind that had carried me so fast to so strange a place.

LADY BIRD JOHNSON

The End of a Presidency

A White House Diary (1970)

If there was anyone ever equipped to deal with emotional beginnings and endings, it was Lady Bird Johnson. And she has certainly had a fair share of each, especially in the five years the Johnsons spent in the White House at the center of Washington life.

Much of Lady Bird's book is highly memorable. She writes as she speaks—about her family, about Lyndon Johnson as a man and as president, about "this great house" that she so loved. One reviewer called this book a "story for America. Part history, part family album, part the self-portrait of an exceptional woman." It is all of that and more. Here are two selections from her White House diary that count as two different kinds of ending. Typically, Lady Bird, with her positive outlook and loving ways, saw both as a new beginning.

Sunday, March 31, 1968

This day began early because Lynda was coming in on "the red-eye special" from California, about 7 a.m., having kissed Chuck good-by at Camp Pendleton last night as he departed for Vietnam.

I wanted to be right there at the door with open arms to meet her, but I begged Lyndon not to get up. "No, I want to," he insisted. So the operator called us in what seemed the gray early morning and both of us were downstairs at the entrance to the Diplomatic Reception Room at 7 when she stepped out of the car. She looked like a ghost—pale, tall, and drooping. We both hugged her and then we all went upstairs. I took her into her room, helped get her clothes off, and put her to bed. She'd had a sedative on the plane, slept a little, not much—and it was, I think, partly emotion and partly the sedative that made her look so detached, like a wraith from another world.

She said, "Mother, they were awful—they kept on pushing and shoving to get to us, and they almost ran over a child. And there were lots of other wives there, saying good-by to their husbands!" She meant the press.

When I went back into Lyndon's room, his face was sagging and there was such pain in his eyes as I had not seen since his mother died. But he didn't have time for grief. Today was a crescendo of a day. At 9 in the evening, Lyndon was to make his talk to the nation about the war. The speech was not yet firm. There were still revisions to be made and people to see. But he began to put on his clothes and got ready to go to church with Luci and Pat, something he does more and more often.

And I, exhausted, went back to bed, where I half-slept for a couple of hours.

On the way home from church, Lyndon stopped to see the Vice President at his apartment. Hubert and Muriel are leaving for Mexico, for a ceremony, sometime during the day. It was a day of coming and going—and it's hard to remember when what happened. Sometime during the morning Buzz came in, took up his place in the Treaty Room, and began to work on the speech. I had spent a good part of Saturday and part of Friday making suggestions on it myself. I read it over again for what was the umpteenth time, and then (I believe it was in his bedroom), Lyndon said to Arthur and Mathilde Krim and me, "What do you think about this? This is what I'm going to put at the end of the speech." And he read a very beautifully written statement which ended, "Accordingly, I shall not seek and I will not accept the nomination of my party for another term as your President."

The four of us had talked about this over and over, and hour after hour, but somehow we all acted and felt stunned. Maybe it was the calm finality in Lyndon's voice, and maybe we believed him for the first time. Arthur said something like, "You can't mean this!" And Mathilde exclaimed in an excited way, "Oh no, no!" Then we all began to discuss the reasons why, and why not, over and over again.

Buzz came in now and again with another page for the main part of the speech. Finally, a little after 2 o'clock Lyndon and I, and Luci and Pat, and Mathilde and Arthur went to the table for lunch. It was Lyndon who thought to call Buzz in from the Treaty Room to have something to eat.

Mathilde's eyes were full of tears, and Luci had obviously been crying forthrightly. Lyndon seemed to be congealing into a calm, quiet state of mind, out of our reach. And I, what did I feel? . . . so uncertain of the future that I would not dare to try to persuade him one way or the other. There was much in me that cried out to go on, to call on every friend we have, to give and work, to spend and fight, right up to the last. And if we lost, well and good—we were free! But if we didn't run, we could be free without all this draining of our friends. I think what was uppermost—what was going over and over in Lyndon's mind—was what I've heard him say increasingly these last months: "I do not believe I can unite this country."

Buzz made a poetic little explanation of the statement saying Lyndon would not run. Lyndon, indeed, was the architect and the planner, but I think it was Buzz who had cloaked it in its final words.

Sometime during the afternoon—the time is very hazy on this day—I think it was around 3 o'clock, Lyndon went to his office, and I talked to Lynda and to Luci. Both of them were emotional, crying and distraught. What does this do to the servicemen? They will think—What have I been sent out here for?—Was it all wrong?—Can I believe in what I've been fighting for? Lynda and Luci seemed to feel that Lyndon has been the champion of the soldiers, and that his getting out would be a blow to them. Lynda said, with an edge of bitterness, "Chuck will hear this on his way to Vietnam."

Later in the afternoon, I talked to Lyndon about what the girls had said. He said, "I called in General Westmoreland last year about that, about how it would affect the morale of the men. He thinks it will not matter appreciably." I felt that Lynda and Luci were looking at it from closer range as the wives of two young soldiers, and pointed that out to him. He looked at me rather distantly and said, "I think General Westmoreland knows more about it than they do."

He was still in the office and it was near 6 o'clock when Walt Rostow, looking gray and weary, arrived on the second floor, with Averell Harriman, who did not look at all weary, and Ambassador Dobrynin. Ambassador Dobrynin was called in because we wanted to make absolutely sure that Hanoi and its friends knew that we were halting the bombing and why we were doing it. Lyndon had told me this morning they were coming to talk about the speech. I took them into the Yellow Room and asked them what they would like to drink. Everyone, I noticed, cautiously took a Coke, in spite of what I've heard about the Russians drinking vodka and trying to toast their opposite numbers under the table. Dobrynin was affable and talkative—I equally so—our subject, safely, the possibility that the Bolshoi Ballet might come to the Hemisfair in San Antonio. Then Lyndon came in with that jaunty step that I've seen him rev up under the most intense tension.

It was a strange afternoon and evening. We would meet in the West Hall by twos or threes, or all of us—Mathilde, Arthur, Buzz, Lynda, Luci, Pat, and I—and look at each other, helplessly, silent, or exploding with talk. I felt as if I ought to do something. I must do something—but what? And how did I dare do anything, with the decision so momentous, one I could by no means implement, or take the responsibility for making turn out right. I remember that I kept on looking at the hands of the clock, and counting the hours until 9 p.m. and the broadcast.

Just before 7, I went over to Lyndon's office with him. He was looking at the news ticker. I told the kitchen we would have some light sandwiches, or snacks, from 8 o'clock on, but that we wouldn't really want to eat until after the speech was over—9:30 or so.

Marvin came in around 8. Lyndon always speaks of him affectionately as "that tough Marine," and so he is. We've shared so much, we've been so close—that I can say about many people here, and that's been the great reward, second only to the sense of achievement. Clark and Marny Clifford came a little past 8. Lyndon had asked me to call them because he especially wanted them with us. And Walt and Elspeth Rostow.

And then about a quarter of 9, Lyndon, Marvin, Walt, and Jim Jones went to Lyndon's office—followed shortly by Luci and Pat. Luci clings to her father these days. It's wonderful to see. She's going to give him every comfort she can.

I went over with Clark and Buzz a few minutes before 9 and Lynda joined us. And there we were in the familiar oval office of the President, the floor a jungle of cables, under the brilliant glare of TV lights. What a stage setting!

Lyndon, very quiet, sat at his desk. The lines in his face were deep, but there was a marvelous sort of repose over-all. And the seconds ticked away.

I went to him and said quietly, "Remember—pacing and drama." It was a great speech and I wanted him to get the greatest out of it—and I did not know what the end would be.

The speech was magnificently delivered. He's best, I think, in the worst of times, calm and strong—those who love him must have loved him more. And those who hate him must at least have thought: "Here is a man."

Then came the end of the speech.

"What we won when all our people united just must not now be lost in suspicion, distrust, selfishness, and politics among any of our people. Believing this as I do, I have concluded that I should not permit the Presidency to become involved in the partisan divisions that are developing in this political year"—and so on. . . .

"I do not believe that I should devote an hour or a day of my time to any personal partisan causes or to any duties other than the awesome duties of this office—the Presidency of your country. Accordingly, I shall not seek, and I will not accept, the nomination of my party for another term as your President."

Lynda and I had been sitting down, behind us Luci and Pat standing. Luci threw her arms around Lyndon. She was obviously holding back the tears, but just barely. Lynda kissed him, and Pat shook hands.

Then there was a great blur of confusion, and we walked out of the President's office and went back to the second floor, with Secretary Clifford, who stood outside the door a little behind us. I looked back at him, and there he was standing, holding his hands behind his back, his head tilted up, with the oddest, most faraway expression on his face.

We gathered on the second floor—Marny and Clark, and the George Christians; Leonard Marks came up, and so did Doug Cater; and Secretary and Mrs. Wilbur Cohen; and Juanita and a few others. Marny had tears in her eyes. Nearly everybody just looked staggered and struck silent—and then the phones began to ring.

I went immediately and called Liz, who was in a state of near shock. I was going to call Bess, when I was called to the phone by Abigail McCarthy, who said, "Bird, Bird, you know what I've always thought of you." And then she said, "When he made the announcement, I could only think of you standing in front of the Wilson portrait . . ." And she didn't have to go on. I know what I always think in front of the Wilson portrait. In that face you see the toll the office and the times extracted. Its message to me is: "A President should have his portrait painted reasonably early in the office."

Dean Rusk called Lyndon, and I got to say a word. And then I talked to Bess. Then Bill Moyers called him, and once more Lyndon put me on the phone. . . . I talked to John and Ivo Sparkman; and to Alice and George Brown, who had Oveta with them, and they seemed stunned but satisfied with his decision. Mary Lasker called and it sounded as if she were crying, but she said, "I know it must be the right thing to do, since the President did it."

About 11, Tom Johnson came over, bringing thirty-five reporters, and Lyndon went into the Yellow Room with them, looking as if a great load had been taken off his shoulders. I believe he made it quite clear to them that his decision was final, and that any talk of a draft was foolishness.

Liz's request to me from the reporters had been, "How would I sum it up?"—what kind of a statement—and I told her, "We have done a lot; there's a lot left to do in the remaining months; maybe this is the only way to get it done."

It must have been one o'clock or later when the last guest left and Lyndon went to bed. And I, too, feeling immeasurably lighter. At last the decision had been irrevocably stated, and as well as any human can, we knew our future!

Lyndon's speech had been, I believe, nobly done, and in its way almost as dramatic as our entrance into this job—although the actual exit is still nine months away, if the Lord lets us live. And to these nine months I'm going to bring the best I possibly can.

I went to sleep planning.

Monday, January 20, 1969

I was up early, the way it was when I was a child and it was the day to go to the County Fair and I didn't want to miss a thing. I had coffee at 7, a small private smile for the big canopied bed that I would not sleep in again, and for the courteous deferential White House butler who brought me the tray. I'm glad I had spent a lot of Saturday afternoon saying good-by and thank you, because there would not be time to do it today.

In my robe with a cup of coffee in my hand, I made a last pilgrimage of my own into all the rooms on the second floor. This was partly the house-wifely need to see whether any personal object had been left anywhere, but mostly just to stand still and absorb the feeling of the Yellow Room and the little Lincoln Sitting Room. I found a whole coffee table full of dirty dishes in the Lincoln Sitting Room which I reported to John. I asked him to please take down the portraits of Lyndon and me, still on the easels in the East Hall, and put them in the care of the Curator. I went into the Queen's Sitting Room and then into the lovely Queen's Room, whose flower arrangements I have loved most of all.

About 9:30 I went up to Ashton's office—one of the last to be dismantled and to stop functioning. It was pandemonium, knee-deep in boxes and files and papers. She said she would be out by noon. And then into Luci's room which looked absolutely hopeless, full of scattered bags, half-opened. We would dispatch Patrick Lyn and Lucinda to the Cliffords' with their nurses about the time we left for the ceremony at the Capitol. Thank Heaven, with one hour of the Secret Service left to Luci, I don't have to handle that!

I went into the Pineapple Bedroom where I found a guest book of the myriad guests who had stayed upstairs with us, and into the rest of the guest rooms and finally into the Solarium—its personality all stripped away and looking cold and clinical now, and what a gay, happy room it had been—the citadel of the young.

Finished, I went back down to my room and put on my peach-pink dress and went down to the Red Room. The floor was alive with butlers and cleaning people and there was a strong smell of ammonia in the air. What a surprising household smell for this place. John assured me that it would be gone in thirty minutes and the fires would be lighted and we would have some sweet rolls with coffee for the new family that will gather here before we ride to the Capitol for the Inauguration.

A couple of times I went into Lyndon's room. He had been on the phone constantly since 7 a.m., talking with aides, dictating, dispatching Jim or Larry for some last thing to be done. Once he showed me a couple of sheets of paper—citations for Mary Lasker and Laurance Rockefeller. He was giving them the Medal of Freedom and these were brief records of their accomplishments for their countrymen. There was a list of about twenty names that we had discussed over a period of months. I was glad he was doing it.

After a while it was time to put on my elegant mink hat—what an indulgence . . . how often will I wear it at Stonewall?—take up my muff, tell Lyndon I was ready and to come as soon as he could, and go down to the Red Room.

For me, in any time of crisis all the real emotions—the leave-takings or whatever-it-is—have already been lived through in a previous, quieter time. By now I was sort of anesthetized—in armor—and still I had the feeling of "going to the Fair" and wanting to absorb and take in everything, remember it, but not feel it.

The day blurs into a montage and I am not sure of sequence. I think Leonard Marks was there all the time and I believe Hubert and Muriel were the first to come. And then, as it so often had happened, we received the message, "They're two minutes away," and Lyndon and I walked out on the North Portico, lined heavily on both sides with cameramen. On the left was an incredible sight! Mr. Traphes Bryant, at his feet a bouncing Yuki, freshly washed and wearing a bright coat that Mrs. Bryant had made for him, and the dogs of the new family—a gray poodle, clipped and brushed and proud, and tucked into Mr. Bryant's coat a miniature of a dog, breed unknown, surveying the scene with bright, alert eyes. Until the human members of this drama arrived, these characters had been willingly filling in for the cameramen!

The big black car rolled up and out stepped the President-elect, growing momentarily more impressive, somehow, and then Pat in a smashing rosy-red outfit, belted, with lapels and a fur hat. Tricia was wearing a powder blue coat with touches of fur. She's tiny and very feminine. And there was Julie, taller, darker, and more vivacious, with David, lanky and smiling that famous Eisenhower smile.

We stopped on the Portico for pictures and then the funny business that so often happens about who should go in the door first happened, until I took Pat's arm firmly and said, "Shall we go in?" Then we were all in the Red Room, the crowd enlarging to include Senator Dirksen,

Speaker McCormack, the Vice President–elect and Mrs. Spiro Agnew and their son, who had been in Vietnam, along with his wife, the Agnews' two daughters, Senator Mansfield, Gerald Ford, Senator Jordan, and Carl Albert, and Lynda and Luci who gravitated at once to the young Nixons. I noticed Luci and Tricia in animated conversation in a corner and Lynda asking David if he really did leave all those notes under the rugs. I was asking John Marriott, the Inauguration Chairman, how he was managing with his thousands of friends who must suddenly have come from the far reaches of the United States, demanding a suite with a large living room.

I remember Leonard Marks saying, "It's time to get into the cars." And Pat and I and Speaker McCormack went out together and took our places in a car. Lyndon and Mr. Nixon were in the lead car and in between were the Secret Service and somewhere behind Lynda and Luci and Leonard.

While everybody was getting in, I looked up at the facade of the White House and there, glued to one of the windows, were the faces of John Fickland and Jerman, and another butler—was it Johnny? . . . And on the steps smiling and blowing kisses were many members of our staff. That was my last view as I drove away from the White House.

We started the parade down Pennsylvania Avenue. It was strange— there were very few people—a little knot here, a small group there. I waved busily and tried to lock eyes whenever I saw an animated face, but mostly they just stood. I did not see a familiar face the whole length of Pennsylvania Avenue. But there was considerable bunting and lots of banners.

Our conversation was desultory and trivial—we were glad it wasn't sleeting—we might even avoid rain although it was a gray brooding day—but it was cold. I said I felt sure that the stands were going to be full by the time they rode back. I felt vaguely sorry that they weren't. Every now and then a booming remark of substance emanated from the Speaker, all the more surprising coming from that gaunt, frail man. We saw a few children with flags and he said, from deep within the well of his thoughts, "I like to see them with flags," and we both looked at the Capitol, he and I. I talked about how, driving in from Virginia on summer afternoons with the other Speaker, Mr. Sam Rayburn, he used to say, "How do you like my Capitol?" And we all said together something like, "We all feel that it's ours!"

Then as we drove up under the portico at that great old building we were met and escorted, with minimum confusion, to the office of Senator Margaret Chase Smith. There was Mrs. Eisenhower in a dark dress with an off-the-face hat, as poised and friendly and lively as she has been in all the more vigorous years I have known her. I was glad to see her and I had one brief minute with her to tell her how much I had always appreciated her coming to the Senate Ladies Luncheons in my time in the White House. She in turn recalled how nice it had been that Mrs. Woodrow Wilson had come to these functions in her day.

Lyndon and Mr. Nixon went to an adjoining office. Presently the orchestrator of all this drama gave us a signal, and together Muriel and I walked out the door and down the great steps of the Capitol under the commanding, handsome, newly built portico—face to face with the great sea of faces that stretched off to the right to the House Office Buildings and to the left to the Senate Office Building and in front of us to the Supreme Court. We went in side by side, and it gave me a warm pleasure that we walked together. Later Muriel said the same. We took our seats in the front row and then turned our heads to watch the next entrance onto the stage of this great quadrennial American pageant. Try as I did to soak everything up, I cannot remember for sure but I think that when Lyndon walked in, they played "Hail to the Chief." And this time truly the last time. He looked very tall and handsome and impressive, and very relaxed too, I thought. Mrs. Nixon came in alone—her bright rose-red dress a dramatic success. And finally, the country's new President.

For all the preparation that had gone into it, it was a brief cere-mony—only about forty-five minutes, I believe. And how to describe it? It was low-keyed, restrained, grave, it seemed to me. Perhaps the times set the mood. None of the youthful ebullience, the poetic brilliance of the Kennedy Inauguration, nor the robust, roaring Jacksonian quality of ours.

Bits and pieces stand out—a special smile between me and Mrs. Warren . . . among the five prayers, one by the head of the Greek Ortho-dox Church who had been my companion on our trip to the funeral of the King of Greece, along with President Truman . . . looking out into the sea of faces and finding so few familiar ones—Allen Drury, I did see—and the personal warm smiles from some of the newspaperwomen down front—Wauhilla La Hay, Betty Beale . . . a murmured remark now and then to Mrs. Agnew who was on my left—something like, "There's going to be so much that you'll enjoy," or "We wish you good luck in all the years ahead." And always, towering in front of us, the camera stand—it seems to get bigger every four years—the great eye of television trained down on us. I remember with corresponding appreciation and dismay that when there was a prayer, or the orchestra broke forth in the "Star-Spangled Banner," in one of the booths one of the commentators rose to his feet, unself-conscious, natural, and in the other booths the commentators sat sprawled around their tables. Perhaps handling their electronic gear required this.

And finally, finally, the Inaugural speech itself. The papers said it was seventeen minutes long and President Nixon delivered it rather quickly, in an even voice. There were no high trumpet calls to action, and probably that is just as well. God knows there's been plenty of striving in the last five, actually the last eight, years. Maybe the country is tired of striving—maybe we just want to hold still—absorb the deluges of change for a while. The address was interrupted by applause from time to time, but there was no great surge of emotion that swept the sea of people in front of us.

Well before one o'clock, President Nixon had finished and we all rose to take our departure. I said good-by to Muriel and to Tricia, in case I did not really get to make a formal good-by to Pat or the new President. As it happened, I didn't.

Then I was swallowed up in the great departing throng going up the stairs, trying to take in every face that I saw, so many of them unfamiliar. The Cabinet was behind President Nixon and over beyond, off the stand, a group of Senators, and then up the stairs on one side the Diplomatic Corps—I gave a last big smile to Sevilla-Sacasa.

Then we were in the big black car—Lyndon and I, and Lynda and Luci—driving with a motorcycle escort away from the Capitol and down the streets, now more filled with people, on toward the Cliffords'. Clark and Marny—foreseeing the situation of an outgoing President—had arranged a farewell luncheon before we left for Texas.

I was prepared for some press coverage outside their house, but not for what we found. It looked as if we had moved backward in time to some particularly homey campaign rally! The Clifford's quiet front lawn, secluded from the highway by a hedge, was jam-packed with people—little boys up the apple trees, babies in arms, high school and college youngsters carrying signs—"We'll Never Forget You, LBJ," "You Did a Good Job," "We Still Love You, Lyndon," "LBJ, You Were Good for the U.S.A." Somebody had a Texas flag and there was a great big U.S. flag waving precariously in front of us across the sidewalk. Marny, without a coat, and Clark were standing at the end of the sidewalk to greet us. We made our way up the sidewalk shaking hands, trying to think of a courteous brief phrase for the microphones that were stuck in front of us, and finally pausing on the front stoop for a picture with the Cliffords. We lost Luci in the crowd, because, of course, her Secret Service agents had departed at the stroke of 12, but I really think she was reveling in it, rather than having difficulty. . . .

The hands of the clock prodded us on. I went down and led the group in loading plates at the sumptuous luncheon table. Emotion and times of great significance do not spoil my appetite—they seem to fuel it. I divided my precious moments between food and the guests, every one of whom meant so much to me. Lucinda made an appearance now and then, regarding us all with solemn big eyes and occasionally a toothless granny grin. Patrick Lyndon, as usual, was weaving among legs while Luci or I retrieved Marny's treasures from the low tables at his approach.

And then, too soon, I got the signal: "Time to go!" I hugged Marny and Clark, not expecting to see them again, although they insisted they were going to race us to Andrews Air Force Base. We stopped on the porch briefly and Lyndon said a few words into Ray Scherer's microphone—how he had been a part of Washington for more than thirty years and loved it and he would come back to visit. And to waves and handshakes and calls of "God bless you, Mr. President," "We'll miss you, Lyndon," we made our way to the car and headed for the helicopter on the grounds of the Bethesda Naval Center. Only en route did I remember that I had left behind my elegant fur muff and my brand new gloves!

There was a small crowd at the helicopter pad. We flew in silence over Washington and landed at Andrews. And there was a big crowd, lining the fence and drawn up around *Air Force One*. Lyndon strode past the lined-up military and began to shake hands at the fence. The band played "Ruffles and Flourishes," and "Auld Lang Syne," and "Yellow Rose of Texas." And there was a salute of guns, I think twenty-one, but anyway, it was total confusion, and dear, and wonderful. Luci was crying—more from the impact of the day than sadness, and saying of Lyn, "He's just lost twenty-one of his best friends," meaning the Secret Service.

In the crowd I glimpsed many familiar and beloved faces. And to my amazement standing at the foot of the steps were none other than Clark and Marny and Dean and Virginia! They had, indeed, raced us and beaten us there, along with a group of the luncheon guests. We mounted the steps of *Air Force One*, Lyndon carrying his faithful companion, Lyn. We stopped at the top, the family, and turned and waved in a good-by tableau, I searching for the eyes of the most dear and most familiar—and there close to the foot of the steps stood Liz with a sign that was an invitation to laughter: "Culpeper Says Thank You, Mr. President." Shades of 1960! The door closed, the motors revved, and we were airborne in the plane.

ELIZABETH DREW

Summer 1974

Washington Journal: The Events of 1973–1974 (1975)

Watergate was many things to many people in Washington—and else-where. Its ripples spread far beyond this city, but the story began and ended here. Its bookends were the break-in at the Democratic National Committee offices in the Watergate complex, in June 1972, and the res-ignation of Richard Nixon as president of the United States, in August 1974. For a large part of that time, this city was held in thrall.

It was clearly a time unlike any other, a period without precedent. Watergate was certainly a central moment in my life—and in the life of The Washington Post. *People in most political and social circles talked of nothing but the latest revelation and rumor, the most recent* Post *article, the possible motives, the connections, the trail to the White House. People lined up in the alley behind the* Post's *building to get the paper as soon as it came out of the mailroom, hot off the presses. I loved that.*

Nixon was always urging the American people to put Watergate behind them and get on with the nation's business, but it turned out that Watergate was the nation's business.

Elizabeth Drew, then a journalist living in Washington, began to keep a journal of the period, which first ran in The New Yorker. *Her book is full of beginnings and endings.*

Ultimately, Watergate became one of the most incredible and dra-matic endings ever associated with the United States of America, and it essentially ended with President Nixon's simple statement: "Therefore I shall resign the presidency effective at noon tomorrow."

THERE is already some talk about what "the historians will say"—the historians, those unknown people who in the future will have the franchise to interpret what is going on now. We tend to assume that out of their years of accumulation of fact they will sift the truth—a truer truth than any we can hope to grasp. They will have many more facts, and they will have what is called "perspective" (which means they will not be trapped in the biases of our day and can freely write in the biases of their day—can find what they are looking for). But I wonder if they will really understand what it was like. Will they know how it felt to go through what we have gone through? Will they know how it felt to be stunned—again and again—as we learned what had been done by people in power? Will they know how it felt to be shocked, ashamed, amused by the revelations—will they understand the difficulty of sorting out the madcap from the macabre? (What was one really to think about someone in the pay of the White House putting on a wig and travelling across the country to visit a sick, disgraced lobbyist?) Can they conceivably understand how it felt as we watched, on our television screen, our President say, "I am not a crook"? Will they be able to understand why, almost two years ago, some very sensible people wondered whether it was the last election? Will they understand how it felt—as it did last fall at the time the President fired Special Prosecutor Cox, and on several later occasions—when it seemed that there were no checks on power? Will they understand how degrading it was to watch a President being run to ground? Will they know how it was to feel in the thrall of this strange man, who seemed to answer only to himself? Knowing the conclusion, as they will, will they understand how difficult, frightening, and fumbling the struggle really was? . . .

The real transfer of power is going on out of sight. Tomorrow, it will be marked by another ceremony, signifying still another beginning. Soon we shall have both a President and Vice-President who were not elected. . . .

August 9

On television this morning, we hear "Hail to the Chief" played for Nixon for the last time. Perhaps it is only in the imagination that it sounds slightly like an echo of itself. Staff members and their wives are seated in chairs in the East Room. The East Room: site of press conferences, religious services, and the naming of Gerald Ford as the next Vice-President. Today, the applause for the President goes on and on. James St. Clair and Raymond Price, a speechwriter who worked on last night's speech, are in a front row, applauding. Henry Kissinger and his new wife and William Simon and Alexander Haig are also in a front row, applauding. They all look grim. One wonders—watching them applaud—how much each of them had to do with bringing this moment about. The President and Mrs. Nixon—in a pink dress—and their daughters and the daughters' husbands stand on a platform in the front of the East Room. A gold curtain is behind them. Nixon looks better than he did last night. Mrs. Nixon is composed, as always. James Schlesinger, the Secretary of

Defense, puffing on his pipe, applauds. Fred Buzhardt applauds. That's all he can do for Nixon now. Rabbi Korff, in a front-row aisle seat, applauds lustily.

Nixon, almost as if he couldn't help himself, begins with a jab at the press, suggesting that the press will be skeptical that this is a "spontaneous" event, and the skepticism "will be so reported in the press, and we don't mind, because they've got to call it as they see it." The President says that he is saying not goodbye but "*au revoir*—we'll see you again." He expressed his gratitude to the unseen staff people—the upstairs people—who keep the White House going. The President seems more human today. Again he is wearing a navy suit and a white shirt, and again a tiny American-flag pin is in his lapel. (What happens to the American-flag pins now?) He is trying to buck up his staff. Then he says some strange things. "Sure we have done some things wrong in this Administration," he says, "and the top man always takes the responsibility, and I've never ducked it." But, he says, "no man or no woman came into this Administration and left it with more of this world's goods than when he came in." Remarkable in several respects that he is standing there and saying that now. He talks of the importance of America's leadership in the world, and gets back to the point that no one in his Administration was "feathering his nest," and that government service is important but so are other careers. ("This country needs good farmers, good businessmen, good plumbers, good carpenters.") Then he talks of his father. Despite the hardships and the business failures, his father was "a great man," he says. "Nobody will ever write a book probably about my mother," he says. (Is he thinking of the book about Rose Kennedy?) Then, his eyes brimming with tears, he says, "My mother was a saint." (My mind flashes back to Egil Krogh telling me, four years ago, about that morning in May, 1970, when there were demonstrations here against the invasion of Cambodia, and the President, at dawn, went to the Lincoln Memorial and talked to the demonstrators about football, and then went to Capitol Hill, where he encountered, in the near-empty corridors, a cleaning woman. Krogh told me that the cleaning woman was carrying a Bible and asked the President to sign it, and as he did so the President told the cleaning woman that his mother had been a saint. "You be a saint," said the President to the cleaning woman.)

Now, choking back sobs, the President tells of his mother's having two sons die of tuberculosis and taking care of four boys not her own so that she could afford to take care of his older brother. One thinks of how often, through all the campaigns, he told us of his hard childhood, how deeply this is still in him. And there are some other touches that are pure Nixon. "I'm not educated, but I do read books," he says, and then he says that he was reading last night, which is hard to believe. In his speech last night, he quoted from Theodore Roosevelt about the importance of being in the arena, of being a man who "if he fails, at least fails while daring greatly." This morning, he reads from Theodore Roosevelt's diary upon the death of Roosevelt's first wife: "And when my heart's dearest died, the light went from my life forever." One thinks of the times Nixon has been Disraeli, Woodrow Wilson, Lincoln, Patton. The Theodore Roosevelt phase seems to be new. (So are the glasses, which he puts on while reading from Roosevelt's book.) This is a very painful sight. Nixon has this emotional side, too, and we have been through so much with him that one cannot help feeling his pain now. Distraught, destroyed, confused, broken, telling himself, because he has to, that this last defeat is "only a beginning." He says some true things about the tests and the strengthening that can come from the deepest disappointments and sadness. He puts it, characteristically, in terms of "the deepest valley" and "the highest mountain." And then one watches, transfixed, as he advises his staff, "Never get discouraged. Never be petty. Always remember others may hate you but those who hate you don't win unless you hate them. And then you destroy yourself." This speech will be much studied. But it shows almost nothing that we did not know about him before. And so the grief that one feels at the moment is for him, this man whose character was his fate, and for us, that we went through so much with and because of him. He did make his ordeal ours.

On the South Lawn of the White House, a red carpet has been rolled out to the waiting helicopter. The helicopter is olive-colored; a flag is painted on its side. President and Mrs. Nixon, together with Vice-President and Mrs. Ford and the Nixon children, walk toward the helicopter. Tricia and Edward Cox are going with the Nixons to California; Julie and David Eisenhower will stay behind to pack. Ron Ziegler is going with the Nixons to California. As the President boards the helicopter, he stands in the doorway, faces the crowd, and shoots his arms in the air, the fingers of both hands shaping the characteristic "V"s. The helicopter lifts off into the gray sky, circles over the Jefferson Memorial, disappears momentarily behind the Washington Monument, and is gone. Nixon seems to have just floated away. Moments later, he will land at Andrews Air Force Base. At twelve o'clock noon, when the President's plane—the *Spirit of '76*—is midway across the country, Nixon's resignation as President will take effect.

ROSALYNN CARTER

Prologue

First Lady from Plains (1984)

Jimmy Carter's beginning as president was an auspicious one. The Carters had planned a simple inauguration, what they called a "people's inauguration," intending for many of those people they'd met during the campaign and those with whom they'd spent the night at various places around the country to come to Washington to participate in different events over several days. Having run against Washington, as most everyone campaigning for president does, Jimmy Carter was quick to take advantage of everything this city has to offer. Miscellaneous activities were planned throughout the city, including musical events, prayer meetings, poetry readings, plays, films, fireworks, children's events, and tours. Mrs. Carter wrote that they had "wanted all 216 million Americans to feel comfortable in Washington. But not all at once! And not at all in the style of Andrew Jackson's famous inaugural, when people had to sleep on pool tables after all the hotel rooms were full, often with five to a bed."

As I do on nearly every inauguration day, I was watching from a window overlooking the parade route from somewhere along Pennsylvania Avenue, between the Capitol and the White House. In fact, in the days when the Post was located on E Street—before 1950—we used to go to the Post building for a ringside seat on the parades, which we could see from my father's office, and later from Phil's. On this particular January day in 1977, there was a palpable sense of excitement in the bone-chilling cold as the crowd spread the word that the new president and his family were walking along part of the parade route. It did sort of take your breath away to realize how right and how democratic that was. Young Amy Carter hopped and skipped along, stopping the parade occasionally while one of her brothers tied her shoes. What could be more American?

I T IS EARLY, too early, when we wake up on January 20, 1977, in Blair House the morning Jimmy is to be sworn in as the thirty-ninth President of the United States. It's dark outside and bone-chilling cold, so cold that the outdoor concert on the Mall last night had to be canceled for fear the mouthpieces of the instruments would stick to the musicians' mouths. In Union Station, the doors on a train filled with people coming to the inauguration froze shut and couldn't be thawed open for several hours.

Now, at 5:30 a.m., Jimmy and I can see the White House dimly across the street, a few lights twinkling in the morning dawn. Already two hundred soldiers are at work along Pennsylvania Avenue, using jackhammers to break up the ice on the sidewalks in preparation for the inaugural parade.

I look at Jimmy, the President-elect, the man for whom the Kennedy Center was filled just last night with some of America's greatest artists performing for him, the one person who would command all the world's attention today. He is still the same person who spent yesterday morning with me, mopping up the garage in Plains after the hot water pipes burst from the cold, the same son who had called Miss Lillian later to admit the motorcade had forgotten to pick her up on the way to the airport. "Stay right there," he told her. "We'll send someone for you."

This morning we are all safely in Washington somewhere, even Misty Malarky Ying Yang, Amy's cat, who had crawled all over the plane on the flight from Plains. Jimmy, Amy, and I have an early breakfast in our bathrobes in the Blair House bedroom. While Jimmy works on his inaugural address, listening to it for the last time on his tape recorder, I fuss over my hair. I had a haircut and a permanent just before we came to Washington, and my hair feels strange . . . and much too short and curly. In a futile attempt to make it look longer, I roll it on big curlers, but it still comes out just as short. It seems incredible that the day my husband is to be sworn in as President, what worries me most is my hair!

And the cold. Jimmy asked me a few days ago what I thought about walking instead of riding from the Capitol to the White House after the inauguration. The Secret Service, he told me, had cleared it if there was no publicity and absolutely no one knew about it ahead of time. Thomas Jefferson had walked to the Capitol for his inauguration, and I thought it was a wonderful idea, a symbol of the open and accessible atmosphere Jimmy hoped to return to the presidency. Now, suddenly, I'm not so sure. Will Amy, at age nine, be able to make it all the way in the cold? Will I have to get in the car and let Jimmy walk without me? And what about Chip's wife, Caron, who is eight months pregnant? But it's too late for second thoughts. It's time to dress, and warmly. For good luck, I put three small crosses on the gold chain around my neck, one each for Amy, our grandson, Jason, and the new grandbaby yet to be born. For warmth, I put on my boots and my knee-length knit underwear. It doesn't seem like the most stylish way to dress for your husband's inauguration, and I laugh at myself a little as I bundle up, but I'm determined to enjoy this day, which may be the most important one of my life, without my teeth chattering.

As the day begins to unfold, I soon forget completely about my hair and almost about the cold. The significance of the events becomes far more important and humbling. Chip, who had been working with the inaugural committee in Washington since the election, had been to several churches in the city and had picked the First Baptist Church as the one he thought we would like to join. Now we assemble there with our family, the Mondales, and several of the Cabinet and staff members for a private prayer service. The Reverend Nelson Price, a special friend from Georgia, invokes the words of President John Adams, words that are inscribed on a White House mantel: "I pray Heaven to bestow the best of blessings on this house and on all that shall hereafter inhabit it. May none but honest and wise men ever rule under this roof." The thoughts Nelson borrowed from Thomas Jefferson are just as pertinent to what Jimmy hopes to bring to his presidency: "Our generation needs persons with hearts like unto that of James Monroe, who was so honest that if you turned his soul inside out, there would not be a spot on it."

It's now Jimmy's turn to live "wisely" under the White House roof, to try to keep his soul as spotless as James Monroe's, to become one of the leaders children will read about in history books. How I wish his father could have been here to see him take the oath of office—my father as well. All these thoughts and more are milling around in my head as I ride in the limousine from the White House, where we all gathered briefly, to the Capitol. Jimmy rides with President Ford and I follow with Mrs. Ford. I'm sure her thoughts are as deep and varied as mine, but like most people, we do not express them. Instead we chat, mostly about Camp David, where the Fords had just spent their last weekend. The food is so delicious there, Mrs. Ford tells me, that she is going to have to go on a diet.

We are met at the Capitol and taken to a small waiting room, where I talk with Happy Rockefeller, Betty Ford, and Joan Mondale. I feel numb. All that Jimmy and I have worked for so hard is about to become a reality. Then it is time, and Joan Mondale and I walk down the aisle between the dignitaries and our families to take our positions on the presidential platform. Dimly I hear applause from the crowd. This is the moment I have anticipated so long, but all I can do is go through the motions. Then it is President Ford's turn to make his way down the aisle, and I tremble slightly as the Marine Band strikes up "Ruffles and Flourishes" and "Hail to the Chief." The next time they play it, it will be for Jimmy.

As the sound of the brass, the vastness of the crowd, and the American flags snapping in the cold wind contribute to the overwhelming sense of pageantry, Amy slips over onto my lap. She is used to big crowds and had been to Jimmy's inauguration as governor of Georgia, but she seems awed by the scene. She is old enough to know what is going on, though, and I am thankful for her presence. She comforts me at this moment as much as I comfort her.

The band plays the Navy Hymn, one of Jimmy's favorites from his days at the Naval Academy, and more memories stir of our Navy days and my sentimental visits with Jimmy to the chapel at Annapolis, when I was young and filled with the anticipation of an exciting and unknown future. The hymn also reminds me of John Kennedy, not only of the excitement and promise he brought to our country, but of his funeral as well, when that excitement was extinguished too soon. I look out at the sea of faces on all sides, as far as the eye can see, and feel the air of expectancy and hope and promise in the crowd. I also feel an awesome responsibility now that Jimmy is about to be President. All these people. And we are responsible to them, and for them.

Jimmy appears, and a sudden hush falls over the crowd before an explosion of applause and cheers. "We love you, Jimmy," someone yells. Then another: "God be with you, Jimmy." I stand to join him at the front of the platform and hold the Bible his mother gave him a few years ago while he takes the oath of office. It is a moment I will never forget. I look right at him, the same person I've looked at so long, and smile, thinking what a wonderful thing this is for our country, what a good, honest, and capable man we are getting for our President, a man who is going to work hard and wisely for all the people of the country, not just the elite few. I have never felt so proud.

Even the words of his inaugural address, one of the shortest in American history, sound fresh and new to me, though I have heard and read them many times before. We studied all the inaugural addresses of past presidents in our den in Plains, and I read the drafts over and over as Jimmy was writing them, surrounded by bits and scraps of paper. I even made a small contribution, suggesting that he add the strengthening of the American family as one of his goals for the presidency. Now these words, so familiar and yet so new, bring tears not only to my eyes, but to the eyes of many around us as well. And the applause of the crowd takes the frost out of the air as he finishes; Jimmy Carter has been inaugurated, and the celebration begins.

PHILIP HAMBURGER

The Inauguration

The New Yorker (1993)

Here is Philip Hamburger once again, this time reporting on Bill Clinton's first inaugural. Far from being jaded, Hamburger still finds great hope in the quiet but unmistakable drama of the inaugural moment, and the importance of the public imprimatur at the beginning of another new presidency.

JUST BACK FROM Washington and largest crush of hopeful humankind in my experience. (This my fourteenth Inauguration, starting with first of Franklin D. Roosevelt, in 1933. Missed only two: FDR's second and third.) Arrived Sunday before Wednesday swearing-in, headed (in mild weather) for huge gathering around Lincoln Memorial Reflecting Pool. Clutched valid invitation to seat near Memorial, for program of pageantry and musical goings on. Fat chance! Thousands upon thousands already there—deep in churned-up mud, lining slippery banks along pool, huddled on quilts and blankets. Many more surging vainly forward, holding equally useless tickets. Had impression *everybody* wearing some sort of button. Buttons of Bill, of Hillary, of White House. Buttons saying "We did it." Thousands of black faces, yellow faces, white faces. No pushing, no shoving. Cynics don't buy this, but there are times when hope is palpable.

Signs everywhere: "First Aid." "Lost Children." Watched small boys scrambling into bare trees for better view of Memorial.

Depth of Depression, first FDR investiture. I'm nineteen, ticketless, facing east façade of Capitol, far away. Spotted leafless tree, climbed branch, shared tree with woman in rags, elderly gentleman in patched tweeds, beautiful redhead. Fitting spot: entire country up tree. Somber, gray, despairing day suddenly electrified by FDR's unforgettable "The only thing we have to fear is fear itself." "I think we'll live," redhead said as we climbed down from citizens' perch. She was right.

Splendid amplification sending forth "Battle Hymn of the Republic." Always showstopper. Booming voice intoning, "And Mr. Lincoln said, 'As I would not be a slave, so I would not be a master.'" Vast crowd fell silent. Voice intoned, "And Mr. Lincoln said, 'Fondly do we hope—fervently do we pray—that this mighty scourge of war may speedily pass away. . . .'"

Stranger beside me said, "I have an unexpected feeling that something good is about to happen to our country."

MONDAY. Breakfast with friend—Thomas H. Allen, former Mayor of Portland, Maine (current member of Portland's City Council). Rhodes Scholar and friend of Clinton's at Oxford. Down for festivities with wife and two daughters. Great admirer of Clinton, especially of his ability—anytime, anyplace—to curl up on bed or sofa, take catnap, regardless of people jabbering, radio blaring in room. "He always woke up refreshed," Allen said. "When he came to Portland last year, he ran us all ragged. He loves reaching out. Always asks more questions than are put to him. An immensely serious man, yet full of fun, and an omnivorous reader." Allen particularly remembers the connection Clinton made with the porters at Oxford. "Other scholars were astounded," Allen said. "They would hear porters swapping stories among themselves about the State of Arkansas—anecdotes told to them by Clinton." Allen's first and continuing impression of Clinton: warmth.

Second Reagan Inauguration. Temperature: 4°F. Fear that whole government would freeze to death, nix next four years, turn Reagan into historic icicle. All outdoor festivities cancelled, my lovely ticket invalid. Roy L. McGhee, then Senate Periodical Gallery superintendent, phoned me at hotel, said, "If you can get here in seven minutes, I have a ticket for you inside the Rotunda for the swearing-in." Unforgettable wild ride to Capitol. Fast-talked way past cadres of Secret Service, clock ticking, and was escorted into Rotunda by McGhee just as Reagan, with experienced actor's impressive gait, strode Presidentially into vast vaulted room to take oath.

Treated myself to yummy crab cake (not Baltimore class, but close), and wandered on to America's Reunion on the Mall. Another mob scene. Holiday spirit (it was Martin Luther King Day), with thousands swarming over grounds, in and out of huge white tents featuring music, exhibits, food: fried trout, buffalo burgers, crawfish Monica, chicken Panang. Multicultured bellies. (Maalox moments to come later.) Approached eighty-eight-foot-long wall entirely covered with hundreds of six-inch colored-paper squares. Concept of Brooklyn visual artist Phyllis Yampolsky, who calls it "The American Town Hall Wall." Markers provided, and people scribbling messages, tacking them onto any available space: "Don't Mess with Bill." "One Race: The Human Race." "Sorry to See You Go, George." "Feed the Hungry Help the Homeless Stop the Killing." I grabbed a square of green paper and wrote "Courage!" but before I could reach wall I was tapped on shoulder by Secret Service man, who said, firmly, "Sit down at this table." He then directed a woman and her daughter to sit beside me. Thought for moment we had been mistaken for Iraqi terrorists. "Just keep seated, and don't rise when Mrs. Clinton comes through," said Secret Service man. Moments later, Hillary Clinton arrived, walked past wall, to frenzied cries of "Hillary! Hillary!" Smart. Serene. Long black coat. Stopped by table where I was sitting. Mother beside me took her hand, said quietly, "We need health and education, Mrs. Clinton. Health and education. And don't let anybody fool your husband." Mrs. Clinton heard her. Handed her my green square that said "Courage!" She read it, smiled, looked directly into my eyes, said "Thank you," and was swept along down Mall, trailed by Secret Service men holding thin yellow rope protecting her from crowds. People again crowded around wall. Un-smiling couple took close look at myriad messages of hope and despair. Man turned to woman and said, "I didn't know there were so many of *them*."

Traffic gridlocked. Cabdrivers unanimous this worst traffic within memory. Kept bumping into friends old and new, many just trying to get across town. Good talk with Haynes Johnson, Pulitzer Prize–winning political writer. He shared my feeling this most important election in sixty years—critical time in nation's history. Said he felt both Justice Department and CIA had become completely politicized, hence vital areas for new administration. Shared my worry about press becoming too aggressive. "I'm worried by a current of cynicism," he said. "An exclusive interview with a high official today would make you appear to be the enemy. If a President calls, you are tainted."

Saw old friend Judy Collins—slim, blue-eyed, excited. All set to sing at one of the balls. Said she'd first met Clintons at Chautauqua in summer of 1991. They had come backstage after hearing her concert. "They evaluate ideas," she said. "They're both so bright, they love good music, they sustain multiple points of view. Artists need support—Clinton seems to understand this." Collins said she hardly believed it when she woke up to find that Clinton had won. She said, " 'It was a Chelsea morning, and the first thing that I heard was a song outside my window. . . .' "

Bumped into disgruntled Republican friend. Fine woman, enamored of the likes of William Bennett. Hated Republican convention, blamed religious right for everything, felt sad to see so many buddies leaving town, and was looking forward to upcoming symposium featuring Cap Weinberger and other disgruntleds. Told her, generally speaking, I was happy that hope springs eternal.

SWEARING-IN DAY. Put on long johns but didn't need them. Cloudless bright-blue sky. Pleased with self for buying Metro ticket ahead: system almost swamped. But, again, no pushing. Unprecedented crowds heading for Capitol. Brisk walk up Capitol Hill. Elaborate security: Secret Service, Marines, electronic checkpoints. Escorted to Seat 53, just below podium. Turned to look back at unending throng far below, stretching onto distant Mall. Official stand behind podium filling up with dignitaries. Marine Band in red dress costume.

FDR's fourth. Wartime. FDR ailing, in wheelchair, unable or unwilling to make trip to Capitol, sworn in on South Portico of White House. Wind up standing next to Archibald MacLeish, then an Assistant Secretary of State, on narrow balcony of old State Department Building, and catch glimpse of FDR, tiny figure through trees, taking oath of office. MacLeish, in strange gesture, keeps running fingers over engraved calling card he holds. "Feel this," he says to me several times.

Kennedy Inauguration. Bitter, bitter cold. Snow, ice everywhere. Robert Frost solemnly reading poem while smoke curled all around him, lightbulb having ignited speech. Aging poet obviously mistook smoke for cold breath in frigid air, plowed ahead with prosody until alert Secret Service man, aware that the entire United States government was about to go up in flames, somehow extinguished blaze.

Last "Hail to the Chief" for Bush. Somber-faced Clinton took place on podium. Disappointed when Associate Justice Byron White, substituting for Thurgood Marshall, administered Vice-Presidential oath to Gore. At close of oath, White said to Gore, "And I *know* you will." Bandmaster had sharp eye on clock, played rousing medleys until precise second of noon, when Clinton took oath of office. Twenty-one-gun salute sounded through entire city, and nation had new President. Throng moved by historic pageant. Glorious voice of Marilyn Horne, singing of children everywhere. Firm, quiet Inaugural Address (pleased that he said, "There is nothing wrong with America that cannot be cured by what is right with America"). Moved by ending of Maya Angelou's poem:

Very simply
With hope—
Good morning

Lost interest in jam-packed, airless Inaugural Balls years ago. Accepted invitation this time to elegant reception at National Gallery. Chance to see exhibit "The Greek Miracle"—classical sculpture from dawn of democracy, fifth century B.C. Thirty-four objects on display, each a treasure. Nike unbinding her sandal, her beautiful body clearly delineated through flowing sculptural gown. Eerie feeling to stand in front of pieces of stone from, say, 410 B.C. and find them so alive. Listened to audiotape of exhibit, narrated by former director of Gallery, J. Carter Brown, who made clear that besides the aesthetic quality of what stood before us there was another message: In Greek thought, individual was free to take charge of his or her destiny but morally subject to needs of the community. Read in catalogue: "Self-knowledge and social responsibility were vivid values that encouraged the development of constitutional democracy."

Something to think about all the way home.

Washington, 2050 A.D.

"Yes, This Is Washington!" (1949)

To end with, I've decided to expose to modern eyes one of a group of bizarre poems that appeared in a little book that first saw the light of day in 1949. Undoubtedly this sonnet—there are sixty-eight poems in all—will strike some as the most eccentric of my choices for inclusion here, but how could I resist resurrecting these "shrines and sonnets of the Potomac shore"? Among the more enticing titles are: "Sans Vote or Voice," "White House Bedtime Story," "Ye Gods of Goods," and "And Yet Fools Say."

George Sanford Holmes was a veteran Washington newsman— hardly a veteran poet—who wrote for the Scripps-Howard staff here in Washington from 1928 to 1938. He then went to work for the government, also here in Washington, as an information officer for the War Department. A poet only by penchant, for many years he wrote a daily column in verse for the Washington Daily News. *What could be more unlikely? In any case, I like this paean to Washington. It made me laugh, and I hope it will make you laugh, too.*

I dreamt I saw you standing in the sun
One hundred years from now, a vision fair
Of bridges new, of subways everywhere
And Dupont Circle underpass nigh done!

I marvelled at those boons so quickly won
And felt indeed a stranger, come to stare,
'Til I espied your tempos rotting there
And breathed again, "Yes, this is Washington!"

And then I dreamed atomic Men from Mars
Had crushed you in the War of Earth and Stars
And left no trace of life nor temple wall
To mark the spot,—yet look! O'er ruined Mall
Your tempos still stood molding, every one,
To tell the world, "Yes, this was Washington!"

Grateful acknowledgment is made to the following for permission to reprint previously published material:

Tyler Abell: "Boiled Bosoms" from *Washington Merry-Go-Round* by Anonymous (Drew Pearson and Robert S. Allen). Copyright © 1931 by Horace Liveright, Inc. "The Capital Underworld" from *More Merry-Go-Round* by Anonymous (Drew Pearson and Robert S. Allen). Copyright © 1932 by Liveright, Inc. Reprinted by permission of Tyler Abell.

Jack Anderson: "Washington's Curious Caste System" from *Washington Exposé* by Jack Anderson. Copyright © 1967 by Jack Anderson. Reprinted by permission of Jack Anderson.

Brandt & Hochman Literary Agents, Inc.: "The Timely Death of President Harding" by Samuel Hopkins Adams from *The Aspirin Age 1919–1941*, edited by Isabel Leighton. Copyright © 1949 by Simon and Schuster, Inc. Reprinted by permission of Brandt & Hochman Literary Agents, Inc., on behalf of Samuel Hopkins Adams. "Washington Is a State of Mind" from *I Write from Washington* by Marquis W. Childs. Copyright © 1942, 1970 by Marquis W. Childs. Excerpt from *Frontier on the Potomac* by Jonathan Daniels. Copyright © 1946, copyright renewed 1974 by Jonathan Daniels. Reprinted by permission of Brandt & Hochman Literary Agents, Inc.

Art Buchwald: Four columns excerpted from *I Chose Capitol Punishment* by Art Buchwald. Copyright © 1962, 1963 by Art Buchwald. Reprinted by permission of Art Buchwald.

Liz Carpenter: "Never Send to Know for Whom the Wedding Bell Tolls" from *Ruffles and Flourishes* by Liz Carpenter. Copyright © 1969, 1970 by Elizabeth Carpenter. Reprinted by permission of Liz Carpenter.

Constance Casey: "Memoirs of a Congressman's Daughter" by Constance Casey. Reprinted by permission of Constance Casey.

Lucy Dos Passos Coggin: "Washington Evening" from *State of the Nation* by John Dos Passos. Copyright © 1944 by John Dos Passos, copyright renewed 1972 by Elizabeth Dos Passos. Reprinted by permission of Lucy Dos Passos Coggin.

Commentary: "Living in Washington, D.C." by Isa Kapp (*Commentary*, July 1997). All rights reserved. Reprinted by permission of *Commentary*.

Condé Nast Publications: "Main Street-on-Potomac" by Jay Franklin (originally published in *Vanity Fair*, March 1933). Copyright © 1933 by Condé Nast Publications. All rights reserved. Reprinted by permission of Condé Nast Publications.

From the files of *The Washington Post*: 109, 182, 246–7, 377, 450, 593, 685, 734

Underwood & Underwood, Washington, D.C.: 8, 322, 380

Courtesy of the Collection of the Estate of Katharine Graham: 66, 587

ALSO BY KATHARINE GRAHAM

PERSONAL HISTORY

Winner of the Pulitzer Prize for Biography, this extraordinarily
frank, honest, and generous book is, as its title suggests, a book
composed of both personal memoir and history. It is the story
of Graham's parents: the multimillionaire father and the formidable, self-absorbed mother. It is the story of Phil Graham,
Kay's brilliant, charismatic husband, whose plunge into manic-
depression, betrayal, and eventual suicide is movingly and
charitably recounted. It is the story of how *The Washington
Post* struggled to succeed—a fascinating and instructive business history as told from the inside. Best of all, it is the story of
Kay Graham herself. Hers is a life that came into its own with
a vengeance—a success story on every level. Populated by a cast
of fascinating characters, including fifty years of presidents,
Graham's book is about learning by doing, about growing and
growing up, about Washington, and about a woman liberated
by both circumstance and her own great strengths.

*"Captivating . . . distinguished by a level of introspection
that ought to be, but rarely is, the touchstone of
autobiography."* —Newsday

Autobiography/0-375-70104-4